CITIES OF THE UNITED STATES

ISSN 0899-6075

CITIES OF THE UNITED STATES
SECOND EDITION

A Compilation of Current Information on
Economic, Cultural, Geographic, and Social Conditions

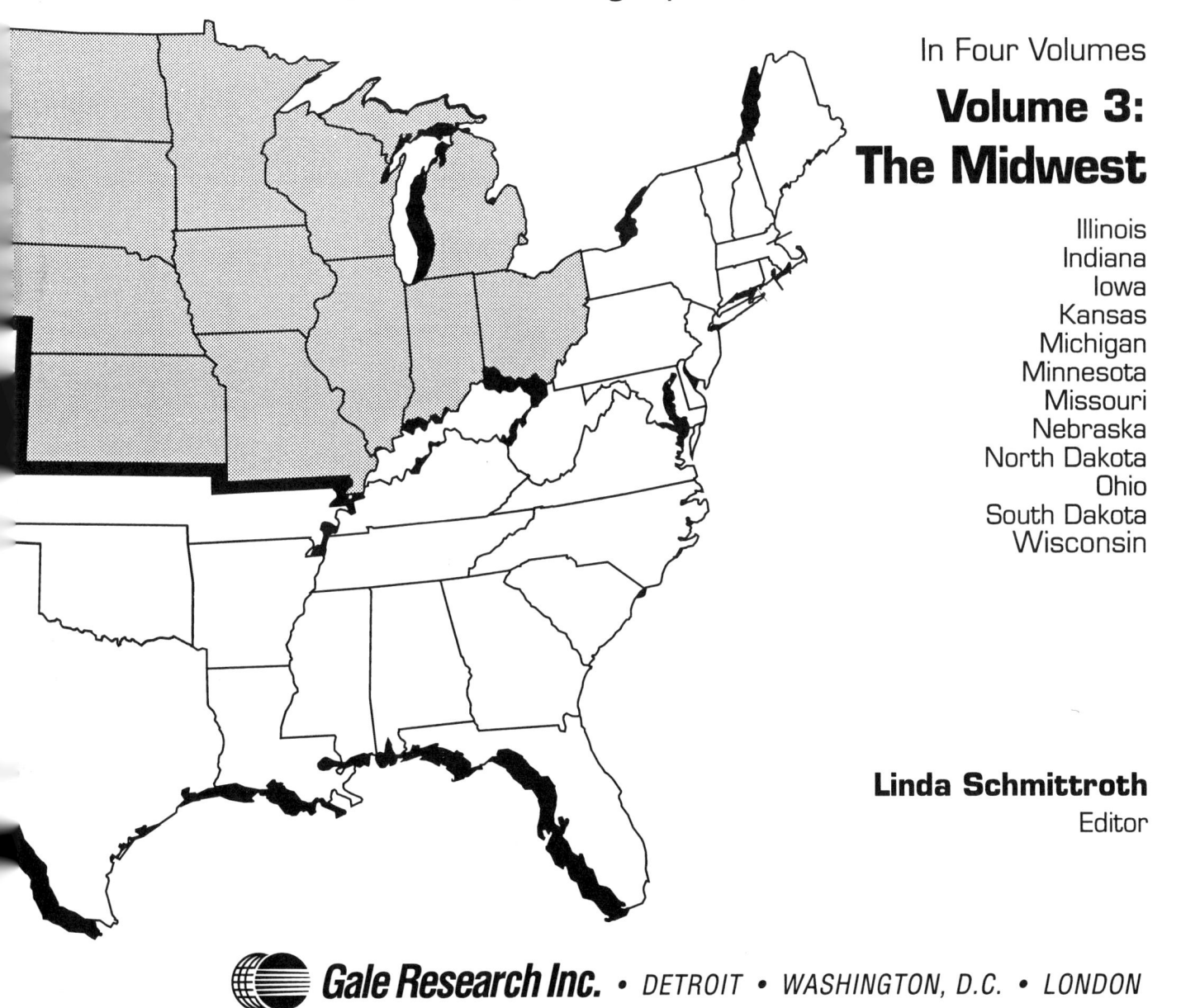

In Four Volumes
Volume 3:
The Midwest

Illinois
Indiana
Iowa
Kansas
Michigan
Minnesota
Missouri
Nebraska
North Dakota
Ohio
South Dakota
Wisconsin

Linda Schmittroth
Editor

Gale Research Inc. • DETROIT • WASHINGTON, D.C. • LONDON

Linda Schmittroth, *Editor*

Gale Research Inc. Staff:

Allison K. McNeill and Carol DeKane Nagel, *Developmental Editors;* Kelle S. Sisung, *Associate Developmental Editor;* Lawrence W. Baker, *Senior Developmental Editor*

Mary Beth Trimper, *Production Director;* Evi Seoud, *Assistant Production Manager;* Mary Kelley, *Production Assistant*

Cynthia Baldwin, *Art Director;* Barbara J. Yarrow, *Graphic Services Supervisor;* Nicholas Jakubiak, *Desktop Publisher;* Willie F. Mathis, *Camera Operator*

> ACCRA Cost of Living Index and ACCRA housing price information reprinted by permission of ACCRA. The ACCRA Cost of Living Index is a measurement of relative price levels for consumer goods and services for a midmanagement standard of living as compared to the national average of 100 for all participating cities. Items priced include groceries, housing, utilities, transportation, health care, and miscellaneous goods and services; taxes are excluded.

While every effort has been made to ensure the reliability of the information presented in this publication, Gale Research Inc. does not guarantee the accuracy of the data contained herein. Gale accepts no payment for listing; and inclusion in the publication of any organization, agency, institution, publication, service, or individual does not imply endorsement of the editors or publisher. Errors brought to the attention of the publisher and verified to the satisfaction of the publisher will be corrected in future editions.

∞™ This book is printed on acid-free paper that meets the minimum requirements of American National Standard for Information Sciences Permanent Paper for Printed Library Materials. ANSI Z39.48-1984.

This publication is a creative work copyrighted by Gale Research Inc. and fully protected by all applicable copyright laws, as well as by misappropriation, trade secret, unfair competition, and other applicable laws. The authors and editors of this work have added value to underlying factual material herein through one or more of the following: unique and original selection, coordination, expression, arrangement, and classification of the information.

Gale Research Inc. will vigorously defend all of its rights in this publication.

Copyright © 1994
Gale Research Inc.
835 Penobscot Bldg.
Detroit, MI 48226-4094

All rights reserved including the right of reproduction in whole or in part in any form.

ISBN 0-8103-7094-8 (4-volume set)
ISBN 0-8103-7095-6 (Volume 1)
ISBN 0-8103-7096-4 (Volume 2)
ISBN 0-8103-7097-2 (Volume 3)
ISBN 0-8103-7098-0 (Volume 4)

Printed in the United States of America
Published simultaneously in the United Kingdom
by Gale Research International Limited
(An affiliated company of Gale Research Inc.)

I(T)P™

The trademark **ITP** is used under license.

10 9 8 7 6 5 4 3 2 1

Volume 3—The Midwest

Contents

Introduction ix

Map and Photo Credits xi

Acknowledgments xiii

ILLINOIS 2
   Chicago 5
   Peoria 23
   Springfield 35

INDIANA 46
   Evansville 49
   Fort Wayne 61
   Gary 73
   Indianapolis 83
   South Bend 99

IOWA 110
   Cedar Rapids 113
   Davenport 127
   Des Moines 137

KANSAS 152
   Kansas City 155
   Topeka 167
   Wichita 179

MICHIGAN 190
   Ann Arbor 193
   Detroit 203
   Grand Rapids 219
   Lansing 231

MINNESOTA 244
   Duluth 247
   Minneapolis 257
   Saint Paul 271

MISSOURI 284
   Kansas City 287
   St. Louis 301
   Springfield 315

NEBRASKA 324
   Lincoln 327
   Omaha 341

NORTH DAKOTA 354
   Fargo 357
   Grand Forks 367

OHIO 378
   Cincinnati 381
   Cleveland 397
   Columbus 409
   Dayton 421
   Toledo 433

SOUTH DAKOTA 446
   Rapid City 449
   Sioux Falls 461

WISCONSIN 472
   Green Bay 475
   Madison 487
   Milwaukee 501
   Racine 515

Cumulative Index 527

Volume 1—The South

Contents

Introduction ix	MISSISSIPPI 270
Map and Photo Credits xi	Jackson 273
Acknowledgments xiii	NORTH CAROLINA 284
	Charlotte 287
ALABAMA 2	Greensboro 301
Birmingham 5	Raleigh 317
Mobile 21	OKLAHOMA 332
ARKANSAS 36	Oklahoma City 335
Little Rock 39	Tulsa 347
DELAWARE 54	SOUTH CAROLINA 360
Wilmington 57	Charleston 363
	Columbia 379
FLORIDA 72	TENNESSEE 394
Jacksonville 75	Chattanooga 397
Miami 89	Knoxville 413
Orlando 105	Memphis 429
St. Petersburg 119	Nashville 445
Tampa 131	TEXAS 462
GEORGIA 146	Austin 465
Atlanta 149	Dallas 479
Marietta 165	Ft. Worth 493
Savannah 179	Houston 507
KENTUCKY 192	San Antonio 523
Lexington 195	VIRGINIA 540
Louisville 209	Richmond 543
	Virginia Beach 559
LOUISIANA 222	WASHINGTON, D.C. 571
Baton Rouge 225	
New Orleans 235	WEST VIRGINIA 584
MARYLAND 252	Charleston 587
Baltimore 255	Cumulative Index 601

Volume 2—The West
Contents

Introduction	ix
Map and Photo Credits	xi
Acknowledgments	xiii
ALASKA	2
Anchorage	5
Fairbanks	17
Juneau	27
ARIZONA	36
Phoenix	39
Scottsdale	51
Tucson	65
CALIFORNIA	78
Anaheim	81
Fresno	93
Los Angeles	103
Oakland	119
Riverside	131
Sacramento	143
San Diego	155
San Francisco	169
San Jose	183
Santa Ana	197
COLORADO	206
Boulder	209
Colorado Springs	219
Denver	231
HAWAII	244
Hilo	247
Honolulu	259
IDAHO	272
Boise	275
MONTANA	286
Billings	289
Butte	299
NEVADA	310
Las Vegas	313
Reno	325
NEW MEXICO	336
Albuquerque	339
Santa Fe	351
OREGON	362
Eugene	365
Portland	373
Salem	385
UTAH	396
Provo	399
Salt Lake City	409
WASHINGTON	422
Seattle	425
Spokane	439
Tacoma	449
WYOMING	460
Cheyenne	463
Cumulative Index	475

Volume 4—The Northeast
Contents

Introduction	ix
Map and Photo Credits	xi
Acknowledgments	xiii

CONNECTICUT 2
   Bridgeport 5
   Danbury 15
   Hartford 25
   New Haven 39
   Stamford 51
   Waterbury 61

MAINE 72
   Augusta 75
   Bangor 85
   Lewiston 97
   Portland 105

MASSACHUSETTS 118
   Boston 121
   Lowell 141
   Springfield 153
   Worcester 165

NEW HAMPSHIRE 176
   Concord 179
   Manchester 191
   Nashua 203
   Portsmouth 213

NEW JERSEY 224
   Atlantic City 227
   Jersey City 239
   Newark 249
   New Brunswick 261
   Trenton 275

NEW YORK 288
   Albany 291
   Buffalo 303
   New York 315
   Rochester 333
   Syracuse 345

PENNSYLVANIA 356
   Allentown 359
   Erie 369
   Harrisburg 379
   Lancaster 391
   Philadelphia 403
   Pittsburgh 419
   Scranton 433

RHODE ISLAND 444
   Newport 447
   Providence 459

VERMONT 472
   Burlington 475
   Montpelier 487
   Rutland 497

Cumulative Index 505

INTRODUCTION

Cities of the United States Is the One-Stop Reference

For information you need on America's top cities, no other single source offers you the coverage *Cities of the United States* provides. To answer your questions about one hundred and fifty-four American urban centers, *Cities of the United States* brings together a wide range of hard-to-locate data in one guide. Each entry, devoted to a single city, organizes descriptions of economic, cultural, geographic, social, and recreational conditions in one place to answer inquiries on a variety of topics. Information about each city's past and present is assembled for you in one handy source. The book's comprehensive scope and in-depth coverage facilitate both quick searches and detailed comparisons.

Key Features Unlock Vital Information

Entries in *Cities of the United States* are arranged under clear headings for easy scanning. You'll find the information you need at a glance. Features include:

- Clearly labeled data sections—The format, which includes sections headed **Geography and Climate, History, Population Profile, Municipal Government, Economy, Education and Research, Health Care, Recreation, Convention Facilities, Transportation,** and **Communications,** makes it easy for you to locate answers to your questions.

- Combined facts and analysis—Fact-packed charts and detailed descriptions bring you the statistics and the rest of the story.

- Enlightening illustrations—Detailed maps help you place cities in their regional contexts while numerous photographs highlight points of interest to you.

- "In Brief" fact sheets—*Cities of the United States* provides you with a concise overview of each state and the cities covered within, presenting essential facts you can absorb at a glance.

Valuable NEW Enhancements

You have responded to the first edition of *Cities of the United States* and, as a result, we have made some changes for the second edition:

- MORE city entries per regional volume—thirty percent more—give you increased coverage in each region.

- NEW directory information at the end of many entry sections provides addresses and phone number for organizations, agencies, and institutions you may need to contact.

- MORE economic information—about such topics as incentive programs, development projects, and largest employers—helps you rate the business climate using criteria that matter to you.

- Extensive NEW indexing guides you not only to main city entries, but also to the hundreds of people and place names that fall within those main entries leading you directly to the information you seek.

- More detailed maps allow you to locate many of the points of interest as described in main city entries. Mileage scales and regional insets allow for greater perspective on the city you are interested in.

- NEW selected bibliography listings suggest fiction and nonfiction titles to read if you wish to learn more about a particular city.

Cities of the United States: A Popular Destination

Whether you are a researcher, traveler, or executive on the move, *Cities of the United States* serves your needs. This is the reference source long sought by a variety of users:

- Business people, market researchers, and other decision-makers will find the current data that helps them stay informed.

- People vacationing, conventioneering, or relocating will consult this source for questions they have about what's new, unique, or significant about where they are going.

- Students, media professionals, and researchers will discover their background work already completed.

Cities Profiled Highlight Yesterday and Today

Published in four volumes, *Cities of the United States* is divided geographically into the South, the West, the Midwest, and the Northeast. The set covers one hundred and fifty-four of the country's largest or fastest-growing cities, or those with a particular historical, political, industrial, or commercial significance.

Entries Compiled With You in Mind

The editors of *Cities of the United States* consulted numerous sources to secure the kinds of data most valuable to you. Each entry gathers together economic information culled in part from the U.S. Department of Labor/ Bureau of Labor Statistics, population figures derived from the U.S. Department of Commerce/Bureau of the Census,* educational and municipal government data supplied by local authorities, historical narrative based on a variety of accounts, and geographical and climatic profiles from the national Oceanic and Atmospheric Administration. Along with material supplied by Chambers of Commerce, Convention and Visitors Bureaus, and other local sources, background information was drawn from periodicals and books chosen for their timeliness and accuracy. *Cities of the United States* saves you time and effort by eliminating the need to piece the picture together bit by bit. *Cities of the United States* provides the whole picture.

Suggestions Are Appreciated

The editors welcome your comments and suggestions. Tell us what you need to find in *Cities of the United States*, and we will shape future editions to best meet the needs of the greatest number of users. Send comments or suggestions to:

> The Editors
> *Cities of the United States*
> Gale Research Inc.
> 835 Penobscot Building
> Detroit, MI 48226-4094

Or, call toll-free at 1-800-347-GALE.

*State mortality and natality figures in this set are from the 1990 U.S. Census; however, city mortality and natality figures are from 1988—the most recent figures available. ACCRA figures are not available for every city.

Map Credits

Regional maps for *Cities of the United States*, 2nd edition, were created by Accurate Art, Inc.

City maps for *Cities of the United States*, 2nd edition, were created by Teresa SanClementi.

★ ★ ★ ★

Photo Credits—Volume 3

Photographs appearing in *Cities of the United States*, 2nd edition, Volume 3—*The Midwest* were received from the following sources:

ILLINOIS:
Chicago—Courtesy Chicago Convention and Tourism Bureau: p. 5, 10, 16, 19;
Peoria—Courtesy Cilco and Peoria Convention and Visitors Bureau: p. 23; and Courtesy Peoria Convention and Visitors Bureau: p. 27, 32;
Springfield—Courtesy Springfield Illinois Convention & Visitors Bureau: p. 35, 43;

INDIANA:
Evansville—Courtesy Evansville Convention & Visitors Bureau: p. 49, 55, 57;
Fort Wayne—Courtesy Fort Wayne Convention and Visitors Bureau: p. 61, 67, 70;
Gary—Courtesy Greater Gary Chamber of Commerce: p. 73, 81;
Indianapolis—Photos by Delores Wright. Courtesy of The Indianapolis Project: p. 83, 87, 93, 97;
South Bend—Courtesy The Chamber of Commerce of St. Joseph County: p. 99, 107;

IOWA:
Cedar Rapids—Courtesy Cedar Rapids Area Convention & Visitors Bureau: p. 113, 117, 122;
Davenport—Courtesy Quad Cities Convention & Visitors Bureau: p. 127, 135;
Des Moines—Courtesy Greater Des Moines Chamber of Commerce Federation: p. 137, 141, 145, 147;

KANSAS:
Kansas City—Courtesy Kansas City Kansas Area Convention and Visitors Bureau, Inc.: p. 155; and Courtesy City of Kansas Information and Research Department: p. 161;
Topeka—Courtesy Greater Topeka Chamber of Commerce: p. 167, 173, 176;
Wichita—Courtesy Wichita Area Chamber of Commerce: p. 179;

MICHIGAN:
Ann Arbor—Photo by Aerial Associates: p. 193;
Detroit—Courtesy City of Detroit Department of Public Information: p. 203, 209, 216;
Grand Rapids—Courtesy Johnson & Dean, Inc.: p. 219; and Courtesy Grand Rapids/Kent County Convention & Visitors Bureau: p. 226;
Lansing—Courtesy Greater Lansing Convention & Visitors Bureau: p. 231, 235, 239;

MINNESOTA:
Duluth—Courtesy Duluth Convention & Visitors Bureau: p. 247;
Minneapolis—Courtesy Greater Minneapolis Convention & Visitors Association: p. 257, 263, 265, 267;
St. Paul—Courtesy Saint Paul Convention and Visitors Bureau: p. 271, 275, 279, 281;

MISSOURI:
Kansas City—Courtesy Kansas City Area Development Council: p. 287, 293, 296;
St. Louis—Courtesy St. Louis Development Corporation: p. 301, 309, 312;
Springfield—Photo by Dan Samples, Ozark Skys Photography: p. 315;

NEBRASKA:
Lincoln—Photo by Tom Tidball: p. 327; Courtesy Lincoln Convention and Visitors Bureau: p. 327, 333, 336;
Omaha—Courtesy Omaha Chamber Services, Inc.: p. 341, 349, 352;

xi

NORTH DAKOTA:
Fargo—Courtesy Fargo Chamber of Commerce: p. 357, 365. Photo by Lowell Wolff: p. 365;
Grand Forks—Courtesy Greater Grand Forks Convention and Visitors Bureau: p. 367, 373, 375;

OHIO:
Cincinnati—Courtesy Greater Cincinnati Convention & Visitors Bureau: p. 381, 387, 391, 393;
Cleveland—Courtesy Convention and Visitors Bureau of Greater Cleveland: p. 397;
Columbus—Courtesy City of Columbus Development Department: p. 409, 415;
Dayton—Photos by UTC Photographic Services, courtesy Dayton Area Chamber of Commerce: p. 421, 429;
Toledo—Courtesy Greater Toledo Convention & Visitors Bureau: p. 433, 439, 442

SOUTH DAKOTA:
Rapid City—Courtesy Rapid City Convention and Visitors Bureau: p. 449, 456;
Sioux Falls—Photo by Antonio Sanchez, p. 461 and photo by Kirby Schultz, p. 469; both courtesy Sioux Falls Convention & Visitors Bureau;

WISCONSIN:
Green Bay—Courtesy Green Bay Area Visitor and Convention Bureau: p. 475, 479, 483, 485;
Madison—Courtesy Greater Madison Convention & Visitors Bureau: p. 487, 491, 493, 499;
Milwaukee—Courtesy Milwaukee Department of City Development: p. 501, 507, 511;
Racine—Courtesy Racine County Convention and Visitors Bureau: p. 515, 519, 524.

Acknowledgments

The editors wish to thank Helen Juntunen, Gail Martin, Mary Reilly McCall, and Virginia Semrow Snyder for their research and proofreading assistance. We are also grateful for the assistance provided by hundreds of helpful Chamber of Commerce and Convention and Visitor Bureau professionals as well as municipal employees for their invaluable generosity and expertise.

CITIES OF THE UNITED STATES

ILLINOIS

Chicago 5
Peoria 23
Springfield 35

The State in Brief

Nickname: Prairie State
Motto: State sovereignty—national union

Flower: Native violet
Bird: Cardinal

Area: 57,918 square miles (1990; U.S. rank: 24th)
Elevation: Ranges from 279 feet to 1,235 feet above sea level
Climate: Temperate, with hot summers and cold, snowy winters

Admitted to Union: December 3, 1818
Capital: Springfield
Head Official: Governor Jim Edgar (R) (until 1995)

Population
  1970: 11,110,285
  1980: 11,427,000
  1990: 11,543,000
  Percent change 1980-1990: Less than 0.5%
  U.S. rank in 1990: 6th
  Percent of residents born in state: 75.4% (1990)
  Density: 205.6 people per square mile (1990; U.S. rank: 11th)
  1991 FBI Crime Index Total: 707,823

Racial and Ethnic Characteristics (1990)
  White: 8,953,000
  Black: 14.8%
  American Indian, Eskimo, Aleut: 0.19%
  Asian and Pacific Islander: 2.50%
  Hispanic (may be of any race): 7.91%

Age Characteristics (1990)
  Population under 5 years old: 887,000
  Population 5 to 17 years old: 2,111,000
  Percent of population 65 years and older: 12.5%
  Median age: 32.8 years
  Voting-age population (1988): 8,636,000 (52.8% of whom cast votes for president; U.S. rank: 22nd

Vital Statistics
  Total number of births (1992): 192,483
  Total number of deaths (1992): 101,590 (1,922 of which were infants under the age of 1 year)
  AIDS cases reported, 1981-1990: 4,298 (U.S. rank: 6th)

Economy
  Major industries: Manufacturing; trade; finance, insurance, and real estate; services
  Unemployment rate: 6.7% (September 1992)
  Per capita income: $15,201 (1989)
  Median household income: $32,252
  Total number of families: 2,944,521 (9.0% of which had incomes below the poverty level; 1989)
  Income tax rate: 3.0%
  Sales tax rate: 5.0%

Chicago

The City in Brief

Founded: 1830 (incorporated 1837)

Head Official: Mayor Richard M. Daley (D) (since 1989)

City Population
 1970: 3,369,000
 1980: 3,005,000
 1990: 2,783,726 (as of 1992, this figure was being challenged)
 Percent change, 1980–1990: −7.4%
 U.S. rank in 1980: 2nd
 U.S. rank in 1990: 3rd (State rank: 1st)

Metropolitan Area Population (CMSA)
 1970: 7,779,000
 1980: 7,937,290
 1990: 8,065,633
 Percent change, 1980–1990: 1.6%
 U.S. rank in 1980: 3rd
 U.S. rank in 1990: 3rd

Area: 227.2 square miles (1990)

Elevation: 578.5 feet above sea level

Average Annual Temperature: 49.2° F

Average Annual Precipitation: 33.34 inches

Major Economic Sectors: Services, wholesale and retail trade, manufacturing, government

Unemployment Rate: 6.2% (September 1992)

Per Capita Income: $12,899 (1989)

1992 (2nd Quarter) ACCRA Average House Price: Not reported

1992 (2nd Quarter) ACCRA Cost of Living Index: Not reported

1991 FBI Crime Index Total: Figures for Illinois were excluded from Uniform Crime Reports

Major Colleges and Universities: University of Chicago; University of Illinois at Chicago; DePaul University; Loyola University of Chicago

Daily Newspapers: *Chicago Tribune; Chicago Sun-Times*

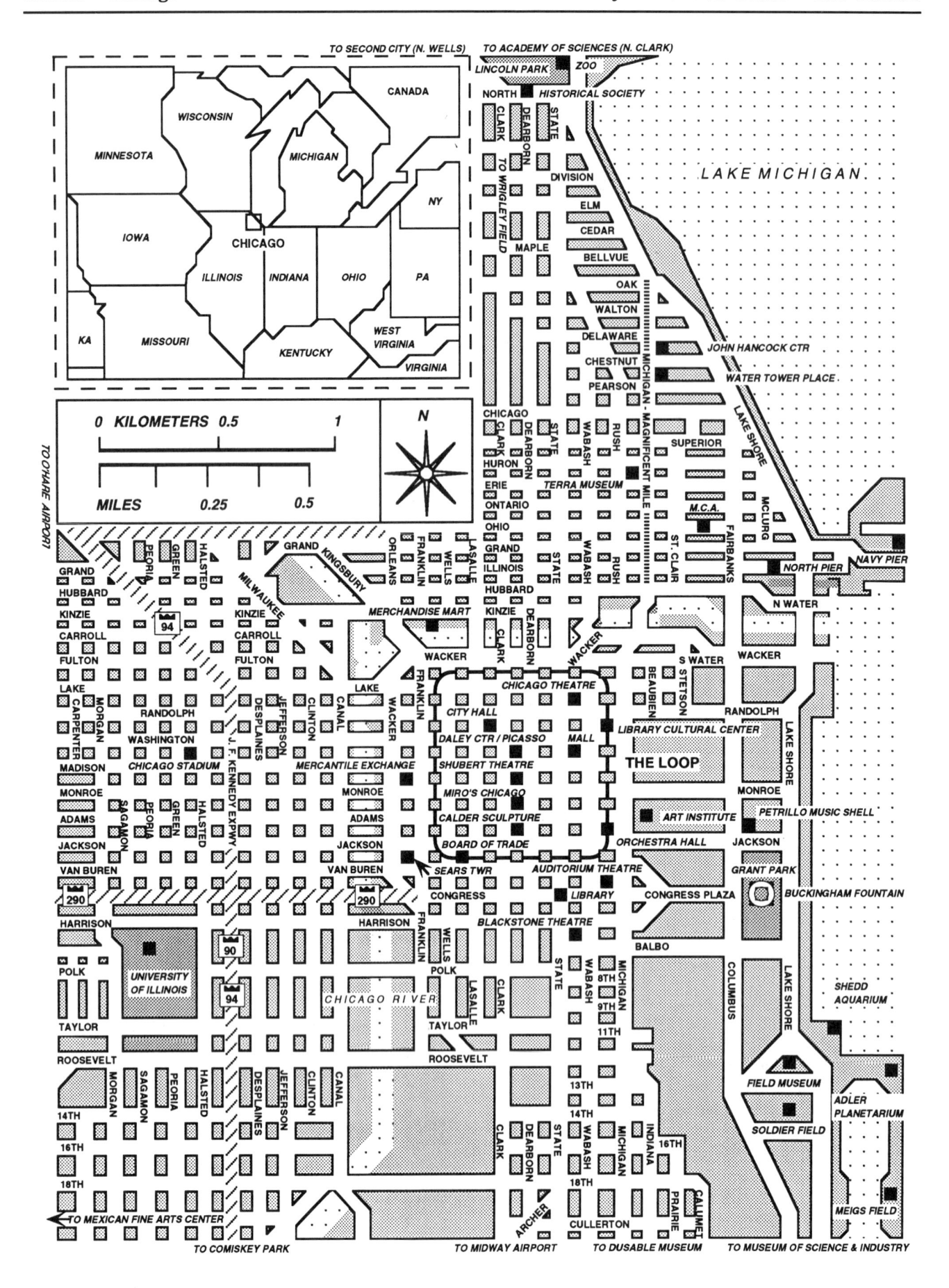

Illinois—Chicago *Cities of the United States • 2nd Edition*

Introduction

Chicago, the seat of Illinois's Cook County and the third largest city in the country, is the focus of a metropolitan statistical area that covers Cook, Du Page, and McHenry counties. "Brawling" was the word Carl Sandburg applied to Chicago in his poem about the city. No longer the "Hog Butcher for the World," in the 1990s Chicago is still an enthusiastically combative city with a fractious political life, although many of the children of the blue-collar work force have entered more genteel occupations. A railroad hub in the latter half of the nineteenth century, when its population had already reached 300,000 people, Chicago became a major force in the nation's development. Today, it is a national transportation, industrial, and financial leader as well as a city of great architectural significance, ethnic diversity, and cultural wealth. The only inland urban area to rank with major East and West Coast metropolises, Chicago has achieved international status through the quality of its cultural institutions and its position as a world financial center.

Geography and Climate

Chicago extends westward on a plain along the southwest shore of Lake Michigan. The climate is continental, with frequently changing weather bringing temperatures that range from relatively warm in the summer to relatively cold in the winter. Temperatures of 96 degrees or higher occur during half the summers; half the winters register a minimum low of minus fifteen degrees. Snowfall near the lake shore is usually heavy because of cold air movement off Lake Michigan. Summer thunderstorms are frequently heavy but variable, as parts of the city may receive substantial rainfall while other sectors will have none. Strong wind gusts in the central business district are caused by the channeling of winds between tall buildings; the nickname "windy city," often applied to Chicago, does not, however, refer to the average wind speed, which is no greater than in many other parts of the country. Chicagoans instead attribute the nickname to their reputed penchant for talking proudly about their city.

Area: 227.2 square miles (1990)

Elevation: 578.5 feet above sea level

Average Temperatures: January, 21.3 F; July, 73.4° F; annual average, 49.2° F

Average Annual Precipitation: 33.34 inches

History

Lakeshore Site Begins With Trading Post, Fort

The earliest known inhabitants of the area they called "Chicaugou" were native Americans of the Illinois tribe. The meaning of the word "Chicaugou" is variously interpreted to mean great, powerful, or strong, depending on the dialect. In the Chippewa dialect the word "shegahg" meant "wild onion"; it is said that an abundance of wild onions grew in the region.

The first people of European descent to reach Chicago were the explorers Father Jacques Marquette and Louis Joliet, who encamped on the Lake Michigan shore at the mouth of the Chicago River in 1673. A century later, in 1783, Jean Baptiste Point Sable, the son of a French merchant from Quebec and a Haitian slave, left New Orleans and established a fur-trading post in the same area. The site was advantageous for transportation, because it afforded a short portage between the Chicago River, part of the Great Lakes waterway, and the Des Plaines River, connected to the Mississippi waterway via the Illinois River. Sable mysteriously vanished in 1800, and John Kinzie, the region's first English civilian settler, took over the trading post. Soon a United States garrison, Fort Dearborn, was built to defend the post. In 1812 angry Potawatomi killed most of the traders, except for the Kinzie family, and destroyed Fort Dearborn, which was rebuilt in 1816.

A survey and plat of the growing settlement were filed in 1830, at which time the area numbered 350 inhabitants. Chicago was chartered as a town in 1833 and rechartered as a city in 1837. The completion of the Illinois-Michigan Canal in 1848 turned the city into a marketing center for grain and food products. The first railroad arrived the same year the canal was opened, and within a decade Chicago was the focal point for 3,000 miles of track. The productive grain industry fed cattle and hogs, and Chicago emerged as the site of a major livestock market and meatpacking industry, surpassing Cincinnati as the nation's pork packer. Cattle merchants formed the Union Stock Yards and Transit Company.

Cyrus McCormick opened a factory in the city in 1847 to manufacture his reaper, leading the way for Chicago to become a farm implements hub. The city also became a leader in the processing of lumber for furniture, buildings, and fencing. Chicago industries outfitted Union troops during the Civil War, when the grain and farm machinery industries also experienced wartime growth. George Pullman began to produce railroad sleeping cars in Chicago in 1867. The next year the city's first blast furnace was built. At this time merchants Potter Palmer, Marshall Field, and Levi Leter began shipping consumer goods to general stores in the Midwest.

Growth Creates Challenges, Opportunities

Chicago's rapid growth resulted in congested residential sectors where the poor were relegated to shabby housing without proper sanitation. Chicago was radically changed, however, on October 8, 1871, by a cataclysmic fire that burned for twenty-seven hours. At that time two-thirds of the city's buildings were made of wood and the summer had been especially dry; high winds spread the fire quickly. Although the stockyards, freight yards, and factory district were spared, Chicago's commercial area was completely destroyed; eight thousand buildings and property valued at just under $200 million were lost. Ninety thousand people were left homeless and three hundred people lost their lives.

Since the city's industrial infrastructure was unscathed by the fire, rebuilding progressed rapidly, and Chicago was essentially rebuilt within a year. When the economic panic of 1873 swept the rest of the nation, Chicago was relatively protected from the ensuing depression. The city's prosperity in the post-fire era was founded on an expansion of its industrial and marketing base. Assembly line techniques were introduced in the meat packing industry, and technological improvements benefitted the steel and farm machinery makers. The United States Steel South Works, based in Chicago, became one of the largest such operations in the world. At that time George Pullman established his Palace Car Company in a nearby town he owned and named after himself, which was later annexed to Chicago.

Chicago celebrated its two decades of growth by sponsoring the World's Columbian Exposition of 1893, which also marked the four hundredth anniversary of Christopher Columbus's discovery of America, and which attracted more than twenty-one million visitors to the city. Chicago at this time was in the forefront of architectural innovation and became known as the birthplace of the skyscraper. Of particular architectural importance is the Chicago Board of Trade, where commodities futures are bought and sold. A politically active city, Chicago underwent a period of reform in the late 1890s. A civil service was inaugurated in 1895, and numerous reform organizations attempted to influence public opinion.

Political Trends Shape City's Future

Five-term Mayor Carter H. Harrison Jr. brought the reform spirit to a high point, but weak law enforcement and other factors allowed gangsters such as Alphonse "Scarface" Capone and John Dillinger to rise to power in the 1920s and 1930s. Chicago was characterized the world over as a gangster headquarters long after Democratic reform Mayor Anton J. Cermak initiated cleanup efforts. He also introduced a style of ward and district politics copied after the New York City Tammany Hall political machine. Cermak was killed by an assassin's bullet intended for President-elect Franklin D. Roosevelt, but Cermak's political organization continued under Mayor Edward J. Kelly.

In 1933 Chicago gained world attention once again when it hosted A Century of Progress, a world exposition that celebrated the city's incorporation as a municipality; Chicago's industrial and financial advances and prosperity were on display despite the era's economic depression. In 1942 scientists working in Chicago produced the first nuclear chain reaction and thus advanced the creation of atomic weaponry and energy. During its history, Chicago has frequently been the site of national political meetings, including the Republican Party gathering to nominate Abraham Lincoln in 1860 and the Democratic Party convention that nominated Hubert H. Humphrey in 1968. The latter brought protestors against the Vietnam War to Chicago's streets and drew national attention to Mayor Richard J. Daley's handling of the demonstrators.

The most powerful symbol of Chicago politics, Daley served as mayor from 1955 until his death in 1976. Daley was a major force in the national Democratic Party and was considered the last "big city boss." His son, Richard M. Daley, ran for Chicago's mayoral office in 1989 in an election that *Time* magazine characterized as "an ethnic power struggle" that divided the city along racial lines. Chicago's first African-American mayor, Harold Washington, had been elected in 1983 and reelected in 1987, but after his death the coalition of blacks and white liberals that had elected him broke down; black voter participation was down from previous elections while, according to *Time*, Daley's "richly financed campaign produced a large turnout among whites. Result: Daley, by 55% to 41%." As mayor of a city known for its widely diverse neighborhoods of Germans, Scandinavians, Irish, Jews, Italians, Poles, Eastern Europeans, Asians, Hispanics, and African-Americans, Daley faces the challenge of uniting the spirit of a divided city entering the 1990s as an internationally important urban center.

Written off for much of his political career as a man capitalizing on his father's name, by 1992 Daley was earning plaudits as a skilled and astute negotiator, with powerful political supporters at the national level.

Chicago made national headlines in 1992 when the Chicago River, polluted by years of dumping by stockyards, the tanning industry, and steel mills, poured through a hole in a tunnel downtown, flooding basements in the city's business district. The city was declared a disaster area.

Historical Information: Chicago Historical Society, Clark Street at North Avenue, Chicago, IL 60614; telephone (312) 642-4600

Population Profile

Metropolitan Area Residents (CMSA)
1970: 7,779,000
1980: 7,937,290
1990: 8,065,633
Percent change, 1980–1990: 1.6%
U.S. rank in 1980: 3rd
U.S. rank in 1990: 3rd

City Residents
1970: 3,369,000
1980: 3,005,000
1990: 2,783,726 (of which, 1,334,705 were males, and 1,449,021 were females) (the population figure was being challenged as of 1992)
Percent change, 1980–1990: –7.4%
U.S. rank in 1980: 2nd
U.S. rank in 1990: 3rd (State rank: 1st)

Density: 12,252.3 persons per square mile (1990)

Racial and ethnic characteristics (1990)
 White: 1,056,048
 Black: 19.2%
 American Indian, Eskimo, Aleut: 0.2%
 Asian and Pacific Islander: 3.2%
 Hispanic (may be of any race): 11.1%

Percent of residents born in state: 72.0% (1990)

Age characteristics (1990)
 Population under 5 years old: 216,868
 Population 18 to 20 years old: 131,754
 Population 21 to 24 years old: 190,642
 Population 25 to 44 years old: 923,994
 Population 45 to 54 years old: 258,532
 Population 55 to 59 years old: 112,421
 Population 60 to 64 years old: 113,497
 Population 65 to 74 years old: 192,202
 Population 75 to 84 years old: 107,458
 Population 85 years and over: 30,552
 Median age: 31.3 years

Births (1988)
 Total number: 56,559

Deaths (1988)
 Total number: 29,671 (of which, 858 were infants under the age of 1 year)

Money income (1989)
 Per capita income: $12,899
 Median household income: $26,301

Total households: 1,020,911
Number of households with income of . . .
  less than $5,000: 108,634
  $5,000 to $9,999: 104,202
  $10,000 to $14,999: 90,406
  $15,000 to $24,999: 183,624
  $25,000 to $34,999: 157,138
  $35,000 to $49,999: 169,045
  $50,000 to $74,999: 130,806
  $75,000 to $99,999: 41,181
  $100,000 to $149,999: 22,556
  $150,000 or more: 13,319
Percent of families below poverty level: 18.3% (62.8% of which were female householder families with related children under 5)
1991 FBI Crime Index Total: Illinois figures were excluded from Uniform Crime Reports.

Municipal Government

The Chicago city government is headed by a strong mayor and a nonpartisan, fifty-member council; the mayor and council members are elected to four-years terms. Mayor Daley has indicated that creating a good climate for business is an essential goal of his administration.

Head Official: Mayor Richard M. Daley (D) (since 1989; current term expires April 1995)

Total Number of City Employees: Approximately 35,000 to 40,000 (1992)

City Information: Municipal Reference Library, City Hall, Room 1004, Chicago, IL 60602; telephone (312)744-4992

Economy

Major Industries and Commercial Activity

Chicago's diversified economy is based on manufacturing, printing and publishing, finance and insurance, and food processing (the city is still considered the nation's "candy capital") as primary sectors. A substantial industrial base and a major inland port contribute to the city's position as a national transportation and distribution center. The source of nationally distributed magazines, catalogs, educational materials, encyclopedias, and specialized publications, Chicago ranks second only to New York in the publishing industry. The city is home to the Federal Reserve Bank, the Chicago Board of Trade, and the Chicago Mercantile Exchange and is in addition the headquarters for forty-three Fortune 500 firms.

Items and goods produced: telephone equipment, musical instruments, surgical appliances, machinery, earth-moving and agricultural equipment, steel, metal products, diesel engines, printing presses, office machines, radios and television sets, auto accessories, chemicals, soap, paint, food products and confections

Incentive Programs—New and Existing Companies

Local Programs—The City of Chicago Department of Planning and Development, consisting of seven divisions, supports business development, economic growth, and job retention. Among the numerous services are: business services and technical assistance in the industrial and commercial sectors; funds for business expansion, relocation, working capital, and other needs; financing for real estate development and physical improvement projects; and opportunities for international trade. Various private entities offer development and funding resources.

State programs—The Illinois Community Development Assistance Program is available to help communities attract or expand local industry. Also available are programs administered by the Illinois Department of Commerce and Community Affairs.

Job training programs—Chicago's world-class educational institutions and research facilities are available to retrain workers. Prairie State 2000 is a state-funded program that assists businesses in retraining employees through low interest loans or grants.

Development Projects

Since 1979 more than $10 billion has been spent on downtown renovation and construction in Chicago, resulting in a thriving center city. The centerpiece of Mayor Daley's economic program is a proposed $10.8 billion airport to be built on the city's southeast side that would permit the existing Midway Airport to become a cargo and freight terminal. It is predicted that this project, which may not be completed until 2005, would bring two-hundred thou-

The trading floor of the Chicago Mercantile Exchange, which was founded in 1919.

sand jobs and $14 billion annually into the local economy.

A contract was awarded in 1991 for renovation of Chicago's Navy Pier. This one-half-mile expanse was built in 1916 and features many handsome landmark structures at its east and west ends. Renovation will augment the pier's recent role as home to several annual expositions and will include a flexible exhibit hall, winter garden, museum, open space, retail shops and restaurants, and parking for eighteen hundred cars, all contained in a series of buildings proceeding along the length of the pier with parks and walkways between them.

Ground was broken in 1992 for the new $55 million home of the Museum of Contemporary Art, a modern, 125,000-square-foot building and one-acre sculpture garden to overlook Lake Michigan.

Sears, Roebuck has renovated parts of the Sears Tower, the world's tallest building, in an effort to lease the more than two million square feet the company is giving up in its move to suburban Chicago. The industrial real estate market in the Chicago area began to pick up somewhat in early 1992 after a series of vacancy rate increases extending to late 1989. Companies continued to move to the suburbs, rental rates in industrial buildings were dropping, and sales prices for industrial property remained flat. Real estate activity by colleges and universities lent a positive note, led by announcement of plans by the University of Chicago's Graduate School of Business to build a 217,000-square-foot downtown facility to house lecture halls, classrooms, a computer center, and reference library. Academic library projects were underway in 1993 and into 1994 at DePaul and Loyola universities.

Economic Development Information: City of Chicago Department of Planning and Development, Long Range Planning Division, 121 N. LaSalle St., Suite 1000, Chicago, IL 60602; telephone (312)744-4445; and Illinois Department of Commerce and Community Affairs, Division of Marketing, State of Illinois Center, 100 Randolph, Suite 3-400, Chicago, IL 60601; telephone (312)917-6659

Commercial Shipping

Since its founding, Chicago has been an important transportation and distribution point; at one time it was a crucial link between the Great Lakes and Mississippi River waterways and today the city ranks among the world's busiest shipping hubs. The city became a world port in 1959 with the opening of the St. Lawrence Seaway, which provides a direct link from the Great Lakes to the Atlantic Ocean. By 1990 Illinois International Port was handling more than one-hundred and fifty overseas ship arrivals annually. The state of Illinois maintains the third-highest combined mileage of railroads and paved highways in the country. Approximately seven hundred and fifty motor freight carriers serve the metropolitan area, and trucking companies ship more than 50 million tons of freight each year; railroads average more than 40 million tons. Chicago's airports handle more than one million metric tons of cargo annually.

Labor Force and Employment Outlook

Chicago has an international reputation as a job market and it continues to attract immigrants from all over the world—one resident in seven is foreign born. As a result of this reputation, Chicago's labor force is growing while employment opportunities are not. The labor force is described as trained, skilled, available, and possessing a good work ethic; more than half of the population has completed high school.

Some two-hundred thousand new jobs are projected for the period 1990–2010. While jobs in finance and insurance continue to open up for the middle class, the less educated, who would have turned to factory work, must now resort to jobs in the less lucrative service industries. As recently as 1960, manufacturing provided thirty-six percent of employment whereas it now accounts for only one job in five.

In a recent Harris poll, Chicago was selected by 404 chief executive officers as the best city in the Midwest for doing business. Downtown Chicago, where industrial spaces are cheaper than in the suburbs, is becoming a mecca for independent businesses. Small, technology-oriented companies are growing.

The following is a summary of data regarding the Chicago metropolitan area labor force as of September 1992.

Size of non-agricultural labor force: 3,114,700

Number of workers employed in . . .
  mining: 1,900
  construction: 122,800
  manufacturing: 529,000
  transportation and public utilities: 198,800
  wholesale and retail trade: 742,200
  finance, insurance, and real estate: 265,300
  services: 884,800
  government: 370,700

Average hourly earnings of production workers employed in manufacturing: $11.73

Unemployment rate: 6.2%

Largest employers (1989)	*Number of employees*
Sears, Roebuck & Co.	38,484
Jewel Food Stores	28,500
A T & T	23,000
Dominick's	18,000
Illinois Bell	18,000
U A L Corp.	17,000
Motorola, Inc.	14,000
First Chicago Corp.	13,466

Cost of Living

In 1992 Chicago imposed a 5.0% tax on out-of-state telephone calls in an effort to replace half of a $49 million cutback in revenue sharing from the state.

The following is a summary of data regarding several key cost of living factors in the Chicago area.

1992 (2nd Quarter) ACCRA Cost of Living Index: Not reported

1992 (2nd Quarter) ACCRA Average House Price: Not reported

State income tax rate: 3.0%

State sales tax rate: 5.0% (a 5.0% tax on out-of-state telephone services is levied by both the city and state)

Local income tax rate: None

Local sales tax rate: 3.0%

Property tax rate: 1.68% per $100,000 of equalized assessed valuation (1989)

Economic Information: Economic Development Commission of the City of Chicago, 1503 Merchandise Mart, Chicago, IL 60654; telephone (312) 744-9550; City of Chicago Department of Planning and Development, Long Range Planning Division, 121 N. LaSalle St., Ste. 1000, Chicago, IL 60602; telephone (312) 744-4445

Education and Research

Elementary and Secondary Schools

The Chicago Public Schools District 299, the largest public elementary and secondary educational system in Illinois, is administered by an eleven-member school board that appoints a superintendent. Because of the city's large foreign-born population, the school system employs bilingual teachers in twenty languages. Special schools include Chicago High School for Agricultural Sciences, situated on the last farm in the city of Chicago, which prepares students for jobs in "anything to do with food and fiber."

The following is a summary of data regarding the Chicago public schools as of the 1992–1993 school year.

Total enrollment: 411,582

Number of facilities
  elementary schools: 523
  high schools: 77

Student teacher ratio: elementary, 20.9:1; high school, 18.7:1

Teacher salaries
  minimum: $27,241
  maximum: $48,467

Funding per pupil: $5,548

Well over one hundred private schools and more than two hundred parochial schools in the Chicago metropolitan area offer educational alternatives at all grade levels, from pre-school through twelfth grade.

Public Schools Information: Chicago Public Schools, 1819 West Pershing Road, Chicago, IL 60609; telephone (312) 535-8080

Colleges and Universities

Chicago-area institutions of higher education include private, state, and religious universities of national note. The University of Chicago, founded with an endowment by John D. Rockefeller in 1891, enjoys an international reputation for pioneering science research and the "Chicago plan" in undergraduate education. The University claims more than sixty Nobel laureates—far more than any other university in the country. The university administers seven professional schools as well as advanced scholarship and research centers, and operates the Argonne National Laboratory. The University of Illinois at Chicago enrolls more than twenty-five thousand students earning bachelor's, master's, and doctoral degrees and first professional degrees in dentistry, medicine, and pharmacy. The city's two leading Catholic institutions are DePaul University, offering undergraduate, master's and doctorate and law programs, and Loyola University of Chicago, which awards bachelor's, master's, and doctoral degrees, first-professional degrees in dentistry, law, and medicine, and a master's degree in divinity. The Illinois Institute of Technology offers professional programs in the sciences, engineering, law, art, and architecture. The Art Institute of Chicago holds national stature in art instruction.

The Chicago City-Wide College offers two-year programs enrolling fifty thousand students a year. Among the city's numerous other institutions of higher learning are Roosevelt University, Chicago State University, Columbia College, Mundelein College, Northeastern Illinois University, and St. Xavier College. Northwestern University is located in nearby Evanston.

Libraries and Research Centers

In late 1991, amid much fanfare and as other cities were cutting back services, Chicago opened the doors of the Harold Washington Library Center, the largest municipal library building in the Western Hemisphere and the culmination of a $175 million project that also included the renovation and construction of several branch libraries in the eighty-four-branch public library system. Named for the city's first African-American mayor, a major supporter of the project, the library features such innovations as drive-up service, a learning center and lunchroom for children, a winter garden, music practice rooms, a restaurant, study alcoves, and a computer center for patrons. The building houses a variety of artwork and is itself considered a work of art. On opening day, the library's collection held about two million books. A 1991 budget of $11 million, said to be the highest in the country, insures the addition of more items to a collection of six million. The special collections department's holdings include Civil War and American history research materials; first editions of local authors; the Chicago Blues Archive; the Jazz, Blues, and Gospel Hall of Fame; a Chicago theater collection; and videos of dance performances. It is projected that the library will serve fourteen thousand patrons a day. Some observers have contended that the new facility has drained resources from the eighty-four branches that serve the majority of the library system's patrons.

The approximately 275 other libraries located in Chicago are affiliated with such entities as government agencies, colleges and universities, cultural and historical societies, professional organizations, research institutes, religious organizations, hospitals and medical associations, private corporations, and law firms.

The University of Chicago, internationally recognized for excellence in education and research, maintains a central library facility with nearly five million volumes, more than fifty-three thousand periodical subscriptions, and special collections in American and British literature, American history, theology and biblical criticism, American and British drama, and Continental literature; six departmental branches include the D'Angelo Law Library. The Newberry Library, founded in 1887, holds more than 1.3 million volumes; among the special collections are materials pertaining to Americana and American Indians.

One of the largest research centers in Chicago is the Center for Research, which houses a library of more than 3.2 million books and periodicals; fields of study include Africa, South Asia, South East Asia, Latin America, and war crime trials. The Lithuanian Research and Studies Center provides resources pertaining to Lithuanian history and culture. The National Opinion Research Center collects current opinion poll reports conducted for commercial television networks, newspapers, state governments, professional pollsters such as Gallop and Harris, and others. The Chicago Historical Society maintains research collections on Chicago, the Civil War, Abraham Lincoln, Illinois, and United States history to 1865.

Chicago-area corporate research centers include those maintained by Bell Labs, Nalco Chemical, the ITT Research Institute, the Institute of Gas Technology, and Motorola. Others include the Illinois State Psychiatric Institute, the Institute for Psychoanalysis, and the Institute on the Church in Urban-Industrial Society.

Public Library Information: Chicago Public Library, 425 North Michigan Avenue, Chicago, IL 60611; telephone (312) 269-2900

Health Care

Chicago ranks among the country's leading centers for health care and referral as well as for medical training and research. In 1990, seventy-eight hospitals in the metropolitan area provided almost twenty-five thousand beds.

The University of Chicago Hospitals, nationally recognized for training and research, are associated with the University of Chicago colleges of medicine, dentistry, nursing, and pharmacy; individual facilities are Bernard Mitchell Hospital, Wyler Children's Hospital, and Chicago Lying-in Hospital. A full range of general and specialized services are available as well as a chemical dependence program, corporate health services, an eating disorders program, geriatric and health evaluation services, and centers for treatment of kidney stones and sexually transmitted diseases.

Among Chicago's major privately-run health care facilities is Rush-Presbyterian—St. Luke's Medical Center, which is affiliated with Rush Medical College and Rush School of Nursing. The hospital operates centers for treatment of cancer, multiple sclerosis, cardiac ailments, sleep disorders, alcohol and substance abuse, Alzheimer's disease, epilepsy, and arthritis. The complex also houses organ and bone marrow transplant units as well as the Chicago and Northeastern Regional Poison Control Center; ten suburban clinic are located throughout the metropolitan area.

The city's largest publicly-operated facility is Cook County Hospital. Other hospitals within the Chicago city limits are Children's Memorial Hospital, Columbus Hospital, Edgewater Hospital, Grant Hospital of Chicago, Holy Cross Hospital, John F. Kennedy Medical Center, Michael Reese Hospital and Medical Center, Mercy Hospital and Medical Center, Norwegian American Hospital, Ravenswood Hospital Medical Center, Roseland Community Hospital, Saint Joseph Hospital and Health Care Center, South Chicago Community Hospital, and Weiss Memorial Hospital. The Rehabilitation Institute of Chicago was selected by doctors in a 1992 *U.S. News & World Report* survey as one of the best facilities of its kind in the country.

Recreation

Sightseeing

Chicago is an ethnically diverse, architecturally important, and culturally rich city. It can be appreciated from the observation floor of the Sears Tower, at 110 stories the country's tallest manmade structure. In fact, three of the world's five tallest buildings are located in Chicago, along with the tallest apartment building, the largest hotel, the largest commercial structure, and the largest post office. Guided sightseeing tours are available for viewing the city's architecture, finance and business districts, ethnic neighborhoods, cultural institutions, and even gangland sites from the Prohibition Era.

The distinctive Chicago School of Architecture, with its aesthetic credo, "form follows function," was shaped by such masters as Louis Sullivan, Frank Lloyd Wright, and a later functionalist architect, Ludwig Mies van der Rohe—all of whom designed buildings in the city and produced in Chicago a veritable living architectural museum. Also important are the city's outdoor sculpture and art works. Pablo Picasso's gift to Chicago, a fifty-foot tall sculpture of rusted steel at the Civic Center Plaza, has become a symbol of the city's modernity. Other works include Claes Oldenburg's *Batcolumn,* Alexander Calder's fifty-three foot high red Flamingo stabile, Marc Chagall's *Four Seasons* mosaic, Louise Nevelson's *Dawn Shadow,* Joan Miro's *Chicago,* and Jean Dubuffet's *Monument with Standing Beast.*

The Shedd Aquarium, the world's largest indoor aquarium, has earned the title "Ocean by the Lake" because it contains more than two hundred fresh- and salt-water exhibits with more than six thousand aquatic animals. A major attraction is the ninety-thousand-gallon coral reef exhibit that features daily feedings. Next to the Shedd Aquarium, the Adler Planetarium sits on a peninsula that juts a half-mile into Lake Michigan; the planetarium offers a spectacular view of the heavens from its Sky Theater. The Museum of Science and Industry is the Midwest's

Chicago's Water Tower Pumping Station, built in 1869 to supply the city with drinking water from Lake Michigan; shown here at night.

leading tourist attraction, housing two thousand exhibits in seventy-five major exhibition halls. Among the attractions are the *Apollo 8* spacecraft, a captured German U-boat, and a sixteen-foot walk-though model of a human heart. The Chicago area's two zoos are the Brookfield Zoo and the Lincoln Park Zoo; the latter is a 35-acre lakeside park with two thousand animals and a multi-story Great Ape House. Just north of the city, the Chicago Botanic Garden features an international collection of flora in twenty garden settings on 300 acres.

Arts and Culture

Chicago's major cultural institutions rank with the best in the world. The Chicago Symphony Orchestra plays a season of concerts at Orchestra Hall from December to June and performs summer concerts at Ravinia Park in Highland Park. Equally prestigious is the Lyric Opera of Chicago, which stages classical and innovative operas at the Civic Opera House. The Chicago Sinfonietta is a mid-sized orchestra that plays the music of Haydn, Mozart, Beethoven, and others at various Chicago locations.

Other musical offerings range from Dixieland jazz imported by the late Louis Armstrong to the electrified urban blues sound of Muddy Waters, frequently referred to as Chicago Blues. All-night jazz and blues clubs are a Chicago tradition. The Ravinia Festival is a summer season of outstanding classical, popular, and jazz concerts performed by well-known artists. The Rosemont Horizon is a showcase for rock concerts.

More than one hundred producing theaters delight Chicago audiences with fare ranging from serious to satirical. The Goodman Theatre, Chicago's oldest and largest professional theater, presents a season of classical and modern dramatic productions. Chicago theater is perhaps best represented by Steppenwolf Theatre, a Tony Award-winning repertory company that focuses on new plays, neglected works, and re-interpretations of masterpieces; several of its actors and directors have worked in New York theater and Hollywood films. Since the mid-1970s Second City, a resident comedy company that produces biting satires, has had a direct influence on American comedy as its members have gone on to star on the "Saturday Night Live" and "SCTV" television programs and in Hollywood movies. Candlelight Dinner Playhouse presents dinner and Broadway musicals. Chicago's historic and architecturally significant theater houses include the De Paul Blackstone Theatre, Chicago Theatre, Shubert Theatre, and Auditorium Theatre, built by Adler and Sullivan in 1889. Chicago's active theater scene includes numerous young companies and dinner theater groups. There are several dance companies in the city.

The Art Institute of Chicago is another local institution with an international reputation. Its collection is recognized for French Impressionist and Post-Impressionist paintings and for comprehensive holdings of American arts and photographs. New galleries of Chinese, Japanese, and Korean art have recently opened there. The Mexican Fine Arts Center Museum is the first Mexican museum in the United States. Chicago's love of art is evidenced in the Loop's parking garage, where famous paintings are reproduced. North of the Loop, a new art district called Su-Hu (located at Superior and Huron streets) contains more than seventy-five art galleries occupying converted manufacturing lofts.

The Field Museum of Natural History, founded in 1893, is rated among the top four natural history museums in the world; its holdings number more than nineteen million artifacts and specimens from the fields of anthropology, botany, geology, and zoology. A scientific research institution, the Field Museum examines life and culture from pre-history to the present time.

The Chicago Academy of Sciences, founded in 1857, features natural science exhibits as well as timely scientific displays. Among the special attractions are lifesize dioramas on natural areas of the Great Lakes and the children's gallery with its lifelike animated dinosaurs and prehistoric creatures. The city's oldest cultural institution is the Chicago Historical Society; its galleries are filled with folk art, furniture, costumes, and manuscripts and a unique audio-visual presentation of the Great Chicago Fire. The DuSable Museum is the nation's first museum dedicated to preserving, displaying, and interpreting the culture, history, and achievements of African-Americans. The Museum of Contemporary Art focuses on contemporary works that are often risk-taking and controversial. The Chicago Public Library Cultural Center presents more than five hundred free programs and exhibitions annually.

Arts and Culture Information: Chicago Council on Fine Arts hotline, telephone (312)346-3278; Curtain Call, telephone (312)977-1755; Jazz Hotline, telephone (312)666-1881; Archicenter, at 330 South

Dearborn, has maps and information on architecture and art tours; telephone (312)922-3432

Festivals and Holidays

The Mayor's Office of Special Events, The Chicago Park District, and the city's major cultural institutions sponsor events throughout the year, but special summer programming is designed to tap into Chicago's heritage and to attract tourists. The Spring Festival of Dance brings renowned companies from throughout the country to Chicago. The Chicago Blues Festival takes place the second weekend in June at the Petrillo Music Shell and brings the best blues musicians to one of the world's blues capitals for concerts, food, and exchange of memorabilia. Viva Chicago, held in September, is a festival celebrating Latino music, food, and arts and crafts at the Petrillo Music Shell. Other music festivals held annually in Chicago include Chicago Gospel Festival (June), Chicago Country Music Festival (July), and Chicago Jazz Festival (September).

Chicago's city parks offer a wealth of free activities in the summer, such as the Grant Park Symphony Orchestra's four weekly concerts at the nation's largest free symphonic music festival.

Festivals Information: Mayor's Office of Special Events, City of Chicago, 121 N. LaSalle, Room 703, Chicago, IL 60602; telephone (312)744-3315; Events Hotline, (312)744-3370

Sports for the Spectator

Chicago fields at least one team in each of the major professional sports and is one of only three cities in the United States with two professional baseball teams in the Major League Baseball Association. The Chicago Cubs compete in the eastern division of the National League and play their home games at Wrigley Field, a turn-of-the-century steel and concrete structure where seats are close to the field. The Chicago White Sox of the western division of the American League play their home games at Comiskey Park on the city's South Side. The Chicago Bears of the National Football League's National Conference compete in central division home games at Soldier Field in Burnham Park. The Chicago Blackhawks of the National Hockey League and the Chicago Bulls of the National Basketball Association play their home schedules at Chicago Stadium.

The Old Style Marathon, one of the world's premier races, follows a course through all of Chicago's major ethnic neighborhoods, finishing in Lincoln Park. Autoracing fans can view competition at Raceway Park in Calumet Park and Santa Fe Speedway in Hinsdale. Horseracing action takes place at Arlington International Racecourse, Balmoral Park, Hawthorne Race Track, Maywood Park Race Track, and Sportsman's Park. Betting action takes place at Winner's Circle.

Sports for the Participant

The Chicago Park District maintains some 550 parks spread out over 7,000 acres, including Lincoln Park, Grant Park, Jackson Park, and Washington Park. Located in the metropolitan area are forest preserves, golf courses, tennis courts, swimming pools and lagoons, and athletic fields. In the summertime Chicago becomes the country's largest beach town as sun fanciers flock to nearly 30 miles of lakefront beaches and yacht clubs to enjoy watersports. The fishing season on Lake Michigan runs year round, while the lake's boating season generally extends from May 15 to October 15; the Park District maintains jurisdiction over the city's eight harbors. A major attraction is the annual Chicago to Mackinac Island sailboat race, during which participants sail the length of Lake Michigan. Kiddieland amusement park offers rides and attractions.

Shopping and Dining

Chicago's commercial district, formerly confined to the area known as The Loop, which was defined by a circuit of elevated trains, now pushes north of the Chicago River to Oak Street. Known as the "Magnificent Mile," the shopping area is considered the Rodeo Drive of the Midwest. Here, in and around buildings of architectural interest, are located some of the world's finest specialty stores. Water Tower Place on North Michigan is a seven-level modern shopping emporium with two major department stores, 125 shops, and eight restaurants. A block away, Chicago Place, an eight-level mall and the newest addition to the shopping scene, features eighty shops anchored by Saks Fifth Avenue, Ann Taylor, and Louis Vuitton. At 900 North Michigan Shops can be found Bloomingdale's, Gucci, and Henri Bendel. Newly refurbished State Street, located nearby, offers a seven-block shopping experience at such landmarks as Marshall Fields and Pirie, Scott & Company. On the waterfront, North Pier mall offers shops as well as museums and art galleries in a renovated warehouse. High fashion is the focus at the boutiques and salons in the Oak Street shopping area.

Field Museum of Natural History, said to be the largest Georgian marble building in the world.

On North Orleans Street are Merchandise Mart, the world's largest wholesale center, and Chicago Apparel Center.

Chicago is served by some of the nation's finest restaurants. Every type of cuisine, from ethnic dishes to traditional American fare, is available at restaurants in metropolitan Chicago. The city's eateries, housed in elegant turn-of-the century hotels, modern chrome and glass structures, and neighborhood cafes, are recognized for consistently high quality. *Food and Wine* magazine's 1992-1993 list of the top twenty-five restaurants in America included Chicago's Ambria; other restaurants judged worthy of the Distinguished Restaurants of North America Award were Benkay, Charlie Trotter's, The Dining Room (Ritz-Carlton Hotel), Entre Nous (Fairmont Hotel), Gordon, Jackie's, La Tour (Park Hyatt), Nick's Fish Market, Restaurant Suntory, Seasons (Four Seasons Hotel), and Yoshi's Cafe. Once known as the city of steak houses by the dozens, Chicago's superior steak restaurants now include Morton's of Chicago, Gibsons Steakhouse, the Palm Restaurant, Eli's The Place for Steak, Chicago Chop House, and The Saloon. The deep-dish style of pizza originated in Chicago.

Visitor Information: Chicago Convention and Tourism Bureau, McCormick Place-on-the Lake, Chicago, IL 60616; telephone (312) 567-8500

Convention Facilities

Chicago, one of the most popular convention cities in the United States, is home to McCormick Place, the largest exhibition center in North America. Set on the edge of Lake Michigan, McCormick Place contains 1.6 million square feet of space, having been augmented in 1986 by North Hall, a two-level expansion that added more than five-hundred thousand square feet. The entire complex consists of four sections, each with exhibition halls and meeting rooms. A planned expansion, scheduled for completion in 1996, will add 1.3 million square feet. McCormick Place East houses the Aries Crown Theatre. Chicago is known for its mix of gracious dowager hotels and modern glass towers with spectacular views of Lake Michigan. As a hotel city, it is constantly expanding, with more than a half-dozen major hotels being constructed in the last few years. The Sheraton Chicago Hotel and Towers, the first new convention hotel to have been built in Chicago in fourteen years, opened in March 1992.

Expocenter/Chicago, located at O'Hare Airport, features 120,000 square feet of exhibit space. The single-level facility can accommodate up to 617 booths; a hotel is on the premises, and parking for five thousand cars is available nearby. Special meeting facilities are available at museums, theaters, stadiums, corporations, and colleges and universities in the Chicago area.

Convention Information: Chicago Convention and Tourism Bureau, McCormick Place-on-the-Lake, Chicago, IL 60616; telephone (312)567-8500

Transportation

Approaching the City

The destination of the majority of air traffic into Chicago is O'Hare International Airport, located 17 miles northwest of downtown, where most major domestic and international commercial carriers schedule more than eight-hundred thousand flights annually. One of the busiest air facilities in the world, O'Hare has been expanded to accommodate the more than sixty million passengers who each year pass through the gates of the architecturally impressive terminal. Several other commuter and general aviation airports are located throughout the Chicago metropolitan area; among them are Midway Airport, twenty minutes from downtown, whose future is uncertain since the demise of Midway Airlines in 1991; and Meigs Field.

Passenger rail service into Chicago is provided by American-European Express and by Amtrak from cities in all regions of the United States; the Chicago South Shore and South Bend is an intercity commuter rail line. The Regional Transit Authority (RTA) operates bus and rapid-transit service into the city from the distant suburbs. Regional rail transportation is available through Metra.

A somewhat complex network of interstate highways facilitates access into the metropolitan area as well as the Loop district. Approaching from the northwest is I-94, which merges with the John F. Kennedy Expressway leading downtown. I-294 (the Tri-State Tollway), an outerbelt on the west side, joins I-80 to the south. Other westerly approaches are: State Road

5, the East-West Tollway, which becomes I-290; I-90, the North-West Tollway, which intersects I-290; and I-55, the Adlai Stevenson Expressway. Approaches from the south include I-94, the Calumet Expressway; I-57; and I-90, the Chicago Skyway; all of these merge with the Dan Ryan Expressway leading into the city. Running south of Chicago is I-80, which connects with I-55, I-57, I-90, and I-94; near the Indiana border I-80 joins I-90 to become the Northern Indiana Toll Road.

Traveling in the City

Chicago streets conform to a consistent grid pattern; major thoroughfares include east-west State Street and north-south Madison Street, which intersect downtown and provide the numerical orientation for all addresses. Lake Shore Drive, affording a scenic view of Lake Michigan and the skyline, extends along the lake from the northern to the southern city limits.

METRA (Metropolitan Rail) runs commuter trains and buses. The Chicago Transit Authority (CTA) operates bus, subway, and elevated train (the "El") routes between the Loop and the nearby suburbs. Cabs are readily available in the downtown area, and a downtown trolley system was in the planning stages in 1992. American Sightseeing conducts four-hour tours daily from the Congress Hotel. Parking in Chicago can be problematic; for this reason several city-run parking garages are available.

Communications

Newspapers and Magazines

Chicago's major daily newspapers are the *Chicago Tribune* and the *Chicago Sun-Times,* both of which are distributed in morning and Sunday editions. A number of African-American newspapers circulate regularly; among them is the *Daily Defender,* established in 1907. More than a hundred community and foreign-language newspapers are published in the city, serving Lithuanian, Polish, Ukrainian, and Hispanic-speaking residents, among others. *Chicago Magazine,* published monthly, covers topics of interest to metropolitan area readers. *The Reader*, published weekly, serves as an alternative newspaper.

Chicago is a national leader in publishing and printing; more than six hundred newspapers and periodical originate in the city, including *Ebony,* which circulates extensively nationwide. Specialized magazines cover a comprehensive range of subjects such as health care, international trade, consumer issues, industry and trade, agriculture, politics, business, and professional information. The University of Chicago is the source of several scholarly journals; among the areas covered are philology, literature, the sciences, ethics, business, labor, history, library science, medicine, and law.

Television and Radio

Chicago is a broadcast media center for a wide region of the Midwest. Television viewers receive programming from thirteen commercial, public, and independent stations based in the Chicago metropolitan area. Nine AM and eleven FM radio stations broadcast a complete selection of formats, including all major types of music, news, talk shows, public interest features, and market reports. Chicago Theatres on the Air is a live radio theater series featuring local companies whose performances are recorded and later aired nationwide.

Media Information: Chicago Tribune, 435 North Michigan, Chicago, IL 60611; telephone (312)222-3232; and, *Chicago Sun-Times,* 401 North Wabash, Chicago, IL 60611; telephone (312)321-3000; and, *Chicago,* 414 North Orleans, Chicago, IL 60610; telephone (312)222-8999

Selected Bibliography

Bellow, Saul, *The Adventures of Augie March* (New York: Avon, 1977, 1953)

Duneier, Mitchell, *Slim's Table: Race, Respectability, and Masculinity* (Chicago: University of Chicago Press, 1992)

Sinclair, Upton, *The Jungle* (Urbana: University of Illinois Press, 1988)

Peoria

The City in Brief

Founded: 1819 (incorporated, 1835)

Head Official: City Manager Thomas Mikulecky (NP) (since 1987)

City Population
 1970: 127,000
 1980: 124,600
 1990: 113,504
 Percent change, 1980–1990: −8.6%
 U.S. rank in 1980: 126th
 U.S. rank in 1990: 157th (State rank: 3rd)

Metropolitan Area Population
 1970: 342,000
 1980: 366,000
 1990: 339,172
 Percent change, 1980–1990: −7.3%
 U.S. rank in 1980: 90th
 U.S. rank in 1990: 108th

Area: 40.9 square miles (1990)
Elevation: 652 feet above sea level
Average Annual Temperature: 50.4° F (mean)
Average Annual Precipitation: 34.89 inches

Major Economic Sectors: Services, trade, manufacturing

Unemployment Rate: 6.0% (September 1992)

Per Capita Income: $14,039 (1989)

1992 (2nd Quarter) ACCRA Average House Price: $127,700

1992 (2nd Quarter) ACCRA Cost of Living Index: 104.6 (U.S. Average = 100.0)

1991 FBI Crime Index Total: Illinois figures were excluded from 1991 Uniform Crime Reports totals

Major Colleges and Universities: Bradley University; Eureka College; Illinois Central College

Daily Newspaper: *Journal Star*

Illinois—Peoria

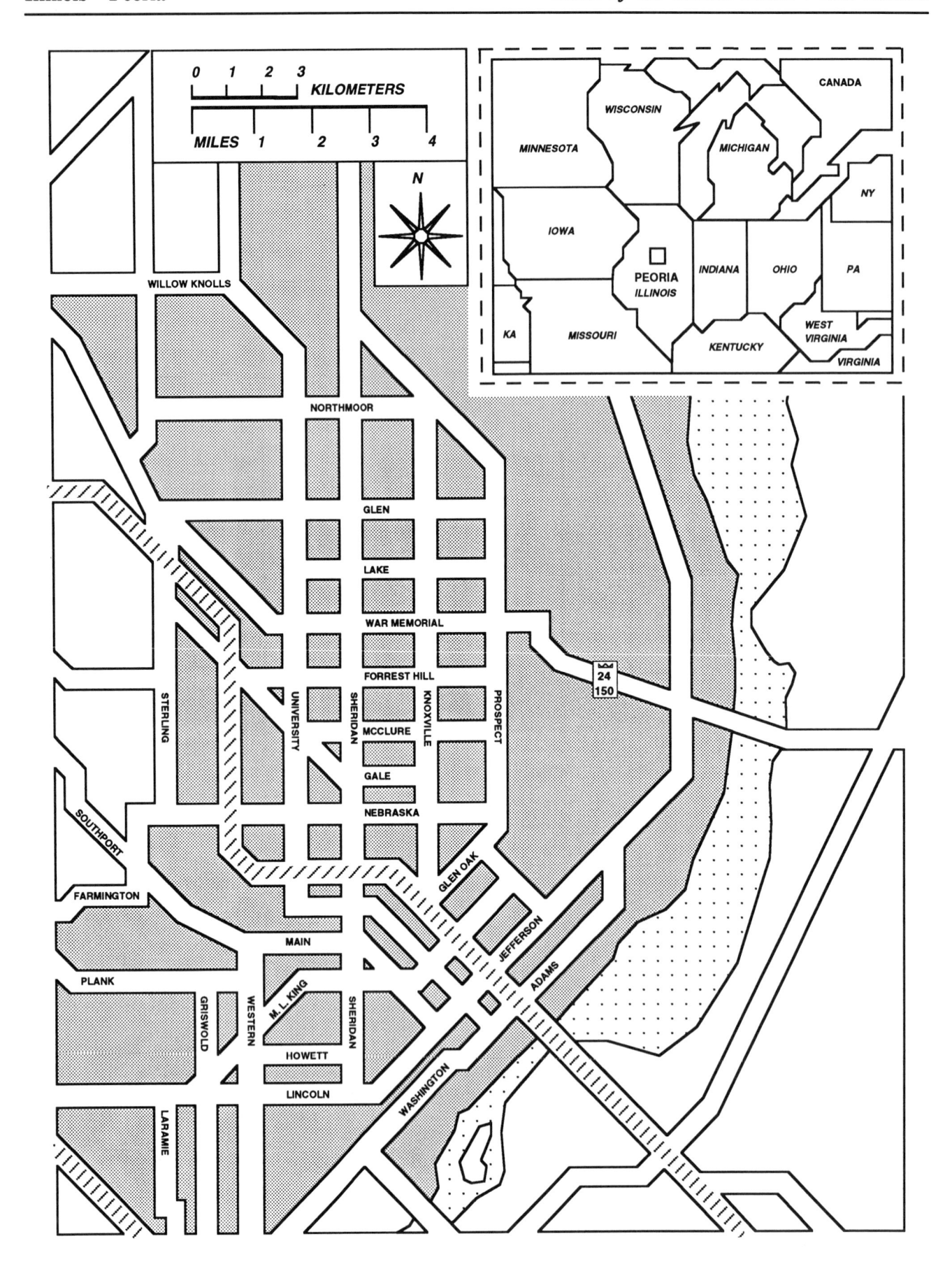

Cities of the United States • 2nd Edition

Introduction

Peoria is the seat of Peoria County and the center of an urban complex consisting of Peoria Heights, West Peoria, Bartonville, Bellevue, East Peoria, Creve Coeur, and Pekin. The city is considered the oldest continuously inhabited American community west of the Allegheny Mountains. Another of Peoria's distinctions is its typicality: in terms of such demographic characteristics as median age and purchasing patterns, the city's general makeup is almost identical to that of the United States as a whole, thus making it an ideal test market for consumer researchers. Peoria was described in the November 1991 *Kiplinger's Personal Finance Magazine* as a super city "where people are moving and opportunity is knocking."

Geography and Climate

Peoria is set in a level tableland surrounded by gently rolling terrain on the Illinois River. The continental climate produces changeable weather and a wide range of temperature extremes. June and September are generally the most pleasant months; an extended period of warm, dry weather occurs during Indian Summer in late October and early November. Precipitation is heaviest during the growing season and lowest in midwinter. Snowfall rarely exceeds twenty inches.

Area: 40.9 square miles (1990)

Elevation: 652 feet above sea level

Average Temperatures: January, 25.4° F; July, 73.0° F; annual average, 50.4° F (mean)

Average Annual Precipitation: 34.89 inches (mean snowfall, 25.8 inches; mean rainfall, 35.13 inches)

History

French Explore Peoria Tribe Territory

The city's name originated from the Peoria native Americans who lived in the region at the time it was first visited by the French explorers Louis Joliet and Pere Marquette in 1673 during their exploration of the Mississippi River. Six years later another French explorer, Robert Cavelier, sieur de La Salle, was forced by inclement weather to land in the area with his party, which included Father Louis Hennepin and Henri de Tonty (Tonti). La Salle built Fort Crevecoeur (Heartbreak) on the east bank of the river before departing for Canada.

In 1682 La Salle returned and opened a trading post at Starved Rock, which was then named Fort St. Louis, located close to the present city of La Salle, Illinois. The fort was renamed Fort Pimiteoui and was moved to the west shore of Lake Peoria in 1691. The French settlement that grew up around the fort came to be known as Old Peoria Fort and Village. Given its excellent river location, the fort prospered as a transportation link to other French outposts in the New World. French settlement continued until 1796 despite control of the region first by Great Britain and then by the United States. In 1778 Jean Baptiste Maillet moved the settlement one mile farther down the river, naming it La Ville de Maillet; however, the French referred to it as Au Pe, or Fort Le Pe.

The town was partly burned and its inhabitants arrested when Captain Thomas E. Craig suspected indirect local support of the British during the War of 1812. The heart of present-day Peoria can be traced to the construction of Fort Clark, named after George Rogers Clark, in 1813. The first American settlers arrived in 1819. Later, New England farmers travelled westward to Peoria in search of new land. Peoria County was created in 1825 and named the county seat, with the French-Indian name of Peoria being officially adopted. Because of the broadness of the river at Peoria, the townsite grew faster than others in north central Illinois. Peoria was incorporated as a town in 1835 and chartered as a city ten years later.

Economic Growth Paired with Historic Events

Early industries that fueled the economy were pork and beef packing, followed by farm implement manufacturing. Peoria is situated over a deep, self-replenishing well system that yields potable water. In 1844 the first distillery opened, and the city soon became a world leader in the manufacture of distilled spirits. Peoria Mineral Springs remains one of the nation's oldest commercial bottling companies as well as a supplier of water to local breweries.

The city of Peoria has been the site of historic events and the home of famous Americans. In 1854 Abraham Lincoln, rebutting a speech by Stephen Douglas, for the first time publicly denounced slavery as incompatible with American institutions; this clash predated the famous Lincoln-Douglas debates by four years. The original mold strain for penicillin was discovered by scientists in Peoria. The first black person to vote in the United States did so in Peoria on April 4, 1870. Peorian Herb Jamison was a medalist in the first modern Olympics in Greece in 1896. A short list of native Peorians include the late Senator Everett Dirksen; Betty Friedan, author of *The Feminine Mystique*; Republican minority leader Robert Michel; and comedian and actor Richard Pryor.

By the early 1990s Peoria was regarded as a boom town, having the image of good labor-management relations. That reputation was damaged in 1992 by a strike by 12,600 United Automobile Workers union members at Caterpillar, Inc., a construction machinery company that employed nearly ten percent of the city's work force. That strike, seen as a new stage in the attack by corporations on unions, had gained national attention when it was abruptly ended by the union five months after it began.

Historical Information: Peoria Historical Society, 942 NE Glen Oak, Peoria, IL 61603; telephone (309)674-1921

Population Profile

Metropolitan Area Residents
1970: 342,000
1980: 366,000
1990: 339,172
Annual average percent change, 1980–1988: −0.9%
U.S. rank in 1980: 90th
U.S. rank in 1990: 108th

City Residents
1970: 127,000
1980: 124,600
1990: 113,504 (of which, 53,586 were males, and 59,918 were females)
Percent change, 1980–1990: −8.6%
U.S. rank in 1980: 126th
U.S. rank in 1990: 157th (State rank: 3rd)

Density: 2,775.2 people per square mile (1990)

Racial and ethnic characteristics (1990)
 White: 86,852
 Black: 23,692
 American Indian, Eskimo, Aleut: Not reported
 Asian and Pacific Islander: 1,906
 Hispanic (may be of any race): 1,813

Percent of residents born in state: 74.9% (1990)

Age characteristics (1990)
 Population under 5 years old: 8,561
 Population 5 to 9 years old: 8,417
 Population 10 to 14 years old: 7,931
 Population 15 to 19 years old: 8,919
 Population 20 to 24 years old: 9,646
 Population 25 to 29 years old: 8,555
 Population 30 to 34 years old: 9,053
 Population 35 to 39 years old: 8,291
 Population 40 to 44 years old: 7,369
 Population 45 to 49 years old: 5,891
 Population 50 to 54 years old: 4,766
 Population 55 to 59 years old: 4,677
 Population 60 to 64 years old: 5,047
 Population 65 to 69 years old: 4,910
 Population 70 to 74 years old: 4,088
 Population 75 to 79 years old: 3,395
 Population 80 to 84 years old: 2,232
 Population 85 years and over: 1,756
 Median age: 32.6 years

Births (1988)
 Total number: 1,796

Deaths (1988)
 Total number: 1,246 (of which, 30 were infants under the age of 1 year)

Money income (1989)
 Per capita income: $14,039
 Median household income: $26,074

Pettengill-Morron House in Peoria is listed on the National Register of Historic Sites.

Total households: 44,883
Number of households with income of . . .
  less than $5,000: 4,390
  $5,000 to $9,999: 5,178
  $10,000 to $14,999: 4,103
  $15,000 to $24,999: 7,996
  $25,000 to $34,999: 6,359
  $35,000 to $49,999: 7,116
  $50,000 to $74,999: 6,082
  $75,000 to $99,999: 1,914
  $100,000 to $149,999: 1,156
  $150,000 or more: 589
Percent of families below poverty level: 15.1% (74.2% of which were female householder families with related children under 5)
1991 FBI Crime Index Total: Illinois figures were excluded from 1991 Uniform Crime Reports totals

Municipal Government

The city of Peoria operates under a council-manager form of government. One council member is elected from each of five districts and five members are elected at large. The mayor heads the council and is elected by the total electorate in a nonpartisan election.

Head Official: City Manager Thomas Mikulecky (NP) (since 1987)

Total Number of City Employees: 750 (1992)

City Information: City of Peoria, 419 Fulton, Peoria, IL 61602; telephone (309)672-8500

Economy

Major Industries and Commercial Activity

Located at the center of a fertile agricultural region, with corn and soybeans as principal crops, Peoria is an important livestock and grain exporting market. Farm production in a three-county area totals more than $290 million yearly; livestock sales, particularly of hogs, consistently rank among the six to eight highest in the nation. Peoria is surrounded by rich bituminous coal fields that hold reserves estimated to last for 150 years and slated for worldwide distribution.

Manufacturing is a major industry: more than two hundred diversified firms make nearly 1,000 different products. Peoria is the headquarters of two of the largest U.S. earth-moving equipment makers, which record an average of $2 billion in shipments annually. Local companies produce more than fourteen percent of the country's internal-combustion engines and about eight percent of all construction machinery in North America. The city is also the base for several distilleries and breweries.

The National Center for Agriculture Research is operated in Peoria by the United States Department of Agriculture; there, soil testing and chemical development are important areas of research. Peoria has recently formed the Biotechnical Research and Development Consortium to allow private development and marketing of the products developed at the center's Agricultural Research Lab and to expand the use of patents into the private sector.

Peoria is a main test market for several national consumer research firms such as Nielsen Data Markets, Inc., which has established one of its six facilities in the city. Health care, education, insurance, finance, and government are the other primary non-manufacturing sectors.

Items and goods produced: tractors, beverages, alcohol and solvents, brick, tile, caskets, castings, cordage, cotton goods, fencing and wire products, nails, animal feeds, food and dairy products, pharmaceuticals, steel, paper, household products, storage batteries, electric motor rails and bases, air-conditioning equipment, furnaces, oil burners, road machinery, heavy graders, strawboard, tools, dies, labels, grease and hides, millworking

Incentive Programs—New and Existing Companies

Local Programs—Business is encouraged in Peoria through a variety of local programs. Among economic incentives are tax increment financing districts, sales and property tax credits and exemptions, and industrial revenue bonds. Six Urban Enterprise Zones have been established in the Peoria metropolitan area; benefits include state tax exemptions and credits, building permit waivers, and property tax abatement.

State programs—The Illinois Community Development Assistance Program is available to help communities attract or expand local industry. The Industrial Training Program and the Central Illinois Private Industry Council provide direct financial assistance. Also available are programs administered by the Illinois Department of Commerce and Community Affairs.

Job training programs—Job training is available through state agencies and educational institutions. Illinois Central College designs customized training programs at the High Tech Training Center, and Bradley University specializes in technical research, prototype development, and market research analysis.

Development Projects

The city of Peoria has adopted a master plan, based on an extensive land-use study, that outlines the complete revitalization of the central business district. Downtown areas will be redeveloped for residential, shopping, and recreational use. Anchoring the project are the twenty-nine-story Twin Towers, a residential and commercial complex completed in 1984, and The Boatworks, a $2.5 million entertainment and recreational development. Projects under construction in 1991, totaling over $90 million, included Hamilton Square, Riverboat Gambling Project, a corporate park, and a $50 million Federal correctional institution.

Economic Development Information: The Economic Development Council for the Peoria Area, 124 SW Adams Street, Suite 300, Peoria, IL 61602-1388; telephone (309)676-7500; and, Illinois Automotive Corridor, P.O. Box 6323, Peoria, IL 61601; telephone 1-800-255-2550

Commercial Shipping

With access to three interstate and four federal highways, metropolitan Peoria is linked to markets nationwide by 168 motor freight carriers, 131 of which maintain local terminals, and thirteen railroads. Air cargo transfer facilities are available at Greater Peoria Regional Airport and two private airfields. Four barge lines transport more than thirty-six million tons during a year-round navigation season through the Peoria Lock and Dam, a major link from the Gulf of Mexico to the St. Lawrence Seaway. Peoria is a Foreign Trade Zone.

Labor Force and Employment Outlook

Peoria workers are recognized for their high productivity, which exceeds the state and national averages. More than half the work force is engaged in white-collar occupations in retail trade, professional services, and government; manufacturing accounts for about twenty-five percent of the work force. Nearly 70% of workers have at least a high school degree. Manufacturers and agribusinesses are said to have been successful in retraining and modernizing the work force through the strong training networks between the private and education sectors. Peoria looks forward to increases in international trade and exporting through the Port of Peoria.

Chemical distillation of grain and corn, paper products and printed material, coal production, and automotive parts are gaining rapidly as major manufacturing areas. Peoria's has always been a strong retail market; further retail development in the downtown area and more strip malls are expected.

The following is a summary of data regarding the Peoria metropolitan area labor force as of September 1992.

Size of non-agricultural labor force: 151,000

Number of workers employed in . . .
  mining: not reported
  construction: 8,100
  manufacturing: 32,600
  transportation and public utilities: 7,200
  wholesale and retail trade: 35,700
  finance, insurance, and real estate: 7,900
  services: 42,600
  government: 16,900

Average hourly earnings of production workers employed in manufacturing: $14.60

Unemployment rate: 6.0%

Largest employers	Number of employees
Caterpillar Tractor Company	12,600
St. Francis Hospital	3,800
Methodist Medical Center of Illinois	3,000
School District 150	2,227
Keystone Steel and Wire Company	1,500
Central Illinois Light Company	1,500
Bradley University	1,054

Cost of Living

The following is a summary of data regarding several key cost of living factors in the Peoria area.

1992 (2nd Quarter) ACCRA Cost of Living Index: 104.6 (U.S. average = 100.0)

1992 (2nd Quarter) ACCRA Average House Price: $127,700

State income tax rate: 3.0%

State sales tax rate: 5.0%

Local income tax rate: None

Local sales tax rate: 2.25% (local and county)

Property tax rate: 9.3174% per $100 assessed valuation (subject to change annually)

Economic Information: Peoria Area Chamber of Commerce, 124 SW Adams, Suite 300, Peoria, IL; telephone (309)676-0755

Education and Research

Elementary and Secondary Schools

The Peoria Public Schools District #150 is the fifth largest public elementary and secondary school system in the state of Illinois. A seven-member, nonpartisan board of education appoints a superintendent by majority vote.

The following is a summary of data regarding the Peoria public schools as of the 1988-1989 school year.

Total enrollment: 16,716

Number of facilities
  primary schools: (kindergarten through grade four): 15
  middle schools: 14
  senior high schools: 4

Student/teacher ratio: primary, 20.82:1; middle, 21.98:1; senior high, 18.45:1

Teacher salaries
  minimum: $18,360
  maximum: $36,607

Funding per pupil: $3,625.95 (1986-1987)

Parochial schools in Peoria enroll more than ten thousand students. There are two private high schools and seven private elementary schools.

Public Schools Information: Peoria Public Schools District 150, 3202 N. Wisconsin Avenue, Peoria, IL 61603

Colleges and Universities

Bradley University, founded in 1897, offers fifty-five undergraduate and thirteen graduate programs in such fields as business and accounting, all major engineering specialties, music, nursing, and teacher education. Eureka College, the alma mater of former President Ronald Reagan, is a four-year liberal arts college. The University of Illinois College of Medicine at Peoria, the Bradley University School of Nursing, and nursing schools at St. Francis Hospital and Methodist Medical Center grant degrees in medical sciences and provide continuing education for health care professionals throughout the Midwest.

Illinois Central College is a two-year institution that schedules courses for more than twelve thousand students in university transfer curricula and vocational and continuing education programs. Among colleges and universities within commuting distance of Peoria are Illinois State University in Normal, Western Illinois University in Macomb, and Carl Sandburg College in Galesburg.

Libraries and Research Centers

The Peoria Public Library maintains a central facility with nearly seven-hundred thousand volumes and more than thirteen hundred periodical titles along with records and audio tapes and video tapes; subject interests include business, census materials, early government documents, genealogy, and local history. The library operates four branches. The city's other major library is the Cullom-Davis Library on the Bradley University campus. Holdings total over 517,000 volumes, and special collections include federal and state documents as well as material pertaining to industrial arts history, Abraham Lincoln, and oral history; the library also houses the Harry L. Spooner Library of the Peoria Historical Society. Ten other libraries in Peoria are associated with colleges, hospitals, churches, corporations, and government agencies.

Bradley University supports research centers in computers and technology, as well as the Institute for Urban Affairs and Business Research. Eureka College also conducts research at its computer center.

Public Library Information: Peoria Public Library, 107 NE Monroe Street, Peoria, IL 61602-1021 (309)672-8835

Health Care

The Peoria metropolitan area is served by seven hospitals supplying more than 2,000 beds. Among health care professionals affiliated with hospitals, clinics, and other facilities are 725 physicians, 173 dentists, and 2,150 nurses. Major hospitals and medical centers include Saint Francis Hospital, Methodist Medical Center of Illinois, Zeller Zone Mental Health Center, and Proctor Community Hospital. Specialized treatment is available at St. Jude's Children's Research Hospital, an affiliate of Methodist Medical Center; the Institute for Physical Medicine and Rehabilitation; and the Allied Agencies Center, which provides research, therapy, and education and training for handicapped patients. Also located in the city are the American Red Cross Peoria Regional Blood Center and Marvin Hult Health Education Center.

Recreation

Sightseeing

A reconstructed fort marks the site of the original Fort Crevecoeur, now an 86-acre park on a bluff overlooking the Illinois River. Glen Oak Park is a 100-acre park with a zoo, conservatory, and gardens; zoo animals range from large cats and marsupials to reptiles and amphibians. The Wildlife Prairie Park, almost 2,000 acres consisting of grazing land, lakes, and woodland, provides a habitat for animals native to Illinois, such as bison, elk, wolves, cougars, bears, waterfowl, and American bald eagles. The park also contains a country store, pioneer area, walking trails, and a miniature railroad that runs through the grounds. The Boatworks complex in downtown Peoria offers paddleboat excursions and a museum of river industry housed in a towboat.

Arts and Culture

The Peoria Area Arts and Sciences Council, now consisting of fifty member organizations, was founded in 1955 to promote the arts and sciences in central Illinois. The council sponsors arts programs in the schools, hospitals, and throughout the community as well as providing a vehicle for local artists. The Lakeview Museum of Arts and Sciences is the council's headquarters; it also houses a permanent collection of art that includes a decorative arts gallery, a planetarium, and the exhibit "Man and Nature: The Changing Relationship."

Peoria performing arts organizations include the Peoria Symphony, Prairie Wind Ensemble, Peoria Ballet Company, Peoria Civic Opera, Peoria Municipal Band, Peoria Area Civic Chorale, and chapters of the Sweet Adelines. The Peoria Art Guild sponsors more than forty events a year. Theater in Peoria is well represented by such organizations as the Broadway Theater League, Community Children's Theatre, Corn Stock Theatre, Peoria Players, Illinois Central College Theater, and Bradley University Theater.

Arts and Culture Information: Peoria Arts and Sciences Council, 11125 West Lake Avenue, Peoria, IL 61614

Festivals and Holidays

Peoria's largest annual event is the Heart of Illinois Fair, which attracts more than 200,000 people. The celebration of Independence Day is capped by the Fourth of July Fireworks display on the riverfront. Rendezvous Days at Fort Crevecoeur re-creates Illinois history with battle re-enactments, tomahawk and knife throws, muzzle-loading competitions, and other events during the last weekend in September. The century-old Santa Parade, the country's longest running event of its kind, takes place each year on Thanksgiving Day. The annual Christmas Art and Craft Show is held each year over Thanksgiving weekend at the Peoria Civic Center. The Peoria Art Guild's Crimson Door Holiday Show runs for one month during the Christmas season at the guild's headquarters.

Sports for the Spectator

The Peoria Chiefs, a Class A minor league farm baseball team, are league leaders each year in home game attendance. David Lamb, author of *Stolen Season,* numbers the Chiefs' new stadium among his ten favorite places to watch a ball game. The Peoria Rivermen, a minor league affiliate of the St. Louis Blues, compete in the International Hockey League and play their home games in a modern indoor facility. The Professional Bowlers Association tour

Illinois—Peoria

Cities of the United States • 2nd Edition

The Spirit of Peoria, sternwheeler excursion boat.

frequently competes in bowling facilities in Peoria, where bowling is a popular sport. Both the Bradley Braves and Illinois Central College field competitive basketball teams. The Steamboat Classic each year attracts world-class middle-distance runners who compete for the $10,000 top prize.

Sports for the Participant

The Peoria Pleasure Driveway and Park District consists of more than 8,000 acres providing facilities for outdoor and indoor sports. Included are five public and four private golf courses, five indoor and four outdoor swimming pools, and fifty public tennis courts. Also available are two artificial ice-skating rinks, an archery range, BMX bicycle racing course, horseshoe pits, shuffleboard courts, and a shooting range. Peoria Lake is available for fishing and boating. The new Great Plains Sports Science and Training Center provides optimal training for potential Midwest Olympic athletes. East Peoria offers riverboat gambling.

Shopping and Dining

Peoria shoppers choose from sixty shopping centers and malls located throughout the greater metropolitan area. Both Peoria and East Peoria are in the process of revitalizing the central business districts by developing shopping areas in conjunction with residential, entertainment, and office facilities.

The dining choices in Peoria feature ethnic food, particularly Chinese and Italian, as well as gourmet cuisine and a variety of well known fast food chains and family-style restaurants. Regional specialties include barbecued ribs and pork tenderloin sandwiches.

Visitor Information: Peoria Convention and Visitors Bureau, 403 N.E. Jefferson Ave., Peoria, IL 61602; telephone (309)676-0303

Convention Facilities

Peoria's principal meeting site is the new Peoria Civic Center, located in the revitalized downtown district, which features a twelve-thousand-seat arena, thirty-three thousand square feet of exhibit space, and a theater with seating for 2,200 people. More than six hundred sleeping rooms are located within four blocks of the complex. Several of the area's eighteen hotels and motels, offering a total of twenty-five hundred lodging rooms, also have convention and meeting accommodations. The largest contains a banquet room for 2,700 persons.

Convention Information: Peoria Convention and Visitors Bureau, 403 N.E. Jefferson Ave., Peoria, IL 61602; telephone (309)676-0303

Transportation

Approaching the City

Eight commercial airlines schedule thirty-two daily flights at the Greater Peoria Regional Airport and two private airfields. Passenger rail transportation into Peoria is available through Amtrak.

Interstate highways 74, 474, 80, and 55 afford easy access into Greater Peoria; the area is also served by four federal highways.

Traveling in the City

Peoria is compact but not crowded. The average commute is ten minutes. Greater Peoria Mass Transit District offers public transportation.

Communications

Newspapers and Magazines

The major newspaper in Peoria is the *Journal Star,* which appears daily and on Sunday morning. Fifteen neighborhood and suburban newspapers circulate weekly, including the *Peoria Heights Herald* and the *Observer.*

A number of special-interest magazines are published in Peoria on such subjects as religion, crafts, guns, helicopters, sewing, and graphic arts.

Television and Radio

Three commercial television network affiliates, the Fox network, and one public television outlet are based in Peoria; cable service is available. Five AM and ten FM radio stations furnish diversified programming.

Media Information: Journal Star, One News Plaza, Peoria, IL 61643; telephone (309) 686-3000

Springfield

The City in Brief

Founded: 1818 (incorporated, 1832)

Head Official: Mayor Ossie Langfelder (D) (since 1987)

City Population
 1970: 92,000
 1980: 99,637
 1990: 105,227
 Percent change, 1980–1990: 5.2%
 U.S. rank in 1980: 171st
 U.S. rank in 1990: 183rd (State rank: 4th)

Metropolitan Area Population
 1970: 171,020
 1980: 187,770
 1990: 189,550
 Percent change, 1980–1990: 0.9%
 U.S. rank in 1980: Not available
 U.S. rank in 1990: Not available

Area: 42.5 square miles (1990)

Elevation: 588 feet above sea level

Average Annual Temperature: 52.6° F

Average Annual Precipitation: 33.78 inches

Major Economic Sectors: Government, services, wholesale and retail trade

Unemployment Rate: 4.3% (September 1992)

Per Capita Income: $14,813 (1989)

1992 (2nd Quarter) ACCRA Average House Price: $101,725

1992 (2nd Quarter) ACCRA Cost of Living Index: 96.1 (U.S. average = 100.0)

1991 FBI Crime Index Total: Illinois figures were excluded from 1991 Uniform Crime Reports

Major Colleges and Universities: Sangamon State University; Southern Illinois School of Medicine; Lincoln Land Community College

Daily Newspaper: *The State Journal Register*

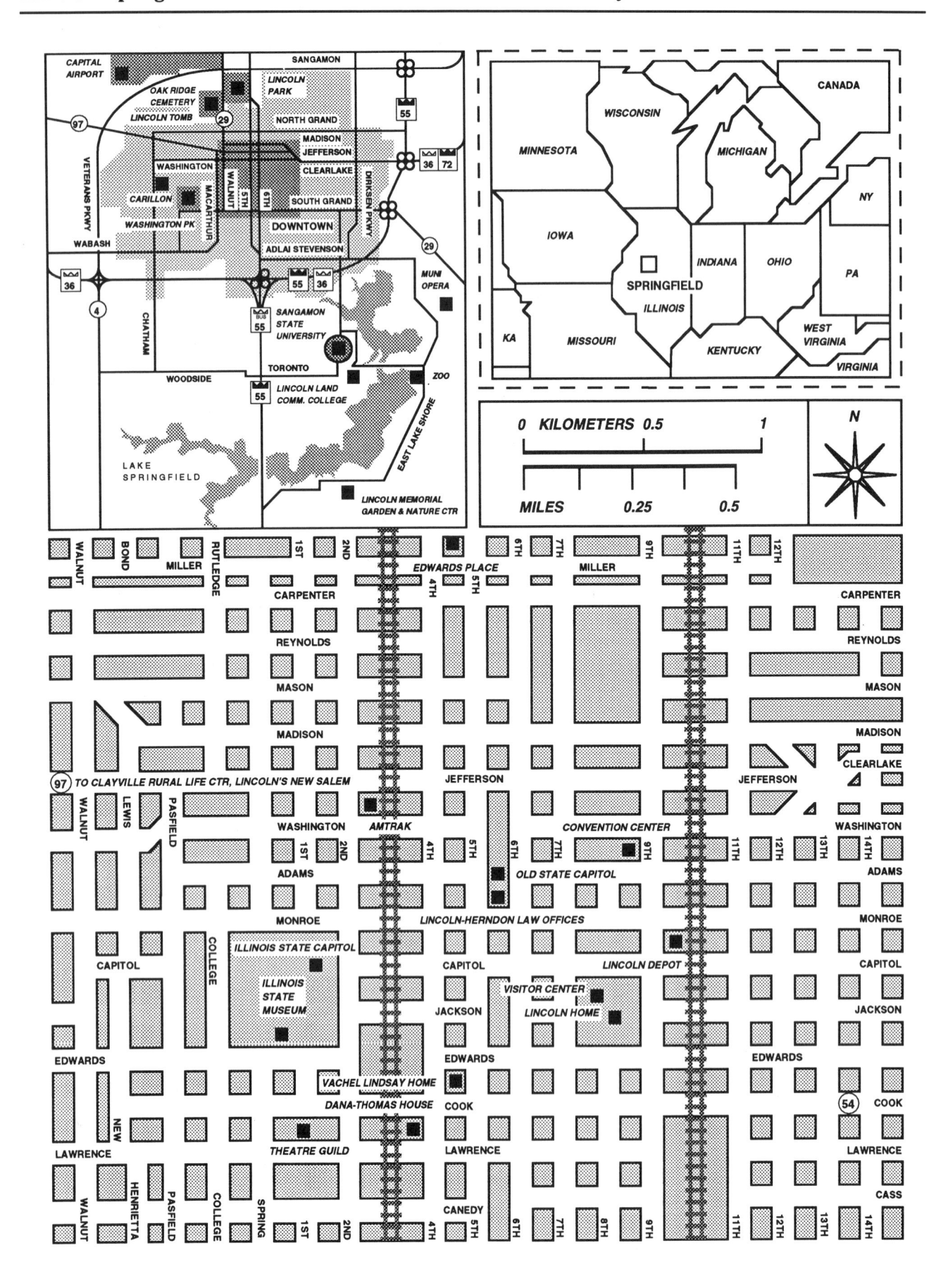

Illinois—Springfield *Cities of the United States • 2nd Edition*

Introduction

Springfield is the capital of Illinois and the seat of Sangamon County, which is included in the Springfield metropolitan area. The city is the commercial, health care, financial, and cultural center for a wide agricultural region. For nearly twenty-four years the home, workplace, and political base of Abraham Lincoln prior to his election as President of the United States, Springfield is also a popular tourist destination.

Geography and Climate

Springfield is located south of the Sangamon River on level to gently sloping terrain in a fertile agricultural region in central Illinois. The city is 190 miles southwest of Chicago, 100 miles northeast of St. Louis, and 195 miles west of Indianapolis. Springfield's climate consists of four seasons, with warm summers and cold winters; snowfall and ice average 21.90 inches a year. Relative humidity measures 64 percent annually.

Area: 42.5 square miles (1990)

Elevation: 588 feet above sea level

Average Temperatures: January, 22.3° F; July, 74.5° F; annual average, 52.6° F

Average Annual Precipitation: 33.78 inches

History

Sangamon River Valley Attracts Settlers

At the time Illinois was admitted to the Union in 1818, the city of Springfield did not exist. In that same year Elisha Kelly of North Carolina, attracted to the fertile Sangamon River valley, built the first homestead at a location that is now the northwest corner of Springfield's Second and Jefferson streets. Other settlers soon arrived and a small settlement began to take shape around the Kelly cabin. When Sangamon County was created in 1821, the Kelly colony was the only one large enough to house county officials. The town was named Springfield in April 1821, the name being derived from Spring Creek and one of the Kelly family's fields. Springfield became the county seat in 1825 and received its incorporation in 1832.

Through the leadership of young Abraham Lincoln, one of the "Long Nine"—seven representatives and two senators whose total height measured fifty-four feet—the state capital of Illinois was transferred from Vandalia to Springfield. Lincoln, who lived in the village of New Salem, 25 miles northwest of the city, moved to the new capital on April 15, 1837; he remained there until he left for Washington, D.C., on February 11, 1861, as the sixteenth president-elect of the United States on the eve of the American Civil War. During Lincoln's twenty-five years in Springfield as a lawyer and politician, the city experienced prosperity and growth, becoming a city in 1840 and recording a population of 9,400 people by 1860.

Monuments Memorialize Lincoln in Springfield

The city of Springfield is a tribute to Lincoln, rivalling Washington, D.C., in the grandeur and significance of its public monuments, shrines, and historic buildings. The Old State Capitol, a Greek Revival style building constructed in 1837, is one of the most historically significant structures west of the Alleghenies. Lincoln delivered his "House Divided" speech on June 16, 1858, and maintained an office as president-elect there. His body lay in state in the Capitol's House of Representatives on May 5, 1865. The Lincoln Tomb and memorial in Oak Ridge Cemetery was dedicated in 1874. The marble burial chamber holds the bodies of Lincoln, his wife Mary, and sons Edward Baker, William Wallace, and Thomas ("Tad"). The Lincoln Memorial Garden and Nature Center, designed by Jens Jensen, reflects the Illinois landscape of Lincoln's time. The Lincoln Home, the Lincoln-Herndon Law Offices, the Lincoln Depot (formerly Great Western depot, where he gave his farewell speech to Springfield), and the Lincoln Family Pew at the First Presbyterian Church complete the sites memorializing Lincoln's life in Springfield.

At the center of Springfield's history and daily life is state politics. After the Civil War, to prevent the removal of the capital to Peoria, Springfield citizens bought the old capitol building for $200,000, which was then used to finance a new structure. Begun in 1868 and finished twenty years later at a cost of $4.5 million, the capitol rises 461 feet above the city and is in the form of a Latin cross with a vast dome in the center capped with stained glass. The building was renovated in 1958.

Springfield Emerges as Regional Center

In 1914 the Russell Sage Foundation picked Springfield for one of its sociological surveys to aid social welfare organizations. The creation of man-made Lake Springfield, the largest civic project in the city's history, was approved in 1930 and financed by a bond issue and federal funds. The city has become a wholesale and retail center for the thriving agricultural region.

Historical Information: Sangamon County Historical Society, 308 East Adams, Springfield, IL 62701; telephone (217) 522-2500; and, Illinois State Historical Society, Old State Capitol, Springfield, IL 62701; telephone (217) 782-2635

Population Profile

Metropolitan Area Residents
1970: 171,020
1980: 187,770
1990: 189,550
Percent change, 1980–1990: 0.9%
U.S. rank in 1980: Not available
U.S. rank in 1990: Not available

City Residents
1970: 92,000
1980: 99,637
1990: 105,227 (of which, 48,440 were males, and 56,787 were females)
Percent change, 1980–1990: 5.2%
U.S. rank in 1980: 171st
U.S. rank in 1990: 183rd (State rank: 4th)

Density: 2,475.9 persons per square mile (1990)

Racial and ethnic characteristics (1990)
  White: 90,069
  Black: 13,687
  American Indian, Eskimo, Aleut: Not reported
  Asian and Pacific Islander: 1,033
  Hispanic (may be of any race): 870

Percent of residents born in state: 79.4% (1990)

Age characteristics (1990)
  Population under 5 years old: 7,765
  Population 5 to 9 years old: 7,385
  Population 10 to 14 years old: 6,743
  Population 15 to 19 years old: 6,229
  Population 20 to 24 years old: 7,366
  Population 25 to 29 years old: 9,603
  Population 30 to 34 years old: 9,439
  Population 35 to 39 years old: 8,648
  Population 40 to 44 years old: 7,526
  Population 45 to 49 years old: 5,323
  Population 50 to 54 years old: 4,576
  Population 55 to 59 years old: 4,346
  Population 60 to 64 years old: 4,646
  Population 65 to 69 years old: 4,457
  Population 70 to 74 years old: 3,714
  Population 75 to 79 years old: 3,295
  Population 80 to 84 years old: 2,288
  Population 85 years and over: 1,878
  Median age: 34.0 years

Births (1988)
  Total number: 1,895

Deaths (1988)
  Total number: 1,131 (of which, 31 were infants under the age of 1 year)

Money income (1989)
  Per capita income: $14,813
  Median household income: $27,995
  Total households: 44,879
  Number of households with income of . . .
    less than $5,000: 2,820
    $5,000 to $9,999: 4,390
    $10,000 to $14,999: 4,249
    $15,000 to $24,999: 8,546
    $25,000 to $34,999: 7,385
    $35,000 to $49,999: 8,230
    $50,000 to $74,999: 6,440
    $75,000 to $99,999: 1,718
    $100,000 to $149,999: 729
    $150,000 or more: 372
  Percent of families below poverty level: 9.7% (63.6% of which were female householder families with related children under 5)
1991 FBI Crime Index Total: Illinois figures were excluded from 1991 Uniform Crime Reports

Municipal Government

Springfield operates under an aldermanic form of municipal government. The ten aldermen and the mayor, who is the head official and a member of council, serve four-year terms.

Head Official: Mayor Ossie Langfelder (D) (since 1987; current term expires April 1995)

Total Number of City Employees: 1,663 (1991)

City Information: Municipal Building, Springfield, IL 62701; telephone (217)789-2000

Economy

Major Industries and Commercial Activity

Springfield's diversified economic base is balanced between the public and private sectors: government, services, and retail trade are the principal industries. A central location and a highly developed transportation and communications network contribute to the city's position as a center of business and professional activity, particularly health care and finance. Springfield is also the headquarters of eight national insurance companies and more than 150 state, regional, and national associations. Manufacturing firms in Sangamon County produce goods for national distribution and international export.

Items and goods produced: tractors, electric meters, radio parts, flour, cereal products, automatic coffeemakers, mattresses, plastic pipe, farm implements, livestock and poultry feeds, yeast, power plant boiler installations, printed circuits, steel storage tanks

Incentive Programs—New and Existing Companies

Local programs—The Sangamon County Department of Community Resources administers the local Job Training Partnership, matching qualified workers with employment opportunities.

State programs—Among the business incentives offered through the Illinois tax system are: a one percent tax investment credit for investment in mining, manufacturing, or retailing; tax districts that rebate property taxes of an industrial or commercial firm moving into the state or a newly created firm within the state; personal property tax exemption for businesses and individuals; and Urban Enterprise Zones that provide extensive sales, property, and income-tax incentives to investors. The Illinois Community Development Assistance Program is available to help communities attract or expand local industry. Also available are programs administered by the Illinois Department of Commerce and Community Affairs.

Development Projects

Infrastructure improvements in Springfield and throughout Sangamon County have encouraged extensive development, with the result that leasable office space as well as residential development continue to grow. Springfield's 59 percent increase in building permit values from 1988 to 1989 ranked it among the country's most rapidly growing cities.

Economic Development Information: Economic Development Department, The Greater Springfield Chamber of Commerce, 3 South Old State Capitol Plaza, Springfield, IL; telephone (217)525-1173

Commercial Shipping

A transportation hub for markets throughout the United States, the Springfield metropolitan area is served by thirty-five intrastate and seventy-four interstate motor freight carriers; forty-one truck terminals are located in the community. Springfield/Sangamon County is linked with major national rail networks via five trunkline railroads, two of which operate facilities in the city, and a local rail company that maintains a switchyard and transports coal in central Illinois.

Labor Force and Employment Outlook

Springfield employers draw from an educated, growing, and productive work force. A diverse economic base produces jobs principally in government, medical care, insurance administration, and services; diversity in the work force, particularly in the services, has enabled the Springfield economy to withstand pronounced shifts. Consistent with a national trend, employment opportunities in industry are expected to decrease while jobs in the service sector will steadily increase.

The following is a summary of data regarding the Springfield metropolitan area labor force as of September 1992.

Size of non-agricultural labor force: 110,100

Number of workers employed in . . .
  mining: not reported
  construction: 4,400
  manufacturing: 3,900
  transportation and public utilities: 4,900
  wholesale and retail trade: 25,100
  finance, insurance, and real estate: 7,900
  services: 30,000
  government: 33,900

Average hourly earnings of production workers in manufacturing: $11.32

Unemployment rate: 4.3%

Largest employers	*Number of employees*
State of Illinois	20,000
St. John's Hospital	3,300
Memorial Medical Center	2,400
U.S. Government	2,100
Springfield School District #186	1,989
City of Springfield	1,663

Cost of Living

With a cost of living level with or below the national average, Springfield residents are reported to have higher disposable income for recreation, savings, and other discretionary expenditures.

The following is a summary of data regarding several key cost of living factors in the Springfield area.

1992 (2nd Quarter) ACCRA Cost of Living Index: 96.1 (U.S. average = 100.0)

1992 (2nd Quarter) ACCRA Average House Price: $101,725

State income tax rate: 3.0%

State sales tax rate: 5.0%

Local income tax rate: None

Local sales tax rate: 2.0% (plus a county tax of 0.25%)

Property tax rate: $1.00 per $100.00 of assessed valuation

Economic Information: The Greater Springfield Chamber of Commerce, 3 South Old State Capitol Plaza, Suite 1, Springfield, IL 62701; telephone (217)525-1173

Education and Research

Elementary and Secondary Schools

Springfield Public School District #186, the seventh largest in the state of Illinois, is administered by a seven-member, nonpartisan board of education that appoints a superintendent.

The following is a summary of data regarding the Springfield public schools as of the 1992–1993 school year.

Total enrollment: 15,765

Number of facilities
  elementary schools: 26
  junior high schools: 3
  senior high schools: 3
  other: 2

Student-teacher ratio: 25.7:1

Teacher salaries
  minimum: $20,671
  maximum: $42,558

Funding per pupil: $3,804.60 (1991–1992)

Springfield is also served by more than twenty private and parochial elementary and secondary schools.

Public Schools Information: Springfield Public School District #186, Superintendent's Office, 1900 West Monroe Street, Springfield, IL 62704; telephone (217)525-3000

Colleges and Universities

Sangamon State University, Lincoln Land Community College, Springfield College in Illinois, and Southern Illinois University (SIU) School of Medicine are located in Springfield. A four-year institution, Sangamon State University grants degrees in such fields as public affairs. Lincoln Land Community College, the area's largest post-secondary institution, offers vocational education, programs for returning students, and a transfer curriculum. Springfield College in Illinois, a two-year private college, provides career training. SIU School of Medicine operates programs in conjunction with area hospitals for the training of physicians and other health care professionals.

Among the technical and vocational schools in Springfield are Capital Area Vocational Center, Brown's Business College, and Robert Morris College.

Libraries and Research Centers

The Lincoln Library, Springfield's public library, holds more than 360,000 books, about one thousand periodical titles, and microfiche, films, audio and video tapes, maps, charts, and art reproductions; special collections pertain to Vachel Lindsay and local history. The library operates three branches and a bookmobile. Springfield is also home to the Illinois State Library, which houses more than two million volumes, and the Illinois State Historical Library, which holds a collection of Abraham Lincoln's letters, documents, and memorabilia. Civil War records are part of the holdings maintained at the library of the Daughters of the Union Veterans of the Civil War. Campus library facilities are maintained by Lincoln Land Community College, Sangamon State University, and Southern Illinois University School of Medicine. In addition to the Illinois State Museum Library, other libraries in the city are affiliated principally with hospitals and with government agencies such as the Illinois State Department of Energy and Natural Resources, the Illinois Environmental Protection Agency, and the Illinois Supreme Court. Sangamon State University research centers conduct research in computing, community and regional studies, and legal studies.

Public Library Information: Lincoln Library, 326 South Seventh Street, Springfield, IL 62701; telephone (217)753-4900

Health Care

Springfield is a primary health care center for the central Illinois region. Three hospitals, forty clinics, and thirty nursing homes provide diagnostic, treatment, and care services. St. John's Hospital, an 800-bed facility, operates trauma, poison, and neo-natal centers. Memorial Medical Center, with 560 beds, maintains burn and rehabilitative medicine units; 177-bed Doctors Hospital provides complete medical facilities. A valuable resource to the Springfield/Sangamon County medical community, which includes more than six hundred practicing physicians and nearly 200 other health care professionals, is Southern Illinois University School of Medicine. Several public and private clinics coordinate counseling and referral services with health care programs.

Recreation

Sightseeing

Historic sites associated with Abraham Lincoln memorialize his presidency and his life in Springfield. The Old State Capitol has been reconstructed and completely furnished to re-create Lincoln's Illinois legislative years; a copy of the "Gettysburg Address" is displayed in the capitol. The Lincoln home, the only house Lincoln ever owned, is located in a four-block historic area administered by the National Park Service. The house, containing many authentic household furnishings, has been restored as closely as possible to its original condition. Neighboring 1850s-era residences have been similarly restored.

The Lincoln Depot, formerly the Great Western, marks the spot where Lincoln bade farewell to the city, and the Lincoln-Herndon law offices recapture the environment in which Lincoln practiced law. The Lincoln tomb at Oak Ridge Cemetery is marked with a sculpture honoring the sixteenth president. The Lincoln Memorial Garden and Nature Center consists of 27 acres of woodland garden along the shore of Lake Springfield devoted to native Illinois plants, trees, and flowers. In nearby New Salem, twenty-three buildings have been restored to depict Lincoln's early life there. The Clayville Rural Life Center, 14 miles northwest of Springfield, demonstrates the rural and urban crafts and trades of nineteenth-century Illinois.

Designed by Frank Lloyd Wright in 1902 for socialite Susan Lawrence Dana, the Dana-Thomas House is the best preserved and most complete of the architect's early Prairie houses; it is finished with furniture, doors and windows, and light fixtures designed by Wright. The Washington Park Botanical Gardens and the Thomas Rees Memorial Carillon in Washington Park are other popular sights in Springfield. Of interest to children are the Henson Robinson Zoo at Lake Springfield, and the two amusement parks and miniature golf course located in the city.

Visitors to Springfield might consider a trip to nearby Fulton County, home of poet Edgar Lee

Masters and to Dickson Mounds Museum, where the excavated remains of a community of prehistoric Mississippians lie in laid-open graves dating to between 1150 and 1350 A.D. This 162-acre park also has extensive Native American remains.

Arts and Culture

Sponsoring a season of plays, the Springfield Theatre Guild features local actors. The Springfield Symphony Orchestra and the Ballet Company perform at Sangamon State University Auditorium and other sites throughout the city and state. During the summer months the Great American People Show stages outdoor drama in a natural amphitheater at New Salem State Park; the production "Your Obedient Servant, A. Lincoln" dramatizes Lincoln's life.

The Illinois State Museum preserves natural, anthropological, and art histories of Illinois with changing and permanent exhibits. The Peoples of the Past exhibit portrays prehistoric Illinois native Americans through life-size dioramas. The Vachel Lindsay Home is a museum and cultural center that pays tribute to one of the state's most famous artist-poets who was known as "the prairie troubadour." The Edwards Place, built in 1833 and the oldest house on its original grounds in Springfield, has been converted to a museum and art gallery. Springfield supports at least two Civil War museums.

Festivals and Holidays

The Springfield Old Capitol Art Fair is considered one of the best art events in the United States, attracting more than two hundred artists who display their work downtown near the Old State Capitol Building on the third weekend in May. A Children's Art Fair accompanies the main attraction. The International Carillon Festival, held seven evenings in June, is considered to be the only one of its kind in the country; international performers play carillon music on the sixty-six bronze bells in the Thomas Rees Memorial Carillon. Lincolnfest, on the Fourth of July weekend, is a free family street festival covering eighteen blocks in downtown Springfield.

The Illinois State Fair, held each August over an eleven-day period, hosts one of the nation's largest livestock shows, farm contests, and one-mile harness racing on a recognized fast track. In late August the Springfield Air Rendezvous attracts a mix of airshow acts from internationally known aerobatics entertainment to warbirds and ultralights. The Springfield International Ethnic Festival on the first week in September brings food, dance, arts, and culture from ten ethnic groups who showcase their cultural heritage in free events held at the Illinois State Fairgrounds. A Festival of Trees in late November and a Christmas Parade in December inaugurate the winter holiday season, which culminates with First Night Springfield on New Year's Eve, featuring varied musical entertainment, arts events, and a midnight fireworks display.

Sports for the Spectator

The Springfield Cardinals, the class A minor league team of the National League St. Louis Cardinals, plays a seventy-game home schedule at Lanphier Stadium. Springfield is also home to several collegiate teams, including the nationally ranked Sangamon State University Prairie Stars Soccer Team. The annual Ladies Professional Golf Association's Rail Charity Golf Classic attracts more than one hundred professional golfers to compete for prizes.

Sports for the Participant

The Springfield Recreation Department and the Springfield Park District maintain thirty parks in the city offering programs and facilities for fishing, hiking, jogging, picnicking, tennis, and softball. Springfield's wildlife sanctuaries provide year-round opportunities to enjoy the countryside of Sangamon County. Lake Springfield, a 4,040-acre, artificially constructed reservoir, is surrounded by eight parks and recreational outlets, including boat launches for canoes, motorboats, pontoons, rowboats, and sailboats.

Recreation information: Park District, telephone (217)544-1751

Shopping and Dining

Springfield is the commercial center for central Illinois, with downtown shops in restored historic buildings. White Oaks Mall offers the largest selection of merchandise in the region. Specialty shops in a nineteenth-century atmosphere make up Vinegar Hill Mall. Illinois Artisans Shop at the Lincoln Home National Historic Site features works by state artists.

Restaurants in the city offer a selection of American, Continental, Chinese, Thai, and Korean menus. The "horseshoe sandwich," a local staple created in Springfield in 1928, consists of a ham slice topped with an English cheddar cheese sauce, and crowned with french fries representing the nails of a horseshoe. Another regional favorite is a special chili

Cities of the United States • 2nd Edition   Illinois—Springfield

Lincoln's Tomb is where the president, his wife, and their three sons are buried. The Lincoln Home is shown at the beginning of this chapter.

recipe served by a local parlor that has spelled chili with an extra "l" since 1909.

Visitor Information: National Park Service Visitors Center, 426 South Seventh Street, Springfield, IL 62705; telephone (217)789-2357; and, Springfield Convention and Visitors Bureau, 109 North Seventh Street, Springfield, IL 62701; telephone (217)789-2360 or 1-800-356-7900 (in Illinois) and 1-800-545-7300; and, The Greater Springfield Chamber of Commerce, 3 Old State Capitol Plaza, Springfield, IL 62701; telephone (217)525-1173

Convention Facilities

The Prairie Capital Convention Center, conveniently located in downtown Springfield, is the city's principal meeting and convention facility. Containing forty-four thousand square feet of space, the exhibit hall can accommodate up to 9,224 participants; seventeen meeting rooms serve the needs of groups ranging from 63 to more than 1,000 people. Thirty-five area hotels and motels provide a total of thirty-three hundred rooms. Major hotels, such as Holiday Inn, Hilton, Ramada, and Sheraton, operate meeting and conference facilities.

Convention Information: Springfield Convention and Visitors Bureau, 109 North Seventh Street, Springfield, IL 62705; telephone (217)789-2360 and 1-800-545-7300

Transportation

Approaching the City

Capital Airport is the major air transportation facility in the Springfield metropolitan area. The airport is served by three commercial carriers; charter service is also available.

The highway system in Springfield/Sangamon County includes three interstate freeways, a limited-access highway, and several state routes. Intersecting Sangamon County, I-55 runs north to south along the eastern boundary of Springfield; I-72 links the city with Champaign-Urbana, Illinois, to the east. U.S. 36 connects with I-55 south of Springfield and continues west to Jacksonville, Illinois. State routes include 4 (north-south), 29 (east-west), 54 (east-west), and 97 (east-west).

Amtrak schedules six trains daily between Springfield, Chicago, and St. Louis, Missouri. Greyhound Bus Lines serve the city.

Traveling in the City

Streets in Springfield are laid out on a grid pattern. Washington Street, bisecting the city from east to west, and Fifth Street and Sixth Street, running parallel north to south, intersect in the center of downtown. The Springfield Mass Transit District operates public bus transportation on regularly scheduled routes Monday through Saturday.

Communications

Newspapers and Magazines

The State Journal-Register is Springfield's major daily newspaper. The *Illinois Times* appears weekly.

Springfield Magazine, published monthly, provides a dining and entertainment guide. Other journals and magazines published in Springfield are directed toward readers with special interests in such subjects as aviation, engineering, Illinois history, health care, education, building trades, and electrical cooperatives. These include *Illinois Aviation, Illinois Dental Journal, Illinois Engineer, Illinois Historical Journal, Illinois Libraries,* and *Illinois Publisher.*

Television and Radio

Three television stations, one commercial, one public, and one independent, are based in Springfield. Broadcasts from two commercial stations in neighboring communities are also received in the city; cable television is available by subscription. Radio programming is provided in Springfield by three AM and six FM stations.

Media Information: The State Journal-Register, One Copley Plaza, P.O. Box 219, Springfield, IL 62705-0219; telephone (217)753-1300; and, *Illinois Times,* 610 S. 7th, Springfield, IL 62708; telephone (217) 753-2226; *Springfield Magazine,* 1620 South 5th, Springfield, IL 62703; telephone (217)544-6564

INDIANA

Evansville 49	Indianapolis 83
Fort Wayne 61	South Bend 99
Gary 73	

The State in Brief

Nickname: Hoosier State
Motto: Crossroads of America

Flower: Peony
Bird: Cardinal

Area: 36,420 square miles (1990; U.S. rank: 38th)
Elevation: Ranges from 320 feet to 1,257 feet above sea level
Climate: Temperate, with four distinct seasons

Admitted to Union: December 11, 1816
Capital: Indianapolis
Head Official: Governor B. Evan Bayh III (D) (until 1997)

Population
  1970: 5,195,392
  1980: 5,490,000
  1990: 5,610,000
  Percent change 1980-1990: 1.0%
  U.S. rank in 1990: 14th
  Percent of residents born in state: 72.3% (1990)
  Density: 154.6 people per square mile (1990; U.S. rank: 16th)
  1991 FBI Crime Index Total: 270,279

Racial and Ethnic Characteristics (1990)
  White: 5,021,000
  Black: 7.8%
  American Indian, Eskimo, Aleut: 0.23%
  Asian and Pacific Islander: 0.68%
  Hispanic (may be of any race): 1.78%
Age Characteristics (1990)
  Population under 5 years old: 406,000
  Population 5 to 17 years old: 1,059,000
  Percent of population 65 years and older: 12.6%
  Median age: 32.8 years
  Voting-age population (1988): 4,111,000 (52.8% of whom cast votes for president)

Vital Statistics
  Total number of births (1992): 83,832
  Total number of deaths (1992): 50,144 (of which, 796 were infants under the age of 1 year)
  AIDS cases reported, 1981-1990: 897 (U.S. rank: 24th)

Economy
  Major industries: Manufacturing, agriculture, mining
  Unemployment rate: 6.2% (September 1992)
  Per capita income: $13,149 (1989)
  Median household income: $28,797 (1989)
  Total number of families: 1,490,130 (7.9% of which had incomes below the poverty level; 1989)
  Income tax rate: 3.4%
  Sales tax rate: 5.0% of adjusted gross income (food, prescription drugs, and items consumed or used in manufacturing are exempt)

Evansville

The City in Brief

Founded: 1818 (incorporated, 1819)

Head Official: Mayor Frank F. McDonald II (D) (since 1985)

City Population
 1970: 139,000
 1980: 130,496
 1990: 126,272
 Percent change, 1980–1990: −3.2%
 U.S. rank in 1980: 121st
 U.S. rank in 1990: 144th

Metropolitan Area Population
 1970: 255,000
 1980: 276,000
 1990: 278,990
 Percent change, 1980–1990: 1.0%
 U.S. rank in 1980: 114th
 U.S. rank in 1990: 121st

Area: 40.7 square miles (1990)
Elevation: 385.5 feet above sea level
Average Annual Temperature: 55.7° F
Average Annual Precipitation: 41.55 inches

Major Economic Sectors: Services, wholesale and retail trade, manufacturing
Unemployment Rate: 6.2% (September 1992)
Per Capita Income: $12,564 (1989)
1992 (2nd Quarter) ACCRA Average House Price: $101,220
1992 (2nd Quarter) ACCRA Cost of Living Index: 94.2 (U.S. average = 100.0)
1991 FBI Crime Index Total: 7,658

Major Colleges and Universities: University of Evansville; University of Southern Indiana

Daily Newspapers: *Evansville Courier; Evansville Press*

Indiana—Evansville

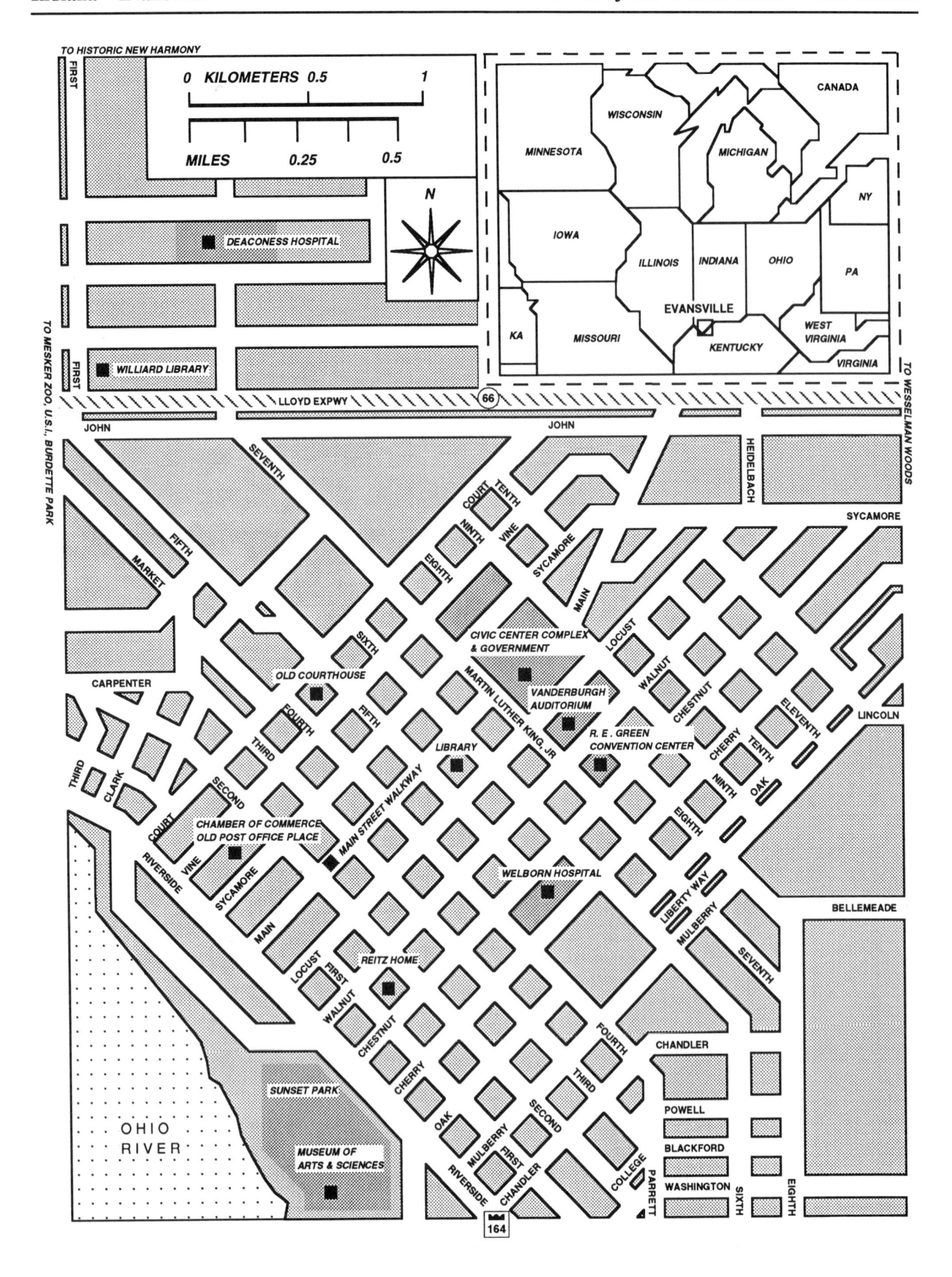

Cities of the United States • 2nd Edition

Introduction

The seat of Vanderburgh County, Evansville is the center of a metropolitan area that includes Warrick and Posey Counties in Indiana and Henderson County in Kentucky. Well-positioned in the days of the steamboat, the city occupies a unique prospect on a U-bend of the Ohio River. Today modern architecture mixes with historic structures to make Evansville an effective blend of the present with the past.

Geography and Climate

Evansville lies along the north bank of the Ohio River in a shallow valley at the southwestern tip of Indiana. Low hills surround flat, rolling land to the north, east, and west; the valley opens onto the river to the south. The city's climate is determined by moisture-bearing low pressure formations that move across the area from the western Gulf of Mexico region northeastward over the Mississippi and Ohio valleys to the Great Lakes and northern Atlantic Coast. These storm systems, which produce considerable variation in seasonal temperatures and precipitation, are especially prevalent during the winter and spring months. The growing season lasts approximately 199 days.

Area: 40.7 square miles (1990)

Elevation: 385.5 feet above sea level

Average Temperatures: January, 30.6° F; July, 78.1° F; annual average, 55.7° F

Average Annual Precipitation: 41.55 inches of rain; 13 inches of snow

History

River Location Draws Flatboat Commerce

The identity of the city of Evansville evolves from its location on the Ohio River at the spot where the river makes a dramatic U-bend. Evansville's founder was Colonel Hugh McGary, who purchased 200 acres from the Federal government and built a cabin at the foot of present-day Main Street, where he started a ferry boat service. Hoping the site would become the county seat, McGary sought the advice of General Robert Evans, a member of the territorial legislature. In 1818 McGary sold a section of land above Main Street to General Evans who replanted the town, which was made the seat of Vanderburgh County and named in honor of Evans. In 1819 it was incorporated as a town.

Evansville prospered from the commerce of Ohio River flatboats that were piloted by colorful frontiersmen who served as both guides and navigators. Theatrical troupes, wandering on the rivers in Ohio, played engagements in Evansville even during its early history, establishing a local theatrical tradition that continues today. But it was the age of the steamboat that brought Evansville economic prosperity.

During the first few decades of the nineteenth century, Evansville experienced a difficult period that jeopardized the physical health of the citizens and the economic stability of the town. First the depression of 1824-1829 hit the city hard and then an epidemic of milk sickness swept through, further weakening an already vulnerable populace. Dr. William Trafton, an Evansville physician, found a cure for the ailment that brought the struggling community national recognition. In the winter of 1831-1832 additional hardship came with the freezing of the Ohio River, which paralyzed river trade, followed by floods that covered the town during the spring thaw. In the summer almost 400 people died of cholera. Then Colonel McGary was charged with horse stealing, and although he explained he had traded horses with a relative, rumors forced him to leave town in disgrace.

Business Growth Brings New Residents

In 1836 Evansville was made the southern terminus of the Wabash & Erie Canal, which was completed in 1853 at the same time the first railroad train arrived in town. Although the canal proved not to be a financial success, it stimulated population growth and business development. European craftsmen immigrated to Evansville to work in the local factories and foundries. By 1890 more than 50,000 people lived in Evansville, which had a population of only 4,000 people when it was incorporated as a city in 1848. Serious floods in 1884, 1913, and 1937 finally led to the construction of a giant levee to protect the city, which today is known as "Plastics Valley" for the many plastics-related companies there. Evansville is regarded as a clean, safe, livable Midwestern city.

Population Profile

Metropolitan Area Residents
1970: 255,000
1980: 276,000
1990: 278,990
Percent change, 1980–1990: 1.0%
U.S. rank in 1980: 114th
U.S. rank in 1990: 121st

City Residents
1970: 139,000
1980: 130,496
1990: 126,272 (of which, 58,620 were males, and 67,652 were females)
Percent change, 1980–1990: -3.2%
U.S. rank in 1980: 121st
U.S. rank in 1990: 144th (State rank: 3rd)

Density: 3,102.5 persons per square mile (1990)

Racial and ethnic characteristics (1990)
  White: 113,090
  Black: 12,031
  American Indian, Eskimo, Aleut: Not reported
  Asian and Pacific Islander: 716
  Hispanic (may be of any race): 732

Percent of residents born in state: 69.8% (1990)

Age characteristics (1990)
  Population under 5 years old: 8,683
  Population 5 to 9 years old: 8,396
  Population 10 to 14 years old: 7,701
  Population 15 to 19 years old: 8,032
  Population 20 to 24 years old: 9,421
  Population 25 to 29 years old: 10,961
  Population 30 to 34 years old: 11,006
  Population 35 to 39 years old: 9,302
  Population 40 to 44 years old: 7,649
  Population 45 to 49 years old: 6,225
  Population 50 to 54 years old: 5,510
  Population 55 to 59 years old: 5,400
  Population 60 to 64 years old: 6,325
  Population 65 to 69 years old: 6,399
  Population 70 to 74 years old: 5,377
  Population 75 to 79 years old: 4,413
  Population 80 to 84 years old: 3,008
  Population 85 years and over: 2,464
  Median age: 34.5 years

Births (1988)
  Total number: 1,980

Deaths (1988)
  Total number: 1,645 (of which, 33 were infants under the age of 1 year)

Money income (1989)
  Per capita income: $12,564
  Median household income: $22,936
  Total households: 53,058
  Number of households with income of . . .
    less than $5,000: 4,394
    $5,000 to $9,999: 6,881
    $10,000 to $14,999: 5,990
    $15,000 to $24,999: 11,201
    $25,000 to $34,999: 8,949
    $35,000 to $49,999: 8,638
    $50,000 to $74,999: 4,834
    $75,000 to $99,999: 1,014
    $100,000 to $149,999: 629
    $150,000 or more: 528
  Percent of families below poverty level: 11.2 (63.1% of which were female householder families with related children under 5)
1991 FBI Crime Index Total: 7,658

Municipal Government

The city of Evansville is governed by a mayor and nine-member Common Council, all of whom are elected to a four-year term. The mayor, who is not a member of the council, and appointive boards oversee all municipal operations; the council approves city appropriations.

Head Official: Mayor Frank F. McDonald II (D) (since 1985; current term expires December 31, 1995)

Total Number of City Employees: 1,158 (1991)

Municipal Information: Evansville City/County Building, One Martin Luther King, Jr. Boulevard, Evansville, IN 47708; telephone (812) 426-5000

Economy

Major Industries and Commercial Activity

Evansville is the industrial, agricultural, retail, and transportation center for a thirty-six-county region in Indiana, Illinois, and Kentucky. The city is situated in the heart of rich coal fields that produce more than 140 tons of coal annually and contain resources of 290 billion tons. Evansville is also located in the Illinois Oil Basin, where 53 million barrels of oil are produced each year; one-hundred and fifty oil companies and oil-related firms are based in the city. Other industries in the area produce appliances, pharmaceuticals, aluminum, equipment and machinery, food products, furniture, pottery, textiles, plastics, metals, and chemicals.

A fertile farming region, part of the Midwest agricultural belt, surrounds Evansville. More than thirty-one thousand farms acres yield corn, soybeans, wheat, oats, barley, melons, apples, peaches, pears, small fruits, potatoes, and various other vegetables. Meat, fruit, and vegetable packing plants operate in the city.

Evansville retail and wholesale trade areas rank second in size in the state of Indiana. The city's financial community also serves the region with nine major banks in addition to brokerage firms, credit unions, consumer finance companies, and the loan production offices of four national and international banks.

Items and goods produced: refrigerators, flour, beer, farm and garden implements, excavating machinery, aluminum, chemicals, furniture, plastics, infant nutritionals, pottery, cigars, textiles

Incentive Programs—New and Existing Companies

Vision 2000, The Evansville Regional Economic Development Corporation works with the Evansville Chamber of Commerce for the economic well-being of the community and is the regional coordinator for economic development. It will assist companies seeking financing and expertise offered through seventeen different programs administered by the Indiana Department of Commerce. One of these programs, the Strategic Development Fund, teams up two or more state businesses in similar markets, offering grants or loans to spur cooperation and creativity between industrial sectors or regions of the state.

Local programs—Three square miles in Evansville are a designated Urban Enterprise Zone, offering tax abatement, real estate, and machinery. The Evansville Industrial Foundation acquires and improves land for nonprofit resale to industrial clients. The city administers a revolving loan fund, and the county is empowered to create Tax Incremental Financing districts.

Economic Development Information: Metropolitan Evansville Chamber of Commerce, Old Post Office Place, Suite 202, 100 N.W. Second Street, Evansville, IN 47708; telephone (812)425-8147; Vision 2000, P.O. Box 20127, Evansville, IN 47708-0127; telephone (812)423-2020

Commercial Shipping

Two public and several private port facilities receive year-round service from five major barge lines operating on the Ohio River. The largest public port is Southwind Maritime Center, a designated Foreign Trade Zone 15 miles west of Evansville at Mt. Vernon, Indiana. The Ohio River connects Evansville with all river markets in the central United States and on the Great Lakes and with international markets through the port of New Orleans. Linking the ports to ground and air transportation networks are four railroads, express and air freight carriers, and more than forty motor freight companies that maintain terminals in Evansville.

A location near the geographic center of the nation and access to inland water transportation contribute to Evansville's position as the second largest warehousing hub in Indiana. Services include modern public warehouses, rail-barge-truck-storage facilities, and storage-in-transit privileges with the three major rail carriers.

Labor Force and Employment Outlook

Evansville boasts a highly productive labor force with a Midwestern work ethic and low absentee rates. Employers often draw from a labor force living within a 50-mile radius of the city. Indiana's workers' compensation insurance rates and unemployment compensation costs are among the lowest in the country.

The following is a summary of data regarding the Evansville metropolitan area labor force as of September 1992.

Size of non-agricultural labor force: 141,900

Number of workers employed in . . .
mining: 1,800
construction: 7,700
manufacturing: 32,800
transportation and utilities: 6,600
wholesale and retail trade: 34,300
finance, insurance, and real estate: 5,700
services: 37,100
government: 15,900

Average hourly earnings of production workers employed in manufacturing: $12.80

Unemployment rate: 6.2%

Largest employers	*Number of employees*
Whirlpool Corp.	4,000
Alcoa	3,900
Bristol-Myers Squibb	3,100
Evansville-Vanderburgh School Corp.	2,841
Deaconess Hospital	2,406
St. Mary's Medical Center	2,200
General Electric	1,600
T. J. Maxx	1,500
Welborn Hospital	1,450
City of Evansville	1,288

Cost of Living

The following is a summary of data regarding several key cost of living factors for the Evansville area.

1992 (2nd Quarter) ACCRA Cost of Living Index: 94.2 (U.S. average = 100.0)

1992 (2nd Quarter) ACCRA Average House Price: $101,220

State income tax rate: 3.4%

State sales tax rate: 5.0% of adjusted gross income (food, prescription drugs, and items consumed or used in manufacturing are exempt)

Local income tax rate: 0.9%

Local sales tax rate: 1.0% food and beverage tax

Property tax rate: 12.0% of assessed value (1992)

Economic Information: Metropolitan Evansville Chamber of Commerce, Old Post Office Place, Suite 202, 100 NW Second Street, Evansville, IN 47708; telephone (812)425-8147; Vision 2000, P.O. Box 20127, Evansville, IN 47708-0127; telephone (812)423-2020

Education and Research

Elementary and Secondary Schools

The Evansville-Vanderburgh School Corporation provides public elementary and secondary education in the Evansville metropolitan area. In addition to honors programs, adult and special education curricula, and apprentice training programs, the school system offers students four semesters of classes relating to Japanese culture and language; two Japanese language teachers are employed. The school board, composed of seven members elected on a nonpartisan basis, selects the superintendent. Eighty-six percent of the teaching staff possesses a Master's degree or higher.

The following is a summary of data regarding Evansville public schools as of the 1991-1992 school year.

Total enrollment: 23,469

Number of facilities
elementary schools: 20
middle schools: 10
senior high schools: 5
other: 7

Student/teacher ratio: 16:3

Teacher salaries
minimum: $22,747
maximum: $42,651

Funding per pupil: $3,598.20

A privately-operated school as well as parochial and other church-affiliated schools and a Montessori Academy offer complete educational programs for students in kindergarten through twelfth grade.

Public Schools Information: Evansville-Vanderburgh School Corporation, Administration Building, One SE Ninth Street, Evansville, IN 47708; telephone (812)426-5053

Colleges and Universities

Evansville is home to two universities and two technical colleges. The University of Evansville,

The John Augustus Reitz house, a French Second Empire style home built in 1871.

founded in 1854, is a private institution granting master's, baccalaureate, and two-year associate degrees in several areas, including arts and sciences, engineering, business, education, fine arts, and nursing and health sciences. The university operates the Harlaxton Study Center in England. The University of Southern Indiana awards baccalaureate and associate degrees in such fields as teacher education, engineering technology, dental hygiene, and radiologic technology.

Ivy Tech Southwest schedules courses in programs leading to associate degrees in science and applied science as well as technical certificates. Business training is available at Business and Industry Training Center and ITT Technical Institute.

Libraries and Research Centers

The main facility of the Evansville-Vanderburgh County Public Library holds more than six-hundred thousand books in addition to periodicals, tapes, films, records, and federal and state documents. The library operates eight branches, one of which is a talking book service. A $2.5 million branch designed to hold forty thousand volumes was underway in 1992. Special interests include agriculture, business and management, economics, education, and religious studies; the Marcus and Mina Ravdin Memorial Collection is devoted to Judaic studies. The Willard Library of Evansville, founded in 1872, specializes in local history and genealogy as well as nineteenth-century periodical literature. Fifteen other libraries in the city are operated by colleges and universities, corporations, the Evansville Museum of Arts and Science, churches, hospitals, and government agencies.

Public Library Information: Evansville-Vanderburgh County Public Library, 22 SE Fifth Street, Evansville, IN 47708; telephone (812)428-8200

Health Care

The Evansville medical community provides health care for the metropolitan region with three general hospitals, numerous diagnostic and rehabilitation clinics, and nursing and convalescent homes; mental health care is a primary specialty offered by several public and private facilities. More than three hundred physicians and specialists and more than one hundred dentists practice in Evansville; approximately 1,500 beds are available in the city's major hospitals, St. Mary's, Welborn, and Deaconess.

Health Care Information: Vanderburgh County Medical Society, 123 NW 4th St., Evansville, IN 47713; telephone (812)425-1200

Recreation

Sightseeing

A visit to Evansville might begin with the Old Vanderburgh County Courthouse, a fine example of Beaux-Arts architecture. Completed in 1891, the courthouse exterior features statuary groups, bas-relief limestone carvings, and a giant clock housed in a bell tower; interior touches include marble floors, wainscoting, oak woodwork, brass handrails, and silverplated hardware. Other buildings of historic interest are the Willard Library, Indiana's oldest public library, which was opened in 1885 and is housed in an Italianate Gothic structure; and the John Augustus Reitz house, a French Second Empire style home built in 1871.

Angel Mounds, one of the best preserved prehistoric native American towns in the eastern United States, dates from a period as early as 1200 A.D. when the Mississippian—as the inhabitants have been named by archaeologists—lived on the Ohio River. Eleven artificially constructed mounds have been identified on the site, including one of the largest prehistoric structures in the eastern half of the country. An interpretative center is located at Angel Mounds. New Harmony, west of Evansville, was founded by the Harmony Society in 1814 as a utopian religious community and sold in 1824 to Robert Owen, who attracted scholars, scientists, and educators to participate in communal living. The buildings of this significant nineteenth-century cultural experiment have been restored. The Atheneum, the visitors' center designed by architect Richard Meier in 1979, is the starting point in learning about the importance of New Harmony.

Mesker Park Zoo, a 67-acre zoological park containing lakes, ponds, and wooded hills, houses more than five hundred exotic and domestic animals. Many animals are free to roam in open areas surrounded by moats; the monkeys live in a lake on a concrete

New Harmony was founded by the Harmony Society in 1814 as a utopian religious community.

replica of the *Santa Maria*. There is a children's contact area and petting zoo. The Wesselman Woods Nature Preserve is comprised of 200 acres of virgin hardwood forest within the city limits. Holiday World Theme Park is an amusement park on 180 acres.

Arts and Culture

The Repertory People of Evansville, a local theater group, performs a four-play season of contemporary and classic drama and comedy at the Old Court House. Specializing in musicals and comedy, the Evansville Civic Theatre includes a talent show in its subscription offerings. Among other local arts organizations are the Philharmonic Orchestra, Philharmonic Chorus, Symphonic Band, Master Chorale, Dance Theatre, and Children's Theatre. Evansville is the national headquarters of Phi Mu Alpha Sinfonia Fraternity, America's largest professional music fraternity.

The Evansville Museum of Arts and Science, located on the Ohio riverfront, exhibits artwork dating from the sixteenth to the twentieth centuries. The Koch Science Center there presents changing and permanent exhibits on science and technology and houses a planetarium; a steam locomotive, tavern car, and caboose are displayed on the grounds. At the Lincoln Boyhood National Memorial and State Park, visitors can see the Young Abe Lincoln Outdoor Drama, a living pioneer farm, and the grave of Lincoln's mother.

Festivals and Holidays

The Freedom Festival, lasting from mid-June to the Fourth of July, is Evansville's biggest celebration. It features a variety of activities for the family, including a fireworks display, ethnic foods, and sporting events. That celebration, and the two-week long Ohio River Arts Festival draw thousands to downtown Evansville each summer. The Reitz Home sponsors Victorian Christmas tours for ten days after Thanksgiving.

Sports for the Spectator

One of the premier hydroplane races in the Midwest is Thunder on the Ohio, which attracts the fastest unlimited hydroplanes for the main event of Evansville's Freedom Festival celebration. Ellis Park, 3 miles south of Evansville, sponsors thoroughbred horse racing June through Labor Day on a track built in 1922 and patterned after Saratoga; parimutuel betting is permitted. The University of Evansville and the University of Southern Indiana field several sports teams.

Sports for the Participant

The Ohio River and state parks in the Evansville area offer camping, fishing, hiking trails, and boating. Burdette Park provides a number of recreational activities for all age groups with an Olympic-size swimming pool, a roller skating rink, batting cages, and camping facilities on 145 acres. City parks maintain an ice skating rink, tennis courts, and athletic fields. Thirteen public and private golf courses are located in Evansville.

Shopping and Dining

Evansville's Downtown Walkway features more than forty shops restaurants. In addition to two modern malls, Evansville offers unique items at the Antique Mall and in retailing areas on North Main and Franklin Street. New Harmony recreates a turn-of-the-century commercial district. Evansville restaurants offer a variety of selections, ranging from fine cuisine served in a restaurant overlooking the Ohio River to homecooked meals in a casual setting. A local Japanese steak house serves American food cooked Japanese style.

Visitor Information: Evansville Convention and Visitors Bureau, 623 Walnut Street, Evansville, IN 47708; telephone (812)425-5402 or (800)433-3025

Convention Facilities

The convention and tourism industry, which brings in millions of dollars annually, is an integral part of the Evansville economy. The Vanderburgh Auditorium Convention Center, located downtown, provides a thirteen-thousand-square-foot exhibit hall; the two-thousand-seat auditorium is ideal for lectures and large-group meetings.

The Robert E. Green Convention Center provides more than fifty-eight-thousand square feet of exhibition space, and Roberts Stadium hosts boat and travel shows and circuses. Seven area hotels and motels maintain meeting and convention facilities, the largest of them accommodating 4,000 people. More than two thousand rooms are available as lodging throughout metropolitan Evansville at twenty-five hotels and motels.

Convention Information: Evansville Convention and Visitors Bureau, 623 Walnut Street, Evansville, IN 47708; telephone (812)425-5402 or (800)433-3025

Transportation

Approaching the City

The newly remodeled terminal at Evansville Regional Airport is served by six airlines and regional carriers that schedule more than forty daily connecting or direct flights from cities in the Midwest, the South, and Pittsburgh. General aviation facilities are maintained at Evansville Regional Airport and at two smaller area airports.

A system of interstate, federal, state, and local highways provides easy access into the city within the Evansville vicinity and from points throughout the nation. Principal routes include I-164; U.S. 41; and Indiana state roads 57, 62, 65, and 66. Interstate passenger service is provided by Greyhound Bus Lines.

Traveling in the City

Metropolitan Evansville Transit System (METS) schedules regular city and suburban bus routes. A motorized trolley also provides transportation along the Downtown Walkway and in the downtown district.

Communications

Newspapers and Magazines

Evansville's major daily newspapers are the morning and Sunday *Evansville Courier,* the evening (Monday-Saturday) *Evansville Press,* and the *Sunday Courier. The Message* is a weekly Catholic magazine published in the city.

Television and Radio

Television programming is available from six stations—three network affiliates, two public, and one independent—based in Evansville. Radio listeners tune into fourteen AM and FM stations that schedule, among other formats, classical, jazz, rock, and contemporary music, religious programs, and news and special interest features.

Media Information: Evansville Courier, P.O. Box 268, Evansville, IN 47702; telephone ((812)424-7711 and *Evansville Press,* P.O. Box 454, Evansville, IN 47703; telephone (812)424-7711

Fort Wayne

The City in Brief

Founded: 1794 (incorporated, 1829)

Head Official: Mayor Paul Helmke (R) (since 1988)

City Population
 1970: 178,000
 1980: 172,196
 1990: 173,072
 Percent change, 1980–1990: 0.4%
 U.S. rank in 1980: 80th
 U.S. rank in 1990: 99th

Metropolitan Area Population
 1970: 335,000
 1980: 354,000
 1990: 363,811
 Percent change, 1980–1990: 2.7%
 U.S. rank in 1980: 93rd
 U.S. rank in 1990: 100th

Area: 62.7 square miles (1990)

Elevation: 790 feet above sea level

Average Annual Temperature: 49.7° F

Average Annual Precipitation: 34.40 inches

Major Economic Sectors: Trade, manufacturing, services

Unemployment Rate: 5.8% (September 1992)

Per Capita Income: $12,726 (1989)

1992 (2nd Quarter) ACCRA Average House Price: $97,240

1992 (2nd Quarter) ACCRA Cost of Living Index: 90.3 (U.S. average = 100.0)

1991 FBI Crime Index Total: 17,104

Major Colleges and Universities: Indiana-Purdue University at Fort Wayne; Saint Francis College; Ivy Tech; Indiana Institute of Technology; International Business College; Taylor University Fort Wayne

Daily Newspaper: *The Journal Gazette; The News-Sentinel*

Indiana—Fort Wayne

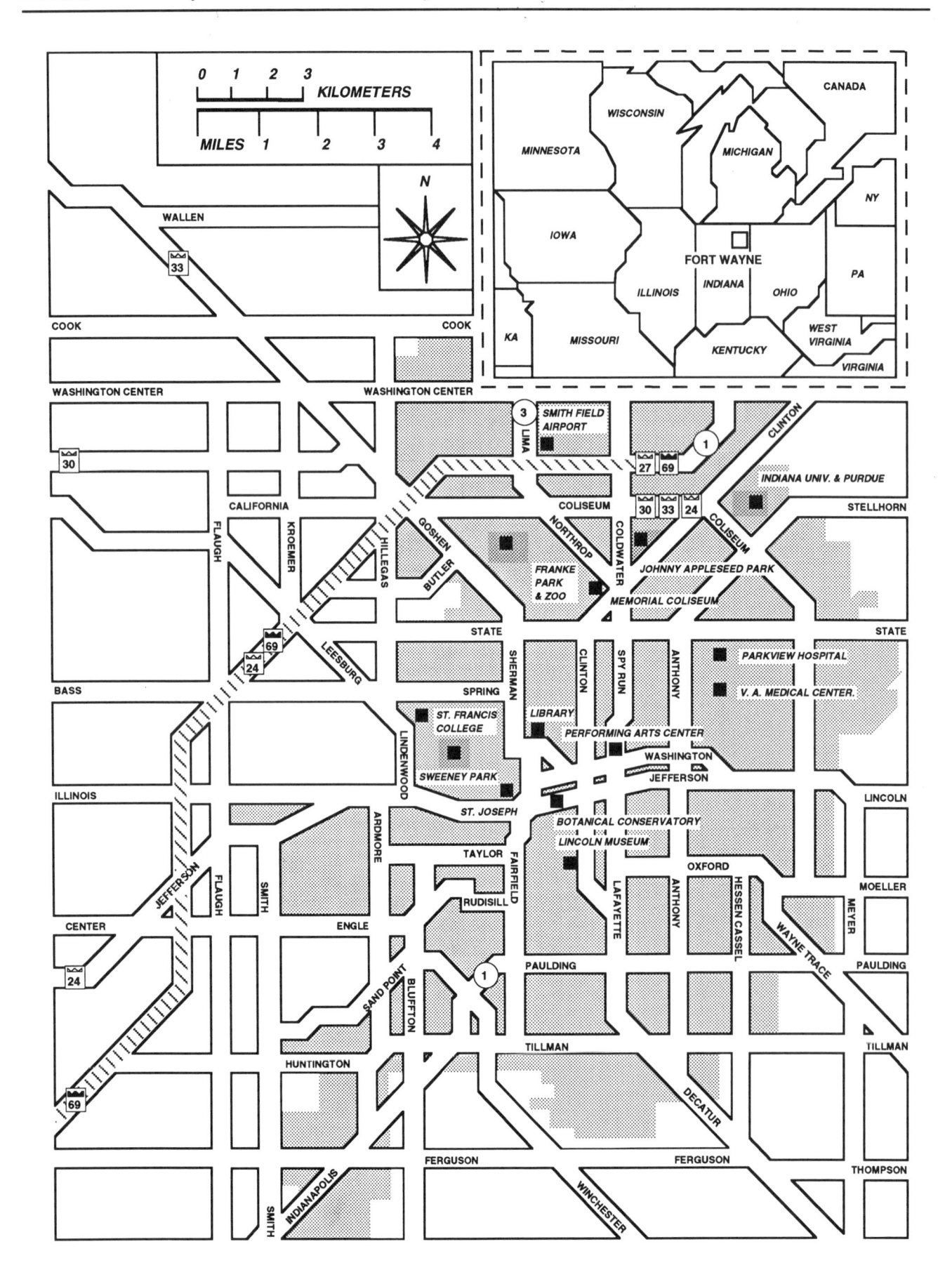

Cities of the United States • 2nd Edition

Introduction

Because of its location at the confluence of three rivers and near the geographic center of the United States, Fort Wayne has from its earliest days been an important marketplace—first as a fur-trading post and now as the headquarters of major corporations. The base of operations for "Mad" Anthony Wayne during the Indian struggles after the Revolutionary War and later the home of John Chapman, known also as Johnny Appleseed, the city figures prominently in the history of the settling of the western frontier. Fort Wayne is the seat of Allen County, which is included in the Fort Wayne standard metropolitan area.

Geography and Climate

Fort Wayne, located at the junction of the St. Marys, St. Joseph, and Maumee rivers in northeastern Indiana, is set in level to rolling terrain. The climate is representative of the midwestern region, with daily high and low temperature differences averaging about twenty degrees. Annual precipitation is well distributed, and the freeze-free period is usually 173 days. Damaging hailstorms occur about once a year; severe flooding also occurs. Snow covers the ground for about thirty days each winter, but heavy snowstorms are infrequent.

Area: 62.7 square miles (1990)

Elevation: 790 feet above sea level

Average Temperatures: January, 23.3° F; July, 73.3° F; annual average, 49.7° F

Average Annual Precipitation: 34.40 inches

History

Miami Territory Opened as Frontier

Ancient North American Indians hunted the mastodon and other wildlife in a hostile environment after the retreat of the glaciers in the area where Fort Wayne now stands. Later, the Moundbuilders constructed an advanced civilization before mysteriously dying out around the time of the European Middle Ages. The Miami native Americans ruled the lower peninsula region, fighting against the Iroquois who were armed by English colonists. In time, the Miami reestablished themselves in the Wabash Valley and built their principal village at the Lakeside district in Fort Wayne, which they named Kekionga, meaning "blackberry patch." Kekionga evolved into Miamitown, a large settlement of native Americans who sided with the British during the American Revolution.

Auguste Mottin de LaBalme, a French soldier fighting for the colonists, captured Miamitown in 1780, only to be defeated by Chief Little Turtle, one of the most feared and respected Miami leaders, in his first major victory. After the revolution, the British encouraged the Miami to attack the new nation, and war parties were sent eastward from Miamitown, prompting President Washington to order armies into the center of Miami territory. Little Turtle defeated the army of General Arthur St. Clair, and President Washington turned to General "Mad" Anthony Wayne, the Revolutionary War hero, to quell the rebellious tribes. General Wayne defeated the Miami at Fort Recovery in Ohio and at Fallen Timbers. Wayne marched on Miamitown and built the first American fort there. Wayne turned the fort over to Colonel John Hamtramck on October 21, 1794, and Hamtramck named it Fort Wayne the next day, which is considered the city's founding date.

Two key figures in Fort Wayne's early history were Chief Little Turtle and Williams Wells, who was kidnapped as a child from his Kentucky family and raised by Little Turtle's family. Wells and Little Turtle signed the Treaty of Greenville, opening up the frontier, and Wells was appointed Indian agent. The two men provided leadership and stability until their deaths in 1812. Potawatomi and Miami factions then invaded Fort Wayne, where order was restored when General William Henry Harrison's army was sent in. At the conclusion of the War of 1812 British influence on native Americans came to a close.

County Seat Becomes Industrial Center

Fort Wayne entered a new stage in its history with the arrival of Judge Samuel Hanna in 1819. Hanna built a trading post and a grist mill, earning himself the name "builder of the city." He was instrumental in realizing the Wabash & Erie Canal and securing Fort Wayne's first railroad. Hanna participated in organizing Allen County in 1824 and helped designate Fort Wayne as the county seat. In 1829, Fort Wayne was incorporated as a town.

Fort Wayne's growth as a midwestern industrial center was helped along by the number of inventions conceived and developed there. In 1871, Dr. Theodore Horton introduced a hand-operated washing machine and later manufactured the first electrically powered domestic washing machine. Joseph and Cornelius Hoagland and Thomas Biddle developed a baking powder formula that proved successful. The Foster Shirtwaist Factory, capitalizing on the popularity of a boy's size-fourteen shirt among women, made the famous Gibson Girl shirtwaist. Other prominent inventions originating in Fort Wayne were the self-measuring pump designed by Silvanus Freelove Bowser and the "arc light" developed by James Jenney.

Electronics and Lincolniana

The first nighttime professional baseball game took place in Fort Wayne in 1883 under Jenney Arc Lights. George Jacobs' discovery of an economical means of coating electrical wiring, which gave rise to the magnet wire industry, made possible modern electrical-powered products such as radios, telephones, automobiles, computers, and appliances. Homer Capehart's company of engineers invented the jukebox, which was sold to the Wurlitzer Company. Philo T. Farnsworth, a pioneer in the invention of television, bought the Capehart Company in 1938, and in time began the mass production of televisions.

Fort Wayne gained a reputation as a city receptive to innovative companies. The Magnavox Company relocated in Fort Wayne in 1928, and became a world leader in acoustical engineering. Also during the 1920s the Lincoln National Life Insurance Company emerged as an innovative insurance company. The company established and endowed the Lincoln Library and Museum, which houses the largest collection of materials on one man other than a biblical personage.

Historical Information: Allen County-Fort Wayne Historical Society, 302 Berry Street, Fort Wayne, IN 46802; telephone (219)426-2882

Population Profile

Metropolitan Area Residents
1970: 335,000
1980: 354,000
1990: 363,811
Percent change, 1980–1990: 2.7%
U.S. rank in 1980: 93rd
U.S. rank in 1990: 100th

City Residents
1970: 178,000
1980: 172,196
1990: 173,072 (of which, 82,311 were males, and 90,761 were females)
Percent change, 1980–1990: 0.4%
U.S. rank in 1980: 80th
U.S. rank in 1990: 99th (State rank: 2nd)

Density: 2,760.3 people per square mile (1990)

Racial and ethnic characteristics (1990)
 White: 139,244
 Black: 28,989
 American Indian, Eskimo, Aleut: 560
 Asian and Pacific Islander: 1,744
 Hispanic (may be of any race): 4,679

Percent of residents born in state: 69.4% (1990)

Age characteristics (1990)
 Population under 5 years old: 13,977
 Population 5 to 9 years old: 12,867
 Population 10 to 14 years old: 11,885
 Population 15 to 19 years old: 12,134
 Population 20 to 24 years old: 13,982
 Population 25 to 29 years old: 16,516
 Population 30 to 34 years old: 15,867
 Population 35 to 39 years old: 13,327
 Population 40 to 44 years old: 10,981
 Population 45 to 49 years old: 8,119
 Population 50 to 54 years old: 6,689
 Population 55 to 59 years old: 6,545
 Population 60 to 64 years old: 7,092
 Population 65 to 69 years old: 6,954
 Population 70 to 74 years old: 5,601
 Population 75 to 79 years old: 4,495
 Population 80 to 84 years old: 3,234
 Population 85 years and over: 2,807
 Median age: 31.5 years

Births (1988)
 Total number: 3,516

Deaths (1988)
  Total number: 1,958 (of which, 50 were infants under the age of 1 year)

Money income (1989)
  Per capita income: $12,726
  Median household income: $26,344
  Total households: 69,345
  Number of households with income of . . .
    less than $5,000: 3,496
    $5,000 to $9,999: 6,861
    $10,000 to $14,999: 7,012
    $15,000 to $24,999: 15,314
    $25,000 to $34,999: 12,906
    $35,000 to $49,999: 13,121
    $50,000 to $74,999: 7,982
    $75,000 to $99,999: 1,603
    $100,000 to $149,999: 675
    $150,000 or more: 375
  Percent of families below poverty level: 8.3% (48.2% of which were female householder families with related children under 5)
1991 FBI Crime Index Total: 17,104

Municipal Government

The head official of the City of Fort Wayne is a strong mayor who administers the government with a nine-member council. The mayor and council members—six elected by district and three elected at large—all serve four-year terms; the mayor is not a member of the council.

Head Official: Mayor Paul Helmke (R) (since 1988; current term expires December 31, 1995)

Total Number of City Employees: 1,734 (1992)

City Information: City of Fort Wayne, Mayor's Office, 1 Main Street, Fort Wayne, IN 46802; telephone (219)427-1111

Economy

Major Industries and Commercial Activity

Health care, manufacturing, and insurance are primary industries in Fort Wayne. The city's three hospitals form a regional medical center that serves three states; sixty-two manufacturing companies employ 100 people or more; and the home offices of several insurance companies are located in Fort Wayne. Lincoln National Life, one of the nation's twelve largest insurance firms, maintains Ft. Wayne headquarters; other national companies with corporate offices in the city are Tokheim, Zollner, Dana, North American Van Lines, and ITT Aerospace Division.

Items and goods produced: electric motors and supplies, trucks, tires, clothing, public speaking systems, televisions and electronic equipment, radios, valves, radio parts, copper wire, diamond wire dies, tools, trailers, aluminum pistons, gasoline pumps, liquid metering equipment, tanks and compressors, automotive axles, plastics, boats, feed, beer, paint, cranes and dredges, paper boxes, precision gears and counters, mobile homes

Incentive Programs—New and Existing Companies

Local programs—The City of Fort Wayne Division of Economic Development serves as the staff for two private development corporations that administer revolving loan programs for manufacturers, small businesses, and minority-owned enterprises; included is the Community Development Corporation of Fort Wayne, which administers the Small Business Administration 504 Loan Program.

State programs—The state of Indiana extends various grants and loans to local governments and companies through such programs as the Industrial Development Infra-Structure Program, Training For Profit, the Basic Industries Re-Training Program, and the Investment Incentive Program. The Federal Government Community Development Block Grant provides monies to support new and expanding businesses by funding infra-structure construction. The Fort Wayne Urban Enterprise Zone offers tax benefits to businesses within a 2.8 square mile radius of the central city area. The International Trade Division of the Indiana Department of Commerce encourages foreign investment locally.

Other state and federal programs provide grants and loans for research, development of business in defense markets, and use of Indiana's natural resources. Also available are job training and technical assistance.

Development Projects

A new General Motors Truck Assembly Plant has had a significant impact on the Fort Wayne economy, increasing employment to more than three thousand workers and generating an equal number of jobs in the non-manufacturing sectors. The Chuo Kagaku Company Ltd., a plastics manufacturer, recently built a $25 million Fort Wayne plant employing between one-hundred and fifty and two hundred workers. The Coca-Cola Bottling Company of Fort Wayne constructed a warehouse/distribution facility as part of a two-phase plan that will result in the creation of up to two hundred jobs. The General Electric Motor Business Group plant underwent a $10 million expansion from 1988 through 1990 under terms of a labor-management joint concession package that will cut labor costs; two-hundred and fifty jobs were to have been created.

Twenty-one projects are completed or under construction as part of Fort Wayne's downtown revitalization program. The centerpiece is Midtowne Crossing, a complex of renovated historic buildings and complementary new construction that houses condominiums, shops and stores, restaurants, and offices; it was completed in 1990. A successor to Midtowne Crossing is the Landing Condominiums in the city's historic commercial district; the Landing is under consideration for placement on the National Register of Historic Places. Another significant project is the Standard Federal Plaza, a thirteen-story office complex, that was completed in 1989. The Patterson Fletcher Building was under construction in 1992.

Economic Development Information: Department of Economic Development, City of Fort Wayne, City County Building, Fort Wayne, IN 46802; telephone (219)427-1127

Commercial Shipping

Fort Wayne International Airport is the national and international air transportation center for northeastern Indiana; it is located fifteen minutes from downtown Fort Wayne. Conrail and Norfolk Southern Railway connect the city with major markets throughout the United States. An excellent highway system is utilized by forty motor freight companies that provide overnight delivery within a 300-mile radius and second day delivery within 700 miles.

Labor Force and Employment Outlook

In spite of an increase in population, Fort Wayne has maintained a low unemployment rate since 1983.

The following is a summary of data regarding the Fort Wayne metropolitan area labor force as of September 1992.

Size of non-agricultural labor force: 198,400

Number of workers employed in . . .
  mining: not available
  construction: 8,600
  manufacturing: 50,000
  transportation and public utilities: 13,000
  wholesale and retail trade: 49,600
  finance, insurance, and real estate: 11,800
  services: 45,800
  government: 19,600

Average hourly earnings of production workers employed in manufacturing: $13.33

Unemployment rate: 5.8%

Largest employers	Number of employees
Magnavox Government & Industrial Electronics Company	3,770
Lincoln National Corp.	5,287
Fort Wayne Community Schools	3,743
Essex Group Inc.	3,700
General Electric Company	3,500
Parkview Memorial Hospital	3,300
General Motors Corporation	3,000
North American Van Lines, Inc.	2,800

Cost of Living

The following is a summary of data regarding several key cost of living factors for the Fort Wayne area.

Historic Fort Wayne is the only fully reconstructed military garrison from the War of 1812.

1992 (2nd Quarter) ACCRA Cost of Living Index: 90.3 (U.S. average = 100.0)

1992 (2nd Quarter) ACCRA Average House Price: $97,240

State income tax rate: 3.4% of adjusted gross income

State sales tax rate: 5.0% of adjusted gross income (food, prescription drugs, and items consumed or used in manufacturing are exempt)

Local income tax rate: 0.004 (county tax)

Local sales tax rate: 1.0% on food and beverages

Property tax rate: $8.45149 per $100 assessed valuation in the city of Fort Wayne and Wayne Township after property tax relief credit

Economic Information: Greater Fort Wayne Chamber of Commerce, 826 Ewing Street, Fort Wayne, IN 46802; telephone (219)424-1435

Education and Research

Elementary and Secondary Schools

The Fort Wayne Community Schools system is the second-largest district in the state of Indiana. The superintendent is selected by a seven-member, non-partisan board of education.

The following is a summary of data regarding the Fort Wayne public schools as of the 1991-1992 school year.

Total enrollment: 31,612

Number of facilities
 preschool: 1
 elementary schools: 33
 middle schools: 11
 senior high schools: 6
 other: 1 career center

Student/teacher ratio: elementary, 1:21.99; middle school, 1:22; senior high, 1:24.5

Teacher salaries
 minimum: $22,507
 maximum: $42,313

Funding per pupil: $3,594

Public Schools Information: Fort Wayne Community Schools, 1200 South Clinton Street, Fort Wayne, IN 46802; telephone (219)425-7227

Colleges and Universities

Enrolling more than ten thousand students, Indiana-Purdue University at Fort Wayne offers a complete range of undergraduate and graduate programs. Saint Francis College is a private liberal arts institution awarding associate, undergraduate, and graduate degrees primarily in business, education, and social sciences. Taylor University Fort Wayne was scheduled to open in 1992. Church-affiliated colleges are Concordia Theological Seminary and Summit Christian College. Vocational and technical training is provided by Ivy Tech, International Business College, ITT Technical Institute, and Indiana Institute of Technology.

Libraries and Research Centers

The main facility of the Allen County Public Library houses extensive holdings—more than two million books in addition to sixty-three hundred periodical titles, records, tapes, films, slides, art reproductions, and compact discs—and special collections in such fields as local history, genealogy, heraldry, fine arts, and federal and state documents. The library operates fourteen branches, a talking book service, and a bookmobile. Indiana-Purdue University at Fort Wayne and other area colleges maintain campus libraries. Specialized libraries include the Allen County-Fort Wayne Historical Society Library as well as libraries affiliated with hospitals, corporations, and government agencies. Indiana University-Purdue University at Fort Wayne supports a Community Research Institute.

Public Library Information: Allen County Public Library, 900 Webster Street, P.O. Box 2270, Fort Wayne, IN 46801-2270; telephone (219)424-7241

Health Care

The largest single industry in Fort Wayne, the health care community employs more than 6,000 people and serves a four-state region. The city's three hospitals, with a total of more than 2,000 beds, are all teaching facilities for Indiana University and provide general care as well as a complete range of specialized services. Parkview Memorial Hospital is the third largest hospital in the state and the largest outside Indianapolis; it offers a degree program in nursing, medical technology, and radiologic technology. Treating more than 75,000 people each year, Parkview operates a twenty-four-hour emergency ward and an intensive care nursery staffed by the only two full-time neonatologists in the area. The hospital also houses the Magnetic Resonance Imaging Center, the Regional Oncology Center, Lindenview Regional Behavior Center, and the Sickle Cell Foundation. In 1989, the hospital finished construction of a seventy-thousand-square-foot, $9 million "Birth Center." It houses forty-six private rooms, two operating suites, and a neonatal intensive care unit with thirty isolettes.

Lutheran Hospital's Renal Dialysis Chronic Outpatient Center is a regional facility for the treatment of kidney disorders. Lutheran, which established the area's first pacemaker clinic, is also known for cardiac care and rehabilitation services; because of its pioneering work in heart transplants, Lutheran is one of six hospitals nationwide to participate in clinical trials of a new advanced heart assist device. St. Joseph's Medical Center, Fort Wayne's first hospital, is recognized for its Regional Burn Center and virus laboratory; other specialties include sports medicine, cardiac care, and nutrition. St. Joseph's conducts degree programs in radiologic technology and medical technology; it is one of the few hospitals in the country to administer a Joint Action Nursing Education (JANE) program, offered in conjunction with Saint Francis College. Among the specialized facilities in Fort Wayne are the Veterans Affairs Medical Center; Park Center, Inc., a community counseling service; the Fort Wayne State Development Center for care of the mentally handicapped; and Charter Beacon Hospital, a psychiatric substance-abuse treatment center for children, adolescents, and adults.

Recreation

Sightseeing

History, animals, and botanical gardens highlight sightseeing in Fort Wayne. Historic Old Fort Wayne, the only fully reconstructed military garrison from the War of 1812, is preserved at its original site downtown where the St. Mary's and St. Joseph rivers merge to become the Maumee. Hosts in period costumes recount the early history of Fort Wayne. The Allen County Courthouse, Fort Wayne's first civic building, was constructed between 1897–1900; it combines Greek and Roman architectural themes and is capped with a rotunda. Its ornately designed interior features Italian marble, granite columns, bright tiles, and murals.

The Fort Wayne Zoo houses Australian Adventure, the largest and most complete Australian exhibit outside Australia. Animals roam free in the zoo's African Veldt; the zoo also contains the Cheetah Conservation Center, a twenty-thousand-gallon marine aquarium, and the Children's Zoo with baby bears, penguins, and macaws. The Foellinger-Freimann Botanical Conservatory preserves rare and exotic tropical plants from around the world, including ancient cycads from the dinosaur era, and desert plants from the Sonoran Desert of southern Arizona and northern Mexico. Lakeside Rose Garden, one of the largest rose gardens in America, features a white pergolas and two reflecting pools.

Arts and Culture

At the center of the performing arts in Fort Wayne is the restored Embassy Theater, considered one of the country's most lavish architectural masterpieces. The Embassy is home to the Fort Wayne Philharmonic, which performs a season of symphony, pops, and chamber music concerts; the theater also hosts touring Broadway shows. The Fort Wayne Ballet presents three major productions in addition to the annual Nutcracker Ballet in December.

The Louis A. Warren Lincoln Library and Museum, endowed by the Lincoln National Life Insurance Company, is a major world museum and research library for Lincolniana. The museum features sixty chronological and thematic displays covering the whole of Lincoln's career, along with three reconstructed period rooms: the Indiana log cabin, the Springfield law office, and the War Department telegraph room. The library has an important pictorial collection that includes oil paintings and original photographs.

The Fort Wayne Museum of Art houses more than one thousand pieces in permanent collections of paintings, prints, and sculpture in three self-contained modern buildings. The Allen County-Fort Wayne Historical Museum is located in the Old City Hall, a local architectural landmark. At the Diehm Museum of Natural History, displays of mounted animals, birds, and fish from North America are

The Australian Adventure Exhibit at Fort Wayne's Children's Zoo.

featured in reproductions of natural habitats. The Fort Wayne Firefighters Museum exhibits antique firefighting equipment and vehicles. In nearby Auburn the Auburn-Cord-Duesenberg Museum houses examples of the world's grandest automobiles.

Festivals and Holidays

Three Rivers Festival, held in mid-July for nine days, features more than two-hundred and fifty events that include a parade, a flotilla of rafts, bed races, and fireworks displays. Forte Festival focuses on the visual and performing arts in a two-day celebration at the end of May. Germanfest recognizes Fort Wayne's largest ethnic group with music, dance, sports, art, and German food for one week in mid-June. On Labor Day weekend in nearby Auburn a prestigious auto auction involving some of the world's finest automobiles takes place in a festive atmosphere. The Johnny Appleseed Festival, held the third weekend in September, brings the early 1800s to life by honoring John Chapman, who introduced apple trees to the Midwest. Holiday Fest from late November to the end of December is a month-long celebration of the Christmas season featuring the Festival of Trees and downtown lighting displays.

Sports for the Spectator

The Fort Wayne Komets, an International Hockey League team, plays a home schedule at Memorial Coliseum. The city's new CBA professional basketball team is dubbed the Fort Wayne Fury. The Hoosier Celebrities Golf Tournament in mid-June brings together top touring professional golfers and sports celebrities. Fort Wayne high schools field football and basketball teams that are competitive on a state level.

Sports for the Participant

Fort Wayne's recreational facilities include fifty tennis courts, thirty-seven softball diamonds, fifteen regulation baseball diamonds, four public swimming pools, four archery ranges, three public golf course, and four ice-skating rinks.

Shopping and Dining

Fort Wayne supports one of the Midwest's largest enclosed malls, which contains four anchor department stores and more than 180 specialty shops and stores. Altogether, shoppers can choose from almost twenty shopping centers and plazas in the Fort Wayne metropolitan area.

The city's four hundred restaurants reflect Fort Wayne's reputation as a restaurant town. One prize-winning establishment, noted for its French and continental cuisine, features aged corn-fed beef, Wisconsin milk-fed veal, and western prime lamb. A local Hungarian restaurant, the leader in ethnic cuisine, serves authentic dishes. In addition to two highly regarded Italian restaurants, other dining choices include regional favorites such as hearty farm-style meals and desserts.

Visitor Information: Fort Wayne Convention and Visitors Bureau, 826 Ewing Street, Fort Wayne, IN 46802; telephone (219)424-1435, ext. 44

Convention Facilities

Fort Wayne offers meeting planners an array of site choices. A major facility is the Grand Wayne Center, a complex that includes the convention center, the Botanical Conservatory, the Embassy Theater, a luxury hotel, and a parking garage. The convention center, which is handicap accessible, contains the multi-purpose Anthony Wayne Exhibition Hall with twenty-five thousand square feet of space that will accommodate more than 130 booths and will seat 1,800 people for a banquet or 27,000 people in a theater setting. The adjacent Embassy Theater is a unique setting for banquets, parties, and receptions.

The Allen County War Memorial Coliseum and Exposition Center, a city landmark, provides versatile facilities for trade shows, concerts, sporting events, stage shows, ice shows, the circus, meetings, and conventions. The arena has a seating capacity up to 10,000 people, ideal for spectator events, and the Exhibition Hall provides twenty-five thousand square feet of display area. Among the other meeting places in Fort Wayne are the Performing Arts Center and the Scottish Rite Masonic Auditorium and Banquet Hall. Area hotels and motels offer accommodations for both large and small group needs.

Convention Information: Fort Wayne Convention and Visitors Bureau, 826 Ewing Street, Fort Wayne, IN 46802; telephone (219)424-1435

Transportation

Approaching the City

The newly renovated terminal at Fort Wayne International Airport is the destination for most air traffic into Fort Wayne. Nine commercial carriers provide regularly scheduled flights from most major cities throughout the United States; connecting flights for international travel are also available. One of the top three revenue sources for the city of Fort Wayne, Fort Wayne International Airport accommodates more than one million passengers and generates over $96 million annually. Fort Wayne International Airport is the base of the 122nd Tactical Fighter Wing of the Air National Guard. Smith Field is a secondary airport for private air traffic.

Amtrak's Broadway Limited makes two daily stops in Fort Wayne, connecting the city with New York, Pittsburgh, and Washington, D.C., to the east and Chicago to the west.

A network of interstate, state, and local highways links Fort Wayne to all parts of the nation. Interstate 69, extending from Flint, Michigan, through Fort Wayne southward to Indianapolis, provides access at various points within 100 miles to other major cities via Interstates 96, 80, 90, 70, 74, and 65. Major north-south highways passing through the city are U.S. 27 and Indiana state roads 1, 37, and 3. Principal east-west routes are U.S. 24 and 30 and Indiana state road 14.

Traveling in the City

The Fort Wayne Public Transportation Corporation (P T C) provides bus service throughout the metropolitan area and in nearby New Haven. P T C also operates trolley cars during special events.

Communications

Newspapers and Magazines

The principal daily newspapers in Fort Wayne are *The Journal Gazette,* published mornings and Sundays, and *The News Sentinel,* published Monday through Saturday evenings.

Special-interest magazines based in the city are *The American Chiropractor, Bowhunter Magazine, Parliamentary Journal,* and *Today's Catholic.*

Television and Radio

Five television stations, including three network affiliates, one independent channel, and a public network outlet, broadcast from Fort Wayne; cable service is available through a local company. Diverse radio programming—such as easy listening, top 40, rock, and country and western music as well as religious features and news and information—is provided by twelve AM and FM stations, one of which is based in neighboring Defiance, Ohio.

Media Information: The Journal Gazette, 600 West Main Street, Fort Wayne, IN 46802; telephone (219)461-8253; and, *The News-Sentinel,* 600 West Main Street, P.O. Box 102, Fort Wayne, IN; telephone (219)461-8222

Selected Bibliography

Kavanaugh, Karen B., *A Genealogist's Guide to the Allen County Public Library, Fort Wayne, Indiana* (Ft. Wayne, IN: The Author, 1981)

Gary

The City in Brief

Founded: 1906

Head Official: Mayor Thomas Barnes (D) (since 1988)

City Population
- 1970: 175,415
- 1980: 151,968
- 1990: 116,646
- Percent change, 1980–1990: −23.2%
- U.S. rank in 1980: 104th
- U.S. rank in 1990: 153rd

Metropolitan Area Population (PMSA)
- 1970: 633,000
- 1980: 643,000
- 1990: 605,000
- Percent change, 1980–1990: 1.6%
- U.S. rank in 1980: 3rd (CMSA)
- U.S. rank in 1990: 3rd (CMSA)

Area: 50.2 square miles (1990)

Elevation: 590 feet above sea level

Average Annual Temperature: 48.9° F

Average Annual Precipitation: 34.66 inches (39.2 inches of snowfall)

Major Economic Sectors: Trade, services, manufacturing

Unemployment Rate: 7.6% (September 1992)

Per Capita Income: $8,994 (1989)

1992 (2nd Quarter) ACCRA Average House Price: Not reported

1992 (2nd Quarter) ACCRA Cost of Living Index: Not reported

1991 FBI Crime Index Total: 11,706

Major Colleges and Universities: Indiana University Northwest

Daily Newspaper: *Post-Tribune*

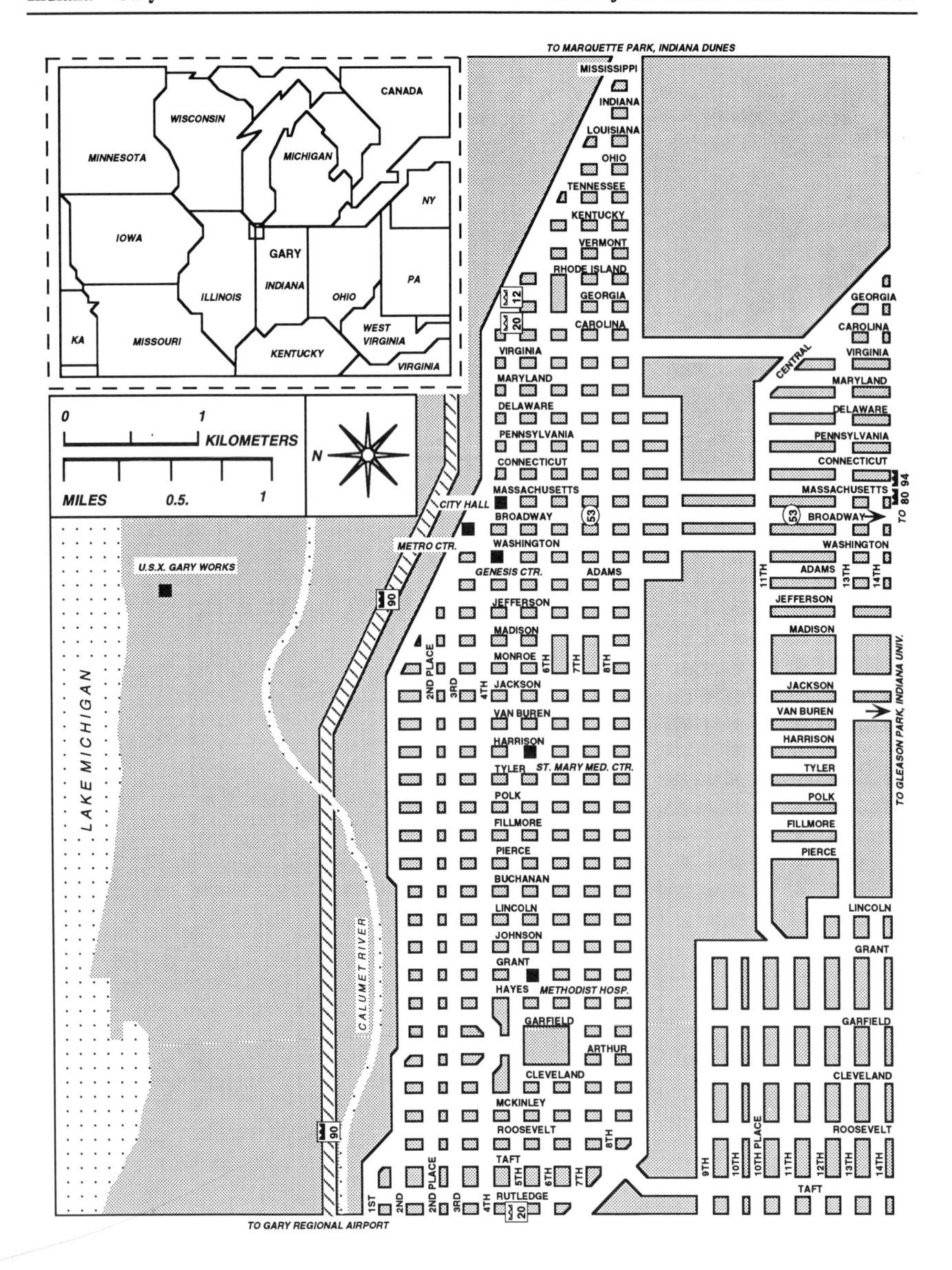

Indiana—Gary *Cities of the United States • 2nd Edition*

Introduction

The fourth largest city in Indiana, Gary is the largest U.S. city founded in the twentieth century. A leading steel producing center, it is often called the *Steel City*. Gary's pristine Lake Michigan beaches, a multimillion dollar marina, and the vast improvement of the once highly polluted skies have been instrumental in the growth of the tourist industry in both Gary and Lake County. The geographical placement of Gary in the Calumet region provides visitors with a vast variety of natural attractions, from the lakeshore to inland protected prairies, nature preserves, numerous parks, and rare wildlife. In 1992 *Money* magazine rated northwest Indiana eighty-first among the top three hundred places to live in the U.S.

Geography and Climate

The city of Gary is located at the southern end of Lake Michigan approximately 28 miles from Chicago in an area called the Calumet region, which includes the northern portions of Lake and Porter counties. Gary is in a region of frequently changeable weather. The climate is predominantly continental, ranging from relatively warm in summer to relatively cold in winter. However, the continental aspect is partially modified by Lake Michigan. Very low temperatures most often occur in air that flows southward to the west of Lake Superior before reaching the Gary area. In summer the higher temperatures result from a south or southwest flow and therefore are not modified by the lake.

Area: 50.2 square miles (1990)

Elevation: 590 feet above sea level

Average Temperatures: January, 24.8° F; July, 73.6° F; annual average, 48.9° F

Average Annual Precipitation: 34.66 inches (39.2 inches of snowfall)

History

Creation of City as Major Steel Center

Miami and Potawatomi native Americans lived in the area of present-day Gary from the 1600s to the 1800s. Few whites settled in the area before 1900, as marshes and sand dunes covered the site. On trips back to France from the New World, Father Marquette used the Calumet Portage between the Little Calumet regions. Tradition holds that Marquette camped at the eastern mouth of the Grand Calumet, the present site of Gary's Marquette Park. In the early 1800s, as many as fifty Potowatomi villages were scattered throughout the area, but by mid-century almost all the tribes had been moved to western reservations.

In 1896, on the shores of Lake Michigan where Gary is now located, the world's first successful sustained flight in a heavier-than-air machine took place. Octave Chanute, a French native and already world famous as a bridge and railroad engineer, first took flight in a glider off the windswept dunes.

The creation of Gary as a major steel center was the dream of Judge Elbert H. Gary, then chairman of the United States Steel Corporation, who wanted to erect the largest steel plant in the world on a lake site midway between the ore fields in Minnesota and the coal fields in the south. He decided on 12,000 acres of unoccupied lands at the southern end of the Lake Michigan. Work on the $100,000 mill began in March 1906, and three and one-half years later the mill began to operate and the first steel was poured. In a few months, the city of Gary was built, providing instant residency for thousands of steel workers and their families.

The steel industry continued to thrive through the decades, and the city grew from 16,800 people in 1910 to 55,000 people by 1920. Gary became a great ethnic melting pot as the attraction of jobs in the mills brought immigrants from Poland, Romania, Serbia, and Hungary, among other places.

City Attracts Unskilled Workers; Laborers Organize

Prior to World War I organized labor failed to gain a foothold among the area's steelworkers, many of whom were immigrants. The post-war period was one of growth for Gary, which by 1920 numbered 55,378 residents and had become the largest city in the

Calumet region. Construction included many apartment buildings and houses, three ten-story buildings, the Hotel Gary, the Gary State Bank, the imposing Knights of Columbus building, and the massive City Methodist Church. Public structures included Gary City Hall, a courthouse, a 10-acre esplanade as well as Marquette Park and Gleason Park. Large numbers of African-Americans were drawn to the city in search of unskilled labor jobs, although a quota system kept the black work force at a level no greater than 15 percent. Most of the region's public accommodations were racially segregated and blacks were contained in the area called "the Patch", the most undesirable housing area in the city. Mexicans, who were originally brought in as strike breakers, also were forced to reside in "the Patch".

The Great Depression of the 1930s had a devastating effect on Gary's economy, with US Steel dropping from 100 percent capacity in 1929 to 15 percent capacity in 1932. The depression also brought the unionization of Gary's industries, with US Steel recognizing the Steelworkers Organizing Committee as the bargaining agent for its workers in 1937. Between 1935 and 1939 steel workers' wages rose nationally some 27 percent, and Gary's workers also benefitted.

During World War II, steel production soared and the tide of prosperity continued for the next two decades. However, manufacturing then began to decline in the region and between 1979 and 1986 northwest Indiana's loss in manufacturing totaled 42.5 percent, largely in the areas of oil and steel. Changes in the world market made U.S. steel more economical by the late 1980s, and the steel industry rebounded to a substantial degree throughout the early 1990s.

Changing Demographics Bring African-American Majority

Since the 1960s, Gary's population has decreased through "white flight" to the suburbs. By 1990 the population was made up of 80 percent African-Americans. Voters elected Gary's first black mayor, Richard G. Hatcher, in 1967 and he was subsequently elected to four more terms. Hatcher's administration improved housing conditions in the city and helped obtain federal job training programs. In 1982 the Genesis Convention Center was built in the heart of Gary's downtown to help in the revitalization of the business district. Hatcher was defeated by Thomas V. Barnes in the 1987 mayoral election.

Gary made great progress during the 1960s and 1970s in reducing its air pollution caused by smoke from factories and steel mills. The amount of impurities in the air dropped nearly 60 percent from 1966 to 1975. The city issued nearly $180 million in revenue bonds to help U S X reduce its pollution at its local facilities.

The loss of population in Gary during the 1980s, nearly 25 percent, was larger than that of any other U.S. city. It is hoped that the development of a $100 million dollar marina complex will breathe new life into this uniquely twentieth century city.

Historical Information: Heritage Gary, Inc., 401 Broadway, Room 200, Gary, IN 46402; telephone (219)881-1398

Population Profile

Metropolitan Area Residents (PMSA)
1970: 633,000
1980: 643,000
1990: 605,000
Average annual percent change, 1980–1988: 0.4%
Percent change, 1980–1990: 1.6%
U.S. rank in 1980: 3rd (CMSA)
U.S. rank in 1990: 3rd (CMSA)

City Residents
1970: 175,415
1980: 151,968
1990: 116,646 (of which 53,602 were males, and 63,044 were females)
Percent change, 1980–1990: −23.2%
U.S. rank in 1980: 104th
U.S. rank in 1990: 153rd (State rank: 4th)

Density: 2,323.6 per square mile (1990)

Racial and ethnic characteristics (1990)
 White: 19,020
 Black: 93,982
 American Indian, Eskimo, Aleut: 175
 Asian and Pacific Islander: 213
 Hispanic (may be of any race): 6,690

Percent of residents born in state: 60.3% (1990)

Age characteristics (1990)
  Population under 5 years old: 9,295
  Population 5 to 17 years old: 27,771
  Population 18 to 20 years old: 5,467
  Population 21 to 24 years old: 5,851
  Population 25 to 44 years old: 32,666
  Population 45 to 54 years old: 11,332
  Population 55 to 59 years old: 5,354
  Population 60 to 64 years old: 5,649
  Population 65 to 74 years old: 8,392
  Population 75 to 84 years old: 3,877
  Population 85 years and older: 992
  Median age: 31.2 years

Births (1988)
  Total number: 2,256

Deaths (1988)
  Total number: 1,330 (of which 40 were infants under the age of 1 year)

Money income (1989)
  Per capita income: $8,994
  Median household income: $19,390
  Total households: 40,752
  Number of households with income of . . .
    less than $5,000: 6,701
    $5,000 to $9,999: 5,670
    $10,000 to $14,999: 4,368
    $15,000 to $24,999: 7,341
    $25,000 to $34,999: 5,344
    $35,000 to $49,999: 5,607
    $50,000 to $74,999: 4,333
    $75,000 to $99,999: 1,117
    $100,000 to $149,999: 214
    $150,000 or more: 57
  Percent of families below poverty level: 26.4% (72.9% of which were female householder families with related children under 5)
1991 FBI Crime Index Total: 11,706

Municipal Government

Gary's city government consists of a mayor and nine councilmen, who are elected to four-year terms.

Head Official: Mayor Thomas Barnes (D) (since 1988; current term expires November 1995)

Total Number of City Employees: 1,602 (1992)

City Information: City of Gary, 401 Broadway, Gary, IN 46402; telephone (219)881-1301

Economy

Major Industries and Commercial Activity

Historically, manufacturing has been the heart of Gary and northwest Indiana. However, the steel production that revived in the late 1980s no longer totally dominates the scene. Gary's economy has been hard hit by decline of the number of people employed in the American steel industry. The Gary Chamber of Commerce points out that although jobs have decreased due primarily to automation, the amount of steel produced in Gary has actually increased as of the early 1990s. The Gary Works of the USX Corporation can produce seven million short tons of steel annually. Three other large steel plants are in the region.

The economy is also exemplified by the following businesses, which are some of the city's major employers: Gary Steel Products Corporation, which produces machinery and air distribution products, Georgia Pacific Corporation, which makes paper products, the women's sports apparel maker Jantus Manufacturing Company, the Lehigh Portland Cement Company, and the Western Engine Company.

In recent years, tourism has become one of the Gary's fastest growing industries. Gary, and Lake County, are becoming increasingly popular for people from Chicago and other urban areas who want to escape the big cities for short vacations and recreational opportunities.

Items and goods produced: steel and steel-finished products including sheet metal, tin plate, tubing, and bridges; hardware, springs, windshield wipers, light fixtures, apparel and bed linens, processed foods

Incentive Programs—New and Existing Companies

The city of Gary, the state, the Gary Urban Enterprises Association, and local business leaders have created the Gary Small Business Incubator for businesses in downtown Gary's Urban Enterprise Zone. The incubator provides tenants with the support necessary to increase their probability of success, as measured in terms of growth in revenue, profits, and number of employees. The Gary Government Contracting Corporation assists companies in obtaining operating capital and in taking advantage of federal, state, and local government contracting opportunities at the state and local level. The Urban Enterprise Zone provides a variety of tax and financial credits, which can result in full forgiveness of any Indiana personal property tax paid on inventory, raw materials, or finished products. Through an employment-expense credit a zone business may receive an annual income tax credit of 10 percent of the wages earned by employers who live in the zone, up to $1,500 credit per employee. To make capital more readily available to zone businesses, the loan interest credit lowers taxes that lenders pay on interest earned on loans to zone businesses. The equity investment credit gives incentive for individual investors to put their money into zone businesses.

Job Training Programs—The Lakeshore Employment Training Partnership (LETP) offers new and expanding businesses the following services at no cost to the employer: supplying a pool of trained people whom they have assisted in developing marketable skills; pre-screening of potential employees for positions needing to be filled by any existing business; conducting occupational and educational testing; writing on-the-job training contracts with employers for training of employees either on-site or at various educational institutions in the area (through the use of federal on-the-job training funds, LETP may reimburse employers up to 50 percent of an individual's wages for as long as that individual is in on the job training up to six months or five hundred hours); and analyzing the tasks and skills required for successful performance of a particular job.

Development Projects

The city of Gary in the 1990s is developing the largest marina on Lake Michigan, estimated at $100 million. The Old Gary Beach Bathing House is being transformed into a $5 million aquatorium that will eventually include a restaurant. In 1993 a multimillion dollar development zone was being constructed at Gary Regional Airport which will include hangars and numerous other buildings.

Economic Development Information: Greater Gary Chamber of Commerce, 504 Broadway, Suite 324, Gary, IN 46402; telephone (219)885-7407

Commercial Shipping

Gary Regional Airport, undergoing expansion in the early 1990s, serves corporate and air cargo operators. Gary has six truck terminals. Railways with service into Gary include Grand Trunk, C & O, B & O, N & W, E. J. & E., C. S. S. & S. B., and Conrail. More than one hundred trucking companies provide overnight service to most major cities within a 300-mile radius.

Labor Force and Employment Outlook

The following is a summary of data regarding the Gary-Hammond metropolitan area labor force as of September 1992.

Size of non-agricultural labor force: 258,300

Number of workers employed in . . .
  mining: not reported
  construction: 19,600
  manufacturing: 54,000
  transportation and public utilities: 18,600
  wholesale and retail trade: 61,800
  finance, insurance, and real estate: 8,500
  services: 62,000
  government: 33,800

Average hourly earnings of production workers employed in manufacturing: $16.40

Unemployment rate: 7.6%

Largest employers	Number of employees
USX/USS Steel Gary Works Division	7,500
Methodist Hospital	2,300
St. Mary's Medical Center	1,781
NBB	813
Indiana Bell	455

Cost of Living

Visitors and residents find that the dollar goes farther in Gary and Northwest Indiana than in most other areas. According to ACCRA, Northwest Indiana offers one of the lowest costs of living of major metropolitan centers within the north central United States.

The following is a summary of data regarding several key cost of living factors for the Gary area.

1992 (2nd Quarter) ACCRA cost of living index: Not reported

1992 (2nd Quarter) ACCRA average house price: Not reported

State income tax rate: 3.4%

State sales tax rate: 5.0% (food, prescription drugs, and items consumed or used in manufacturing are exempt)

Local income tax rate: none

Local sales tax rate: none

Property tax rate: $23.42 per $100 of assessed valuation, assessment ratio = 33.33% for residential

Economic Information: Greater Gary Chamber of Commerce, 504 Broadway, Suite 324, Gary, IN 46402; telephone (219)885-7407

Education and Research

Elementary and Secondary Schools

Besides the conventional schools, the Gary Community School System has three special education facilities, one career center, the Lincoln Achievement Center, Martin Luther King, Jr. Academy, and a Visual and Performing Arts Center.

The following is a summary of data regarding Gary's public schools as of the 1992-1993 school year.

Total enrollment: 23,902

Number of facilities
 elementary schools: 28
 junior high/middle schools: 6
 senior high schools: 5
 other: 7

Teacher salaries
 minimum: $23,126
 maximum: $40,258

Funding per pupil: $4,304.96 (1990-1991) $5,481 (1991-1992)

Public Schools Information: Gary Community School District, 620 East Tenth Place, 46402; (219)886-6400

Colleges and Universities

Indiana University Northwest offers degrees in business, technical studies, and medical education for more than five thousand students.

Libraries and Research Centers

The Gary Public Library has nearly five-hundred thousand volumes, nearly fifteen thousand items of graphic materials, and more than 1,375 audio-visuals and films. The library has five branches and one bookmobile. Its special collections focus on Gary and Indiana history.

At Indiana University Northwest's Laboratories for Environmental Research, activities focus on recycling of byproduct materials for basic industries.

Public Library Information: Gary Public Library, 220 West Fifth Avenue, Gary, IN 46402-1270; telephone (219)886-2484

Health Care

Gary is the home of Methodist Hospital and St. Mary Medical Center. Methodist Hospital's specialties include cancer research, diagnosis, and treatment; maternal and child health; gerontology; and cardiac rehabilitation. Methodist is the regional center for treatment and care for spinal injuries. The Lakeshore Health System is the result of cooperation between St. Catherine Hospital in East Chicago and St. Mary Medical Centers in Gary and Hobart. A leader in occupational-health services, the system offers a variety of preventive programs. The city is served by 475 doctors. Other special health facilities include mental health clinics, alcohol treatment clinics, medical clinics, and a drug treatment center.

Recreation

Sightseeing

Gary's Genesis Convention Center, a modern structure featuring rounded corners and an imposing glass wall across the front, is well worth a viewing. Built in 1921, the Gary Bathing Beach Aquatorium, one of the first examples of modular block construction in the world, is undergoing restoration in the early 1990s. Other notable buildings include the City Methodist Church, a massive Gothic structure of limestone completed in 1926, and the old westside neighborhood historic district, part of the company town built by U S Steel Corporation in 1906, which reflects a variety of architectural styles.

Tours of the U S X Gary Works, one of the largest steel plants in the world, are available by appointment. The Chanute Glider, a glider airplane which took its first flight off the Indiana sand dunes in 1896, is on display at the Gary Regional Airport. Orville Wright credited Octave Chanute with building the prototype of the plane which the Wright Brothers flew four years later, under power for the first, time at Kitty Hawk, NC.

The Indiana Dunes extend intermittently along the lakeshore from Gary to Michigan City, Indiana. Poet Carl Sandburg described the dunes as being "to the Midwest what the Grand Canyon is to Arizona and Yosemite is to California. They constitute a signature of time and eternity." The dunes, home to woodland hiking and miles of sandy beach, have been recognized as a national treasure by the U.S. Congress. The Paul H. Douglas Environmental Center at Indiana Dunes National Lakeshore provides an opportunity to learn about the disciplines of ecology and environmental science. Also at the dunes are the Bailly Homestead, which offers a look at pioneer and native American life, and the Chellberg Farm, where visitors may catch a glimpse of turn-of-the-century farming. The Brunswick Park savanna, a 49-acre park on the city's west side, features rare plants such as black oak, bluejoint grass, and prairie sunflowers that have been safeguarded in the preserve, as well as tennis courts and picnic areas.

In nearby Hammond is one of the country's largest marinas, Hammond Marina, which has more than eleven hundred wet slips, five launch ramps, and fishing piers. The Marina is Home to the SS *Milwaukee Clipper,* a 361-foot steam-powered passenger ship built in 1905. Also in Hammond is the Little Red Schoolhouse, built in 1869 in Hessville to replace a log school, which is operated as a living museum. The building features the original tower bell, desks, and other period furnishings. Visiting children are invited to attend classes conducted in a nineteenth century manner.

Festivals and Holidays

The last weekend in April is the time for Northwest Indiana Black Expo. July's Lakefront Festival at Gleason Park is held the first week in July. The city of Gary Old Fashioned Carnival Picnic takes place at Gilroy Stadium during the third weekend in August. September's Duneland Harvest Festival at Chellberg Farm offers crafts, music, and exhibits.

Sports for the Spectator

Gary residents have the advantage of being a short drive from Chicago, which boasts major teams in baseball, basketball, hockey, and many other sports.

Sports for the Participant

Lake Etta Park offers 70 acres of open space with a stocked fishing lake, a fish cleaning station, a fishing pier, concessions, a swimming beach, a playground, picnic shelters, walking trails, and paddle boats. Gary has fifty-one other parks including North Gleason Park, Marquette Park and Beach, and Wells Street Beach. Northwest Indiana has more than one hundred privately and publicly run golf courses, including Gary's Calumet Golf Club and South Gleason Golf Course. The Indiana Dunes National Lakeshore Park preserves over 12,000 acres in its natural splendor, and offers swimming, fishing, hiking, picnicking, and horseback riding along the miles of sandy beaches on Lake Michigan.

Shopping and Dining

Lake County contains a variety of antique shops and specialty stores, as well as major shopping malls that feature many popular chain stores.

A variety of foods, from Chicago-style polish sausage, homemade pierogies (a Polish dumpling), or some of the best seafood in the Midwest can be found in area restaurants. Gary's eateries range from moderate family style to ethnic cafes, bakery lunchrooms, and ethnic establishments.

Visitor Information: Lake County Convention and Visitors Bureau, 5800 Broadway, Suite S, Merrillville, IN 46410; telephone (219)980-1617

The Genesis Convention Center, an impressive example of contemporary architecture, is the site of many important local events.

Convention Facilities

Genesis Convention Center, with its striking contemporary design, can accommodate nearly 9,000 people for conventions with eleven meeting rooms that seat 40 to 400 persons. The concourse area provides ample room for registration and information centers.

Convention Information: Lake County Convention and Visitors Bureau, 5800 Broadway, Suite S, Merrillville, IN 46410; telephone (219)980-1617

Transportation

Approaching the City

Located about 28 miles southeast of Chicago, Gary is accessible from Interstate 65, which runs north and south, and I-94/80, which runs east and west. The Indiana Toll Road I-90 connects the Chicago Skyway to the west and the Ohio Turnpike to the east. Greyhound Trailways, Indiana, and Tri-State operate bus service into Gary. Gary Regional Airport, 4 miles east of the city on U.S. 12, houses Direct Air, which provides passenger service to Pittsburgh, Cleveland, Detroit, and Fort Wayne. Chicago's Midway airport is a thirty-minute drive while Chicago's O'Hare Airport is a one-hour drive from Gary.

Traveling in the City

Local bus transportation is provided by the Gary Public Transportation Corporation.

Communications

Newspapers and Magazines

Gary's newspapers include the daily *Post-Tribune, The Gary Crusader,* and *Info Newspaper.*

Media Information: Post-Tribune, 1065 Broadway, Gary, IN 46402; telephone ((219)881-3000

Selected Bibliography

Poinsett, Alex, *Black Power: Gary Style: The Making of Mayor Richard Gordon Hatcher* (Chicago, Johnson Pub. Co., 1970)

Indianapolis

The City in Brief

Founded: 1816 (incorporated, 1847)

Head Official: Mayor Steve Goldsmith (R) (since 1992)

City Population
 1970: 737,000
 1980: 701,000
 1990: 731,327
 Percent change, 1980–1990: 4.4%
 U.S. rank in 1980: 12th
 U.S. rank in 1990: 13th

Metropolitan Area Population
 1970: 1,111,000
 1980: 1,167,000
 1990: 1,249,822
 Percent change, 1980–1990: 7.1%
 U.S. rank in 1980: 30th
 U.S. rank in 1990: 31st

Area: 361.7 square miles (1990)

Elevation: Ranges from 645 to 910 feet above sea level

Average Annual Temperature: 52.1° F

Average Annual Precipitation: 40 inches of rain; 23 inches of snow

Major Economic Sectors: Trade, services, manufacturing

Unemployment Rate: 4.8% (September 1992)

Per Capita Income: $14,605 (1989)

1992 (2nd Quarter) ACCRA Average House Price: $101,250

1992 (2nd Quarter) ACCRA Cost of Living Index: 97.0 (U.S. average = 100.0)

1991 FBI Crime Index Total: 36,005

Major Colleges and Universities: Indiana University-Purdue University at Indianapolis; Butler University; University of Indianapolis; Ivy-Tech; Marian College

Daily Newspaper: *Indianapolis Star; Indianapolis News*

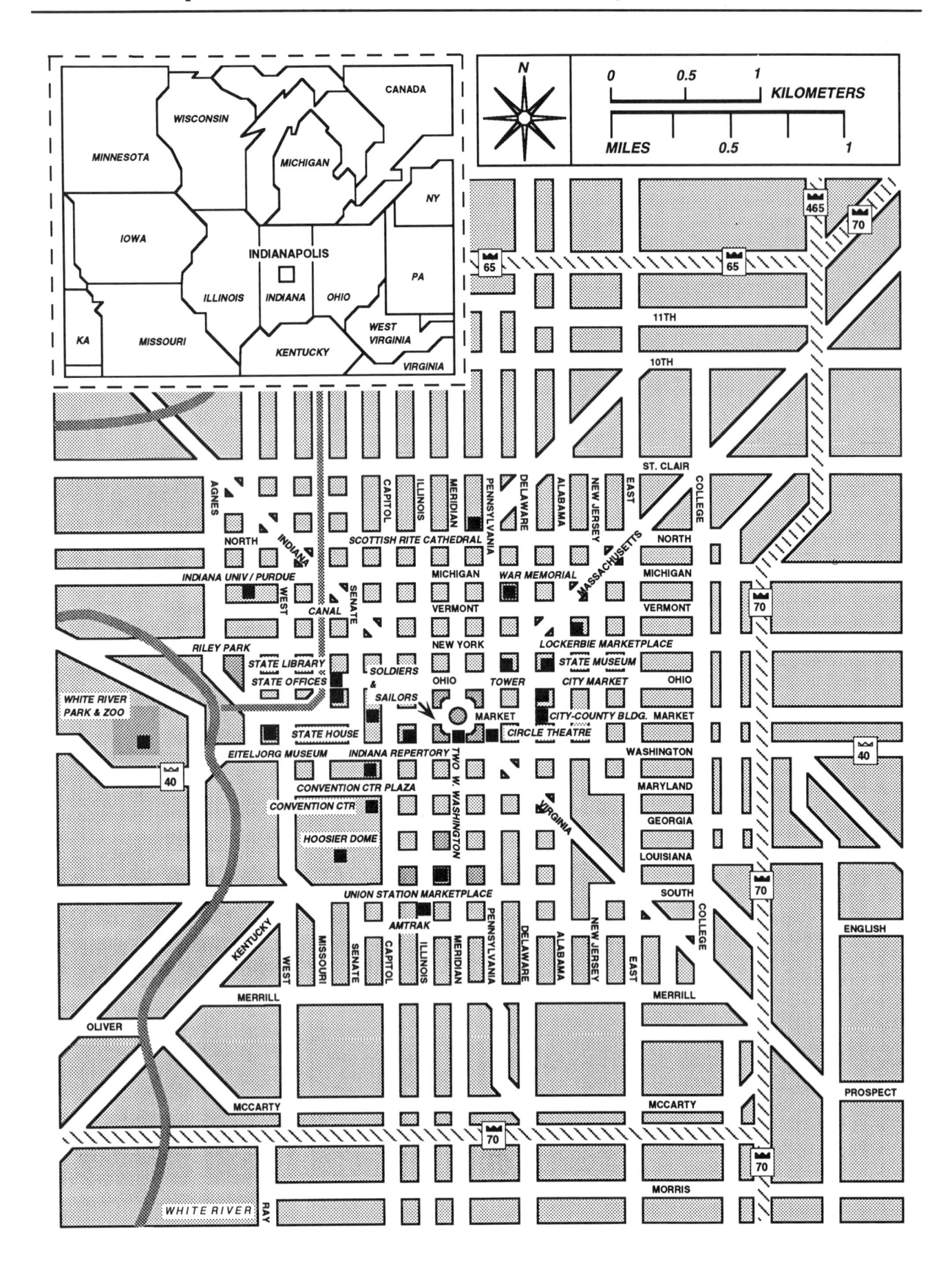

Indiana—Indianapolis *Cities of the United States • 2nd Edition*

Introduction

Indianapolis is the capital of Indiana and the seat of Marion County; the Indianapolis metropolitan statistical area includes Boone, Hamilton, Hancock, Hendricks, Johnson, Morgan, and Shelby counties. Decreed by proclamation in the nineteenth century as the state capital and carved out of the wilderness where only a settlers' camp had previously stood, Indianapolis is redefining itself in the late twentieth century. The city is currently undergoing a renaissance of far-ranging proportions through development and improvement projects that are transforming both the image and the character of the downtown area. Building on the fame of the annual Indianapolis 500 automobile race, the city has become a national center for amateur sports and athletics; it is also a major financial, industrial, commercial, and transportation center for the Midwest. In 1991 the editors of *Inc* magazine selected Indianapolis as one of the country's best cities for growing a business, offering a safe, pleasant quality of life.

Geography and Climate

Situated on level or slightly rolling terrain in central Indiana east of the White River, Indianapolis has a temperate climate; because of even distribution of precipitation throughout the year, there are no pronounced wet or dry seasons. Summers are very warm, and the invasion of polar air from the north often produces frigid winter temperatures with low humidity. Two to three times each winter, snowfalls average three inches or more.

Area: 361.7 square miles (1990)

Elevation: 645 feet to 910 feet above sea level

Average Temperatures: January, 28.0° F; July, 75.0° F; annual average, 52.1° F

Average Annual Precipitation: 40 inches of rain; 23 inches of snow

History

Site Chosen for Central Location

The city of Indianapolis was established not by settlers but by proclamation when Indiana was granted statehood in 1816. The United States Congress set aside four sections of public land for the site of the capital of the Union's nineteenth state. In January 1820, the Indiana legislature picked ten commissioners and charged them with the mandate to locate the new capital as near as possible to the center of the state, the purpose being to take advantage of western migration. The following February, George Pogue and John McCormick settled with their families on land that was to become the site of Indianapolis. Other settlers soon arrived and by the summer of 1820 a dozen families had built cabins along the river bank in a settlement named Fall Creek. In June 1820, the commissioners selected for the capital a location that was close to the exact center of the state; on that spot was the cabin of John McCormick.

After the legislature approved the site in 1821, the name Indianapolis, a combination of Indiana plus the Greek word *polis* for city, was chosen. Four squares miles were allotted for the city, but the chief surveyor, E. P. Fordham, plotted an area of only one square mile because it seemed inconceivable that the capital would ever be any larger. Alexander Ralston, who previously had helped plot the District of Columbia, was hired to design the future city. He decided to model it on the nation's capital, with four broad avenues branching out diagonally to the north, south, east and west from a central circle.

In 1821, Indianapolis became the county seat of the newly configured Marion County, and four years later, when the state legislature met for the first time, Indianapolis boasted one street and a population of 600 people. By the time the town was incorporated in 1832 the population had reached only 1,000 people. Growth was slow because Indianapolis—which now holds the distinction of being one of the world's most populous cities not situated near navigable waters—lay on the banks of the White River, which was too shallow for commerce.

Road/Rail Transport Create a Regional Center

The construction of the Central Canal from Broad Ripple to Indianapolis seemed to solve the problem temporarily, but the canal turned out to be useless when water volume decreased. The routing of the national highway through the center of Indianapolis in 1831 provided a more permanent solution, fulfilling the original purpose of the city's location. In 1847, the year Indianapolis was incorporated as a city, the Madison & Indianapolis Railroad arrived, soon to be followed by seven additional major rail lines, which gave the city access to the Ohio River.

On the eve of the Civil War the population, aided by an influx of German immigrants, had increased to 18,611 people; the city now provided modern services and supported a stable, manufacturing-based economy. With twenty-four army camps and a large ammunition plant, Indianapolis became a major wartime center for Union campaigns on the western front. Progress continued into the postwar period only to be set back by the inflationary recession of 1873. During the last two decades of the nineteenth century, Indianapolis experienced a period of growth known as the "golden age." It became, in 1881, one of the first American cities to install electric street lighting. Many downtown landmarks were erected in an explosion of public architecture that helped establish the city's identity. A new market, a new statehouse, and Union Station were completed in the late 1880s. The neglected Circle Park had deteriorated and was revived when the Soldiers' and Sailors' Monument was constructed in honor of the people who served in the Civil War. During this period, wealthy citizens built palatial Victorian homes on North Meridian Street, and as the result of the growth of new neighborhoods and suburbs along tree-lined avenues, Indianapolis became known as the "city of homes."

At the turn of the century Indianapolis was a leader in the burgeoning automobile industry. Local inventor Charles H. Black is credited with building in 1891 the first internal combustion gasoline engine automobile, which eventually proved to be impractical because its ignition required a kerosene torch. Sixty-five different kinds of automobiles were in production before World War I, including Stutz, Coasts, Duesenberg, and Cole. Other Indianapolis industrialists originated many innovations and improvements in automotive manufacturing, including four-wheel brakes and the six-cylinder engine.

Sporting Events Attract International Attention

The most significant development was the Indianapolis Motor Speedway, a 2.5-mile oval track, which was inaugurated in 1911 when an Indianapolis-made car named the Marmon won the first race. The Indianapolis 500, held on Memorial Day weekend each year, has since become one of the premier international sporting events, drawing world-wide attention. Indianapolis was a major industrial center by 1920, with a population of more than 300,000 people, yet retained much of its small-town ambience.

A pivotal event in the total transformation of Indianapolis from a manufacturing to a sporting town occurred in 1969, when a change in federal tax laws required charitable foundations to spend more money. The Lilly Endowment, a local foundation based on the Eli Lilly drug fortune (with assets of more than $2.1 billion) decided to concentrate on Indianapolis. The result was a massive capital infusion promoting sport business in the city and leading to the conversion of the city's convention center into a sixty-one-thousand-seat football stadium.

In 1970 the creation of UniGov combined city government with Marion County government, immediately making Indianapolis the eleventh largest city in the nation. The city made dramatic strides in its national reputation through initiatives implemented by the UniGov structure. Indianapolis renovated its core historical structures, built new sports facilities, and invested in the arts and entertainment. The city positioned itself as an international amateur sports capital when, in 1987, it invested in athletic facilities and hosted both the World Indoor Track and Field Championships and the Pan American Games, second in importance only to the summer Olympics. Civic leaders have set the goal of transforming Indianapolis into a modern American city that is progressive in vision while faithful to its conservative midwestern values.

Historical Information: Indiana Historical Society, 315 West Ohio Street, Indianapolis, IN 46202; telephone (317)232-1882

Population Profile

Metropolitan Area Residents
1970: 1,111,000

Soldiers' and Sailors' Monument in Indianapolis's Monument Circle.

1980: 1,167,000
1990: 1,249,822
Percent change, 1980–1990: 7.1%
U.S. rank in 1980: 30th
U.S. rank in 1990: 31st

City Residents
1970: 737,000
1980: 701,000
1990: 731,327 (of which, 347,418 were males, and 383,909 were females)
Percent change, 1980–1990: 4.4%
U.S. rank in 1980: 12th
U.S. rank in 1990: 13th (State rank: 1st)

Density: 2,021.9 people per square mile (1990)

Racial and ethnic characteristics (1990)
  White: 554,423
  Black: 165,570
  American Indian, Eskimo, Aleut: 1,574
  Asian and Pacific Islander: 6,852
  Hispanic (may be of any race): 7,681

Percent of residents born in state: 70.9% (1990)

Age characteristics (1990)
  Population under 5 years old: 58,270
  Population 5 to 9 years old: 53,555
  Population 10 to 14 years old: 47,594
  Population 15 to 19 years old: 48,276
  Population 20 to 24 years old: 57,205
  Population 25 to 29 years old: 76,265
  Population 30 to 34 years old: 71,094
  Population 35 to 39 years old: 59,095
  Population 40 to 44 years old: 47,803
  Population 45 to 49 years old: 36,757
  Population 50 to 54 years old: 31,447
  Population 55 to 59 years old: 30,172
  Population 60 to 64 years old: 30,166
  Population 65 to 69 years old: 27,959
  Population 70 to 74 years old: 20,817
  Population 75 to 79 years old: 15,938
  Population 80 to 84 years old: 10,409
  Population 85 years and over: 8,505
  Median age: 31.6 years

Births (1988)
  Total number: 13,670

Deaths (1988)
  Total number: 6,752 (of which, 172 were infants under the age of 1 year)

Money income (1989)
  Per capita income: $14,605
  Median household income: $29,083
  Total households: 296,599
  Number of households with income of . . .
    less than $5,000: 17,317
    $5,000 to $9,999: 25,583
    $10,000 to $14,999: 26,758
    $15,000 to $24,999: 56,578
    $25,000 to $34,999: 50,225
    $35,000 to $49,999: 55,661
    $50,000 to $74,999: 42,656
    $75,000 to $99,999: 12,112
    $100,000 to $149,999: 5,759
    $150,000 or more: 3,950
  Percent of families below poverty level: 9.7% (51.5% of which were female householder families with related children under 5)
1991 FBI Crime Index Total: 36,005

Municipal Government

In 1970, Indianapolis and Marion County consolidated governmental functions to form Unigov, with jurisdiction including all of Marion County except the town of Speedway and the cities of Beech Grove, Lawrence, and Southport. The mayor, who serves a four-year term, holds executive powers; the twenty-nine members of City-County Council are elected to four-year terms by district and at large. A six-department city government administers Unigov programs. *Business Month* magazine selected Indianapolis in 1989 as one of the ten best-managed municipalities in the country for its ability to deliver services while keeping taxes relatively low.

Head Official: Mayor Steve Goldsmith (R) (since 1992; current term expires November 1995)

Total Number of City-County Employees: 5,300 (1990) (does not include schools, libraries, and other municipal corporations such as Metro Bus, Airport)

City Information: City Center, 201 South Capitol Ave., Indianapolis, IN 46225; telephone (317)237-5200

Economy

Major Industries and Commercial Activity

Indianapolis is a primary industrial, commercial, and transportation center for the Midwest. Situated in proximity to the vast agricultural region known as the corn belt and to the industrialized cities of the upper Midwest and the East, Indianapolis is supported by a diversified economic base. Prior to the 1980s, the city's principal industry was manufacturing, which has been displaced by retailing and services. Having made a conscious decision to achieve prosperity through sports, Indianapolis quadrupled its tourism trade and doubled its hotel space during the period 1984-1991, largely by hosting amateur sporting events. Each major sporting event pumps tens of millions of dollars into the economy, contributing $1.1 billion to the tourism trade in 1990, and leading to expanded business opportunities, more jobs, and increasing tax payments to the city.

The insurance industry has long been established in Indianapolis; several insurance companies have located their headquarters and regional offices in the city. With the largest stockyards east of Chicago, Indianapolis is also an important meatpacking center.

Items and goods produced: food and allied products, furniture and woodworking, paper and allied products, printing and publishing, chemicals, petroleum and allied products, rubber and plastic products, primary metals, fabricated metal products, machinery, electrical and electronics equipment, transportation equipment, instruments, medical and optical goods, knitted garments, bricks

Incentive Programs—New and Existing Companies

A principal goal of Unigov is stimulation of business growth through a broader distribution of the tax base, streamlined business access to government services, and expansion of city boundaries. The Greater Indianapolis Progress Committee, an independent adjunct of the mayor's office, and the Corporate Community Council facilitate public and private business cooperation. Local business incentive programs include industrial revenue bonds, tax abatements and reductions, job training, and the Greater Indianapolis Foreign Trade Zone. The state grants loans and administers such programs as the Small Business Administration 7A Program, the Indiana Business Modernization and Technology Corporation, the Corporation for Innovation Development, and the Indiana Corporation for Science and Technology (research and development grants).

Development Projects

A significant factor in the vitality of the Indianapolis economy is the downtown renaissance. In 1980 the city drew up a blueprint called the Regional Center Plan, which was to guide downtown growth and development through the year 2000. With over $2 billion in publicly and privately funded projects already completed by 1987 and another $2 billion in various stages of planning and construction by 1991, the plan objectives were realized ten years earlier than expected. By 1990, one-quarter of downtown buildings were either new or renovated. Ongoing projects scheduled for completion in the 1990s are the Canal Improvement Project ($14 million), the White River State Park ($200 million), Indiana Government Center ($200 million), IUPUI Science/ Engineering and Technology Building ($40 million), Library Building ($32 million), Eli Lilly Technology Center ($540 million), Eli Lilly Corporate Office Center ($415 million), Circle Centre Mall ($941 million), and a downtown corporate park ($250 million).

Economic Development Information: Indianapolis Economic Development Corporation, 320 North Meridien, Suite 906, Indianapolis, IN 46204; telephone (317)236-6262

Commercial Shipping

Indianapolis is a major transportation and distribution hub for the Midwest. As the most centrally located of the largest one hundred cities in the United States, Indianapolis is within 650 miles of 55 percent of all Americans, or more than 50 million households. The city is served by four interstate highways, five railroads, an international airport, and a foreign trade zone. The Indianapolis market benefits from low state-wide transportation costs: Indiana ranks among the five least costly states in most categories of manufacturing production and maintains the lowest costs in the transportation of all but two commodities. Continued expansion of the wholesale sector and the entry of more than forty-eight hundred businesses into the local economy since 1980 contribute to Indianapolis's position as a primary distribution center.

An extensive rail network, consisting of the three largest railroads east of the Mississippi River, connects Indianapolis with ports on the Great Lakes and the Ohio River and seaports on the Mississippi and on the East Coast. More than one-hundred thousand freight car and piggyback shipments are processed through Indianapolis each year. Among the largest rail operations is the Conrail Big Four yard, one of only three such facilities in the Midwest, which handles liquid and dry bulk commodities, provides piggyback service for coordinated rail-highway transport, and maintains warehouses with direct connections to national steel markets.

The express freight industry expanded during the late 1980s in Indianapolis. C. F. Air Freight, a subsidiary of Consolidated Freightways, operates a national sorting hub that handles more than a million tons of cargo daily; Federal Express has also established a facility to serve a radius of up to 700 miles. The U.S. Postal Service's Express Mail hub was granted to Indianapolis in 1991.

Labor Force and Employment Outlook

Indianapolis boasts a skilled labor force; trained personnel are available from the area's higher education institutions. The population has increased and that growth is projected to continue. The total number of jobs has steadily increased since 1986, while unemployment has remained low. Service businesses are the city's major employers. With central Indiana becoming less dependent on the automobile industry, manufacturing nevertheless continues to be a strong economic sector in Indianapolis. In 1990, more than eighteen hundred manufacturing firms employed 110,300 workers, or 16 percent of the labor force, generating 30 percent of total wage and salary income. Federal, state, and local government is also a principal employer of the metropolitan labor force.

United Airlines' $800 million maintenance hub, scheduled for completion in 1994, brings a potential seventy-one hundred new jobs to the city. More than $165 million invested in world-class sports facilities will attract events, as will a planned $85 million Family Entertainment Center at White River State Park. Development projects such as the half-billion-dollar Circle Centre and the convention center addition will generate jobs throughout the 1990s.

The following is a summary of data regarding the Indianapolis metropolitan area labor force as of September 1992.

Size of non-agricultural labor force: 696,300

Number of workers employed in . . .
  mining: 700
  construction: 39,500
  manufacturing: 109,500
  transportation and utilities: 44,600
  wholesale and retail trade: 177,200
  finance, insurance, and real estate: 51,900
  services: 166,200
  government: 106,600

Average hourly earnings of production workers employed in manufacturing: $13.47

Unemployment rate: 4.8%

Largest employers	*Number of employees*
Federal Government	33,400
State of Indiana	31,485
City-County Government	29,465
Allison Gas Turbine Operations, GMC (gas turbine engines)	7,200
Eli Lilly and Company (mfg./ pharmaceutical products)	6,900
Indiana Bell Telephone Co., Inc.	6,700
Allison Transmissions, GMC	6,000
Methodist Hospital of Indiana, Inc.	5,100
Community Hospital of Indianapolis	4,000

Cost of Living

State taxes are consistently rated among the lowest in the country in terms of total state and local tax collections per capita. Utility costs are also relatively low. Overall cost of living consistently ranks at or below the national average.

The following is a summary of data regarding several key cost of living factors in the Indianapolis area.

1992 (2nd Quarter) ACCRA Cost of Living Index: 97.0 (U.S. average = 100.0)

1992 (2nd Quarter) ACCRA Average House Price: $101,250

State income tax rate: 3.4% of adjusted gross income

State sales tax rate: 5.0% (food, prescription drugs, and items consumed or used in manufacturing are exempt)

Local income tax rate: 0.06%

Local sales tax rate: 1.0% (on food and beverages, downtown only)

Property tax rate: $8.85 per $100.00 (1991)

Economic Information: Research Department, Indianapolis Chamber of Commerce, 320 North Meridian Street, Indianapolis, IN 46204-1777; telephone (317)464-2238; and, The Indianapolis Project, Inc., One Hoosier Dome, Suite 110, Indianapolis, IN 46225; telephone (317)639-4773

Education and Research

Elementary and Secondary Schools

The Indianapolis Public Schools system is the largest district in the state of Indiana. A nonpartisan, seven-member school board appoints a superintendent.

The following is a summary of data regarding the Indianapolis public schools as of the 1989-1990 school year.

Total enrollment: 48,000

Number of facilities
  elementary schools: 69
  junior high schools: 10
  senior high schools: 7

Student/teacher ratio: elementary (not available); junior high, 17.5:1; senior high, 23.97:1

Teacher salaries
  minimum: $17,994
  maximum: $38,283

Funding per pupil: $4,539.26

Forty parochial schools, including thirty-four elementary schools, four interparish high schools, and two private high schools, operate within the Indianapolis school district.

Public Schools Information: Indianapolis Public Schools, Superintendent's Office, 120 East Walnut Street, Indianapolis, IN 46204; telephone (317)266-4411

Colleges and Universities

Several public and private institutions of higher learning are located in Indianapolis. Affiliated with the two major state universities is Indiana University-Purdue University at Indianapolis; nearly thirty-three thousand students are enrolled in associate, baccalaureate, master's, and doctorate programs. Areas of specialization include art, engineering technologies, dentistry, law, medical technology, nursing, occupational therapy, and social work. Butler University and the University of Indianapolis, both private institutions, award undergraduate and graduate degrees in such fields as music, pharmacy, nursing, education, and physical therapy.

Among the colleges and technical schools in the Indianapolis metropolitan region are Marian College, offering a liberal arts curriculum, and Indiana Vocational Technical College (Ivy Tech), one of a network of thirteen state training and education centers.

Libraries and Research Centers

In addition to its main branch downtown, the Indianapolis-Marion County Public Library operates twenty-one branches throughout the city. The library, with holdings of nearly 1.7 million volumes, has an annual circulation of more than seven million items and maintains special collections of first editions of Indiana authors, early textbooks, and the poetry of James Whitcomb Riley, and is a U.S. document depository.

The Indiana State Library, also located downtown, houses federal and state documents; special collections include hymn books, oral history, and the Indiana Academy of Science Library. The Indiana State Library Division for the Blind and Physically Handicapped offers extensive holdings in Braille books, audio cassettes and discs, and large-print books. The Indiana Historical Society Library specializes in the Civil War, early North American travel accounts, and the history of Indiana and the Northwest Territory.

The University Library at Indiana University-Purdue University at Indianapolis, completed in 1992 at a cost of $32 million, has a book volume capacity approaching one million. One of the country's first major libraries designed for the electronic information age, it is expected to become a national model. Other area colleges and universities maintain campus libraries.

Indianapolis is home to more than seventy special libraries and research centers. Among them is the Hudson Institute, the internationally renowned policy research organization. State agencies, such as the Indiana Department of Commerce, the Indiana Department of Education, and the Indiana Department of Environmental Management also operate libraries. Local businesses and corporations, including the American United Life Insurance Company and Union Carbide, maintain research and information centers. Other specialized libraries are affiliated with law firms, hospitals, newspapers, publishing houses, museums, and churches and synagogues. Of unique interest are the Indianapolis Zoo Library, the Children's Museum of Indianapolis Library, and the Hurty-Peck Library of Beverage Literature.

Research is conducted at Indiana University-Purdue University's Indianapolis Center for Advanced Research in such fields as ultrasound, urban technology, technology transfer, computer engineering, automated manufacturing, and advanced electronics. The Butler University (BU) Holcolm Research Institute researches water science, while BU's International Ground Water Modeling Center researches groundwater contaminants. At Indiana/World Skating Academy and Research Center's Human Performance Lab, skaters' abilities as they relate to physical conditioning are tested. The U.S. Navy's new Electronics Manufacturing Productivity Facility is the first to be built at the Near North Science and Technology Park.

Public Library Information: Indianapolis-Marion County Public Library, 40 East St. Clair Street, Indianapolis, IN 46206-0211; telephone (317)269-1700

Health Care

A major health care center for the state of Indiana, Indianapolis is home to nearly three thousand licensed physicians and thirteen general hospitals providing more than 7,500 beds. Several specialized facilities, clinics, nursing homes, research laboratories, pharmaceutical manufacturers, and administrative offices of state and local health agencies are also located in the city. Research and training programs of five area hospitals support surgical specialization in heart, other organ, and bone marrow transplant; clinical specialties include the treatment of spinal cord injuries and sleep disorders.

A significant force in the regional medical community is the Indiana University Medical Center, affiliated with the second-largest medical school in the nation. The center operates ninety clinics that concentrate in such fields as DNA banking, location of gene markers for genetic diseases, and testicular cancer. The university plans to build a $34 million clinical research center designed to house a library and to enhance the international standing of the medical school.

Based in Indianapolis are the national headquarters of two major physical fitness organizations, the American College of Sports Medicine and the Association for Fitness in Business. Local hospitals and private groups offer a diversity of health and fitness programs, ranging from stress management to nutrition and biofeedback therapy.

Recreation

Sightseeing

Easily within driving distance for more than half of the country's population, Indianapolis has set out to make itself an attractive tourist destination by combining diverse cultural opportunities with first-class hotels and fine shopping and dining. Revitalization of the downtown core, where modernized nineteenth-century buildings stand adjacent to futuristic structures, has made Indianapolis an architecturally interesting city.

The street grid, modeled after Washington, D.C., makes the center-city Mile Square a compact and convenient area for walking tours. In Monument Circle the Soldiers' and Sailors' Monument observation platform offers a panoramic view of the city and the surrounding countryside. The Indiana War Memorial Plaza, a five-block downtown mall providing

The Eiteljorg Museum of American Indian and Western Art.

urban green space, contains a one-hundred-foot granite monolith, flags from all fifty states, and a fountain at University Square. The plaza houses the national headquarters of the American Legion; a museum of martial history is located in the Memorial Shrine building.

Capitol Commons contains the Indiana Statehouse, which celebrated its centennial in 1988; it houses the governor's office and the General Assembly. Garfield Park, home of Garfield Park Conservatory, features more than five hundred examples of tropical flora, rare carnivorous plants, and tropical birds; the park contains formal gardens, fountains and limestone bridges. The Lilly Center, located at the corporate headquarters of Eli Lilly & Co., schedules a multivision theater presentation and maintains computerized exhibits on topics such as diabetes, antibiotics, and electronic medical instrumentation. The Scottish Rite Cathedral, built of Indiana limestone, is the largest Masonic temple in the world; its fifty-four-bell carillon can be heard city wide.

Victorian architecture enthusiasts can visit the well-preserved James Whitcomb Riley Home; built in 1872, it was the residence—during the last twenty-three years of his life—of the Hoosier dialect poet who created Little Orphan Annie. The President Benjamin Harrison Home is a sixteen-room Italianate mansion, completed in 1875, where much of the original Harrison family furniture is displayed. The Massachusetts Avenue Historic Fire Station was restored in 1988 as a museum equipped with a children's fire safety laboratory.

The Indianapolis Zoo, the first urban zoo to be built in several decades, houses more than two thousand animals. The zoo is located on 64 acres in the urban White Water State Park. The whale and dolphin pavilion presents shows with bottlenose dolphins, beluga whales, and false killer whales. Piranha and giant snakes live in a simulated Amazon forest; the desert conservatory, covered by an acrylic dome, features plant and animal life from the world's arid regions.

Arts and Culture

The Indianapolis renaissance is most evident in the city's dedication to the renewal of its cultural life. A number of historically significant nineteenth-century buildings have been refurbished in order to present local arts organizations in the best possible environment.

The Indianapolis Symphony Orchestra, founded in 1930, performs year-round in the restored historic Circle Theatre and at parks and elsewhere throughout the city and state. The Indianapolis Jazz Club is one of the country's largest such organizations and promotes all forms of jazz music. The Indiana Opera Theatre produces three modern or rarely performed pieces each year. The Indianapolis Children's Choir has received international acclaim. The Madame Walker Urban Life Center, honoring the country's first female self-made millionaire, houses the Walker Theatre, where "Jazz on the Avenue" concerts are held on Fridays.

The Indianapolis Ballet Theatre is a professional resident troupe that performs at Butler University's Clowes Memorial Hall, also the home of the Indianapolis Opera Company. Dance Kaleidoscope is the city's contemporary dance troupe and Dans Ethnik focuses on international dance.

An active theater community contributes to Indianapolis cultural life. The Indianapolis Civic Theatre, the nation's oldest continuously active civic theater group, performs at a seven-hundred-seat facility located in the Museum of Art. The Indiana Repertory Theatre, the state's only professional resident theater, presents more than three-hundred performances annually and is housed in the restored Indiana Theatre. European-style performances are the specialty of American Cabaret Theatre, formerly of New York City. Beef and Boards Dinner Theatre presents Broadway shows, concerts, and dinner. Off-Broadway plays are staged by Phoenix Theatre, presenting sixteen shows annually at Chatham Arch, a restored church. Two annual productions are staged at Garfield Park by the Indianapolis Shakespeare Festival. NAPI REP, founded in 1987, brings quality black theatrical productions to several city venues.

The Indianapolis Museum of Art, renovated and expanded in 1990, is located in a 154-acre wooded cultural park; also in the park are a botanical garden designed by William Law Olmstead, four pavilions, and greenhouses, one of which features six-hundred varieties of orchids. On the grounds is the Lilly Pavilion, an eighteenth-century French-style chateau, formerly the residence of J. K. Lilly Jr. and now the site of decorative arts exhibits. The Museum of Art holds the largest American collection of works by the nineteenth-century British landscape artist J. M. W. Turner. The J. W. Holliday Collection of Neo-impressionist art, extensive Chinese art holdings, and the Robert Indiana *Love* painting, with a matching outdoor sculpture in large rusted letters, round out one of the most impressive collections in the Midwest.

The Children's Museum is the world's largest museum of its type and one of the twenty most-visited museums in the country. The five-level facility features a variety of hands-on exhibits and touchable scientific experiments as well as a planetarium. Favorite exhibits include an Egyptian mummy, a Victorian carousel, and the largest public collection of toy trains. In "Passport to the World" children learn about foreign cultures through toys from around the world and a clothes simulation exhibit. The Eli Lilly Center for Exploration at the museum allows children to explore and experiment with current issues.

The award-winning Conner Prairie Pioneer Settlement, a living history museum, presents an authentic recreation of Hoosier life in 1836. The Indiana State Museum chronicles the history and culture of the state and features a Museum of Sports and a living history exhibit of lifestyles of free blacks in the year 1870. The city's newest museum, the National Art Museum of Sports, contains ancient and modern art depicting sports motifs. Other museums in the city are Indiana Medical History Museum, Hook's Historic Drug Store and Pharmacy, and Indianapolis Motor Speedway and Hall of Fame Museum.

The Eiteljorg Museum of the American Indian and Western Art, considered one of the finest of its kind, was opened in 1989. The Indianapolis Transportation Museum, in nearby Noblesville, preserves the city's past; volunteers have restored horse-drawn carriages, fire engines, and more than sixty railroad cars and locomotives.

Festivals and Holidays

Each year Indianapolis presents a host of festivals and fairs that celebrate the city's history, traditions, and ethnic heritage. The most elaborate is the month-long annual Indianapolis 500 Festival in May, which combines events associated with the race as well as enjoyable activities that are totally unrelated to racing. The St. Benno Fest in March celebrates the city's German heritage. Midwestern artists present their crafts and art work in June at the Talbot Street Art Fair. The Lockerbie Summer A'Fair offers tours of restored Victorian homes in historic Lockerbie Square.

Oktoberfest takes place in early September, followed by Penrod Arts Fair, a commemorative celebration of Indianapolis author Booth Tarkington's most famous character, with art exhibits and entertainment at the Indianapolis Museum of Art. A three-day International Festival is held in late October at the Convention Center. The 1760 Rendezvous recaptures a typical day of that era held at Eagle Creek Park, site of the Days in the Country Festival, around Halloween time. The Romantic Festival at Butler University presents music by Romantic composers and other related activities. The Madrigal Dinners ring in the year-end holiday season on the campus of Indiana University-Purdue University at Indianapolis with a grand banquet that recreates the customs, dress, and songs of medieval England.

Sports for the Spectator

Sports Travel calls Indianapolis the hottest sports city in the nation. Best known for the Indianapolis 500, Indianapolis made a conscious and successful effort in the 1980s to become an amateur sports capital and a major league city. Its 60,500-seat Hoosier Dome is home to the Indianapolis Colts of the National Football League (NFL). The Hoosier Dome has been the site of the National Collegiate Athletic Association's Final Four Championships, which return there in 1997, the World Gymnastics, and other championships; it houses the National Track & Field Hall of Fame.

The Indiana Pacers of the National Basketball Association (NBA) play in the Market Square Arena, which is also the site of national and international competitions of various kinds. Professional tennis and golf take place at the Indianapolis Sports Center. The Indianapolis Ice, a minor league affiliate for the Chicago Black Hawks, play hockey at Indiana State Fairgrounds Pepsi Coliseum. The Indianapolis Indians, a farm team for the Montreal Expos, play professional baseball at Bush Stadium.

The premier sporting event in Indianapolis takes place every Memorial Day weekend at the Indianapolis Motor Speedway. The Indianapolis 500-Mile Race attracts more than 350,000 spectators who watch the "Greatest Spectacle in Racing." An international field of professional race car drivers compete in the most sophisticated and technologically advanced racing machines at speeds that average above 200 miles per hour.

Sports for the Participant

Indianapolis's commitment to sponsor world-class amateur athletic competition has made available excellent facilities to the public. The Major Taylor Velodrome—named for the first Afro-American to win a world championship in any sport—is a state-of-the-art oval bicycle track with a twenty-eight-degree banked concrete surface; it is open to the public from March to October. Joggers can try out the track at the Indiana University Track & Field Stadium; the university's natatorium offers public facilities, including swimming pools, weight rooms, and a gymnasium. The Indianapolis Sports Center makes twenty-four tennis courts available for public use.

The Indianapolis Parks and Recreation Department maintains more than 10,000 acres of land comprising 167 parks; among them is the 5,100-acre Eagle Creek Park, the country's largest municipally owned and operated park, which features a competition-quality rowing course. The park system includes fifteen community centers, 140 tennis courts, twelve golf courses, seventy-one softball diamonds, twenty-four football and twenty-nine soccer fields, forty-six baseball diamonds, and seventeen swimming pools.

Shopping and Dining

A main attraction among the sixty-six shopping centers in Indianapolis is Union Station, across from the Hoosier Dome. A Romanesque Revival style train station built in 1887, this massive structure, reopened in 1986 after a $52 million facelift, contains more than one-hundred specialty shops and restaurants. Another imposing nineteenth-century building is the Indianapolis City Market, first opened in 1886, which provides continuity with the city's past. Known for its fresh vegetables and meats, the market is a favorite spot for downtown workers who lunch at small specialty shops. Circle Centre Mall, scheduled to open in the fall of 1994 in downtown Indianapolis, will be anchored by three major stores and will contain more than one-hundred small shops. Broad Ripple Village, known as the "Greenwich Village of Indianapolis," is a renovated neighborhood of antique and other shops, art galleries, and nightclubs; a canal runs through it. Recent years have seen a revitalization of Massachusetts Avenue, a Soho-like downtown area of art galleries and dining establishments.

Indianapolis enjoys its share of good restaurants serving a variety of ethnic and traditional food, ranging from Nouvelle American cuisine with a Hoosier touch to authentic German and French specialties. For the adventurous diner, a local ribs restaurant serves rattlesnake, lion, giraffe, and alligator fillets along with more traditional fare. Indiana Dinner Train offers dining and theme excursions in newly renovated passenger cars.

Visitor Information: Indianapolis City Center, 201 South Capitol Avenue, Indianapolis, IN 46225; (317)237-5206; and, The Indianapolis Project, Inc., One Hoosier Dome, Suite 110, Indianapolis, IN 46225; telephone (317)639-4773 or 1-800-323-INDY

Convention Facilities

Indianapolis is gaining in prominence as a convention destination. The number of convention delegates grew from 147,150 in 1984 to 655,926 in 1991. The principal meeting facility is the Indiana Convention Center/Hoosier Dome (ICC/HD). The convention center provides more than 300,000 square feet of column-free exhibit space. A $35 million expansion scheduled for completion in 1993 would add thirty-six thousand square feet and improve the existing space; skywalks would connect the center with more than one-thousand hotel rooms. The Hoosier Dome, opened in 1984, features ninety-thousand square feet of space. The complex, consisting of five exhibit halls and the multi-use Dome floor, is the site of trade shows, banquets, sporting events, and concerts.

More than one-hundred hotels in the metropolitan area, providing almost 16,000 rooms, offer convention and meeting space. Among them is the University Place Executive Conference Center on the downtown Indiana University-Purdue University at Indianapolis campus; the recently completed Westin Convention Center Hotel is also located downtown. As part of the second phase of the Circle Centre Mall project, Sheraton Suites plans to open a 250-room hotel. Indiana Room Ballroom in the restored Indiana Theatre Building offers meeting space in a unique setting.

Convention Information: Indianapolis Convention and Visitors Association, One Hoosier Dome, Suite 100, Indianapolis, IN 46225; telephone (317)639-4282

Indianapolis's century-old Union Station was reopened in 1986 as a "festival marketplace."

Transportation

Approaching the City

The Indianapolis International Airport, operated by the Indianapolis Airport Authority, is located 8 miles southwest of the downtown area and is accessible to the city via the Airport Expressway and I-70. Fourteen airlines schedule 203 daily departures to forty-eight non-stop destinations. Four reliever airports for smaller aircraft, also operated by the airport authority, are located in the metropolitan area.

Indianapolis is linked with points throughout the nation by a network of interstate highways. Intersecting the city from east to west is I-70; I-65 passes through the downtown area from the northwest to the southeast. I-69 approaches from the northwest. All of these routes connect with I-465, which encircles the metropolitan area. Amtrak carries rail passengers into Union Station.

Traveling in the City

Streets in Indianapolis are laid out on a grid pattern. The main north-south thoroughfare is Meridian Street, which is intersected in the center of downtown by Washington Street.

Public transportation is provided by Indiana Public Transportation Corp. (METRO); special service for handicapped persons is available through Metro Transit Open Door. Metro Trolley also maintains bus routes.

Communications

Newspapers and Magazines

The major daily newspapers in Indianapolis are the *Indianapolis Star* (morning) and the *Indianapolis News* (evening). The *Indianapolis Business Journal*, the *Indianapolis Recorder*, a newspaper with an ethnic orientation, and several neighborhood and suburban newspapers are published weekly. *Indianapolis Monthly* is a magazine featuring articles on local and state topics.

A number of magazines and special-interest journals are published in the city. Among the nationally-known magazines are *The Saturday Evening Post, Jack and Jill,* and *Humpty Dumpty's Magazine.* Topics covered by other Indianapolis-based publications—a total of nearly eighty—include art, religion, medicine, nursing, law, banking, computers, accounting, insurance, real estate, farming, mining, trucking, gymnastics, and auto racing.

Television and Radio

Ten television stations—four commercial, one public, and five independent—broadcast from Indianapolis. The city is served by eight AM and twelve FM radio stations providing a variety of formats such as jazz, gospel, country, and classical music; easy listening; educational and religious programs; network news; and farm reports.

Media Information: Indianapolis News and *Indianapolis Star*, 307 North Pennsylvania Street, Indianapolis, IN 46204; telephone (317) 633-1240

Selected Bibliography

Berry, S.L., *Indianapolis* (Minneapolis, MN: Dillon Press, 1990)

South Bend

The City in Brief

Founded: 1820 (incorporated, 1835)

Head Official: Mayor Joseph E. Kernan (D) (since 1988)

City Population
- 1970: 125,580
- 1980: 109,727
- 1990: 105,511
- Percent change, 1980–1990: −3.8%
- U.S. rank in 1980: 143rd
- U.S. rank in 1990: 182nd (State rank: 5th)

Metropolitan Area Population
- 1970: 244,827
- 1980: 241,617
- 1990: 247,052
- Percent change, 1980–1990: 2.2%
- U.S. rank in 1980: Not available
- U.S. rank in 1990: Not available

Area: 36.4 square miles (1990)

Elevation: 773 feet above sea level

Average Annual Temperature: 49.5° F

Average Annual Precipitation: 36.14 inches of rain; 72.1 inches of snow

Major Economic Sectors: Services, wholesale and retail trade, manufacturing

Unemployment Rate: 6.2% (September 1992)

Per Capita Income: $11,949 (1989)

1992 (2nd Quarter) ACCRA Average House Price: $95,533

1992 (2nd Quarter) ACCRA Cost of Living Index: 94.0 (U.S. average = 100.0)

1991 FBI Crime Index Total: Not reported

Major Colleges and Universities: University of Notre Dame; Indiana University at South Bend

Daily Newspaper: *South Bend Tribune*

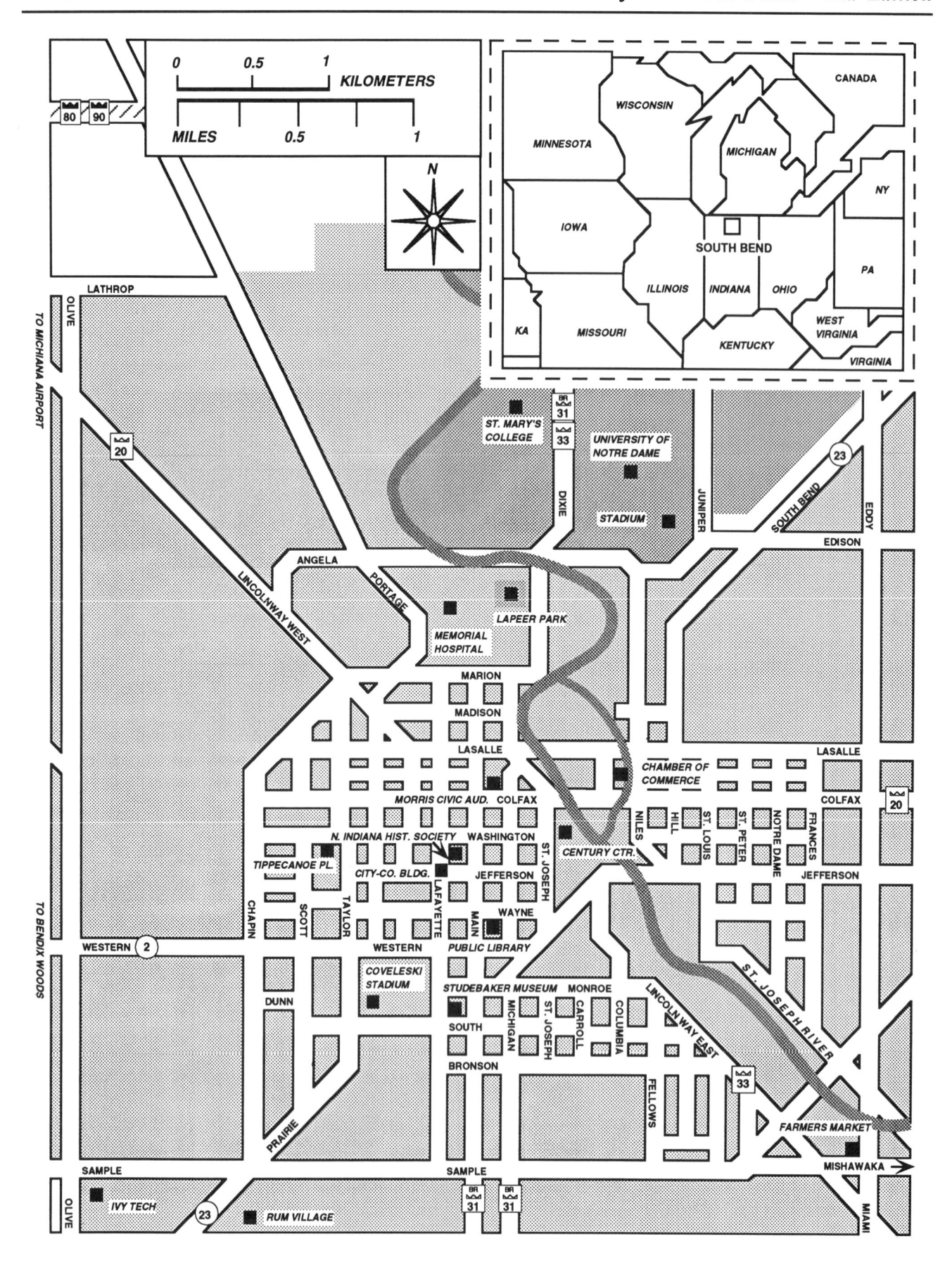

Indiana—South Bend — *Cities of the United States • 2nd Edition*

Introduction

South Bend is the seat of St. Joseph County and the focus of a region known as "Michiana" that extends over six counties in Indiana and two counties in Michigan. Mishawaka lies to the east of South Bend; the two cities comprise a metropolitan statistical area and are in the heart of the nation's industrial belt. With a location on the beautiful St. Joseph River, South Bend is home to the University of Notre Dame, which is nationally recognized for its academic excellence and for "The Fighting Irish," its winning football teams.

Geography and Climate

South Bend is located on the Saint Joseph River on mostly level to gently rolling terrain and some former marshlands. The proximity of Lake Michigan—the city is within twenty miles of the nearest shore—produces a moderating effect on South Bend's climate. Temperatures of one hundred degrees or higher are rare and cold waves are less severe than at other locations at the same latitude. Distribution of precipitation is relatively even throughout the year; the greatest amounts occur during the growing season, May to October. Winter is characterized by cloudiness and high humidity, with frequent periods of snow. Heavier snowfalls are often borne into the area by a cold northwest wind passing over Lake Michigan.

Area: 36.4 square miles (1990)

Elevation: 773 feet above sea level

Average Temperatures: January, 24.2° F; July, 73.3° F; annual average, 49.5° F

Average Annual Precipitation: 36.14 inches of rain; 72.1 inches of snow

History

French Exploration Establishes South Bend

The first European explorer to reach the region surrounding present-day South Bend was Rene Robert Cavelier, sieur de La Salle, who in 1679 passed near the spot where today the University of Notre Dame's administration building is located. Two years later, La Salle met with Miami and Illinois chiefs under a tree named Council Oak in what was then the heart of the Miami nation; they signed a peace treaty that involved a pledge from the Miami and the Illinois to fight the Iroquois. LaSalle, protected by the treaty, was free to explore the Mississippi River region in which present-day South Bend is included; he then claimed the territory for France, naming it Louisiana.

Pierre Freischutz Navarre, an educated Frenchman married to a Potawatomi woman, established the first trading post for the American Fur Company in 1820 near South Bend's future site. But Alexis Coquillard is credited with founding South Bend; the town's name was derived from his trading post, which was called "The Bend," and noted its southerly location on the St. Joseph River. Coquillard's business rival and friend, Colonel Lathrop M. Taylor, renamed the settlement St. Joseph in 1827 and then Southold. The U.S. Post Office officially named it South Bend. Coquillard and Taylor worked together to develop the settlement and encouraged settlers with gifts of land and money. The city was platted and named the county seat in 1831, incorporated in 1835, and chartered in 1865.

Industry and Scholarship Enhance the City

In 1852 Henry and Clement Studebaker arrived in South Bend and opened a blacksmith and wagon shop. They built farm wagons, carriages, prairie schooners, and then a gasoline engine automobile in 1904, transforming the company into an automobile plant that remained in business until 1966. James Oliver came to South Bend in 1855, founding the Oliver Chilled Plow Works, which manufactured a superior farm plow that revolutionized farming and introduced a manufacturing process that replaced iron with chilled and hardened steel. The Singer Cabinet Works began production in 1868 in South Bend to take advantage of the proximity of Indiana hardwood forests, emerging as the world's largest cabinet factory by 1901.

The most significant event in the city's history was the arrival of Father Edward Sorin, the founder of the University of Notre Dame, who reached the future site of the university on November 26, 1842, with seven Brothers of the Congregation of the Holy Cross. Bishop Hailandiere of the diocese of Vincennes had given Father Sorin 600 acres to found a college for seminary and secular students as well as to start a mission for the Potawatomi native Americans. The college's first student was Alexis Coquillard. Enrollment picked up with the arrival of the Lake Shore Railroad in 1851. A fire destroyed the campus in 1879, and the Neo-Gothic Administration Building, with its golden dome topped by a figure of the Virgin Mary, was opened later that year. The golden dome, a tradition of academic excellence, and winning football teams have become familiar symbols of this famous university, which is today a significant part of life in South Bend.

Historical Information: Northern Indiana Historical Society, 112 South Lafayette Boulevard, South Bend, IN 46601; telephone (219) 284-9664

Population Profile

Metropolitan Area Residents
1970: 244,827
1980: 241,617
1990: 247,052
Percent change, 1980-1990: 2.2%
U.S. rank in 1980: Not available
U.S. rank in 1990: Not available

City Residents
1970: 125,580
1980: 109,727
1990: 105,511 (of which, 49,812 were male, and 55,699 were female)
Percent change, 1980-1990: -3.8%
U.S. rank in 1980: 143rd
U.S. rank in 1990: 182nd (State rank: 5th)

Density: 2,898.7 people per square mile (1990)

Racial and ethnic characteristics (1990)
  White: 80,221
  Black: 22,049
  American Indian, Eskimo, Aleut: Not reported
  Asian and Pacific Islander: 916
  Hispanic (may be of any race): 3,546

Percent of residents born in state: 68.7%

Age characteristics (1990)
  Population under 5 years old: 8,520
  Population 5 to 9 years old: 7,862
  Population 10 to 14 years old: 7,102
  Population 15 to 19 years old: 6,469
  Population 20 to 24 years old: 7,823
  Population 25 to 29 years old: 9,198
  Population 30 to 34 years old: 8,907
  Population 35 to 39 years old: 8,056
  Population 40 to 44 years old: 6,239
  Population 45 to 49 years old: 4,546
  Population 50 to 54 years old: 3,732
  Population 55 to 59 years old: 4,151
  Population 60 to 64 years old: 5,166
  Population 65 to 69 years old: 5,375
  Population 70 to 74 years old: 4,395
  Population 75 to 79 years old: 3,611
  Population 80 to 84 years old: 2,427
  Population 85 years and over: 1,932
  Median age: 33.2 years

Births (1988)
  Total number: 2,005

Deaths (1988)
  Total number: 1,322 (of which, 28 were infants under the age of 1 year)

Money income (1989)
  Per capita income: $11,949
  Median household income: $24,131
  Total households: 42,000
  Number of households with income of . . .
    less than $5,000: 3,012
    $5,000 to $9,999: 4,863
    $10,000 to $14,999: 4,753
    $15,000 to $24,999: 9,048
    $25,000 to $34,999: 7,246
    $35,000 to $49,999: 7,009
    $50,000 to $74,999: 4,134
    $75,000 to $99,999: 1,283
    $100,000 to $149,999: 447
    $150,000 or more: 205
  Percent of families below poverty level: 11.2% (60.8% of which were female householder families with related children under 5)
1991 FBI Crime Index Total: Not reported

Municipal Government

The city of South Bend operates under a mayor-council form of government. The mayor and nine council members are elected to four-year terms; the mayor is not a member of council.

Head Official: Mayor Joseph E. Kernan (since 1988; current term expires December 31, 1995)

Total Number of City Employees: 1,300 (1991)

City Information: Office of the Mayor, 1400 County-City Building, South Bend, IN 46601; telephone (219)235-9261

Economy

Major Industries and Commercial Activity

South Bend's diversified economic base consists principally of wholesale and retail trade, manufacturing, services, and government. About fifty-seven hundred non-agricultural businesses are located in St. Joseph County; about 86 percent of those businesses employ fewer than 25 persons. Manufacturing industries include non-electrical machinery, transportation equipment, and rubber and various plastic products. Several construction firms that conduct business nationwide are located in the area.

South Bend is a retail center for the "Michiana" region, with a total market penetration of sixteen counties; sales average more than $5 billion per year. From 1979 to 1985, retail sales increased by 48.4 percent per household in St. Joseph County alone. South Bend is also emerging as a center for professional, financial, and business support services as well as marketing, telecommunications, and computer and data processing. Another primary industry in St. Joseph and Elkhart counties is tourism, which generates a significant number of jobs and revenues reaching $250 million in 1987.

Items and goods produced: airplanes and auto parts, aluminum castings, fixtures, lawn tractors, blasting equipment, conveyor components, electronic controls, machine tools, dies, drills, fabricated steel products, military vehicles, vinyl siding, office furniture, pet food, plastic coated fabrics, corrugated boxes and cartons, windows and doors, printing rollers and inks, paints, food, condiments, metal stampings, wire and cable processing

Incentive Programs—New and Existing Companies

The state of Indiana encourages a climate favorable to business through low taxes, workers' compensation insurance rates, and unemployment compensation, all of which rank among the lowest in the country. The city of South Bend offers special tax advantages to businesses and industries locating in urban enterprise zones and other targeted areas. Among those advantages are state tax exemptions, credits, abatements, and increment financing.

Further incentives include industrial parks that have been established in St. Joseph County, each providing full utility and shipping services. To promote industrial growth, major banks and savings and loan associations make available financing and capital and provide data processing services.

Job training programs—Customized training and consultants are available from a number of state and local providers. Funding to cover training costs is available in some cases.

Other programs and incentives—Enterprise Development Fund makes loans to help "nontraditional entrepreneurs" establish or maintain businesses.

Development Projects

Work continues on the Airport 2010 Project, one of the largest developments in state history. Infrastructure improvements were begun in the early 1990s. That project is expected to create or retain twenty-seven thousand jobs by the year 2010 and to add $680 million in private investment to the local economy. Dozens of local firms, as well as colleges and universities, have announced plans for expansion, renovation, and new construction.

Economic Development Information: Department of Economic Development, 1200 County-City Building, South Bend, IN 46601; telephone (219)284-9371; and, Project Future, 401 East Colfax Avenue, P.O. Box 1677, South Bend, IN 46634; telephone (219)234-6590

Commercial Shipping

Designated a Foreign Trade Zone, South Bend is a center for manufacturer suppliers and vendors throughout the United States and abroad. Six air freight carriers ship goods through Michiana Regional Airport. A network of interstate highways, including I-80 and I-90, the nation's major east-west axis routes, provides access to more than seventy motor freight carriers. Four major rail freight lines include Conrail, which links metropolitan South Bend with Chicago, Detroit, New York, and Boston; two privately-owned railroads offer regional service. About sixty-thousand tons of freight annually are transported by four bus lines.

Labor Force and Employment Outlook

According to a local survey, labor-management relations are considered cooperative. Skilled and semi-skilled labor is said to be available, affordable, and reliable. The wage structure is competitive with other industrial communities. A good educational system is in place; South Bend and environs boast the highest concentration of educational institutions per capita in the Midwest. Small companies will account for most job openings.

The following is a summary of data regarding the South Bend metropolitan area labor force as of September 1992.

Size of non-agricultural labor force: 123,900

Number of workers employed in . . .
 mining: not reported
 construction: 8,400
 manufacturing: 21,000
 transportation and public utilities: 5,500
 wholesale and retail trade: 30,500
 finance, insurance, and real estate: 6,800
 services: 39,400
 government: 12,200

Average hourly earnings of production workers employed in manufacturing: $12.16

Unemployment rate: 6.2%

Largest employers	Number of employees
Allied-Signal Divisions (Bendix)	2,500
Memorial Health System	2,400
South Bend Community Schools	2,300
Saint Joseph's Care Group	1,900
City of South Bend	1,300
L T V Missiles & Electronics	1,100
St. Joseph County	900

Cost of Living

The following is a summary of data regarding several key cost of living factors in the South Bend area.

1992 (2nd Quarter) ACCRA Cost of Living Index: 94.0 (U.S. average = 100.0)

1992 (2nd Quarter) ACCRA Average House Price: $95,533

State income tax rate: 3.4% of adjusted gross income

State sales tax rate: 5.0% (food, prescription drugs, and items consumed or used in manufacturing are exempt)

Local income tax rate: None

Local sales tax rate: None

Property tax rate: Ranges from $11.59 to $13.85 per $100 valuation, assessed at 33-1/3% of true value (1990)

Economic Information: Chamber of Commerce of St. Joseph County, Commerce Center, 401 East Colfax Avenue, P.O. Box 1677, South Bend, IN 46634; telephone (219)234-0051

Education and Research

Elementary and Secondary Schools

Public elementary and secondary schools in South Bend, the state's fifth largest district, are administered by the South Bend Community School Corporation. Average achievement scores at each level tend to exceed state and national norms. The district has a strong technology program with more than two-thousand microcomputers in classrooms. Cooperative (on-the-job) training is in place at all high schools. About 80 percent of high school seniors continue on to higher education. School building projects under way in 1992 exceeded $18 million, with considerably more planned over the following five years.

The following is a summary of data regarding South Bend public schools as of the 1991–1992 school year.

Total enrollment: 21,500

Number of facilities
elementary schools: 25
middle schools: 5
high schools: 6

Student/teacher ratio: 15:1

Teacher salaries
minimum: $20,456
maximum: $44,799

Funding per pupil: $4,361 (including transportation)

Twenty-one private and parochial schools offer educational alternatives to South Bend area students. Among them are a Roman Catholic elementary and high school system with an enrollment of nearly five-thousand students, as well as Hebrew schools and the Stanley Clark School, a private institution with a limited enrollment.

Public Schools Information: South Bend Community School Corporation, 635 South Main Street, South Bend, IN 46601; telephone (219)282-4145

Colleges and Universities

South Bend/Mishawaka is home to eight colleges and universities. The University of Notre Dame, affiliated with the Roman Catholic Church and founded in 1842 as a college for men, is now coeducational, with an enrollment of nearly ten-thousand students. The university offers graduate and undergraduate degrees in the arts and sciences, engineering, business administration, and law. A unique feature of the curriculum is the "Executive M.B.A." program for working professionals. Saint Mary's College is a liberal arts college for women, sharing an academic co-exchange with Notre Dame and maintaining a campus in Italy as well as a special program in Ireland.

Indiana University at South Bend (IUSB), the third largest in the state's eight-university system, grants associate through master's degrees in more than eighty fields, such as business and management, education, and library and archival science. IUSB operates a continuing education division that provides evening, weekend, and off-campus instruction. Holy Cross Junior College, adjacent to Notre Dame, prepares students for education at four-year colleges. Bethel College in Mishawaka is a four-year liberal arts college affiliated with the United Missionary Church; Bethel offers a range of programs, with emphasis on teacher education.

Purdue Statewide Technology Program at IUSB offers associate degrees in engineering technology and other areas plus associate and bachelor degrees in organizational leadership and supervision. Technical and vocational training is also available at a number of other colleges and specialized schools. Among them are Indiana Vocational Technical College-North Central (IVY Tech), Michiana College of Commerce, Davenport College, and Lake Michigan College.

Libraries and Research Centers

The central facility of the St. Joseph County Public Library houses more than 448,000 volumes, 1,020 periodical subscriptions, computer software, microfiche, films, records, audio and video tapes, slides, art reproductions, and sculptures. Special collections include large type books, genealogical materials, and state documents. The library operates seven branches. Local colleges and universities maintain campus libraries. Other specialized libraries in the city are associated with hospitals, government agencies, and the Studebaker National Museum.

The University of Notre Dame supports centers conducting research on gerontology, the environment, radiation chemistry, biology, the philosophy of religion, American Catholicism, international studies, urban studies, Latin American studies, Soviet and East European studies, law and government, and multinational corporations and Third World Development. A study and research center for wetland ecology is located at Spicer Lake Nature Preserve.

Public Library Information: St. Joseph County Public Library, 304 South Main, South Bend, IN 46601; telephone (219)282-4600

Health Care

Four general and acute care hospitals in South Bend and Mishawaka collectively provide over 1,500 beds and offer complete medical services that include standard health care, advanced surgery, and specialized treatment such as patient rehabilitation programs, urgent care, sports medicine, and fitness. The medical community is comprised of 380 physicians, fourteen-hundred registered nurses, and eighty-seven dentists, among other health care professionals and support staff.

Saint Joseph's Medical Center, South Bend's first hospital and a regional kidney dialysis center, operates units for cardiac, cancer, and pediatric care as well as regional sleep disorder and pain rehabilitation centers. The Medical Center also maintains clinics that are conveniently located for residents in surrounding communities.

Memorial Hospital of South Bend is the region's largest hospital and primary referral center. Memorial has established the Memorial Health System, consisting of five affiliates that offer care and service at all levels, including staffing and home care, medical equipment and supplies, management and consulting, insurance claims processing, pharmacies, rural family practice, and mobile mammography and magnetic resonance imaging facilities. Part of the system are four Med-Point emergency centers throughout South Bend. Other general and specialty hospitals are Michiana Community Hospital and Madison Center, which provides mental health care and recently opened an $8 million, 60-bed facility. Home health services, nursing homes, substance abuse programs, mental health services, and public-supported care programs are also available.

The National Center for Senior Living consists of housing, medical research centers, offices, recreational facilities, and light assembly factories for senior citizens.

Health Care Information: St. Joseph County Medical Society, 2015 West Western Avenue, Suite 333, South Bend, IN 46634; telephone (219)284-9711

Recreation

Sightseeing

South Bend is noted for the University of Notre Dame, for its industrial heritage, and for its municipal parks. The University of Notre Dame's golden-domed Administration Building is the campus's central symbol; inside, the walls are lined with murals depicting the life of Christopher Columbus by Vatican artist Luigi Gregori. Also on the campus are a reproduction of France's Grotto of Lourdes and the Snite Museum of Art, which displays rare religious art and holds more than seventeen-thousand pieces in its permanent collection.

Studebaker Archives Center in Century Center traces the history of the Studebaker Company from its days as a maker of horse-drawn carriages to its innovations in the manufacture of automobiles. Among the exhibits is the carriage in which President Lincoln rode to Ford's Theater on the night he was assassinated. The Northern Indiana Historical Society Museum charts local history through industry, individuals, clothing, and even toys. Historic mansions open to the public are Tippecanoe Place, which was the home of Studebaker Company president Clement Studebaker and resembles a feudal castle, and Beiger Mansion, residence of Martin Beiger, founding partner of Mishawaka Woolen Manufacturing Company. Amish Acres is a small farm designed to explain the customs, beliefs, and work habits of the Amish people. The Potawatomi Park Zoo and Botanical Gardens are on 60 acres; the zoo has been remodeled and the conservatory exhibits tropical and desert gardens.

Arts and Culture

Century Center is South Bend's modern convention and cultural facility, which includes a theater, art center, and the Discovery Hall Museum featuring exhibits on the city's major industries. The South Bend Symphony, the Broadway Theatre League, and other community arts groups perform at the Morris Civic Auditorium, Indiana's oldest historic theater. A $2.5 million renovation will permit large shows to play at Morris Civic Auditorium after 1993. The Mishawaka Children's Museum is one of two children's museums in the state. Among its hands-on exhibits are mastodon bones, Indiana artifacts, and antique musical instruments.

Festivals and Holidays

South Bend's parks are the location for many of the city's festivals and special events. Bendix Woods hosts Winter Celebration in January and Sugar Camp Days during the second weekend in March; St. Patrick's Park presents the Firefly Festival, a weekend outdoor music and theater program throughout the summer. The Baubaugo Station Rendezvous presents life in pioneer South Bend at the Ferrettie-Baugo Creek County Park on Labor Day weekend. Among the major events at Leeper Park are an art fair the last weekend in June and a river run in May. Merrifield Park hosts a Summerfest. Autumn Fest takes place at Rum Village Park in October. South

An aerial view of downtown South Bend, the St. Joseph River, and Stanley Coveleski Regional Stadium. The photograph at the beginning of this chapter shows the University of Notre Dame campus.

Bend is the site of the Fischoff National Chamber Music Competition in March. The city's Ethnic Festival usually takes place on the Fourth of July.

Sports for the Spectator

The University of Notre Dame Fighting Irish football team is among the most famous college teams in the world. Legendary coach Knute Rockne began the school's success in the 1920s with the "Four Horsemen" and "Seven Mules." Throughout Notre Dame's history, the Fighting Irish have been known for great players, outstanding coaches, and a schedule of games against the nation's best football teams. The home schedule is played on Saturday afternoons in the fall on the Notre Dame campus in Knute Rockne Stadium; the Fighting Irish also field competitive teams in basketball and other sports.

The Stanley Coveleski Regional Stadium is the home field of the Chicago White Sox Class A minor league franchise that competes in the Midwest League. The East Race, the only artificial whitewater course in North America and one of three in the world, hosts world-class whitewater slaloms and United States World Cup Team trials.

Sports for the Participant

Recreation opportunities abound at parks in and around South Bend. Among them is Merrifield Park, which has an olympic-size swimming pool, ice rink, ball fields, boat launch, lighted tennis courts, and volleyball and basketball courts. The South Bend-Mishawaka area boasts highly rated public golf courses. South Bend's biggest attraction is East Race, which offers innertubing, canoeing, kayaking, and rafting in the summer. An exercise trail borders the waterway and is part of a 5-mile trail that runs through the city's downtown parks.

Shopping and Dining

South Bend-Mishawaka balances its shopping districts between four enclosed malls and small independent specialty shops. The 100 Center Complex, a shopping and entertainment center, is in the renovated Kamm & Schellinger Brewery in Mishawaka, a structure built in 1853 and now providing space for stores, galleries, and restaurants. Farmer's Market in South Bend offers the wares of more than 125 merchants.

Amish Acres serves authentic Amish food in a converted barn. Northern Indiana is known for regional food specialties such as frog legs, pan-fried perch, and relishes, including bean salad, cabbage salad, and pickled beets.

Visitor Information: Chamber of Commerce of St. Joseph County, Commerce Center, Suite 310, 401 East Colfax Avenue, P.O. Box 1677, South Bend, IN 46634-1677; telephone (219)234-0051

Convention Facilities

The principal meeting site in South Bend is the Century Center, situated on an 11-acre downtown riverfront park with direct access to major hotels and 5 miles from Michiana Regional Airport. The complex has been integrated with theaters, parks, art galleries, and a museum. Century Center consists of a convention and exhibition hall, a great hall, a thrust-stage theater, and a recital hall. The twenty-five-thousand-square-foot Convention Hall, which will accommodate 155 booths and banquet space for 1,800 people, can be subdivided into two areas that can then be partitioned into eleven meeting rooms for groups of 48 to 237 people. The Great Hall, overlooking Island Park and White Water Rapids, hosts receptions, exhibits, and meetings; also available are eleven river-level meeting room suites. The 166-seat Recital Hall and the 694-seat Bendix Theatre are suitable for performances and meetings; both offer sound and lighting systems. The Morris Civic Auditorium, the oldest theater in Indiana, features a 2,486-seat auditorium that can be used for lectures, meetings, and conferences; an expansion is planned for completion after 1993. Additional convention facilities can be found on the University of Notre Dame campus at the Athletic and Convocation Center and the Center for Continuing Education. Among area hotels and motels featuring meeting and banquet rooms for groups of 16 to 600 people are the South Bend Marriott Hotel, Holiday Inn—Downtown, Holiday Inn-South Bend, Howard Johnson's Motor Lodge, and Ramada Inn. Approximately twenty-seven hundred lodging rooms are available in the South Bend/Mishawaka area.

Convention Information: Convention and Tourism Division, Chamber of Commerce of St. Joseph County, Commerce Center, Suite 310, 401 East Colfax Avenue, P.O. Box 1677, South Bend, IN 46634-1677; telephone (219)234-0079

Transportation

Approaching the City

Eight commercial airlines schedule more than one-hundred direct and connecting daily flights into South Bend at the Michiana Regional Airport from all major United States cities and points abroad. The closest major airport is O'Hare in Chicago, about 120 miles away.

Passenger rail transportation is available by Amtrak from Boston, New York, and Chicago. The South Shore Line, the nation's only remaining interurban rail service, connects the Chicago Loop with South Bend and Mishawaka.

An efficient highway system—including Interstates 80 and 90, U.S. 20 and 31/33, and State Routes 2 and 23—affords access into the South Bend metropolitan area.

Traveling in the City

South Bend is laid out on a grid system, the main thoroughfares within the city being north-south Main Street and Michigan Street (U.S. 31/33) and east-west Colfax Avenue (U.S. 20).

Transpo, the municipal bus service, schedules regular routes in both South Bend and Mishawaka. Commuting time in South Bend is considered low in comparison to other urban regions of comparable size.

Communications

Newspapers

The South Bend daily newspaper is the *South Bend Tribune*. Two weekly newspapers circulate throughout a multi-county region.

Television and Radio

South Bend, Mishawaka, and neighboring communities receive broadcasts from five area-based television stations—three commercial network affiliates, one public broadcasting outlet, and one independent station—and have access to five Chicago and Elkhart stations, as well as cable. Six FM and two AM radio stations serve a listener population of 297,500 households with music, news and information, and religious programming.

Media Information: South Bend Tribune, 225 West Colfax Avenue at Lafayette Blvd., South Bend, IN 46626; telephone (219)233-6161

IOWA

Cedar Rapids 113
Davenport 127
Des Moines 137

The State in Brief

Nickname: Hawkeye State
Motto: Our liberties we prize and our rights we will maintain

Flower: Wild rose
Bird: Eastern goldfinch

Area: 56,276 square miles (1990; U.S. rank: 25th)
Elevation: Ranges from 480 feet to 1,670 feet above sea level
Climate: Continental, with extremes in temperature (30 degrees in winter, 100 degrees in summer)

Admitted to Union: December 28, 1846
Capital: Des Moines
Head Official: Governor Terry E. Branstad (R) (until 1995)

Population
  1970: 2,825,368
  1980: 2,914,000
  1990: 2,795,000
  Percent change 1980–1990: −4.7%
  U.S. rank in 1990: 30th
  Percent of residents born in state: 78.8% (1990)
  Density: 49.7 people per square mile (1990; U.S. rank: 33rd)
  1991 FBI Crime Index Total: 115,546

Racial and Ethnic Characteristics (1990)
  White: 2,683,000
  Black: 1.7%
  American Indian, Eskimo, Aleut: 0.26%
  Asian and Pacific Islander: 0.92%
  Hispanic (may be of any race): 1.18%

Age Characteristics (1990)
  Population under 5 years old: 193,000
  Population 5 to 17 years old: 532,000
  Percent of population 65 years and older: 15.4%
  Median age: 32.9 years
  Voting-age population (1988): 2,125,000 (57.7% of whom cast votes for president)

Vital Statistics
  Total number of births (1992): 38,120
  Total number of deaths (1992): 27,002 (of which, 296 were infants under the age of 1 year)
  AIDS cases reported, 1981–1990: 187 (U.S. rank: 40th)

Economy
  Major industries: Manufacturing; finance, insurance, and real estate; trade; services
  Unemployment rate: 3.8% (September 1992)
  Per capita income: $12,422 (1989)
  Median household income: $26,229 (1989)
  Total number of families: 746,331 (8.4% of which had incomes below the poverty level; 1989)
  Income tax rate: Ranges from 0.4% to 9.98% of taxable income over $45,000; includes deduction of 100% of federal income taxes
  Sales tax rate: 4.0% on personal property except food, prescription drugs, and medical devices

Cedar Rapids

The City in Brief

Founded: 1841 (incorporated, 1856)

Head Official: Mayor Larry Serbousek (NP) (since 1992)

City Population
  1970: 111,000
  1980: 110,243
  1990: 108,751
  Percent change, 1980–1990: −1.4%
  U.S. rank in 1980: 141st
  U.S. rank in 1990: 174th

Metropolitan Area Population
  1970: 163,213
  1980: 169,775
  1990: 168,767
  Percent change, 1980–1990: −0.6%
  U.S. rank in 1980: Not available
  U.S. rank in 1990: Not available

Area: 53.5 square miles (1990)

Elevation: 733 feet above sea level

Average Temperatures: Winter, 23.7° F; summer, 72.6° F

Average Annual Precipitation: 30.2 inches of snow; 33.7 inches of rain

Major Economic Sectors: Services, trade, manufacturing

Unemployment Rate: 4.0% (September 1992)

Per Capita Income: $15,246 (1989)

1992 (2nd Quarter) ACCRA Average House Price: $114,482

1992 (2nd Quarter) ACCRA Cost of Living Index: 97.0 (U.S. average = 100.0)

1991 FBI Crime Index Total: Not reported

Major Colleges and Universities: Coe College; Mount Mercy College

Daily Newspaper: *The Cedar Rapids Gazette*

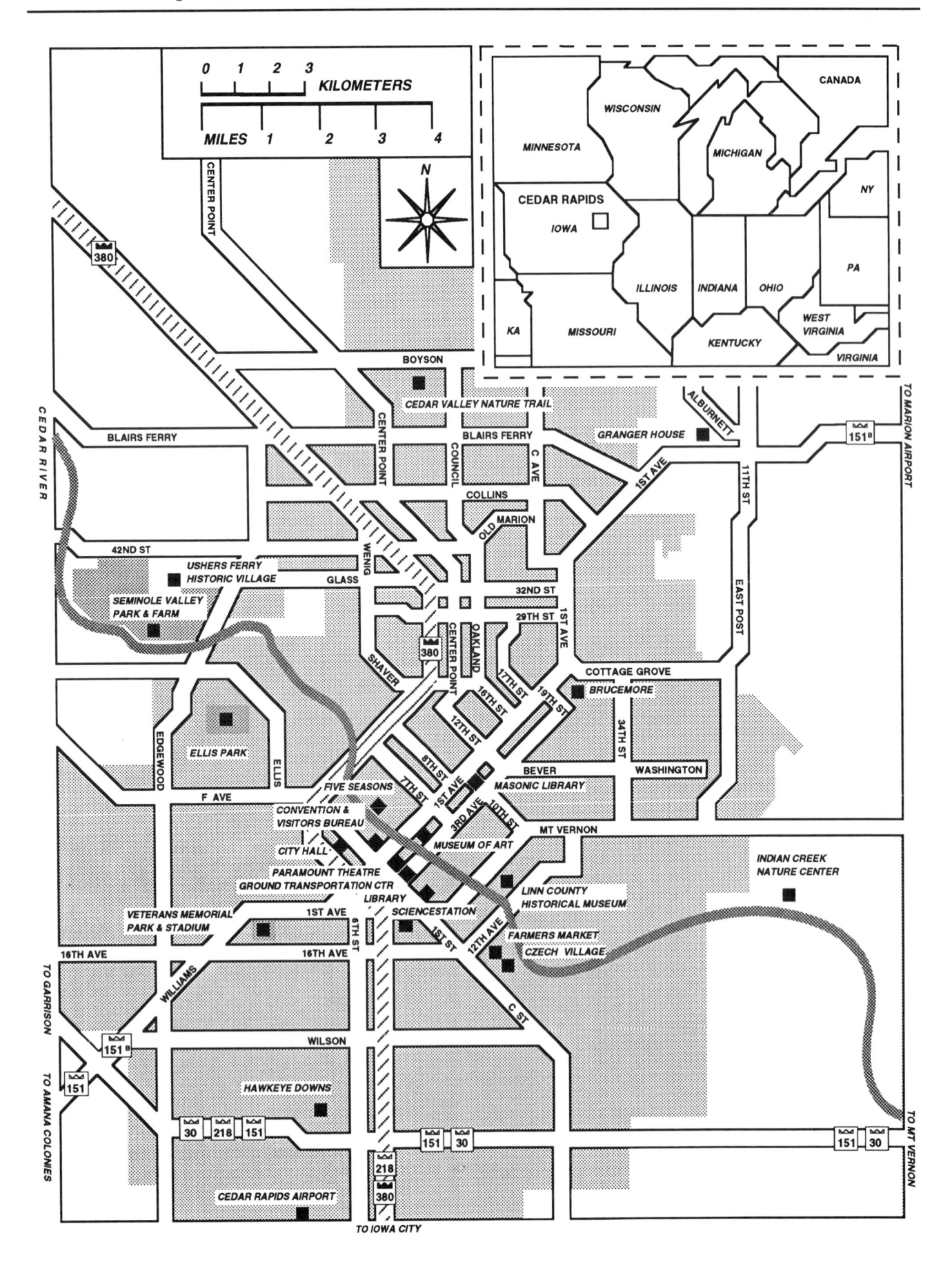

Iowa—Cedar Rapids *Cities of the United States • 2nd Edition*

Introduction

Cedar Rapids preserves a small-town atmosphere in a metropolitan setting. The industrial and cultural center of eastern Iowa, the city has undergone growth and development as it gains prominence in high-technology industries and in export trade. Expansion has been carefully monitored by civic leaders, however, so that international business may be conducted at an unhurried pace and residents may maintain their midwestern traditions. Cedar Rapids is the seat of Linn County and adjoins the city of Marion.

Geography and Climate

Cedar Rapids is situated on the Cedar River, which flows through the city, on rolling terrain in eastern Iowa. The surrounding area is laced with rivers and lakes and dotted with limestone bluffs. The climate consists of four distinct seasons, with warm days and cool nights in spring and autumn. Winter snowfall averages seven inches.

Area: 53.5 square miles (1990)

Elevation: 733 feet above sea level

Average Temperatures: winter, 23.7° F; summer, 72.6° F

Average Annual Precipitation: 30.2 inches of snow; 33.7 inches of rain

History

Cedar River Supports Settlement

The Sac and the Fox, native American tribes, hunted and trapped along the Cedar River before the arrival of Osgood Shepherd, the area's first permanent settler of European descent. Shepherd built a cabin on the river's east side in 1838 at what is now the location of First Avenue and First Street. A survey was made in 1841 and the newly formed town was named Rapids City after the rapids on the Cedar River; the name was changed to Cedar Rapids in 1848. In the early 1840s a dam was built across the river to provide power for the grist and lumber industries. Cedar Rapids was incorporated as a city in 1856; the town of Kingston, located on the west side of the river, was annexed to Cedar Rapids in 1870.

The early history of Cedar Rapids was highlighted by colorful characters and events. An island—now named Municipal Island—in the channel of the Cedar River was until 1851 the headquarters of the Shepherd gang, notorious horse thieves. Local residents built the steamer *The Cedar Rapids* in 1858 and used it for round trips to St. Louis; however, a collision on the Mississippi River and the arrival of the railroad ended river transportation.

Czechoslovakians, known as Bohemians, have made lasting contributions to the Cedar Rapids community. Czechs began arriving in 1852 to work in local packing plants, and soon a "Little Bohemia" was established in the southwest sector of the city. Josef Sosel, the first Czech lawyer in the United States, was smuggled out of his native country in a barrel after he was accused of revolutionary activities; Sosel settled in Cedar Rapids where he played a prominent role in the Czech community. In 1869 Czechs established The Reading Society, which evolved into a Little Theater movement, as well as the Light Guard Band. The Czech-language *Cedar Rapids Listy* began publication in 1906.

Industry and Arts Flourish

The economic growth of Cedar Rapids was spurred in 1871 with the arrival, from Ireland, of T. M. Sinclair, who established one of the nation's largest meatpacking companies, T. M. Sinclair Company, now known as Farmstead Foods. Some other major local industries that date from the same era are Cherry-Burrell and the world's largest cereal mill, Quaker Oats. Cultural development was simultaneous with economic expansion, as many Cedar Rapids arts and educational institutions were formed during this period. Greene's Opera House was dedicated in 1880, the same year the Cedar Rapids Business College opened its doors. Among the school's first faculty members was Austin Palmer, the inventor of the Palmer Method of Penmanship.

For more than sixty years city fathers challenged nearby Marion for designation as the county seat; in 1919, voters endorsed a move to Cedar Rapids. The county courthouse and the Memorial Building, dedicated in 1928 to Americans who have fought in the nation's wars, were built on Municipal Island. Thus Cedar Rapids came to share with Paris, France, the unusual distinction of its seat of government being located on an island. Grant Wood, the Iowa artist, designed the stained glass window in the Memorial Building and supervised its construction in Munich, Germany.

The artistry of Wood, one of the leading practitioners of midwestern regionalism, is felt throughout the city. Wood grew up in Cedar Rapids and taught in the community junior high school; after studying in France he returned to the city and, supported by a local patron, set up a studio. Wood's "American Gothic" caused a sensation in the art world for its uncompromising realism when it was unveiled in 1930. Wood's daring work led to success and he was hired in 1934 to teach art at the University of Iowa.

Telecommunications Help Shape City's Future

Private enterprise, a principal force in the city's economic history, continued to be important during the first half of the twentieth century. Another Cedar Rapids native, Arthur Collins, started Collins Radio Company with eight employees during the Great Depression; the small electronics firm soon established a reputation as a leader in the industrial radio business. The company supplied electronic equipment to all branches of the armed services during World War II. Collins Radio, a major employer in the Cedar Rapids area, became a part of Rockwell International in 1973. Today the Cedar Rapids metropolitan area is a telecommunications and transportation center, performing an important role in the nation's economy and defense.

Historical Information: Linn County Historical Museum, 101 Eighth Ave SE, Cedar Rapids, IA 52401; telephone (319)362-1501

Population Profile

Metropolitan Area Residents
 1970: 163,213
 1980: 169,775
 1990: 168,767
 Percent change, 1980-1990: -0.6%
 U.S. rank in 1980: Not available
 U.S. rank in 1990: Not available

City Residents
 1970: 111,000
 1980: 110,243
 1990: 108,751 (of which, 52,235 were males, and 56,516 were females)
 Percent change, 1980-1990: -1.4%
 U.S. rank in 1980: 141st
 U.S. rank in 1990: 174th (State rank: 2nd)

Density: 2,032.7 people per square mile (1990)

Racial and ethnic characteristics (1990)
 White: 103,884
 Black: 3,127
 American Indian, Eskimo, Aleut: Not reported
 Asian and Pacific Islander: 1,067
 Hispanic (may be of any race): 1,243

Percent of residents born in state: 77.0% (1990)

Age characteristics (1990)
 Population under 5 years old: 7,615
 Population 5 to 9 years old: 7,473
 Population 10 to 14 years old: 7,106
 Population 15 to 19 years old: 7,632
 Population 20 to 24 years old: 8,754
 Population 25 to 29 years old: 9,729
 Population 30 to 34 years old: 9,558
 Population 35 to 39 years old: 8,752
 Population 40 to 44 years old: 7,750
 Population 45 to 49 years old: 5,749
 Population 50 to 54 years old: 4,988
 Population 55 to 59 years old: 4,678
 Population 60 to 64 years old: 4,643
 Population 65 to 69 years old: 4,408
 Population 70 to 74 years old: 3,500
 Population 75 to 79 years old: 2,740
 Population 80 to 84 years old: 1,944
 Population 85 years and over: 1,732
 Median age: 33.1 years

Births (1988)
 Total number: 1,694

Deaths (1988)
 Total number: 926 (of which, 26 were infants under the age of 1 year)

Brucemore, built between 1884 and 1886, preserves the lifestyle of a prominent midwestern family over several generations.

Money income (1989)
  Per capita income: $15,246
  Median household income: $31,458
  Total households: 43,490
  Number of households with income of . . .
    less than $5,000: 2,108
    $5,000 to $9,999: 3,735
    $10,000 to $14,999: 3,594
    $15,000 to $24,999: 7,435
    $25,000 to $34,999: 7,646
    $35,000 to $49,999: 9,337
    $50,000 to $74,999: 6,685
    $75,000 to $99,999: 1,657
    $100,000 to $149,999: 726
    $150,000 or more: 567
  Percent of families below poverty level: 6.6% (50.1% of which were female householder families with related children under 5)
1991 FBI Crime Index Total: Not reported

Municipal Government

Cedar Rapids is administered by a commission-mayor form of government. The five council members and the mayor, who is a member of the council, are elected to two-year terms.

Head Official: Mayor Larry Serbousek (NP) (since 1992; current term expires 1994)

Total Number of City Employees: 1,200 (1993)

City Information: City Hall, 50 Second Avenue Bridge, Cedar Rapids, IA 52401; telephone (319)398-5012

Economy

Major Industries and Commercial Activity

The economy of Cedar Rapids has been traditionally based on the manufacture and processing of agricultural and food products, steel fabricating, tool and die making, and radios and electronics. Manufacturing, which continues to be an important economic sector, has been augmented by high-technology industries and transportation. The Cedar Rapids-Iowa City "Corridor of Technology" is one of the leading centers in the country for the defense electronics industry; the fastest-growing segment of the metropolitan area economy is telecommunications and telemarketing. Advanced research and development laboratories, an educated and productive labor force, and a mid-continent location are increasingly attracting new business and industry to Cedar Rapids.

Cedar Rapids is one of the largest exporting cities per capita in the United States, with local industries conducting commerce with points in all parts of the world. The International Trade Bureau, based in the area for more than forty years, draws its membership from banking, translation, consulting and documentation services, and marketing. Cedar Rapids is establishing trade connections with the Soviet Union, and the telemarketing expertise of local firms will be employed to identify and penetrate other foreign markets.

The city's association with high technology dates to the early years of Collins Radio Company. Today, Collins is part of Rockwell International, employing more than 7,000 people in the Cedar Rapids-Iowa City region. Major Collins projects include spacecraft communications equipment, advanced navigation systems for the NASA Space Shuttle program, communications products and systems for the defense department and U.S. allies, and Navstar Global Positioning System equipment. The University of Iowa in Iowa City has also been involved in space research since 1958, generating a direct impact on the Cedar Rapids economy.

The "Corridor of Technology" is a vital link in the nation's fiber optic industry. Local firms provide a variety of services such as electronic design and consultation, systems planning, equipment manufacturing, and telemarketing. The Technology Innovation Center at the University of Iowa is the base for companies involved in developing and marketing computer-assisted design, nuclear imaging, and electronic speech reproduction products.

Items and goods produced: cereal, syrup, sugar, dairy, mining, and road machinery, boxboard and containers, automotive tools and machinery, radio electronics and avionics equipment, oil burners, furniture, pumps, gravel crushers, cranes, snow plows, electric-powered shovels, trailer parts, candy, office and drainage equipment, rubber goods, plastic bags, medical and chemical products, plumbing supplies, auto parts and toys, furnaces, livestock feed, structural steel, compressed gas, pharmaceuticals, avionics and earth-moving equipment, telecommunications equipment, home appliances

Incentive Programs—New and Existing Companies

State programs—Part of the private/public partnership Cedar Rapids fosters is evident in such state programs as state lottery revenues for business development, state tax abatements on new research and manufacturing facilities, and state tax credits for new job creation. In addition, no sales or use taxes are assessed on equipment or computers and open port warehousing is available.

Local programs—The Cedar Rapids Area Chamber of Commerce and its divisions are active in implementing growth plans, helping existing businesses, and recruiting companies from throughout the world. Kirkwood Community College's New Business Center provides an incubator program for developing businesses.

Development Projects

The millions of dollars invested in attracting and developing high-technology firms and the hundreds of acres of land that have been developed in Cedar Rapids have resulted in the location there of Kodak's $70 million biotechnology complex, Kroenert's (Germany) first American plant for the manufacturing of laminating machinery, P M X Industries' $150 million copper and brass mill, and Genecor International's $50 million bioproducts plant. Building permits in Cedar Rapids tripled over five years to a high in 1989 of more than $90 million. Increasing numbers of single-family homes continue to be built.

Economic Development Information: Economic Development Department, Cedar Rapids Area Chamber of Commerce, P.O. Box 74860, Cedar Rapids IA 52402; telephone (319)398-5317

Commercial Shipping

A central location, efficient access, and low supply and distribution costs have contributed to the development of Cedar Rapids as a primary transportation hub in the Midwest and as the number one exporting city in the country. More than one-hundred area companies are involved in world markets, and Cedar Rapids is a designated Foreign Trade Zone. Cedar Rapids Municipal Airport's ten air cargo carriers transport more than twenty-thousand tons annually. The airport was chosen by United Parcel Service (UPS) as a "central input point" for overnight service in the continental United States. Iowa is the only state bordered by two navigable rivers, and many area exports leave via water.

Three railroads, providing piggyback ramp service, move freight through Cedar Rapids to markets throughout the nation. Approximately thirty-four motor carriers, operating more than twenty local terminals, transport cargo border to border via a network of interstate highways surrounding the city. Cedar Rapids is also an important link in the emerging "information transport" industry; area companies are part of a nationwide fiber optic tele-transportation system that furnishes digital telecommunication service.

Labor Force and Employment Outlook

With an educated, available, and skilled workforce, Cedar Rapids maintains a productivity rate that is substantially above the national average; job turnover rate and absenteeism are among the lowest in the country. Business and industry draw from a high population of engineers, medical professionals, academics, and skilled technicians. As a result of the preeminence of Cedar Rapids in data base telemarketing, experienced personnel can also be found in the telemarketing sector. One out of six jobs in manufacturing is associated with import and export trade.

The following is a summary of data regarding the Cedar Rapids metropolitan area labor force as of September 1992.

Size of non-agricultural labor force: 94,100

Number of workers employed in . . .
  mining: not available
  construction: 4,700
  manufacturing: 20,600
  transportation and public utilities: 5,500
  wholesale and retail trade: 22,800
  finance, insurance, and real estate: 5,000
  services: 24,100
  government: 11,400

Average hourly earnings of production workers employed in manufacturing: $14.90

Unemployment rate: 4.0%

Largest employers	*Number of employees*
Collins Group, Rockwell International	7,189
Amana Refrigeration, Inc.	2,142

Largest employers	Number of employees
Cedar Rapids Community Schools	2,032
St. Luke's Hospital	1,787
Iowa Electric Light & Power Company	1,707
Quaker Oats Company	1,340
Mercy Medical Center	1,211
M C I Communications	1,150
Rockwell Graphic Systems	1,015

Cost of Living

Cedar Rapids's property taxes are the lowest of the state's seven largest cities.

The following is a summary of data regarding several key cost of living factors in the Cedar Rapids area.

1992 (2nd Quarter) ACCRA Cost of Living Index: 97.0 (U.S. average = 100.0)

1992 (2nd Quarter) ACCRA Average House Price: $114,482

State income tax rate: Ranges from 0.4% to 9.98% of taxable income over $45,000; includes deduction of 100% of federal income taxes

State sales tax rate: 4.0% on personal property except food, prescription drugs, and medical devices

Local income tax rate: None

Local sales tax rate: None

Property tax rate: $32.539 per $1,000 of assessed valuation (1991-1992)

Economic Information: Cedar Rapids Area Chamber of Commerce, P.O. Box 74860, Cedar Rapids, IA 52402; telephone (319) 398-5317

Education and Research

Elementary and Secondary Schools

The Cedar Rapids Community School District is the third largest district in the state of Iowa, which is one of only eight states allowing students to attend school in any district in the state. Average ACT composite scores rank Iowa first in the nation; Cedar Rapids's scores are higher than the state's. Computer instruction is available from kindergarten through high school; there is one computer for every twelve students. High schools graduate 94 percent of students entering ninth grade, well above the national average of 71 percent. Sixty percent of high school graduates enroll in post-secondary education. Forty-eight percent of teachers have master's degrees.

The following is a summary of data regarding the Cedar Rapids public schools as of the 1991-1992 school year.

Total enrollment: 17,000

Number of facilities
elementary schools: 23
middle schools: 6
senior high schools: 4

Student/teacher ratio: elementary, 24:1; middle, 26:1; senior high, 25:1

Teacher salaries (1988-1989)
minimum: $18,000
maximum: $34,280

Funding per pupil: $3,900 (1988-1989)

Cedar Rapids is also served by nearly twenty private schools that offer alternative educational opportunities.

Public Schools Information: Cedar Rapids Community School District, Superintendent's Office, 346 Second Avenue SW, Cedar Rapids, IA 52404; telephone (319)398-2000

Colleges and Universities

Six institutions of higher learning are located in the Cedar Rapids area. Coe College, founded in 1851, and Mount Mercy College are private colleges awarding baccalaureate degrees in such fields as biological sciences, nursing, business and management, education, social sciences, and fine and applied arts. The curricula of both schools feature evening classes, study abroad, and cooperative programs with local colleges and with universities throughout the United States. In nearby Iowa City, the University of Iowa, with an enrollment of more than twenty-eight thousand students, offers undergraduate and graduate education through special study programs and law, business, dental, and medical schools. Cornell College in neighboring Mount Vernon is a four-year liberal arts college under the auspices of the United Methodist Church with accreditation in teacher education.

Kirkwood Community College, serving a seven-county region, provides sixty-five vocational and technical programs, thirty-three arts and sciences transfer programs, and community education. Hamilton Business College offers vocational training.

Libraries and Research Centers

The Cedar Rapids Public Library operates an architecturally impressive main facility as well as two other branches in the city. Library holdings consist of more than three-hundred thousand books, more than twenty thousand bound periodicals, twelve thousand films, and recordings, tapes, slides, maps, and charts. The library is a depository for state documents and houses the Iowa Substance Abuse Information Center. Cedar Rapids is also served by the Coe College and Kirkwood Community College libraries. Among special libraries are the Iowa Masonic Library (housing the best Masonic collection in the world), the Cedar Rapids Gazette Library, the East Central Regional Library, and the Linn County Law Library; others are affiliated with the Museum of Art, hospitals, corporations, and religious groups.

The University of Iowa was recently the beneficiary of a collection of more than eleven thousand cookbooks and culinary writings dating back to 1499. University of Iowa research facilities such as the Laser Research Center and Human Biology Research Facility receive more than $120 million annually in grants and contracts. A Genealogical Research Center is maintained by the Linn County Heritage Society.

Public Library Information: Cedar Rapids Public Library, 500 First Street SE, Cedar Rapids, IA 52401; telephone (319)398-5123

Health Care

Four hospitals, providing nearly 2,000 beds, serve the metropolitan Cedar Rapids area; the medical community includes nearly three-hundred practicing physicians. St. Luke's Hospital maintains centers specializing in such fields as emergency and trauma care, heart care, birth and pediatric care, rehabilitative and psychiatric services, and mobile diagnostic services. St. Luke's also operates a school of nursing. Mercy Hospital's facilities include the Eastern Iowa Center for Cancer Detection, Treatment and Research, a part of the Mayo Clinic, and the Neuroscience Center, one of seven centers in the country using the Kelly stereotactic neurosurgical system. In addition, the hospital provides cardiopulmonary diagnosis and care, substance abuse treatment, pediatric care, residential care, and various community health and safety programs. The health care needs of Cedar Rapids's residents are also attended to at University of Iowa Hospital and Clinics and Veterans Affairs Medical Center.

Health Care Information: St. Luke's Hospital, 1026 A Avenue NE, Cedar Rapids, IA; telephone (319)369-7211

Recreation

Sightseeing

A trip to Cedar Rapids might include a visit to Brucemore Mansion and Gardens, one of only seventeen house museums in the country on the National Trust for Historic Preservation. A twenty-one room Queen Anne-style mansion on a 26-acre estate, Brucemore is the ancestral home of the founder of the Quaker Oats Company. It is both an important architectural structure and a community cultural center, the site of dance and drama performances as well as seasonal events such as a Victorian Christmas. Capturing the splendor of a by-gone era, the mansion is enhanced by a porch designed by Grant Wood and is surrounded by grounds with formal gardens and a duck pond.

The Czech and Slovak Museum and Library preserves the city's ethnic heritage; shops and stores feature authentic crafts and foods. On the Cedar River a colonnaded observation tower rises from the seven-story Municipal Building; the building's focal point is the stained glass window—illuminated from within nightly—designed by Grant Wood, featuring an allegorical depiction of Victory. The Science Station, housed in the refurbished Central Fire Station, offers hands-on science and technology exhibits for children and adults. At the Indian Creek Nature Center, located on a 140-acre preserve with hiking trails, natural history exhibits are displayed in a remodelled dairy barn featuring an observatory in the silo.

The Cedar Rapids Museum of Art, opened in 1989, encompasses a restored Beaux Arts building and a newly constructed gallery.

Several points of interest are within driving distance of Cedar Rapids. The Amana Colonies, 19 miles from the city, is Iowa's primary tourist attraction. The Herbert Hoover Presidential Library and National Historic Site is in West Branch, 25 miles from Cedar Rapids.

Arts and Culture

An important part of cultural life in Cedar Rapids is the Museum of Art, which moved into a new facility in 1989. The $10 million building, which features a glass winter garden, was designed to complement the Carnegie Library Building that is a part of the museum. The museum houses the world's largest collection of works by Grant Wood, Marvin Cone, and Mauricio Lasansky.

The city's cultural community presents a variety of concerts and shows and hosts visiting international performance groups. The renovated Paramount Theatre, with a hall of mirrors and Broadway-style marquee, is the home of the Cedar Rapids Symphony. The symphony performs a full season of classical, pop, and chamber music concerts. The Paramount also houses the Cedar Rapids Community Association, which books touring artists and music and theatre productions. The internationally recognized Marion Community Concert and Jazz Band presents summer performances in Marion's City Park.

Theatre Cedar Rapids presents seven mainstage shows in a repertoire ranging from musicals to drama at its downtown theater on Third Street during a September to July season. Children's Theatre of Cedar Rapids presents three performances annually. The Ole Creamery Theatre Company in nearby Garrison is a professional group that tours in the winter and performs a May to December season at the Amana Colonies. Area colleges sponsor a host of cultural programs. Among them is the Summer Rep series at the University of Iowa University Theatres, which features works each season by a single playwright. The university's Hancher Auditorium brings international artists and performing groups to the vicinity.

Czech and Slovak Museum and Library is located in a restored immigrant home, and the furnishings of a prosperous nineteenth-century middle class family are preserved at Granger House. Turn-of-the-century farm life can be relived at Seminole Valley Farm; small-town life is recreated at Ushers Ferry Historic District.

Festivals and Holidays

A festival, parade, or show is scheduled nearly every weekend of the year in Cedar Rapids. The Maple Syrup Festival at Indian Creek Nature Center in March is one of the more popular seasonal events. St. Nicholas Day, also in March, and Houby Days in May celebrate the heritage of the city's Czech population. All Iowa Fair in mid-June at Hawkeye Downs pays tribute to the Iowa farming industry. The Arts Festival at Brucemore in June presents visual and performing artists. Brucemore also holds a Dixieland Jazz Festival in July. The Freedom Festival on the Fourth of July weekend consists of a number of events including a softball spectacular. Pioneer Days in July at Usher's Ferry Pioneer Village recreates the life of the nineteenth century buckskinner. The Czech Village Festival welcomes the fall season.

Sports for the Spectator

The Cedar Rapids Reds, a Class A farm club of the National League Cincinnati Reds professional baseball club, play a full home schedule in the Midwest League at Veterans Memorial Park. The Cedar Rapids Silver Bullets play professional basketball at Five Seasons Center from November through March. For automobile-racing enthusiasts Hawkeye Downs Speedway hosts a number of sanctioned racing events in a spring to fall schedule. The full range of major college sports is presented at the University of Iowa in nearby Iowa City, where the Hawkeyes engage in Big Ten competition. Coe College, Mount Mercy College, and Kirkwood Community College in Cedar Rapids, and Cornell College in Mount Vernon compete in a number of sports.

Sports for the Participant

Seventy-eight parks on over 4,000 acres of land provide facilities for a variety of recreational activities in Cedar Rapids. The Cedar Rapids Recreation Commission maintains five heated pools, fifty ball fields, nineteen playgrounds, twenty pre-school tot lots, fifty tennis courts, and municipal golf courses, one of which was the first in the nation equipped with lights for nighttime play. Mays Island in the Cedar River offers a host of recreational activities, and camping is possible at Seminole Valley Park and Farm. Cedar Valley Nature Trail, once a railroad bed, offers 52 miles of trails for biking, hiking, and skiing through recreation areas, along riverbanks, and through small towns.

Recreation Information: Cedar Rapids Recreation Commission, telephone (319)398-5065

Shopping and Dining

Cedar Rapids offers many shopping and dining attractions found in a large city, but on a smaller scale. Coventry Gardens Mall downtown is connected via a skywalk system to a fifteen-block area offering more than 130 stores. Czech Village and the Amana Colonies offer an assortment of specialty shops. Dining choices in Cedar Rapids consist of a mix of ethnic and traditional cuisines, with some of the best food being served in the downtown hotels. The only Czech restaurant in the state and an excellent family bakery can be found at Czech Village.

Visitor Information: Cedar Rapids Area Convention and Visitors Bureau, P.O. Box 5339, 119 First Avenue SE, Cedar Rapids, IA 52406-5339; telephone (319)398-5009. A visitor information center is located at Cedar Rapids Airport.

Convention Facilities

The multipurpose Five Seasons Center, in downtown Cedar Rapids, is accessible via skywalks to shopping, dining, entertainment, lodging, and transportation. The facility accommodates up to 10,000 people; it can seat 1,800 people in a banquet setting. The center, providing more than twenty-eight thousand square feet of exhibit space, is part of a complex that includes two hotels, a ballroom, and parking facilities.

Hotels and motels in metropolitan Cedar Rapids offer accommodations for a range of meeting and convention needs. More than two-thousand rooms are available.

Convention Information: Cedar Rapids Convention and Visitors Bureau, P.O. Box 5339, 119 First Avenue SE, Cedar Rapids, IA 52406-5339; telephone (319)398-5009

Transportation

Approaching the City

The Cedar Rapids Airport, 7 miles south of the center of the city, offers direct service to ten cities on an average of seventy-four commercial flights daily. Business travelers have access to the airport's Information Center. It is estimated that the airport will board 803,000 passengers annually by the year 2006.

Cedar Rapids is linked with points throughout the nation by two interstate highways, I-380 (north-south) and I-80 (east-west). Federal highways are 30/218, which runs east to west through the south sector Cedar Rapids, and 151, which intersects the city diagonally northeast to southwest. State routes include 150, running parallel with I-380, and east-west 94.

Traveling in the City

The Cedar River divides Cedar Rapids into east and west sectors; for address purposes, streets are designated according to quadrants: northeast, northwest, southeast, and southwest. The City Bus Department and taxis are headquartered in the new Ground Transportation Center on Fourth Avenue. Linn County LIFTS provides service to the elderly and handicapped with specially-equipped buses.

Communications

Newspapers and Magazines

The major daily newspaper in Cedar Rapids is *The Cedar Rapids Gazette*. Also published in the city is a weekly agricultural newspaper, *Iowa Farmer Today*. The *Fraternal Herald* (*Bratrsky Vestnik*) is a monthly benefit society magazine.

Television and Radio

Four television stations affiliated with major commercial networks are received in Cedar Rapids, and cable service is available. Eleven AM and FM radio stations schedule musical, special interest, and news and public affairs programming. Listeners also receive radio stations out of Iowa City.

Media Information: The Cedar Rapids Gazette, 500 Third Avenue, SE, P.O. Box 511, Cedar Rapids, IA 52401; telephone (319)398-8211

Davenport

The City in Brief

Founded: 1808 (incorporated 1836)

Head Official: City Manager Charles Mallory (since 1989)

City Population
 1970: 98,469
 1980: 103,264
 1990: 95,333
 Percent change, 1980–1990: −7.7%
 U.S. rank in 1980: 158th
 U.S. rank in 1990: 212th

Metropolitan Area Population
 1970: 363,000
 1980: 384,000
 1990: 350,861
 Percent change, 1980–1990: −8.8%
 U.S. rank in 1980: 158th
 U.S. rank in 1990: 104th

Area: 61.4 square miles (1990)

Elevation: Ranges from 579 to 700 feet above sea level

Average Annual Temperature: 50.1° F

Average Annual Precipitation: 32.79 inches

Major Economic Sectors: Trade, services, manufacturing, government

Unemployment Rate: 6.5% (September 1992)

Per Capita Income: $12,557 (1989)

1992 (2nd Quarter) ACCRA Average House Price: Not reported

1992 (2nd Quarter) ACCRA Cost of Living Index: Not reported

1991 FBI Crime Index Total: Not reported

Major Colleges and Universities: St. Ambrose University; Teikyo Marycrest University

Daily Newspaper: *Quad-City Times*

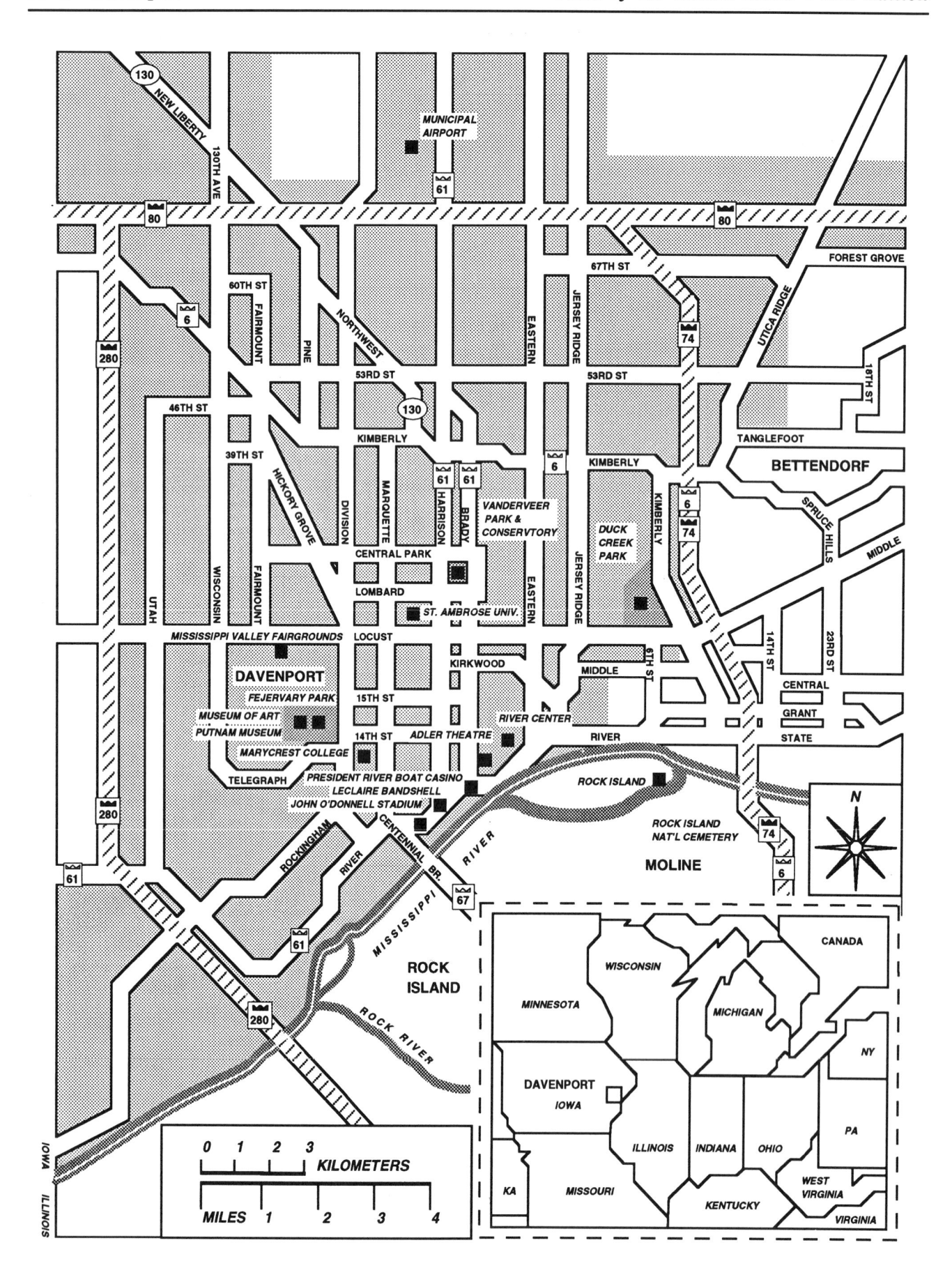

Iowa—Davenport *Cities of the United States • 2nd Edition*

Introduction

Davenport is the seat of Scott County and the largest of four cities in Iowa and Illinois that comprise the Quad Cities metropolitan area; the other three cities are Bettendorf, Iowa, Rock Island, Illinois, and Moline, Illinois. Because of its location on the Mississippi River, Davenport played an important role in western expansion during the nineteenth century; along with the other Quad Cities, Davenport continues to be a world leader in the production of farm equipment. With the introduction of riverboat gambling in the 1990s, Davenport is emerging as a top Midwestern tourist destination.

Geography and Climate

Davenport is set on a plain on the north bank of the Mississippi River, where the river forms the boundary between Iowa and Illinois. Davenport's section of the generally north-to-south-flowing river flows from east to west. Located in the heart of an agricultural region, the city is within 300 miles of most other major midwestern cities. Davenport's position near the geographic center of the country produces a temperate, continental climate that is characterized by a wide range in temperatures. Summers are short and hot; winters are usually severe, with an average annual snowfall of approximately 30 inches.

Area: 61.4 square miles (1990)

Elevation: 579 feet to 700 feet above sea level

Average Temperatures: winter, 23.7° F; summer, 72.6° F; annual average, 50.1° F

Average Annual Precipitation: 32.79 inches

History

Westward Expansion Targets Davenport Townsite

In the early 1800s the land now occupied by the city of Davenport was the site of bloody fighting between native Americans and settlers from the eastern United States. This location was valuable in the westward expansion beyond the Mississippi River, serving as a trading center of the American Fur Company. Early treaties specified that the Sac tribe could remain in their villages until the land was surveyed and sold to settlers; warfare resulted, however, after Chief Black Hawk and his followers refused to leave the land on the order of the United States Government agent at Fort Armstrong. In the fall of 1832, Black Hawk was captured and returned to Fort Armstrong where he signed a treaty, known as the Black Hawk Purchase, that conveyed to the United States 6 million acres of land west of the Mississippi River.

Two figures stand out in the period that predates the formation of Davenport. The city was named for Colonel George Davenport, an Englishman who had served in the United States Army and then established a fur trading post in the vicinity. Antoine LeClaire, an interpreter who was fluent in three languages and several native American dialects, served as interpreter for the Black Hawk Purchase. For his efforts the federal government, at the request of Chief Keokuk, awarded him a section of land opposite Rock Island and another section at the head of the rapids above Rock Island where the treaty was negotiated. In 1833, in a claim dispute over land he owned, LeClaire settled for a quarter-section bounded by Davenport's present-day Harrison Street, Warren Street, and Seventh Street. In 1835 Colonel Davenport and six other men formed a company to survey a townsite; they purchased this section from LeClaire, who succeeded in having the new town named after his good friend Davenport. The town was incorporated in 1836.

The initial sale of lots attracted few buyers and in the first year only a half dozen families relocated to the new town. LeClaire and Davenport erected a hotel on the corner of Ripley and First Streets, naming it the Hotel Davenport. By the spring of 1837, the population was growing; a town retailer, for instance, served customers who traveled hundreds of miles to buy goods from his inventory, valued at $5,000. In December of that year the Wisconsin Territorial Legislature authorized the creation of Scott County, named after General Winfield Scott. A dispute subsequently broke out between Davenport and neighboring Rockingham for the right to be the county seat. The matter was decided, after three elections, in favor of Davenport; in time, Rockingham was absorbed by the larger city. Davenport received its first city charter in 1839.

Industry and Culture Establish Traditions

During the decade before the Civil War Davenport increased its population more than fivefold, with an influx of immigrants from Germany that continued unabated into the 1890s. These new residents imported music and other cultural interests to Davenport, creating institutions such as the Davenport Public Museum and the Municipal Art Gallery. The first railroad bridge to span the Mississippi River was completed in 1856 between Davenport and Rock Island, contributing to the development of the western frontier. The Rock Island Arsenal opened in 1861 to help Union war efforts; the arsenal eventually grew to become one of the largest in the world. In the post-Civil War era Davenport prospered as a riverboat town and as a burgeoning industrial center for the manufacture of cement, steel and iron products, and leather goods.

By the turn of the twentieth century Davenport was considered the "Washing Machine Capital of the World"—the revolutionary home appliance was invented in the city—and the "Cigar Making Capital of the Midwest." The cigar industry flourished in Davenport until World War II. Davenport counts among its former citizens a number of prominent Americans. B. J. Palmer, the inventor of chiropractics, and his son, D. D. Palmer, were lifelong residents; the younger Palmer used his radio station to introduce Americans to his new medical practice and to Davenport. Buffalo Bill Cody grew up in the rural Davenport area; Dixieland jazz great Bix Beiderbecke was born in the city; and two Pulitzer Prize winners, Charles Edward Russell and Susan Glaspell, once lived there.

Davenport and the Quad Cities region, having invested tens of millions of dollars in the 1990s on lavish riverboat casinos, look forward to being designated Riverboat Gambling Capital of the World.

Historical Information: Rock Island County Historical Society, 822 11th Avenue, Moline, IL 61265; telephone (309)764-8590

Population Profile

Metropolitan Area Residents
1970: 363,000
1980: 384,000
1990: 350,861
Average annual percent change, 1980–1988: −0.7%
Percent change, 1980–1990: −8.8%
U.S. rank in 1980: 158th
U.S. rank in 1990: 104th

City Residents
1970: 98,469
1980: 103,264
1990: 95,333 (of which, 45,686 were males, and 49,647 were females)
Percent change, 1980–1990: −7.7%
U.S. rank in 1980: 158th
U.S. rank in 1990: 212th (State rank: 3rd)

Density: 1,552.7 people per square mile (1990)

Racial and ethnic characteristics (1990)
  White: 84,968
  Black: 7,521
  American Indian, Eskimo, Aleut: Not reported
  Asian and Pacific Islander: 1,001
  Hispanic origin (may be of any race): 3,300

Percent of residents born in state: 65.4% (1990)

Age characteristics (1990)
  Population under 5 years old: 7,700
  Population 5 to 9 years old: 7,535
  Population 10 to 14 years old: 7,018
  Population 15 to 19 years old: 6,506
  Population 20 to 24 years old: 7,576
  Population 25 to 29 years old: 8,256
  Population 30 to 34 years old: 8,446
  Population 35 to 39 years old: 7,572
  Population 40 to 44 years old: 6,282
  Population 45 to 49 years old: 4,622
  Population 50 to 54 years old: 4,091
  Population 55 to 59 years old: 3,779
  Population 60 to 64 years old: 3,802
  Population 65 to 69 years old: 3,850
  Population 70 to 74 years old: 2,964
  Population 75 to 79 years old: 2,303
  Population 80 to 84 years old: 1,655
  Population 85 years and over: 1,376
  Median age: 31.7 years

Births (1988)
  Total number: 1,634

Deaths (1988)
  Total number: 864 (of which, 16 were infants under the age of 1 year)

Money income (1989)
  Per capita income: $12,557
  Median household income: $26,218
  Total households: 37,069
  Number of households with income of . . .
    less than $5,000: 2,815
    $5,000 to $9,999: 3,986
    $10,000 to $14,999: 3,748
    $15,000 to $24,999: 7,127
    $25,000 to $34,999: 6,330
    $35,000 to $49,999: 6,254
    $50,000 to $74,999: 4,938
    $75,000 to $99,999: 1,187
    $100,000 to $149,999: 436
    $150,000 or more: 248
  Percent of families below poverty level: 12.4% (77.0% of which were female householder families with related children under 5)
1991 FBI Crime Index Total: Not reported

Municipal Government

Davenport, the seat of Scott County, is administered by a council-mayor form of government. Ten aldermen—eight chosen by ward and elected at large—and the mayor serve two-year terms; a city administrator is appointed. Davenport is the only city in Iowa to hold partisan political elections.

Head Official: City Manager Charles Mallory (since 1989)

Total Number of City Employees: 830 (1991)

City Information: City Hall, telephone (319)326-7763

Economy

Major Industries and Commercial Activity

The Davenport economic base is diversified, with a relatively equal distribution among the manufacturing, wholesale and retail, and services sectors. Manufacturing has traditionally been a principal industry in the city. Davenport is also a primary retail and wholesale trade center, drawing from a market area encompassing a radius of up to 100 miles; retail sales have totalled nearly $7 million annually. Business and industry in Davenport benefit from the Quad City financial community. Forty-four area banks and lending institutions, in conjunction with the state of Iowa, have established a fiscal atmosphere favorable to new business and the expansion of existing firms through progressive and conventional financing procedures. Thirteen industrial islands are located within the Davenport city limits.

Items and goods produced: agricultural implements, construction machinery, military equipment, airplane parts, chemicals, meat and food products, lumber and timber, sheet aluminum, metal products, cement and foundry products, electronic parts, clothing, printing and publishing products

Incentive Programs—New and Existing Companies

The public and private sectors help insure a healthy business climate for companies located in Davenport. The state of Iowa's industrial revenue bonds, tax exemption for manufacturing improvements, and job training and re-training legislation are joined by the Eastern Iowa Community College District's New Jobs Training Program in creating conditions favorable to business. Scott County also initiates planning and development programs, as does the City of Davenport Division of Community and Economic Development.

Development Projects

Perhaps the most significant development in Davenport and environs in the 1990s has been the introduction of riverboat casino gambling. Tens of millions of dollars have been poured into these ventures and tourists have been responding. Another recent development is the new *Quad-City Times* facility, built at a cost of nearly $24 million. New housing starts have been on the rise.

Economic Development Information: Eastern Iowa Economic Development Council, c/o Eastern Iowa Community College District, 306 West River Drive, Davenport, IA 52801-1221; telephone (319)322-5015, ext. 263

Commercial Shipping

Davenport's mid-continent location is favorable to freight distribution, with one-day delivery by highway and rail to points throughout the Midwest. As a U.S. Customs Port of Entry and a Foreign Trade Zone (FTZ), Davenport is also a center for national and international commerce. Its Quad Cities Container Terminal works with the FTZ to permit materials to be shipped around the world without being unpacked or passing through customs until they reach their final destination. The Quad City area comprises the largest market of any major metropolitan region with a population over 300,000 people between Chicago and California. Nine airfreight carriers process cargo through the Quad City Airport. Nearly 150 motor freight companies maintain 130 warehouses in the Quad Cities. Five railroads, three of them mainline, provide daily piggyback, transloading, rail-barge transit, and special-purpose car services. Twenty-six private and two public river terminals operate on the Mississippi River, offering fleeting, bulk commodity transfer, and short- and medium-line towing. The river provides a 9-foot channel and a ten-month season for barge-based commerce.

Labor Force and Employment Outlook

Davenport claims a productive, skilled labor force that can be employed at a lower cost than the national average. The service sector is the fastest-growing, led by the proliferation of gambling casinos and attendant industries catering to tourists.

The following is a summary of data regarding the Davenport metropolitan area labor force as of September 1992.

Size of non-agricultural labor force: 166,100

Number of workers employed in . . .
  mining: Not reported
  construction: 7,600
  manufacturing: 28,000
  transportation and public utilities: 7,900
  wholesale and retail trade: 48,700
  finance, insurance, and real estate: 7,900
  services: 40,100
  government: 25,900

Average hourly earnings of production workers employed in manufacturing: $14.29

Unemployment rate: 6.5%

Largest employers	Number of employees
Deere & Company (farm/ industrial equipment)	9,000
Rock Island Arsenal (artillery weapons)	8,500
Aluminum Company of America (aluminum products)	3,000
Davenport Schools	2,257
Oscar Mayer and Company (meat packers)	771
Eagle Food Centers	1,550

Cost of Living

Davenport offers tax-exempt housing mortgage revenue bonds to prospective homeowners. Health care costs are relatively low.

The following is a summary of data regarding several key cost of living factors in the Davenport area.

1992 (2nd Quarter) ACCRA Cost of Living Index: Not reported

1992 (2nd Quarter) ACCRA Average House Price: Not reported

State income tax rate: Ranges from 0.4% to 9.98% of taxable income over $45,000; includes deduction of 100% of federal income taxes

State sales tax rate: 4.0% on personal property except food, prescription drugs, and medical devices

Local income tax rate: None

Local sales tax rate: 1.0%

Property tax rate: $34.794 per $1,000 assessed valuation (1990–1991)

Economic Information: Davenport Chamber of Commerce, 112 East Third Street, Davenport, IA 52801; telephone (319)322-1706

Education and Research

Elementary and Secondary Schools

Public elementary and secondary schools in Davenport are part of the Davenport Community School District. A seven-member, nonpartisan board selects a superintendent. Iowa is one of only eight states allowing students to attend school in any district in the state. Average ACT composite scores rank Iowa first in the nation.

The following is a summary of data regarding the Davenport public schools as of the 1991–1992 school year.

Total enrollment: 18,245

Number of facilities
  elementary schools: 23
  junior high schools: 6
  senior high schools: 3

Student/teacher ratio: Kindergarten–1st grade, 26:1; grades 2 and 3, 28:1; grades 4–12, 30:1

Teacher salaries
  minimum: $19,300
  maximum: $40,530

Funding per pupil: $3,203 ($2,198 of which is paid by the state)

Several private and parochial schools offer education alternatives in the Davenport metropolitan region.

Public Schools Information: Davenport Community School District, Superintendent's Office, 1001 Harrison Street, Davenport, IA 52803; telephone (319)323-9951

Colleges and Universities

Among the institutions of higher learning located in Davenport are Teikyo Marycrest and St. Ambrose Universities, coeducational liberal arts colleges affiliated with the Catholic Church; both grant a master's degree in addition to baccalaureate degrees. The Palmer College of Chiropractic provides a four-year course of study toward the doctor of chiropractic degree. Eastern Iowa Community College, which awards associate degrees, offers continuing education and vocational and technical training. The Quad Cities Graduate Study Center represents a consortium of eight Iowa and Illinois institutions; the center coordinates course offerings and applies credit toward advanced degrees.

Among colleges and universities within commuting distance of Davenport are Augustana College in Rock Island, Illinois; the University of Iowa in Iowa City; and Knox College in Galesburg, Illinois.

Libraries and Research Centers

The Davenport Public Library operates two branches and a bookmobile. Its main facility holds about 222,000 volumes as well as periodicals, tapes, slides, films, maps, charts, and art reproductions. The library, a depository for state and federal documents, maintains special collections on chess, Iowa authors. Also based in Davenport is Southeastern Library Services, which provides libraries in the region with reference back-up, continuing education classes, and library development and support services.

Specialized libraries and research centers in Davenport are affiliated with colleges, museums, corporations, and the Scott County Bar Association.

Public Library Information: Davenport Public Library, 321 Main Street, Davenport, IA 52801-1490; telephone (319)326-7832

Health Care

Davenport is a health care center for the Quad City metropolitan area. Located in the city are three hospitals, providing more than 650 beds: St. Luke's Hospital, Mercy Hospital, and Davenport Medical Center. Palmer College operates four chiropractic clinics in the city. Other medical facilities accessible from Davenport include Franciscan Medical Center in Rock Island, Illinois, Illini Hospital in Silvis, and United Medical Center in Moline, Illinois. The Quad Cities medical community is comprised of nearly seven-hundred practicing physicians, osteopaths, chiropractors, and dentists.

Health Care Information: Health Care Information Referral and Assistance Service of Scott and Rock Island Counties, telephone (319)324-0625

Recreation

Sightseeing

The Village of East Davenport was founded in 1851 and prospered from the logging industry along the Mississippi River, playing a significant role in western migration. Today, the village is sixty square blocks of more than five-hundred preserved and redeveloped homes and businesses; small shops, new businesses, and one-family residential homes are combined in a variety of historical styles. An elaborate recreation of nineteenth-century America at Christmas time takes place in the village each year on the first Friday and Saturday of December.

Sightseeing cruises on Davenport-based Mississippi riverboats are a popular attraction. Among other historic sites are the Buffalo Bill Cody homestead in nearby McCausland, the Buffalo Bill Museum in LeClaire, and the Rock Island Arsenal, where Colonel George Davenport's home is located. Tram ride tours of the arsenal are available. Another sightseeing attraction near Davenport is located on a 1,000-acre site that overlooks the Rock River Valley in Moline, Illinois, where the Deere & Company Administrative Center—the company's world headquarters—was designed by Eero Saarinen, the celebrated Finnish architect.

Arts and Culture

The Quad City Symphony Orchestra, founded in 1914, is housed in the Adler Theatre, a restored art-deco movie palace; the orchestra performs a six-concert season with international guest artists. The Adler is also the home of the Broadway Theatre League, which hosts touring shows. Other organizations that sponsor musical events are the Friends of Chamber Music, the Handel Oratorio Society, and the American Guild of Organists. New to Davenport's performing arts scene is the Cassandra Manning Ballet Theatre.

The Putnam Museum, situated on a bluff overlooking the Mississippi River, houses exhibits on natural science, tribal cultures, ancient civilizations, and the Mississippi River valley. A recently added permanent exhibit, "River, Prairie and People," illustrates the history of the Quad Cities from prehistoric times to the present. The Davenport Museum of Art, Iowa's first municipal art museum, is located next door to the Putnam. Its Regionalist Collection includes the Grant Wood Display, a permanent collection of the works of Iowa's most famous artist. Other collections include European Old Masters, Mexican Colonial Art, and Haitian Art.

The Hauberg Indian Museum, part of Blackhawk State Park in Rock Island, Illinois, preserves the heritage of the Sac and Fox tribes. Local history can be explored at Bettendorf Children's Museum.

Festivals and Holidays

The Mississippi River is the focal point for many of Davenport's annual events. The Great River Ramble, held on the Fourth of July holiday, features the Mississippi Valley Blues Festival and a nighttime lighted boat parade. The musical genius of Mozart is celebrated at various locations in June. The weeklong Great Mississippi Valley Fair, featuring a carnival and entertainment, begins in late July. Top Dixieland bands from around the world flock to the Bix Beiderbecke Memorial Jazz Festival in July. The Civil War Muster & Mercantile Exposition is held on the third weekend in September at Lindsay Park, formerly Camp McClellan, where recreated Civil War battles and other events are staged.

Sports for the Spectator

The Quad-City Angels, a Midwest League Class A professional baseball affiliate of the California Angels of the American League, play a home schedule of seventy baseball games at John O'Donnell Stadium in Davenport. The Quad-City Downs in East Moline sponsors live harness racing from March through November. The *Quad-City Times* Bix 7 Run is held in late July when more than seventeen-thousand runners—including nationally known competitors—challenge the hills of Davenport. A Professional Golfers' Association golf classic is also held locally. Basketball action is provided by the Quad City Thunders, members of the Continental Basketball Association, who play twenty-eight home games from November through March at Wharton Field House in Rock Island.

Sports for the Participant

The Davenport Parks and Recreation Department manages seventy sites, on 2,200 acres of parks and public facilities, for golf, tennis, swimming, jogging, and softball. Scott County Park, 6 miles north of Davenport on more than 1,000 acres of land, features picnic grounds and an Olympic-size pool. Davenport's proximity to the Mississippi River provides easy access for boating and various other water sports; riverboat casino gambling out of Davenport and Bettendorf is offered November through March. Wacky Waters is a 30-acre amusement park with water rides and a 5-acre swimming lake. Skiing is possible from December to March in Taylor Ridge.

Shopping and Dining

Davenport's Northpark Mall is Iowa's largest mall; anchored by five major stores, it houses more than 165 specialty shops. Thirty-five specialty and gift shops, clothing stores, restaurants, and taverns are located in the historic Village of East Davenport. American and family dining is the focus of the majority of local restaurants, with a sampling of Chinese cuisine, pubs, and delis also offered.

Visitor Information: Quad Cities Convention and Visitors Bureau, P.O. Box 3097, Rock Island, IL

The RiverCenter in Davenport offers an exhibit hall, meeting rooms, and a hotel under one roof.

61204-3097; telephone (309)788-7800 or (800)747-7800

Convention Facilities

The RiverCenter, located in downtown Davenport and accessible to the airport and interstate highways, is a complex consisting of an exhibition hall, a theater, and a luxury hotel. The exhibition hall contains 13,500 square feet of multi-purpose space to accommodate up to 1,800 participants in convention, trade show, banquet, and concert settings. Separate meeting rooms, with customizing features, are designed for groups ranging from 20 to 250 people. Attached to RiverCenter are the twenty-five-hundred-seat Art Deco-style Orpheum Theatre and the Blackhawk Hotel.

Hotels and motels in Davenport offer meeting facilities; among them is the Davenport Holiday Inn, with six meeting rooms, a ballroom, and two conference halls; 35,228 square feet of space accommodates up to 1,500 participants. Accommodations are available at traditional hotels and motels as well as bed-and-breakfasts located in historic riverfront homes, mansions, and farmhouses.

Convention Information: Quad Cities Convention and Visitors Bureau, P.O. Box 3097, Rock Island, IL 61204-3097; telephone (309)788-7800 or (800)747-7800

Transportation

Approaching the City

The Quad City Airport, fifteen minutes from downtown Davenport in Moline, Illinois, is served by eight airlines. Davenport Municipal Airport, in Mt. Joy, Iowa, handles corporate aircraft and acts as a reliever airport for Quad City Airport.

Three interstate and three primary highways connect Davenport with points throughout the Midwest and across the United States. I-280 is an outerbelt around the Quad City region. I-80 passes through the city from New York to San Francisco; I-74 links Davenport with Indianapolis and Cincinnati to the east. U.S. 61 runs north-south, from Minneapolis-St. Paul; U.S. 67 extends south to St. Louis; and U.S. 6 connects Davenport with the East and West Coasts.

Traveling in the City

Corresponding to a grid pattern, Davenport's north-south streets are named and east-west streets are numbered. River Drive follows the waterfront of the Mississippi River.

Citibus operates regularly scheduled bus routes in Davenport on weekdays and Saturday. Special bus service is available for the elderly and handicapped.

Communications

Newspapers and Magazines

The Davenport daily newspaper is the *Quad-City Times*. Weekly newspapers include the *Catholic Messenger* and the *Farm Bureau News*. *Classic Images* is a monthly tabloid magazine covering classic films for movie buffs and collectors.

Television and Radio

Two commercial television stations are based in Davenport; viewers receive broadcasts from four other stations in Rock Island and Moline, Illinois. Cable television service is available by subscription. Radio listeners can tune to nineteen AM and FM stations that offer a variety of programs.

Media Information: Quad City Times, 500 E. Third, Davenport, IA 52801; telephone (319) 383-2250

Des Moines

The City in Brief

Founded: 1843 (incorporated, 1857)

Head Official: Mayor John Dorrian (D) (until 1994)

City Population
 1970: 201,000
 1980: 191,000
 1990: 193,187
 Percent change, 1980–1990: 1.1%
 U.S. rank in 1980: 74th
 U.S. rank in 1990: 80th

Metropolitan Area Population
 1970: 340,000
 1980: 368,000
 1990: 392,928
 Average annual percent change, 1980–1988: 0.8%
 U.S. rank in 1980: 86th
 U.S. rank in 1990: 94th

Area: 75.3 square miles (1990)

Elevation: 838 feet above sea level

Average Annual Temperature: 49.7° F

Average Annual Precipitation: 22.1 inches of rain; 22.7 inches of snow

Major Economic Sectors: Services; trade; finance, insurance, and real estate; government; manufacturing

Unemployment Rate: 3.5% (September 1992)

Per Capita Income: $13,710 (1989)

1992 (2nd Quarter) ACCRA Average House Price: $117,800

1992 (2nd Quarter) ACCRA Cost of Living Index: 101.5 (U.S. average = 100.0)

1991 FBI Crime Index Total: Not reported

Major Colleges and Universities: Drake University; Grand View College

Daily Newspaper: *Des Moines Register*

Iowa—Des Moines

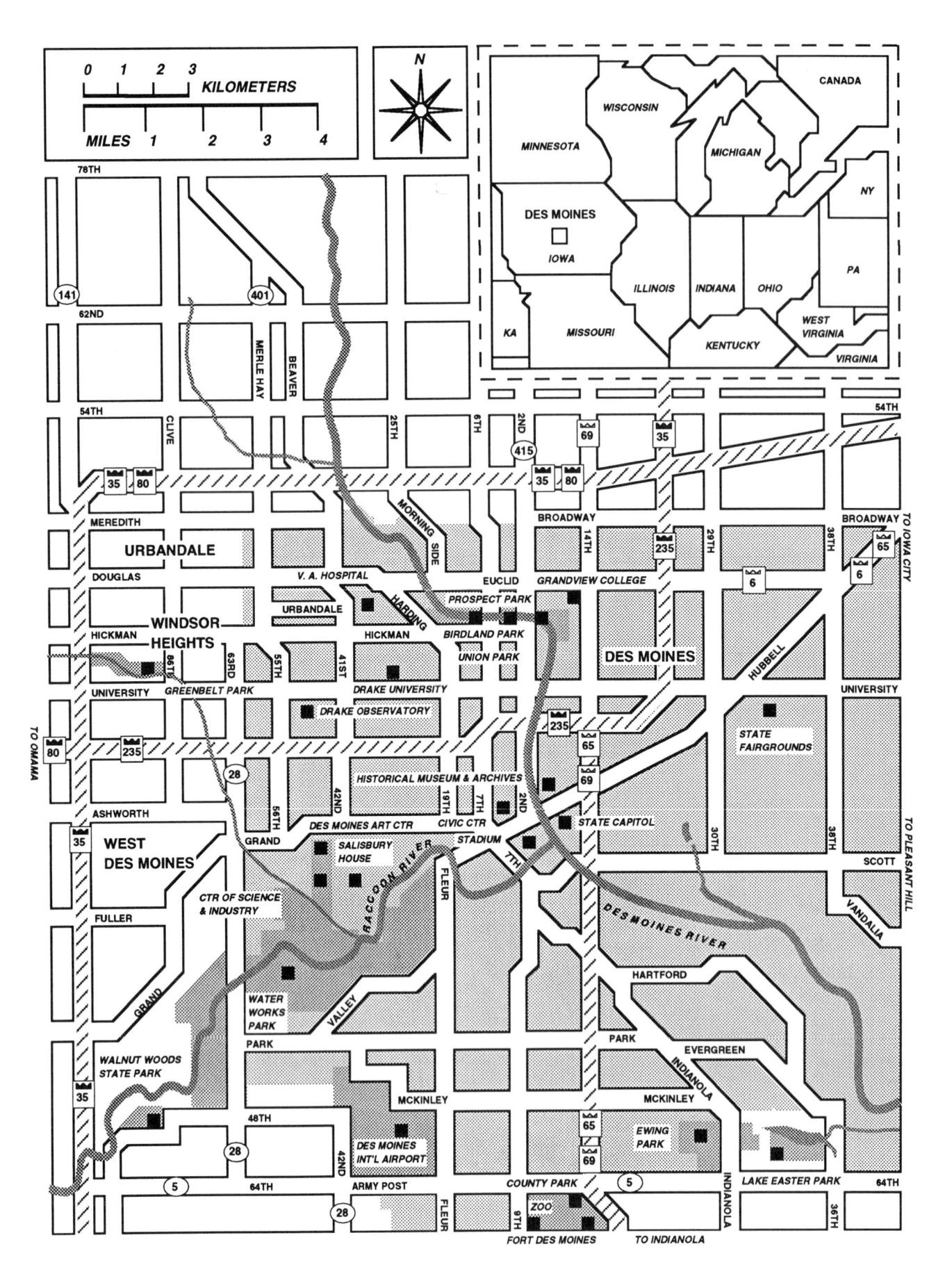

Introduction

Des Moines is the capital of Iowa, the seat of Polk County, and the center of a metropolitan area consisting of West Des Moines, Urbandale, and Pleasant Hill. Des Moines is fixed in the national consciousness as the place where the Presidential race begins every four years. It is also acquiring a new identity as a "post-industrial urban center," a term used by experts to describe midwestern communities that, like Des Moines, have acquired the characteristics of East and West Coast cities—impressive skylines, bustling commercial centers, suburban growth—but have at the same time retained their rural, agrarian roots.

Geography and Climate

Des Moines is situated on rolling terrain in south-central Iowa along the banks of the Des Moines River, the longest river in the state and an important tributary of the Mississippi River. Good drainage to the southwest produces fertile farm land, which is surrounded by coal fields. Marked seasonal changes occur in both temperature and precipitation. During winter, snowfall averages 22.7 inches; drifting snow often impedes transportation but sub-zero temperatures are relatively uncommon. The growing season extends from early May to early October; approximately 60 percent of the annual precipitation occurs during this time, with maximum rainfall in late May and June. Autumn is generally sunny and dry, producing favorable conditions for drying and harvesting crops.

Area: 75.3 square miles (1990)

Elevation: 838 feet above sea level

Average Temperatures: January, 18.6° F; July, 76.3° F; annual average, 49.7° F

Average Annual Precipitation: 22.1 inches of rain; 22.7 inches of snow

History

River Fort Becomes State Capital

The city of Des Moines originated with the building of Fort Des Moines in 1843, at the confluence of the Raccoon and Des Moines rivers, as a military garrison to protect the rights of Sak and Fox tribes. Debate surrounds the correct origin of the name of Iowa's largest city. The Moingonia, a native group, had located a village on the river and it appeared on the map of Jacques Marquette, the French explorer. The French expression "la riviere des moines" translates to "the river of the monks," but may approximate the name of the Moingonia, who inhabited the riverbank. "De Moyen," meaning "middle," was understood as a reference to the Des Moines River being the middle distance between the Mississippi and Missouri rivers.

The Iowa River Valley was opened to new settlers in 1845; a year later, when Iowa gained statehood, the population of Fort Des Moines numbered 127 residents. After the city charter was adopted in 1857, the word Fort was dropped from the name. Des Moines officially became the state capital—and its future growth was guaranteed—in January 1858 when two oxen-driven bobsleds hauled the state's archives into the city from Iowa City.

Des Moines played an active role in the Civil War. In May 1864 Des Moines women signed a petition pledging to replace working men to free them to fight for the Union cause, but enough male recruits were found to fill the quotas. After the Civil War, in 1875, Des Moines was the site of a nationally significant speech by President Ulysses S. Grant to a reunion of the Army of Tennessee, wherein he reiterated a commitment to universal equality.

During the last quarter of the nineteenth century wood-frame buildings in Des Moines underwent extensive construction and renovation. The impressive state capitol building, situated on an 80-acre park and featuring a gold-gilded central dome of the revived classical Roman style, was completed in 1884. In the 1880s and 1890s, local businessmen built mansions and the city's cultural life continued to flourish.

Hospitality and Development Shape Des Moines

The history of Des Moines is filled with colorful events such as the arrival, in the spring of 1894, of

Kelly's Army, one-thousand unemployed men on their way to Washington, D.C., and led by Charles T. Kelly, "King of the Commons." Citizens greeted them with hospitality to prevent trouble. When Kelly's Army seemed reluctant to leave, however, the townspeople bought lumber to construct an "industrial fleet" of one hundred fifty flatboats, under local union direction, to transport the men out of the city. Each man was issued a small American flag, and the waving of the flags was the last sight of Kelly's Army. Among them was the American writer Jack London.

Des Moines has distinguished itself in various ways throughout its history. The Des Moines Plan, one of the first of its kind in the nation, streamlined municipal government and charted development, taking into consideration the city's natural setting. Fort Des Moines, dedicated as a calvary post in 1903, became the first training center for the Women's Army Corps, which gained national attention. The economic base of Des Moines was substantially expanded when the city became a national insurance and publishing center. In 1949, Des Moines was named an All-American City by the National Municipal League. The honor was repeated in 1971, then again in 1981 after Des Moines had addressed urban renewal issues by committing $313 million to the restoration of the historic districts of Court Avenue and Sherman Hills. Since 1981, more than $1 billion has been spent on new downtown construction.

The city of Des Moines was immobilized in the summer of 1993 by flooding of the Mississippi River. The state of Iowa was declared a national disaster area, and preliminary estimates indicated the city alone suffered more than $253 million in damages.

Historical Information: Polk County Historical Society, 317 SW 42nd Street, Des Moines, IA 50312; telephone (515)255-6657; and, State Historical Society of Iowa, 600 East Locust Street, Des Moines, IA 50309; telephone (515)281-5111

Population Profile

Metropolitan Area Residents
1970: 340,000
1980: 368,000
1990: 392,928
Annual average percent change, 1980–1988: 0.8%
U.S. rank in 1980: 89th
U.S. rank in 1990: 94th

City Residents
1970: 201,000
1980: 191,000
1990: 193,187 (of which, 91,074 were males, and 102,113 were females)
Percent change, 1980–1990: 1.1%
U.S. rank in 1980: 74th
U.S. rank in 1990: 80th (State rank: 1st)

Density: 2,565.6 people per square mile (1990)

Racial and ethnic characteristics (1990)
  White: 172,417
  Black: 13,741
  American Indian, Eskimo, Aleut: 699
  Asian and Pacific Islander: 4,602
  Hispanic (may be of any race): 4,629

Percent of residents born in state: 77.4% (1990)

Age characteristics (1990)
  Population under 5 years old: 15,157
  Population 5 to 9 years old: 13,339
  Population 10 to 14 years old: 11,715
  Population 15 to 19 years old: 12,781
  Population 20 to 24 years old: 16,648
  Population 25 to 29 years old: 18,975
  Population 30 to 34 years old: 17,668
  Population 35 to 39 years old: 15,159
  Population 40 to 44 years old: 12,653
  Population 45 to 49 years old: 9,510
  Population 50 to 54 years old: 7,854
  Population 55 to 59 years old: 7,769
  Population 60 to 64 years old: 8,075
  Population 65 to 69 years old: 7,748
  Population 70 to 74 years old: 6,414
  Population 75 to 79 years old: 5,130
  Population 80 to 84 years old: 3,539
  Population 85 years and over: 3,053
  Median age: 32.2 years

Births (1988)
  Total number: 3,518

Deaths (1988)
  Total number: 1,913 (of which, 45 were infants under the age of 1 year)

The Court Avenue Historic District in Des Moines.

Money income (1989)
  Per capita income: $13,710
  Median household income: $26,703
  Total households: 78,587
  Number of households with income of . . .
    less than $5,000: 4,685
    $5,000 to $9,999: 8,012
    $10,000 to $14,999: 8,051
    $15,000 to $24,999: 15,881
    $25,000 to $34,999: 14,657
    $35,000 to $49,999: 14,261
    $50,000 to $74,999: 9,055
    $75,000 to $99,999: 2,161
    $100,000 to $149,999: 914
    $150,000 or more: 910
  Percent of families below poverty level: 9.5% (58.0% of which were female householder families with related children under 5)
1991 FBI Crime Index Total: Not reported

Municipal Government

Des Moines operates under a city manager/council form of government. The seven-member council is comprised of six council persons and a manager, who are elected to staggered terms in non-partisan elections. The manager serves a term of indefinite length at the pleasure of the council.

Head Official: Mayor John Dorrian (D) (until 1994)

Total Number of City Employees: Approximately 1,700 (1991)

City Information: Des Moines City Action Center, East First and Locust, Des Moines, IA 50307; telephone (515)283-4944

Economy

Major Industries and Commercial Activity

The Des Moines economy consists of a balance among the manufacturing, services, government, wholesale and retail trade, and agribusiness sectors. Manufacturing, while comprising a relatively small percentage of the city's total employment base, has a significant impact on the area economy. Manufacturing firms buy many of their supplies locally, generating more secondary jobs than any other industry. In addition, most of the goods produced are shipped outside the metropolitan area, and 8 to 10 percent of manufacturing production is exported, thus contributing to the development of the local shipping industry. The city's economic diversity helped it surmount hard times in the 1980s.

With the headquarters of nearly 70 insurance companies and the regional offices of one-hundred other firms located in the metropolitan area, Des Moines is the third largest international insurance center after London, England, and Hartford, Connecticut. Other service businesses, including the health care industry, employ nearly one fourth of the work force. Many area firms are active in biotechnology, conducting research in such fields as human, plant, and animal disease cures; safer pesticides and herbicides; and new, higher crop yields.

A statewide employer based in Des Moines is Meredith Corporation, a diversified communications company specializing in printing, publishing, broadcasting, and real estate. An emerging industry in the Greater Des Moines area is fiber optics telecommunications, which is expected to replace conventional communications systems. Government employs a substantial portion of the city's work force, with the state of Iowa being the largest employer.

Items and goods produced: flour, cosmetics, furnaces, stove and furnace parts, agricultural implements, automotive and creamery equipment, leather products, medicine, brick, food items, paint, electric switches, and elevators

Incentive Programs—New and Existing Companies

Local programs—The Greater Des Moines Chamber of Commerce Federation will assist firms with an interest in applying for economic development financial assistance programs. A corporation intending to create one-hundred jobs may be eligible to receive a $400,000 low interest or forgivable loan to help reduce its relocation cost. Financial and incentive programs include: Community Betterment Account; City of Des Moines Action Loan Fund; Economic Development Set-Aside; Private Activity Revenue Bonds; Urban Renewal; and Urban Revitalization Tax Abatement.

Golden Circle Business Center, an incubator on the campus of Des Moines Area Community College in Ankeny, provides space and support services for entrepreneurs. The center is also home to Drake University's Small Business Development Center and a Small Business contract procurement center.

Development Projects

During the 1980s Des Moines underwent extensive development as the result of a ten-year plan created in 1980 by the Des Moines Development Commission, a coalition of local businesses. More than $1 billion has been invested in commercial, residential, and civic construction downtown; among the projects have been a civic performing arts center, a convention and meeting center, and several office and retail buildings. In addition to new construction has been the renovation of historic buildings, the conversion of the Rock Island Depot to office space, and the revitalization of the Court Avenue District; suburban expansion has also increased dramatically. Several Fortune 500 service industries have located in the city, building new facilities and creating jobs. Des Moines has become a regional center for retail trade, with retail sales per capita ranking higher than the national average. More than one third of Iowa's tourism dollars are spent in Des Moines.

Economic Development Information: Economic Development Council, Greater Des Moines Chamber of Commerce Federation, 601 Locust, Suite 100, Des Moines, IA 50309; telephone (515) 286-4978

Commercial Shipping

Des Moines is served by four major railroads that provide full-time switching and piggyback ramp service. Eighty-five motor freight carriers provide overnight and one- to five-day shipping to points throughout the United States; fifty-five terminals are maintained in the community. Commercial air carriers handled nearly twenty-seven thousand metric tons of cargo at Des Moines International Airport in 1986.

Labor Force and Employment Outlook

Des Moines employers draw from an educated, skilled, and motivated work force. Worker productivity ranks well above the national average; the unemployment rate remains low in comparison with other major urban centers. Union and management maintain a cooperative relationship in firms where organized labor is present. The manufacturing sector produces the highest payroll per worker of any industry in the city. Des Moines has been experiencing problems finding enough workers to fill entry-level positions in its rapidly expanding service-oriented economy.

The following is a summary of data regarding the Des Moines metropolitan area labor force as of September 1992.

Size of non-agricultural labor force: 238,600

Number of workers employed in . . .
  mining: Not reported
  construction: 10,700
  manufacturing: 25,700
  transportation and public utilities: 11,900
  wholesale and retail trade: 60,700
  finance, insurance, and real estate: 33,800
  services: 63,700
  government: 32,100

Average hourly earnings of production workers employed in manufacturing: $12.72 (September 1992)

Unemployment rate: 3.5% (September 1992)

Largest employers	Number of employees
Principal Financial Group	6,020
Mercy Medical Center	4,200
Iowa Methodist Medical Center	3,225
Younkers, Inc. (department stores)	1,877
US West Communications and subsidiaries	1,793
Neodata (fulfillment services)	1,300
R. R. Donnelly & Sons (printing)	1,100
Meredith Corporation (diversified media)	1,000

Cost of Living

The cost of living in Des Moines is near the national average and on par with that of other cities in the Midwest. State and local taxes are lower than the U.S. average. The city was ranked the fifth most affordable area for housing in the country in 1990.

The following is a summary of data regarding several key cost of living factors in the Des Moines area.

1992 (2nd Quarter) ACCRA Cost of Living Index: 101.5 (U.S. average = 100.0)

1992 (2nd Quarter) ACCRA Average House Price: $117,800

State income tax rate: Ranges from 0.4% to 9.98% of taxable income over $45,000; includes deduction of 100% of federal income taxes

State sales tax rate: 4.0% on personal property except food, prescription drugs, and medical devices

Local income tax rate: None

Local sales tax rate: None

Property tax rate: $40.39 per $1,000 of assessed valuation

Economic Information: Greater Des Moines Chamber of Commerce, 601 Locust, Suite 100, Des Moines, IA 50309; telephone (515)286-4978

Education and Research

Elementary and Secondary Schools

The Des Moines Independent School District, considered among the best urban districts in the country, is governed by a seven-member board of directors who are elected at large to three-year staggered terms. The head administrator is the superintendent of schools.

Iowa is one of only eight states allowing students to attend school in any district in the state. In Des Moines, so many affluent and white students elected to leave the school district that in 1992 the school board decided it would no longer let white students transfer from the district. That decision was being appealed to the state.

The following is a summary of data regarding Des Moines public schools as of the 1992–1993 school year.

Total enrollment: 31,524

Number of facilities
 elementary schools: 42
 middle schools: 3
 senior high schools: 8
 alternative and magnet schools: 3

Student/teacher ratio: 20.9:1

Teacher salaries
 minimum: $19,374
 maximum: $40,040

Funding per pupil: $3,404

Four private and parochial school districts providing the Des Moines metropolitan area with educational alternatives are Des Moines Christian, Diocese of Des Moines Catholic Schools, Grandview Park Baptist, and Mount Olive Lutheran.

Public Schools Information: Des Moines Independent Community School District, 1800 Grand Avenue, Des Moines, IA 50309; telephone (515)242-7911

Colleges and Universities

Drake University, a private institution founded in 1881, grants undergraduate and graduate degrees in a range of disciplines through the College of Arts and Sciences, the College of Business Administration, the School of Journalism and Mass Communication, the College of Pharmacy and Health Sciences, and the Law School. Drake operates a work experience program that includes cooperative education and internships.

Grand View College, a private liberal arts school, awards associate and baccalaureate degrees in several fields of study; cross-registration with Drake University and Des Moines Area Community College is available. The University of Osteopathic Medicine and Health Sciences offers baccalaureate, master's, and first-professional degrees in a variety of health care areas such as osteopathic medicine and surgery, podiatric medicine and surgery, health care administration, and physical therapy.

Vocational, technical, and pre-professional education in Des Moines is provide by Des Moines Area Community College and the American Institute of Business. Within commuting distance of the city are Iowa State University, an undergraduate and graduate institution in Ames, Iowa, and Simpson College, a four-year liberal arts college in Indianola, Iowa.

Nollen Plaza in downtown Des Moines.

Libraries and Research Centers

The Public Library of Des Moines houses more than 544,000 volumes and about 771 periodical subscriptions in addition to recordings, tapes, films, slides, and art reproductions. The library system includes five branches; services for the blind and hearing impaired are available. A depository for federal and state documents, the library maintains the Iowa History Collection. The State Library of Iowa is also located in downtown Des Moines; holdings include more than 331,000 volumes as well as a complete range of audio-visual materials and special collections on state of Iowa publications, attorney general opinions, and bar association proceedings. The library is a depository for state and patent documents.

The Iowa Regional Library for the Blind and Physically Handicapped provides Braille books, large print books, and cassettes and disks. The Drake University Library houses extensive holdings in all major department areas; the law library maintains an Iowa legal history collection. The Grand View College Library also serves the community.

Approximately twenty-five specialized libraries and research centers located in the city are affiliated with hospitals, corporations, government agencies, and law firms; the Blank Park Zoo and the Des Moines Art Center also maintain libraries.

Public Library Information: Public Library of Des Moines, 100 Locust Street, Des Moines, IA 50309; telephone (515)283-4152

Health Care

Providing all levels of care in more than fifty specialty fields, the health care network in metropolitan Des Moines consists of eight hospitals providing 2,614 beds, four skilled-care facilities, and thirty-seven immediate-care facilities. A regional trauma center and a helicopter ambulance service are also based in Des Moines. The medical community includes 530 physicians, 140 osteopaths, 25 chiropractors, and 225 dentists.

Iowa Methodist Medical Center, with 710 beds, is the city's largest medical facility. The complex includes Blank Memorial, a children's hospital; Powell Center, a general and convalescent care center; and Younkers Rehabilitation Center. Mercy Hospital Medical Center, a 500-bed facility, and Veterans Hospital provide general care; Des Moines General Hospital offers osteopathic treatment in addition to general care. Broadlawn Medical Center and Iowa Lutheran Hospital are both general and psychiatric hospitals.

Recreation

Sightseeing

The starting point for a tour of Des Moines is the State Capitol, one of the nation's most beautiful public buildings and one of the largest of its kind. The 275-foot main dome is covered with 23-karat gold leaf and is flanked by four smaller domes. The capitol's interior features more than ten different wood grains mixed with twenty-nine types of marble in detailed stone and wood carvings, ornately painted ceilings, and mosaics and murals. Another popular site is Terrace Hill, the present residence of Iowa's governor; considered to be one of the finest examples of Second Empire architecture in the country, Terrace Hill was designed by W.W. Boyington, architect of the Chicago Water Tower. Donated to the state by the Frederick M. Hubbell family, the mansion has been refurbished to is original Victorian elegance.

In both the Courthouse and Sherman Hill districts of Des Moines, residential and commercial buildings dating to 1850 reflect changing tastes and styles in architecture; especially interesting are doorway and entrance designs. The Hoyt Sherman Place, home of one of Des Moines's most successful businessmen and an example of ornate Victorian design, is now owned by the city and open for tours. The Iowa State Historical Building, completed in 1987 and housing the State Historical Library, is dedicated to Iowa's past with exhibits on natural history, Indian lore, and pioneer life. A large outdoor neon sculpture named *Plains Aurora* is displayed on top of the building.

The Des Moines Botanical Center cultivates plants and flowers under one of the biggest geodesic domes in the nation. The Center preserves a permanent collection of more than one-thousand different species of tropical and subtropical plants and cultivars, growing in their natural cycle; six thematic displays are presented each year. Living History Farms, a 600-acre agricultural museum, focuses on the history and future of farming in the Midwest; buildings, planting

A rowing regatta in Des Moines.

methods, and livestock are authentic to the five time periods represented. At Adventureland Park, an amusement park with the theme of 1900 Iowa, rides and activities combine with permanent exhibits germane to Iowa. Salisbury House, a reconstruction of a country manor, patterns itself after King's House of Salisbury, England, duplicating Renaissance luxury and splendor; it is owned by the Iowa State Education Association, which arranges tours. The Science Center of Iowa covers all fields of science; of special interest are a miniature railroad exhibit and live animals native to Iowa in animal den houses. At Blank Park Zoo, where four-hundred animals from five continents inhabit 15 acres, special attractions include the Australian and African walk-through displays.

Arts and Culture

One beneficiary of Des Moines's development has been the city's cultural life. Funds have been invested to house the city's cultural institutions in architecturally significant facilities. The most impressive is the Des Moines Art Center, designed by international architects Eliel Saarinen, I. M. Pei, and Richard Meier. Housing art of the nineteenth and twentieth centuries in a permanent collection, the Center also sponsors international exhibits, educational programs, and film and music series. Nollen Plaza, adjacent to the Civic Center of Greater Des Moines, is a block-square amphitheater and park with a tree-lined "peace garden," a waterfall, and a reflecting pool; Claes Oldenburg's sculpture *The Crusoe Umbrella* is on view in the plaza.

The Des Moines Symphony and the Des Moines Ballet perform at the Civic Center. The Des Moines Playhouse produces a main stage season of drama, musicals, and light drama as well as Theatre in the Ground shows and Theatre for Young People. The Ingersoll Dinner Theater presents a ten-show season, which features local and guest artists in Broadway musicals and plays in addition to special attractions.

Festivals and Holidays

In February the downtown skywalk is transformed into a 54-par putt-putt golf course for a tournament with more than thirteen-hundred players competing for prizes. The Drake Relays Festival, a week-long celebration in April, pits city corporations against one another in sanctioned relays; other festival events include a whimsical "most beautiful bulldog" contest, a collegiate golf tournament, and musical entertainment. The Court Avenue River Party in the city's historic district, nicknamed "the Carp Festival," involves a day of family events, food, and entertainment held the third Saturday in May. The Sports Car Club of America sponsors a sanctioned Grand Prix for three days in early July, with Trans Am, Super Vs, and Corvette challenge races. The Festival of Trees raises money for a local hospital with the decorating of one-hundred downtown trees in November during Thanksgiving week.

Sports for the Spectator

The Drake Relays hold the distinction of being the country's largest such event, with more than two-hundred colleges and universities participating from forty-seven states. The relays, held in Jim Duncan Stadium at Drake University the last weekend in April, sell out each year; the competition also includes track and field events. The relays take the place of a football game for the university's homecoming weekend; more than fifty other events are held throughout the city, making the Relays the focal point for an entire festival.

The Iowa Cubs, the National League Chicago Cubs's top farm team, compete in baseball's Triple A international professional baseball league at Sec Taylor Stadium.

Sports for the Participant

Seventy-three parks are located in the Des Moines metropolitan area. The Des Moines Parks and Recreation Departments sponsor year-round public programs in parks with such facilities as softball fields, horseshoe pits, volleyball courts, tennis courts, fitness and bicycle trails, play equipment, and swimming pools. The city offers free swimming and tennis lessons and arts and crafts programs. Softball, volleyball, and tennis leagues are also sponsored by the recreation department. Des Moines maintains eighty-seven public tennis courts, eleven public golf courses, and six public swimming pools. Both indoor and outdoor sports can be enjoyed during the winter at community center gyms and at fifteen ice rinks. Swimming, water skiing, fishing, and motorboating are available at local rivers and lakes. Seventy private country clubs dot the community.

Shopping and Dining

Des Moines's downtown shopping district is twenty square blocks connected by a second-level skywalk system that encompasses 150 shops. Altogether, more than forty shopping squares and plazas serve shoppers throughout the metropolitan area, including four major enclosed malls, one of which is located downtown.

Des Moines's restaurants offer choices ranging from American and midwestern fare to ethnic and continental cuisine. The city is ranked fourteenth per capita nationally in its number of restaurants. Prime rib and steak entrees are specialties at a number of the better restaurants. Chinese cuisine is another local favorite. A local seafood restaurant is considered to have one of the largest selections of fresh seafood in the Midwest. Imported Italian pasta is the specialty at one of the city's oldest and most popular eateries.

Visitor Information: Greater Des Moines Convention and Visitors Bureau, 601 Locust, Suite 200H, Des Moines, IA 50309-2285; telephone (515)286-4960 or (800)451-2625

Convention Facilities

Four meeting and convention facilities serve Des Moines. Opened in 1985, the Des Moines Convention Center is the newest of the four as well as the largest multi-purpose meeting complex in the state. Three levels furnish space for trade shows, conventions, meetings, banquets, and other activities. The upper level contains a thirty-thousand-square-foot exhibit hall; the second level assembly hall, with twenty-thousand square feet, can be divided into ten meeting rooms; and the lower level features twenty-five meeting rooms. The Convention Center accommodates groups ranging in size from 10 to 4,000 people; parking for twenty-five hundred cars is available.

The newly remodeled Veterans Memorial Auditorium provides seating for 7,200 to 14,000 people; a total of ninety-eight thousand square feet of space can be used for exhibitions, sporting events, and entertainment. Two other principal meeting places in the city are the Civic Center, located downtown, and the Iowa State Fairgrounds. Area hotels and motels maintain banquet and meeting facilities for large and small groups. More than six-thousand rooms are available for lodgings in metropolitan Des Moines.

Convention Information: Greater Des Moines Convention and Visitors Bureau, 601 Locust, Suite 200H, Des Moines, IA 50309-2285; (515)286-4960 or (800)451-2625

Transportation

Approaching the City

Des Moines International Airport, ten minutes from downtown, is served by thirteen commercial airlines with daily flights handling nearly two million passengers annually. Rail transportation into the city is provided by Amtrak.

Principal highways that intersect northeast of the city are I-80, running east to west, and I-35, extending north to south. Federal highways include east-west U.S. 6 and north-south U.S. 69.

Traveling in the City

Downtown Des Moines is laid out on a grid pattern; in the northeast sector, streets near the Des Moines River, still conforming to a grid, follow the configuration of the river. North-south streets are numbered and east-west streets are named.

Des Moines is noted for its 2.6-mile skywalk system, which makes the city virtually "weatherproof." Forty-four climate-controlled, glass-enclosed bridges provide access to thirty blocks that comprise the downtown core.

Public transportation is provided by the Des Moines Metropolitan Transit Authority, locally known as The Metro; special service for the handicapped is available.

Communications

Newspapers and Magazines

The daily newspaper in Des Moines is the *Des Moines Register,* fifteen times a Pulitzer Prizewinner. *The Business Record,* a weekly newspaper, covers local business news; several suburban newspapers are also distributed weekly. *Des Moines Skywalker* is also published weekly.

Home to the Meredith Corporation and other printing and publishing firms, Des Moines is a major center for the publication of nationally-circulated magazines. Among the popular magazines produced in the city are *Better Homes and Gardens, Better Homes and Gardens Building Ideas, Country Home, Midwest Living,* and *Successful Farming.* A wide range of special-interest publications based in Des Moines are directed toward readers with interests in such subjects as religion, agriculture, hunting, education, and crafts.

Television and Radio

Five television stations—three commercial, one independent, and one public—broadcast in the metropolitan Des Moines region. Cable service is available. Radio listeners receive programming from fifteen AM and FM stations.

Media Information: Des Moines Register, 715 Locust St., Des Moines, IA 50309; telephone (515)284-8000

KANSAS

Kansas City 155
Topeka 167
Wichita 179

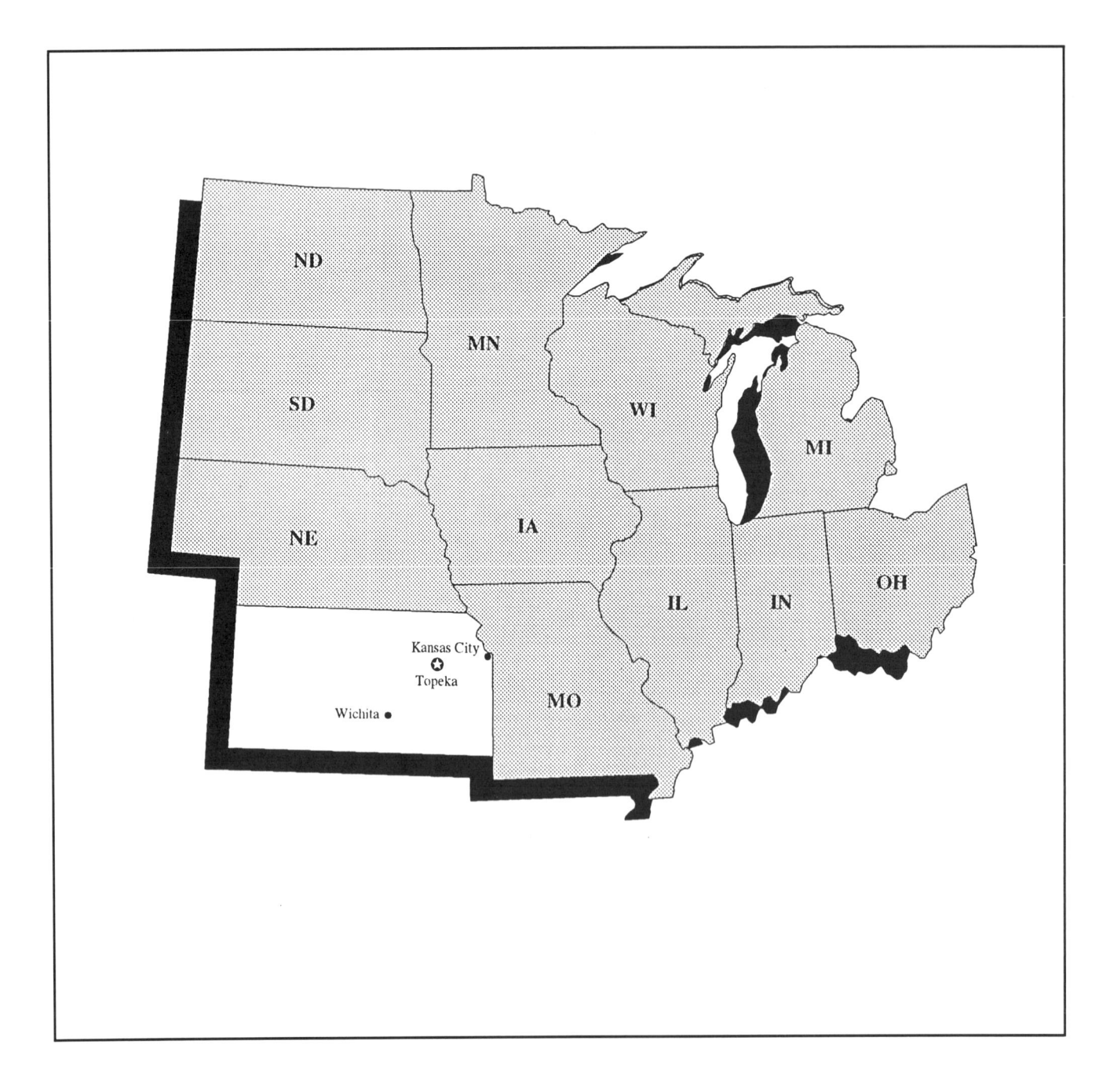

The State in Brief

Nickname: Sunflower State
Motto: *Ad astra per aspera* (To the stars through difficulties)

Flower: Native sunflower
Bird: Western meadowlark

Area: 82,282 square miles (1990; U.S. rank: 14th)
Elevation: Ranges from 680 feet to 4,039 feet above sea level
Climate: Temperate, but with seasonal extremes of temperature as well as blizzards, tornadoes, and severe thunderstorms; semi-arid in the west

Admitted to Union: January 29, 1861
Capital: Topeka
Head Official: Governor Joan Finney (D) (until 1995)

Population
 1970: 2,249,071
 1980: 2,364,000
 1990: 2,495,000
 Percent change 1980–1990: 4.8%
 U.S. rank in 1990: 32nd
 Percent of residents born in state: 62.9% (1990)
 Density: 30.3 people per square mile (1990; U.S. rank: 39th)
 1991 FBI Crime Index Total: 138,081

Racial and Ethnic Characteristics (1990)
 White: 2,232,000
 Black: 5.8%
 American Indian, Eskimo, Aleut: 0.89%
 Asian and Pacific Islander: 1.28%
 Hispanic (may be of any race): 3.78%

Age Characteristics (1990)
 Population under 5 years old: 190,000
 Population 5 to 17 years old: 482,000
 Percent of population 65 years and older: 13.9%
 Median age: 34.0 years
 Voting-age population (1988): 1,848,000 (53.7% of whom cast votes for president)

Vital Statistics
 Total number of births (1992): 37,484
 Total number of deaths (1992): 22,160 (of which, 313 were infants under the age of 1 year)
 AIDS cases reported, 1981–1990: 396 (U.S. rank: 33rd)

Economy
 Major industries: Agriculture, oil production, mining
 Unemployment rate: 4.1% (September 1992; Kansas City, MO)
 Per capita income: $13,300 (1989)
 Median household income: $27,291 (1989)
 Total number of families: 664,668 (8.3% of which had incomes below the poverty level; 1989)
 Income tax rate: Graduated from 3.65% to 9.0%
 Sales tax rate: 4.25%

Kansas City

The City in Brief

Founded: 1843 (incorporated, 1859)

Head Official: City Manager David Isabell (since 1985)

City Population
 1970: 168,213
 1980: 161,148
 1990: 149,767
 Percent change, 1980–1990: −7.1%
 1992: 151,521 (following annexation of part of Wyandotte County)
 U.S. rank in 1980: 93rd
 U.S. rank in 1990: 115th

Metropolitan Area Population
 1970: 1,373,000
 1980: 1,433,000
 1990: 1,566,280
 Percent change, 1980–1990: 9.3%
 U.S. rank in 1980: 25th
 U.S. rank in 1990: 25th

Area: 127.85 square miles (1992)

Elevation: 726 feet above sea level

Average Annual Temperature: 54.1° F

Average Annual Precipitation: 35.2 inches

Major Economic Sectors: Services, trade, government, manufacturing

Unemployment Rate: 5.1% (September 1992; Kansas City, MO)

Per Capita Income: $10,478 (1989)

1991 (2nd Quarter) ACCRA Average House Price: $99,000

1991 (2nd Quarter) ACCRA Cost of Living Index: 95.5 (U.S. average = 100.0)

1991 FBI Crime Index Total: 17,944

Major Colleges and Universities: Kansas City Kansas Community College; University of Kansas Medical Center

Daily Newspaper: *Kansas City Kansan*

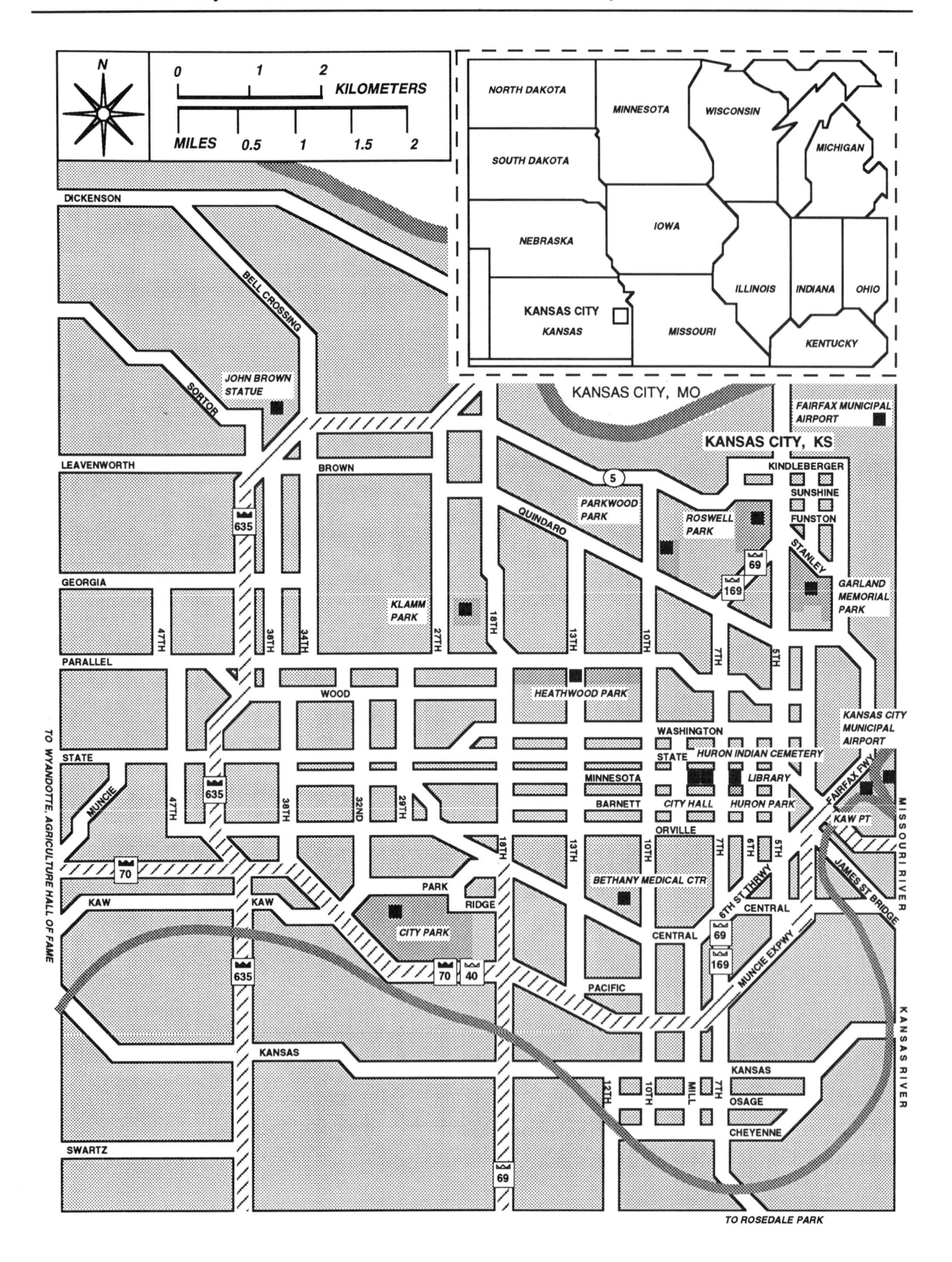

Kansas—Kansas City *Cities of the United States • 2nd Edition*

Introduction

Kansas City, Kansas is part of a metropolitan complex that also includes Kansas City, Missouri. The seat of Wyandotte County, Kansas City is the center of a metropolitan statistical area that covers the counties of Johnson, Leavenworth, Miami, and Wyandotte in Kansas, plus six Missouri counties. The most industrialized of the two Kansas Cities, it nevertheless is bordered by rich farmland and serves as an agricultural trade center. Established by Wyandot native Americans, Kansas City was the site of the drafting of the state constitution and played a crucial role in the slavery issue in the Civil War.

Geography and Climate

Gently sloping terrain and forested hills surround Kansas City, which is located on the Kansas Missouri border at the confluence of the Kansas and Missouri Rivers. The area is laced with lakes, streams, and small rivers. A four-season climate prevails, with a substantial range in temperatures; the average annual snowfall is 14.2 inches.

Area: 127.85 (following 1992 annexation of part of Wyandotte County)

Elevation: 726 feet above sea level

Average Temperatures: January 25.8° F; July, 78.5° F; annual average, 54.1° F

Average Annual Precipitation: 35.2 inches

History

Wyandot Tribe Establishes Townsite

Kansa native Americans were the first inhabitants to occupy land near both banks of the Kansas (Kaw) River at its confluence with the Missouri River, the site of Kansas City. The explorers Meriwether Lewis and William Clark camped on Kaw Point, the land between the two rivers and now part of Kansas City, in 1804 during their exploration of the Louisiana Purchase. The land became part of the Delaware Indian reservation in 1829, and the Delaware sold the land in 1843 to the Wyandot.

The Wyandot, an integrated tribe of native Americans and whites from western Lake Erie and the last of the migrating tribes, founded a town called Wyandott in the eastern part of the Wyandott Purchase. An educated and cultured agrarian society, they built the first free school in Kansas and reestablished their Ohio church; they also opened a community-owned store. The Wyandot, knowing their land would be highly prized by white settlers, decided to approach Congress on the issue of establishing a Territory, and elected Abelard Guthrie, a white member of the tribe by marriage, as a delegate to the Thirty-Second Congress. Guthrie was not admitted but Wyandot leaders decided to organize Kansas-Nebraska into a provisional territory on July 26, 1853, thus focussing national attention on their community.

Slavery Issue Dominates Territory

The next year Congress passed the Kansas-Nebraska Act, which inflamed sectional sentiments on the issue of slavery in the territories and helped to contribute to the outbreak of the Civil War. The Wyandot petitioned for and received the rights of citizenship, which enabled them to divide their land among the individual members of the tribe and open the reserve to settlement. The Wyandott City Town Company was formed in 1856 to plat and develop the town, which was incorporated as a town in 1858 and as a city the next year. In July 1859, members of a convention at Wyandott wrote the state constitution by which Kansas became the thirty-fourth state of the Union. The state was known as Bleeding Kansas in the decade before the Civil War, when people in Missouri stirred up support for slavery in Kansas. Wyandott citizens became active in antislavery efforts and after the Civil War, blacks moved to the region, their migration reaching a peak between 1878 and 1982. Growth in the region was spurred by settlers on both sides of the slavery controversy.

Beginning in 1860, when James McGrew opened the first slaughter house, and continuing when eight years later Edward Patterson and J. W. Slavens started a packing house, the city was a meat processing center. This industry received its biggest boost when Charles Francis Adams, descendant of two former presidents, built the first stockyards in the city and convinced Plankington and Armour to relocate their meat packing business from Missouri in 1871.

Stockyards Contribute to City's Growth

Small towns around Wyandotte such as old Kansas City, Armstrong, and Armourdale sprouted up near the rail lines and packing houses. Through consolidation and legislative annexation, the city of Kansas City was created in 1886 when these towns combined with the larger Wyandotte, which vied for the naming of the new city after itself. The name Kansas City was picked, however, because it would be a more attractive inducement for the selling of municipal bonds. Argentine became part of Kansas City via petition in 1909, and Rosedale followed suit by legislative enactment in 1922. Quindaro Township, once a town named after Guthrie's Wyandot wife, was absorbed through expansion. Turner was added in 1966, thus continuing the expansion of Kansas City's borders. In 1992, the city annexed part of Wyandotte County.

Kansas City was one of the nation's first cities to locate a model industrial park away from residential areas, the Fairfax Industrial District. The city completed a two-decade urban renewal project in 1980.

Historical Information: Historic Kansas City Foundation, 20 West Ninth Street, Suite 450, Kansas City, MO 64105; telephone (816)471-3391; and, Kansas City Museum, 3218 Gladstone Boulevard, Kansas City, MO 64123; telephone (816)483-8300

Population Profile

Metropolitan Area Residents
1970: 1,373,000
1980: 1,433,000
1990: 1,566,280
Average annual percent change, 1980-1988: 1.1%
U.S. rank in 1980: 25th
U.S. rank in 1990: 25th

City Residents
1970: 168,213
1980: 161,148
1990: 149,767 (of which, 71,361 were males, and 78,406 were females)
Percent change, 1980-1990: −7.1%
1992: 151,521 (following annexation of part of Wyandotte County)
U.S. rank in 1980: 93rd
U.S. rank in 1990: 115th (State rank: 2nd)

Density: 1,389.3 people per square mile (1990)

Racial and ethnic characteristics (1990)
 White: 97,356
 Black: 43,834
 American Indian, Eskimo, Aleut: 1,025
 Asian and Pacific Islander: 1,854
 Hispanic (may be of any race): 10,705

Percent of residents born in state: 59.7% (1990)

Age characteristics (1990)
 Population under 5 years old: 12,563
 Population 5 to 9 years old: 12,592
 Population 10 to 14 years old: 11,166
 Population 15 to 19 years old: 10,466
 Population 20 to 24 years old: 10,745
 Population 25 to 29 years old: 13,353
 Population 30 to 34 years old: 12,931
 Population 35 to 39 years old: 11,054
 Population 40 to 44 years old: 9,011
 Population 45 to 49 years old: 7,333
 Population 50 to 54 years old: 6,225
 Population 55 to 59 years old: 6,349
 Population 60 to 64 years old: 6,490
 Population 65 to 69 years old: 6,172
 Population 70 to 74 years old: 5,009
 Population 75 to 79 years old: 3,827
 Population 80 to 84 years old: 2,459
 Population 85 years and over: 2,022
 Median age: 31.4 years

Births (1988)
 Total number: 2,863

Deaths (1988)
 Total number: 1,661 (of which, 38 were infants under the age of 1 year)

Money income (1989)
 Per capita income: $10,478
 Median household income: $23,307
 Total households: 57,058
 Number of households with income of . . .
  less than $5,000: 4,927
  $5,000 to $9,999: 7,230
  $10,000 to $14,999: 6,156
  $15,000 to $24,999: 12,098
  $25,000 to $34,999: 10,207
  $35,000 to $49,999: 9,381
  $50,000 to $74,999: 5,615
  $75,000 to $99,999: 1,068
  $100,000 to $149,999: 285
  $150,000 or more: 91
 Percent of families below poverty level: 14.6% (62.0% of which were female householder families with related children under 5)

1991 FBI Crime Index Total: 17,944

Municipal Government

Kansas City established a mayor/council/city administrator form of government in 1983. Council elections take place during odd-numbered years; six council members from geographic districts are elected to four-year terms. The council and the mayor, the seventh council member and titular head of government, appoint a city administrator who is responsible for day-to-day governmental operations.

Head Official: City Manager David Isabell (since 1985)

Total Number of City Employees: 1,650 (1992)

City Information: Municipal Office Building, 701 North Seventh Street, Kansas City, KS 66101; telephone (913)573-5000

Economy

Major Industries and Commercial Activity

The diversified economy of Wyandotte County, which constitutes the metropolitan Kansas City area, is based on heavy industry, manufacturing, wholesaling and retailing, and transportation. Principal industrial activity includes grain processing, flour milling, railroads, bakery products, meat processing, and the manufacture of automobiles and allied products, soap and detergent, and insulation. Agriculture continues to be important in the rural area west of the city.

Items and goods produced: fiberglass, cement, creamery products, soap, fiber box, brick, tile, automobiles

Incentive Programs—New and Existing Companies

Business development and expansion is actively promoted in Kansas City and Wyandotte County. Seventeen banks and four savings and loan associations, with assets totalling nearly $17 billion, provide various forms of financing; in addition, state and local governments offer tax incentives to new and expanding projects.

State programs—The state of Kansas has designated a major portion of Kansas City as a state enterprise zone. Companies located within the enterprise zone receive tax credits on new investment in plant and non-movable capital equipment and on new jobs created for Kansas residents; a sales tax exemption is also allowed on construction materials and capital equipment. Additional incentives are provided through the Kansas Industrial Training Program, a state-funded program that is tailored to the participating manufacturing operation.

Local programs—The City Council of Kansas City adopted a policy in 1988 whereby tax abatements may be granted, through negotiation with the City Department of Development, to projects that produce substantial economic benefits in the community. Several areas and businesses within Wyandotte County have been designated as Foreign Trade Zones, wherein foreign goods are not subject to restrictions such as duties, quotas, and *ad valorem* (in proportion to the value) taxes under certain conditions. Among the companies operating in these zones are General Motors Corporation, Inland Industries Underground Warehouse, and Americold Distribution Center.

Development Projects

In 1988 an excursion riverboat operation negotiated a long-term lease with the city for operations on the Kaw Point grounds. The Kaw Point area has recently been renamed River City U.S.A. The River City U.S.A. operation transported more than 110,000 passengers on dinner and entertainment cruises in 1989 and more than 135,000 passengers in 1990. For the 1990 season a new $2 million, 800-passenger riverboat, the *America,* joined the 600-passenger riverboat, the *Missouri River Queen,* at the River City U.S.A. riverfront. A riverwalk now adds to the numerous scenic attractions along the riverfront and all of the parking facilities have been landscaped and paved. In addition, the River City development is the home port of the USS *William S. Mitchell,* a historic dredge vessel that is being converted into a riverfront museum. Plans call for the development of additional historic, restaurant and entertainment facilities, as well as an aquarium and a monument worthy of the site. River City U.S.A. has added new recreation facilities including several amusement park rides.

The local economy has benefitted from the construction of the General Motors assembly plant, which employs nearly four-thousand workers, east of downtown Kansas City. More than three-hundred wholesale establishments and nearly eight-hundred retail outlets maintain a combined annual payroll of more than $250 million. Local, state, and federal government accounts for a substantial percent of the Wyandotte County economy.

A new $35 million U.S. Federal Courthouse began construction in the city's downtown area in June 1991. This facility will bring two-hundred new jobs, adding to the more than four-hundred jobs added in 1990 by the expansion of the Environmental Protection Agency local offices and the relocation of the regional Department of Housing and Urban Development offices to the city.

Economic Development Information: Department of Development, 701 North Seventh Street, Kansas City, KS 66101; telephone (913)573-5730

Commercial Shipping

Kansas City is one of the largest transportation hubs in the nation. Local firms provide a complete range of intermodal services, including rail, air, truck, and water, for the receiving and shipping of goods. With 176 daily rail freight movements, the city is a primary center for interstate rail transportation. Eleven main line railroads operate in the city; six of these maintain loading and unloading facilities. In addition to piggyback service and reciprocal switching, in-transit storage privileges are available for most commodities shipped through a Kansas City plant.

The Kansas City business community profits from commercial freight activity at Downtown Airport, a general aviation facility in neighboring Kansas City, Missouri. During a ten-month period in 1991, for example, 1.7 million pounds of cargo were shipped into and out of Kansas City. A trans-shipment point for more than two hundred motor freight carriers, Kansas City is part of the Kansas City Commercial Zone, where exemption from Interstate Commerce Commission tariff supervision is granted to shipments originating from and received within this region. Shippers and motor carriers independently negotiate rates. A number of warehouses are maintained in the area.

Thirty-five wharves in the Missouri River channel accommodate barges with loads of up to twelve-hundred tons. Four major barge lines provide direct service from Kansas City to New Orleans during an eight-month shipping season.

Labor Force and Employment Outlook

The following is a summary of data regarding the Kansas City, Kansas–Kansas City, Missouri metropolitan area labor force as of September 1992.

Size of non-agricultural labor force: 776,500

Number of workers employed in . . .
  mining: not reported
  construction: 30,600
  manufacturing: 105,000
  transportation and public utilities: 63,900
  wholesale and retail trade: 196,000
  finance, insurance, and real estate: 59,000
  services: 200,500
  government: 121,500

Average hourly earnings of production workers employed in manufacturing: $13.22 (Kansas City, MO)

Unemployment rate: 5.1% (Kansas City, MO)

Largest employers: Bethany Medical Center (services), General Motors (automotive assembly plant), City of Kansas City, Kansas (local government), International Paper Co. (paper products), Providence St. Margaret Health Center (services), Santa Fe Railroad (transportation), Unified School District #500 (education), Union Pacific Railroad (transportation), University of Kansas Medical Center (education, services), Associated Wholesale Grocers (headquarters warehouse division), Board of Public Utilities (municipal utility), Certain-Teed Products Corp. (insulation products), Colgate-Palmolive Co. (soaps and detergents), Lady Baltimore Foods, Inc. (food broker), Owens Corning Fiberglas Corp. (thermal insulation), Sunshine Biscuits, Inc. (crackers and cookies), Wyandotte County (county government), Champ Service Line (auto replacement parts), Continental Can (plastic products), Coopers Animal Health, Inc. (veterinarian supplies), Environmental Protection Agency (government), Fairbanks Morse (water pumps), Midwest Conveyor (steel fabrication), Proctor and Gamble Manufacturing (soaps and detergents), Sealright (containers), Sewell Plastics (plastic products), Southwestern Bell Telephone Co. (communications), Swift-Eckrich (meat processing), Thompson-Hayward Chemical Co. (chemicals), Turner Unified School District #202 (education)

Cost of Living

The following is a summary of data regarding several key cost of living factors in the Kansas City area.

The Rosedale Arch in Kansas City, Kansas.

1992 (2nd Quarter) ACCRA Cost of Living Index: 95.5 (U.S. average = 100.0)

1992 (2nd Quarter) ACCRA Average House Price: $99,000

State income tax rate: Graduated from 3.65% to 9.0%

State sales tax rate: 4.25%

Local income tax rate: None

Local sales tax rate: city, 1.0%; county, 1.0%

Property tax rate: 64.902 mills (total levy property and school district)

Economic Information: Department of Development, 701 North 7th Street, Kansas City, KS 66101, telephone (913)573-5730

Education and Research

Elementary and Secondary Schools

The Kansas City, Kansas Board of Education's Five-Year School Improvement Plan, adopted in 1987, was hailed by the International Society for Educational Planning for "bold vision and extensive involvement of staff and community." As a result of the plan, one of the district's elementary schools was one of only fifteen in the nation to be funded in the first year of the Nabisco Next Century Schools project. The district's drug and alcohol education program, which begins in kindergarten, is recognized as a national model.

The following is a summary of data regarding Unified School District 500 as of the 1992-1993 school year.

Total enrollment: 22,048

Number of facilities
 elementary schools: 33
 middle schools: 8
 senior high schools: 4
 other: 2 alternative high schools; 1 magnet school; a Summer Academy of Arts and Science; 1 vocational technical school

Student/teacher ratio: 23:1

Teacher salaries
 minimum: $22,247
 maximum: $43,685

Funding per pupil: $3,600

Fifteen private and parochial schools provide educational alternatives in Wyandotte County.

Public Schools Information: Kansas City, Kansas Public Schools, 625 Minnesota Avenue, Kansas City, KS 66101; telephone (913)551-3200

Colleges and Universities

The University of Kansas Medical Center, a teaching and research hospital, grants associate, baccalaureate, first-professional, master's, and doctorate degrees in a variety of fields, including allied health education and administration, nursing, medicine, and pharmacology. Two-year curricula are provided by Kansas City, Kansas, Community College and Donnelly College. The Central Baptist Theological Seminary awards a degree in theology.

Libraries and Research Centers

The main facility of the Kansas City Kansas Public Library is located downtown; two branches are operated within the system. Holdings total more than four-hundred thousand books in addition to subscriptions to more than twelve-hundred periodicals and newspapers, and microfiche, films, records, tapes, and art reproductions. Special collections include state documents and the Connelley Collection on Wyandotte Indians. The Archie R. Dykes Library of the Health Sciences is the largest health sciences library in Kansas. Housing the working collection of the University of Kansas Medical Center, the library supports the academic programs at the center as well as the University of Kansas Hospital. It is also a resource library for health care and educational institutions throughout Kansas and the Midwest. Other specialized libraries and research centers in Kansas City are affiliated with educational institutions, hospitals, and government agencies.

Public Library Information: Kansas City Kansas Public Library, 625 Minnesota Avenue, Kansas City, KS 66101; telephone (913)551-3200

Health Care

As the home of the University of Kansas Medical Center and two other hospitals, Kansas City is a regional leader in health care. The medical center, a teaching hospital for the University of Kansas Medical School, contains a 524-bed hospital and operates the Mid-American Radiation Therapy Center for research and treatment of cancer as well as the Mid-America Poison Control Center and the Level I Trauma Center. Other areas of specialization include osteoporosis, burn care, infant illness and deformity, and diagnostic radiology.

Bethany Medical Center, a 426-bed hospital, provides cancer treatment, surgery, chemical dependency programs, maternity care, and psychiatric care, among other services. Providence-St. Margaret Health Center, with 400 beds, specializes in treatment and care of cardiac, respiratory, and kidney disorders. Health service facilities in metropolitan Kansas City offer approximately thirty hospitals from which to choose; ancillary care is available at seventy-five clinics and two state-supported mental health centers. Five hundred physicians and seventy-five dentists practice in Wyandotte County.

Health Care Information: Kansas City, Kansas, Area Chamber of Commerce, P.O. Box 171337, Kansas City, KS 66117; telephone (913)371-3070

Recreation

Sightseeing

The Agricultural Hall of Fame and National Center was chartered by Congress in 1960 to honor the nation's farmers. Funded by private contributions, the hall is on a 270-acre site housing, in three major buildings, exhibits that trace the history of agriculture in the United States, including exhibits on rural life, customs, and material culture. The National Farmers Memorial in front of the hall was dedicated in 1986.

The Huron Indian Cemetery located in the heart of downtown is the burial ground of the Wyandots, the founders of the first town in the evolution of Kansas City. White Church Christian Church was founded by the Methodist Church in 1832 as a Delaware Indian Mission and maintains the Delaware Indian Cemetery next to the church. The John Brown Statue at 27th Avenue and Sewell pays tribute to the Brown-led antislavery movement from Quindaro, Kansas. In council chambers at City Hall the history of Kansas City is told through stained-glass windows and a large mural. The Rosedale Arch, built in 1924 as a memorial to World War I soldiers, replicates the Arch of Triumph in Paris and was rededicated to Kansas City, Kansas, citizens killed in service to their country. The Grinter House, built in 1857 and furnished with authentic period furniture, is the restored home of one of the first white settlers in Kansas City, Moses Grinter, who operated a ferry across the Kaw (Kansas) River.

Children will be interested in the Kansas City Zoo and Worlds of Fun, an international-theme park with 115 rides. Both are located in nearby Kansas City, Missouri.

Arts and Culture

The Kansas City metropolitan area is home to a number of theater companies. The American Heartland is a new professional company performing Broadway shows and musicals in the Crown Center Complex in Kansas City, Missouri, also home to Folly Theatre, a restored 1900 burlesque house, presenting drama and concerts. The Midland Center for the Performing Arts in Kansas City, Missouri, is the home of Theater League productions and concerts. Summer theater is performed at Sandstone Amphitheater, a natural amphitheater in Bonner Springs that sponsors top recording acts. Starlight Theatre, an outdoor amphitheater in Kansas City, Missouri's Swope Park, hosts musicals and concerts during the summer.

The era of pipe organs and silent movies comes alive at Kansas City, Kansas's Granada Theatre, home of the Grande Barton Theatre pipe organ, one of the most impressive instruments of its kind, weighing more than twenty tons and rising over two stories in height. The Granada Theatre sponsors an annual pipe organ pops series that brings some of the world's most famous pipe organists to perform while audiences watch silent movies. Built in 1928–1929 by Boller Brothers in a Spanish-Mediterranean style, the Granada Theatre was restored in 1986 and is now a performing arts center.

The Kansas City Museum, located in Kansas City, Missouri, features regional history displays, a natural history hall, a planetarium, and a recreated 1910-era corner drugstore. Kansas City, Missouri's Market Square is the home of the Arabia Steamboat Museum. The boat, which sank in 1856, was excavated along with its cargo in 1988 and 1989. Because the river's course had changed, excavation was done on dry land and much of the ship's cargo was preserved. The Harry S. Truman Library and Museum in nearby Independence, Missouri, contains documents and memorabilia of the Truman presidency, including a reproduction of Truman's White House office. The Jesse James Bank Museum, site of the first daylight bank robbery in the nation's history, contains the original 1858 vault and safe and other artifacts.

Neighboring Kansas City, Missouri, is the home of the nationally renowned William Rockhill Nelson Gallery of Art and Museum. The Wyandotte County Historical Museum in Bonner Springs exhibits local and regional displays, including native American relics and other items from the county's early history. The Strawberry Hill Museum, located in the former St. John's Children's Home, originally the home of railroad magnate James A. Cruise, is Kansas City's newest cultural center; it promotes Croatian and other ethnic cultures. The Children's Museum at the Indian Springs Shopping Center is an educational hands-on experience.

Festivals and Holidays

Kansas City is nicknamed the "City of Festivals." The city and Wyandotte County recognize history, culture, tradition, and ethnic heritage with annual events in which crafts, foods, and music play an important part. The biggest event is the Renaissance Festival that spans six fall weekends beginning on Labor Day weekend. Ethnic festivals include the Polish Constitution Day in May, Mexican fiestas in May and September, and the Festival International on the third weekend in June. The Piper Prairie Days in May combine good food with family fun. The Indian Club Pow-Wow features native American items at the Wyandotte County Fairgrounds on the third weekend in July. The Kansas City Spirit Festival takes place each year in Kansas City, Missouri, with a full array of events on the third weekend in September. Grinter House is the location of a number of special events, including the quilt show and spin in April, the Applefest in October, and the annual Christmas gift bazaars and old-fashioned Christmas days.

Sports for the Spectator

One of the fastest-growing spectator sports in the nation came to Kansas City, Kansas, in 1989. Greyhound racing, the sixth largest spectator sport in the country, and thoroughbred and quarterhorse racing take place at the $70 million dual-track Sunflower Racing Inc. complex. The privately funded racetrack includes two separate enclosed spectator facilities, a 1-mile-circumference horse track with a straightaway for thoroughbreds and quarterhorses, and a greyhound track suitable for year-round racing.

The American Royal, the world's largest combined livestock show, horse show, and rodeo, takes place for two full weeks in November at the American Royal Arena and Kemper Arena in the stockyard district in Kansas City, Missouri. Sports enthusiasts are just twenty minutes away from the Harry S. Truman Sports Complex in nearby Kansas City, Missouri, where the Kansas City Chiefs play in the National Football League at Arrowhead Stadium, and the Kansas City Royals compete in the Western Division of professional baseball's American League at Royals Stadium. The Kansas City Attack play indoor soccer at Municipal Auditorium, and the Kansas City Blades compete in the International Hockey League at Kemper Arena.

Sports for the Participant

The Kansas City Parks and Recreation Department manages forty-seven parks and eight recreational centers and twenty-two playgrounds that have facilities for tennis, golf, and picnicking. Wyandotte County maintains several large parks with boating, fishing, and outdoor activities available. Wyandotte County Lake has excellent fishing. Private facilities are available for a variety of individual and team sports. Oceans of Fun, adjacent to Worlds of Fun in Kansas City, Missouri, offers a number of water sports and activities. Wyandotte County has three first-rate golf courses; Dub's Dread, once the longest course in the United States, is known for its competitive challenges. The city's own municipal golf course, Sunflower Hills, is considered the premier public course in the metropolitan area.

Shopping and Dining

Indian Springs Shopping Center is Kansas City's largest shopping center, with more than seventy shops and restaurants and a ten-theater movie complex. Country Club Plaza and Crown Center are located in Kansas City, Missouri. City Market, also in Missouri, is a colorful farmers' market open on Wednesdays and weekends. Kansas City restaurants are known for their barbecue, steaks, chicken, and ethnic cuisine, including Mexican, Greek, Asian, and Italian.

Visitor Information: Kansas City Kansas Area Convention and Visitors Bureau, 753 State Ave., Suite 101, Kansas City, KS 66101, telephone (913)321-5800; and, The Kansas City Kansas Area Chamber of Commerce, P.O. Box 171337, Kansas City, KS 66117; telephone (913)371-3070

Convention Facilities

The Reardon Civic Center in downtown Kansas City is the site of conferences, meetings, banquets, and conventions. Accommodating up to 1,400 participants, the facility contains twenty-thousand square feet of exhibit space with twelve meeting rooms and sixty booth spaces. Soldiers and Sailors Memorial Hall, located near The Reardon Center, hosts meetings and conventions as well as sports events and concerts. Fifteen hotels and motels in the area also maintain meeting and banquet rooms.

Convention Information: Reardon Civic Center, Fifth and Minnesota, Kansas City, KS 66101; telephone (913)371-1610

Transportation

Approaching the City

Kansas City International Airport, 16 miles north of downtown in Kansas City, Missouri, is served by thirteen commercial airlines.

A network of interstate highways links Kansas City with points throughout the nation. I-35 runs from Duluth, Minnesota, southward through Kansas City to Laredo, Texas. I-29, originating in North Dakota, terminates in Kansas City; the Kansas Turnpike, I-70, bisects the city and extends to St. Louis and Denver, Colorado. I-435, an outerbelt, spans western Wyandotte County and connects Kansas City with the airport to the north.

Traveling in the City

North-south streets in Kansas City are numbered and labelled "street;" east-west streets are named and designated "avenue." Public bus transportation in the city is operated by the Kansas City Area Transit Authority and a city-operated bus system. These two bus systems are tied together and provide public transportation Monday through Saturday.

Communications

Newspapers

The Kansas City, Kansas daily newspaper is *The Kansas City Kansan.* The metropolitan daily is the *Kansas City Star.* Numerous neighborhood, ethnic, and suburban newspapers are distributed weekly and monthly, including *Wyandotte West.*

Television and Radio

Kansas City television viewers receive broadcasts from seven stations—three commercial network affiliates and four independent and public—based in Kansas City, Missouri; cable service is available locally. Thirty-two metropolitan area AM and FM radio stations provide a complete range of music, news, and special interest programming.

Media Information: The Kansas City Kansan, 901 North Eighth, Kansas City, KS 66101; telephone (913)371-4300; and, *Wyandotte West,* Wyandotte West Communications Inc., 7735 Washington Ave., P.O. Box 12003, Kansas City, KS 66112-0003; telephone (913)788-5565

Selected Bibliography

Hemingway, Ernest, *Ernest Hemingway, Cub Reporter; Kansas City Star Stories* (Pittsburgh: University of Pittsburgh Press, 1970)

Topeka

The City in Brief

Founded: 1854 (incorporated, 1857)

Head Official: Mayor Harry "Butch" Felker (R) (since 1989)

City Population
 1970: 125,000
 1980: 118,690
 1990: 119,883
 Percent change, 1980–1990: 1.0%
 U.S. rank in 1980: 136th
 U.S. rank in 1990: 149th

Metropolitan Area Population (Shawnee County)
 1970: 155,322
 1980: 154,916
 1990: 160,976
 Percent change, 1980–1990: 3.9%
 U.S. rank in 1980: Not available
 U.S. rank in 1990: Not available

Area: 55.2 square miles (1990)

Elevation: Ranges from 876 feet to 971 feet above sea level

Average Annual Temperature: 54.1° F

Average Annual Precipitation: 33.0 inches of rain; 21.0 inches of snow

Major Economic Sectors: Services, government, trade, manufacturing

Unemployment Rate: 4.3% (September 1992)

Per Capita Income: $13,680 (1990)

1992 (2nd Quarter) ACCRA Average House Price: Not reported

1992 (2nd Quarter) ACCRA Cost of Living Index: Not reported

1991 FBI Crime Index Total: 12,598

Major Colleges and Universities: Washburn University of Topeka

Daily Newspaper: *Topeka Capital-Journal*

Kansas—Topeka

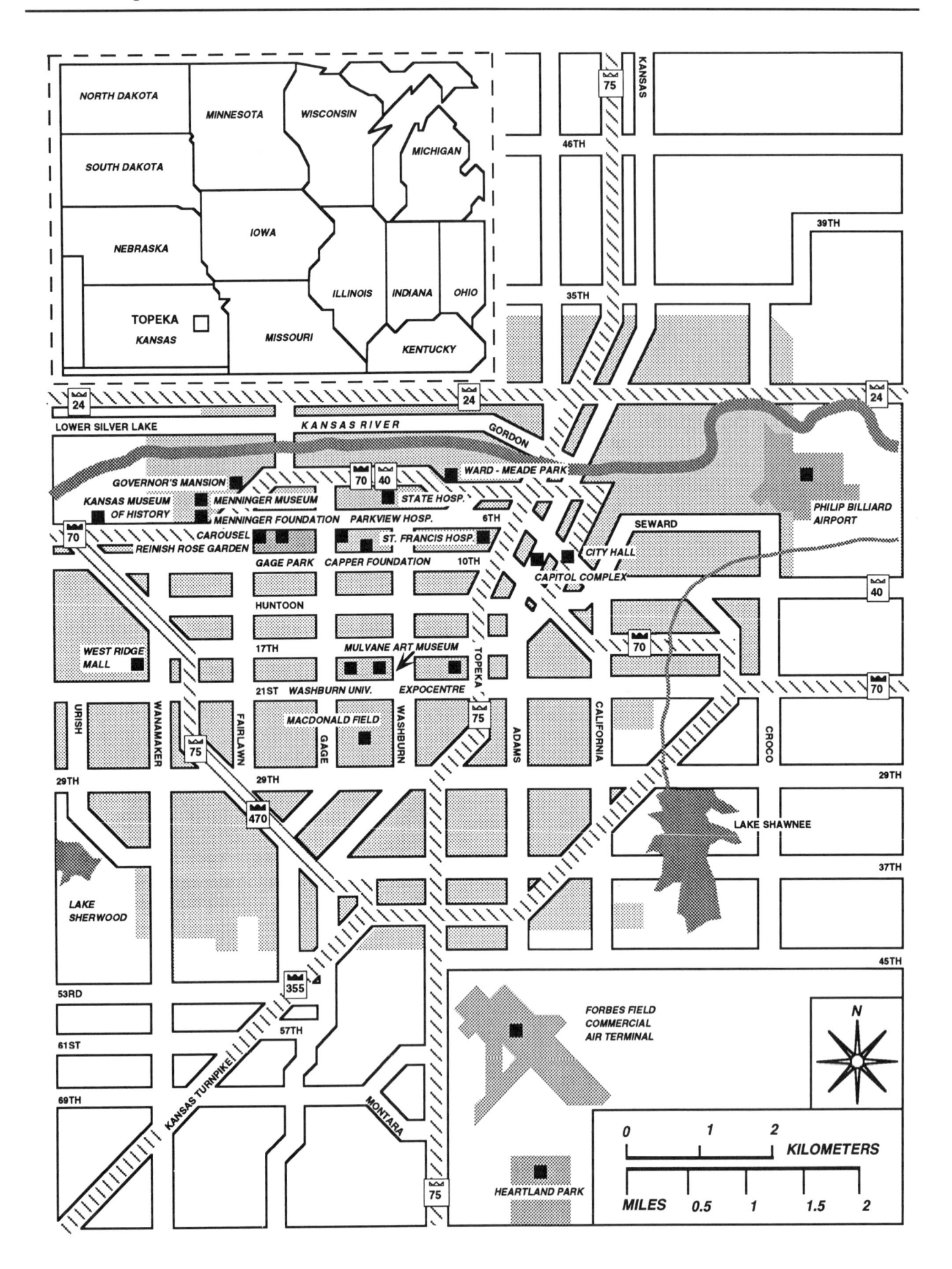

Introduction

Topeka is the seat of Shawnee County, the capital of Kansas, and center of a metropolitan statistical area that includes the rest of Shawnee County. Throughout its history, Topeka has been at the forefront of progress: created as a principal link in the westward expansion of the railroad and settled by New England antislavery supporters in the nineteenth century, the city has in the twentieth century been a world leader in the treatment of mental illness. In the 1980s Topeka became a commercial hub for northwestern Kansas.

Geography and Climate

Topeka lies on both banks of the Kansas River about 60 miles upriver from the point where the Kansas joins the Missouri River. Two tributaries of the Kansas River, Soldier and Shunganunga Creeks, flow through the city. The valley near Topeka, bordered by rolling prairie uplands of two-hundred to three-hundred feet, ranges from 2 to 4 miles in width. Seventy percent of the annual precipitation falls from April through September. Heavy rains pose the threat of flooding, but the construction of dams has reduced the problem. Summers are usually hot, with low humidity and southerly winds; periods of high humidity and oppressively warm temperatures are of short duration. Winter cold spells are seldom prolonged; winter precipitation is often in the form of snow, sleet, or glaze. Severe or disruptive storms occur infrequently.

Area: 55.2 square miles (1990)

Elevation: Ranges from 876 feet to 971 feet above sea level

Average Temperatures: January, 26.0° F; July, 78.6° F; annual average, 54.1° F

Average Annual Precipitation: 33.0 inches of rain; 21.0 inches of snow

History

Westward Expansion Targets Kaw River Valley

Two historic nineteenth-century movements combined to create the city of Topeka—one was the antislavery issue and the other was the westward expansion made possible by the railroad, which connected the East with the vast unsettled territory in the West. Before the Kansas frontier was opened by the federal government to settlement, the first people of European descent to live on the site of present-day Topeka were two French-Canadians, Joseph and Louis Pappan. They each married a woman from the Kaw tribe in 1842 and opened a ferry service across the Kaw River. The ferry was temporarily replaced in 1857 when bridge builders ignored warnings from the local native Americans, who insisted that structures built too close to the Kaw would not be secure against flood waters. The bridge was destroyed in a flood the following year.

Colonel Cyrus K. Holliday, a native of Pennsylvania, came to the Kansas Territory in 1854 with funding from Eastern investors to build a railroad. Holliday and a few pioneers had walked 45 miles from Kansas City to Lawrence, where Holliday approached Dr. Charles Robinson, agent of the New England Emigrant Aid Company, an antislavery organization, about his plan. Then Holliday and Robinson travelled 21 miles to Tecumseh, but businessmen there wanted too much money for their land. Holliday located a spot 5 miles from Tecumseh along the river and purchased land from Enoch Chase, who had previously bought it from the Kaws.

Holliday formed a company, naming himself as president and the Lawrence contingent and Chase as stockholders. Holliday wanted to name the town Webster after Daniel Webster, but the others preferred a name whose meaning was local; they chose Topeka, a native American word meaning "smokey hill," according to one version, or "a good place to dig potatoes," according to another. Dr. Robinson attracted antislavery New Englanders to settle in Topeka, thus counteracting the influence of a proslavery group in Tecumseh. A Free State constitutional convention was held in Topeka but federal troops arrested the new legislators when they tried to meet on July 4, 1855.

Kansas Statehood Brings Capital to Topeka

The Kansas constitution was framed at Wyandotte (later named Kansas City), and Kansas was admitted to the Union in 1861. The constitution specified that the state capital would be selected by election. Dr. Robinson ran for governor, favoring Topeka over Lawrence as the site for the capital; he also supported the Atchison, Topeka & Santa Fe Railway system, which began laying its westward track in 1869. Holliday served as the company's first president, with general offices and machine shops located in Topeka. Topeka's population increased from 700 people in 1862 to 5,000 people in 1870; it then made another dramatic population jump in the late 1880s when investors were misled by land speculators, later ushering in a depression in the 1890s.

The Kaw River flooded in the spring of 1903, submerging the industrial district of North Topeka; 29 people lost their lives in this disaster, which caused over $2 million in property damage. Dikes were built after this flood, holding firm against high waters that came again in 1908, 1923, and 1935.

Foundation in Topeka Gains International Fame

Topeka is known internationally as the home of the Menninger Foundation, a nonprofit organization dedicated to the study of mental illness and founded by Karl Menninger and his father, Charles. In 1920 the Menningers opened a group psychiatric practice that they named the Menninger Clinic; they were joined in 1925 by William, Charles's younger son. The Menningers opened the Topeka Institute of Psychoanalysis in 1938 after the brothers had studied formally in Chicago. The family is credited with introducing psychiatry to America. Karl Menninger's *The Human Mind* was the first book on psychiatry to become a bestseller. The Menningers opened, in 1941, the nonprofit Menninger Foundation the world's largest psychiatric training center.

Historical Information: Kansas State Historical Society—Center for Historical Research, 120 West Tenth, Topeka, KS 66612; telephone (913)296-3251

Population Profile

Metropolitan Area Residents (Shawnee County)
1970: 155,322
1980: 154,916
1990: 160,976
Percent change, 1980-1990: 3.9%
U.S. rank in 1980: Not available
U.S. rank in 1990: Not available

City Residents
1970: 125,000
1980: 118,690
1990: 119,883 (of which, 57,054 were males, and 62,829 were females)
Percent change, 1980-1990: 1.0%
U.S. rank in 1980: 136th
U.S. rank in 1990: 149th (State rank: 3rd)

Density: 2,171.8 people per square mile (1990)

Racial and ethnic characteristics (1990)
 White: 101,550
 Black: 12,761
 American Indian, Eskimo, Aleut: 1,538
 Asian and Pacific Islander: 948
 Hispanic (may be of any race): 6,930

Percent of residents born in state: 70.9% (1990)

Age characteristics (1990)
 Population under 5 years old: 8,864
 Population 5 to 9 years old: 8,654
 Population 10 to 14 years old: 7,672
 Population 15 to 19 years old: 7,277
 Population 20 to 24 years old: 8,917
 Population 25 to 29 years old: 11,030
 Population 30 to 34 years old: 10,591
 Population 35 to 39 years old: 9,445
 Population 40 to 44 years old: 7,770
 Population 45 to 49 years old: 5,987
 Population 50 to 54 years old: 4,981
 Population 55 to 59 years old: 5,278
 Population 60 to 64 years old: 5,736
 Population 65 to 69 years old: 5,412
 Population 70 to 74 years old: 4,211
 Population 75 to 79 years old: 3,387
 Population 80 to 84 years old: 2,571
 Population 85 years and over: 2,100
 Median age: 33.5 years

Births (1988)
 Total number: 2,071

Deaths (1988)
  Total number: 1,254 (of which, 16 were infants under the age of 1 year)

Money income (1989)
  Per capita income: $13,680
  Median household income: $26,774
  Total households: 49,839
  Number of households with income of . . .
    less than $5,000: 2,771
    $5,000 to $9,999: 4,623
    $10,000 to $14,999: 4,981
    $15,000 to $24,999: 10,614
    $25,000 to $34,999: 9,679
    $35,000 to $49,999: 8,582
    $50,000 to $74,999: 6,026
    $75,000 to $99,999: 1,447
    $100,000 to $149,999: 716
    $150,000 or more: 400
  Percent of families below poverty level: 9.3% (55.0% of which were female householder families with related children under 5)
1991 FBI Crime Index Total: 12,598

Municipal Government

Topeka adopted a strong mayor-council-administrator form of government in 1984. Council members from each of nine districts are elected to staggered four-year terms; the mayor, who is a member of council, also serves for four years. The administrator is responsible to the mayor.

Head Official: Mayor Harry "Butch" Felker (R) (since 1989; current term expires 1997)

Total Number of City Employees: 1,500 (1992)

City Information: City Hall, 215 SE Seventh Street, Topeka, KS 66603; telephone (913)295-3867

Economy

Major Industries and Commercial Activity

Government and services comprise more than 50 percent of the metropolitan Topeka economy: total state, county, and city government employment accounts for over one-fourth of the work force, and more than 20 percent of area workers are on the service industry payroll. Wholesale and retail trade employs more than 20 percent of the work force. Among the Fortune 500 companies that have established manufacturing or distribution facilities in Topeka are American Bakeries; Armco, Inc.; Atchison, Topeka & Santa Fe Railway; Essex Group; Frito-Lay, Inc.; Georgia Pacific; Goodyear Tire & Rubber; and Hill's Pet Products.

Topeka Quaker (Quaker Oats Company), among the most technologically advanced pet food processors in the world, is considered an industry-wide model for management-employee cooperation. Self-regulating work teams and hiring and training procedures account for the success of the "Topeka System."

Other principal industries located in Topeka include flour mills, printing and publishing companies, iron foundries, creameries, and meat, poultry, and egg packing plants.

Items and goods produced: flour, dairy products, meats and poultry, pet foods, cellulose goods, tires, tents, awnings, serum, farm machinery, steel fixtures, culverts, tanks, medicines, steel jetties

Incentive Programs—New and Existing Companies

The state of Kansas and the city of Topeka offer a range of incentives for business expansion, including a state-maintained "first-stop clearinghouse," tax credits and exemptions, utility rate discounts, fee waivers, and loan assistance. Organizations such as Topeka-Shawnee County Development Corporation and Kansas Venture Capital, Inc. promote development in the metropolitan area. Job training programs are also available through agencies such as KAW Area Technical School and Topeka Technical School.

The state of Kansas was one of two states to receive funding in 1991 for a Manufacturing Technology Center. Forty million dollars was to be spent on the state's technology infrastructure, preparing manufacturers to compete internationally.

Development Projects

The Topeka Performing Arts Center opened in 1991. A local manufacturer, Jostens, makers of products that recognize achievements (such as class rings and sports awards) has invested millions in recent years on state-of-the-art printing equipment at its Topeka plant.

Economic Development Information: Greater Topeka Chamber of Commerce, Three Townsite Plaza, 120 East Sixth Street, Topeka, KS 66603; telephone (913)234-2644

Commercial Shipping

Topeka is a shipping and distribution hub that links the corn- and wheat-growing region of northeastern Kansas and the cattle-producing states of the Southwest with markets throughout the country via an efficient transportation network. The three rail freight carriers, offering piggyback service within a 60-mile radius, are the Santa Fe Railway Company, Union Pacific, and St. Louis-Southwestern. Twenty trucking companies provide overnight and second-morning delivery to major cities in the Midwest and the West. Nine air carriers operate parcel and freight facilities at Forbes Field.

Labor Force and Employment Outlook

The following is a summary of data regarding the Topeka metropolitan area labor force as of September 1992.

Size of non-agricultural labor force: 91,200

Number of workers employed in . . .
  mining: not reported
  construction: 3,800
  manufacturing: 9,000
  transportation and public utilities: 5,900
  wholesale and retail trade: 20,100
  finance, insurance, and real estate: 6,300
  services: 23,900
  government: 22,200

Average hourly earnings of production workers employed in manufacturing: $13.69

Unemployment rate: 4.3%

Largest employers	Number of employees
State of Kansas	12,110
Goodyear Tire & Rubber	2,125
Unified School District #501	2,100
Stormont-Vail Regional Medical Center	1,800
Atchison, Topeka, & Santa Fe Railway	1,785
St. Francis Hospital & Medical Center	1,709

Cost of Living

According to Coldwell Banker, the average home price in Topeka in 1992 was $128,975.

The following is a summary of data regarding several key cost of living factors in the Topeka area.

1992 (2nd Quarter) ACCRA Cost of Living Index: Not reported

1992 (2nd Quarter) ACCRA Average House Price: Not reported

State income tax: Graduated from 3.65% to 9.0%

State sales tax rate: 4.25%

Local income tax rate: Ranges from 3.65% to 5.95% depending on marital status and federal tax deduction status

Local sales tax rate: 1.0% (5.0% transient guest tax on hotel/motel rooms)

Property tax rate: 167.03 mills per $1,000 of assessed value (1990)

Economic Information: Greater Topeka Chamber of Commerce, Three Townsite Plaza, 120 East Sixth Street, Topeka, KS 66603; telephone (913)234-2644

Education and Research

Elementary and Secondary Schools

Public elementary and secondary schools within the Topeka corporation limits are administered by United School District #501. The school superintendent is appointed by a nonpartisan, seven-member board of education.

The Topeka Public Schools claim national recognition for excellence as exemplified in frequent selection by the National School Recognition Award Program and other national and state organizations. Iowa Basics test scores are usually at or near the seventieth percentile. Special educational opportunities offered include full-day kindergarten classes for "at-risk" students, education and treatment of physically handicapped students, a hands-on Adventure Center, use of telecommunications equipment and computers in classrooms, emphasis on "writing

The copper-domed Kansas State Capitol Building features native oak, cherry wood, and marble from Tennessee, Italy, and Belgium.

across the curriculum," and special education for gifted and exceptional students.

The following is a summary of data regarding the Topeka public schools as of the 1991-1992 school year.

Total enrollment: 14,164

Number of facilities
  elementary schools: 26
  middle schools: 6
  senior high schools: 3
  other: 9

Student/teacher ratio: elementary, 14.4:1; middle, 13.5:1; senior high, 15.9:1

Teacher salaries
  minimum: $21,632
  maximum: $47,398

Funding per pupil: $3,749.66

Educational alternatives are offered by seven parochial and six private schools in Topeka. Special schools include the Capper Foundation for Crippled Children, the Institute of Logopedics Speech Center, and the Topeka Association for Retarded Children.

Public Schools Information: Topeka Unified School District #501, Office of the Superintendent, 624 West 24th Street, Topeka, KS 66611; telephone (913)233-0313

Colleges and Universities

Washburn University of Topeka, a public institution, offers forty-five programs leading to baccalaureate, first-professional, and master's degrees is such fields as business and management, health professions, public affairs, and social sciences, among others. Washburn is comprised of a College of Arts and Sciences and schools of law, business, nursing, and applied and continuing education. Vocational/technical schools located in the Topeka area include Kaw Area Vocational-Technical School and Topeka Technical College. Kansas University is located 20 miles east of Topeka.

Libraries and Research Centers

Topeka is home to several major libraries. The Topeka Public Library main branch holds nearly 370,000 books in addition to more than eleven-hundred periodical subscriptions, plus films, records, tapes, slides, art reproductions, and compact discs. The Subregional Library for the Blind and Physically Handicapped is also housed there. Special service is provided to Red Cross meal sites, retirement complexes, adult care homes, and individuals who are unable to visit the library.

The Kansas State Library contains nearly fifty-five thousand books; special collections include government operations, public administration, and social and behavioral sciences. The library maintains a Talking Book collection, serves as a depository for federal and state documents, and operates a division for the blind and physically handicapped in Emporia. The Kansas State Historical Society Library contains an extensive state archival collection as well as archaeological and genealogical materials, manuscripts, and federal documents.

The Menninger Foundation houses a library for professional research in such fields as behavioral sciences, family therapy, psychiatry, clinical psychiatry, psychoanalysis, and psychotherapy. Special services include literature searching, document delivery, and reference verification. Washburn University's Mabee Library and Law Library, the Kansas Supreme Court Law Library, the Kansas Neurological Institute professional library, and libraries associated with corporations, hospitals, and state agencies are also located in Topeka.

Public Library Information: Topeka Public Library, 1515 West Tenth Street, Topeka, KS 66604-1374; telephone (913) 233-2040

Health Care

The Topeka medical community has expanded with renovation and new construction at the city's major facilities, which include two general and seven specialized hospitals that provide a total of nearly 3,000 beds. Having completed extensive building projects, St. Francis Hospital and Medical Center and Stormont-Vail Regional Medical Center both operate emergency departments and offer care through state-of-the-art technology. The Colmery-O'Neil Veterans Administration Medical Center is a general care facility with more than 800 beds for veterans. Over 379 physicians practicing in fifty-six specialties and ninety licensed dentists are among the health care professionals working in Topeka.

As the headquarters of the Menninger Foundation, Topeka has historically been a center for specialized treatment. The C.F. Menninger Memorial Hospital and the Children's Hospital, with a total of 230 long- and short-term beds, offer psychiatric care for adults and children. In a survey of more than one-thousand leading doctors conducted by *U.S. News & World Report* and reported in June 1992, Menninger was chosen best facility in the country for psychiatric care. The Topeka State Hospital, a public psychiatric facility, serves thirty-one counties, and the Kansas Neurological Institute is recognized for its programs for the mentally retarded. The nonprofit Capper Foundation provides education and rehabilitative care for physically handicapped children, and Parkview Hospital treats emotional and behavioral disorders.

Recreation

Sightseeing

Historic Ward-Meade Park overlooks the Kansas River valley from its position on a bluff. At the center of the park is the ancestral home of the Anthony Ward family, a Victorian mansion restored during the United States Bicentennial in 1976. Also on the grounds are the Ward frontier log cabin, a country schoolhouse, botanical gardens, and a restored 1900s Kansas town called Prairie Crossings.

The Topeka Zoo, located on 160 acres in Gage Park, features a gorilla encounter habitat—providing for close observation of great apes through a glass partition—and an Indonesian tree house, home of orangutans born in captivity. Among the zoo's wide variety of animals on display are venomous snakes of northeast Kansas. Also at Gage Park are the Reinish Rose Garden and Carousel in the Park.

Topeka's copper-domed state Capitol building is well known for its frescoes and woodworking, but it is the Kansas Murals that give the Capitol its artistic focal point; these murals by John Steuart Curry capture dramatic events in the state's history that proved so controversial at the time they were executed that the project was not finished. The Menninger Museum traces the history of mental health and the contribution of the Menninger family. Potwin Place is an exclusive section of Topeka with Italianate, Victorian, and nineteenth-century farmhouse-style homes.

Two public school buildings are worth noting: Topeka High School displays the mast spar from *Old Ironsides* on its lawn, and the Sumner School was involved in the 1954 *Brown* v. *Topeka Board of Education* Supreme Court decision that integrated American public schools.

Arts and Culture

Musical entertainment in Topeka is provided by the Topeka Symphony Orchestra, Community Concert Association, Topeka Opera Society, Fine Arts Society, and Jazz Workshop, performing at Kansas Expocentre and elsewhere. Ballet Midwest performs an annual production of *The Nutcracker* amid a season of classical ballet.

The Topeka Performing Arts Center, which opened in 1991, presents Broadway musicals and other entertainment. The Topeka Civic Theater, as the winner of Festival of American Community Theater awards, is recognized as one of the nation's most highly regarded dinner theaters. Other Topeka theater companies include Helen Hocker Theater in Gage Park and the Washburn University Players.

More than twenty art galleries as well as public buildings and businesses and corporations in Topeka display an array of art. Among the more outstanding pieces are John Steuart Curry's *John Brown* in the State Capitol, Peter Felton's *Amelia Earhart* in the rotunda of the State Capitol, and Louis Comfort Tiffany's *The Ascension Window,* a stained glass window in the sanctuary of the First Presbyterian Church. The Mulvane Art Museum on the campus of Washburn University exhibits works by Duerer, Goya, Picasso, and Dali in its permanent collection. The Kansas Museum of History focuses on the history of Kansas and uses an interactive approach that involves museum visitors with exhibits covering the state's history from the earliest native cultures to the present. The Combat Air Museum at Forbes Field displays airplanes and aircraft memorabilia dating back to 1939 and including the *Columbia* space shuttle. The museum restores and displays American wartime military aircraft, maintaining them in flying condition.

Festivals and Holidays

Kansas Day Celebration in late January commemorates Kansas's admission into the Union. The Arab Shrine Circus is the main event in February. The featured attraction in March is the St. Patrick's Day Parade and Street Fair. The Sunflower Music Festi-

The Combat Air Museum features artifacts spanning the period from the Spanish American War to the space age.

val brings professional performers to Washburn University in June. The KSNT Go 4th Festival, Mexican Fiesta, and Kansas River Valley Art Fair make for an active July. Railroad Days celebrate Topeka's rail legacy, and the Huff 'N' Puff Balloon Rally and Superbatics Air Show are also popular September events. Apple Festival held at Historic Ward-Meade Park celebrates Kansas's folk life. A parade is held on Columbus Day. The Festival of Carols and the Festival of Trees take place in November and December respectively.

Sports for the Spectator

Washburn University, fielding teams in intercollegiate competition in a number of sports, hosts the National American Association of Universities' Basketball Tournament in April. The Great Plains Rowing Championship, also in April, pits men's and women's rowing teams for medals and trophies. The Kansas State High school Rodeo Championships are held at the Topeka Expocentre Livestock Arena in early June. Drag racing action takes place at Heartland Park in Topeka.

Sports for the Participant

The Topeka parks department maintains eighty-seven parks equipped with shelter houses, picnic tables, tennis courts, swimming pools, and softball fields. Five eighteen-hole public golf courses are located in the city. East of Topeka is Lake Shawnee, providing opportunities for swimming, fishing, boating, water skiing, and sailing. The recreation department sponsors programs for all age groups and maintains facilities for tennis, racquetball, handball, soccer, and baseball and softball. Gage Park, in addition to being the home of the Topeka Zoo, features recreational facilities. The Topeka Tinman Triathlon takes place at Lake Shawnee the third weekend in June, when men and women compete in a variety of events.

Shopping and Dining

The one-million-square-foot West Ridge Mall, which opened in 1988, and Hypermart USA doubled retail shopping space in Topeka. More than thirty-eight other shopping areas range from enclosed malls to neighborhood shopping centers.

Steakhouses serving Kansas beef are the main attraction in Topeka. Other dining choices include French, Mexican, Oriental, and Cajun Creole. Topeka's most popular family restaurants specialize in traditional American fare such as Southern fried chicken, country fried steaks, barbecued ribs, and homemade pies and pastries.

Visitor Information: Topeka Convention and Visitors Bureau, Three Townsite Plaza, 120 East Sixth, Topeka, KS 66603; telephone (913)234-2644

Convention Facilities

The Kansas Expocentre, a multi-purpose complex that accommodates meetings, conventions, trade shows, and entertainment events, houses an arena, a concert hall, and a convention center. The arena, seating up to 10,000 people, contains 210,000 square feet of unobstructed space. Parking for twenty-five hundred vehicles is provided on the site and catering service is available. Twenty-seven hotels and motels, several of which offer complete meeting facilities, total more than twenty-two hundred rooms for lodgings.

Convention Information: Kansas Expocentre, One Expocentre Drive, Topeka, KS 66612-1442; telephone (913)235-1986

Transportation

Approaching the City

Four major commercial airlines schedule flights into Forbes Field, where the Air Terminal is slated for expansion, 7 miles south of downtown Topeka. Daily commuter service is available from Kansas City. The destination for general and business aviation traffic is Phillip Billiard Field, 3 miles northeast of the city. Passenger rail service to Topeka is provided by Amtrak.

An efficient highway network facilitates access into Topeka. Three interstate and three U.S. highways converge in Topeka: I-70, I-470, and I-335; and U.S. 24, U.S. 40, and U.S. 75.

Traveling in the City

Downtown Topeka is laid out on a grid pattern. Streets running east to west are numbered; streets running north to south are named. The Topeka Metropolitan Transit (Topeka Transit) schedules fourteen public bus routes in the city Monday through Saturday; the company's Lift Service accommodates the transportation needs of the handicapped and the elderly. During weekday mornings and afternoons, Topeka Transit operates the Topeka Trolleys, a downtown shuttle and lunchtime circulator service.

Communications

Newspapers and Magazines

Topeka's major daily newspaper is the *Topeka Capital-Journal*. The city is also a center for magazine publishing. Among the widely circulated periodicals based in Topeka is *Capper's,* a biweekly human interest magazine established in 1879. Other publications pertain to agriculture, commerce and industry, psychiatry, and rural living. Of unique appeal is *Lefthander Magazine,* which publishes articles of interest to left-handed individuals.

Television and Radio

Topeka television viewers select programming from four stations, including three commercial network affiliates and one public station; cable service is available through subscription. Three AM and six FM radio stations schedule a variety of formats such as contemporary, country and western, and top-40s music; news; religious programming; and public interest features.

Media Information: Topeka Capital-Journal, 616 Jefferson Street, Topeka, KS 66607; telephone (913)295-1111

Wichita

The City in Brief

Founded: 1868 (incorporated, 1871)

Head Official: City Manager Chris Cherches (since 1985)

City Population
  1970: 277,000
  1980: 279,838
  1990: 304,011
  Percent change, 1980–1990: 8.6%
  U.S. rank in 1980: 51st
  U.S. rank in 1990: 51st

Metropolitan Area Population
  1970: 417,000
  1980: 442,000
  1990: 485,270
  Percent change, 1980–1990: 9.7%
  U.S. rank in 1980: 75th
  U.S. rank in 1990: 75th

Area: 115.5 square miles (1990)
Elevation: 1,300 feet above sea level
Average Annual Temperature: 56.4° F
Average Annual Precipitation: 28.61 inches of rain; 15.0 inches of snow

Major Economic Sectors: Services, manufacturing, trade
Unemployment Rate: 4.6% (September 1992)
Per Capita Income: $14,516 (1989)
1992 (2nd Quarter) ACCRA Average House Price: $111,917
1992 (2nd Quarter) ACCRA Cost of Living Index: 98.7 (U.S. average = 100.0)
1991 FBI Crime Index Total: 30,113

Major Colleges and Universities: The Wichita State University; University of Kansas School of Medicine—Wichita; Friends University; Kansas Newman College

Daily Newspaper: *The Wichita Eagle-Beacon*

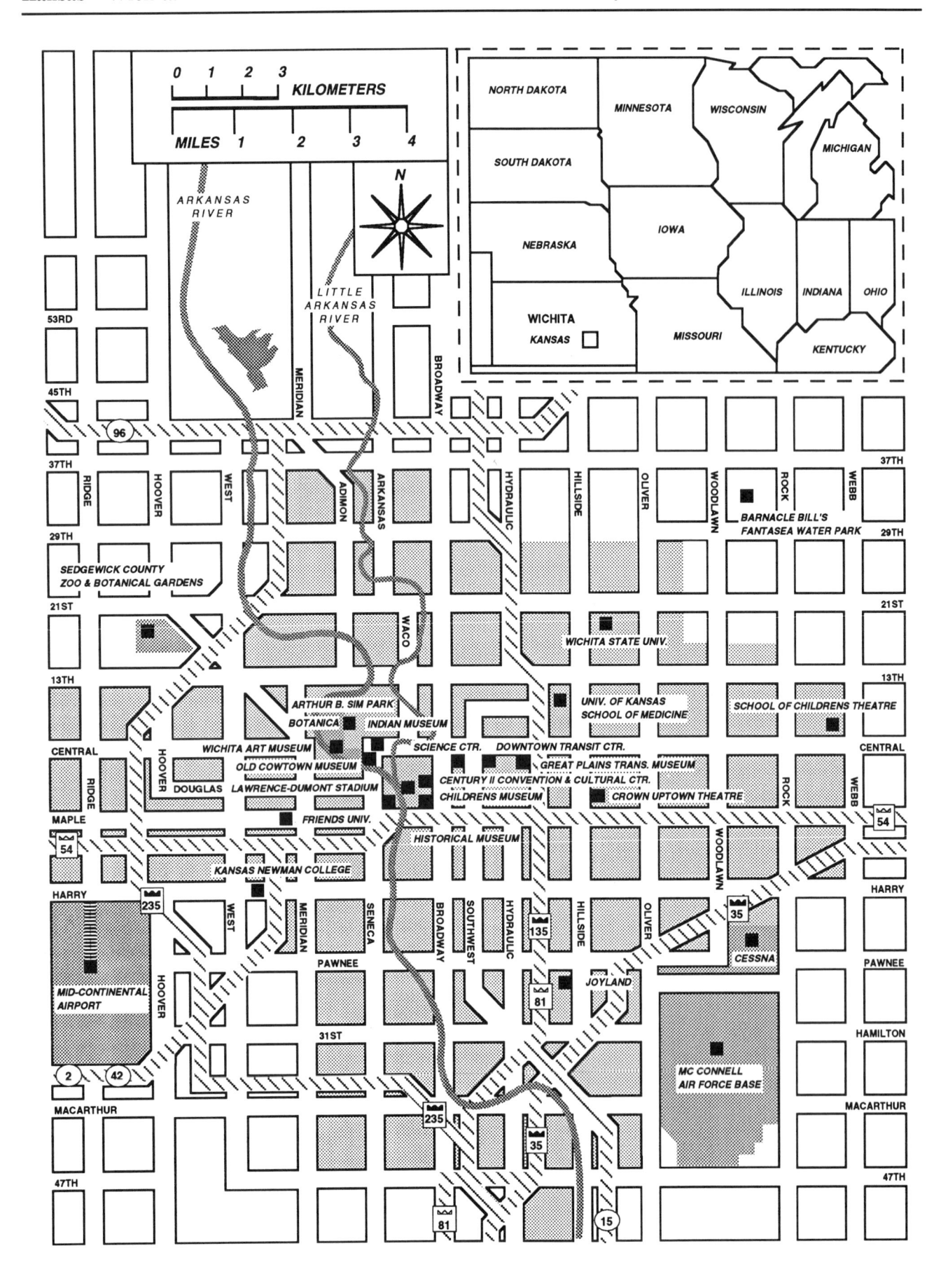

Kansas—Wichita *Cities of the United States • 2nd Edition*

Introduction

Wichita, the largest city in Kansas and the seat of Sedgwick County, is the focus of a metropolitan statistical area that includes Butler and Sedgwick counties. The city's history reflects the major stages of western U.S. development. The primary stop on the Chisholm trail, Wichita flourished first as a cattle town, then as a rail link and milling center for Kansas grain. Prosperity continued with the discovery of oil near the city limits. Today Wichita is an important center in the aircraft industry.

Geography and Climate

Wichita is located on the Arkansas River in the Central Great Plains. The collision of moist air from the Gulf of Mexico with cold air from the Arctic produces a wide range of weather in the Wichita area. Summers, which are generally warm and humid, can often be hot and dry; winters are mild, though cold periods are not infrequent. Temperature variations are extreme, reaching above 110 degrees in the summer and below minus twenty degrees in the winter. Spring and summer thunderstorms can be severe, accompanied by heavy rain, hail, strong winds, and tornadoes. Protection against floods is provided by the Wichita-Valley Center Flood Control Project.

Area: 115.5 square miles (1990)
Elevation: 1,300 feet above sea level
Average Temperatures: January, 29.6° F; July, 81.3° F; annual average, 56.4° F
Average Annual Precipitation: 28.61 inches of rain; 15.0 inches of snow

History

The city of Wichita is named after the native American Wichita tribe, who settled on the site of present-day Wichita along the banks of the Arkansas River during the U.S. Civil War to avoid conflict with pro-Southern tribes in Oklahoma. James R. Mead and Jesse Chisholm, who was part Cherokee, opened a trading post next to the Wichita's village. Chisholm, on a return trip from the Southwest where he had ventured on a trading expedition, was traveling through a rain storm, and the wheels of his wagon carved deep tracks into the prairie soil. Thus the famous Chisholm Trail was blazed, and the route was used in subsequent years by cattlemen driving cattle to their eventual market destinations.

After the relocation of the Wichita tribe to Oklahoma in 1867, the Mead trading post became a center of commerce. As Texas cattlemen drove their longhorn steer up the Chisholm Trail to Abilene, the settlement around the trading post provided a stop on the way. The "first and last chance saloon" was opened there for thirsty cowboys. The settlement, named Wichita, was platted in 1870 and incorporated in 1871. When rail transport reached the town in 1872 and 350,000 cattle were driven in from the grazing ranges, Wichita became the "cow capital" of eastern Kansas. Wichita was a rough place despite signs posted at the corporation limits that warned visitors to check their guns before entering town.

Boom times lasted until 1880 when the Chisholm Trail was blocked by barbed-wire fences protecting land planted with wheat, which prevented drovers from bringing their cattle to Wichita. Businessmen who made their livelihood from cattle relocated to Dodge City, and Wichita land values temporarily tumbled. But revenues from grain quickly outdistanced cattle when farmers brought their harvest to Wichita, transforming the city into a trading and milling center. Whereas the cattle business had supported dance halls and gambling houses, the wheat industry brought the civilizing forces of churches and schools.

Wichita's population steadily increased in the twentieth century, and new forms of wealth and business opportunity emerged. A major oil deposit discovered in Butler County in 1915 earned the nickname "door-step pool" because of its proximity to the city limits. During the 1920s Wichita became known as the "Air Capital of America" in recognition of the number of airplane factories located there. Today it is a leading manufacturer of aircraft and aerospace equipment.

Historical Information: Wichita Sedgwick County Historical Museum Library, 204 South Main Street, Wichita, KS 67202; telephone (316) 265-9314

Population Profile

Metropolitan Area Residents
1970: 417,000
1980: 442,000
1990: 485,270
Average annual percent change, 1980–1988: 1.1%
U.S. rank in 1980: 75th
U.S. rank in 1990: 75th

City Residents
1970: 277,000
1980: 279,838
1990: 304,011 (of which, 147,659 were males, and 156,352 were females)
Percent change, 1980–1990: 8.6%
U.S. rank in 1980: 51st
U.S. rank in 1990: 51st (State rank: 1st)

Density: 2,641.3 people per square mile (1990)

Racial and ethnic characteristics (1990)
   White: 250,176
   Black: 34,301
   American Indian, Eskimo, Aleut: 3,527
   Asian and Pacific Islander: 7,773
   Hispanic (may be of any race): 15,250

Percent of residents born in state: 63.6% (1990)

Age characteristics (1990)
   Population under 5 years old: 26,122
   Population 5 to 9 years old: 23,411
   Population 10 to 14 years old: 20,155
   Population 15 to 19 years old: 18,757
   Population 20 to 24 years old: 23,839
   Population 25 to 29 years old: 29,525
   Population 30 to 34 years old: 29,481
   Population 35 to 39 years old: 24,427
   Population 40 to 44 years old: 19,590
   Population 45 to 49 years old: 14,647
   Population 50 to 54 years old: 11,917
   Population 55 to 59 years old: 12,368
   Population 60 to 64 years old: 12,117
   Population 65 to 69 years old: 12,402
   Population 70 to 74 years old: 9,581
   Population 75 to 79 years old: 7,198
   Population 80 to 84 years old: 4,580
   Population 85 years and over: 3,894
   Median age: 31.7 years

Births (1988)
   Total number: 6,398

Deaths (1988)
   Total number: 2,645 (of which, 60 were infants under the age of 1 year)

Money income (1989)
   Per capita income: $14,516
   Median household income: $28,024
   Total households: 123,682
   Number of households with income of . . .
     less than $5,000: 7,747
     $5,000 to $9,999: 10,962
     $10,000 to $14,999: 11,621
     $15,000 to $24,999: 24,136
     $25,000 to $34,999: 21,838
     $35,000 to $49,999: 22,694
     $50,000 to $74,999: 16,833
     $75,000 to $99,999: 4,367
     $100,000 to $149,999: 2,101
     $150,000 or more: 1,383
   Percent of families below poverty level: 9.5% (63.2% of which were female householder families with related children under 5)

1991 FBI Crime Index Total: 30,113

Municipal Government

The city of Wichita operates under a council-manager form of government, with six council members and a mayor being elected to four-year terms.

Head Official: City Manager Chris Cherches (since 1985)

Total Number of City Employees: 2,719 (1992)

City Information: telephone (316)268-4351

Economy

Major Industries and Commercial Activity

During the early 1980s, the Wichita economy underwent setbacks caused by declines in agriculture, oil exploration, and durable goods manufacturing. Since 1987, however, growth in manufacturing has maintained a rate of 2.5 to 3.0 percent annually, particularly in the aviation sector; the services industry has also undergone expansion. Retail sales have risen steadily; in fact, in 1987 Wichita was ranked the thirtieth most affluent market in the United States. Primary areas of production are wheat growing, meat packing, flour milling, grain storage, oil refining, high technology, and telecommunications.

The aircraft industry has long been established in Wichita, and today the city is headquarters of some of the nation's leading aerospace firms. Boeing Military Airplanes is the second-largest division of the Boeing Company and Kansas's largest employer; it is also the world's largest private aerospace complex at a single site. Boeing announced in early 1993 the projected loss of up to thirty-thousand jobs industry-wide; about five-thousand workers at Wichita plants were among this number. The Cessna Aircraft Company is the world's leading maker of light aircraft and corporate jets. Founded in Wichita in 1932, the Beech Aircraft Corporation manufactures business and general aviation craft. Learjet Corporation headquarters and manufacturing facilities are also located in Wichita. Nearby McConnell Air Force Base, one of only four bases in the country that house the B-1 bomber, is the headquarters of the Kansas Air National Guard—the third largest in the nation—and also contributes to the local economy.

Several Wichita companies are leaders in their respective fields. Vulcan Chemicals ranks among the country's top producers of chlorinated solvents used to make such products as plastics, film, soft drinks, and electronic circuitry. Cargill, one of the nation's major agribusiness corporations, operates processing facilities in Wichita; the Excel Corporation, a subsidiary of Cargill, is the second-largest beef packer in the United States. N C R Engineering and Manufacturing-Wichita, part of the N C R multinational network, makes advanced computer products. The Coleman Company, pioneers in the production of outdoor recreational gear, was founded in the city in the early twentieth century. Coleman announced a 1987-1991 foreign growth rate exceeding 30 percent a year. Other companies based in Wichita include Pizza Hut, Rent-A-Center, the Pioneer Balloon Company, and Chance Rides, Inc., the world's largest designer and manufacturer of amusement rides.

Items and goods produced: airplanes, airplane supplies, heating and air conditioning units, agricultural and auto equipment, machinery, dairy products, household appliances

Incentive Programs—New and Existing Companies

Local programs—The Wichita/Sedgwick County Partnership for Growth, a nonprofit corporation, establishes economic development policy for the metropolitan area, oversees its implementation, and coordinates all economic development activity. The organization is comprised of representatives from city and county government, higher education, area businesses, and the Chamber of Commerce. Blueprint 2000, a five-year economic development plan designed to attract industry, investment, and jobs to the area, is being implemented by Wichita/Sedgwick County partnership for Growth.

Area colleges and universities work with the business community to promote economic development and expansion through education, technical assistance, and job training. Among the programs are the Center for Productivity Enhancement, the Program Control Center for the Kansas Small Business Development Center, the Center for Entrepreneurship and Small Business Management, and the Institute for Aviation Research and Development and the new Center for Technology Application at Wichita State University.

State programs—The state of Kansas was one of two states to receive funding in 1991 for a Manufacturing Technology Center. Forty million dollars was to be spent on the state's technology infrastructure, preparing manufacturers to compete internationally.

Development Projects

Downtown redevelopment of Wichita continued in the 1990s with $75 million earmarked for that purpose. A $3.9 million Transit Center was scheduled to open in 1993, as was the downtown location consolidating all Wichita-area offices of the state of Kansas. A developer was selected for a $100 million project to include a four-hundred-room convention hotel, stores, restaurants, marina, and casino. At least five downtown restaurants opened in Wichita in 1992.

A $2.65 billion Comprehensive Highway Bill passed in 1989 will expand and upgrade the city's highway system.

Economic Development Information: Wichita/Sedgwick County Partnership for Growth, 350 West Douglas, Wichita, KS 67202; telephone (316)265-2095

Commercial Shipping

Air cargo service is provided by thirteen freight companies based at Wichita's Mid-Continent Airport. Nine trucking companies ship goods nationwide; nine others offer intrastate delivery; and an additional seventy independent carriers are available on a contract basis. Three major railroads—Union Pacific, Burlington Northern, and Atchison, Topeka, & Santa Fe—link the city with most major continental markets.

Labor Force and Employment Outlook

Community leaders envision a healthy economic future for Wichita, with new highways, a new biomedical research center, a rejuvenated educational system, and increased technological sophistication of local manufacturers.

The following is a summary of data regarding the Wichita metropolitan area labor force as of September 1992.

Size of non-agricultural labor force: 242,800

Number of workers employed in . . .
  mining: 1,600
  construction: 10,800
  manufacturing: 60,200
  transportation and public utilities: 11,200
  wholesale and retail trade: 56,100
  finance, insurance, and real estate: 10,900
  services: 62,300
  government: 29,700

Average hourly earnings of production workers employed in manufacturing: $13.90

Unemployment rate: 4.6%

Largest Employers (1992)	Number of Employees
The Boeing Co.*	20,300
Beech Aircraft Corp.	6,450
Unified School District #259	5,266
Cessna Aircraft Co.	5,171
United States Government (including civilian employment at McConnell AFB)	3,858
State of Kansas	3,520

*Boeing announced industry-wide layoffs of up to 30,000 people nationally in early 1993.

Cost of Living

The following is a summary of data regarding several key cost of living factors in the Wichita area.

1992 (2nd Quarter) ACCRA Cost of Living Index: 98.7 (U.S. average = 100.0)

1992 (2nd Quarter) ACCRA Average House Price: $111,917

State income tax rate: Graduated from 3.65% to 9.0%

State sales tax rate: 4.25%

Local income tax rate: None

Local sales tax rate: 1.0% county tax

Property tax rate: $146.640 per $1,000 assessed valuation

Economic Information: Wichita Area Chamber of Commerce, 350 West Douglas Avenue, Wichita, KS 67202-2970; telephone (316)265-2095

Education and Research

Elementary and Secondary Schools

Unified School District #259 of the Wichita Public Schools is the state's largest elementary and secondary public education system. It is administered by a nonpartisan, seven-member board that contracts a superintendent.

The following is a summary of data regarding Wichita public schools as of the 1991–1992 school year.

Total enrollment: 49,149

Number of facilities
  elementary schools: 69
  middle schools: 15
  senior high schools: 13

Student/teacher ratio: elementary, 23:1; junior high, 23:1; senior high, 23:1 (1988–1989)

Teacher salaries
  minimum: $22,563 (1992–1993)
  maximum: $35,892 (1992–1993)

Funding per pupil: $3,312 (1988–1989)

Sedgwick County is served by twenty-eight private and parochial elementary and secondary schools.

Public Schools Information: Wichita Public Schools, 217 North Water, Wichita, KS 67202; telephone (316)833-4000

Colleges and Universities

The Wichita State University is an undergraduate and graduate institution with an enrollment of approximately seventeen thousand students, 72 percent of whom are nontraditional students living and working in the community. Nearly two-hundred academic areas are offered, including several doctoral programs in such fields as communicative disorders and sciences (logopedics), engineering, mathematics, and chemistry. The university operates the Institute of Logopedics, the only therapy center of its kind in the nation, founded in 1934 by the late Dr. Martin Palmer.

The University of Kansas School of Medicine-Wichita, at one time affiliated with The Wichita State University and now a separate facility, provides medical education in most fields of specialization. The university maintains cooperative programs with four hospitals and operates the Division of Research, Planning, and Development, which conducts clinical research and consultation.

Friends University, affiliated with the Society of Friends church and the largest independent college in Kansas, grants baccalaureate and master's degrees in business and management, communications, and interdisciplinary studies, among other areas. Kansas Newman College is a four-year, coeducational liberal arts institution associated with the Roman Catholic Church. Webster University in St. Louis, Missouri, operates a graduate learning center at McConnell Air Force Base. Butler Community College in neighboring El Dorado offers two-year degree programs.

Libraries and Research Centers

Twenty libraries maintained principally by public institutions and agencies, hospitals, and corporations, are located in Wichita. The Wichita Public Library—with holdings of more than 616,000 volumes, more than one-thousand periodical subscriptions, plus tapes, films, records, maps, and art reproductions—operates twelve branches in addition to a main facility. Among special collections are the Driscoll Piracy Collection, Kansas and local history, genealogy, motor manuals, music scores, and state documents. The Wichita State University operates a substantial campus library with more than nine-hundred thousand volumes, more than four-thousand periodical subscriptions, and numerous special collections on a range of subjects pertaining primarily to Kansas and American history. Also based at the university are the Milton Helpern International Center of Forensic Sciences, which specialized in materials relating to crime and forensic problems, and the recently completed Institute for Aviation Research.

Among other libraries and research centers in the city are those affiliated with Friends University, Kansas Newman College, the Wichita Art Museum, the *Wichita Eagle,* the Midwest Historical and Genealogical Society, the Wichita Sedgwick County Historical Society, the Institute of Logopedics, and Boeing Military Airplane Company.

Public Library Information: Wichita Public Library, 223 South Main, Wichita, KS 67202; telephone (316)262-0611

Health Care

Wichita is a regional center for medical treatment and referral as well as training and research employing more than fifteen-thousand health care professionals. Many medical workers and allied staff are educated at the University of Kansas School of Medicine—Wichita, which maintains training programs at four local hospitals. Wichita is home to the Women's Research Institute, the only combined clinic and research organization of its type in the country. The Wesley Foundation, based in Wichita, has $250 million in assets, the major portion of which goes to basic medical research.

St. Francis Regional Medical Center operates centers for organ transplants, burn treatment, diabetes care, and treatment of epilepsy; other areas of specialization include cardiology, oncology, emergency and trauma care, and psychiatric services. The H C A Wesley Medical Center houses a regional women's hospital with an *in vitro* fertilization lab and is the base for the largest air ambulance system in the state; major inpatient and outpatient care and services are provided.

Among other health care facilities in the city is St. Joseph Medical Center, which operates centers for teaching, chemical dependence treatment, stress management, back-pain treatment, family practice, and emergency care. Riverside Hospital is a general care facility, and C P C Great Plains Hospital and Charter Hospital of Wichita treat psychiatric and behavioral disorders as well as alcohol and drug abuse. Military facilities include the 384th Strategic Hospital at McConnell Air Force Base and the Veterans Administration Medical Center. Five other hospitals and medical complexes, forty-one nursing homes, an emergency ambulance service, more than one-hundred health care clinics, and fifteen fitness centers are located in the Wichita metropolitan area.

Health Care Information: Medical Society of Sedgwick County, telephone (316)683-7557

Recreation

Sightseeing

Wichita has retained its frontier roots while developing a cosmopolitan ambiance. The Old Cowtown Museum capitalizes on Wichita's past as a stop on the Chisholm Trail with forty-four original, restored, or replica buildings and displays depicting life between 1865 and 1880, along with programs celebrating Wichita's cattle-driving beginnings. Wichita turned the Arkansas River into a cultural asset by redesigning the riverside for public recreation and for popular events such as River Festival. Wichita's sophistication is evident in the city's outdoor sculptures, which now number more than 125 and include such works as the large Joan Miro mosaic mural at Wichita State University. Price Woodward Park is located between Century II and the Arkansas River; on the park grounds are several sculptures.

The Botanica, or Wichita Gardens, is located near the banks of the Arkansas River and is the state's only such garden. The Olive W. Garvey Center for the Improvement of Human Functioning is housed at the Pyradomes, eight geodesic domes designed by R. Buckminster Fuller. The Omnisphere and Science Center offers hands-on science exhibits for all ages, and the Lake Afton Public Observatory with its sixteen-inch telescope is open on weekends for astronomy enthusiasts. At the Sedgwick County Zoo and Botanical Garden animals roam an imitation veldt, birds fly in a tropical rain forest, and nocturnal creatures live in a herpetarium that switches night for day. Children enjoy Barnacle Bill's Fantasea and Joyland Amusement Park.

Arts and Culture

Wichita supports more than fifty organizations in the fine, performing, and visual arts. Century II, the city's center for cultural activities, houses the major performance organizations. The Wichita Symphony Orchestra plays a season of classical, chamber, and pops concerts in Century II's concert hall. A highlight of the symphony orchestra season is the performance of P. I. Tchaikovsky's *1812 Overture* that concludes the River Festival. The Wichita Pops series features the performances on the "mighty" Wurlitzer organ, which was housed in the New York Paramount Theater. The Metropolitan Ballet's season of concerts always includes a staging of Tchaikovsky's popular *Nutcracker Ballet* during the Christmas season.

Live theater is popular in Wichita. Music Theater of Wichita features Broadway guest artists performing with a resident company at Century II; the summer season includes five productions in all. Wichita Community Theater presents drama and in the summer creates "Comedia" spoofs of current local and national events. The Crown-Uptown Dinner Theater hosts professional performances of Broadway shows. Wichita Children's Theater sponsors shows performed by children for children.

Museums in the Wichita area include the Children's Museum of Wichita, the Fellow-Reeve Museum at Friends University, the Great Plains Transportation Museum, and the Indian Center Museum. The Wichita Art Museum holds the Murdock collection of American art and a sculpture deck; the Ulrich Museum of Art is on The Wichita State University campus.

Festivals and Holidays

The Wichita River Festival, the city's major event, schedules more than seventy events in a ten-day celebration centered on the Arkansas River in May. Held in conjunction with the festival is an art and book fair that features arts and crafts from more than two hundred participating artists. Also scheduled for May is the three-day Kansas Polkatennial. The Old Cowtown Museum presents music and 1870s saloon shows on the weekends from June to Labor Day; the museum also sponsors the 1876 Independence Day Celebration during the last weekend in June with patriotic music, a parade, and political oratory. The Fourth of July Celebration culminates with a musical synchronized fireworks show at Cessna Stadium. Traditional native American dancing is featured at the Indian Pow-wow in July. A Saturday is selected each summer on which citizens can pretend they are oceanside: tons of sand are dumped outside the convention center, firehoses are turned on, and a bodybuilding contest is held.

The Wichita Arts Festival is a weekend event in September celebrated with dance, theater, music, and art. The Mexican Independence Day Celebration is held in September followed by the Wichita Asian Festival in October. At the Old Cowtown Museum in October the Old Sedgwick County Fair recreates a 1870s Wichita fair. Oktoberfest is a three-day festival featuring German food, drink, entertainment, Volksmarch, and sporting events. The International Holiday Festival takes place in November. A Victorian Christmas celebration is held at Cowtown Museum from Thanksgiving through Christmas. Wichita has been hosting the Miss USA Pageant since 1990.

Sports for the Spectator

Wichita's two professional sports teams are the Wichita Wings, an indoor soccer team that plays at the Kansas Coliseum, and the Wichita Pilots, a semi-professional Double-A minor league baseball team in the Texas League that plays its home schedule at the Lawrence-Dumont Stadium. The Wichita State University baseball team consistently earns national ranking and holds the record for most victories in a season. Wichita State also fields winning basketball teams in National Collegiate Athletic Association play. The National Baseball Congress is the nation's largest amateur baseball tournament and has been held in Wichita since 1931.

The Wichita International Raceway sponsors drag racing on Saturdays during the summer while 81 Speedway features auto races on Saturday and Sunday evenings. Parimutuel greyhound racing action takes place at Wichita Greyhound Park. Wichita has been the choice for the Coleman International Ski Tournament on the Arkansas River. Wichita is also one of the cities on the Virginia Slims Tour, a women's professional tennis competition. The Kansas Special Olympics brings twenty-five hundred athletes to Wichita each summer. Lake Afton is the site of the annual Grand Prix automobile racing team competition.

Sports for the Participant

Wichita maintains 136 municipal parks on 2,990 acres for such activities as volleyball, croquet, softball, and soccer. One hundred seven public tennis courts are augmented by two private clubs; Riverside Tennis Center has been named one of the best public complexes in the country by the U.S. Tennis Association. For golfers, eleven public and seven private courses are located in the area. Fishing and boating are permitted in authorized areas (El Dorado Lake is said to be the spot for prime bass fishing), and water skiing is allowed at Nims Bridge, North Riverside Park. A free fitness trail with twenty exercise stations is maintained in Sim Park. Cycling and rollerskating can be enjoyed in designated areas along the Arkansas River. The Soccer Club operates a regulation size indoor field for practice and league play.

Shopping and Dining

The Wichita area's sixty-one shopping centers and malls include the state's two largest malls and the world's largest western store. Wichita is an antiques center; a number of antique stores and shops are located in historic houses and in the downtown district. Wichita Old Town, a historic warehouse district, has been restored and offers shops and restaurants. Shoppers enjoy the Downtown Farm and Art Market in the summer. Wichita restaurants are famous for steaks, prime rib, and barbecue beef, but dining choices also include international cuisine such as Italian, French, Chinese, Mexican, and Indian.

Visitor Information: Wichita Convention and Visitors Bureau, 100 South Main, Suite 100, Wichita, KS 67202; telephone (316)265-2800

Convention Facilities

The principal meeting and convention facility in Wichita is the Century II Convention Center, which houses four multipurpose halls and a six-hundred-seat theater. The complex contains a total of 198,500 square feet of open floor space that will accommodate 750 exhibit booths; the Convention Hall seats 5,244 people, and twenty-four meeting rooms seat from 30 to 5,244 people. Utilized separately or combined with the Convention Hall is the forty-five-thousand-square-foot Exhibition Hall; the Expo Hall, with ninety-three thousand square feet, also opens onto the Convention Hall. The Century II Concert Hall can be used as a large convention meeting room. Banquet facilities and adjacent parking are available.

Additional meeting accommodations can be found at hotels and motels in the metropolitan area.

Convention Information: Wichita Convention and Visitors Bureau, 100 South Main, Suite 100, Wichita, KS 67202; telephone (316)265-2800

Transportation

Approaching the City

Mid-Continent Airport, a twelve-minute drive from downtown, is the destination for most air travelers to Wichita. Served by about ten commercial carriers with daily direct and connecting flights from most cities throughout the United States, the airport has recently been renovated. Seven general aviation facilities are located within a 25-mile radius of the city.

A network of interstate, federal, and state highways links Wichita with the East and West Coasts as well as the Canadian and Mexican borders. Interstates I-35 and I-135 pass directly through metropolitan Wichita, connecting the city with I-40, I-44, and I-70. Major U.S. highways are 54 and 81; state routes include K-42, K-2, K-15, K-254, K-96, and the Kansas Turnpike.

Amtrak passenger service is available at the nearby Newton depot.

Traveling in the City

Public bus transportation on Starline Transit Services is operated by the Metropolitan Transportation Authority, providing routes within a quarter of a mile of 90 percent of city residents; handicapped service is available. A new Transit Center was scheduled to open in 1993.

Communications

Newspapers and Magazines

Wichita's daily newspaper is *The Wichita Eagle-Beacon,* which appears mornings and Sunday. The *Wichita Business Journal* is the city's weekly business newspaper. Special-interest newspapers and magazines published in Wichita focus on a variety of topics, such as business and economics, aging, antiques and art collectibles, aviation for farmers, shopping news, and community affairs.

Television and Radio

Three television stations affiliated with the major commercial networks and one public television station are received in Wichita; residents also receive programming from a station based in neighboring Hutchinson. Cable service is available. Twenty-three AM and FM radio stations serve the Wichita metropolitan area with music, news, information, and public interest features.

Media Information: The Wichita Eagle-Beacon, 825 East Douglas, 825 E. Douglas, Wichita, KS 67209; telephone (316)268-6000

MICHIGAN

Ann Arbor 193
Detroit 203
Grand Rapids 219
Lansing 231

The State in Brief

Nickname: Wolverine State; Great Lakes State
Motto: *Si quaeris peninsulam amoemam circumspice*
(If you seek a pleasant peninsula, look about you)

Flower: Apple blossom
Bird: Robin

Area: 96,810 square miles (1990; U.S. rank: 11th)
Elevation: 572 feet to 1,980 feet above sea level
Climate: Temperate with well-defined seasons, tempered by surrounding water; colder in upper peninsula

Admitted to Union: January 26, 1837
Capital: Lansing
Head Official: Governor John Engler (R) (until 1995)

Population
  1970: 8,881,826
  1980: 9,262,000
  1990: 9,368,000
  Percent change 1980–1990: 0.4%
  U.S. rank in 1990: 8th
  Percent of residents born in state: 77.8%
  Density: 163.6 people per square mile (1990; U.S. rank: 14th)
  1991 FBI Crime Index Total: 575,013

Racial and Ethnic Characteristics (1990)
  White: 7,756,000
  Black: 13.9%
  American Indian, Eskimo, Aleut: 0.60%
  Asian and Pacific Islander: 1.13%
  Hispanic (may be of any race): 2.17%

Age Characteristics (1990)
  Population under 5 years old: 717,000
  Population 5 to 17 years old: 1,767,000
  Percent of population 65 years and older: 11.9%
  Median age: 33.6 years
  Voting-age population (1988): 6,805,000 (53.9% of whom cast votes for president)

Vital Statistics
  Total number of births (1992): 138,968
  Total number of deaths (1992): 79,307 (of which, 1,459 were infants under the age of 1 year)
  AIDS cases reported, 1981–1990: 1,795 (U.S. rank: 15th)

Economy
  Major industries: Manufacturing; trade; finance, insurance, and real estate; services
  Unemployment rate: 8.5% (September 1992)
  Per capita income: $14,154 (1989)
  Median household income: $31,020 (1989)
  Total number of families: 2,458,481 (10.2% of which had incomes below the poverty level; 1989)
  Income tax rate: 4.6% of all taxable income
  Sales tax rate: 4.0%

Ann Arbor

The City in Brief

Founded: 1824 (incorporated, 1833)

Head Official: Mayor Ingrid Sheldon (R) (since 1993)

City Population
 1970: 100,000
 1980: 107,966
 1990: 109,592
 Percent change, 1980–1990: 1.5%
 U.S. rank in 1980: 146th
 U.S. rank in 1990: 170th

Metropolitan Area Population (PMSA)
 1970: 234,103
 1980: 264,740
 1990: 283,000
 Percent change, 1980–1990: 6.9%
 U.S. rank in 1980: 6th (CMSA)
 U.S. rank in 1990: 6th (CMSA)

Area: 25.9 square miles (1990)
Elevation: 802 feet above sea level
Average Annual Temperature: 49.2° F
Average Annual Precipitation: 30.67 inches (mean)

Major Economic Sectors: Government, services, manufacturing, trade
Unemployment Rate: 5.0% (September 1992)
Per Capita Income: $14,684 (1989)
1992 (2nd Quarter) ACCRA Average House Price: Not reported
1992 (2nd Quarter) ACCRA Cost of Living Index: Not reported
1991 FBI Crime Index Total: 6,991

Major Colleges and Universities: University of Michigan

Daily Newspaper: *Ann Arbor News*

Michigan—Ann Arbor

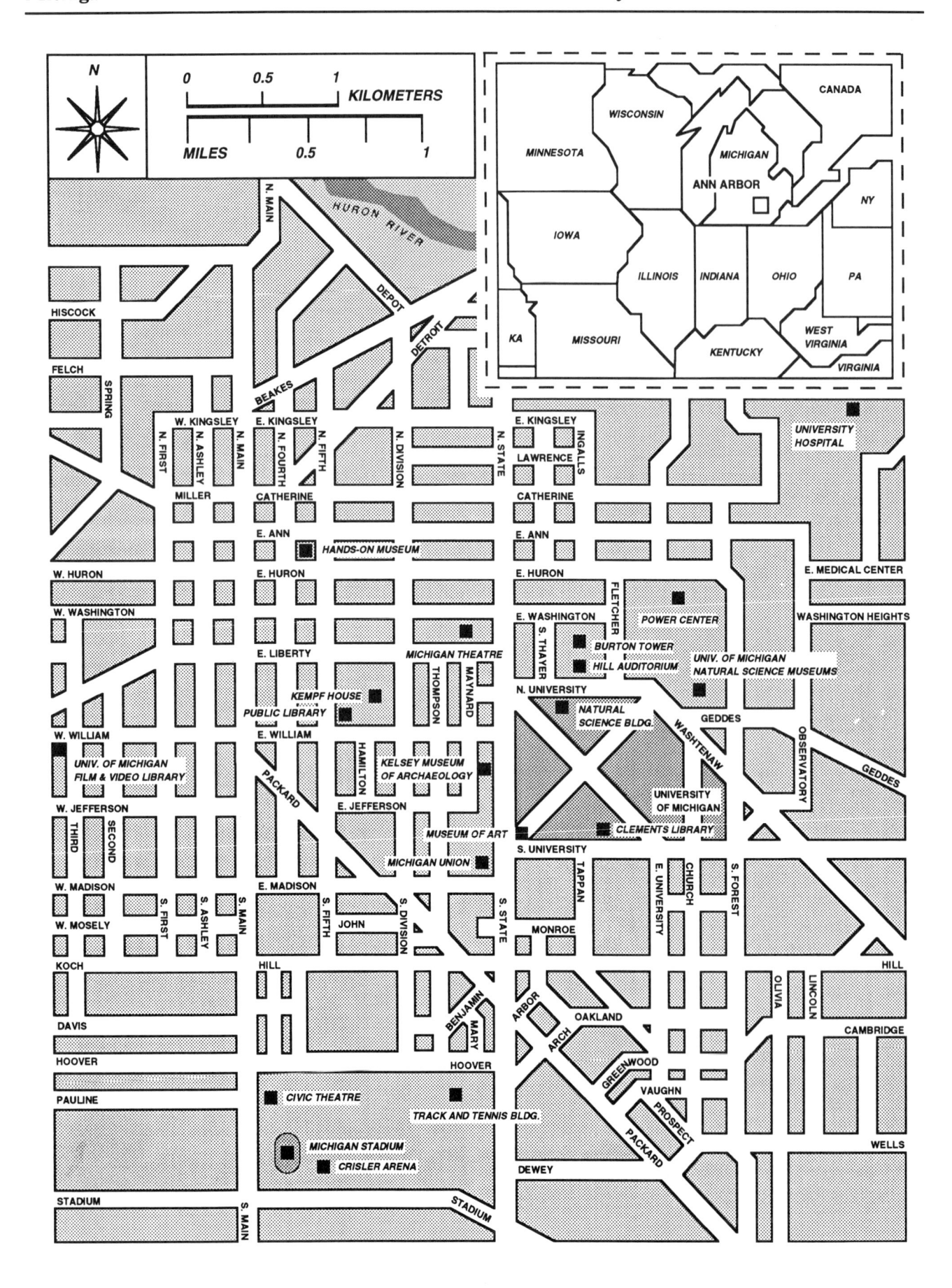

Introduction

The seat of Washtenaw County, Ann Arbor is part of a metropolitan statistical area that includes Detroit. Ann Arbor is the home of the University of Michigan, nationally recognized for a tradition of excellence in education. Having gained prominence in high-technology research and development, Ann Arbor is among the fastest-growing cities in the state of Michigan.

Geography and Climate

Ann Arbor is located on the Huron River approximately 40 miles west of Detroit in the heart of southeastern Michigan, surrounded by rivers, lakes, forests, and farmland. The continental climate is characterized by four distinct seasons.

Area: 25.9 square miles (1990)

Elevation: 802 feet above sea level

Average Annual Temperature: 49.2° F

Average Annual Precipitation: 30.67 inches (mean)

History

Easterners Found Settlement; Industry Attracts Immigrants

By some accounts, Virginians John and Ann Allen and New Yorkers Elisha and Ana Rumsey arrived in the southeastern Michigan Territory in 1824 at a place named Allen's Creek. The men built an arbor for the wild grapevines they found there and named their settlement Anns' Arbor in honor of their wives. According to an unsubstantiated story, however, the settlement was named after a mysterious young woman guide named Ann D'Arbeur who led parties from Detroit westward into the wilderness as early as 1813. Local native Americans called the settlement "Kaw-goosh-kaw-nick" after the sound of John Allen's gristmill. Settlers from Virginia and New York and immigrants from Ireland and Germany soon arrived as other mills, a tannery, and a general store were opened. Ann Arbor was made the seat of Washtenaw County in 1827; it was incorporated as a village in 1833 and chartered as a city in 1851. Ann Arbor's strategic location on the Huron River, the Territorial Road, and the Michigan Central Railroad contributed to its development as a trading center.

City Becomes Site of Major American University

The most significant event in the city's history was the relocation of the University of Michigan from Detroit to Ann Arbor in 1841 by the new state legislature after Ann Arbor citizens effectively lobbied for the move. But it was not until 1852 that the university's first president, Henry Philip Tappan, was appointed. President Tappan broke from academia's traditional classical curriculum and introduced a scientific program and elective courses. Erastus Otis Haven, the university's second president, secured an annual state subsidy to bring the institution's finances under control while President James Burrill Angell's administration added new buildings and programs during a thirty-eight-year tenure. Today the University of Michigan is regarded as one of the nation's top public universities, noted for its undergraduate education, research and graduate programs, and athletic teams that compete in the Big Ten Conference.

The university has been the site of historically significant political announcements. Senator John F. Kennedy introduced his plan for a Peace Corps on the steps of the university's Student Union during his 1960 presidential campaign, and President Lyndon Baines Johnson unveiled his Great Society program at commencement exercises there in 1964. A high proportion of Michigan graduates have become astronauts; in fact, during the *Apollo 15* flight a flag was planted on the moon in recognition of University of Michigan alumni astronauts. The influence of the University of Michigan is such that Ann Arbor is the highest ranked community in the United States for the educational and medical facilities available to its residents.

High-technology research and development has contributed to the growth in Ann Arbor's population, which also includes an increasing number of residents who commute to work in the Detroit area.

Historical Information: Washtenaw County Historical Society, P.O. Box 3336, Ann Arbor, MI 48106; telephone (313)662-9092

Population Profile

Metropolitan Area Residents (PMSA)
1970: 234,103
1980: 264,740
1990: 283,000
Average annual percent change, 1980–1988: 0.1%
U.S. rank in 1980: 6th (CMSA)
U.S. rank in 1990: 6th (CMSA)

City Residents
1970: 100,000
1980: 107,966
1990: 109,592 (of which, 54,204 were males, and 55,388 were females)
Percent change, 1980–1990: 1.9%
U.S. rank in 1980: 146th
U.S. rank in 1990: 170th (State rank: 7th)

Density: 4,231.4 people per square mile (1990)

Racial and ethnic characteristics (1990)
  White: 89,841
  Black: 9,905
  American Indian, Eskimo, Aleut: Not reported
  Asian and Pacific Islander: 8,424
  Hispanic (may be of any race): 2,827

Percent of residents born in state: Not available

Age characteristics (1990)
  Population under 5 years old: 6,357
  Population 5 to 9 years old: 5,378
  Population 10 to 14 years old: 4,533
  Population 15 to 19 years old: 11,461
  Population 20 to 24 years old: 21,120
  Population 25 to 29 years old: 12,768
  Population 30 to 34 years old: 9,956
  Population 35 to 39 years old: 8,691
  Population 40 to 44 years old: 7,238
  Population 45 to 49 years old: 4,972
  Population 50 to 54 years old: 3,410
  Population 55 to 59 years old: 3,058
  Population 60 to 64 years old: 2,769
  Population 65 to 69 years old: 2,508
  Population 70 to 74 years old: 1,851
  Population 75 to 79 years old: 1,514
  Population 80 to 84 years old: 1,018
  Population 85 years and over: 990
  Median age: 27.1 years

Births (1988)
  Total number: 1,311

Deaths (1988)
  Total number: 410 (of which, 10 were infants under the age of 1 year)

Money income (1989)
  Per capita income: $14,684
1991 FBI Crime Index Total: 6,991

Municipal Government

The City of Ann Arbor operates under a mayor-city manager form of government. Eleven council members, from whose number a mayor is appointed, are elected to two-year terms.

Head Official: Mayor Ingrid Sheldon (R) (since 1993; current term expires April 1997)

Total Number of City Employees: 1,598 (1993)

City Information: City of Ann Arbor, Office of the City Administrator, 100 North Fifth Avenue, P.O. Box 8647, Ann Arbor, MI 48107; telephone (313)994-2650

Economy

Major Industries and Commercial Activity

The Ann Arbor metropolitan area economic base is distributed among the manufacturing, non-manufacturing, and education and government sectors. Since 1970 manufacturing has declined (although it still provides 30 percent of employment) reflecting a decreased dependence on automobile manufacturing. At the same time services and high technology industries (more than one-hundred companies) have increased; more than one-thousand new jobs have been created annually in these industries since 1980.

Ann Arbor is now the western anchor of high-technology corridors extending from Detroit along I-94 and M-14. Aiding the increase in firms involved in research, development, or testing is the proximity of the University of Michigan and Eastern Michigan University in Ypsilanti, which provide technical resources and an educated workforce. Principal high-technology industries include business services, computer and data processing, and instrument development.

Items and goods produced: ball bearings, springs, baling presses, drill heads, tapping and reaming machinery, advertising novelties, precision instruments, awnings

Incentive Programs—New and Existing Companies

State programs—Incentives on the state level include tax abatements, tax-exempt revenue bonds, public loans, and grants. State-sponsored job training programs, recently revamped through the $25 million Michigan Adult Education Training Initiative, include the Job Training Partnership Act, Displaced Homemakers program, summer youth employment programs, and pre-college programs in engineering and sciences. The State Department of Commerce administers a $1.2 million Training Incentive Fund, which provides assistance to employers wishing to upgrade the skills of their current work force. Other programs include Targeted Jobs Tax Credits, and adult and vocational education.

Local programs—The Washtenaw Development Council is a centralized, free information source for expanding industrial, technological, and major commercial businesses. The Ann Arbor Area Chamber of Commerce operates an incubator for start-up businesses among other services. Also available locally are customized job training programs.

Economic Development Information: Washtenaw County Metropolitan Planning Commission, 305 County Building, Ann Arbor, MI 48107; telephone (313)994-2435

Development Projects

With the economic slowdown of the late 1980s and early 1990s, development in Ann Arbor focused on small projects and the expansion of existing buildings rather than large projects. Projects completed included the building of a 44,500-square-foot office building near downtown; South Main Market at 20,000 square feet; a 127,000-square-foot retail development anchored by Kroger's; a 70,000-square-foot Art Van furniture store; the Atrium, a 100,000-square-foot office building in the Briarwood Mall; and Michigan Health, a 65,000-square-foot research facility. Projects pending or approved in 1993 included a restaurant/bank complex at the Saline Road/I-94 intersection; the expansion of student housing at the University of Michigan; a senior housing project proposed by Zion Lutheran Church; and Arbor Hills, a residential area consisting of 250 single-family units.

According to the Washtenaw County Metropolitan Planning Commission, future growth in the area will concentrate in and around existing cities and villages; one aim is to enhance the viability of established central business districts.

Commercial Shipping

Air cargo service is available locally at Willow Run Airport and within a short drive at Detroit Metropolitan Airport. Conrail and three other railroads provide rail freight shipping, and the city is served by six trucking companies. Within a fifty-minute drive are the international port facilities of Detroit and Monroe.

Labor Force and Employment Outlook

Ann Arbor employers draw on a pool of well-educated, highly skilled, reasonably priced workers who indulge in few work stoppages. These workers include University of Michigan graduates reluctant to leave the city after graduation and willing to work for less money in exchange for the high quality of life in a small-town setting experienced there. The population is expected to increase by 50 percent over the period 1990–2015. The outlook for technology companies serving the electronics, medical, and education markets is very good.

The following is a summary of data regarding the Ann Arbor metropolitan area labor force as of September 1992.

Size of non-agricultural labor force: 172,500

Number of workers employed in . . .
  mining: not reported
  construction: 4,000
  manufacturing: 36,000
  transportation and public utilities: 5,200
  wholesale and retail trade: 32,100
  finance, insurance, and real estate: 5,000
  services: 38,400
  government: 51,600

Average hourly earnings of production workers employed in manufacturing: $15.93

Unemployment rate: 5.0%

Largest employers	Number of employees
University of Michigan	16,643
General Motors Corp.	12,434
University of Michigan Medical Center	10,132
Ford Motor Company	7,202
Catherine McAuley Health Center	3,220

Cost of Living

Health care costs in Ann Arbor are well above the national norm, a reflection of the high-cost, high-technology care available at the University of Michigan Medical Center. According to local real estate experts, the median house value in Ann Arbor in 1990 was $96,000.

In July 1993 the Michigan legislature passed a bill cutting residents' property taxes an average of 60 to 65 percent, beginning with the summer 1994 tax bills. The tax cut, the largest in Michigan history, was to be accomplished by eliminating local and intermediate school district operating millages. The legislature was then considering a number of options to restore money for schools, including sales taxes on services and entertainment, an increase in the state sales tax, or a statewide millage.

The following is a summary of data regarding several key cost of living factors in the Ann Arbor area as of mid-1993.

1992 (2nd Quarter) Cost of Living Index: Not reported

1992 (2nd Quarter) ACCRA Average House Price: Not reported

State income tax rate: 4.6% of all taxable income

State sales tax rate: 4.0%

Local income tax rate: None

Local sales tax rate: None

Property tax rate: $38.70 per $1,000 of assessed value (July 1991); assessed twice yearly

Economic Information: Washtenaw County Metropolitan Planning Commission, 305 County Building; Ann Arbor, MI 48107; telephone (313)994-2435

Education and Research

Elementary and Secondary Schools

The Ann Arbor school district is administered by a nine-member nonpartisan board that appoints a superintendent. The major emphasis of the system is on early childhood education, mathematics, science, and technology.

The following is a summary of data regarding the Ann Arbor public schools as of the 1991–1992 school year.

Total enrollment: 14,564

Number of facilities
  elementary schools: 20
  junior high schools: 5
  senior high schools: 4 (2 comprehensive and 2 alternative)

Student/teacher ratio: kindergarten, 20.5:1; grades 1–5, 23.9:1; middle school, 17.8:1; high school, 19.2:1

Teacher salaries
  minimum: $25,350
  maximum: $55,160

Funding per pupil: $7,052

The Ann Arbor area is also served by several private and religiously affiliated schools.

Public Schools Information: Ann Arbor Public Schools, 2555 South State Street, South, Ann Arbor, MI 48104; telephone (313)994-2200

Colleges and Universities

In Ann Arbor education extends to all facets of life: social, cultural, and economic. The city is home to the University of Michigan and Concordia College; located in neighboring Ypsilanti are Eastern Michigan University, Cleary College, and Washtenaw Community College.

At the heart of the Ann Arbor community is the University of Michigan, recognized as one of the nation's foremost public institutions of higher learning; twelve of its departments have been ranked among the top ten in the country by the American Council on Education. The university offers a complete range of programs leading to associate, baccalaureate, master's, and doctorate degrees in seventeen schools and colleges. Primary areas of study include liberal arts, architecture and planning, art, business administration, education, engineering, music, natural resources, nursing, pharmacy, dentistry, law, medicine, information and library studies, public health, and social work. Concordia College, affiliated with the Lutheran Church-Missouri Synod, provides associate and undergraduate programs in such fields as business management, education, and theology. Eastern Michigan University houses the College of Technology, and Washtenaw Community College specializes in vocational and technical training and is the site of a Robotics Repair Program.

Libraries and Research Centers

Approximately twenty-five libraries and research centers, maintained by a variety of organizations and agencies, are located in Ann Arbor. The Ann Arbor Public Library, part of the public school system and recently expanded at a cost of $9.3 million, maintains holdings of more than 450,000 volumes in addition to more than one-thousand periodicals, plus tapes, films, and compact discs. The library operates three branches and a bookmobile, serves as a depository for state documents, and houses special collections in black studies and basic education, among others fields. The Washtenaw County Library is the headquarters of the Huron Valley Library System. With holdings of more than forty thousand volumes, the library houses a facility for the blind and the physically handicapped; special services include a low-vision center, various aids for the handicapped, homebound service, volunteer taping, and a video library.

The Gerald R. Ford Library and Museum contains materials pertaining to the life and career of Gerald R. Ford, former President of the United States. The non-circulating collection, which is open to the public, includes nine-thousand books, films, audio and video tapes, manuscripts, and oral history records.

The University of Michigan library system, one of the largest research library systems in the country, includes facilities for all colleges within the university as well as for individual academic departments. Holdings of the University Libraries total more than 6.5 million volumes; nearly forty special collections include such subjects as American, British, and European literature, radical protest and reform literature, manuscripts, theater materials, and United States and Canadian government documents. The University of Michigan School of Business Administration maintains the Kresge Library; among the nine facilities within the Kresge Library system are the Law Library, the Bentley Historical Library, and the Transportation Institute Library.

Other libraries in Ann Arbor are affiliated with Concordia College, Washtenaw Community College, and corporations, hospitals, and churches.

Research centers are associated primarily with state and federal government agencies. Among the major research centers are the Environmental Research Institute of Michigan, the Institute for Social Research Library, the Michigan Department of Natural Resources Institute for Fisheries Research Library, the National Oceanic and Atmospheric Administration Great Lakes Environmental Research Laboratory, and the Van Oosten Library of the United States Fish and Wildlife Service.

Public Library Information: Ann Arbor Public Library, 343 South Fifth Avenue, Ann Arbor, MI 48104-2293; telephone (313)994-2333

Health Care

A vital part of the metropolitan Ann Arbor health care community is the University of Michigan Medical Center, a treatment, referral, and teaching complex that houses several facilities: University Hospital, Women's Hospital, Mott Children's Hospital, Holden Perinatal Hospital, Taubman Health Center, and the Medical School as well as emergency services, an adult psychiatric hospital, an anatomical donations program, a burn center, an outpatient psychiatric unit, and an eye care center. In a survey of more than one-thousand leading doctors conducted by *U.S. News & World Report* and reported in June 1992, the University of Michigan Medical Center was rated best in the country for care in otolaryngology. The staff includes more than 1,550 physicians and 1,700 nurses.

Offering general care are Catherine McAuley Health Center, which operates the Hospice of Washtenaw, home health services, and an Alzheimer's Care and Treatment Center; and St. Joseph Mercy Hospital, which maintains branch clinics in the city and the county. Public and private chemical dependency, mental health, urgent care, physical therapy, and fitness programs are also available in Ann Arbor.

Health Care Information: Washtenaw County Medical Society, telephone (313)668-6241

Recreation

Sightseeing

A number of museums as well as buildings of architectural significance are located on the University of Michigan campus. The Rackham Auditorium, which covers two city blocks, is made of Indiana limestone, with bronze window and door frames, a copper-sheathed roof, and art-deco interior. The Museum of Natural Science houses the state's largest collection of dinosaur bones, including a fifteen-foot-tall dinosaur that was the forerunner of the Tyrannosaur, and more than two-hundred species of birds native to Michigan. The most popular exhibit is the Michigan Mastodon, an elephant-like creature that became extinct more than six thousand years ago.

The Kelsey Museum of Ancient and Medieval Archaeology in Newberry Hall exhibits artifacts, statues, and glass discovered on university excavations in Egypt and Iraq. The Museum of Art in Alumni Memorial Hall exhibits a diverse permanent collection that includes a number of works by James Abbott McNeill Whistler. The Burton Memorial Tower is the world's third-largest carillon and presents weekly concerts during the summer.

The Ann Arbor Hands-On Museum displays 170 participatory exhibits on the sciences and arts; it is housed in a century-old former fire house. The U-M Exhibit Museum, a natural science museum devoted to Michigan's prehistoric past, maintains exhibits on minerals and biology, a hall of evolution, and a planetarium. Matthaei Botanical Garden, the university's conservatory and outdoor garden, is a favorite winter oasis.

Domino's Farms Center for Local History, paying tribute to Frank Lloyd Wright and other interests of Tom Monaghan, Domino's Pizza chief executive office, Cobblestone Farm, and Kempf House are among the area's other tourist attractions. Ann Arbor is rich in architectural history; among some of the city's distinctive buildings are St. Andrew's Church and several homes dating from the early to mid-nineteenth century. In nearby Ypsilanti at Willow Run Airport, the Yankee Air Museum maintains a women in aviation exhibit as well as displays tracing the history of aviation, including both World Wars, the Korean conflict, and the Vietnam conflict.

Arts and Culture

The city of Ann Arbor and the University of Michigan offer a broad selection of music, dance, theater, and cinema. The university's Hill Auditorium is considered to rank with the Kennedy Center in Washington, D.C., and Carnegie Hall in New York City as one of the nation's premier performing arts facilities. Built in 1913 and featuring excellent acoustics and an innovative cooling and heating system, Hill Auditorium houses the Henry Freize Pipe Organ, which was originally unveiled at the 1883 Chicago World's Fair. The University Musical Society, founded in 1879, schedules music and dance concerts featuring international artists and performing groups.

The Ann Arbor Symphony Orchestra plays a season of concerts at the newly renovated Michigan Theater, where the Ann Arbor Chamber Orchestra also presents a series of concerts of classical and contemporary music featuring young artists. Ars Musica performs Baroque music; The Comic Opera Guild is a local amateur company that is the only one of its kind to tour nationally. The university's Gilbert and Sullivan Society presents light opera productions in the spring and winter.

The Ann Arbor Civic Theatre, drawing on experienced local artists, stages six dramatic productions a season. The Young People's Theater, recruiting young people from across the country, is an outlet for students to write and perform their own works. Since 1954 the Ann Arbor Civic Ballet has programmed dance performances. The Performance Network is a local studio and theater space for original work by local artists creating theater, film, video, music, and dance. Ann Arbor supports twelve local art galleries and seven film theaters, including the Miehigan Theater, which shows classic film. In addition, eight film societies are active in the city.

Festivals and Holidays

The Ann Arbor Film Festival is a week-long event held in March. The juried Spring Art Fair brings together hundreds of artists in all media at the University of Michigan Track and Tennis Building on an early April weekend; a Winter Art Fair is held in November. More than three-hundred dealers gather at the Ann Arbor Antiques Market to sell antiques and collectibles every Sunday from April through November. More than four-hundred dealers participate in the Saline Antique Show in nearby Saline, held thrice-yearly in April, July, and October.

"Taste of Ann Arbor" on Main Street on a Sunday in June offers specialties from participating Ann Arbor restaurants. The Summer Festival, taking place over several weeks in June and July, presents mime, dance, music, and theater.

The Summer Art Fair brings artists from around the country to Ann Arbor to exhibit and sell their work in three separate fairs running simultaneously for four days in July. Held at several locations in the city, the Medieval Festival features authentic Medieval music, dance, and costumes. One hundred fifty artists participate in the Christmas Art Fair at the University of Michigan Coliseum on Thanksgiving weekend.

Sports for the Spectator

The University of Michigan fields some of the finest college sports teams, which compete in the Big Ten athletic conference. The Michigan Wolverines football team plays home games at Michigan Stadium, the largest college-owned stadium in the country, and compete each season for the Big Ten championship and a berth in the Rose Bowl. Other University of Michigan team sports include basketball, wrestling, baseball, hockey, and swimming. Professional sporting events in nearby Detroit feature the Tigers (baseball), Pistons (basketball), Lions (football), Red Wings (hockey), and Express (soccer) competing in their respective leagues.

Sports for the Participant

Among the popular participatory sports that can be enjoyed in Ann Arbor are cycling, ice skating, racquetball, paddleball, handball, roller skating, downhill and cross-country skiing, swimming, and tennis. The Ann Arbor Department of Recreation and Parks maintains the city's more than 120 parks and sponsors programs for all age groups. The Dexter-Ann Arbor Half-Marathon and 10-K Run is sponsored by the Ann Arbor Track Club and held on a Saturday in May. Ann Arbor is one of the ten best cycling cities in North America, and the Ann Arbor Bicycle Touring Society is the state's largest group for cyclists. The Huron River can be fished and canoed, and golf is played at city and university-owned courses.

Shopping and Dining

Ann Arbor's Main Street area, consisting of several blocks of specialty shops and restaurants, forms the central commercial district. State Street, the university's major business district, consists of a cluster of retail stores, restaurants, and several record and book shops that include one of the nation's best independent book stores. Nickels Arcade, built in 1915 and modelled after a European arcade, houses shops and galleries. Kerrytown and the Farmers' Market are three restored historic buildings in the Kerrytown district that contain thirty-four semi-enclosed shops and other stores offering farm-fresh produce, baked goods, and craft items. Ann Arbor and nearby Ypsilanti are considered an antiques center.

The presence of a major state university in Ann Arbor helps explain the city's many fine restaurants and varied cuisines. Ann Arbor restaurants offer New American cuisine, traditional American fare, Northern Italian, French, Greek, and German menus; numerous other ethnic establishments serve diners as well. A number of restaurants are located in historic or unusual buildings, such as a train depot. Cafe, deli, and pub settings are also popular choices.

Visitor Information: Ann Arbor Convention and Visitors Bureau, 211 East Huron, Suite 6, Ann Arbor, MI; telephone (313)995-7281

Convention Facilities

The major convention and meeting facilities in metropolitan Ann Arbor are situated on the University of Michigan campus. The ballroom of the Michigan Union, containing more than six-thousand square feet of space, can accommodate thirty exhibit booths and seat 450 people for a banquet and 600 people in a theater setting. The union provides twenty-one meeting rooms that can be used as breakout rooms. The Rackham Auditorium and Amphitheater seat 1,129 people and 240 people respectively; galleries totalling nearly four-thousand square feet of space hold twenty-five exhibit booths; and the Assembly Hall hosts receptions for up to three-hundred participants. The Towsley Center for Continuing Medical Education in the medical complex offers two auditoriums, four meeting rooms, a reception area, and a dining room. The Chrysler Center for Continuing Education houses a 225-seat auditorium and four meeting rooms. Among other campus meeting sites for large and small groups are Crisler Arena, Hill Auditorium, Power Center for the Performing Arts, and the Track and Tennis Building.

Additional meeting facilities are available at the Corporate Training Center on the campus of Eastern Michigan University in Ypsilanti, Domino's Farms, and at several area hotels and motels. Nearly three-thousand hotel and motel rooms are available.

Convention Information: Ann Arbor Convention and Visitors Bureau, 211 East Huron, Suite 6, Ann Arbor, MI 48104; telephone (313)995-7281

Transportation

Approaching the City

The destination of the air traveler to Ann Arbor is most likely Detroit Metropolitan Airport, which is only twenty-five minutes east of the city; served by fourteen major commercial airlines, Detroit Metropolitan is the largest airport in Michigan. Local general aviation facilities include Ann Arbor City Airport and Willow Run Airport. Passenger rail transportation is available from Chicago three times daily.

Principal highways leading into Ann Arbor are east-west I-94 and M-14 and north-south U.S. 23.

Traveling in the City

Ann Arbor Transit Authority buses link all parts of the city. Downtown, Main Street, and the University of Michigan campus are easily explored on foot.

Communications

Newspapers and Magazines

The *Ann Arbor News,* which appears evenings Monday through Saturday and on Sunday morning, is Ann Arbor's daily newspaper. The *Ann Arbor Observer* is a monthly magazine offering features, profiles, historical articles, business items, restaurant reviews, and a listing of events and exhibits; it also publishes an annual City Guide. *Current,* available free at many locations, lists entertainment events.

Car and Driver, a popular magazine for automobile enthusiasts, is published monthly in Ann Arbor. Other special-interest magazines and scholarly journals cover such subjects as health care, Michigan history, religion, and Asian studies.

Television and Radio

With one television station broadcasting from the city, Ann Arbor receives several additional channels from surrounding cities such as Lansing and Detroit, three national affiliates, PBS, and three independents (including one that is black-owned and operated).

Seven AM and FM radio stations based in Ann Arbor furnish diverse programming choices, including jazz, rock, and contemporary music, news and information, and farm reports, as well as public broadcasting. Listeners also choose from stations in Detroit and other cities, including a Windsor (Ontario) station that broadcasts British Broadcasting Corporation programming, and five stations that broadcast classical music twenty-four hours a day.

Media Information: Ann Arbor News, 340 Huron Street, Ann Arbor, MI 48104; telephone (313)994-6989; *Ann Arbor Observer,* 201 Catherine, Ann Arbor, MI 48104; telephone (313)769-3175; and *Current,* 415 Detroit St., Ann Arbor, MI 48104; telephone (313)668-4404

Detroit

The City in Brief

Founded: 1701 (incorporated, 1815)

Head Official: Mayor Coleman A. Young (D) (since 1974)

City Population
 1970: 1,514,000
 1980: 1,203,339
 1990: 1,027,974
 Percent change, 1980–1990: −14.6%
 U.S. rank in 1980: 6th
 U.S. rank in 1990: 7th

Metropolitan Area Population
 1970: 4,788,000
 1980: 4,753,000
 1990: 4,665,236
 Percent change, 1980–1990: −1.8%
 U.S. rank in 1980: 6th
 U.S. rank in 1990: 6th

Area: 138.7 square miles (1990)

Elevation: 633 feet above sea level

Average Annual Temperature: 48.6° F

Average Annual Precipitation: 30.97 inches

Major Economic Sectors: Services; trade; manufacturing; finance, insurance, and real estate

Unemployment Rate: 8.9% (September 1992)

Per Capita Income: $9,443 (1989)

1992 (2nd Quarter) ACCRA Average House Price: Not reported

1992 (2nd Quarter) ACCRA Cost of Living Index: Not reported

1991 FBI Crime Index Total: 127,080

Major Colleges and Universities: Wayne State University; University of Detroit-Mercy

Daily Newspapers: *Detroit Free Press*; *Detroit News*

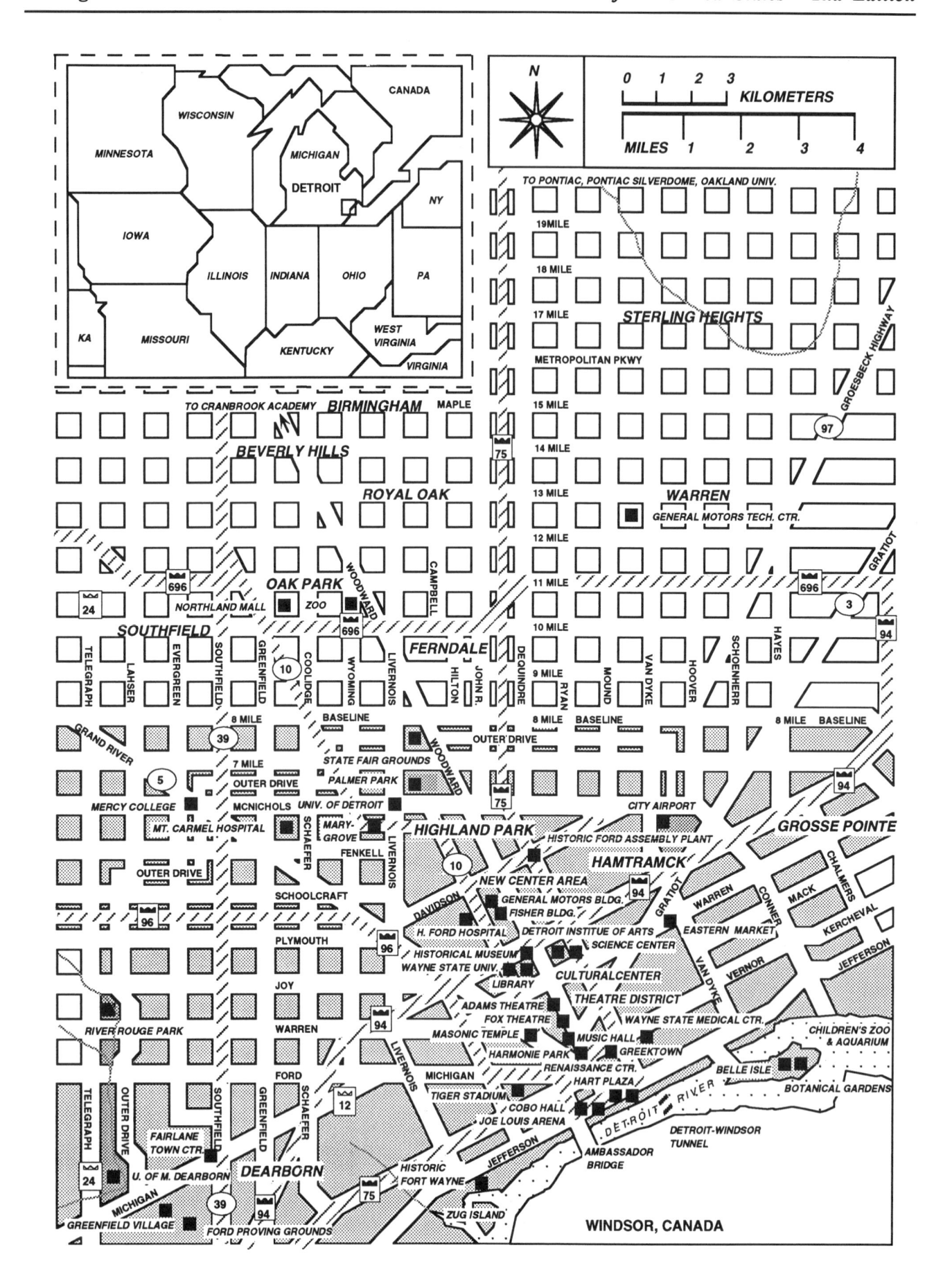

Michigan—Detroit *Cities of the United States • 2nd Edition*

Introduction

Detroit is the seat of Michigan's Wayne County and the center of a consolidated metropolitan statistical area that includes Ann Arbor. One of the oldest settlements in the Midwest, Detroit played an instrumental role in the development of the Northwest Territory. During the War of 1812 Detroit became the only major American city ever to surrender to a foreign power; in 1847 the city lost its status as state capital when the legislature moved the state headquarters to Lansing. Detroit was a leading regional economic power in the nineteenth century. The invention of the automobile and its mass production in Detroit headed by Henry Ford changed American and world culture. Today Detroit's position as the automobile capital of the world is being challenged by foreign competition.

Geography and Climate

Detroit is set on the Detroit River; the metropolitan area includes the St. Clair River, Lake St. Clair, and the west end of Lake Erie. The land is nearly flat, rising gently northwestward from the waterways, then becoming rolling terrain. The climate is influenced by the city's location near the Great Lakes and its position in a major storm track; climatic variations also arise from the urban heat island, the effect becoming most apparent at night, when temperatures downtown will remain significantly higher than those in suburban locations. Winter storms can bring combinations of rain, snow, freezing rain, and sleet with heavy snowfall possible at times. During the summer, storms pass to the north, allowing for intervals of warm, humid weather with occasional thunderstorms that are followed by days of mild, dry weather. Air pollution coming from heavy industry in the area is said to have been minimized with state-of-the-art pollution control efforts.

Area: 138.7 square miles (1990)

Elevation: 633 feet above sea level

Average Daily Temperatures: January, 28.1° F; July, 72.3° F; annual average, 48.6° F

Average Annual Precipitation: 30.97 inches

History

Riverside Stronghold Established by French

In July 1701, Antoine de la Mothe Cadillac and his party landed at a riverbank site chosen because the narrow strait there seemed strategically situated for protecting French fur trading interests in the Great Lakes. The river was called d'Etroit, a French word meaning "strait." Cadillac and his men built Fort Pontchartrain on the site, naming the fort after Comte de Pontchartrain, French King Louis XIV's minister of state; soon a palisaded riverfront village developed nearby. Cadillac named the settlement "ville d'etroit," or city of the strait. Eventually the name was simplified to Detroit.

The control of Detroit changed hands three times during the eighteenth century. At the conclusion of the French and Indian War, the resulting treaty specified the surrender of Detroit to Great Britain. Under Henry Hamilton, the settlement's British governor, armies of native Americans were encouraged to scalp frontier settlers for rewards, earning Hamilton the sobriquet, "Hair Buyer of Detroit." France's tribal allies, led by Ottawa chief Pontiac, plotted to capture Detroit; when the plot failed, they continued their siege of the fort.

At the end of the American Revolution, the United States claimed lands west of the Alleghenies by treaty, but the British refused to leave Detroit and other western forts, encouraging allied tribes to attack settlers. It was not until two years after General Anthony Wayne defeated the native Americans at the Battle of Fallen Timbers in 1796 that the British finally left Detroit. During the War of 1812 General William Hull turned Detroit's fort over to the British without a fight, thus making Detroit the only major American city ever to be occupied by a foreign power. The United States regained control of the settlement in 1813 following Oliver H. Perry's victory in the Battle of Lake Erie.

Manufacturing Center Becomes Automobile Capital

Detroit was incorporated as a town in 1802 and as a city in 1815. In 1805 Detroit was selected the capital of the newly created Michigan territory. On June 11, 1805, a fire totally destroyed the city, and while all residents survived, two-hundred wood structures were reduced to ashes. Local Catholic leader Father Gabriel Richard observed at the time, "Speramus meliora; resurget cineribus (We hope for better things; it will arise from the ashes)." His statement became the city's motto. Augustus B. Woodward, one of the new territory's judges, awarded a larger piece of land to each citizen who had lost his home. To create a street design for Detroit, Woodward selected Pierre Charles L'Enfant's plan for Washington, D.C.: a hexagon with a park in the middle and wide streets radiating outward in a hub-and-spoke pattern. As Detroit grew, additional hexagons could be added parallel to the original one. This idea was adopted then eventually abandoned and a grid street pattern was superimposed over the hexagonal design. Michigan gained statehood in 1837; ten years later, fearing Detroit's vulnerability to foreign invasion, the young legislature relocated Michigan's capital from Detroit to Lansing.

Detroit's early economic development was spurred by a combination of factors: the opening of the Erie Canal in 1826, the city's Great Lakes location, the increasing use of rail transport, the growing lumber and flour-milling industries, and the availability of a skilled labor force. The Detroit Anti-Slavery Society was organized in 1837 and the city was a station on the Underground Railroad. Abolitionist John Brown brought slaves to Detroit in 1859 and there purportedly planned with Frederick Douglass the notorious raid on Harpers Ferry, Virginia. During the Civil War Detroit provided supplies and provisions to the Union cause. By the end of the century Detroit had emerged as an important industrial and manufacturing center.

In 1896 Charles B. King determined Detroit's destiny when he drove a horseless carriage on the city streets. Soon Henry Ford introduced his own version of the conveyance, and Detroit was on its way to becoming the automobile capital of the world. Along with Ford, such automotive pioneers as W.C. Durant, Walter P. Chrysler, Ransom Olds, Henry Leland, and the Dodge brothers laid the foundation for the companies that emerged as the Big Three auto makers—Ford, General Motors, and Chrysler—by the latter half of the twentieth century.

Development Brings New Challenges

The automotive industry brought thousands of immigrants into Detroit during the 1920s. Then during the Great Depression the industry was severely shaken, leaving one-third of the workforce out of jobs in 1933. The rise of the union movement under the leadership of Walter Reuther led to the sit-down strikes in Detroit and Flint in 1937, resulting in anti-union violence. Federal legislation helped the United Automobile Workers win collective bargaining rights with General Motors and Chrysler in 1937 and with Ford Motor Company in 1941. During World War II, Detroit turned its energies to the war effort as Ford opened a bomber factory and Chrysler a tank plant, leading to a new nickname for Detroit—"the arsenal of democracy."

Detroit's racial tension, traceable to a race riot in 1863, erupted in 1943 when violence resulted in the death of thirty-five people and injury to more than one thousand. Much progress was made in solving Detroit's race problems after the 1943 outbreak. Like many urban areas in the late 1960s, however, the city was forced to confront the issue once again when civil disturbances exploded in July 1967: forty-three people were killed, hundreds injured, and entire city blocks burned to the ground. The organization New Detroit was founded as an urban coalition to resolve issues of education, employment, housing, and economic development, which were seen as the root causes of race problems.

In 1970 a group of business leaders formed Detroit Renaissance to address questions of Detroit's future. The following year the group, restructured under chairman Henry Ford II, announced plans for construction of the Renaissance Center, the world's largest privately financed project, as a symbol of the new Detroit. In 1974 Coleman A. Young, Detroit's first mayor of African-American descent, was elected to office; in 1993 he announced that he would not seek a sixth term.

Historical Information: Detroit Historical Museum, 5401 Woodward Avenue, Detroit, MI 48202; telephone (313)833-1805

Population Profile

Metropolitan Area Residents
1970: 4,788,000
1980: 4,753,000
1990: 4,665,236
Percent change, 1980–1990: –1.8%
U.S. rank in 1980: 6th
U.S. rank in 1990: 6th

City Residents
1970: 1,514,000
1980: 1,203,339
1990: 1,027,974 (of which, 476,814 were males, and 551,160 were females)
Percent change, 1980-1990: -14.6%
U.S. rank in 1980: 6th
U.S. rank in 1990: 7th (State rank: 1st)

Density: 7,411.5 people per square mile (1990)

Racial and ethnic characteristics (1990)
  White: 21.6%
  Black: 75.7%
  American Indian, Eskimo, Aleut: 0.4%
  Asian and Pacific Islander: 0.8%
  Hispanic (may be of any race): 2.8%

Percent of residents born in state: 68.0% (1990)

Age characteristics (1990)
  Population under 5 years old: 93,109
  Population 5 to 9 years old: 79,646
  Population 10 to 14 years old: 78,865
  Population 15 to 19 years old: 85,856
  Population 20 to 24 years old: 80,422
  Population 25 to 29 years old: 82,689
  Population 30 to 34 years old: 86,700
  Population 35 to 39 years old: 78,823
  Population 40 to 44 years old: 66,783
  Population 45 to 49 years old: 49,401
  Population 50 to 54 years old: 39,467
  Population 55 to 59 years old: 38,994
  Population 60 to 64 years old: 42,286
  Population 65 to 69 years old: 41,574
  Population 70 to 74 years old: 32,464
  Population 75 to 79 years old: 24,161
  Population 80 to 84 years old: 14,228
  Population 85 years and over: 12,506
  Median age: 30.7 years (1990)

Births (1988)
  Total number: 19,729

Deaths (1988)
  Total number: 12,617 (of which, 414 were infants under the age of 1 year)

Money income (1989)
  Per capita income: $9,443
  Median household income: $18,724
  Total households: 373,857
  Number of households with income of . . .
    less than $5,000: 60,104
    $5,000 to $9,999: 60,692
    $10,000 to $14,999: 40,846
    $15,000 to $24,999: 61,515
    $25,000 to $34,999: 48,501
    $35,000 to $49,999: 50,922
    $50,000 to $74,999: 36,093
    $75,000 to $99,999: 10,524
    $100,000 to $149,999: 3,685
    $150,000 or more: 975
  Percent of families below poverty level: 29.0% (71.8% of which were female householder families with related children under 5)
1991 FBI Crime Index Total: 127,080

Municipal Government

The government of the city of Detroit is administered by a mayor and a nine-member council; the mayor, who is not a member of council, and councilpersons are elected to four-year terms.

Head Official: Mayor Coleman A. Young (D) (since 1974; current term expires December 31, 1993)

Total Number of City Employees: 19,751 (1991)

City Information: City Government Telephone Number Assistance, telephone (313)224-3270

Economy

Major Industries and Commercial Activity

Automobile manufacturing continues to be a primary force in the Detroit economy, and Detroit is the nation's only older city that is home to a state-of-the-art auto assembly plant. In recent years, however, dependence on the auto industry has decreased—the city lost 39 percent of its manufacturing jobs in the 1980s—while the services sector has increased. More than 70 percent of the labor force is employed in non-manufacturing jobs in such areas as research and development; accounting, law, and financial services; computer services; and personnel and clerical support. The Henry Ford Health System is the sixth largest employer in the state and is a major research center. Detroit ranks among the five major financial centers in the United States; offices of all the "Big Eight" accounting firms are also located there. Among the nineteen Fortune 500 companies with headquarters in metropolitan Detroit are the General Motors Corporation, the Ford Motor Company, and Kmart; and, consistent with the city's prominent position in the international marketplace, more than four-hundred foreign firms are represented in Greater Detroit.

Items and goods produced: automobiles and automobile products, gray iron, machine tools and fixtures, ranges and heating devices, computing machines, foundry products, paints, varnishes, lacquers, chemicals, pleasure boats, paper and twine, air conditioning equipment, aircraft bearings and cushions, bolts, screws, nuts, boilers, tanks, ball bearings, tools, steel plates, flues and tubes, rubber goods

Incentive Programs—New and Existing Companies

Local programs—The Greater Detroit/Southeast Michigan Business Attraction and Expansion Council (BAEC) is a coalition of leaders in the public and private sectors, established in 1980 with the goal of coordinating regional economic development efforts. BAEC is currently implementing its Strategic Plan for the Economic Development of Southeast Michigan, adopted in 1984—in direct response to an economic recession, a high crime rate, and a negative national image of Detroit—which involves eight specific goals tied to economic improvement in Southeastern Michigan. According to a 1991 progress report, most of the goals are being met. Among BAEC's main functions is providing assistance to other economic development agencies in the form of research, marketing materials, and business attraction and expansion programs.

Also encouraging economic development is the Metropolitan Center for High Technology, a business and research incubator offering 160,000 square feet of leasable space, which is located five minutes north of the central business district.

State programs—Incentives on the state level include tax abatements, tax-exempt revenue bonds, public loans and grants. State-sponsored job training programs, recently revamped through the $25 million Michigan Adult Education Training Initiative, include the Job Training Partnership Act, Displaced Homemakers program, summer youth employment programs, and pre-college programs in engineering and sciences. The State Department of Commerce administers a $1.2 million Training Incentive Fund, which provides assistance to employers wishing to upgrade the skills of their current work force. Other programs include Targeted Jobs Tax Credits, and adult and vocational education.

Development Projects

One of the most dynamic changes in the area's economy is the addition of more than 24 million square feet of office space in office towers, parks, and downtown centers during the period 1986–1991. This represents a potential of 117,000 jobs added to the workforce, many in high-paying professions and services such as legal, financial, and research. Other projects completed in downtown Detroit in recent years include a small luxury hotel, an expansion that has doubled the exhibit areas of Cobo Convention Center, the addition of a third twenty-one-story tower to the Riverfront Apartments complex, and restoration of the historic Fox Theatre and Office Building. In the 1980s more than 110 new office, industrial, technical, and research parks were developed in the Detroit metropolitan area. Developments in the 1990s include the redevelopment of the Theater District and Harmonie Park (to include art galleries, residential units, and shops), and the opening of Victoria Park, the city's first new subdivision in decades. A Master Plan for the expansion of Detroit City Airport projects the expenditure of $378 million by the completion date of 2008. Southeastern Michigan's biggest construction project, the $250 million, government-funded Veterans Administration Hospital in Detroit's Medical Center district, was scheduled to open in the mid-1990s. Much of the construction that took place in Detroit during the 1980s and early 1990s was built with government aid.

Economic Development Information: Detroit Economic Growth Corporation, 600 First National Building, Detroit, MI 48226; telephone (313)963-2940; and, Central Business District Association, 700 Penobscot Building, Detroit, MI 48226; telephone (313)961-1403; and, Detroit Community and Economic Development Department, City of Detroit, 150 Michigan Avenue, Detroit, MI 48226; telephone (313)224-2560; and, Detroit/Wayne County Port Authority or Greater Detroit Foreign Trade Zone,

Cities of the United States • 2nd Edition   **Michigan—Detroit**

Downtown Detroit's People Mover.

Inc., Tower 200, Renaissance Center, Suite 650, Detroit, MI 48243; telephone (313)841-6700

Commercial Shipping

Detroit is a major international market. The Greater Detroit Foreign Trade Zone, the largest zone in the country, processes $1.65 billion in goods annually. The passage in 1989 of the United States/Canada Free Trade Agreement established the largest free trading block in the world, further expanding the parameters of the Detroit market. Detroit is adjacent to Windsor, Ontario, Canada.

The Port of Detroit, one of the busiest on the Great Lakes, has direct access to world markets via the Great Lakes/St. Lawrence Seaway System. The Port is comprised of seven privately-owned terminals with thirteen berths on the Detroit and Rouge Rivers. All types of cargo can be processed through port facilities; in 1990 cargo volume totalled more than three million tons. Service is provided by four tug and barge lines as well as two auxiliary companies, one of which operates a mail boat that is the only boat in the United States with its own zip code.

More than seven-hundred motor freight carriers utilize Greater Detroit's extensive highway system to transport goods to points throughout the United States and Canada. Trucking service is coordinated with that provided by the four rail lines maintaining facilities in Detroit. Air cargo service is available at Detroit Metropolitan Airport and Detroit City Airport.

Labor Force and Employment Outlook

A high percentage of Detroit's workers are professionals and technicians. While the city struggles to create jobs for the many unemployed, service jobs in the suburbs have expanded. Automobiles are expected to continue to be the primary economic influence. With the advent of the Free Trade Agreement, Detroit is seen as a logical major import-export point for American-Canadian goods.

The following is a summary of data regarding the Detroit metropolitan area labor force as of September 1992.

Size of non-agricultural labor force: 1,840,500

Number of workers employed in . . .
  mining: 500
  construction: 61,800
  manufacturing: 430,200
  transportation and public utilities: 87,000
  wholesale and retail trade: 432,900
  finance, insurance, and real estate: 107,000
  services: 506,300
  government: 214,800

Average hourly earnings of production workers employed in manufacturing: $16.38

Unemployment rate: 8.9%

Largest employers	*Number of employees*
Chrysler Corp. (automotive)	18,800
Detroit Medical Center	10,260
General Motors Corp. (automotive)	9,368
Henry Ford Health Care Corp.	7,765
NBD Bankcorp Inc. (bank holding company)	7,200
Wayne State University	5,060
Detroit Edison (utility)	4,035

Cost of Living

In July 1993 the Michigan legislature passed a bill cutting residents' property taxes an average of 60 to 65 percent, beginning with the summer 1994 tax bills. The tax cut, the largest in Michigan history, was to be accomplished by eliminating local and intermediate school district operating millages. The legislature was then considering a number of options to restore money for schools, including sales taxes on services and entertainment, an increase in the state sales tax, or a statewide millage.

The following is a summary of data regarding several key cost of living factors in the Detroit area as of mid-1993.

1992 (2nd Quarter) ACCRA Cost of Living Index: Not reported

1992 (2nd Quarter) ACCRA Average House Price: Not reported

State income tax rate: 4.6% of taxable income

State sales tax rate: 4.0%

Local income tax rate: 3.0% residential; 1.5% non-residential

Local sales tax rate: None

Property tax rate: $80.16 per $1,000 assessed valuation

Economic Information: Greater Detroit Chamber of Commerce, 600 West Lafayette, Detroit, MI 48226; telephone (313)964-4000

Education and Research

Elementary and Secondary Schools

The Detroit Public Schools is the largest school district in Michigan. The school board is composed of eleven nonpartisan members—seven elected by geographic district and four elected at large—who select a superintendent.

The district's autonomy program allows schools to manage their own budgets and permits parents, staff, and students to choose curricula, programs, and services. The district spent $4 million in 1992 to make available schools of choice, where programs range from a Spanish/English academy to math and science studies at the Detroit Science Center.

The following is a summary of data regarding the Detroit public schools as of the 1992–1993 school year.

Total enrollment: 169,819

Number of facilities
  elementary schools: 165
  junior high schools: 46
  senior high schools: 27
  other: 18 (including African-centered academies)

Student/teacher ratio: grades 1–3, 30:1; grades 4–5, 34:1; grades 6–8, 34:1; grades 9–12, 34:1 (1988–1989)

Teacher salaries
  minimum: $27,132
  maximum: $50,229

Funding per pupil: $4,195

Several private and parochial school systems offer educational alternatives at pre-school, elementary, and secondary levels. The Roman Catholic Archdiocese initiated Cornerstone Schools in 1991; these are Christian schools that do not preach a particular doctrine. Specialized curricula have been designated by the Japanese Society of Detroit Hashuko-Saturday School, Burton International School, Liggett and Waldorf schools, Friends School, and W. E. B. DuBois Preparatory School.

Public Schools Information: Detroit Public Schools, 5057 Woodward Avenue, Detroit, MI 48202; telephone (313)494-1010

Colleges and Universities

Wayne State University is Detroit's largest institution of higher learning, enrolling approximately thirty-four thousand students in thirteen schools and colleges, including the colleges of medicine, nursing, and pharmacy and allied health, and the law school. Strong programs are offered in the college of engineering and the school of fine and performing arts, which includes a nationally recognized drama program. Wayne State is one of ninety-eight universities nationwide to be designed a Carnegie One Research University. The University of Detroit-Mercy, a Roman Catholic institution, enrolls six-thousand students in baccalaureate, master's, and doctorate programs in the arts and sciences; the university also administers schools of law and dentistry. The Detroit College of Law operates a juris doctor program.

Other undergraduate and graduate institutions affiliated with the Roman Catholic Church are Marygrove College, Madonna University (in Livonia), and Sacred Heart Seminary College. Colleges located in neighboring suburbs include Detroit College of Business in Dearborn, Lawrence Technological University in Southfield, the Dearborn campus of the University of Michigan, Cranbrook Academy of Art in Bloomfield Hills, and Oakland University in Rochester. Greater Detroit has a wide selection of community colleges, including Henry Ford Community College, Highland Park Community College, Wayne County Community College, Macomb Community College, Monroe County Community College, and Oakland Community College. Central

Michigan University maintains centers throughout metropolitan Detroit.

Libraries and Research Centers

The Detroit Public Library, founded in 1865 and the city's largest library, maintains twenty-five branches and five bookmobiles. The main facility houses over 2.7 million book volumes and bound periodicals, in addition to 7,190 periodical subscriptions, over 738,000 microfiche and microfilms, plus recordings and videos. Special collections include materials pertaining to national automotive history, Michigan, the Great Lakes, the Northwest Territory, and Black Americans in the performing arts. The Wayne State University Libraries system is comprised of a central facility with over 2.6 million volumes and four departmental libraries with separate holdings. A United States documents depository, the library has special collections in oral history, children and young people, photography, social studies, chemistry, and women and the law.

The University of Detroit-Mercy Library maintains collections on such subjects as humor and local color; it is a depository for federal, state, and southeastern Michigan county government documents. The Smithsonian Institution operates the Archives of American Art Midwest Center, housed at the Detroit Institute of Arts; it holds a microfilm history of the visual arts in the United States. Other specialized libraries in the city are associated with corporations, hospitals, law firms, cultural organizations, and federal agencies.

Research centers affiliated with Wayne State University conduct activity in such fields as labor and urban affairs, ethnic studies, folklore, bioengineering, human growth and development, automotive research, manufacturing, and technology. At centers affiliated with the University of Detroit-Mercy, research is conducted in aging and polymer technologies. The Budd Company, an engineering and manufacturing resource specializing in automotive design, has recently opened four research and development centers in southeastern Michigan.

Public Library Information: Detroit Public Library, 5201 Woodward Avenue, Detroit, MI 48202-4093; telephone (313)833-1000

Health Care

Detroit is the primary medical treatment and referral center for southeastern Michigan. Vital factors in the health care industry are the education, training, and research programs conducted by the city's institutions of higher learning. The Wayne State University and University of Michigan schools of medicine, nursing, and pharmacy and allied health services provide area hospitals and clinics with medical professionals and support staff. The University of Detroit-Mercy offers programs in dentistry, nursing, and medical technology, and Madonna University provides a baccalaureate program in nursing. In 1990, nineteen hospitals in the city furnished 6,783 beds and forty-six nursing homes provided 5,922 beds. More than thirty-three hundred physicians practicing in all areas of specialization served Detroit in 1990. The metropolitan area is served by seventy-four hospitals.

The Detroit Medical Center, one of the city's largest health care facilities, is affiliated with Wayne State University; the complex includes Children's Hospital of Michigan, Detroit Receiving Hospital, Grace Hospital, Harper Hospital, Hutzel Hospital, Kresge Eye Institute, Michigan Cancer Foundation, and the Rehabilitation Institute. A 503-bed Veterans Hospital was under development in 1993. Another major facility is Henry Ford Hospital, which operates twenty-seven centers and clinics; among them are oncology, renology, and a host of therapy and research facilities, an alcoholism treatment center and home health care programs. Joining the Ford Hospital Group in 1991 were Mercy Hospitals and Health Services of Detroit, which operate the 587-bed Mount Carmel Hospital, Mercy Family Care Centers, and the 375-bed Mercy Hospital. The Henry Ford Health System recently affiliated with the medical school of Case Western Reserve University of Cleveland.

Detroit Macomb Hospital and Saratoga offer general and surgical care; principal suburban hospitals are Beaumont, St. Joseph Mercy, and Providence, which provide a range of specialties. Michigan Osteopathic Medical Center and Detroit Osteopathic Hospital furnish both general and specialized treatment. Among other health care facilities located in Wayne County are Brent General Hospital, Detroit Riverview Hospital, Holy Cross Hospital, Sinai Hospital of Detroit, St. John's, Oakwood, and St. Mary's hospitals.

Health Care Information: Detroit Medical Center Referral Service, telephone (313)745-5000

Recreation

Sightseeing

Signs of Detroit's revitalization are especially apparent in the downtown district. The most recent innovation is the People Mover, an elevated computerized rail transit system opened in 1987. Each of thirteen stations features artwork characteristic of the neighborhood and can be viewed from the train cars. Hart Plaza, named in honor of the late Senator Philip A. Hart, stands adjacent to Detroit's most visible symbol of renewal—the recently renovated Renaissance Center. Hart Plaza includes the Dodge Memorial Fountain, designed by sculptor Isamu Noguchi. Nearby at the foot of Woodward Avenue, is mounted Robert Graham's sculpture "The Fist, "commemorating fighter Joe Louis and considered the city's most controversial piece of art.

The Detroit Zoo in Royal Oak was the first zoo in the United States to make extensive use of barless exhibits; the zoo is home to more than twelve-hundred animals representing four-hundred different species. The new chimpanzee exhibit covers four acres of naturalistic habitat. Other popular exhibits are the penguinarium, reptile house, free-flying aviary, and elephant and rhinoceros houses.

Belle Isle, located in the Detroit River two miles from downtown, was purchased from the Chippewa and Ottawa native Americans and was landscaped as a 1,000-acre city park in 1879 by Frederick Law Olmsted. Belle Isle is the home of the Anna Scripps Whitcomb Conservatory, a nature center, a zoo, the nation's oldest fresh water aquarium, the Dossin Great Lakes Museum, the Scott Fountain, and the Floral Clock.

Boblo Island is located in the Detroit River near the entrance to Lake Erie. Visitors can be transported to this popular amusement park from the Detroit area by ferry boat. Among Boblo's attractions are a historic carousel, a nineteenth-century blockhouse and lighthouse, and a monument erected to the memory of Great Lakes sailors.

Detroit is graced by a number of mansions built by automobile industrialists that are now open to the public. Meadow Brook Hall, a one-hundred-room mansion on a 1,400-acre estate on the campus of Oakland University in Rochester, was built by auto baron John Dodge in 1926. Henry Ford's final home, fifty-six-room Fair Lane, is located on the University of Michigan's Dearborn campus. The Edsel and Eleanor Ford House, overlooking Lake St. Clair in Grosse Pointe Shores on a 90-acre estate, is built with an authentic Cotswold stone roof and leaded glass windows with heraldic inserts. The Fisher mansion on the Detroit River features original Eastern art works, Italian Renaissance and vintage Hollywood architecture, and more than two-hundred ounces of pure gold and silver leaf on the ceilings and moldings.

Other historic structures in Detroit include Moross House, Old Mariners Church, Sibley House, and Pewabic Pottery, where ceramic Pewabic tiles were first developed. The International Institute of Metropolitan Detroit is an agency for the foreign-born founded by the Young Women's Christian Association (YWCA) in 1919, with a "gallery of nations" featuring the arts and crafts of forty-three nations.

Arts and Culture

The Detroit Symphony, one of the country's few orchestras with international stature, plays a September-to-May season of classical and pops concerts at Orchestra Hall as well as a summer season at Meadow Brook, an outdoor amphitheater in Rochester. Michigan Opera Theatre produces classical grand opera, operetta, and musical theater in seasons at the Fisher Theater and at the Masonic Temple Theatre; the group planned to move into the restored Grand Circus Theater in the fall of 1994. The Detroit Concert Band, the nation's only professional concert band, specializes in marches, patriotic tunes, and popular music.

Detroit supports an active theater community. The Attic Theatre specializes in plays by new playwrights and performed by a resident professional company. One of the city's oldest professional companies is the Detroit Repertory Theatre, which stages comedies, dramas, and musicals. The Fox Theatre, the largest movie theater in the United States, was designed by movie palace architect C. Howard Crane in 1928; it has undergone renovation to preserve its "Siamese Byzantine" interior featuring Far Eastern, Egyptian, Babylonian, and Indian themes and is the site of performing arts events. Another opulent theater facility is the Fisher Theatre, designed by Albert

Kahn; it sponsors Broadway shows. A developing theater district includes the Fox, the State and the Gem theaters. Second City, the comedy troupe, is to establish a presence nearby in the fall of 1993.

Both the Music Hall Center for the Performing Arts and the Birmingham Theatre bring professional touring theater companies to Detroit audiences. Actor's Alliance Theatre Company performs various theatrical works at different locations in the city. Meadow Brook Theatre at Oakland University presents an eight-play season of musicals, classics plays, and new works. Wayne State University's Hilberry Theatre produces classic drama performed by graduate student actors; undergraduate productions are staged at the Bonstelle Theatre. The Cranbrook Performing Arts Theatre in Bloomfield Hills offers orchestra, band, and vocal concerts, in addition to dance and drama, by high school students at the Cranbrook Educational Community. Detroit Youtheatre at the Music Hall presents family entertainment. Other venues for the performing arts are Chene Park Riverfront Theatre, Detroit Center for the Performing Arts, Joe Louis and Cobo arenas, Macomb Center for the Performing Arts, Oakland University Center for the Arts, and the Palace of Auburn Hills.

The Detroit Institute of Arts, established in 1885, is one of the nation's major art museums. Art treasures from throughout the world and covering a historical period of five thousand years, are housed in more than one-hundred galleries. Among the institute's most prized holdings is the four-wall mural *Detroit Industry* by Diego Rivera. Also known worldwide is the Henry Ford Museum and Greenfield Village in Dearborn, which Henry Ford founded in 1929 to document America's growth from a rural to an industrial society by exhibiting objects from the nation's material culture. Henry Ford Museum is a fourteen-acre complex housing major collections in transportation, industry, agriculture, and the domestic arts; the museum features one of the world's most comprehensive car collections. Greenfield Village, a 240-acre outdoor museum, gathers on a single site one of the largest collections of historic American homes, workplaces, and communities; among them are Thomas Edison's Menlo Park laboratory, the Wright brothers' bicycle shop, and Noah Webster's Connecticut home.

The Detroit Historical Museum in the Detroit Cultural Center was founded in 1928 as an archive of the history and customs of Detroiters. The museum's collection of more than 250,000 urban historical artifacts is one of the largest such collections in the country. An educational unit of the Detroit Public Schools, the Children's Museum displays collections that focus on African musical instruments, the Inuit, and American folk crafts and toys. The Museum of African American History is dedicated to the contributions of African-Americans in the humanities and creative arts. The Motown Museum is quartered in the former home of Berry Gordy, Jr., Motown's founder, and preserves the music studio and recording equipment used in pioneering the Motown Sound. A gift from singer Michael Jackson in 1987 built the room named for him at Motown Museum. Fort Wayne is home to the National Museum of the Tuskegee Airmen, an all-black unit of World War II fighter pilots.

Festivals and Holidays

Detroit's downtown riverfront is the scene of a program of ethnic festivals and the Downtown Hoedown from April until Labor Day. June events include the Annual Heritage Fair at the Dearborn Historical Museum; Art on the Pointe, a juried art show at the Ford Estate; and the Muzzle Loaders Festival at Greenfield Village. The International Freedom Festival, begun in 1959, is a summer celebration of the friendship between Canada and the United States; it attracts more than 3 million people and culminates in a large fireworks display on the Detroit River.

On the Fourth of July weekend the Colonial Music and Military Muster at Greenfield Village features uniformed American and British troops in simulated encampment activities. Also in July at Greenfield Village is the Fire Engine Muster with hand-pulled rigs and horse-drawn pumpers in a re-creation of early fire-fighting techniques. The Blues Festival of Detroit, the Henry Ford Day at the Fair Lane Mansion, and the Wyandotte Street Art Fair conclude July activities. The Michigan State Fair at the State Fairgrounds, the nation's oldest state fair, takes place in August, as does the Spirit of Detroit Car Show and the Swap Meets at Historic Fort Wayne. The Montreux-Detroit International Jazz Festival over Labor Day weekend brings together over 100 international artists and local jazz musicians in one of the nation's largest jazz festivals. The Autumn Harvest Festival in Dearborn, the Detroit Festival of the Arts, the Hamtramck Polish Festival, and the Old Car Festival at Greenfield Village are major activities in September.

A major event in November is the Michigan Thanksgiving Day Parade, which presents more than seventy floats, fifteen helium balloons, twenty-five marching bands, more than nine-hundred costumed marchers, and Santa Claus in one of the nation's largest Thanksgiving Day parades. Other November events include the Detroit Aglow and Symphony Sing-a-Long and the Festival of Trees and Christmas Carnival at Cobo Conference Center. Christmas at Greenfield Village in December features Christmas past and present at over two dozen historic village sites, with yuletide meals cooked at open hearths. Other seasonal shows are Noel Night at the Detroit Cultural Center, the Wassail Feast at the Detroit Institute of Arts, and the Christmas dinner at the Fair Lane Manor.

Sports for the Spectator

Detroit supports professional franchises in all the major sports. The Detroit Tigers, the city's oldest team, play their home games in historic Tiger Stadium. The Tigers compete in the eastern division of the American League in the Major League Baseball Association. The Detroit Lions are in the central division of the National Conference of the National Football League. The Lions' home games are held at the Pontiac Silverdome, the nation's largest air-support domed stadium. The Detroit Pistons of the central division of the eastern conference of the National Basketball Association play their home games at the Palace of Auburn Hills, a twenty-thousand-seat arena. The Detroit Red Wings of the Norris Division of the Clarence Campbell Conference of the National Hockey League host visiting competitors at Joe Louis Arena located downtown on the riverfront. The Detroit Drive also play their football home games at Joe Louis Arena.

The Detroit Grand Prix, the United States' only Formula One race, brings Grand Prix auto racers from around the world for an event held in Detroit since 1981. The Spirit of Detroit-Budweiser Thunderboat Championship brings super-power hydroplanes to race on the Detroit River in June. Harness Racing is on view at the Hazel Park Harness Raceway, Northville Downs, and Ladbroke Detroit Race Courses in Livonia, which also offers thoroughbred racing.

Sports for the Participant

The Detroit Department of Parks and Recreation oversees 6,000 acres of park land. More than 350 city parks contain a total of 318 baseball diamonds, 257 tennis courses, six golf courses, and two marinas. Detroit has developed four downtown riverfront parks. Outdoor sports such as swimming, boating, hiking, skiing, fishing, and skating are available at metropolitan parks.

Shopping and Dining

The most visible symbol of Detroit's downtown revitalization is the Renaissance Center, which projects one-eighth of a mile onto the city skyline. This multi-function complex houses eighty retail stores and restaurants and a new centralized shopping area on the first level with public access from Jefferson Avenue. Detroit's New Center Area consists of sixty blocks forming a "city within a city." Eastern Market, the largest flower-bedding market in the world and an outlet for fresh meats and produce, attracts farmers from the Midwest and Canada. Adjacent to Eastern Market are specialty stores selling fresh meat, poultry, gourmet foods, and wines.

Greektown and International Center, a popular Detroit tourist spot, features bakeries, restaurants, bars, and coffeehouses. Trappers Alley, first established by Taugott Schmidt in the 1850s, is today a five-level mall in the heart of Greektown with more than seventy-five fashion stores, gift boutiques, and ethnic restaurants. Bricktown, located in a refurbished sector of downtown, is anchored by an art gallery selling Oriental vases, Persian rugs, and antique furniture.

In recent years a number of venerable Detroit dining institutions have been forced to close their doors and have given way to less formal—and less pricey—establishments. However, elegant dining experiences are still possible in such settings as a restored forty-two-room mansion, a brick fish house, and at Opus One, selected by *Food and Wine* magazine as a 1992-1993 Distinguished Restaurant of North America. Detroit is home to some outstanding Italian restaurants; Creole, Japanese, Chinese, Lebanese, Ethiopian, Thai, Indian, and Turkish cuisine are included among the other ethnic choices.

Visitor Information: Metropolitan Detroit Convention and Visitors Bureau, 100 Renaissance Center, Suite 1950, Detroit, MI 48243-1056; telephone (313)259-4333; City Activities and Events, telephone (313)224-3755; Detroit Dept. of Public Information, 608 City-County Building, Detroit, MI 48226; telephone (313)224-3755

Trappers Alley, built in the 1850s, is today a five-level mall in the heart of Greektown.

Convention Facilities

Detroit's principal meeting facilities are clustered in the Detroit Civic Center, which stands at the edge of the Detroit River on the approximate site where the city's founder embarked in 1701. The Civic Center consists of five complexes: Cobo Conference/Exhibition Center, Cobo Arena, Joe Louis Arena, Hart Plaza, and the Veterans Memorial Building.

Completed in 1989, Cobo Conference/Exhibition Center contains a total of seven-hundred thousand square feet of meeting and exhibit space in five halls. The adjacent Cobo Arena, with a seating capacity of 11,000 people, is used for conventions and shows as well as large functions such as concerts and sports events. Joe Louis Arena, named for the heavyweight boxing champion, was the site of the 1980 Republican National Convention and hosts major events. The Veterans Memorial Building, the original Civic Center structure built in 1950, houses a ballroom and meeting rooms.

Convention and meeting facilities are also available at the Detroit Historical Museum, the Detroit Institute of Arts, the Detroit Fox Theatre, Orchestra Hall, the Renaissance Club, the Michigan Exposition and Fairgrounds, and even Tiger Stadium, as well as at Henry Ford Museum, the Detroit Zoo, restored estates and historic sites, suburban civic centers, college and university campuses, and on yachts and riverboats. All major downtown and suburban hotels and motels offer meeting accommodations for both large and small functions.

Convention Information: Metropolitan Detroit Convention and Visitors Bureau, 100 Renaissance Center, Suite 1950, Detroit, MI 48243-1056; telephone (313)259-4333

Transportation

Approaching the City

Detroit Metropolitan Airport (Metro), one of the busiest in the United States, is located 22 miles from downtown in Romulus. Served by seventeen airlines with one-thousand daily flights, Metro is the major hub for Northwest Airlines. Commercial service is also available into Detroit City Airport on the city's east side, 6 miles from downtown; destinations for charter and private air traffic are Willow Run Airport and Oakland-Pontiac Airport. Amtrak provides passenger rail transportation to Detroit from Chicago; a two-hour route on "bullet trains" was being sought in late 1992.

Six interstate highways and several limited-access expressways serve the Greater Detroit area. Interstate-75, with its northern terminus in Michigan's Upper Peninsula, extends through the city from north to southwest; north of downtown it is called the Chrysler Freeway, and southwest of downtown it is the Fisher Freeway. Interstate-375 connects the Fisher and Chrysler Freeways. East-west I-94, known as the Ford Freeway, is the primary connection from Detroit Metropolitan Airport. West-northwest I-96, the Jeffries Freeway, approaches Detroit from Muskegon, Grand Rapids, and Lansing. Interstate-696, the Walter Reuther Freeway, is the main east-west route across the northern suburbs in Macomb and Oakland counties. Interstate-275 is a north-south bypass on the city's west side, linking I-75 and I-96. Other major routes leading into Detroit are north to west U.S. 10 (Lodge Freeway) and north-south S.R. 39 (Southfield Freeway). Canadian Highway 401 enters Detroit from Windsor via the Detroit/Windsor International Tunnel and the Ambassador Bridge.

Traveling in the City

Most Detroit streets conform to a grid system. East-west streets are labelled "mile road" in ascending order northward; north-south streets are named. The northern boundary of the city is Eight Mile Road. Superimposed on the downtown grid are hubs and squares, the focal point being Kennedy Square and Cadillac Square in the center of the business district. Radiating from this hub are east-west Michigan Avenue, northeast Monroe Street, and east-west Fort Street. The largest hub is Grand Circus Park, which is bisected by Woodward Avenue, a main north-south thoroughfare. Jefferson Avenue follows the curve of the Detroit River and Lake St. Clair past Belle Isle through the Grosse Pointes into Harrison Township and downriver past Wyandotte to Grosse Ile.

Detroit is served by two public transportation systems: the Detroit Department of Transportation (D-DOT) and the Suburban Mobility Authority for Regional Transport (SMART). The People Mover, a 2.9-mile elevated rail circuit, provides travel to major downtown sites from thirteen stations. Old-time trolleys run shuttle routes between Grand Circus

Park and Cobo Conference/Exposition Center and the Renaissance Center.

Communications

Newspapers and Magazines

The Detroit News (evening) and the *Detroit Free Press* (morning) are the city's two major daily newspapers; they publish joint editions on Saturday, Sunday, and holidays. *Detroit Monthly,* with a circulation of nearly 100,000 readers, is a magazine that reports on issues and events of local interest.

A number of nationally circulated periodicals originate in Detroit. Among them are *Solidarity,* a monthly publication of the United Automobile Workers; *Better Investing, Manufacturing Engineering, Autoweek,* a weekly magazine for car enthusiasts; and *Automotive News* and *Auto World,* auto industry magazines. *Football News* publishes twenty issues during the football season.

Television and Radio

Detroit television viewers receive broadcasts from eight stations: three national networks affiliates, three independent, one public, and one Canadian. Pay and cable television services are available in the Detroit metropolitan area. Fifty-five AM and FM radio stations schedule a full range of formats. The most popular is adult contemporary music; other formats include adult-oriented rock, black and black contemporary, motown, classic rock, easy listening, jazz, middle of the road, modern country, news and news-talk, pop, oldies, sold gold and urban contemporary rhythm and blues. Two of the AM stations with 50,000-watt capacity enjoy a longstanding popularity throughout the Midwest; one FM station was the first in the country to offer a full-time news-talk format.

Media Information: Detroit News and *Detroit Free Press*, 615 Lafayette Blvd., Detroit, Michigan 48231; telephone (313)222-2300; and, *Detroit Monthly,* 1400 Woodbridge, Detroit, MI 48231; telephone (313)446-6000

Selected Bibliography

Arnow, Harriette Louisa Simpson, *The Dollmaker* (New York: Avon Books, 1972, 1954)

Avery, Joan, *Angel of Passage* (Harper, 1993)

Chafets, Ze'Ev, *Devil's Night And Other True Tales of Detroit* (New York: Random House, 1990)

Henrickson, Wilma Wood, ed., *Detroit Perspectives: Crossroads and Turning Points* (Detroit: Wayne State University Press, 1991)

Lindsay, Paul, *Witness to the Truth: A Novel of the FBI* (New York: Random House, 1992)

Grand Rapids

The City in Brief

Founded: 1831 (incorporated, 1850)

Head Official: City Manager Kurt Kimball (since 1987)

City Population
 1970: 198,000
 1980: 181,843
 1990: 189,126
 Percent change, 1980–1990: 4.0%
U.S. rank in 1980: 75th
U.S. rank in 1990: 83rd
Metropolitan Area Population
 1970: 539,000
 1980: 602,000
 1990: 688,399
 Percent change, 1980–1990: 14.4%
U.S. rank in 1980: 56th

U.S. rank in 1990: 57th

Area: 44.4 square miles (1990)

Elevation: Ranges from 785 to 1,075 feet above sea level

Average Annual Temperature: 47.4° F

Average Annual Precipitation: 36.0 inches of rain, 64.0 inches of snow

Major Economic Sectors: Manufacturing, trade, services

Unemployment Rate: 6.9% (September 1992)

Per Capita Income: $12,070 (1989)

1992 (2nd Quarter) ACCRA Average House Price: $160,950

1992 (2nd Quarter) ACCRA Cost of Living Index: 113.4 (U.S. average = 100.0)

1991 FBI Crime Index Total: 17,494

Major Colleges and Universities: Grand Valley State University

Daily Newspaper: *Grand Rapids Press*

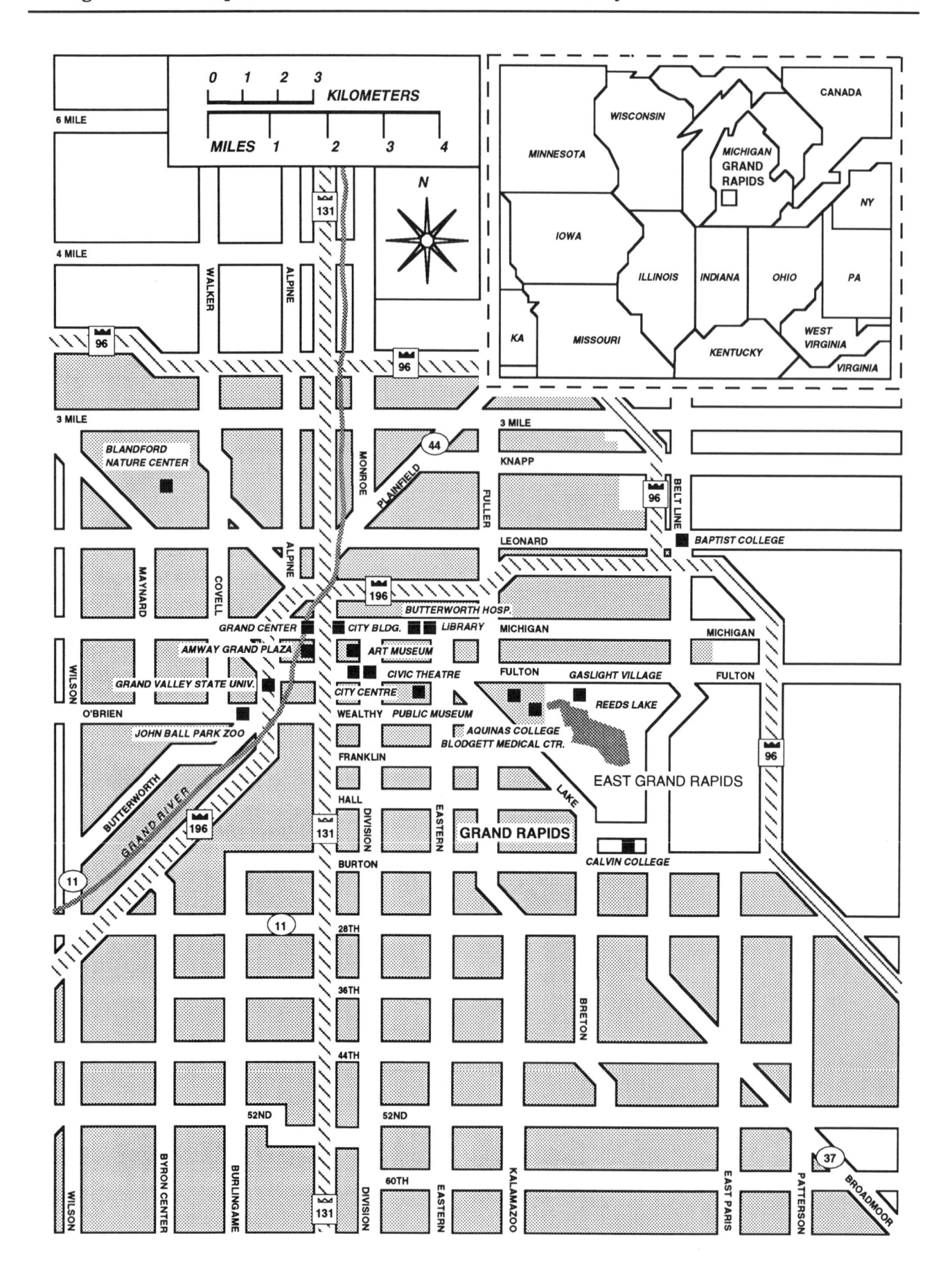

Michigan—Grand Rapids *Cities of the United States • 2nd Edition*

Introduction

The seat of Kent County, Michigan, Grand Rapids is the center of a metropolitan statistical area that includes both Kent and Ottawa counties. The Grand River, on which the city is located, shaped the future of Grand Rapids first as a leader in the logging industry and then as one of the world's primary furniture manufacturing centers. The city's identity also was determined by thousands of Dutch immigrants who settled in Grand Rapids to work in the furniture factories. Today Grand Rapids is a mid-sized midwestern city with innovative cultural institutions, a revitalized downtown core, a diverse economy, and high marks for quality of life factors. *Kiplinger's Personal Finance Magazine* singled out Grand Rapids as a 1991 Super City, "Where People Are Moving and Opportunity is Knocking."

Geography and Climate

Bisected by the Grand River, Michigan's longest river, Grand Rapids is located in the Grand river valley approximately 30 miles east of Lake Michigan. The city's climate is influenced by the lake, which tempers cold waves from the west and northwest during the winter and produces a regulating effect on both frost and vegetation during the growing season. Seasonal extremes are infrequent, although hot, humid weather can be expected for about three weeks during the summer and drought occasionally occurs for a short duration; snow cover sometimes remains throughout the winter. Two mid-winter thaws, in January-February and in March-April, can cause the Grand River to reach the flood stage, but the overflow is usually limited to the flood plain.

Area: 44.4 square miles (1990)

Elevation: Ranges from 785 feet to 1,075 feet above sea level

Average Temperatures: January, 22.0° F; July, 71.4° F; annual average, 47.4° F

Average Annual Precipitation: 36.0 inches of rain, 64.0 inches of snow

History

Grand River Valley Site of Land Feud

Trails established by the Ottawa tribe converged at the west bank of the Grand River at the site of present day Grand Rapids, where native peoples hunted and fished. A Baptist mission building was completed in the vicinity in 1826, the same year Frenchman Louis Campau settled in the Grand Valley. In 1827, Campau established a fur-trading post on the river bank along which Huron Street now runs. Four years later Campau bought a large tract of land where the center of Grand Rapids is now located.

Campau subsequently engaged in a land feud with Lucius Lyon, who purchased land north of Campau's. The two men platted their ground at the disadvantage of one another: Campau blocked Lyon's streets to keep them from extending to the river and Lyon platted foreshortened and oddly angled streets. Campau Square, land at the center of Grand Rapids that was overlooked in the squabble, is the permanent legacy of this turbulent beginning. Lyon even had the name of the village changed to Kent, but Campau, nicknamed "The Fox" by local native Americans, maneuvered to have it changed back. Grand Rapids was incorporated as a village in 1838 and as a city in 1850.

Logging Fuels Grand Rapids Development

Grand Rapids began a period of rapid development in the 1850s when logs were floated down the Grand River to the city's new mills. Upstream mill owners stole the logs headed for Grand Rapids in a practice called "hogging." To prevent hogging, the mills hired men called river drivers, who rode the logs downstream to their rightful destination. The result was boom times for Grand Rapids, but along with the river drivers came prostitution, gambling, and basement bars concentrated around Campau Square. To help prevent slipping off floating logs the river drivers wore caulked boots with projections on the soles; these boots damaged flooring and boardwalks, leading one hotel owner to supply carpet slippers to all river drivers who entered his hotel.

River ice and log jams proved to be a continual problem for Grand Rapids. A series of floods or heavy rains that launched runaway logs caused repeated damage to the town, notably in 1838, 1852, 1883, and 1904, occasions when flood damage to property exceeded $1 million. Despite these problems, the river and the logging industry remained the city's most valuable resources. The first hydro-electric plant in the Midwest was built in Grand Rapids. In 1881 when the Wolverine Chair Company experimented with a sixteen-light brush arc machine, the Grand Rapids hydro-electric plant became the first to furnish commercial electric service of any kind.

Furniture Craftsmanship Gains World Attention

Furniture had been manufactured in Grand Rapids as early as 1838, but it was not until the Philadelphia Centennial Exposition in 1876 that the city gained national recognition for its furniture craftsmanship. Two years later, Grand Rapids held its first furniture marts, attracting buyers worldwide. By 1895, more than one hundred Eastern buyers travelled each year to Grand Rapids, which had become the nation's principal producer of furniture. Immigrants from the Dutch provinces of Zeeland, Friesland, and Groningen settled in Grand Rapids to work in the furniture industry. They gathered in distinct sections of the city that they modelled after their communities in Holland.

The practice of importing foreign labor at what amounted to indenture—now illegal—resulted in serious problems for the Grand Rapids's furniture industry. These difficulties culminated in the strike of 1911 during which fifty plants were closed and sixty-five hundred workers manned the picket lines. The anti-union Citizens' Alliance became involved and a major riot resulted. The strike finally ended when workers voted to return to work.

Grand Rapids began to diversify its economy during World War I with the development of the metal trades, and today the city has a multi-level economic base that includes the manufacture of automotive and household products.

Historical Information: Grand Rapids Historical Society, c/o Grand Rapids Public Library, 60 Library Plaza NE, Grand Rapids, MI 49503; telephone (616)456-3640

Population Profile

Metropolitan Area Residents
1970: 539,000
1980: 602,000
1990: 688,399
Annual average percent change, 1980–1988: 0.2%
U.S. rank in 1980: 56th
U.S. rank in 1990: 57th

City Residents
1970: 198,000
1980: 181,843
1990: 189,126 (of which, 89,855 were males, and 99,271 were females)
Percent change, 1980–1990: 4.0%
U.S. rank in 1980: 75th
U.S. rank in 1990: 83rd (State rank: 2nd)

Density: 4,269.2 people per square mile (1990)

Racial and ethnic characteristics (1990)
  White: 144,464
  Black: 35,073
  American Indian, Eskimo, Aleut: 1,573
  Asian and Pacific Islander: 2,164
  Hispanic (may be of any race): 9,394

Percent of residents born in state: 77.6% (1990)

Age characteristics (1990)
  Population under 5 years old: 17,740
  Population 5 to 9 years old: 15,339
  Population 10 to 14 years old: 12,274
  Population 15 to 19 years old: 13,358
  Population 20 to 24 years old: 17,470
  Population 25 to 29 years old: 19,328
  Population 30 to 34 years old: 17,535
  Population 35 to 39 years old: 14,455
  Population 40 to 44 years old: 10,300
  Population 45 to 49 years old: 7,521
  Population 50 to 54 years old: 6,008
  Population 55 to 59 years old: 6,117
  Population 60 to 64 years old: 6,970
  Population 65 to 69 years old: 6,855
  Population 70 to 74 years old: 5,801
  Population 75 to 79 years old: 4,852
  Population 80 to 84 years old: 3,695
  Population 85 years and over: 3,508
  Median age: 29.8 years

Births (1988)
  Total number: 4,227

Deaths (1988)
  Total number: 1,893 (of which, 44 were infants under the age of 1 year)

Money income (1989)
  Per capita income: $12,070
  Median household income: $26,809
  Total households: 69,452
  Number of households with income of . . .
    less than $5,000: 4,204
    $5,000 to $9,999: 7,800
    $10,000 to $14,999: 6,918
    $15,000 to $24,999: 13,380
    $25,000 to $34,999: 12,435
    $35,000 to $49,999: 12,784
    $50,000 to $74,999: 8,578
    $75,000 to $99,999: 2,016
    $100,000 to $149,999: 872
    $150,000 or more: 465
  Percent of families below poverty level: 12.6% (64.0% of which were female householder families with related children under 5)
1991 FBI Crime Index Total: 17,494

Municipal Government

Grand Rapids operates under a "weak mayor," commission-manager form of government, in which the seven council members—one of whom serves as mayor—are elected to four-year terms. The city manager, who runs the government, is appointed.

The Metropolitan Council, formed in 1990, is a voluntary coalition of thirteen participating units of government assigned to plan the region's major capital investments.

Head Officials: City Manager Kurt Kimball (since 1987)

Total Number of City Employees: 1,600 (1993)

City Information: City Hall, 300 Monroe NW, Grand Rapids, MI 49503; telephone (616)456-3010

Economy

Major Industries and Commercial Activity

The furniture industry has been a mainstay of the Grand Rapids economy since the late 1800s. Today the metropolitan area is home to five of the world's leading office furniture companies: Herman Miller, Haworth, American Seating, Westinghouse, and Steelcase, Inc. Several firms also continue to produce residential furniture. The Grand Rapids manufacturing base, consisting of more than thirteen-hundred companies that employ nearly one-third of the work force, has expanded to include nineteen of the twenty primary U.S. industries. General Motors, an automotive manufacturer, and Amway, manufacturer of home care products, are among the city's largest employers.

The core of the Grand Rapids manufacturing sector is made up of family-owned or small businesses. Among the national firms that began as family operations are the Bissell Company, carpet sweeper makers; the Howard Miller Clock Company, the world's largest manufacturer of grandfather clocks, in neighboring Zeeland; and Wolverine World Wide, makers of Hush Puppies shoes. The ten largest companies in the area employ among them more than forty-thousand workers, yet 90 percent of local businesses employ fewer than 50 persons.

Advertising, graphic arts, and printing comprise a substantial portion of the economic base; Grand Rapids is the sixth-largest printing community in the country. International business also plays an important role, with twenty-two foreign-owned firms located in the city and more than two-hundred local firms involved in international trade. Tourism is an emerging industry in the Grand Rapids area as Kent County increasingly becomes a popular vacation and convention destination. Agriculture continues to be an economic mainstay in Kent County, which is the largest apple-producing region in the state and a source for Christmas trees, dairy products, fruits and vegetables, and nursery products.

Items and goods produced: automobile parts, office furniture, leather products, home care products, fabricated metal products, home appliances, food, plastics

Incentive Programs—New and Existing Companies

Organized to promote economic expansion in western Michigan, the Research and Technology Institute (RTI) is a nonprofit corporation of member companies and area educational institutions (Grand Valley State University, Michigan State University, and Western Michigan University). RTI provides engineering education and assistance, research and development programs, technical assistance, and technology training to companies in the metropolitan region.

The Right Place Program, founded in 1985, is an organization headed by business and government leaders with the purpose of encouraging economic development. The Right Place Program assists existing companies in retention and expansion of business while marketing the Grand Rapids area to other domestic and foreign firms.

Business growth in Grand Rapids is also encouraged through such incentives as state tax write-offs for new capital investment and tax savings on new industrial plant or rehabilitation programs, for which out-of-state and overseas manufacturing firms are eligible.

Job training programs—State-sponsored job training programs, recently revamped through the $25 million Michigan Adult Education Training Initiative, include the Job Training Partnership Act, Displaced Homemakers program, summer youth employment programs, and pre-college programs in engineering and sciences. The State Department of Commerce administers a $1.2 million Training Incentive Fund, which provides assistance to employers wishing to upgrade the skills of their current work force. Grand Rapids's new $27 million Applied Technology Center provides skilled graduates and retrained employees to the business community.

Development Projects

A $100 million pipeline completed in 1992 brings clean water from Lake Michigan to the region. Recent business growth in Grand Rapids includes a $20 million, one-hundred-thousand-square-foot facility built by a West German manufacturer of interior wood trim for luxury automobiles; a $20 million, sixty-five-thousand-square-foot production facility for a manufacturer of hardware supplies for the office furniture industry; and D L P Inc.'s new $23 million facility.

Economic Development Information: Grand Rapids Area Chamber of Commerce, The Right Place Program, 17 Fountain Street NW, Grand Rapids, MI 49503; telephone (616)459-7221; Economic Development Information Center, Consumers Power Company, 200 E. Michigan Ave., Kalamazoo, MI 49007

Commercial Shipping

Because of its strategic location—more than 50 percent of the United States population is within a twelve-hour drive—Grand Rapids is no more than two delivery days away from all Midwest, East Coast, mid-south, and eastern Canadian markets. Ground transportation is available through more than forty motor carriers, several of which operate terminals in Grand Rapids, and three rail freight systems providing a range of services such as piggyback shipments, bulk handling, and refrigeration. Twelve air cargo companies and a deep-water port on Lake Michigan, 35 miles away in Muskegon, link Grand Rapids with world markets.

Labor Force and Employment Outlook

Employers in the Grand Rapids area have access to a young and growing population with a Midwestern work ethic (Grand Rapids ranked fifth in the nation among cities most often moved to in 1990). Employer relations are said to be excellent and work stoppages rare. The service and trade industries are expanding. A Foreign Trade Zone was in the development states in 1992, which will place the region at the forefront of worldwide competition.

The following is a summary of data regarding the Grand Rapids metropolitan area labor force as of September 1992.

Size of non-agricultural labor force: 365,700

Number of workers employed in . . .
  mining: not reported
  construction: 16,300
  manufacturing: 101,800
  transportation and public utilities: 13,800
  wholesale and retail trade: 96,800
  finance, insurance, and real estate: 16,200
  services: 85,800
  government: 35,000

Average hourly earnings of production workers employed in manufacturing: $12.59

Unemployment rate: 6.9%

Largest employers	Number of employees
Steelcase Inc.	10,100
General Motors Corporation	6,200

Largest employers	Number of employees
Amway Corporation	4,500
Wolverine World Wide	2,000
Smiths Industries	1,800
Keeler Brass Company	1,500
Lescoa, Inc.	1,300

Cost of Living

In July 1993 the Michigan legislature passed a bill cutting residents' property taxes an average of 60 to 65 percent, beginning with the summer 1994 tax bills. The tax cut, the largest in Michigan history, was to be accomplished by eliminating local and intermediate school district operating millages. The legislature was then considering a number of options to restore money for schools, including sales taxes on services and entertainment, an increase in the state sales tax, or a statewide millage.

The average cost per hospital admission in Grand Rapids is 34 percent lower than the U.S. average and 44 percent lower than the state average.

The following is a summary of data regarding several key cost of living factors in the Grand Rapids area as of mid-1993.

1992 (2nd Quarter) ACCRA Cost of Living Index: 113.4 (U.S. average = 100.0)

1992 (2nd Quarter) ACCRA Average House Price: $160,950

State income tax rate: 4.6% of all taxable income

State sales tax rate: 4.0%

Local income tax rate: 1.0% for residents; 0.5% for non-residents

Local sales tax rate: None

Property tax rate: 5.735% combined city, county, and school taxes

Economic Information: Grand Rapids Area Chamber of Commerce, 17 Fountain Street NW, Grand Rapids, MI 49503; telephone (616)771-0300

Education and Research

Elementary and Secondary Schools

The Grand Rapids community, including local businesses, is deeply committed to the education of its young. Public elementary and secondary education is provided by Grand Rapids Public Schools, the largest school district in Kent County. Fifty-five percent of high school graduates in the Grand Rapids area pursue a college education. The Tech Program is a four-year program incorporating the last two years of high school with two years of junior college to prepare students for advanced technical training.

The following is a summary of data regarding Grand Rapids public schools as of the 1992–1993 school year.

Total enrollment: 31,000

Number of facilities
  elementary schools: 50
  middle schools: 5
  high schools: 4
  other: 10

Student/teacher ratio: Elementary, 27:1; secondary, 32:1

Teacher salaries
  minimum: $25,498
  maximum: $45,358

Funding per pupil: $4,150

Parochial, private, church-affiliated, alternative, and specialty schools offer educational curricula from pre-school through grade twelve in the Grand Rapids area.

Public Schools Information: Grand Rapids School District, 143 Bostwick NE, Grand Rapids, MI 49503; telephone (616) 771-2182

Colleges and Universities

Six institutions of higher learning, offering undergraduate and graduate degrees, are located in Grand Rapids: Grand Valley State University, Calvin College, Aquinas College, Davenport College of Business, Grand Rapids Baptist College and Seminary, and Kendall College of Art and Design. Two-year programs are available at Grand Rapids Community College and Jordan College. Among colleges and seminaries providing religious training are Grace

A Grand Rapids highlight is Alexander Calder's *La Grand Vitesse,* **located in the center of the city.**

Bible College, Grand Rapids School of Bible and Music, Reformed Bible College, and Calvin Theological Seminary.

Three state universities—Ferris State University, Michigan State University, and Western Michigan University—maintain extension services for undergraduate and graduate curricula in Grand Rapids. Vocational schools in the city are ITT Technical Institute, Grand Rapids Educational Center, and Kent Skills Centers.

Libraries and Research Centers

The Grand Rapids Public Library operates five branches in addition to its main facility, which is a depository for federal and state documents. Library holdings consist of more than 636,000 books and more than one-thousand periodicals, plus records, tapes, films, maps, and compact discs; special collections cover several fields, such as furniture, Michigan history, landscape architecture and gardening, and the history of the Old Northwest Territory.

Also located downtown is the main branch of the Kent County Library System, which houses over 626,000 books and 1,650 periodicals, and maintains twenty additional branches in the city and in area communities. The Lakeland Library Cooperative, serving a regional population of over 900,000 people, is based in Grand Rapids. Twenty-four other libraries are affiliated with entities such as the *Grand Rapids Press,* the Grand Rapids Art Museum, colleges and universities, hospitals, corporations, and churches.

Research is conducted at Grand Valley State College in facilities management, human factors of environmental design, and work environments. At Steelcase Inc.'s $111 million think tank, behavioral scientists, designers, and engineers study emerging trends such as ergonomics and translate them into office products. Studies are also conducted to find more efficient ways to develop new products and speed up delivery to customers.

Public Library Information: Grand Rapids Public Library, 60 Library Plaza NE, Grand Rapids, MI 49503-3093; telephone (616)456-3600

Health Care

Grand Rapids is a western Michigan regional center for medical diagnosis, treatment, and care. Four full-service hospitals, eight specialized hospitals, mental health facilities, nursing homes, and numerous emergency medical centers and rehabilitative clinics form the working environment for health care professionals practicing in every major specialty. The 500-bed Butterworth Hospital, the city's largest general care facility, operates a kidney stone lithotriper program, a sleep disorder center, an ambulatory care clinic, and a physical therapy department in addition to a regional perinatal center and an emergency helicopter service.

Blodgett Memorial Medical Center, founded in 1847, maintains a surgical suite of fourteen operating rooms and provides acute care and emergency treatment. Blodgett is a teaching hospital affiliated with medical education and nursing programs at area colleges and universities; among the fields of specialization are Reye's Syndrome treatment, diabetes control, *in vitro* fertilization, burn care, and back pain treatment. Metropolitan Hospital houses a ventilator dependency unit and alcohol and drug rehabilitation program. Saint Mary's Health Services is a regional kidney dialysis and transplant center, and its Heartside Clinic furnishes basic health care to the homeless.

Ferguson Hospital, Forest View Psychiatric Hospital, Kent Community Hospital, Mary Free Bed Hospital and Rehabilitation Center, Michigan Veterans' Facility, and Pine Rest Christian Hospital Association are the specialized facilities located in Grand Rapids. Altogether, nearly four-hundred health care organizations function in the metropolitan area.

Health Care Information: Kent County Medical Society, telephone (616)458-4157

Recreation

Sightseeing

The Gerald R. Ford Museum in Grand Rapids honors the thirty-eighth President of the United States; permanent exhibits, including a replica of the Oval Office, highlight the significant events of the

Ford presidency, such as the Bicentennial celebration, President Nixon's resignation, and the Cambodian conflict. The contributions of Betty Ford as First Lady are also represented. The Grand Rapids Public Museum concentrates on Michigan mammals, archeology, birds, furniture, and costumes; an 1890s gaslight village and native American artifacts are part of the museum's holdings.

Heritage Hill, a historic district near downtown, contains more than thirteen-hundred structures built in sixty different architectural styles, including Frank Lloyd Wright's Meyer May house. A Grand Rapids highlight is Alexander Calder's *La Grand Vitesse* (The Grand Rapids), a large-scale outdoor sculpture located in the center of the city. Another Calder work, an abstract painting, has been installed atop the County Building adjacent to the sculpture. Joseph Kinnebrew's *Fish Ladder* sculpture has been placed at the Sixth Street dam.

The John Ball Zoological Garden features more than five-hundred animals from around the world, a freshwater aquarium, a snake house, and an assortment of tropical plants. The Blandford Nature Center, sited on 143 acres, provides self-guided trails through fields and forests; a pioneer farmstead, a one-room schoolhouse, a working farm, an interpretive building, and a wild-animal hospital are on the grounds.

Arts and Culture

The arts in Grand Rapids are celebrated for three days each June when a major arts festival fills the city with more than one-half million attendees. During the regular season, the Grand Rapids Symphony, an award-winning orchestra recognized for its innovative programming, presents a program of classical, pops, and family concerts. Opera Grand Rapids sponsors two fully staged productions each year featuring guest artists of international stature plus a jazz concert. The Grand Rapids Ballet presents *The Nutcracker* in December and two other ballet productions each year. Founded in 1883 and designated as a Landmark of American Music, the St. Cecilia Music Society presents public programs and educational opportunities for youth and adults. Other organizations perform at DeVos Hall and at Welsh Auditorium, which is part of the new Grand Center.

Grand Rapids Civic Theatre, Michigan's oldest community theater and one of the nation's most highly rated, presents six main stage productions and two children's plays annually. Community Circle Theatre, one of the county's largest summer community theaters, presents productions at the John Ball Park Pavilion during the summer. National touring companies entertain Grand Rapids audiences under the auspices of the Broadway Theater Guild. Spectrum Theatre, located downtown at Grand Rapids Junior College, is the performance home for Actors' Theatre, Robeson Players, and Grand Rapids Players.

The Urban Institute for Contemporary Arts provides exhibition and performance space for concerts, performance art, lectures, and readings. The Grand Rapids Art Museum, opened in 1913 and renovated in 1981, houses a permanent collection of paintings, sculpture, and graphic and decorative arts in ten galleries; the furniture-design wing features period furniture from the Renaissance to the present time.

Arts and Culture Information: Arts Council of Greater Grand Rapids, Waters Building, Suite 205-B, 161 Ottawa NW, Grand Rapids, MI (616) 459-2787

Festivals and Holidays

The major festival in Grand Rapids is a three-day arts celebration in June that initiates the summer season and attracts over one-half a million visitors; it is the nation's largest festival run entirely by volunteers. Ethnic festivals take place nearly every summer weekend: the Irish, Italians, Polish, Germans, native Americans, and Mexicans celebrate their cultural heritage with song, food, art, and costumes. The summer season concludes with the Celebration on the Grand during the second weekend in September. Other important events are the Winter Carnival and Snow Sculpture Contest in January, the Fourth of July Celebration, Pulaski Days, and Red Flannel Days in October.

Sports for the Spectator

The Grand Rapids Hoops team competes in the semi-professional Continental Basketball League. Both Calvin College and Hope College in nearby Holland, Michigan, field competitive basketball teams. Berlin Raceway features stock car racing, and Gratton Raceway presents auto, motorcycle, and go-cart races.

In 1993 it was announced that professional baseball would be coming to the Grand Rapids area. The Madison Muskies, a Wisconsin Single A team, will play in a privately financed new $5.5 million stadium in Plainfield Township, five minutes north of downtown Grand Rapids. The first pitch is to be thrown in the spring of 1994.

Sports for the Participant

Sports enthusiasts are provided numerous opportunities to enjoy the outdoors in Grand Rapids and the vicinity. Cross-county ski trails wind through scenic apple orchards and across golf courses. The Winter Sports Center in nearby Muskegon provides the longest lighted ski trail in the Midwest; the center also maintains a six-hundred-meter chute for luge, one of only four in the nation. Three local resorts feature downhill skiing. Year-round fishing is another popular sport; charter boats on Lake Michigan are available for salmon and lake trout fishing. Swimmers and sunbathers populate the miles of sandy beaches of Lake Michigan during the summer. Rowers are often seen on the Grand River; so are salmon fishers in October and November. The Old Kent Bank River Run, a 25K event, attracts runners from around the country.

Recreational facilities include twenty-six public and eight private golf courses, twenty-one inland lakes, and dozens of tennis courts and baseball fields. The Grand Rapids recreation department sponsors four-hundred softball teams in league competition, as well as programs in swimming, soccer, baseball, basketball, tennis, golf, scuba diving, and social dancing.

Shopping and Dining

City Centre, Grand Rapids's downtown shopping mall, is a four-level complex anchored by a department store that is surrounded by specialty stores and a variety of restaurants at the International Food Court. One independent store sells woolen garments made in Iceland. An indoor monorail train and a centralized fountain are added attractions. The Gaslight Village in East Grand Rapids is a residential district where fine shops are located in period homes.

The city's best restaurants are clustered downtown. An award-winning Chinese restaurant serves both Mandarin and Szechwan cuisine prepared by a chef from mainland China. One of the most popular eateries offers fresh fish with a changing daily menu; another specializes in prime rib. The major hotel restaurants are also rated highly.

Visitor Information: Grand Rapids/Kent County Convention and Visitors Bureau, 245 Monroe Avenue NW, Grand Rapids, MI; telephone (616)456-3922; and, Grand Rapids Area Chamber of Commerce, Chamber of Commerce Building, 17 Fountain Street NW, Grand Rapids, MI 49503; telephone (616)771-0300 or (800)678-9859

Convention Facilities

Grand Rapids was one of the first cities in the country to build a convention center and in 1987 reported a record $100 million in convention receipts. Constructed in 1933, the art-deco style Civic Auditorium, now a downtown landmark, has since been renamed Welsh Auditorium and was in 1981 incorporated into a riverfront complex that also features the Grand Center, a convention facility; DeVos Hall, a performing arts center; and the Amway Grand Plaza Hotel. Welsh Auditorium and the Grand Center contain a combined total of 117,000 square feet of meeting and exhibit space; seating for 4,516 people is available in the auditorium and for 2,446 people in DeVos Hall. Twenty-nine meeting and banquet rooms are located in the hotel.

Four thousand six hundred rooms are available for lodgings in more than fifty hotels and motels, many of which also provide meeting and convention accommodations.

Convention Information: Grand Center, 245 Monroe Avenue NW, Grand Rapids, MI 49503; telephone (616)456-3922

Transportation

Approaching the City

Michigan's second largest airport, Kent County International Airport, is located twenty minutes from downtown Grand Rapids. Five major airlines and six commuter services schedule 126 daily direct and connecting flights from cities in the United States, Canada, Mexico, Europe, and the Far East. More than a million passengers are enplaned and deplaned each year at the newly expanded facility.

A network of interstate, federal, and state highways provides access into Grand Rapids from surrounding communities as well as points throughout the United States and Canada. Interstate highways serving the metropolitan area are I-96, I-196, and I-296. U.S. highways extending through the city are 16 and 131; state routes include 11, 44, 50, 21, and 37. Daily rail passenger transportation from Chicago is provided by Amtrak.

Traveling in the City

Grand Rapids Area Transportation Authority (GRA-TA) schedules public bus service in the metropolitan area. Go Bus provides door-to-door transportation for the elderly and disabled; the Gus Bus, a commuter shuttle, operates from near-downtown parking lots to the downtown district.

Communications

Newspapers and Magazines

The *Grand Rapids Press* is the city's daily newspaper. Other newspapers circulating in the community include the *Grand Rapids Business Journal* and *Grand Valley Labor News*. *Grand Rapids Magazine* is a monthly publication that features articles of regional interest. Several special-interest magazines are also published in Grand Rapids; a number of them focus on religious topics.

Television and Radio

Nine television stations and cable service are received in Grand Rapids. Nearly thirty radio stations are received; several of them broadcast Christian inspirational programming.

Media Information: Grand Rapids Press, Booth Newspapers, Inc., 155 Michigan Street NW, Grand Rapids, MI 49503; telephone (616)459-1400; and, *Grand Rapids Magazine,* Gemini Publications, 40 Pearl Street NW, Trust Building, Suite 1040, Grand Rapids, MI 49503; telephone (616)459-4545

Lansing

The City in Brief

Founded: c. 1835 (incorporated, 1849)

Head Official: Mayor James A. Crawford (NP) (since 1992)

City Population
 1970: 131,000
 1980: 130,414
 1990: 127,321
 Percent change, 1980–1990: −2.4%
 U.S. rank in 1980: 122nd
 U.S. rank in 1990: 142nd

Metropolitan Area Population
 1970: 378,00
 1980: 420,000
 1990: 432,674
 Percent change, 1980–1990: 3.1%
 U.S. rank in 1980: 81st
 U.S. rank in 1990: 83rd

Area: 32.8 square miles (1990)

Elevation: 830 feet above sea level

Average Annual Temperature: 47.1° F

Average Annual Precipitation: 31 inches of rain; 48 inches of snow

Major Economic Sectors: Government, trade, services, manufacturing

Unemployment Rate: 5.7% (September 1992)

Per Capita Income: $12,232 (1989)

1992 (2nd Quarter) ACCRA Average House Price: $137,185

1992 (2nd Quarter) ACCRA Cost of Living Index: 105.2 (U.S. average = 100.0)

1991 FBI Crime Index Total: 10,340

Major Colleges and Universities: Michigan State University (in East Lansing), Lansing Community College

Daily Newspaper: *Lansing State Journal*

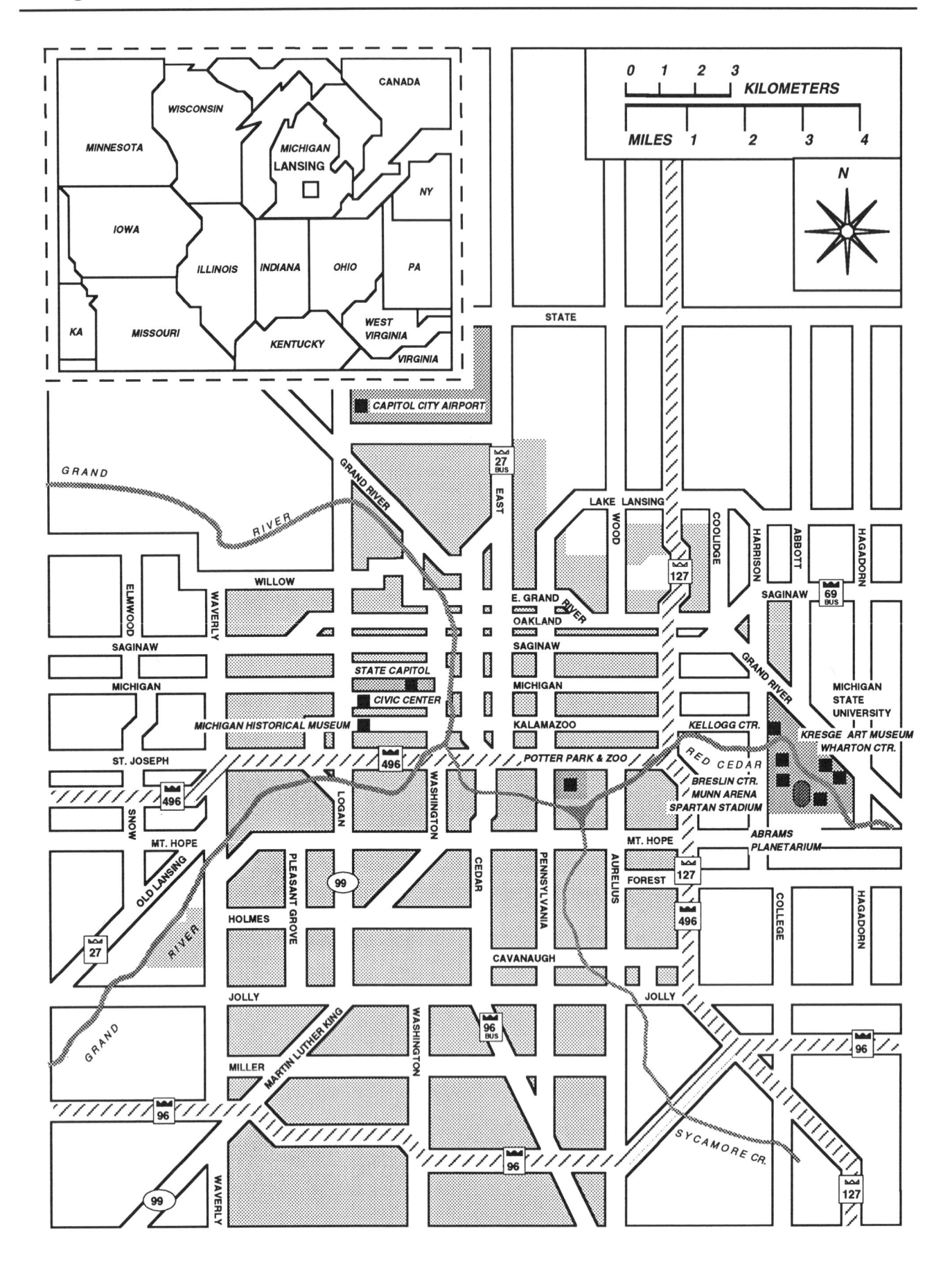

Michigan—Lansing *Cities of the United States • 2nd Edition*

Introduction

Lansing, the capital of Michigan, is the focus of a metropolitan statistical area that includes the city of East Lansing and Clinton, Eaton, and Ingham counties. Virtually a wilderness when the site was designated for the building of the state capital, Lansing was slow to develop until the arrival of the railroad. The nation's first land grant college was founded in Lansing, and the city became a world leader in the automotive industry through the pioneering work of the Olds Motor Vehicle Company. Today Lansing's status as the state capital, its industrial base, and the presence of Michigan State University in East Lansing contribute to the city's strength.

Geography and Climate

Lansing is located on the Grand River at its junction with the Red Cedar. The area climate alternates between continental and semi-marine. When little or no wind is present, the weather becomes continental, producing pronounced fluctuations in temperature. The weather turns semi-marine with a strong wind from the Great Lakes. Snowfall averages about forty-eight inches annually. Tornadoes occur occasionally, as do thunder and wind storms. Flooding is likely one year out of three; floods cause extensive damage one year out of ten.

Area: 32.8 square miles (1990)

Elevation: 830 feet above sea level

Average Temperatures: January, 21.6° F; July, 71.7° F; annual average, 47.1° F

Average Annual Precipitation: 31 inches of rain; 48 inches of snow

History

Wilderness Site Chosen for State Capital

The original settlers of Lansing arrived at the junction of the Grand and Red Cedar rivers expecting to find New Settlement, a city that turned out to exist only on paper. Most of the pioneers were from the village of Lansing, New York, and some decided to settle the area, deciding to call it Lansing Township in honor of their former home. James Seymour, another resident of New York State, migrated to Detroit in the mid-1830s and acquired land holdings in the Michigan interior for purposes of speculation. Seymour was aware that the Michigan constitution of 1835 specified that a permanent site be found by 1847 for the state capital, which was then temporarily located in Detroit. The legislators feared Detroit's proximity to Canada would make it susceptible to foreign invasion, as had been the case in the War of 1812. Since no mutually agreed-upon township could be found, Seymour pressed the idea of Lansing as the site, but his suggestion initially evoked laughter from the legislators. Seymour's persistence finally prevailed and Lansing, a wilderness spot with one log house and a sawmill, became the new center of Michigan's government.

By December 1847, a frame capitol building had been built, and the creation of a business district had begun at the point where Main Street and Washington Avenue now meet. In 1849, Lansing was incorporated with a population of fifteen hundred inhabitants. In 1854, a new brick capitol was constructed. Small agricultural implement industries began to introduce mechanical farming techniques to combat the manpower shortage caused by the Civil War. Development, however, was slowed by lack of transportation and the uncertainty of retaining the state capital at Lansing. But the arrival of the railroad boosted the economy by linking Lansing with the rest of the state. The legislature appropriated funding for a new capitol, which was completed in 1878 on a 10-acre park next to the Grand River in the center of the city.

Industry and Education Join Government

Automotive innovator Ransom E. Olds, who used gasoline power instead of steam, founded the Olds Motor Vehicle Company in 1897. Olds is credited with building the first practical automobile, and by the turn of the century his company was the world's largest car manufacturer and had earned a reputation for high quality. Olds's company lives on as the Oldsmobile Division of General Motors. By 1904 Lansing was the base of more than two-hundred manufacturing businesses and a world leader in the production of agricultural implements, automobiles, and gasoline engines.

Farmers had created the Michigan Agricultural Society in 1850 as a means to be heard in the state legislature. Many of the settlers from the East placed high value on education and culture; they petitioned the state legislature through the Agricultural Society for a college of agriculture to be founded separately from the University of Michigan in Ann Arbor. The nation's oldest land-grant institution, created as part of Michigan's state constitution of 1850, was thus granted authorization in 1855. The agricultural college was founded on nearly 700 acres in the woods three miles east of Lansing in present-day East Lansing, which was granted a city charter in 1907. The name of the college was changed to Michigan State College of Agriculture and Applied Sciences in 1923, and became a university upon its centennial celebration in 1955.

Historical Information: Library of Michigan, 735 East Michigan Avenue, P.O. Box 30007, Lansing, MI 48909; telephone (517)373-1593; and, Friends of Michigan Women's Historical Center, 213 Main, Lansing, MI 48909; telephone (517)484-1880

Population Profile

Metropolitan Area Residents
1970: 378,000
1980: 420,000
1990: 432,674
Annual average percent change, 1980–1988: 0.2%
U.S. rank in 1980: 81st
U.S. rank in 1990: 83rd

City Residents
1970: 131,000
1980: 130,414
1990: 127,321 (of which, 60,351 were males, and 66,970 were females)
Percent change, 1980–1990: –2.4%
U.S. rank in 1980: 122nd
U.S. rank in 1990: 142nd (State rank: 5th)

Density: 3,740.9 people per square mile (1990)

Racial and ethnic characteristics (1990)
  White: 94,135
  Black: 23,626
  American Indian, Eskimo, Aleut: 1,295
  Asian and Pacific Islander: 2,263
  Hispanic (may be of any race): 10,112

Percent of residents born in state: 75.9% (1990)

Age characteristics (1990)
  Population under 5 years old: 11,702
  Population 5 to 9 years old: 9,966
  Population 10 to 14 years old: 8,543
  Population 15 to 19 years old: 8,361
  Population 20 to 24 years old: 11,993
  Population 25 to 29 years old: 13,795
  Population 30 to 34 years old: 12,856
  Population 35 to 39 years old: 10,600
  Population 40 to 44 years old: 8,270
  Population 45 to 49 years old: 5,812
  Population 50 to 54 years old: 4,625
  Population 55 to 59 years old: 4,359
  Population 60 to 64 years old: 4,268
  Population 65 to 69 years old: 3,935
  Population 70 to 74 years old: 3,153
  Population 75 to 79 years old: 2,333
  Population 80 to 84 years old: 1,545
  Population 85 years and over: 1,205
  Median age: 29.7 years

Births (1988)
  Total number: 2,617

Deaths (1988)
  Total number: 1,018 (of which, 20 were infants under the age of 1 year)

Money income (1989)
  Per capita income: $12,232
  Median household income: $26,398
  Total households: 50,835
  Number of households with income of . . .
    less than $5,000: 3,971
    $5,000 to $9,999: 5,553
    $10,000 to $14,999: 4,905
    $15,000 to $24,999: 9,582
    $25,000 to $34,999: 8,775
    $35,000 to $49,999: 9,643
    $50,000 to $74,999: 6,270
    $75,000 to $99,999: 1,504
    $100,000 to $149,999: 538
    $150,000 or more: 94
  Percent of families below poverty level: 16.5% (66.0% of which were female householder families with related children under 5)
1991 FBI Crime Index Total: 10,340

The Michigan State Capitol Building.

Municipal Government

Lansing city government is administered by an eight-member council and a mayor, who does not serve as a member of council; all are elected to a four-year term.

Head Official: Mayor James A. Crawford (NP) (since 1992; current term expires December 31, 1993)

Total Number of City Employees: 1,200 (1993)

City Information: City Hall, 124 West Michigan, Lansing, MI 48933; telephone (517)483-4141

Economy

Major Industries and Commercial Activity

Services, wholesale and retail trade, and manufacturing (primarily of transportation products) comprise the economic base of the Lansing metropolitan area. The number of service firms in the region increased by 50 percent during the 1980s and employment rose 44 percent. Health care accounts for the largest share of the services sector, followed by business services and trade associations. Twelve insurance companies have corporate or regional offices in Lansing; four are headquartered there. Other important sectors are government, education, and transportation and public utilities.

Nearly six-hundred wholesalers employing 8,400 people are located in the Lansing region, reflecting an 18 percent increase in the number of firms and a 9 percent increase in employment since 1980. Because of the region's large share of professional workers, the retailing market showed robust growth throughout the 1980s.

The Lansing region is an important notch in the Midwest manufacturing belt. There are 430 manufacturers in the region; forty auto-related manufacturers account for 70 percent of manufacturing jobs. Industrial leaders such as the General Motors Buick-Oldsmobile-Cadillac Group Lansing Product Team adapt progressive manufacturing processes and new technology. Many firms are following the General Motors lead to institute advanced materials-handling techniques and to encourage participatory management, with the goal of improving product quality and increasing competitiveness. A small but rapidly growing sector is the instruments industry, reflecting a variety of high-technology firms spawned at Michigan State University.

Incentive Programs—New and Existing Companies

Financial institutions and economic development corporations in metropolitan Lansing work together to provide lower-cost financing and tax incentives to encourage new and expanding businesses. Fifteen banking and trust firms, three savings and loan companies, and twenty-two credit unions facilitate access to nearly $38 billion in funds. Property tax abatements are available. Among them are the exemption from Michigan tax of personal property such as inventories, jigs and fixtures, and pollution control equipment; industrial property tax abatements for expansion projects; and tax increment financing.

The Economic Development Resource Center at Michigan State University, a single point of contact for businesses, provides resources and information to assist firms in starting, locating, expanding, and prospering in mid-Michigan.

Job training programs—State-sponsored job training programs, recently revamped through the $25 million Michigan Adult Education Training Initiative, include the Job Training Partnership Act, the Displaced Homemakers program, summer youth employment programs, and pre-college programs in engineering and sciences. The State Department of Commerce administers a $1.2 million Training Incentive Fund, which provides assistance to employers wishing to upgrade the skills of their current work force. Other programs include Targeted Jobs Tax Credits, and adult and vocational education.

Development Projects

The downtown facelift that Lansing has undergone in recent years includes new office buildings, a convention center, a State Library, a paved Riverwalk at Riverfront Park, and the refurbishment of the Capitol building. That structure, considered a fine example of the Gilded Age of public building construction, underwent a three-year, $58 million restoration to a like-new, authentic condition that won it the 1992 National Trust for Historic Preservation Honor Award. It was rededicated in 1992.

Economic Development Information: Lansing Regional Chamber of Commerce, 510 West Washtenaw,

P.O. Box 14030, Lansing, MI 48901; telephone (517)487-6340

Commercial Shipping

The Grand Trunk & Western, C S X, and Conrail rail freight lines serve Lansing. Fifty-seven motor freight carriers transport goods from the city to markets throughout the country. Air cargo is handled by several companies at Capital City Airport. Four interstate highways connect the area to all major North American markets, including Canada.

Labor Force and Employment Outlook

Lansing area employers draw from a large, stable pool of highly skilled, professional workers. Due to the restructuring of the manufacturing sector, labor is plentiful. Michigan State University's thousands of graduates add to the pool; 32 percent of the labor force has at least an undergraduate degree; 26 percent has some vocational/technical training. State government has been downsized in recent years, MSU employees are holding on to their jobs longer, and employers have not been filling vacancies. Nevertheless, local analysts predict that the tri-county region will retain its share of U.S. employment within 1 percent based on trends since 1970. Manufacturing employment will continue to decline, but the number of manufacturing firms is expected to increase.

The following is a summary of data regarding the Lansing metropolitan area labor force as of September 1992.

Size of non-agricultural labor force: 210,800

Number of workers employed in . . .
  mining: not reported
  construction: 5,600
  manufacturing: 30,400
  transportation and public utilities: 6,300
  wholesale and retail trade: 48,000
  finance, insurance, and real estate: 12,200
  services: 44,600
  government: 63,700

Average hourly earnings of production workers employed in manufacturing: $16.29

Unemployment rate: 5.7%

Largest employers	Number of employees
BOC Lansing Auto Division	20,500
State of Michigan	15,600
Michigan State University	9,000
Meijer Inc.	4,000
Sparrow Hospital	3,500
Lansing School District	2,400
Lansing Community College	2,000

Cost of Living

In July 1993 the Michigan legislature passed a bill cutting residents' property taxes an average of 60 to 65 percent, beginning with the summer 1994 tax bills. The tax cut, the largest in Michigan history, was to be accomplished by eliminating local and intermediate school district operating millages. The legislature was then considering a number of options to restore money for schools, including sales taxes on services and entertainment, an increase in the state sales tax, or a statewide millage.

The following is a summary of data regarding several key cost of living factors in the Lansing area as of mid-1993.

1992 (Second Quarter) ACCRA Cost of Living Index: 105.2 (U.S. average = 100.0)

1992 (2nd Quarter) ACCRA Average House Price: $137,185

State income tax rate: 4.6% of all taxable income

State sales tax rate: 4.0%

Local income tax rate: 1.0% resident, 0.5% non-resident

Local sales tax rate: None

Property tax rate: 15.40 mills per $1,000 assessed value

Economic Information: Lansing Regional Chamber of Commerce, 510 West Washtenaw, P.O. Box 14030, Lansing, MI 48901; telephone (517)487-6340

Education and Research

Elementary and Secondary Schools

The Lansing School District, the fourth largest in the state of Michigan, is administered by a nine-member, nonpartisan board of education that appoints a superintendent.

The following is a summary of data regarding the Lansing public schools as of the 1992–1993 school year.

Total enrollment: 22,865

Number of facilities
 elementary schools: 33
 middle schools: 4
 senior high schools: 3
 other: 2

Teacher salaries
 minimum: $26,282
 maximum: $52,039

Funding per pupil: $4,614.16

Public Schools Information: Lansing School District, 519 West Kalamazoo Street, Lansing, MI 48933; telephone (517) 374-4071

Colleges and Universities

Michigan State University in East Lansing is the largest institution of higher learning in the area, with an enrollment of more than forty-thousand students. Granting degrees in four colleges at all educational levels, the university has gained an international reputation for research. It is the only U.S. university with three medical colleges. Cooley Law School in Lansing serves working professionals with a program leading to a Juris Law degree. Great Lakes Bible College offers undergraduate programs in theology, fine arts, and interdisciplinary studies. Lansing Community College in downtown Lansing provides vocational and technical curricula as well as training programs in more than three-hundred areas of study. Other schools in the three-county region are Olivet College, Davenport College, Capital Area Career Center, and Harry Hill Vocational Center.

Libraries and Research Centers

At least twenty libraries located in Lansing are maintained by educational institutions, government agencies, and hospitals. The Lansing Public Library houses 275,00 books and nearly five-hundred periodical titles in addition to records, films, maps, and art reproductions. Materials pertaining to local history are among the special collections; the library operates two branches and a bookmobile. The Library of Michigan maintains holdings of well over 5 million volumes and special collections in such fields as Michigan local and family history and eighteenth- and nineteenth-century periodicals. The library also provides Braille and large-type books and serves as a depository for federal and state documents. Thomas M. Cooley Law School, Lansing Community College, and Great Lakes Bible College maintain campus libraries.

Michigan State University (MSU), working closely with more than a dozen private companies, formulates new technology in various fields. With research centers of international stature, MSU operates facilities for study in a range of fields. In addition to institutes that work in cooperation with private firms, MSU operates the National Super Conducting Cyclotron Laboratory, the MSU-Department of Energy Plant Research Laboratory, the Case Center for Computer Aided Design (CAD) Artificial Language Laboratory, and the Computerized Pattern Recognition Lab. Research in electron optics, spectroscopy, and packaging technology is also conducted at the university.

The Composite Materials and Structure Center is a research partner with the Michigan Molecular Institute, the National Science Foundation, the Ford Motor Company, and the U.S. Department of Defense. The Pesticide Research Center works with pesticides and pest control. The Michigan Biotechnology Institute, a non-profit corporation, applies recombinant deoxyribonucleic acid, plant tissue culture, and immobilized enzymes to the commercialization of biotechnology in the state of Michigan.

The state-supported Research Excellence and Education Fund makes available $25 million annually for basic and applied research at public universities in areas relevant to economic development.

Public Library Information: Lansing Public Library, 401 South Capitol Avenue, Lansing, MI 48933; telephone (517)374-4600

Health Care

Seven hospitals, with a total of more than 1,200 beds, serve metropolitan Lansing. Several facilities based in the city are noted for research as well as treatment and care. Sparrow Hospital maintains a burn unit, a dialysis unit, and a family practice center; the hospital's Department of Laboratories conducts research in multiple sclerosis, AIDS, and treatment of cancer through bone marrow transplants. St. Law-

Michigan Library and Historical Center.

rence Hospital operates a poison control center, a health service for persons without physicians, and an alcohol detoxification and counseling unit; hospital researchers have successfully used infusion pumps for cancer treatment.

Ingham Medical Center provides, among other services, care for lung disease, heart surgery, pediatric and adult intensive care, and psychiatric care; Lansing General Hospital is noted for substance abuse and sports medicine programs. All major facilities in the city offer twenty-four-hour emergency care and maintain maternity units. Michigan State University provides medical education and training through the College of Human Medicine and the College of Osteopathic Medicine; it also operates an outpatient clinic open to the public.

Recreation

Sightseeing

Lansing's Capitol, completed in 1879 and one of the first state edifices built to emulate the nation's Capitol, is the center of attraction in Lansing's downtown sector. Two blocks southwest of the Capitol is the new Michigan Library and Historical Center, a modern facility with an outdoor courtyard. The museum traces the history of Michigan from its remote past to the twentieth century, including the evolution of the state's economy in agriculture, timber, mining, and manufacturing to the rise and dominance of the automobile. Impression Five Science Museum, Michigan's largest participatory science museum with two-hundred exhibits, stimulates the senses with interactive displays. Next to Impression Five is the R. E. Olds Transportation Museum, a major transportation museum recognizing the contribution of R. E. Olds to the automotive industry and the evolution of transportation in Lansing.

Michigan State University in neighboring East Lansing provides numerous sightseeing opportunities beginning with Beal-Garfield Botanical Gardens, the oldest, continuously operated garden of its type in the country with over five-thousand species of plants. Abrams Planetarium presents programs on space science topics in the sky theater, and the MSU Cyclotron is an international center for research in nuclear science and accelerator instrumentation physics. The Michigan State Museum houses displays on cultural and scientific development. The Michigan State Dairy Barn offers daily tours at milking time.

Michigan Women's Historical Center and Hall of Fame pays tribute to the contributions of Michigan women. The Lansing-North Lansing Electric Railroad Museum contains models of the original electric trolley and interurban steam and diesel locomotives that operated in Lansing until 1929. Potter Park Zoo places animals in natural settings, with a special display on Michigan animals; the aviary houses exotic species and the fish exhibit features a glass floor.

At the Rose Lake Wildlife Research Center, 3,000 acres of woods and marsh are accessible via hiking trails; Woldumar Nature Center stresses environmental education and is open to the public for hiking. Fenner Arboretum maintains self-guided trails leading to a prairie scene with live bison. Red Cedar, Sanford, and Baker Woodlot Natural Areas are islands of wilderness on the Michigan State University campus. The Ledges in Grand Ledge, 10 miles west of Lansing, is named for its rock formations, which rise along the Grand River and are over 300 million years old.

Arts and Culture

Many of Lansing's cultural events take place at the Wharton Center for Performing Arts on the campus of Michigan State University. The Greater Lansing Symphony Orchestra presents a season of classical and pops concerts. Lansing is particularly strong in theater. The nationally known BoarsHead Theater, a residential professional company based at the Wharton Center, presents a season of modern and classical drama and comedy as well as Winterfare, a festival of new plays. Other local theater companies are the Lansing Civic Players Guild, the Community Circle Players at Riverwalk Theatre, and Children's Ballet Theatre, which stages *The Nutcracker* and a spring performance annually. The Michigan State University Department of Theater sponsors performances and cultural events on campus.

Festivals and Holidays

The BoarsHead Theater Winterfare festival of new American plays begins in January. The Sugar Bush Festival at Fenner Arboretum takes place in March. The East Lansing Art Fair is held the third weekend in May followed by the Lansing Art Fair the second weekend in June. One of the year's major annual events is the Michigan Festival, held for ten days in August on the Michigan State University campus; major performing arts events are staged both indoors and outdoors. Riverfest on Labor Day weekend features a lighted boat parade on the Grand River and a fireworks display at Riverfront Park.

Sports for the Spectator

The Michigan State Spartans compete in the Big Ten athletic conference and field nationally competitive teams. The football team plays its home games in the seventy-six-thousand-seat Spartan Stadium. Munn Ice Arena seats sixty-five hundred fans and is the home of the Spartan hockey team. The Jack Breslin Student Events Center, which opened in 1991 and seats 15,000 people, is the home of the MSU basketball program. One of the nation's premier women's softball teams, the Lansing Laurels, enjoy a large local following. Each August the Ladies Professional Golf Association competes in the Oldsmobile classic. The Spartan Speedway attracts super stocks and hobby stocks racing on Friday nights from mid-May through September. Jackson Harness Raceway features seasonal parimutuel racing at night in nearby Jackson.

Sports for the Participant

Lansing municipal softball leagues field three-hundred softball teams, and a men's baseball league schedules daily games with many former collegiate athletes participating. Golf is particularly popular at three private clubs and twenty-five public and municipal courses of varying difficulty. More than twenty-five golf tournaments are held in the summer. There are more than one-hundred neighborhood parks in the city, and Lansing maintains public tennis courts at city parks and public school locations. Forty courts are located behind Spartan Stadium on the Michigan State University campus. Public outdoor pools are located throughout greater Lansing, and lakes with beaches are nearby in Holt and Haslett. Ice skating facilities are available at Washington Park and Munn Arena at Michigan State University, and at the Lansing Ice and Gymnastic Centre. River Trail presents a canoeing route that follows the banks of the Grand and Red Cedar rivers through urban and natural environments and the campus of Michigan State University.

Shopping and Dining

In East Lansing, near the Michigan State University campus, specialty shops that cater to students are clustered among exclusive clothing stores, small restaurants, bookstores, and record shops. The Lansing City Market offers a large selection of fresh fruits and vegetables. Several new, upscale restaurants are located near the university; older, more established eateries in the Capitol district include two popular Italian restaurants, one of them displaying an extensive Tiffany lamp collection. A family-owned sandwich shop near the Capitol serves a patented oliveburger.

Visitor Information: Convention and Visitors Bureau of Greater Lansing, Civic Center, Suite 302, Lansing, MI 48933; telephone (517)487-6800

Convention Facilities

Meeting and convention planners may choose among several facilities in the Lansing area. Opened in 1987, the Lansing Center is situated downtown on the Grand River and Riverwalk near the Capitol Complex. The center adjoins the Radisson Hotel and a sixteen-hundred-car parking area via an enclosed walkway. Accommodating up to 5,000 people, the exhibit halls and meeting rooms function as separate units or in multiple combinations. The Lansing Civic Arena, also downtown, contains a main auditorium, several meeting rooms, and an exhibition hall; the complex will seat up to 5,400 people in a theater or meeting setting and as many as 2,000 people for a banquet.

The indoor arena of the Ingham County Fairgrounds is available for horse shows, exhibitions, trade shows, and other large events. In downtown Lansing the Center for the Arts adjoins an art gallery and provides barrier-free space for functions with up to 240 participants. In East Lansing, Michigan State University maintains meeting facilities in the Kellogg Center, the Breslin Center, the Hannah Center Ballroom, and the Wharton Center for the Performing Arts. Hotels and motels, containing a total of almost four-thousand rooms for lodgings, also offer banquet and meeting rooms.

Convention Information: Convention and Visitors Bureau of Greater Lansing, Civic Center, Suite 302, Lansing, MI 48933; telephone (517)487-6800

Transportation

Approaching the City

Seven commercial airlines schedule regular daily flights into Capital City Airport, located fifteen minutes from downtown Lansing. Daily rail service to Lansing is provided by Amtrak.

An efficient highway system facilitates access to Lansing and its environs. Part of a beltway circling the southern half of the city, I-96 is intersected by several major and secondary routes; east-west I-69 completes the beltway around the northern sector. I-496 bisects the downtown area westward from north-south U.S. 127 in East Lansing. Other principal highways are U.S. 27 and M 99, both running north-south, and east-west M 43.

Traveling in the City

Downtown Lansing streets are laid out on a strict grid system with the Capitol Complex as the center of orientation; the web of one-way streets can be confusing. Public bus transportation is provided by Capital Area Transportation Authority (CATA), which operates twenty-five routes seven days a week in Lansing and East Lansing as well as to points throughout the metropolitan region. CATA's Fast Trak Park & Shuttle Service to downtown Lansing and the Capital Loop reduces rush-hour traffic and parking congestion in central city areas. Special service for elderly, handicapped, commuting, and rural patrons is available.

Communications

Newspapers and Magazines

The major daily newspaper in Lansing is the *Lansing State Journal*. A monthly magazine focusing on business news is the *Greater Lansing Business Monthly*. Other publications include *Lansing City Magazine, Lansing Metropolitan Quarterly,* and *State News,* a daily published by Michigan State University.

Television and Radio

One independent and three commercial television stations are based in Lansing; a public channel broadcasts from Michigan State University. Cable television service is available from three area companies. Lansing radio listeners receive broadcasts from six FM, four AM, and four FM/AM radio stations in the city and seven additional stations in the neighboring communities of East Lansing, Williamston, St. Johns, Jackson, Albion, and Midland. Musical programming includes country, classical, rock and roll, religious, top 40, and easy listening.

Media Information: Lansing State Journal, 120 East Lenawee, Lansing, MI 48919; telephone (517)377-1000

Selected Bibliography

Celizic, Mike, *The Biggest Game of Them All: Notre Dame, Michigan State, and the Fall of '66* (New York: Simon & Schuster, 1992)

MINNESOTA

Duluth 247
Minneapolis 257
Saint Paul 271

The State in Brief

Nickname: North Star State
Motto: *L'etoile du nord* (Star of the north)

Flower: Pink and white lady's slipper
Bird: Common loon

Area: 86,943 square miles (1990) (U.S. rank: 12th)
Elevation: Ranges from 602 feet to 2,301 feet above sea level
Climate: North part of state lies in the moist Great Lakes storm belt; western border is at the edge of the semi-arid Great Plains; spring is brief; summer is short, hot, and humid; winter is long and severe with heavy snowfall.

Admitted to Union: May 11, 1858
Capital: Saint Paul
Head Official: Governor Arne Carlson (R) (until 1995)

Population
   1970: 3,806,103
   1980: 4,076,000
   1990: 4,432,000
   Percent change, 1980–1990: 7.3%
   U.S. rank in 1990: 20th
   Percent of residents born in state: 75.6% (1990)
   Density: 55 people per square mile (1990; U.S. Rank: 31st)
   1991 FBI Crime Index Total: 199,274

Racial and Ethnic Characteristics (1990)
   White: 4,130,000
   Black: 2.2%
   American Indian, Eskimo, Aleut: 1.14%
   Asian and Pacific Islander: 1.78%
   Hispanic (may be of any race): 1.23%

Age Characteristics (1990)
   Population under 5 years old: 338,000
   Population 5 to 17 years old: 851,000
   Percent of population 65 years and older: 12.5%
   Median age: 33.0 years
   Voting-age population (1988): 3,201,000 (65.5% of whom cast votes for president)

Vital Statistics
   Total number of births (1992): 65,477
   Total number of deaths (1992): 34,909 (of which, 458 were infants under the age of 1 year)
   AIDS cases reported, 1981–1990: 747 (U.S. rank: 26th)

Economy
   Major industries: Manufacturing; trade; finance, insurance, and real estate; services
   Unemployment rate: 4.4% (September 1992)
   Per capita income: $14,389 (1989)
   Median household income: $30,909 (1989)
   Total number of families: 1,138,581 (7.3% of which had incomes below the poverty level; 1989)
   Income tax rate: 8.5%
   Sales tax rate: 6.5%

Duluth

The City in Brief

Founded: 1852 (chartered, 1870)

Head Official: Mayor Gary L. Doty (NP) (since 1992)

City Population
 1970: 100,578
 1980: 92,811
 1990: 85,493
 Percent change, 1980–1990: −7.9%
 U.S. rank in 1980: 184th
 U.S. rank in 1990: 243rd (State rank: 4th)

Metropolitan Area Population
 1970: 265,350
 1980: 266,650
 1990: 239,971
 Percent change, 1980–1990: −10.0%
 U.S. rank in 1980: Not available
 U.S. rank in 1990: Not available

Area: 67.6 square miles (1990)

Elevation: Ranges from 605 to 1,485 feet above sea level

Average Annual Temperature: 38.1° F

Average Annual Precipitation: 29.68 inches; average annual snowfall, 76.9 inches

Major Economic Sectors: Services, trade, government

Unemployment Rate: 6.0% (September 1992)

Per Capita Income: $12,484 (1989)

1992 (2nd Quarter) ACCRA Average House Price: Not reported

1992 (2nd Quarter) ACCRA Cost of Living Index: Not reported

1991 FBI Crime Index Total: 4,886

Major Colleges and Universities: University of Minnesota—Duluth

Daily Newspaper: *Duluth News-Tribune*

Minnesota—Duluth

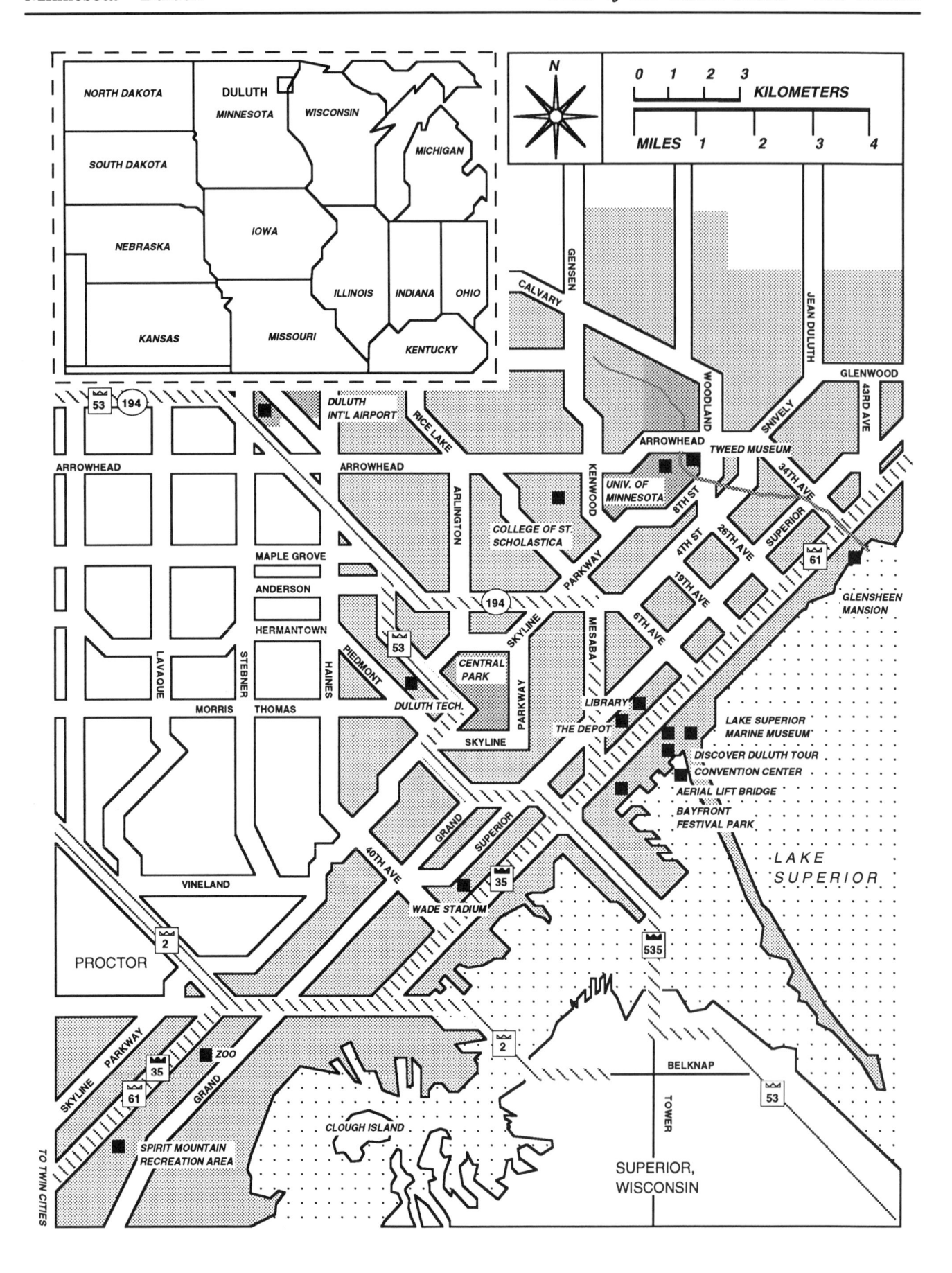

Cities of the United States • 2nd Edition

Introduction

The seat of St. Louis County in Minnesota, Duluth is the focus of a metropolitan statistical area comprised of both St. Louis County and Wisconsin's Douglas County. The city has developed into the second largest port on the Great Lakes and is the commercial, industrial, and cultural center of northern Minnesota. Duluth is noted for its dramatic geographic setting. Steep inclines, dotted with buildings that seem to pop out of hillsides, provide the backdrop for Duluth's famous Skyline Parkway, which winds above the city.

Geography and Climate

Duluth is located on a natural harbor at the western tip of Lake Superior and at the base of a range of hills overlooking the St. Louis River. This position below high terrain and along the lake permits easterly winds to cool the area automatically, thus earning Duluth the nickname of the "Air-Conditioned City." During the summer a westerly wind flow abates at night, and the cool lake air moves back in toward the city. High and low pressure systems and proximity to Lake Superior, the coldest of the Great Lakes, have an important influence on the climate, which is predominantly continental. Summer temperatures are thus cooler and winter temperatures warmer; the frequency of severe storms—wind, hail, tornadoes, freezing rain, and blizzards—is also low in comparison to other areas at a distance from the lake. Fall is an especially pleasant season in Duluth, as the changing leaves produce a striking combination of reds, yellows, and browns.

Area: 67.6 square miles (1990)

Elevation: Ranges from 605 to 1,485 feet above sea level

Average Temperatures: January, 6.3° F; July, 65.2° F; annual average, 38.1° F

Average Annual Precipitation: 29.68 inches; average annual snowfall, 76.9 inches

History

Harbor, Timber, and Ore Attract Development

The western Lake Superior area was originally occupied by members of the Sioux and Chippewa tribes. One of the first explorers of European descent to arrive in the area now occupied by Duluth was Frenchman Pierre Esprit Radisson, who explored the region in the 1650s or 1660s. The city was ultimately named, however, for Daniel Greysolon, Sieur du Lhut (variously spelled Dulhut, Derhaut, and du Luth), who visited the southern shore of Lake Superior in 1679 in an attempt to make peace between the Ojibway and Sioux tribes and to secure trading and trapping rights. A fur trading outlet remained in the area until 1847. The site's first permanent resident was George P. Stuntz, who was attracted by the beautiful wilderness landscape surrounding Lake Superior and settled there in 1852.

In 1854 and 1855 settlers flocked to the unnamed town hoping to discover copper deposits, although the Grand Portage and Fon du Lac people had not yet signed the Treaty of La Pointe that relinquished their mineral rights. In 1856 the village was named Duluth and designated the seat of St. Louis County. Almost immediately Duluth was beset by troubles: the panic of 1857 devastated the economy, and in 1859 a scarlet fever epidemic caused a further setback to the community. By the end of the Civil War, only two houses remained occupied in Duluth.

The town's fortunes were quickly reversed when geologists found iron ore and gold-bearing quartz at nearby Lake Vermillion. Then the Eastern financier Jay Cooke selected Duluth as the northern terminus of the Lake Superior & Mississippi Railroad. Adding to the boom, Maine woodsmen relocated to the region to establish a lumber industry. By 1869 the population of Duluth had grown to thirty-five hundred residents, and the city received its first charter a year later.

Growth Includes New Immigrants

The new prosperity was short-lived, however, as bank and real estate failures hurt the economy and plunged the city government into debt. Duluth was forced to revert to village status. The city's topsy-turvy early history reversed itself once again, however, when the lumbering industry was revitalized and grain business fueled the economy. By 1887 Duluth's population reached twenty-six thousand residents, and the state legislature granted permission for reclassification as a city. Six lakeshore communities were absorbed into the city by the end of the nineteenth century.

Among the settlers who had made Duluth home were immigrants from the Scandinavian countries and Finland, who settled in the city's West End. These people possessed a commitment to cooperative undertakings, a strong sense of individualism, and a respect for organizational arrangements—qualities that have shaped the city's character. In addition to its residents, Duluth is defined by its topography. The natural harbor is the base of the economy and the source of the city's scenic beauty.

Historical Information: St. Louis County Historical Society, 506 West Michigan, Duluth, MN; telephone (218)722-8011

Population Profile

Metropolitan Area Residents
1970: 265,350
1980: 266,650
1990: 239,971
Percent change, 1980–1990: −10.0%
U.S. rank in 1980: Not available
U.S. rank in 1990: Not available

City Residents
1970: 100,578
1980: 92,811
1990: 85,493 (of which, 40,302 were males, and 45,191 were females)
Percent change, 1980–1990: −7.9%
U.S. rank in 1980: 184th
U.S. rank in 1990: 243rd (State rank: 4th)

Density: 1,264.7 people per square mile (1990)

Racial and ethnic characteristics (1990)
  White: 95.9%
  Black: 0.9%
  American Indian, Eskimo, Aleut: 2.1%
  Asian and Pacific Islander: 0.9%
  Hispanic (may be of any race): 0.2%

Percent of residents born in state: 77.8% (1990)

Age characteristics (1990)
  Population under 5 years old: 5,449
  Population 5 to 9 years old: 5,669
  Population 10 to 14 years old: 5,375
  Population 15 to 19 years old: 6,628
  Population 20 to 24 years old: 8,236
  Population 25 to 29 years old: 6,278
  Population 30 to 34 years old: 6,459
  Population 35 to 39 years old: 6,657
  Population 40 to 44 years old: 5,617
  Population 45 to 49 years old: 4,182
  Population 50 to 54 years old: 3,357
  Population 55 to 59 years old: 3,214
  Population 60 to 64 years old: 3,721
  Population 65 to 69 years old: 3,746
  Population 70 to 74 years old: 3,605
  Population 75 to 79 years old: 3,154
  Population 80 to 84 years old: 2,188
  Population 85 years and over: 1,908
  Median age: 35.7 years

Births (1988)
  Total number: 1,197

Deaths (1988)
  Total number: 1,082 (of which, 10 were infants under the age of 1 year)

Money income (1989)
  Per capita income: $12,484
  Median household income: $23,370
  Total households: 34,646
  Number of households with income of . . .
    less than $5,000: 2,130
    $5,000 to $9,999: 5,245
    $10,000 to $14,999: 3,928
    $15,000 to $24,999: 6,956
    $25,000 to $34,999: 5,532
    $35,000 to $49,999: 5,275
    $50,000 to $74,999: 3,786
    $75,000 to $99,999: 1,063
    $100,000 to $149,999: 446
    $150,000 or more: 285
  Percent of families below poverty level: 10.5% (63.1% of which were female householder families with related children under 5)
1991 FBI Crime Index Total: 4,886

Municipal Government

The city of Duluth operates under a mayor-council form of government. The mayor and nine council members are elected to a four-year term. The city's mandatory arrest in domestic violence cases program is a national model.

Head Official: Mayor Gary L. Doty (NP) (since 1992; current term expires January 1, 1996)

Total Number of City Employees: 950 (1993)

City Information: City Hall, Mayor's Office, Room 403, 411 West First St., Duluth, MN 55802; telephone (218)723-3295

Economy

Major Industries and Commercial Activity

Principal industrial firms in Duluth include heavy and light manufacturing plants, food processing plants, woolen mills, lumber mills, cold storage plants, fisheries, grain elevators, and oil refineries. The city is a also a regional center for banking, retailing, and medical care for northern Minnesota, northern Wisconsin, northern Michigan, and northwestern Ontario, Canada. Arts and entertainment offerings as well as year-round recreation in a natural environment have contributed to expansion of the tourist industry in Duluth.

Items and goods produced: air reduction equipment, farm machinery, tractors, mining and heavy construction equipment, frozen food, canned goods and preserves, wood and wire products, Mackinaw cloth and heavy woolens

Incentive Programs—New and Existing Companies

The city of Duluth, St. Louis County, and the state of Minnesota administer several programs that provide low-interest incentive loans, reduced property and sales taxes, grants for infrastructure improvement and economic development, and job training and employment assistance. The Minnesota Power Company, the Northeast Entrepreneur Fund, and the Northstar Community Development Corporation are among the private organizations that offer various forms of incentives and assistance to industry and businesses operating in the region.

Development Projects

Of major importance to the local economy is construction of a $400 million paper mill by Lake Superior Paper Industries, a joint venture of subsidiaries of Minnesota Power in Duluth and Pentair Inc. in Saint Paul. Among other major developments are expansion of the Miller Hill Mall, construction of the Duluth Entertainment Convention Center and the addition of about 290 hotel rooms, extension of an interstate highway for downtown and waterfront access, and renovation of the historic waterfront. Further investment is taking place in electronics, publishing, and the financial sector.

Economic Development Information: Duluth Business Ombudsman, 325 Harbor Drive, Duluth, MN 55802; telephone (218)722-5501

Commercial Shipping

A vital part of the Duluth economy is the Port of Duluth-Superior, which is designated a Foreign Trade Zone and ranks among the top twelve ports in the country in total volume of international and domestic cargo shipped in a ten-month season. An average of 40 million tons of cargo is handled at Duluth-Superior each year; the impact on the local economy in 1990 was $248 million. Containing over 19 square miles of water at an average depth of 27 feet, the harbor is lined by 113 docks and nearly 50 miles of commercial waterfront development. Approximately ninety-five ocean vessels and more than twelve-hundred Great Lakes ships passed through the port in 1990. Duluth-Superior operates one of the largest grain-handling facilities in the world. Grain is the primary export product; domestic shipments consist mainly of iron ore and taconite, in addition to metal products, twine, machinery, coal, cement, salt, newsprint, lumber, and general cargo.

Connecting the port and the city of Duluth with inland markets are five railroads—Burlington Northern, Duluth Missabe & Iron Range, Chicago & Northwestern, Duluth Winnipeg & Pacific, and Soo Line—and nineteen motor freight carriers. Air cargo carriers serving Duluth International Airport with daily flights are Federal Express, United Parcel Service, Northwest Airlines Other Service, and U.S. Customs, Immigration, and Agriculture Services.

Labor Force and Employment Outlook

The following is a summary of data regarding the Duluth metropolitan area labor force as of September 1992.

Size of non-agricultural labor force: 98,400

Number of workers employed in . . .
  mining: 5,400
  construction: 3,800
  manufacturing: 8,100
  transportation and public utilities: 6,200
  wholesale and retail trade: 24,800
  finance, insurance, and real estate: 3,500
  services: 26,000
  government: 20,600

Average hourly earnings of production workers employed in manufacturing: $11.89

Unemployment rate: 6.0%

Largest employers: City of Duluth; Independent School District #709; St. Louis County; St. Mary's Medical Center; Beckley-Cardy, Inc. (school supply distributor); Edgell Communications, Inc. (publisher); Minnesota Power; St. Luke's Hospital; United States Government; University of Minnesota—Duluth; The Duluth Clinic, Ltd.; Duluth, Missabe & Iron Range Railway Co.; Minnesota State Government; Miller Dwan Medical Center; Minnesota Air National Guard; Minnesota Department of Transportation; United States Postal Service

Cost of Living

The following is a summary of data regarding several key cost of living factors in the Duluth area.

1992 (2nd Quarter) ACCRA Cost of Living Index: Not reported

1992 (2nd Quarter) ACCRA Average House Price: Not reported

State income tax rate: 8.5%

State sales tax: 6.5%

Local income tax rate: None

Local sales tax rate: 1.0% (food, clothing, and prescription drugs exempt)

Property tax rate: Single family homestead property—1.0% times the first $72,000 of estimated market value (EMV) plus 2.0% times the next $43,000 of EMV, plus 3.0% times the remainder over $115,000 EMV (a credit of 1.17% of the first $72,000 EMV is applied against the property tax bill of homestead property)

Economic Information: Duluth Area Chamber of Commerce, 325 Harbor Drive, Duluth, MN 55802; telephone (218)722-5501

Education and Research

Elementary and Secondary Schools

In the first experiment of its kind in the nation, Duluth's local school board handed over control of the school district to a private company, Education Alternatives Inc. of Minneapolis, in 1992. The goal was to redirect money out of the parts of the system not directly related to education and funnel it back into the classroom. Eventually, officials planned to introduce the Tesseract system, a teaching method that stresses children's individual learning styles and requires two teachers per classroom.

The following is a summary of data regarding Duluth public schools as of the 1992–1993 school year.

Total enrollment: 14,500

Number of facilities
  elementary schools: 18
  junior high schools: 3
  senior high schools: 3
  other: 1

Student/teacher ratio: elementary, 25:1; junior high, 21:1; senior high, 23.8:1 (1988–1989)

Teacher salaries
  minimum: $21,656
  maximum: $43,311

Funding per pupil: $3,050

Six area parochial elementary schools and a Hebrew school supplement the educational offerings.

Public Schools Information: Duluth Public Schools, Independent School District #709, 215 North First Avenue East, Duluth, MN 55802; telephone (218)723-4150

Colleges and Universities

The University of Minnesota—Duluth (UMD) is one of five campuses of the University of Minnesota. With an enrollment of more than seven-thousand students, UMD offers seventy-six majors including sixteen pre-professional programs, leading to baccalaureate and master's degrees, and the first two years of medical school. The College of St. Scholastica, a private four-year institution, has gained recognition in the areas of nursing, physical therapy, gerontology, health information administration, and early music. Duluth Business University grants diplomas in eight fields. Vocational training is available through the Duluth Technical Institute, and associate's degrees in nursing and radiologic technology, liberal education, and applied science are offered at Duluth Community College.

Libraries and Research Centers

The Duluth Public library houses more than 366,000 volumes, about 638 periodical subscriptions, and films, prints, maps, charts, art reproductions, compact discs, and microsoftware; special collections relate to Duluth, the Great Lakes region, and Minnesota. The library, a depository for federal documents, operates three branches. An addition to the library was planned for completion in 1992. The University of Minnesota—Duluth (UMD) and the College of St. Scholastica maintain substantial campus libraries. Duluth is home to the Saint Louis County Health Department Library, the Saint Louis County Law Library, the Environmental Protection Agency library, and the Northeast Minnesota Historical Center Archives, in addition to the libraries of health service and religious organizations.

The Natural Resources Research Institute, affiliated with UMD and staffed by scientists, engineers, and business consultants, conducts research and development projects in fields such as forest products and the environment.

Public Library Information: Duluth Public Library, 520 West Superior Street, Duluth, MN 55802; telephone (218)723-3802

Health Care

Duluth is a regional health care center for the northern sections of Minnesota, Wisconsin, and Michigan and for northwestern Ontario, Canada. Three hospitals, with a bed capacity of nearly 800, provide complete medical services. St. Mary's Medical Center, staffed by more than 330 physicians and dentists, operates the Regional Heart Center and provides cardiac surgery, cancer care, orthopedic surgery, intensive care, and level three prenatal care. St. Mary's offers twenty-four-hour emergency treatment and maintains trauma and poison information units in addition to outpatient services, home care, and community education programs.

St. Luke's Hospital, a regional neurosurgical center, also houses the federally-designated Emergency Medical Service Regional Trauma Center. A full range of general services is supplemented by such specialties as psychiatry, oncology, physical medicine, hospice care, high cholesterol treatment, occupational health services, lithotripsy, and magnetic resonance imaging. More than 300 physicians and dentists are on St. Luke's staff. Miller-Dwan Medical Center administers the largest mental health program in the region and operates a burn clinic along with hemodialysis, medical rehabilitation, rheumatic disease, and radiation therapy units. Area clinics include The Duluth Clinic, which operates four neighborhood centers and six affiliated clinics, and Polinsky Medical Rehabilitation Center, which specializes in work injury management.

Recreation

Sightseeing

The St. Louis County Heritage and Arts Center is housed in the 1892 Union Depot, a renovated railroad depot with four levels of history and arts exhibits. On display are antique doll and toy collections, a Victorian parlor, Indian crafts, and Depot Square, a recreation of 1910 Duluth that contains twenty-four old-time stores, a silent movie theater, and an ice-cream parlor. The old immigration room that once processed immigrants is preserved in its original condition. Railroad cars and locomotives, including the first locomotive in Minnesota and one of the largest steam locomotives ever built, are on exhibit.

The Canal Park Marine Museum houses exhibits on the history of Lake Superior Shipping while the Lake Superior Museum of Transportation maintains one of the nation's finest collections of historical railroad equipment. At Lake Superior Zoological Gardens animals from around the world can be viewed in facilities that include a nocturnal house and a children's zoo. Located on the shore of Lake Superior, Glensheen is a Jacobean-style mansion featuring original furnishings and a collection of carriages and sleighs.

The Skyline Parkway, a 16-mile boulevard above Duluth, provides a dramatic view of the city, the harbor, and Lake Superior. Lake Shore Drive parallels Lake Superior from Duluth to Thunder Bay and is considered one of the most scenic coastal highways in the nation. The Aerial Lift Bridge, which connects Minnesota Point with the mainland and spans Duluth harbor, is one of Duluth's most popular tourist attractions. The present bridge, built in 1930, is the world's largest and fastest lift bridge.

Arts and Culture

Union Depot now houses eight of Duluth's major arts and cultural institutions. The Duluth Art Institute sponsors major exhibitions in addition to its instructional programs. Rooted in classical ballet with contemporary dance influences, the Duluth Ballet stages three major performance series annually. The Duluth Playhouse, founded in 1914 and one of the nation's oldest community theaters, produces a variety of theatrical presentations. Organized in 1932, the Duluth-Superior Symphony Orchestra presents seven concerts a season, as well as three Pops performances and an annual holiday concert. The Matinee Musicale, Duluth's oldest cultural organization, promotes promising young musicians. The Tweed Museum of Art at the University of Minnesota—Duluth presents historical and contemporary exhibitions in nine galleries and is home to the Sax Sculpture Conservatory.

Festivals and Holidays

The summer season in Duluth features the Park Point Art Fair in June, the Fourth Fest in July, and Taste North Food Festival and Bayfront Blues Festival, both in August. The Duluth Aviation Expo takes place during odd-numbered years. The International Folk Festival presents music, ethnic foods, and dance at Bayfront Park in August.

Sports for the Spectator

The University of Minnesota—Duluth competes nationally in Division I hockey, playing a twenty-home game schedule at the Convention Center. The facility is home to the Ice Capades, a professional ice skating troupe, which practices there prior to its national tours. The Beargrease Sled Dog Marathon, the nation's premier dog race in the lower forty-eight states, is a 500-mile wilderness race held in early January. The race's route, from Duluth to Grand Portage and back, includes fourteen checkpoints along Lake Superior's North Shore.

The Duluth Winter Sport Festival begins at the same time as the Beargrease and runs until the end of January. The Duluth Yacht Club sailboat races from Duluth and Port Wing take place on Labor Day weekend. Also scheduled for Labor Day weekend is the Great North Arabian Horse Show at the County Fairgrounds.

Sports for the Participant

Spirit Mountain Recreation Area offers downhill skiing, cross-country trails, tennis, camping, and hiking. Duluth maintains, on 11,000 acres of land, 105 municipal parks and playgrounds, two twenty-seven-hole golf courses, forty-one tennis courts, twenty baseball and softball fields, and twenty-two community recreation centers. In addition are 44 miles of snowmobile trails, seven hiking trails, and five cross-country ski trails maintained by the city. Residents and visitors can compete in Grandmother's Marathon, which is run along the North Shore the second weekend in June. The recently completed $7 million

Fond-Du-Luth Gaming Casino is another popular attraction.

Shopping and Dining

The development of Duluth's historic waterfront downtown and the conversion of a local brewery into a hotel, restaurant, and shopping complex on the shore of Lake Superior have modernized Duluth's shopping milieu. Duluth restaurants offer freshwater fish from Lake Superior. Ethnic cuisine consists principally of Greek, Italian, and Chinese dishes.

Visitor Information: Duluth Convention and Visitors Bureau, Endion Station, 100 Lake Place Drive, Duluth, MN 55892; telephone (218)722-4011 or 1-800-4-DULUTH; and, Duluth Area Chamber of Commerce, 325 Harbor Drive, Duluth, MN 55082; telephone (218)722-5501

Convention Facilities

The Duluth Entertainment Convention Center is the site of conventions and a wide range of other functions. Attracting more than a million visitors a year, the complex houses two-hundred thousand square feet of meeting and exhibit space and an eight-thousand-seat arena and a twenty-four-hundred-seat auditorium. An addition to the center was completed in 1990, offering a twenty-six-thousand-square-foot ballroom, fifteen meeting rooms, and exhibit space. Fifty hotels and motels, several of them with meeting facilities, provide more than twenty-eight hundred rooms for lodgings in the Duluth area.

Convention Information: Duluth Convention and Visitors Bureau, Endion Station, 100 Lake Place Drive, Duluth, MN 55802; telephone (218)722-4011

Transportation

Approaching the City

The Duluth International Airport, located six miles from downtown, is the destination for most air traffic into the city. Domestic and international commercial carriers schedule daily flights into the passenger terminal.

Duluth is the terminus point for Interstate 35, which extends from the United States-Mexico border into northern Minnesota; federal highways providing easy access into the city include U.S. 53, 61, and 2. State routes running through Duluth are 23, 39, and 194.

Traveling in the City

Duluth Transit Authority (DTA) provides public bus transportation throughout the metropolitan area; among the DTA's special services are A Special Transit Ride (STRIDE) for handicapped passengers and carpool and rideshare programs. The DTA operates the "Discover Duluth" sightseeing tour and the Port Town Trolley, a downtown circulator, during the summer months. Visitors may also explore the city on horse-drawn carriages.

Communications

Newspapers and Magazines

Duluth's major daily newspaper is the *Duluth News-Tribune.* Several suburban newspapers and shopping guides circulate weekly. *Labor World,* a labor newspaper established in 1895, appears biweekly. *The Duluthian Magazine,* a bimonthly, is published with a business and community orientation. A number of special-interest magazines are published in the city on such subjects as mining and mineral processing, the restaurant industry, and the dental profession.

Television and Radio

Four television stations, representing the three major commercial networks and the public network, are received in Duluth; cable programming is available by subscription. Seven AM and fifteen FM radio stations offer a variety of formats, including classical, contemporary, and country music, religious programming, news, and public interest features.

Media Information: Duluth News-Tribune, 424 West First Street, Duluth, MN 55802; telephone (218)723-5281; and, *The Duluthian Magazine,* Duluth Area Chamber of Commerce, 325 Harbor Drive, Duluth, MN 55802; telephone (218)722-5501

Minneapolis

The City in Brief

Founded: 1849 (incorporated, 1866)

Head Official: Mayor Donald M. Fraser (D) (since 1980)

City Population
 1970: 434,000
 1980: 370,951
 1990: 368,383
 Percent change, 1980–1990: −0.7%
 U.S. rank in 1980: 34th
 U.S. rank in 1990: 42nd

Metropolitan Area Population
 1970: 1,982,000
 1980: 2,137,000
 1990: 2,464,124
 Percent change, 1980–1990: 15.3%
 U.S. rank in 1980: 17th
 U.S. rank in 1990: 16th

Area: 54.9 square miles (1990)

Elevation: Ranges from 687 feet to 1,060 feet above sea level

Average Annual Temperature: 44.7° F

Average Annual Precipitation: 26.36 inches

Major Economic Sectors: Services, trade, manufacturing, government

Unemployment Rate: 4.3% (September 1992)

Per Capita Income: $14,830 (1989)

1992 (3rd Quarter) ACCRA Average House Price: $120,030

1992 (3rd Quarter) ACCRA Cost of Living Index: 100.2 (U.S. average = 100.0)

1991 FBI Crime Index Total: 42,115

Major Colleges and Universities: University of Minnesota—Twin Cities

Daily Newspaper: *Star Tribune*

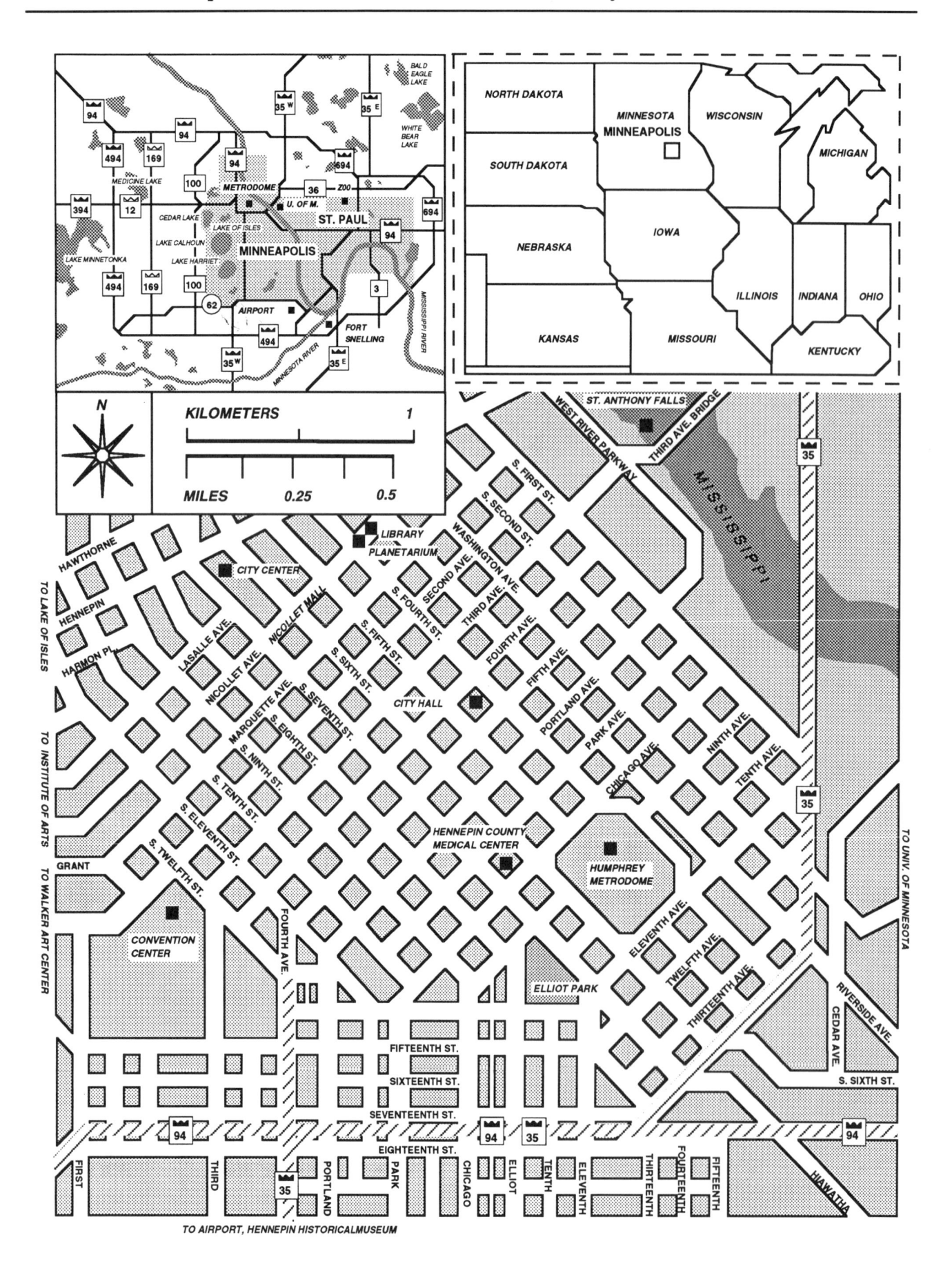

Minnesota—Minneapolis *Cities of the United States • 2nd Edition*

Introduction

The largest city in Minnesota, Minneapolis is the seat of Hennepin County and the sister city of Saint Paul, with which it forms the Twin Cities metropolitan statistical area that includes ten counties in Minnesota and St. Croix County in Wisconsin. Strategically located on the navigable head of the Mississippi River, Minneapolis traces its history to the early exploration of the Northwest Territory. The city encompasses within its boundaries twenty-two lakes (said to have been formed by Paul Bunyan's footprints) and is noted for its natural beauty and parklands. First a milling and lumbering center, Minneapolis today has one of the largest concentrations of high-technology firms in the nation. The combined cities of Minneapolis and Saint Paul were chosen in 1991 by *Inc.* magazine as one of the best places in the country for growing a business and in 1992 by *Money* magazine as the fourth-best place to live in America.

Geography and Climate

Minneapolis, sharing geographic and climatic characteristics with Saint Paul, is situated at the point where the Minnesota River joins the Mississippi River on flat or gently rolling terrain. Twenty-two lakes are located within the city limits; the largest, at nearly 15,000 acres, is Lake Minnetonka. The other lakes are small and shallow, covered by ice in the winter. The city's climate is continental, with large seasonal temperature variations and a favorable growing season of 166 days. Severe weather conditions, such as blizzards, freezing rain, tornadoes, and wind and hail storms are fairly common; winter recreational weather is excellent, however, because of the dry snow, which reaches average depths of six to ten inches.

Area: 54.9 square miles (1990)

Elevation: Ranges from 687 feet to 1,060 feet above sea level

Average Temperatures: January, 11.2° F; August, 70.6° F; annual average, 44.7° F

Average Annual Precipitation: 26.36 inches

History

Falls Provide Townsite and Waterpower

The area where Minneapolis is now located was farmed and hunted by the Sioux tribe before the arrival of Father Louis Hennepin, a French Franciscan missionary who explored the Mississippi River in 1680. Father Hennepin discovered the future site of Minneapolis at a waterfall on the navigable head of the Mississippi River; the falls, which he named after St. Anthony, have since played a crucial role in the city's development. Permanent settlement came in 1820, when Federal troops under the command of Colonel Josiah Snelling built Fort St. Anthony on a bluff overlooking the confluence of the Minnesota and Mississippi Rivers. Renamed Fort Snelling in 1825, it safeguarded fur traders from the warring Sioux and Chippewa and served as a trading center and outpost to the Upper Midwest.

The St. Anthony Falls provided the source of power for lumber and flour milling, the two industries that fueled the city's rapid growth. Soldiers built the first flour mill in 1823 and the first commercial sawmill was in operation in 1841. Attracting settlers from New England, particularly lumbermen from Maine, the rich land was ready for settlement. A geographical fault discovered at the falls in 1869 nearly led to economic disaster and the demise of these industries, but an apron built with federal funding secured the source of waterpower and helped the city to grow in wealth and prosperity.

In 1849 the village of All Saints was founded on the west side of the falls and nine years later settlers who squatted on U.S. military reservation land were awarded patent rights. Also in 1855, the village of St. Anthony on the east side of the falls was incorporated. In 1856 the name of All Saints was changed to Minneapolis, which was derived from the Sioux "minne" for water and the Greek "polis" for city. St. Anthony was chartered as a city in 1860 and Minneapolis six years later. Then in 1872 the two cities become one, spanning both sides of the Mississippi River, with the name of the larger being retained.

Flour, Lumber Industries Attract New Residents

Immigrants from Northern Europe, particularly Sweden but also Norway, Denmark, and Finland, flocked to Minneapolis to work in the new industries. A shoemaker named Nils Nyberg is credited as being the first Swede to settle, having arrived in St. Anthony in 1851. The wave of Scandinavian immigration after the Civil War was felt in every aspect of life in Minneapolis.

In one short generation Minneapolis emerged as a great American city. The original New England settlers platted the streets to reflect order and prosperity, with the boulevards lined with oak and elm trees. The Mississippi River divided the city and served as the focal point of the street grid. The city's rapid population growth and booming economy were attributable in part to the perfection of the Purifer, a flour-sifting device, that made possible the production of high-quality flour from inexpensive spring wheat and led to the construction of large flour mills.

A mill explosion in 1878 that destroyed half the flour mill district prompted residents to research methods to reduce mill dust. Minnesota emerged as the world's leading flour-milling center by 1882. Steam-powered machinery propelled the lumber industry and during the period 1899 to 1905 Minneapolis was the world's foremost producer of lumber. Production was so high that logs actually jammed the river from the timberlands of the north in 1899. Minneapolis became a rail transportation center during this period, further contributing to economic prosperity.

Progressive Programs Revitalize City

The lumber industry in Minneapolis declined once the great forest lands of the north were exhausted, and the large milling companies were forced to relocate some of their plants in other cities to combat the high cost of transportation, which further hurt the economy. After World War II Minneapolis rebounded and became a national leader in the manufacture of computers, electronic equipment, and farm machinery. It established a reputation as a progressive city, undertaking an ambitious urban development project that improved the downtown core and revitalized the economic base. The innovative Nicollet Mall, with a skywalk system, was one of the first of its kind in a major city. Minneapolis and its twin city, Saint Paul, emerged as one of the nation's fastest-growing metropolitan areas in the 1960s and 1970s. Minneapolis's successful transformation inspired other cities to find solutions to the problems of urban decay.

Historical Information: Hennepin County Historical Society, 2303 Third Avenue, South, Minneapolis, MN 55404; telephone (612)870-1329

Population Profile

Metropolitan Area Residents
1970: 1,982,000
1980: 2,137,000
1990: 2,464,124
Annual average percent change, 1980–1988: 1.3%
U.S. rank in 1980: 17th
U.S. rank in 1990: 16th

City Residents
1970: 434,000
1980: 370,951
1990: 368,383
Percent change, 1980–1990: –0.7%
U.S. rank in 1980: 34th
U.S. rank in 1990: 42nd (State rank: 1st)

Density: 6,710.1 people per square mile (1990)

Racial and ethnic characteristics (1990)
  White: 288,967
  Black: 47,948
  American Indian, Eskimo, Aleut: 12,335
  Asian and Pacific Islander: 15,723
  Hispanic (may be of any race): 7,900

Percent of residents born in state: 65.6% (1990)

Age characteristics (1990)
  Population under 5 years old: 27,114
  Population 5 to 9 years old: 21,984
  Population 10 to 14 years old: 17,241
  Population 15 to 19 years old: 20,799
  Population 20 to 24 years old: 38,598
  Population 25 to 29 years old: 44,867
  Population 30 to 34 years old: 40,960
  Population 35 to 39 years old: 33,614
  Population 40 to 44 years old: 24,426
  Population 45 to 49 years old: 16,022
  Population 50 to 54 years old: 12,296
  Population 55 to 59 years old: 10,802
  Population 60 to 64 years old: 11,942
  Population 65 to 69 years old: 12,307
  Population 70 to 74 years old: 11,071
  Population 75 to 79 years old: 9,604
  Population 80 to 84 years old: 7,261
  Population 85 years and over: 7,475
  Median age: 31.5 years

Births (1988)
  Total number: 6,484

Deaths (1988)
　Total number: 3,866 (of which, 73 were infants under the age of 1 year)

Money income (1989)
　Per capita income: $14,830
　Median household income: $25,324
　Total households: 160,531
　Number of households with income of . . .
　　less than $5,000: 10,108
　　$5,000 to $9,999: 20,399
　　$10,000 to $14,999: 17,063
　　$15,000 to $24,999: 31,739
　　$25,000 to $34,999: 25,313
　　$35,000 to $49,999: 26,006
　　$50,000 to $74,999: 19,060
　　$75,000 to $99,999: 5,702
　　$100,000 to $149,999: 3,253
　　$150,000 or more: 1,888
　Percent of families below poverty level: 14.1% (68.3% of which were female householder families with related children under 5)
1991 FBI Crime Index Total: 42,115

Municipal Government

Minneapolis, the seat of Hennepin County, is governed by a mayor and a thirteen-member council, all of whom are elected to four-year terms. The mayor, who is not a member of council, shares equally-distributed powers with council members.

Head Official: Mayor Donald M. Fraser (D) (since 1980; current term expires January 1994)

Total Number of City Employees: 6,774 (1993)

City Information: City Hall, 350 South Fifth Street, Minneapolis, MN 55415; telephone (612)673-3000

Economy

Major Industries and Commercial Activity

Manufacturing is the primary industry in Minneapolis's diversified economic base. Principal manufacturing areas are electronics, milling, machinery, medical products, food processing, and graphic arts. Fifteen Fortune 500 industrial companies maintain headquarters in the Twin Cities, which is among the largest commercial centers between Chicago and the West Coast.

Also integral to the local economy are high-technology industries. With the University of Minnesota and other colleges and technical schools providing applied research and well-trained scientists and engineers, one of the largest concentrations of high-technology firms in the nation—more than thirteen-hundred—developed in metropolitan Minneapolis-Saint Paul. An accompanying expansion of the services sector, especially health services, has attracted seventeen Fortune 500 service companies to the two cities.

Among the banks and other financial institutions that make the Twin Cities the financial center of the Upper Midwest, seven of the largest are based in Minneapolis. In addition, the headquarters of the Ninth Federal Reserve District Bank is located in the city. Local banks, savings and loan companies, venture capital concerns, and insurance companies play a major role in the economic development of the region.

Items and goods produced: electronics, food and dairy products, computers, structural steel, thermostatic controls, conveyor systems, medical electronics equipment, farm machinery, ball bearings, tools, construction machinery, boilers, tanks, burglar alarms, underwear and hosiery, packaging, garden tools, lawn mowers, sprinklers

Incentive Programs—New and Existing Companies

The Minneapolis economy benefits from a variety of incentive programs available to new and existing businesses and corporations. Most of the programs—which involve loans and grants, tax credits and exemptions, research and development assistance, foreign income deductions, and job training—are administered through the state of Minnesota or the federal government.

Development Projects

Fueling the local economy is the redevelopment of downtown Minneapolis. Since the expansion of the now-famous Nicollet Mall in 1982 and the initiation of the innovative skyway system, more than $2 billion have been invested in construction projects, which have continued into the 1990s. Included in revitalization plans are the building of new hotels, office buildings, and housing complexes, and the restoration of historic structures along the Mississippi riverfront.

Part of the downtown development is the new City Center, already completed, which contains stores, restaurants, a hotel, and the International Multifoods Tower. Recently completed was an arena for Minnesota's National Basketball Association (NBA) team; slated for construction are three parking garages. Two 1920s-era theaters have been renovated.

Economic Development Information: Greater Minneapolis Chamber of Commerce, Chamber of Commerce Building, Young Quinlan Building, 81 South Ninth Street, Suite 200, Minneapolis, MN 55402; telephone (612)370-9132; and, Minneapolis Community Development Agency, Marketing and Business Services, Midland Square, 331 Second Avenue South, Minneapolis, MN 55401; telephone (612)342-1378

Commercial Shipping

An important factor in the Minneapolis economy is the Minneapolis-Saint Paul International Airport, which is served by four air cargo carriers and forty air freight forwarders. The airport handles more than 170,000 tons of freight yearly. The Twin Cities area is also linked with major United States and Canadian markets via a network of seven railroads, including the Soo Line, which is based in Minneapolis.

Considered one of the largest trucking centers in the nation, Minneapolis-Saint Paul is served by 150 motor freight companies that provide overnight and four- to five-day delivery in the Midwest and major markets in the continental United States. Vital to the Twin Cities' role as a primary transportation hub is the port of Minneapolis, which together with the port of Saint Paul processes annually more than eleven million tons of cargo to and from domestic and foreign markets.

Labor Force and Employment Outlook

The Minneapolis labor force is well educated. The unemployment rate in the Twin Cities remains substantially below the national average. During 1989-1991 Minneapolis-Saint Paul tallied an increase of nine-thousand wage and salary jobs. The suburban Mall of America, which opened in 1992, is expected to have a major economic impact on the entire metropolitan area.

The following is a summary of data regarding the Minneapolis metropolitan area labor force as of September 1992.

Size of non-agricultural labor force: 1,402,500

Number of workers employed in . . .
  mining: 400
  construction: 52,500
  manufacturing: 260,100
  transportation and public utilities: 79,200
  wholesale and retail trade: 333,500
  finance, insurance, and real estate: 100,300
  services: 392,200
  government: 184,300

Average hourly earnings of production workers employed in manufacturing: $12.93

Unemployment rate: 4.3%

Largest employers	Number of employees
Dayton-Hudson Corporation (retail trade)	21,650
Health One Corp.	11,000
Honeywell Inc.	11,000
Lifespan	8,800
Norwest Corp.	8,151

Cost of Living

The following is a summary of data regarding several key cost of living factors in the Minneapolis area.

1992 (3rd Quarter) ACCRA Average House Price: $120,030

1992 (3rd Quarter) ACCRA Cost of Living Index: 100.2 (U.S. average = 100.0)

State income tax rate: 8.5%

State sales tax rate: 6.5%

Local income tax rate: None

Local sales tax rate: 3.0%

Property tax rate: $120.20 per $1,000 assessed value

Economic Information: Greater Minneapolis Chamber of Commerce, Young Quinlan Building, 81 South Ninth Street, Suite 200, Minneapolis, MN 55402; telephone (612)370-9132

Cities of the United States • 2nd Edition   Minnesota—Minneapolis

Lake Calhoun.

Education and Research

Elementary and Secondary Schools

Education receives high priority in Minnesota; the state has the highest graduation rate in the nation. Of persons twenty-five years or older in Minneapolis and Saint Paul, 89 percent are high school graduates. Minnesota was the first state in the nation to offer open enrollment in all public schools.

Elementary and secondary public schools in Minneapolis are part of the Special Independent #1 District, the largest system in the state. Seven nonpartisan school board members select a superintendent.

The following is a summary of data regarding the Minneapolis public schools as of the 1992–1993 school year.

Total enrollment: 36,368

Number of facilities
 elementary schools: 46
 junior high schools: 6
 senior high schools: 7

Student/teacher ratio: 14:1

Teacher salaries (1988–1989)
 minimum: $20,324
 maximum: $44,794

Funding per pupil: $5,638

Hennepin County is served by forty-five private schools offering alternative educational curricula.

Public Schools Information: Greater Minneapolis Chamber of Commerce, 200 Young Quinlan Building, 81 South Ninth Street, Minneapolis, MN 55402; telephone (612)370-9197

Colleges and Universities

The University of Minnesota—Twin Cities, a state institution with an enrollment of more than forty-thousand students, is located in Minneapolis. Five degree levels—baccalaureate, first-professional, master's, intermediate, and doctorate—are available in over 250 fields, including architecture, medicine, engineering, journalism, teacher education, public health, and music. Former students and faculty members have been awarded twelve Nobel Prizes in physics, medicine, chemistry, economics, and peace. Augsburg College and North Central Bible College, private religious institutions, award associate, baccalaureate, and master's degrees. The Minneapolis College of Art and Design offers four-year programs in fine and applied arts. Community and technical colleges in the metropolitan area include Minneapolis Community College, Minneapolis Technical College, and Hennepin Technical College.

Libraries and Research Centers

The main branch of the Minneapolis Public Library and Information Center is located downtown; fourteen additional branches are maintained throughout the city. Library holdings total nearly two million volumes, about 4,560 periodical subscriptions, and microfilm, audio and video tapes, and slides. Services for the deaf are available. A Municipal Information Library is housed at City Hall. Among the library's special collections are Huttner Abolition and Anti-Slavery papers, the Adams collection of Lincolniana, and literature pertaining to the North American native American. The library is a U.S. documents depository.

The University of Minnesota Libraries—Twin Cities, also located in Minneapolis, have total holdings of nearly five million volumes in major academic departments. Special collections include literature on ballooning, the Hess Dime Novel Collection, the Charles Babbage Institute, the A. Conan Doyle Collection, and the Performing Arts Archives. The library is a depository for federal and state documents. The Immigration History Research Center at the university houses one of the nation's most comprehensive collections of the immigrant past.

Seventy-six special libraries and research centers serve the city. Most are affiliated with state and county government agencies, businesses and corporations, hospitals, churches and synagogues, and arts organizations.

Public Library Information: Minneapolis Public Library, 300 Nicolett Mall, Minneapolis, MN 55401-1992; telephone (612)372-6633 or 372-6500

Health Care

Minneapolis has one of the country's highest rates of health maintenance organization membership, available for over twenty years. A vital force in the

Spoonbridge and Cherry by Claes Oldenburg and Coosje van Bruggen is one of more than fifty-five works featured in the Minneapolis Sculpture Garden.

medical community is the University of Minnesota Hospital, where the first open heart surgery was performed in 1954. The hospital is also known as a leading organ transplant center. Among the other major hospitals in Minneapolis are the Minneapolis Children's Medical Center, Shriner's Hospital, the Veteran's Administration Medical Center, the Hennepin County Medical Center, and the Abbott-Northwestern/Sister Kenny Institute. The Mayo Clinic is located 75 miles southeast of Minneapolis, in Rochester.

Health Care Information: Healthwise Connection referral service, telephone (612)371-6200

Recreation

Sightseeing

Sightseeing in Minneapolis might begin with the Chain of Lakes—Lake of the Isles, Lake Calhoun, and Lake Harriet—just a few miles west of downtown; in all, twenty-two lakes are located within the city limits and more than one-thousand are in close proximity. Minnehaha Falls, the point at which Minnehaha Creek plunges into the Mississippi River, was made famous by Henry Wadsworth Longfellow in his poem *The Song of Hiawatha*. A lifesize statue of Hiawatha holding his wife Minnehaha is located on an island just above the falls.

For those with an interest in Minneapolis's historical roots, the American Swedish Institute maintains a turn-of-the-century thirty-three room mansion that displays Swedish immigrant artifacts as well as traveling exhibits. The Ard Godrey House, built in 1849 and the oldest existing frame house in the city, features authentic period furnishings. Minneapolis's early history and development are captured at the Hennepin County Historical Society Museum.

Fort Snelling, an historic landmark dating from 1820 in Fort Snelling National Park, has been restored to its frontier-era appearance and is open six months a year. At the Minnesota Zoo, which occupies 408 acres, six trails lead to exhibits in natural settings. The Minneapolis Planetarium, with a forty-foot dome, projects over two-thousand stars. Six hundred seventy-five acres cultivated with numerous varieties of trees, flowers, and shrubs make up the Minnesota Landscape Arboretum.

Arts and Culture

In both Minneapolis and Saint Paul business and the arts go hand-in-hand. The Five Percent Club consists of local businesses and corporations that donate five percent of their pre-tax earnings to the arts, education, or human services. This investment results in such high-quality institutions as the Guthrie Theater, named for Sir Tyrone Guthrie, which ranks as one of the best regional and repertory theater companies in the United States. The Walker Art Center exhibits progressive modern art in an award-winning building designed by Edward Larrabee Barnes, which has been judged among the best art exhibition facilities in the world. The center, housing a permanent collection that represents major twentieth-century movements, also sponsors a program of music, dance, film, theater, and educational activities.

The Minnesota Orchestra, performing at Orchestra Hall on Nicollet Mall and at Ordway Music Theater in Saint Paul, presents a season of concerts that includes a great performers series, the weekender series, a pop series, and a summer festival. Family holiday concerts are performed at Christmas time. The Minnesota Opera performs traditional and new works at the newly reopened 1921 Historic State Theater as well as at the Ordway and World theaters in Saint Paul. Touring Broadway musicals and musical stars perform at the restored Orpheum Theater. The Children's Theater Company offers a world-class theater education program for young people. International theater professionals work with student actors and technicians to present productions of the highest quality. Musical and comedic entertainment of all kinds is presented at Mississippi Live, a downtown complex housing fifteen clubs under one roof.

The Minneapolis Sculpture Garden, adjacent to the Walker Art Center, was designed by Barnes and landscape architect Peter Rothschild; it consists of four symmetrical square plazas that display more than fifty-five works by Henry Moore, George Segal, and Deborah Butterfield, among others. The Minneapolis Institute of Arts showcases world art in a collection of more than seventy-thousand objects from every period and culture.

Festivals and Holidays

Minneapolis celebrates March with a St. Patrick's Day Parade and a Spring Flower Show. The Minneapolis Aquatennial, established in 1940, is a ten-day extravaganza held in late July with a special theme

Nicollet Mall, featuring a skywalk system, was one of the first of its kind in a major city.

each year; the Aquatennial Association programs over 250 free events that focus on the city's proximity to water. Many Minneapolis festivals honor the city's Scandinavian heritage. Other festivals celebrate ethnic cultures with music, dance, food, arts, and crafts. Uptown Art Fair, one of the largest such events in the country, is held in August. Main Street Bazaar is an outdoor festival that takes place from May through December, featuring music, dancing, storytelling, and more.

Sports for the Spectator

The Hubert H. Humphrey Metrodome is home to two of the city's major sports franchises; the Minnesota Twins of the western division of baseball's American League and the Minnesota Vikings of the central division of the National Football League play their home games in this domed stadium, conveniently located downtown. Professional hockey was represented by the Minnesota North Stars of the National Hockey League from 1967 to 1993, when the team moved to Dallas. The National Basketball Association's Timberwolves play at the new Target Center. Sports fans can also attend major and minor sporting events at the University of Minnesota—Twin Cities, which fields Big Ten teams like the Gophers, who play to sellout crowds.

Sports for the Participant

Minneapolis is one of the country's most naturally beautiful cities, enhanced by twenty-two lakes within the city limits. The abundance of easily accessible water makes possible a full range of water sports and activities in both summer and winter. Four thousand acres of city park land are available for swimming, canoeing, sailing, windsurfing, waterskiing, rollerskating, and biking along with softball, tennis, and golf. Winter sports include skating, skiing, snowshoeing, ice fishing, and camping.

Shopping and Dining

Minneapolis is the originator on a grand scale of the "second floor city" concept, integrating essentially two downtowns—a sidewalk-level traditional downtown and a second city joined by an elaborate skywalk system. Nicollet Mall, completed in 1967, redefined the urban downtown and eliminated the element of weather as a deterrent to the shopper. This all-weather skywalk system connects an indoor shopping center whose four major department stores and hundreds of specialty shops cover thirty-four city blocks. Shopping activity is also a part of the new City Center. St. Anthony Main and Riverplace, two new developments along the historic Mississippi riverfront, consist of old warehouses and office buildings converted to shopping centers. Suburban Bloomington is home to the largest mall in North America, the new Mall of America.

Elegant dining is possible at The 510 Restaurant, Goodfellow's, and Rosewood Room, named by *Food and Wine* magazine as Distinguished Restaurants of North America for 1992–1993. Dinner cruises on the Mississippi River are offered during the summer.

Visitor Information: Greater Minneapolis Convention and Visitors Association, 1219 Marquette Avenue, Minneapolis, MN 55403; telephone (612)348-4313; Twin Cities Tourism Attractions Association, telephone (612)338-6427

Convention Facilities

The primary meeting and convention site in Minneapolis is the Minneapolis Convention Center, which opened in 1990.

Convention Information: Minneapolis Convention Center, telephone (612)348-8300

Transportation

Approaching the City

Located southeast of downtown Minneapolis, the Minneapolis-Saint Paul International Airport is served by thirteen commercial airlines and eight regional carriers. The airport's service links Minneapolis with eighty other major U.S. cities; direct international flights connect the Midwest with primary foreign cities. The airport, numbered among the safest in the country, has been expanded to provide more efficient service. Six reliever airports are also located in the metropolitan area. Amtrak runs a major east-west line from Chicago and the East into Saint Paul.

Two major interstate highways serve Minneapolis: I-94 (east-west) and I-35 (north-south). Two belt-line freeways, I-494 and I-694, facilitate travel around the Twin-City suburbs. Seven federal and thirteen state highways link the city with points throughout the United States and Canada.

Traveling in the City

Minneapolis is laid out on a grid pattern, with streets south of Grant Street intersecting on a north-south axis and those north of Grant running diagonally northeast-southwest. The Minneapolis Skywalk System connects major downtown public buildings and retail establishments with elevated, covered walkways.

Serving Minneapolis, Saint Paul, and the surrounding suburbs is the Metropolitan Transit Commission (MTC), the second largest bus system in the United States. Additional bus service is provided by five private operators, including Gray Line, which conducts sightseeing tours, stopping at Nicollet Mall and at various hotels in Minneapolis and Saint Paul. The city is noted for efficiency of commuting time: the freeway system, moderate population density, and two central business districts contribute to high levels of mobility during peak and non-peak hours.

Communications

Newspapers and Magazines

The major daily newspaper in Minneapolis is the *Star Tribune.* Several neighborhood and suburban newspapers are distributed weekly in the city.

Mpls. St.Paul is a magazine focusing on metropolitan life in the Twin Cites. A popular publication with a national distribution is *The Utne Reader.* Other special interest magazines based in Minneapolis pertain to such subjects as religion, aviation, business, entertainment, hunting and conservation, minority issues, medicine, politics, and computers.

Television and Radio

Seven television stations—four commercial network affiliates, two public network outlets, and an independent station—serve the Minneapolis-Saint Paul metropolitan region. Cable television channels are also available. Radio listeners in the Twin Cities can choose from at least nineteen AM and FM stations. Programming includes ethnic music, jazz, gospel, classical music, easy listening, and news and public affairs.

Media Information: Star Tribune, 425 Portland Avenue, Minneapolis, MN 55488; telephone (612)372-4343

Saint Paul

The City in Brief

Founded: 1846 (incorporated, 1849)

Head Official: Mayor James Scheibel (NP) (since 1990)

City Population
 1970: 310,000
 1980: 270,230
 1990: 272,235
 Percent change, 1980–1990: 0.7%
U.S. rank in 1980: 54th
U.S. rank in 1990: 57th (State rank: 2nd)
Metropolitan Area Population
 1970: 1,981,951
 1980: 2,137,133
 1990: 2,464,124
 Percent change, 1980–1990: 15.3%
 U.S. rank in 1980: 17th
 U.S. rank in 1990: 16th

Area: 52.8 square miles (1990)
Elevation: 834 feet above sea level
Average Annual Temperature: 44.7° F
Average Annual Precipitation: 26.36 inches

Major Economic Sectors: Services, trade, manufacturing, government
Unemployment Rate: 4.3% (September 1992)
Per Capita Income: $13,727 (1989)
1992 (2nd Quarter) ACCRA Average House Price: $125,000
1992 (2nd Quarter) ACCRA Cost of Living Index: 101.3 (U.S. average = 100.0)
1991 FBI Crime Index Total: 21,765

Major Colleges and Universities: University of Minnesota—Twin Cities; Metropolitan State University; Macalester College; University of St. Thomas; College of St. Catherine; Hamline University; William Mitchell College of Law

Daily Newspaper: *Saint Paul Pioneer Press*

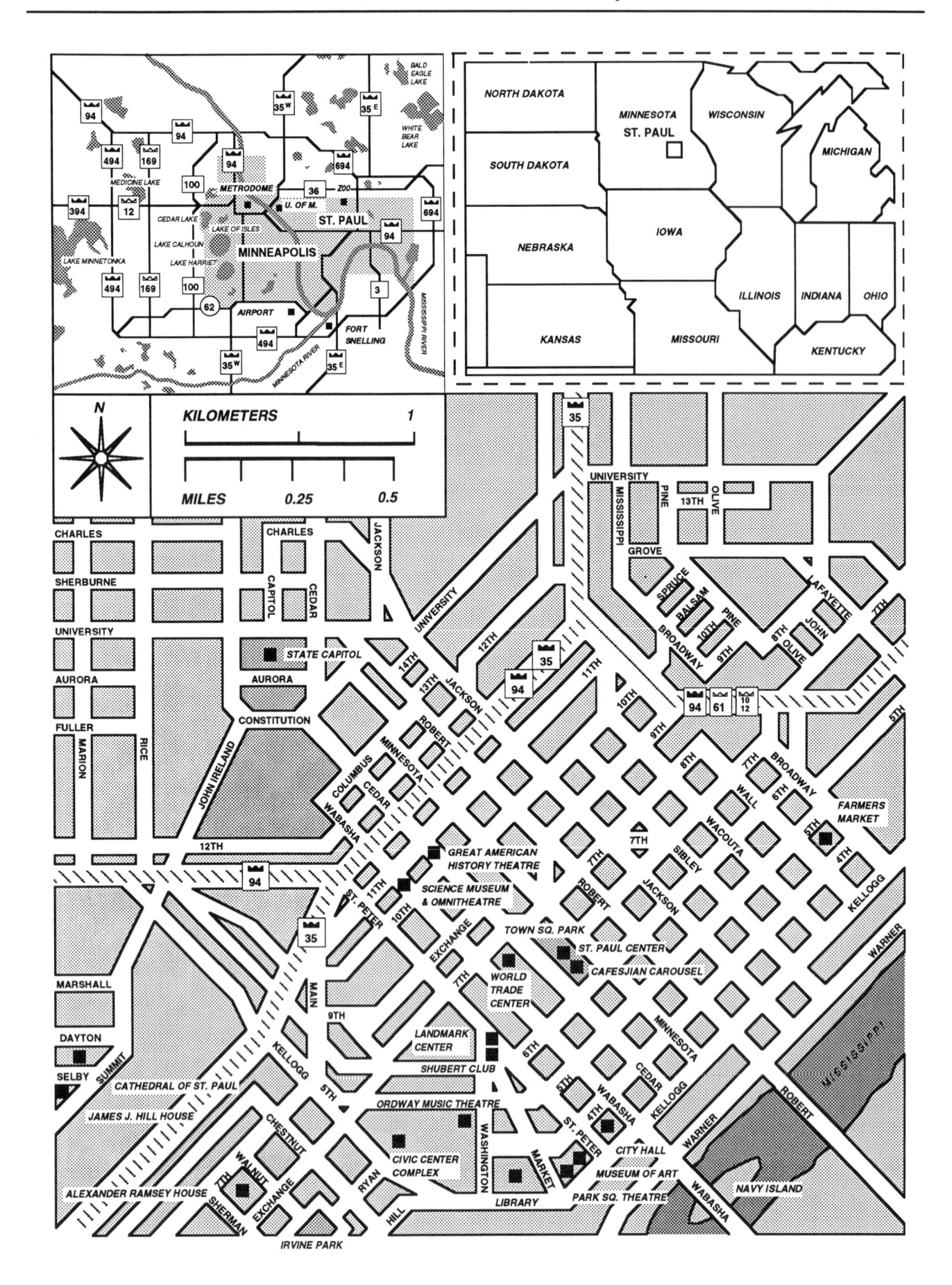

Minnesota—Saint Paul

Cities of the United States • 2nd Edition

Introduction

Saint Paul is the capital of Minnesota and the seat of Ramsey County. Along with Minneapolis, it occupies the center of the Twin Cities metropolitan statistical area comprised of ten counties in Minnesota and St. Croix County in Wisconsin. The city developed in the late nineteenth century through the efforts of railroad baron James Hill and religious leader Archbishop John Ireland. In addition to being a primary transportation and distribution hub, Saint Paul has gained a national reputation for its effective local government, attractive architecture, rich cultural environment, and quality of life. The combined cities of Minneapolis and Saint Paul were chosen in 1991 by *Inc.* magazine as one of the best places in the country for growing a business and in 1992 by *Money Magazine* as the fourth-best place to live in America.

Geography and Climate

Saint Paul is located with Minneapolis at the confluence of the Mississippi and Minnesota Rivers over the heart of an artesian water basin. The surrounding terrain is flat or rolling and dotted with lakes. The climate is predominantly continental with wide seasonal temperature variations, ranging from minus thirty degrees to one-hundred degrees and above. During the spring snow melt and periods of excessive rainfall, or as the result of an ice jam, flooding occurs on the Mississippi River. The flood problem is especially complicated for Saint Paul because, unlike Minneapolis, the city is located downriver from the emptying of the Minnesota River into the Mississippi River, which creates a greater potential for high water or flooding.

Area: 52.8 square miles (1990)

Elevation: 834 feet above sea level

Average Temperatures: January, 11.2° F; July, 70.6° F; annual average, 44.7° F

Annual Average Precipitation: 26.36 inches

History

River Fort Draws Traders, Settlers

Jonathan Carver, a New Englander, was attempting to find a northwest passage to the Pacific Ocean in the winter of 1766 when he stopped near the future site of Saint Paul, where he discovered an native American burial ground (now known as Indian Mound Park). When the Louisiana Purchase became part of United States territory in 1803, federally-financed expeditions explored the new territory, which included present-day Saint Paul. In 1805 Lieutenant Zebulon M. Pike camped on an island later named Pike Island and entered into an unofficial agreement with the Sioux tribe for land at the confluence of the Mississippi and Minnesota rivers; also included in the pact was land that became the site of Fort Snelling.

In 1819, Colonel Henry Leavenworth built an army post on the Minnesota River on a spot named Mendota south of present-day Saint Paul; the next year the fortress was moved across the river where Colonel Josiah Snelling constructed Fort Anthony, which was later renamed Fort Snelling. The presence of the fort allowed an Indian agency, fur trading post, missionaries, and white settlers to gain a foothold there. Settlers living on federal land were eventually expelled, and Pierre "Pig's Eye" Parrant, a French Canadian, joined others in building a settlement named after Parrant's colorful nickname near Fort Snelling. In 1841, Father Lucian Galtier named a log chapel in Pig's Eye after his patron saint, Saint Paul, and persuaded others to accept the name for their emerging community, as well.

Saint Paul was platted in 1847; two years later it was named the capital of the Minnesota Territory and incorporated as a town. Saint Paul received its city charter in 1854 and when Minnesota became a state in 1858, the city retained its status as state capital. By the start of the Civil War, 10,000 people lived in Saint Paul.

Rail Transport and New Residents Shape City

Two men had major roles in the development of Saint Paul in the post-Civil War period. The railroad magnate James J. Hill used the city and the Great Northern Railroad to accumulate great individual wealth and to wield immense political power. Hill envisioned his adopted city of Saint Paul as the base for an empire in the northwest, built on his railroad holdings. The other major influence on Saint Paul's development was Catholic Archbishop John Ireland, a native of Ireland who settled in Saint Paul at the age of fourteen and, as an adult, established a religious base for community endeavors. He brought thousands of destitute Irish families to Saint Paul, where they relocated in colonies and started a new life. The Catholic influence in the shaping of Saint Paul can be traced to the pioneering efforts of Archbishop Ireland.

In the nineteenth century a number of distinct population groups contributed to the character of Saint Paul. One was from the New England states and New York; these transplanted Easterners brought their educational values and business experiences to the prairie community. Another consisted of immigrants from Germany and Ireland who flocked to the United States by the tens of thousands. Among the professional groups were German physicians and Irish politicians and lawyers. German musical traditions and beer-making practices found a new home in Saint Paul. Scandinavians also immigrated to the city, but in fewer numbers than those who settled in neighboring Minneapolis.

Historical Information: Minnesota History Center, 345 Kellogg, Saint Paul, MN 55102; telephone (612)726-9430

Population Profile

Metropolitan Area Residents
1970: 1,981,951
1980: 2,137,133
1990: 2,464,124
Annual average percent change, 1980-1988: 1.3%
U.S. rank in 1980: 17th
U.S. rank in 1990: 16th

City Residents
1970: 310,000
1980: 270,230
1990: 272,235 (of which, 128,606 were males, and 143,629 were females)
Percent change, 1980-1990: 0.7%
U.S. rank in 1980: 54th
U.S. rank in 1990: 57th (State rank: 2nd)

Density: 5,156.0 people per square mile (1990)
Racial and ethnic characteristics (1990)
 White: 223,947
 Black: 20,083
 American Indian, Eskimo, Aleut: 3,697
 Asian and Pacific Islander: 19,197
 Hispanic (may be of any race): 11,476
Percent of residents born in state: 73.2% (1990)
Age characteristics (1990)
 Population under 5 years old: 22,850
 Population 5 to 9 years old: 19,703
 Population 10 to 14 years old: 15,600
 Population 15 to 19 years old: 17,021
 Population 20 to 24 years old: 25,571
 Population 25 to 29 years old: 28,477
 Population 30 to 34 years old: 26,520
 Population 35 to 39 years old: 22,276
 Population 40 to 44 years old: 16,920
 Population 45 to 49 years old: 11,637
 Population 50 to 54 years old: 9,484
 Population 55 to 59 years old: 9,025
 Population 60 to 64 years old: 9,739
 Population 65 to 69 years old: 9,950
 Population 70 to 74 years old: 8,817
 Population 75 to 79 years old: 7,757
 Population 80 to 84 years old: 5,579
 Population 85 years and over: 5,309
 Median age: 31.2 years
Births (1988)
 Total number: 5,125
Deaths (1989)
 Total number: 2,573 (of which, 58 were infants under the age of 1 year)
Money income (1989)
 Per capita income: $13,727
 Median household income: $26,498
 Total households: 110,608
 Number of households with income of . . .
  less than $5,000: 5,871
  $5,000 to $9,999: 13,753
  $10,000 to $14,999: 10,717
  $15,000 to $24,999: 21,848
  $25,000 to $34,999: 18,219
  $35,000 to $49,999: 19,560
  $50,000 to $74,999: 13,961
  $75,000 to $99,999: 3,957
  $100,000 to $149,999: 1,669
  $150,000 or more: 1,053
 Percent of families below poverty level: 12.4% (63.8% of which were female householder families with related children under 5)
1991 FBI Crime Index Total: 21,765

Cities of the United States • 2nd Edition   Minnesota—Saint Paul

The Minnesota State Capitol building, designed by noted architect Cass Gilbert, features the world's largest unsupported dome.

Municipal Government

Saint Paul, the seat of Ramsey County, operates under a mayor-council form of government, with strong power being delegated to the mayor, who serves for four years. The seven council members are elected by ward to two-year terms.

Head Official: Mayor James Scheibel (NP) (since 1990; current term expires January 1994)

Total Number of City Employees: 2,987 plus 569 part-time (1992)

City Information: City Hall, 14 West Kellogg Blvd., Saint Paul, MN 55102; telephone (612)298-4012

Economy

Major Industries and Commercial Activity

The principal economic sectors in Saint Paul are services, wholesale and retail trade, manufacturing, and government. Along with Minneapolis, Saint Paul is the site of one of the largest concentrations of high-technology firms in the United States and ranks among the major commercial centers between Chicago and the West Coast. The city is also among the two or three largest livestock and meatpacking centers in the nation. Eleven Fortune 500 industrial and fifteen Fortune 500 service companies have established headquarters in the Twin Cities. Local companies are involved in the manufacture of super computers, electronics, medical instruments, milling, machine production, food processing, and graphic arts. Of the thirty-four World Trade Centers in the world, only nine are located in the United States; one of those nine, and the only inland facility, is located in Saint Paul. The arts contribute more than $392 annually to the regional economy.

Items and goods produced: hoists and derricks, rugs, computers, food products, medical products, machinery

Incentive Programs—New and Existing Companies

Various programs are available for small business incentive and expansion; among them are the Small Business Development Loan Program, offering fixed-rate low-interest direct loans, and tax credits for corporations that assist small businesses. State business tax incentives include research and development credits, foreign income deductions, and sales tax exemptions and reductions. In addition, the state of Minnesota offers, through a network of five job-training programs, assistance to businesses in locating and training employees.

Development Projects

Downtown Saint Paul has undergone extensive revitalization, with investment in development projects exceeding $1 billion. The city has also profited from the Neighborhood Development Program, a unique redevelopment initiative that has gained Saint Paul national recognition. Economic expansion has been spurred by five industrial parks, including Energy Park, a 218-acre mixed-use project that combines $250 million in industrial, commercial, and residential development to create five-thousand new jobs. An academic library was added to Northwestern College in 1992.

Economic Development Information: Metro East Development Partnership, 101 Norwest Center, 55 East 5th St., Saint Paul, MN 55101; telephone (612)224-3278

Commercial Shipping

Saint Paul is a Foreign Trade Zone with duty free facilities. The ports of Saint Paul and Minneapolis are served by nine barge lines operating on the Mississippi, Minnesota, and St. Croix rivers; together the ports handle more than eleven million tons of cargo annually. Considered one of the largest trucking centers in the United States, the Twin Cities are a hub for over 150 motor freight companies that provide overnight and four- to five-day delivery throughout the country. Six rail lines are integrated with both the United States and Canadian railway systems. Air transportation is available at Minneapolis-Saint Paul International Airport from sixteen air cargo carriers and thirty-seven air freight forwarders.

Labor Force and Employment Outlook

Local educational institutions assure employers of well-trained workers, particularly in high-technology areas, where engineers, scientists, researchers, and technicians are in demand. The service sector is expected to continue to show the greatest increase, together with wholesale trade. Manufacturing employment will continue to decrease.

The following is a summary of data regarding the Saint Paul metropolitan area labor force as of September 1992.

Size of non-agricultural labor force: 1,402,500

Number of workers employed in . . .
  mining: 400
  construction: 52,500
  manufacturing: 260,100
  transportation and public utilities: 79,200
  wholesale and retail trade: 333,500
  finance, insurance, and real estate: 100,300
  services: 392,200
  government: 184,300

Average hourly earnings of production workers employed in manufacturing: $12.93

Unemployment rate: 4.3%

Largest employers	*Number of employees*
Northwest Airlines	17,500
3M Corporation	13,000
Unisys	7,200
Healtheast	5,300
West Publishing	4,300
Andersen Corporation	3,800

Cost of Living

The following is a summary of data regarding several key cost of living factors in the Saint Paul area.

1992 (2nd Quarter) ACCRA Cost of Living Index: 101.3 (U.S. average = 100.0)

1992 (2nd Quarter) ACCRA Average House Price: $125,000

State income tax rate: 8.5%

State sales tax rate: 6.5%

Local income tax rate: None

Local sales tax rate: None

Property tax rate: 17.0% of first $68,000 of market value; 27.0% over $68,000

Economic Information: The Saint Paul Area Chamber of Commerce, 101 Norwest Center, 55 East Fifth St., Saint Paul, MN 55101; telephone (612)223-5004

Education and Research

Elementary and Secondary Schools

Public schools in Saint Paul are administered by Independent School District 625, the second largest school system in Minnesota. A superintendent is chosen by a seven-member, nonpartisan board of education.

The following is a summary of data regarding the Saint Paul public schools as of the 1992–1993 school year.

Total enrollment: 31,995

Number of facilities
  elementary schools: 39
  junior high schools: 8
  senior high schools: 7

Student/teacher ratio: 15:1

Teacher salaries
  minimum: $22,352
  maximum: $51,184

Funding per pupil: $5,206

There are thirty-seven private schools in Saint Paul enrolling more than twelve-thousand students.

Public Schools Information: Saint Paul Public Schools, 360 Colborne Street, Saint Paul, MN 55102; telephone (612)293-5280

Colleges and Universities

Saint Paul is home to several colleges and universities. The University of Minnesota—Twin Cities operates a main campus in Saint Paul as well as in Minneapolis. An important research institution with a total enrollment of about forty-one thousand students, the university awards a full range of undergraduate and graduate degrees in 250 fields of study, including first-professional degrees in dentistry, law, medicine, pharmacy, and veterinary medicine. University of Minnesota faculty and graduates have been awarded twelve Nobel Prizes for physics, medicine, chemistry, economics, and peace.

Metropolitan State University, part of the Minnesota State University system, offers undergraduate and graduate programs in liberal arts, nursing, and management; the administrative offices of Minnesota State University are located in Saint Paul. The

William Mitchell College of Law is a privately operated professional school devoted solely to the study of law. A fine arts curriculum leading to a baccalaureate degree is offered by the School of the Associated Arts.

Hamline University, affiliated with the United Methodist Church, provides undergraduate and graduate programs in such areas as chemistry, law, music, and teacher education. Bethel College and Seminary is a four-year institution associated with the Baptist General Conference. The four-year Concordia College is operated by the Lutheran Church-Missouri Synod. Lutheran Northwestern Seminary is the divinity school for the American Lutheran Church and the Lutheran Church in America. Other church-related colleges include Northwestern College and Macalester College, which is associated with the Presbyterian Church. The College of St. Catherine, the College of St. Thomas, and the Saint Paul Seminary School of Divinity are Roman Catholic institutions.

Vocational and technical training is available at community colleges and specialized schools in Saint Paul and Minneapolis; among them is Saint Paul Technical Vocational Institute. In all, the Twin Cities support thirteen colleges and universities, six state-supported comprehensive community colleges, and nine publicly supported technical institutions.

Libraries and Research Centers

Nearly seventy public and private libraries are based in Saint Paul. The Saint Paul Public Library system includes a main facility, thirteen branches, and a bookmobile. The main library, which is a depository for federal and city documents, houses more than 920,000 volumes as well as more than one-thousand periodicals, and films, maps, and other items. Special collections include Babylonian and Sumerian tablets, books by or pertaining to F. Scott Fitzgerald, rare books, and oral history. Adjacent to the Saint Paul Public Library is the James J. Hill Reference Library; its business and economic collection is open to the public. The Minnesota Historical Society maintains an extensive reference library with subject interests in genealogy, Minnesota history, and Scandinavians in the United States among other areas. Most colleges and universities in Saint Paul operate campus libraries, the largest being the University of Minnesota system, which consists of a main facility and four department libraries; its collection numbers more than four million catalogued volumes.

3M Information Services is a major corporate library open to the public by advance notice and a 3M visitor's pass. Eleven branches contain such holdings as manufacturers' catalogs, research and development information, and vendors' information as well as special collections relating to a broad range of technical fields, including biochemistry, chemistry, medicine, physiology, electronics, micrographics, optics, metallurgy, and textiles.

Among the larger state agency libraries in the city are the Minnesota State Law Library, the Minnesota State Agency Library, and the Minnesota Legislative Reference Library. Other specialized libraries are associated primarily with corporations, churches, and hospitals.

Research centers in the Twin Cities affiliated with the University of Minnesota include the Center for Urban Design; the Hubert H. Humphrey Institute of Public Affairs; the Industrial Relations Center; the Laboratory for Research in Scientific Communication; the Center for Research in Learning, Perception, and Cognition; the Minnesota Technology Corridor; the Underground Space Center; the Immigration History Research Center; and the Minnesota Center for Twin and Adoption Research.

Public Library Information: Saint Paul Public Library, 90 West Fourth Street, Saint Paul, MN 55102-1668; telephone (612)292-6311

Health Care

Minneapolis-Saint Paul is a regional health care center. Seven hospitals are based in Saint Paul. The largest facility is Saint Paul-Ramsey Medical Center, a teaching and research hospital that specializes in trauma and critical care, Alzheimer's research and treatment, poison information and treatment, and burn treatment. Saint Paul-Ramsey also houses an ambulatory care clinic and provides general medical, surgical, pediatric, psychiatric, and chemical dependency services. Gillette Children's Hospital is a teaching and referral center specializing in orthopedics and epilepsy; it is located on the Saint Paul-Ramsey campus.

Midway Hospital provides orthopedic, hospice, and maternity care. Children's Hospital, a teaching and referral center for infants and children with pediatric

Jonathan Padelford, one of two sternwheeler riverboats offering narrated sightseeing cruises and dinner and dancing excursions on the Mississippi River.

disorders, includes among its specialties open heart surgery and cardiac catheterization, and infant apnea diagnosis. Other hospitals in Saint Paul include St. John's, St. Joseph's, Washington County District Memorial, Lakeview Memorial, and Bethesda Healtheast.

Health Care Information: Children's Hospital free health information line, telephone (612)220-6868

Recreation

Sightseeing

Landmark architectural structures provide unique space for Saint Paul's arts institutions. The state Capitol was designed by Cass Gilbert in 1904 and blends Minnesota stones with imported marbles; paintings, murals, and sculptures represent the state's history. A trip to Saint Paul might include a visit to Saint Paul Cathedral, which is modelled after St. Peter's in Rome. Landmark Center, once a Federal Courts Building, is now the city's arts center and winner of a national restoration award.

Historic Fort Snelling has been restored to its original state; costumed guides tell about the fort's early history as the first non-native American settlement in the Saint Paul area. The Alexander Ramsey House was the home of Minnesota's first territorial governor. Reflecting the opulence of Saint Paul's most famous nineteenth-century railroad baron, the thirty-two room James J. Hill House was at one time the largest home in the Midwest. A 5-mile stretch of Summit Avenue is lined with Victorian homes.

Como Park, Zoo, and Conservatory features a children's zoo, a large cats house, an aquatic house, and the newly renovated conservatory. Town Square Park in Saint Paul Center, the largest indoor public park in the world, cultivates more than one-thousand plants and trees. The Children's Museum features hands-on exhibits.

Arts and Culture

Like Minneapolis, Saint Paul enjoys a national reputation in the performing arts. The Ordway Music Theater is the home of the Saint Paul Chamber Orchestra and the Minnesota Opera Company. The Landmark Center is a Romanesque Revival building whose south tower is modeled after Boston's Trinity Church. The Schubert Piano Club and Keyboard Instruments Museum and a branch of the Minnesota Museum of Art are located in the center. The other branch of the museum is at Kellogg Boulevard and houses contemporary and Asian art as well as sculpture, paintings, photography, and drawings.

The Science Museum of Minnesota hosts programs on space and science at the Omnitheater, which as the world's largest floor-to-ceiling domed screen. The museum also mounts displays on the natural sciences, technology, and anthropology. The Minnesota History Center presents interpretations of the state's history through exhibits and material objects.

Saint Paul's theater companies include the Park Square Theater, which concentrates on classic plays; the Great North American History Theater, which presents local historical drama; and Penumbra Theater, a professional black theater company.

Arts and Culture Information: Metropolitan Council Regional Arts Council, 300 Metro Square Bldg., Saint Paul, MN 55101; telephone (612)291-6571

Festivals and Holidays

The Saint Paul Winter Carnival is the largest winter celebration in the nation. This annual festival, held the last weekend in January through the first weekend in February, features parades, ice and snow sculpture, fine arts performances, a ball, unusual winter sporting events, and a re-enactment of the legend of King Boreas. Saint Paul hosts the largest celebration of St. Patrick's Day outside of New York City. The Festival of Nations in late April celebrates the food and cultures of more than fifty countries. Grand Old Day on an early June Sunday begins with a parade on a one-mile stretch of Grand Avenue and includes entertainment, food, and crafts. Taste of Minnesota on the Fourth of July weekend is held on the Minnesota State Capitol Mall and concludes with a fireworks display on Independence Day. The Minnesota State Fair, one of the largest state fairs in the country, runs for ten days ending on Labor Day at the Minnesota State Fairgrounds.

Sports for the Spectator

The Twin Cities is home to four professional sports teams. The Minnesota Vikings compete in the National Football Conference in the Midwest Division; the Minnesota Twins are in the western division of baseball's American League; the Minnesota Timberwolves are in the National Basketball Association;

Winter Carnival in Saint Paul.

and the Minnesota North Stars are in the National Hockey League. The baseball and football teams play home games in the Hubert H. Humphrey Metrodome in downtown Minneapolis. The North Stars play their home games at the Metropolitan Sports Center in Bloomington, and the Timberwolves compete at the new Target Center in downtown Minneapolis. University of Minnesota teams compete in the Big Ten in football, baseball, hockey, and basketball. Thoroughbred horses run at Canterbury Downs Racetrack in Shakopee in a late April to November season; the Saint Paul Derby is held there on the last weekend in June.

Sports for the Participant

Outdoor sports in the Saint Paul area include fishing, swimming, boating, and water skiing in the summer and ice fishing, ice skating, cross-country skiing, and hockey in the winter. The Twin Cities Marathon is an annual event that attracts as many as six-thousand runners and is usually held the first or second Sunday in October.

Shopping and Dining

Saint Paul boasts the world's longest public skyway system; it consists of 4.7 miles of second-level walkways that link downtown hotels, restaurants, stores, and businesses. The Saint Paul World Trade Center is four-square blocks of more than one-hundred retail and dining establishments; at the center is the Town Square Park, which is an enclosed, year-round park housing the Cafesjian Carousel. The Farmers Market is an old-world open market selling home-grown foods and crafts. Historic Grand Avenue is lined with private homes, retail shops, boutiques, and antique stores. A local shopping square is housed in a turn-of-the-century railroad building. There are antique stores as well as specialty stores promoting Minnesota goods located throughout the Twin Cities.

Saint Paul restaurants stress American home cooking and Midwest cuisine; ethnic choices range from Afghan and Vietnamese menus to continental and French restaurants. Fresh fish, prime rib, and sixteen-ounce steaks are local favorites. Scandinavian dishes can be sampled at the daily buffet at the Deco Restaurant in the Minnesota Museum of Art. For diners in search of novelty, a local cafe develops a 1950s motif with waitstaff on rollerskates. Dinner cruises on the Mississippi River are offered. The quaint river town of Stillwater, 25 miles east of Saint Paul, also offers dining and shopping opportunities.

Visitor Information: Saint Paul Convention and Visitors Bureau, 600 NCL Tower, 101 Norwest Center, 55 East Fifth St., Saint Paul, MN 44101; telephone (612)297-6985 or 1-800-627-6101

Convention Facilities

The Saint Paul Civic Center, providing a total of 180,000 square feet of exhibit space and eighteen meeting rooms, accommodates events such as seminars, banquets, and conventions. The Arena seats 19,000 people and the newly renovated Roy Wilkins Auditorium offers space for up to 5,700 people. The World Theater, the city's oldest standing theater, provides seating for over nine-hundred people for meetings and various kinds of presentations in a two-balcony hall. The Minnesota State Fair Grounds maintains thirteen indoor facilities, ranging from 2,000 to 100,000 square feet, for use outside fair season. Film in the Cities, a non-profit media arts organization, offers its 260-seat theater for daytime and occasional evening events. Four conference sites, accommodating from 100 to 4,000 people, and lodging rooms for 1,000 people are available on the Macalester College campus.

Several hotels and motels offering meeting and banquet facilities for both large and small groups. A total of forty-seven hundred lodging rooms can be found in Saint Paul.

Convention Information: Saint Paul Convention and Visitors Bureau, 101 Norwest Center, 55 East Fifth Street, Saint Paul, MN 55101; telephone (612)297-6991 or 1-800-627-6101

Transportation

Approaching the City

The principal destination of most air travelers to Saint Paul is the Minneapolis-Saint Paul International Airport, fifteen minutes from downtown Saint Paul. Twelve commercial airlines and seven regional carriers schedule daily flights to 103 United States cities; direct international flights area also available. There are six reliever airports in the Saint Paul area.

An efficient highway system permits easy access into Saint Paul. Interstate-94 intersects the city from east to west and I-35 from north to south. I-494 and I-694 form a beltway circling the north, east, and west perimeters. Serving metropolitan Minneapolis-Saint Paul are seven federal and thirteen state routes.

Passenger rail service to Saint Paul from Chicago and Seattle is provided by Amtrak. Bus service is by Greyhound.

Traveling in the City

Saint Paul's freeway system, moderate population density, and two business districts facilitate high levels of traffic mobility throughout Minneapolis-Saint Paul during both peak and non-peak hours. The average commuting time from home to workplace is seventeen minutes. The Twin Cities' Metropolitan Transit Commission (MTC), one of the largest bus transportation systems in the country, operates regularly scheduled routes in Saint Paul as well as Minneapolis and the surrounding suburbs.

Communications

Newspapers and Magazines

Saint Paul's major daily newspaper is the *Saint Paul Pioneer Press*. Other newspapers appearing daily in the Twin Cities area are the *Minneapolis State and Tribune, Minnesota Daily,* and *Finance and Commerce. Minnesota Monthly* is a magazine focusing on topics of state and regional interest.

More than forty magazines, journals, and newsletters originate in the metropolitan area. Among those with the widest circulation are *Catholic Digest, The Family Handyman,* and *Farm Industry News, The Farmer/The Dakota Farmer,* and other agriculture-related monthlies. Member or special interest publications for professional associations, religious organizations, trade groups, and fraternal societies are also based in the city.

Television and Radio

Six commercial and two public television stations broadcast in the Minneapolis-Saint Paul area; cable service is also available. Thirty-five AM and FM radio stations furnish music, news, and information programming. The headquarters of the Minnesota Public Radio Network, an affiliate of National Public Radio, is located in Saint Paul. Minnesota Public Radio produces "Saint Paul Sunday Morning," a popular program that is broadcast live nationally from Saint Paul.

Media Information: Saint Paul Pioneer Press Dispatch, 345 Cedar Street, Saint Paul, MN 55101; telephone (612)222-5011; and, *Minnesota Monthly,* Minnesota Monthly Publications, Inc., 45 East Seventh Street, Saint Paul, MN 55104; telephone (612)290-1500

Selected Bibliography

Fitzgerald, F. Scott, *Taps at Reveille* (New York: C. Scribner's Sons, 1935)

MISSOURI

Kansas City 287
St. Louis 301
Springfield 315

The State in Brief

Nickname: Show Me State
Motto: *Solar populi suprema lex esto* (The welfare of the people shall be the supreme law)

Flower: Hawthorn
Bird: Bluebird

Area: 69,709 square miles (1990; U.S. rank: 19th)
Elevation: Ranges from 230 feet to 1,722 feet above sea level
Climate: Continental, with seasonal extremes; affected by cold air from Canada, warm moist air from the Gulf of Mexico, and dry air from the Southwest

Admitted to Union: August 10, 1821
Capital: Jefferson City
Head Official: Governor Mel Carnahan (D) (until 1997)

Population
  1970: 4,677,623
  1980: 4,917,000
  1990: 5,158,000
  Percent change, 1980–1990: 4.1%
  U.S. rank in 1990: 15th
  Percent of residents born in state: 70.8% (1990)
  Density: 74.3 people per square mile (1990; U.S. rank: 27th)
  1991 FBI Crime Index Total: 279,340

Racial and Ethnic Characteristics (1990)
  White: 4,486,000
  Black: 10.7%
  American Indian, Eskimo, Aleut: 0.39%
  Asian and Pacific Islander: 0.81%
  Hispanic (may be of any race): 1.21%

Age Characteristics (1990)
  Population under 5 years old: 378,000
  Population 5 to 17 years old: 962,000
  Percent of population 65 years and older: 14.1%
  Median age: 32.5 years
  Voting-age population (1988): 3,840,000 (54.5% of whom cast votes for president)

Vital Statistics
  Total number of births (1992): 75,437
  Total number of deaths (1992): 50,447 (of which, 680 were infants under the age of 1 year)
  AIDS cases reported, 1981–1990: 1,624 (U.S. rank: 17th)

Economy
  Major industries: Manufacturing; trade; finance, insurance, and real estate; services
  Unemployment rate: 5.9% (September 1992)
  Per capita income: $12,989 (1989)
  Median household income: $26,362 (1989)
  Total number of families: 1,378,020 (10.1% of which had incomes below the poverty level) (1989)
  Income tax rate: Graduated from 1.5% to 6.0%
  Sales tax rate: 4.225%

Kansas City

The City in Brief

Founded: 1821 (incorporated, 1853)

Head Official: Mayor Emanuel Cleaver (D) (since 1991)

City Population
 1970: 507,000
 1980: 448,159
 1990: 435,146
 Percent change, 1980–1990: −2.9%
 U.S. rank in 1980: 27th
 U.S. rank in 1990: 31st

Metropolitan Area Population
 1970: 1,373,000
 1980: 1,433,000
 1990: 1,566,280
 Percent change, 1980–1990: 9.3%
 U.S. rank in 1980: 25th
 U.S. rank in 1990: 25th

Area: 311.5 square miles (1990)

Elevation: 742 feet above sea level

Average Annual Temperature: 56.3° F

Average Annual Precipitation: 35.16 inches of rain; 20.3 inches of snow

Major Economic Sectors: Services, wholesale and retail trade, government, manufacturing

Unemployment Rate: 5.1% (September 1992)

Per Capita Income: $13,799 (1989)

1992 (2nd Quarter) ACCRA Average House Price: $99,000

1992 (2nd Quarter) ACCRA Cost of Living Index: 95.5 (U.S. average = 100.0)

1991 FBI Crime Index Total: 57,834

Major Colleges and Universities: University of Missouri at Kansas City

Daily Newspapers: *Kansas City Star*; *Kansas City Times*

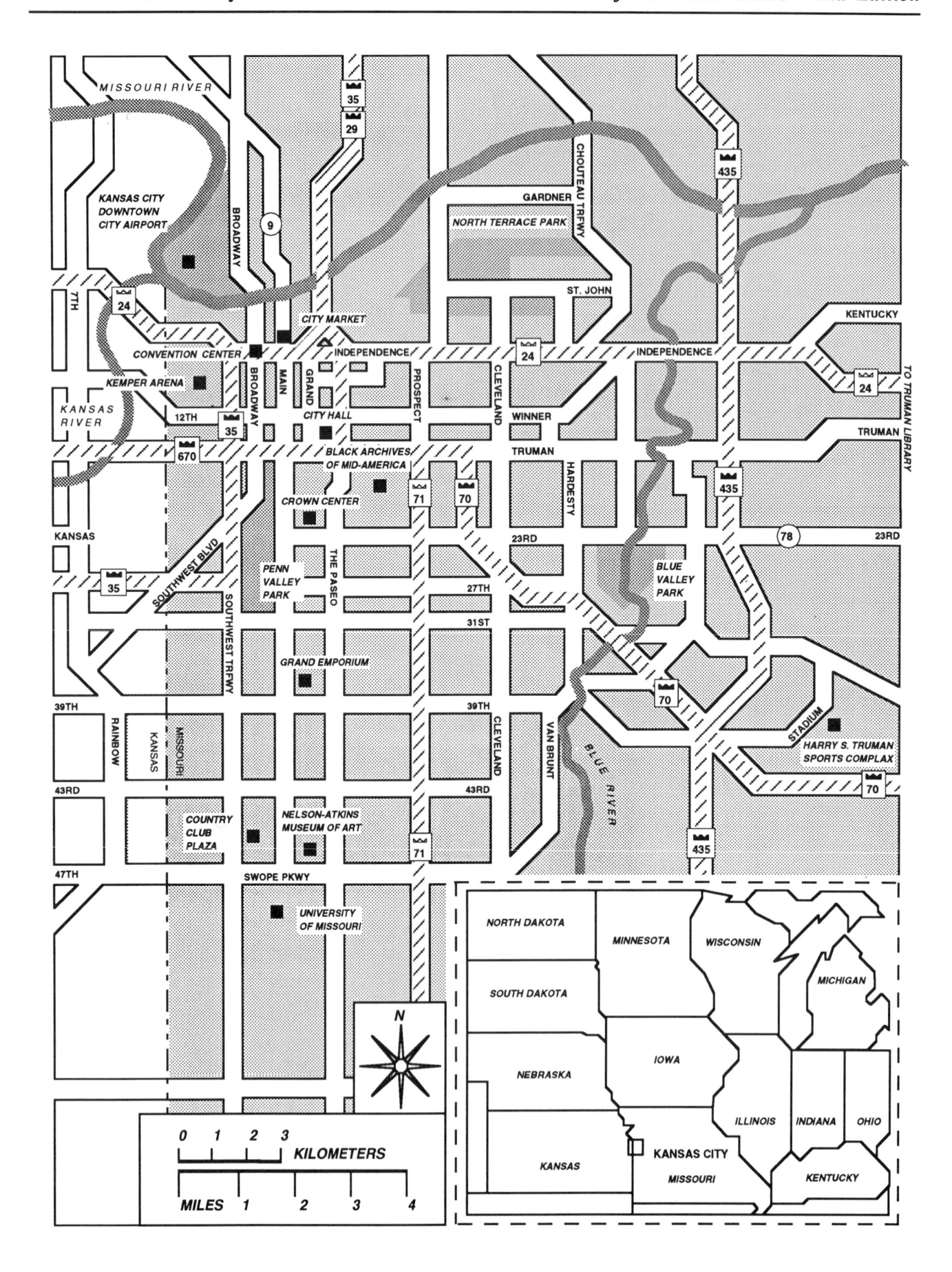

Missouri—Kansas City

Cities of the United States • 2nd Edition

Introduction

Kansas City, the largest city in Missouri, is the center of a metropolitan statistical area that includes Cass, Clay, Jackson, Platte, and Ray counties in Missouri and Johnson and Wyandotte counties in Kansas. First a trading post and river port settlement, the city after the Civil War developed as a link in the intercontinental railroad network, which led to prosperous grain, livestock, and meat-packing industries. During the twentieth century Kansas City has garnered a national reputation for its distinctive architecture, boulevard system, and innovations in urban redevelopment. *Fortune* magazine named Kansas City the fourth-best city for business in the United States in 1991.

Geography and Climate

Surrounded by gently rolling terrain, Kansas City is located near the geographical center of the United States. It is situated on the south bank of the Missouri River at the Missouri-Kansas state line. The climate is modified continental, with frequent and rapid fluctuations in weather during early spring. Summer is characterized by warm days and mild nights; fall days are mild and the nights cool. Winter is not severely cold, the occurrence of snowfall of more than ten inches being rare.

Area: 311.5 square miles (1990)

Elevation: 742 feet above sea level

Average Temperatures: January, 28.4° F; July, 80.9° F; annual average, 56.3° F

Average Annual Precipitation: 35.16 inches of rain; 20.3 inches of snow

History

Riverside Site Aids Westward Expansion

The area along the Missouri River now occupied by Kansas City was originally territory within the domain of the Kansa (Kaw) native Americans. The first persons of European descent to enter the region were Meriwether Lewis and William Clark, who camped at the confluence of the Kansas and Missouri rivers in 1804 while on their Louisiana Purchase expedition. Several years later, in 1821, Francois Chouteau opened a depot for the American Fur Company on the site; after a flood destroyed his warehouse in 1830, he relocated to a spot where a ferry boat service was in operation and where the town of Kansas eventually developed.

In 1832 John Calvin McCoy settled nearby and built a store; the following year he platted the town of Westport, offering lots for establishing businesses. Westport was soon competing with neighboring Independence, the seat of Jackson County, to be chosen as the eastern terminus of the Santa Fe Trail. Meanwhile Chouteau's settlement, Kansas, developed more slowly; in 1838 the Kansas Town Company was formed to sell property near Chouteau's warehouse. Both Westport and Kansas Town prospered under westward migration until at the height of the Gold Rush, in 1849, an epidemic of Asiatic cholera reduced the local population by one-half and drove business elsewhere.

The Kansas Town settlement remained substantial enough, however, to be incorporated in 1850 as the Town of Kansas and then as the City of Kansas in 1853. By 1855 overland trade had returned and the city began to prosper once again. Nevertheless the nation's conflict over the issue of slavery, which led Southern and Northern forces to vie for dominance in the Kansas Territory, disrupted life in the new city. Kansas border ruffians invaded Wyandotte County, creating havoc in the City of Kansas, which fell into disrepair and underwent economically difficult times with the outbreak of the Civil War. Wartime became even bleaker when opposing forces met nearby; the Union Army resisted a Confederate Army attack at the Battle of Westport in October of 1864.

Rail Center Develops Architectural Refinement

By 1865, when the Missouri Pacific Railroad arrived there, the City of Kansas at the confluence of the Kansas and Missouri rivers was found to be a perfect location for a railroad distributing center. The first stockyards were opened in 1870 and, after the grasshopper plagues in 1874, the City of Kansas emerged as a wheat and grain exchange center. Since the city had been expanding, the economy was further stimulated when the first bridge was built across the Kansas River in 1866, followed by the construction of the Hannibal Bridge across the Missouri River in 1869. Kansas City adopted its current name in 1889; Westport became a part of Kansas City in 1897.

The figure who had the greatest impact in transforming Kansas City into a beautiful metropolis was William Rockhill Nelson, an Indiana native who settled in Kansas City in 1880 to become owner and editor of the *Kansas City Star*. Nelson, shaping the future of the city much as the founding fathers had shaped the country, used his position to persuade the community's elite to commit themselves to civic betterment. Through Nelson's constant nudging, a residential development project was begun, turning a rundown neighborhood into the exclusive Country Club district that contained the internationally acclaimed business section, Country Club Plaza. This enclave was carefully landscaped with parks, fountains, and European statuary—and remains so today. Through Nelson's influence as well, George E. Kessler planned Kansas City's much-admired boulevard system that helps define its distinctive character. The city also contains innumerable architecturally significant buildings, especially in the Art Deco style; much of the credit goes to Nelson's ability to convince people to express their civic pride through architecture, landscaping, and city planning.

In the 1920s Democrat Thomas J. Pendergast introduced machine politics to Kansas City, with mixed blessings. Although civic improvements were initiated, Kansas City developed a reputation for a corrupt government that functioned under "boss rule," a reputation that continued until 1940 when reformers were voted into office. Kansas City has continued to prosper through urban redevelopment projects. Crown Center, Hallmark Cards' "city within a city," is the latest in a long history of significant architectural projects. Some felt the Crown Center drew development away from Kansas City's downtown, while others credited the project with halting the drain of business into the suburbs. In 1981 two skywalks at the Crown Center's Hyatt Hotel collapsed, killing more than 100 people. Hallmark Cards subsequently pledged to contribute $6.5 million to Kansas City charitable causes as a "healing gesture." The Crown Center remains a Kansas City landmark.

Historical Information: Historic Kansas City Foundation, 20 West Ninth Street, Suite 450, Kansas City, MO 64105; telephone (816)471-3391; and, Kansas City Museum, 3218 Gladstone Boulevard, Kansas City, MO 64123; telephone (816)483-8300

Population Profile

Metropolitan Area Residents
1970: 1,373,000
1980: 1,433,000
1990: 1,566,280
Annual average percent change, 1980-1988: 1.1%
U.S. rank in 1980: 25th
U.S. rank in 1990: 25th

City Residents
1970: 507,000
1980: 448,159
1990: 435,146 (of which, 206,985 were males, and 228,181 were females)
Percent change, 1980-1990: -2.9%
U.S. rank in 1980: 27th
U.S. rank in 1990: 31st (State rank: 1st)

Density: 1,396.9 people per square mile (1990)

Racial and ethnic characteristics (1990)
  White: 290,572
  Black: 128,768
  American Indian, Eskimo, Aleut: 2,144
  Asian and Pacific Islander: 5,239
  Hispanic (may be of any race): 17,017

Percent of residents born in state: 60.9% (1990)

Age characteristics (1990)
  Population under 5 years old: 33,656
  Population 5 to 9 years old: 30,750
  Population 10 to 14 years old: 27,652
  Population 15 to 19 years old: 27,666
  Population 20 to 24 years old: 32,088
  Population 25 to 29 years old: 42,744
  Population 30 to 34 years old: 41,649
  Population 35 to 39 years old: 34,687
  Population 40 to 44 years old: 28,886
  Population 45 to 49 years old: 22,540
  Population 50 to 54 years old: 19,085
  Population 55 to 59 years old: 18,646
  Population 60 to 64 years old: 18,931
  Population 65 to 69 years old: 18,167
  Population 70 to 74 years old: 13,563
  Population 75 to 79 years old: 10,600
  Population 80 to 84 years old: 7,443
  Population 85 years and over: 6,393
  Median age: 32.7 years

Births (1988)
  Total number: 7,960

Deaths (1988)
  Total number: 4,608 (of which, 105 were infants under the age of 1 year)

Money income (1989)
  Per capita income: $13,799
  Median household income: $26,713
  Total households: 177,157
  Number of households with income of . . .
    less than $5,000: 14,936
    $5,000 to $9,999: 16,864
    $10,000 to $14,999: 16,784
    $15,000 to $24,999: 33,988
    $25,000 to $34,999: 29,828
    $35,000 to $49,999: 30,575
    $50,000 to $74,999: 22,866
    $75,000 to $99,999: 6,246
    $100,000 to $149,999: 3,328
    $150,000 or more: 1,742
  Percent of families below poverty level: 11.7% (57.0% of which were female householder families with related children under 5)
1991 FBI Crime Index Total: 57,834

Municipal Government

Kansas City operates under a council-manager form of government, with the mayor and twelve council members all elected to four-year terms. The city manager serves at the pleasure of the mayor and council. According to *Fortune* magazine, Mayor Cleaver, a black elected by a white majority, "has launched a new era of race relations."

Head Official: Mayor Emanuel Cleaver (D) (since 1991; current term expires April 1995)

Total Number of City Employees: 4,212 (full-time, not including police department; 1992)

City Information: City Hall, 414 East Twelfth, Kansas City, MO 64106; telephone (816)274-2222

Economy

Major Industries and Commercial Activity

Because of its location near the center of the United States, Kansas City has long been a manufacturing, commercial, transportation, distribution, and storage hub for the Midwest. The fastest growing economic sector is service; increased employment is attributed to lower than national-average operating costs. The service sector is closely followed by wholesale and retail trade, influenced in part by the area's rising disposable income. Government, traditionally one of the area's largest employers, is the fourth largest employment sector. In 1990 over twenty-three hundred manufacturing firms in the area accounted for nearly 14 percent of employment. Transportation, communications, and utilities, which have long played a key role in the economy, continue to do so, led by major employers such as U.S. Sprint and AT&T. The construction industry and agribusiness also contribute to the economy.

Items and goods produced: food products, automobiles, trucks, agricultural chemicals, airplane accessories, ammunition, paints, wire goods, industrial uniforms, electrical equipment, valve fittings, pipes, dental supplies, work garments, clothing, refrigerators, fire apparatus, tile and brick, beverages, malt syrup, furniture, caskets, mattresses, motor cars, stationery, drugs

Incentive Programs—New and Existing Companies

The Kansas City Area Development Council, founded in 1976, is a coalition of business, government, development, and chambers of commerce leaders. The council acts as a facilitator to prospective business and industrial firms seeking information about the Kansas City area.

Businesses relocating to the Kansas City area have available to them tax credits, abatements, and exemptions; revenue and general obligation bonds; and six general purpose foreign trade zone sites. The Greater Kansas City Chamber of Commerce places its major focus on economic growth, job retention and creation, and small enterprise and minority business development through a variety of services and benefits.

Development Projects

Announced capital improvements for the Kansas City area in the 1990s total over $900 million. Among these projects are a $100 million expansion of the city's major convention center, intended to extend the facility over Interstate I-70 and scheduled for completion in late 1993; a $50 million Phase I expansion of the Kansas City Zoo; and a ten-year, $330 million improvement of the airport. Kansas

City is investing $600 million in improvements to its inner-city school system.

Economic Development Information: Kansas City Area Development Council, 920 Main, Suite 600, Kansas City, MO 64105-2049; telephone (816)221-2121

Commercial Shipping

Located at the juncture of five interstate and eight federal highways and served by 250 motor freight carriers, Greater Kansas City is one of the country's primary trucking centers. The site of twelve mainline railroads carrying three-hundred rail transports each day, it also ranks nationally as the second-largest rail hub. Kansas City is connected via the Kansas and Missouri rivers to the nation's inland water system and is served by eleven regulated barge lines; as an important inland port, it maintains one of the largest foreign trade zones in the United States. Air cargo facilities are available at Kansas City International Airport. Kansas City is one of a few U.S. cities served by three interstate highways.

Labor Force and Employment Outlook

The Kansas City area labor force is described as well-educated—more than 70 percent of persons over age twenty-five are high school graduates—and as motivated and highly productive. Two-thirds of workers are white collar.

Fortune magazine has selected Kansas City as one of the top cities in the country for doing business. Growth is projected in all sectors of the economy through 1995, led by wholesale and retail trade, services, manufacturing, and government. Total employment is expected to increase 8.6 percent by 1995. Construction employment will benefit from the more than $900 million in announced capital improvements. The number of international companies located in Kansas City tripled between 1985-1990, and this trend is expected to continue. Economists predict that Kansas City will be more stable than most cities due to a capital improvements boom, a strong agribusiness economy, and steady employment.

The following is a summary of data regarding the Kansas City metropolitan area labor force as of September 1992.

Size of non-agricultural labor force: 776,500

Number of workers employed in . . .
mining: not reported
construction: 30,600
manufacturing: 105,000
transportation and public utilities: 63,900
wholesale and retail trade: 196,000
finance, insurance, and real estate: 59,000
services: 200,500
government: 121,500

Average hourly earnings of production workers employed in manufacturing: $13.22

Unemployment rate: 5.1%

Largest employers	Number of employees
State and local government	85,300
Federal government	31,800
Hallmark Cards, Inc.	8,774
Trans World Airlines	6,800
Allied Signal Aerospace	6,787
United Telecom and U.S. Sprint	6,500
A T & T	6,200

Cost of Living

The following is a summary of data regarding several key cost of living factors in the Kansas City area.

1992 (2nd Quarter) ACCRA Cost of Living Index: 95.5 (U.S. average = 100.0)

1992 (2nd Quarter) ACCRA Average House Price: $99,000

State income tax rate: graduated from 1.5% to 6.0%

State sales tax rate: 4.225%

Local income tax rate: 1.0% of total income

Local sales tax rate: 1.5%

Property tax rate: $9.86 per $1,000 of assessed valuation

Economic Information: Kansas City Area Development Council, 920 Main, Suite 600, Kansas City, MO 64105-2049; telephone (816)221-2121

Cities of the United States • 2nd Edition Missouri—Kansas City

The J. C. Nichols Fountain at Country Club Plaza.

Education and Research

Elementary and Secondary Schools

School District 33 of Kansas City, Missouri, is the major provider of public elementary and secondary education in Kansas City. The school system is administered by a nine-member board that selects a superintendent. Kansas City is investing $600 million in its school system, an expenditure ordered by a federal court in a desegregation suit. A $32 million high school has been built; a magnet school offers computer and robotics training and a Jesuit-inspired curriculum including Greek, Latin, and Olympic sports training.

The following is a summary of data regarding the Kansas City public schools as of the 1991-1992 school year.

Total enrollment: 36,007

Number of facilities
  elementary schools: 52
  junior high schools: 11
  senior high schools: 10

Student/teacher ratio: kindergarten to grade 3, 22:1; grades 4 and 5, 27:1; junior and senior high school, 25:1

Teacher salaries
  minimum: $22,215
  maximum: $44,430

Funding per pupil: reported as "$4.96 per $100"

More than 150 private and parochial schools operate in the metropolitan area.

Public Schools Information: Kansas City School District 33, 1211 McGee, Kansas City, MO 64106; telephone (816)871-7000

Colleges and Universities

Kansas City is home to several colleges and universities. The largest institution is the University of Missouri at Kansas City, with an enrollment of nearly twelve-thousand students. Granting baccalaureate, first-professional, master's, and doctorate degrees, the university operates a College of Arts and Sciences, a conservatory of music, a computer science division, and schools of business and public administration, education, pharmacy, dentistry, law, medicine, and basic life sciences.

Undergraduate and graduate degrees are awarded in specialized and professional areas by a number of the area's colleges. The Kansas City Art Institute, which began as a sketch club in 1885, offers a four-year fine and applied arts curriculum.

Church-related colleges in the city include Avila College, Mid America Nazarene College, and Rockhurst College.

Two-year vocational and college transfer programs are available at Penn Valley Community College and Maple Woods Community College. In all, nearly twenty multi-purpose colleges and universities and affiliates within a 50-mile radius offer educational advancement opportunities.

Libraries and Research Centers

Approximately fifty libraries are maintained in Kansas City by public agencies, educational institutions, private corporations, cultural organizations, hospitals, and churches and synagogues. The Kansas City Public Library, with holdings of over 1.6 million volumes and more than sixteen hundred periodical subscriptions in its central facility, operates seven branches. Special collections include black history, Missouri Valley history and genealogy, oral history, and federal and state government documents. Also based in the city is the Northeast Missouri Library Service, which houses 111,800 books; five branches, with collections ranging from 10,632 to 18,440 volumes, are located in communities throughout the region.

The Linda Hall Library is one of the largest privately endowed libraries of its kind in the country, holding more than 677,000 volumes and 12,500 periodicals. Special collections include National Aeronautics and Space Administration and Department of Energy technical reports, Soviet and European scientific and technical publications, United States patent specifications, and the holdings of the Archie R. Dykes Library of Health Sciences and the University of Missouri Health Science Library. The Kansas City Branch of the National Archives and Records Administration holds records of various federal government agencies. The University of Missouri—Kansas City operates an extensive campus library facility and operates the Institute for Community Studies.

The C. J. Patterson Memorial Library of the Midwest Research Institute is devoted to the fields of biology, chemistry, and environmental studies. The Research

Medical Center also houses a library specializing in materials on the health sciences.

Public Library Information: Kansas City Public Library, 311 East Twelfth Street, Kansas City, MO 64106-2454; telephone (816)221-2685

Health Care

Among the primary health care facilities in Kansas City-Jackson County are approximately nineteen hospitals providing more than 4,800 beds and sixty-four nursing homes furnishing more than 5,000 beds. In addition to health care professionals and allied staff, the Kansas City medical community is comprised of around fifteen hundred physicians practicing in most specialties.

Research Medical Center, founded in 1896 and one of the city's major employers, offers general and specialized care in such areas as arthritis, cardiac, and pulmonary rehabilitation, pain management, and speech and hearing disorders. The Research Psychiatric Center provides a complete range of psychiatric treatment for adults and adolescents. St. Luke's Hospital operates the Mid-America Heart Institute and a school of nursing. Truman Medical Center is affiliated with the University of Missouri—Kansas City schools of medicine, dentistry, pharmacy, and nursing. Other major health care facilities located in the city include Menorah Medical Center, St. Joseph Hospital, St. Mary's Hospital, and the Children's Mercy Hospital. A number of public and private special clinics, chemical dependency centers, mental health centers, and fitness centers also serve Kansas City.

Health Care Information: Metropolitan Medical Society, telephone (816)531-8432 (for information regarding Health Phone)

Recreation

Sightseeing

Kansas City is regarded as one of the most cosmopolitan cities of its size in the United States. Second only to Rome, Italy, in the number of its fountains, Kansas City streets total more miles of boulevards than Paris, France. More than one-thousand of the city's structures are included on the National Register of Historic Places; among them are the Scarritt Building and Arcade, the *Kansas City Star* Building, Union Station, and the Kansas City Power and Light Building. The Mutual Musicians Foundation, a hot-pink bungalow acquired by the Black Musicians Union Local 627 in 1928, received a National Historic Landmark designation.

A unique feature of the city is a system of underground limestone caves that were formerly quarries. This twenty-million-square-foot "subterropolis," is now a commercial complex used for offices and warehouses. The Hallmark Visitors Center showcases the history and most recent developments of the Hallmark Greeting Card Company. The Harry S Truman Library and Museum in Independence, Missouri, captures Truman's political career and years as thirty-third President of the United States. One of the nation's largest urban parks, Swope Park includes the Kansas City Zoo and a braille trail.

The towns around Kansas City are full of historic homes and sites, including the home of Harry S Truman in Independence. Among some of the more unusual sites is the Jesse James Bank Museum in Liberty, the site of the first daylight bank robbery in the United States. The Marshal's House, Jail and Museum in Independence, dating from 1859, once held Frank James and William Quantrill.

Sports fans will enjoy a tour of the National Collegiate Athletic Association Visitors Center, opened in September 1990 to commemorate great moments in intercollegiate athletics through multi-image and video presentations and displays and exhibits.

Arts and Culture

Kansas City's Nelson-Atkins Museum of Art, one of the largest museums in the United States, maintains a permanent collection that represents arts from all civilizations and periods, from Sumeria to the present. Opened in 1933, the museum covers 20 landscaped acres, and is home to the only Henry Moore Sculpture Garden outside the artist's native England. The Liberty Memorial Museum, conceived as a "monument to peace," is the nation's only museum devoted to World War I and America's involvement in that conflict. Its dedication in 1921 brought together five Allied commanders who met for the first and only time in their lives. The Kansas City Museum of History and Science concentrates on

The Truman Sports Complex.

native North American artifacts and includes a natural history hall, a planetarium, and reconstructed corner drugstore. The Toy and Miniature Museum of Kansas City is one of only three museums of its kind in the country. Other museums in the city include the Black Archives of Mid-America, the Federal Reserve Bank Visitors Center, and the home and studio of the late painter, Thomas Hart Benton.

Kansas City is noted for a distinctive jazz musical style, which consists of a two-four beat, predominance of saxophones, and background riffs; it has been played by musicians in local clubs since the early 1900s. The late Count Basie and Charlie "Bird" Parker, regarded as two of the greatest practitioners of the genre, began their careers in Kansas City. The Landmark Commission sponsors a walking tour of the jazz district, where nearly forty nightspots host Kansas City jazz, including the Grand Emporium Saloon, named the country's best blues club by the National Blues Foundation.

Kansas City ranks as the third largest theater city in the Midwest, boasting more than twenty equity and community theater companies. The Missouri Repertory Theatre performs a seven-show season, hosting nationally known actors and performing a stage adaptation of Charles Dickens's *A Christmas Carol* each holiday season. Among the other theater companies in Kansas City are Theatre for Young America, the Coterie, American Heartland Theatre, Tiffany's Attic, Waldo Astoria, Vaudeville Company, New Directions Theatre Company, Quality Hill Playhouse, Unicorn Theatre, and Actors' Ensemble Saloon Theatre.

Folly Theatre, a former burlesque house refurbished in 1981, is the first theater to appear on the National Historic Register; it hosts professional theater productions. The Midland Center for the Performing Arts, also on the National Historic Register, is a 1920s movie palace that was refurbished and reopened in 1981; the Theater League presents Broadway shows in this ornate structure, which is decorated with gold leaf overlays, Tiffany glass, and bronze chandeliers.

The Lyric Theater is the home of the Kansas City Symphony and Lyric Opera, which presents all of its performances in English, as well as the headquarters of the State Ballet of Missouri. Music Hall, Kansas City's largest theater, hosts ballets, symphony concerts, and musical theater productions. Ranked among the nation's largest outdoor amphitheaters, the Starlight Theater is located in Swope Park and presents musicals and concerts in the summer.

Festivals and Holidays

Kansas City celebrates the Fourth of July for two days during the Spirit Festival. Music and dance fests are held on the lawn at the Nelson-Atkins Museum of Art during the summer. The Kansas City Jazz Festival is held in August and draws upon the city's rich jazz tradition. Also in August the Plaza's art fair brings nationally known artists to Kansas City for a juried two-day event, and the Ethnic Enrichment Festival celebrates the heritage of forty different nationalities. A Renaissance Festival is held in autumn, and artists from across the country bring their works to the Plaza Art Fair in September. The American Royal Livestock, Horse Show, and Rodeo is held each year over a sixteen-day period in November at Kemper Arena, combining horse shows and rodeo competition in the nation's premier event of its kind. Events begin in October with the Barbecue Cook-off Kick-off, followed by the National Royal Cookoff and then the Barbecue and Diddy-Wa-Diddy Sauce Contest. Events in November begin with the quarter horse show and American Royal parade and end with the 4-H horse show. The Concert for Champions combines a horse show with classical music performed by the Kansas City Symphony. Country Club Plaza's lighting of 45 miles of Christmas lights on Thanksgiving night attracts 100,000 people.

Sports for the Spectator

Kansas City athletes compete in three of the most modern sports facilities in the United States. The Harry S Truman Sports Complex consists of Arrowhead Stadium, home of the Kansas City Chiefs in the Western Division of the American Conference of the National Football League, and Royals Stadium, home of the Kansas City Royals of the Western Division of baseball's American League. The dual complex is the only one of its kind in the country. Kemper Arena in downtown Kansas City is an award-winning circular and pillarless structure that allows unobstructed and intimate viewing from all locations. The Kansas City Comets of the Major Indoor Soccer League play home games at Kemper Arena. Kansas City is also headquarters of the National Collegiate Athletic Association (NCAA), National Association of Intercollegiate Athletics (NAIA), the Big 8 Conference, and the Fellowship of Christian Athletes. Professional golfer Tom Watson, a Kansas City native, is affectionately known as the city's "fourth sports franchise."

Sports for the Participant

The beautiful and popular Kansas City parks offer an outlet for sports enthusiasts who enjoy fishing, golf, hiking, jogging, swimming, boating, ice skating, or tennis. Swope Park, one of the largest city parks in the nation, provides two eighteen-hole golf courses, a swimming pool, and a braille trail. Shawnee Mission Park is one of the best spots for sailing and canoeing. Fishing and sailing are available at nine public access lakes within an hour's drive. The area has facilities for professional and amateur auto racing as well as horse- and dog-race tracks.

Shopping and Dining

City Market, at the north end of Main Street, offers shopping in a bazaar-like atmosphere. A Saturday morning trip to City Market for produce is a local tradition. Further south on Main Street, the Country Club Plaza, developed by Jessie Clyde Nichols in 1922, enjoys the distinction of being "America's Original Shopping Center." Located 5 miles south of downtown, the Plaza covers 55 acres and contains almost two-hundred retail and service businesses, including forty restaurants. The plaza, with its tile-roofed, pastel-colored buildings and imported filigree ironwork, borrows heavily from Hispanic architecture in honor of Seville, Spain, Kansas City's sister city. The European ambiance is enhanced with a number of fountains and horse-drawn carriages. The city's most popular tourist attraction, the plaza inaugurated America's outdoor Christmas lighting tradition in 1926.

Crown Center, described as a city within a city, is a one-half billion-dollar downtown complex of shops, restaurants, hotels, offices, apartments, and condominiums over 85 acres developed by the Hallmark Company. The Crown Center Shops occupy three levels topped by Halls Crown Center, a one-hundred-thousand-square-foot specialty store. Crown Center revitalized the inner city by creating a downtown suburb where families can live and work. The Town Pavilion, a tri-level shopping complex at the base of the A T & T building downtown, is connected by a walkway to two major department stores. Westport, Kansas City's historic district, features boutiques, restaurants, and nightly entertainment.

Kansas City barbecue is one of America's premier contributions to world cuisine. Dating from the 1920s when Henry Perry, the "father of K.C. Barbecue," first started selling slabs of barbecued meat cooked on an outdoor pit and wrapped in newspaper, Kansas City barbecue is now a fashionable food. The process requires that the meat be cooked slowly over wood, preferably hickory, for as long as eighteen hours. More than seventy Kansas City barbecue establishments serve ribs, pork, ham, mutton, sausage, and even fish. Each establishment prides itself on its own unique recipe for sauce; many of the sauces can be purchased. The barbecue restaurant owned by the legendary Arthur Bryant has been described by food critic Calvin Trillin as "the single, best restaurant in the world."

Elegant dining is also possible in Kansas City at establishments like Cafe Allegro, The Grill, Jasper's, and Peppercorn Duck Club, all selected by *Food and Wine* magazine as 1992–1993 Distinguished Restaurants of North America.

Visitor Information: Convention and Visitors Bureau of Greater Kansas City, City Center, 1100 Main, Suite 2550, Kansas City, MO; telephone (816)221-5242

Convention Facilities

Kansas City is a popular convention destination, ranking among the top twenty meeting centers in the nation. The Kansas City Convention Complex, site of most major functions in the city, consists of H. Roe Bartle Hall and Municipal Auditorium and covers a four-block downtown area that includes Barney Allis Plaza. The two buildings are linked by an underground walkway that is also connected to a parking garage and to three hotels. A $100 million expansion was scheduled for completion in late 1993. That expansion would bring total square footage of Bartle Hall to four-hundred thousand and total square footage of the complex to 670,000. A cable-supported lighted roof structure will rise two-hundred feet above the building. Historically significant Municipal Auditorium, built in 1935 and considered an outstanding example of art deco architecture, was recently remodeled. Barney Allis Plaza, the city's newest park, can be used for parties and receptions.

Located near the Convention Center is the American Royal Center, a 14-acre complex that includes Kemper Arena, the American Royal Arena, and Jack

Reardon Civic Center. Home of the Kansas City Comets, Kemper Arena is the site of large functions such as political conventions. The American Royal Arena, with seating for 5,600 people, is the site of the annual American Livestock and Horse Show.

Additional convention facilities for both large and small groups can be found at metropolitan area hotels and motels, where more than fourteen thousand rooms are available.

Convention Information: Convention and Visitors Bureau of Greater Kansas City, City Center Square, 1100 Main, Suite 2550, Kansas City, MO 64105; telephone (816)221-5242 or (800)523-5953

Transportation

Approaching the City

Kansas City International Airport, 17 miles northwest of downtown, is served by fourteen commercial carriers with daily direct and connecting flights from all major United States cities and from points abroad.

Primary highway routes into Kansas City are north-south I-35 and I-29, which join U.S. 71 leading into the city. The I-435 bypass links with east-west I-70 from the south.

Amtrak provides passenger rail service to two stops in the metropolitan area.

Traveling in the City

Kansas City's streets are laid out in a basic grid pattern except in areas contiguous with the Kansas and Missouri rivers, where one-way streets predominate. The principal downtown thoroughfare is Main Street, which runs north to south. Beginning at the Missouri River, east-west streets are numbered in ascending order southward through the city. State Line Road separates Kansas City from its sister city, Kansas City, Kansas; the two cities are connected via I-70.

The Kansas City Area Transportation Authority operates the Metro, a public bus system that serves most metropolitan area cities. The Kansas City Trolley transports shoppers from Country Club Plaza to the downtown area, with stops at Westport and Crown Center.

Communications

Newspapers and Magazines

The major daily newspapers in Kansas City are the *Kansas City Star* and the *Kansas City Times.* The *Kansas City Business Journal* is a weekly newspaper focusing on local business events and issues. Several community newspapers also circulate weekly and monthly. *Kansas City Magazine* features articles on topics of interest to metropolitan readers.

A number of magazines and journals are published in Kansas City. Among them is the nationally distributed *Flower and Garden Magazine* (the magazine's demonstration garden is also located in Kansas City); others address such subjects as medicine, nursing, the livestock industry, banking, business, religion, history and genealogy, the building trades, literature, office machines, and electrical power.

Television and Radio

Seven television stations—three major network affiliates, three independents, and one public—are received in Kansas City. Broadcasts are also received from stations in neighboring Fairway, Kansas, and Shawnee Mission, Kansas. Thirty-two AM and FM radio stations in metropolitan Kansas City schedule a range of program formats, including music, news, and information.

Media Information: Kansas City Star Company, 1729 Grand Avenue, Kansas City, MO 64108; telephone (816)234-4141; and, *Kansas City Magazine,* Sutherland Media, Inc 3401 Main Street, Kansas City, MO 64111; telephone (816)561-0444

Selected Bibliography

Christo, *Wrapped Walk Ways, Loose Park, Kansas City, Missouri, 1977–78: Essay by Ellen R. Goheen; photos by Wolfgang Volz* (New York: H.N. Abrams, 1978)

Hemingway, Ernest, *Ernest Hemingway, Cub Reporter; Kansas City Star Stories* (Pittsburgh: University of Pittsburgh Press, 1970)

St. Louis

The City in Brief

Founded: 1763 (incorporated, 1822)

Head Official: Mayor Raymond Bosley (D) (since 1993)

City Population
 1970: 622,000
 1980: 453,085
 1990: 396,685
 Percent change, 1980–1990: −12.4%
 U.S. rank in 1980: 26th
 U.S. rank in 1990: 34th

Metropolitan Area Population
 1970: 2,429,000
 1980: 2,377,000
 1990: 2,444,099
 Percent change, 1980–1990: 2.8%
 U.S. rank in 1980: 14th
 U.S. rank in 1990: 17th

Area: 61.9 square miles (1990)

Elevation: 535 feet above sea level

Average Annual Temperature: 55.4° F

Average Annual Precipitation: 33.91 inches

Major Economic Sectors: Services, wholesale and retail trade, manufacturing, government

Unemployment Rate: 5.8% (September 1992)

Per Capita Income: $10,798 (1989)

1992 (2nd Quarter) ACCRA Average House Price: $101,504

1992 (2nd Quarter) ACCRA Cost of Living Index: 96.5 (U.S. average = 100.0)

1991 FBI Crime Index Total: 64,103

Major Colleges and Universities: Washington University; Saint Louis University

Daily Newspaper: *St. Louis Post-Dispatch*

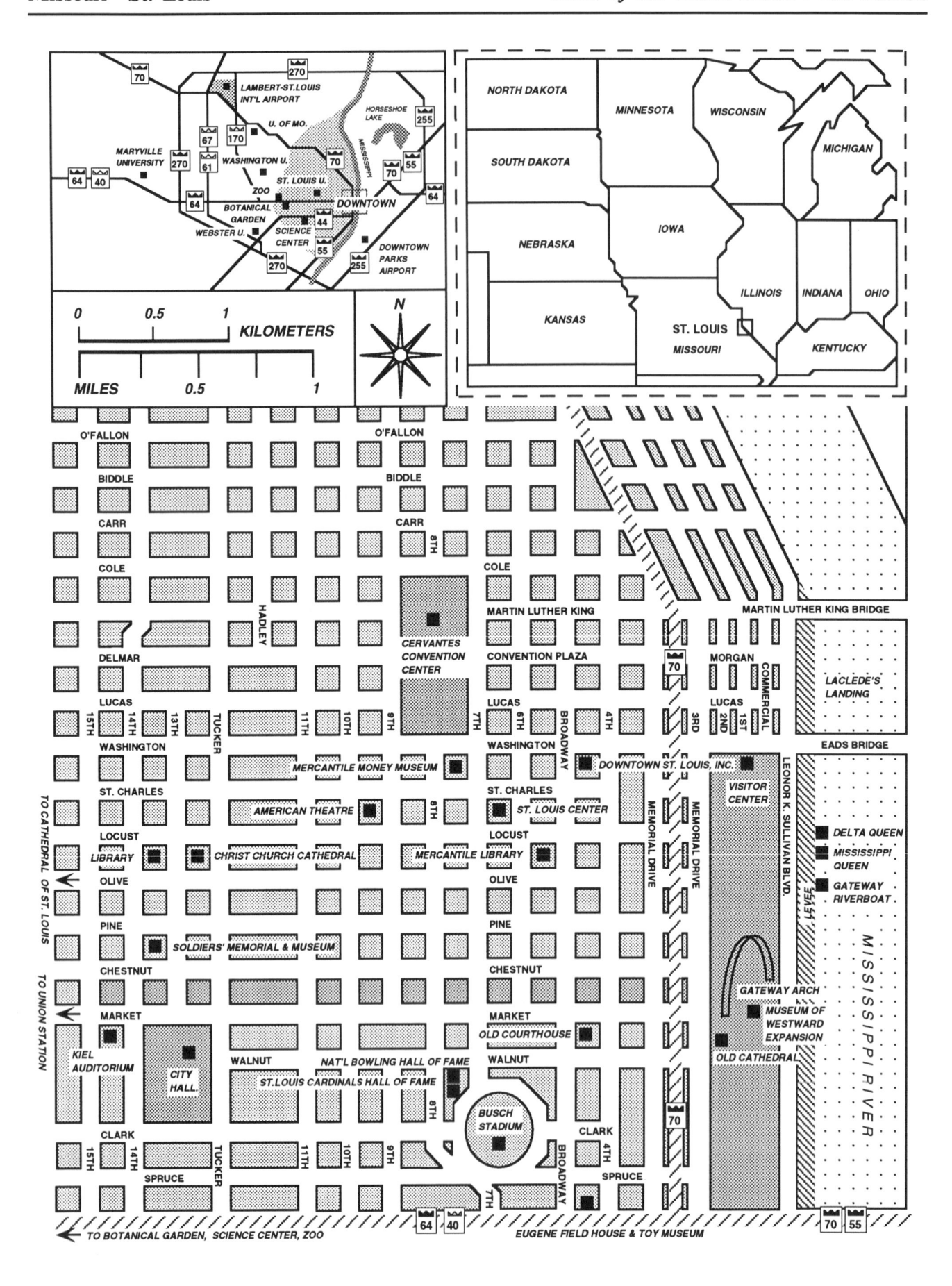

Missouri—St. Louis *Cities of the United States • 2nd Edition*

Introduction

St. Louis, the second largest city in Missouri, is the focus of the metropolitan statistical area comprised of Franklin, Jefferson, St. Charles, and St. Louis counties in Missouri and Clinton, Jersey, Madison, Monroe, and St. Clair counties in Illinois. Since its founding St. Louis has undergone several significant stages of development, which parallel the nation's westward expansion, symbolized by the city's famous Gateway Arch. St. Louis enjoys a rich and culturally diverse life and a revitalized downtown commercial district. As one of the first regions in the country to confront defense cutbacks in the 1990s and develop plans for dealing with them, the St. Louis area is emerging as a national laboratory for the post-cold-war economy.

Geography and Climate

Located at the confluence of the Mississippi and Missouri rivers, St. Louis is near the geographic center of the United States. Its modified continental climate is characterized by four seasons without prolonged periods of extreme heat or high humidity. Alternate invasions of moist air from the Gulf of Mexico and cold air masses from Canada produce a variety of weather conditions. Winters are brisk and seldom severe; annual snowfall averages about eighteen inches. Hot days with temperatures of one hundred degrees or higher occur on the average of five days per year. Severe storms are often accompanied by hail and damaging winds, and tornadoes have caused destruction and loss of life.

Area: 61.9 square miles (1990)

Elevation: 535 feet above sea level

Average Temperatures: January, 28.8° F; July, 78.9° F; annual average, 55.4° F

Average Annual Precipitation: 33.91 inches

History

Fur Trade Establishes St. Louis Townsite

The first known attempted settlement near present-day St. Louis was the Jesuit Mission of St. Francis Xavier, established in 1700 at the mouth of the Riviere des Peres (River of the Fathers). Two native American bands settled at the site with the Jesuit party, but within three years the mission was abandoned and no permanent settlement was attempted again in that area for more than sixty years.

Around 1760 the New Orleans firm of Maxent, Laclede & Company secured exclusive rights from France to trade with native Americans in the Missouri River Valley and the territory west of the Mississippi River as far north as the St. Peter River. Pierre Laclede Liguest selected the present site of St. Louis for a trading post in December 1763. Laclede said his intent was to establish "one of the finest cities in America." The village was named for the patron saint of France's King Louis XV. North of the village were Native American ceremonial mounds; these mounds stood outside the original village boundary but were eventually leveled as the city expanded. The largest, known as Big Mound, was located at the present-day St. Louis intersection of Mound and Broadway streets.

In its early years St. Louis was nicknamed *Pain Court* (short of bread) because of the absence of local agriculture to supply such staples as bread flour. Laclede's fur business prospered but in time France lost control of the territory and the ruling Hispanic government withdrew Laclede's exclusive fur-trading rights. This opened the city to new settlers and new businesses. During the American Revolutionary War, the Mississippi-Ohio River route was protected when soldiers and townsmen successfully rebuffed an attack by British General Haldimand's troops; this victory secured the strategic importance of St. Louis. After the Revolution Mississippi River pirates disrupted trade on the river but in 1788 boats carrying fighting crews from New Orleans defeated the pirates. St. Louis quickly emerged as a trading center as the village grew into an oasis of wealth, culture, and privilege.

American Influence Brings Westward Expeditions

This early period of splendor ended in 1803 when France, which had regained control of the surrounding territory, sold the vast tract of land to the new government of the United States in a land deal known as the Louisiana Purchase. American migrants soon brought gambling, violence, and mayhem into the community. Nearby Bloody Island gained a national reputation as a place of infamous duels, such as the one in 1817 when Thomas Hart Benton shot and killed a man. The rough-and-tumble village life eventually stabilized itself; the *Missouri Gazette,* St. Louis's first newspaper, and the opening of the first English school helped to improve the local environs.

St. Louis-based fur trappers and traders were the source of great local wealth; the Missouri Fur Company was founded in 1809 and dominated the Missouri Valley for the next forty years. The city became a logical point of departure for explorers setting off on westward journeys. The most famous of these undertakings is the Lewis and Clark expedition of 1804 to 1806. Eventually as many as fifty wagons a day crossed the Mississippi River at St. Louis on the trek westward, and the arrival of the first steamboat from New Orleans in 1817 was the first sign of the city's importance as a river trading center.

St. Louis was incorporated as a village in 1808 and as a city in 1822. The city asserted its political dominance early in Missouri's public life, but tension between businessmen and farmers in outlying areas resulted in the election of Alexander McNair as the state's first governor and the eventual establishment of the state government in Jefferson City.

Industry and Immigration Prompt Development

St. Louis's first manufacturing enterprises were operated by craftsmen in small shops, but by mid-century the city was an industrial center as the development of flour mills, ironworks, and factories for the production of foodstuffs and manufactured goods fueled the economy. Between 1832 and 1850 more than thirty thousand German immigrants started new lives in St. Louis. As industry brought another wave of new wealth, many of the city's existing civic, educational, and cultural institutions were established. During this period, credit for introduction of the highball, Southern Comfort, and Planter's Punch was attributed to local bartenders.

Serious damage to the city's downtown resulted when a fire on the steamboat *White Cloud* in 1849 spread to the wharf district and destroyed fifteen blocks in the commercial district; estimates of property damage ran as high as $6 million. St. Louis rebuilt by replacing log and wood buildings with masonry; public health issues such as sewage disposal and contaminated water were also addressed.

At the outset of the Civil War St. Louis was divided in its sympathies. The city's role was decided when General Nathaniel Lyon led the Union Army action, surrounding Missouri state troops at Camp Jackson. St. Louis became a base of Federal operations, and the city benefitted from the purchase of manufactured goods by the Chief Quartermaster that totalled $180 million. St. Louis's industrial capability increased by almost 300 percent in the decade between 1860 and 1870.

Prosperity, Culture Draw World Notice

In the post-Civil War period railroads replaced steamboats as the primary transportation mode, and a new route to the east was opened. The Eads Bridge, the world's first arched steel truss bridge, was completed in 1874 and the city's first Union Station was built in 1878. The new prosperity was diverted in part to cultural enrichments such as the Missouri Botanical Gardens and Tower Grove Park. The St. Louis Symphony Orchestra, the nation's second oldest, was founded in 1880. The Mercantile Library Association, which opened in 1846, began purchasing and commissioning original art works. Joseph Pulitzer's *Globe-Democrat* and Carl Schurz's *Westliche Post* were two of many newspapers that reported on the political and social issues of the day. St. Louis was, in 1876, the first city west of the Mississippi River to host a national political convention. In 1877 St. Louis's city charter separated it from the county and freed the city from state government control except for general laws.

By the turn of the century St. Louis had a population of 575,000 residents. In 1904 the city hosted the Louisiana Purchase Exposition, which focused national and world attention on St. Louis. Many European nations were represented in yearlong festivities that were considered a success. The first Olympiad to be held in the United States took place in St. Louis in 1904. The ice cream cone, the hot dog, and iced tea mark their beginnings at this world's fair. In 1926 an $87 million bond issue improved the city's infrastructure and financed the construction of new public buildings. A second bond issue in 1934 continued the improvements. New industrial initiatives in the late 1930s helped St. Louis pull out of the Great Depression.

In 1965 the Gateway Arch became a part of the St. Louis skyline, marking the spot where Laclede first established St. Louis. After failing to solve public housing problems in the 1950s, 1960s, and 1970s, the city emerged in the 1980s as a model for urban housing renewal, with stable neighborhoods of rehabilitated structures. A renovated warehouse district near the Gateway Arch called Laclede's Landing attracts tourists to the historic roots of modern St. Louis.

In the summer of 1993 St. Louis suffered extensive damage from flooding when the Missouri and Mississippi rivers joined forces just north of the city and swept down over its protective levees in some of the worst flooding in the country's history. Damage in the flood region was then estimated at over $10 billion.

Historical Information: Historical Association of Greater St. Louis, 3601 Lindell Boulevard, St. Louis, MO 63108; telephone (314)658-2588; Missouri Historical Society, P.O. Box 11940, St. Louis, MO 63112-0040; telephone (314)746-4599

Population Profile

Metropolitan Area Residents
 1970: 2,429,000
 1980: 2,377,000
 1990: 2,444,099
 Annual average percent change, 1980–1988: 0.4%
 U.S. rank in 1980: 14th
 U.S. rank in 1990: 17th

City Residents
 1970: 622,000
 1980: 453,085
 1990: 396,685 (of which, 180,680 were male and 216,005 were female)
 Percent change, 1980–1990: -12.4%
 U.S. rank in 1980: 26th
 U.S. rank in 1990: 34th (State rank: 2nd)

Density: 6,408.5 people per square mile (1990)

Racial and ethnic characteristics (1990)
 White: 202,085
 Black: 188,408
 American Indian, Eskimo, Aleut: 950
 Asian and Pacific Islander: 3,733
 Hispanic (may be of any race): 5,124

Percent of residents born in state: 74.3% (1990)

Age characteristics (1990)
 Population under 5 years old: 31,335
 Population 5 to 9 years old: 28,366
 Population 10 to 14 years old: 25,405
 Population 15 to 19 years old: 26,150
 Population 20 to 24 years old: 30,186
 Population 25 to 29 years old: 36,841
 Population 30 to 34 years old: 35,827
 Population 35 to 39 years old: 29,125
 Population 40 to 44 years old: 21,614
 Population 45 to 49 years old: 16,504
 Population 50 to 54 years old: 15,401
 Population 55 to 59 years old: 16,030
 Population 60 to 64 years old: 17,880
 Population 65 to 69 years old: 18,153
 Population 70 to 74 years old: 15,275
 Population 75 to 79 years old: 13,998
 Population 80 to 84 years old: 10,186
 Population 85 years and over: 8,389
 Median age: 32.7 years

Births (1988)
 Total number: 8,018

Deaths (1988)
 Total number: 5,895 (of which, 117 were infants under the age of 1 year)

Money income (1989)
 Per capita income: $10,798
 Median household income: $19,458
 Total households: 164,404
 Number of households with income of . . .
  less than $5,000: 20,613
  $5,000 to $9,999: 25,173
  $10,000 to $14,999: 20,238
  $15,000 to $24,999: 33,999
  $25,000 to $34,999: 24,366
  $35,000 to $49,999: 20,726
  $50,000 to $74,999: 13,780
  $75,000 to $99,999: 3,310
  $100,000 to $149,999: 1,419
  $150,000 or more: 780
 Percent of families below poverty level: 20.6% (71.2% of which were female householder families with related children under 5)
1991 FBI Crime Index Total: 64,103

Municipal Government

St. Louis functions via a mayor-council form of government; the mayor and twenty-nine aldermen are elected to four-year terms. Voters choose a mayor in the April of odd-numbered years; half the number of aldermen, each from a single ward, are selected every two years. Established as both a city and a county, the city of St. Louis operates under home rule, but St. Louis County, without home rule, conforms to Missouri's state requirements for county government.

Head Official: Mayor Raymond Bosley (D) (since 1993; current term expires April 1997)

Total Number of City Employees: 8,946 (1993)

City Information: City of St. Louis, Office of the Mayor, 200 City Hall, Tucker and Market Streets, St. Louis, MO 63103; telephone (314)622-3201

Economy

Major Industries and Commercial Activity

St. Louis is the headquarters of about ten Fortune 500 companies as well as a primary banking and financial center for the region. Second only to Detroit in automobile production, St. Louis supports a strong manufacturing sector; the three major American automakers—General Motors, Chrysler, and Ford—operate assembly plants in the area. St. Louis is also the base for the Eighth Federal Reserve District Bank and several national insurance and brokerage firms.

St. Louis is emerging as a center for advanced technology. More than ninety thousand scientists, engineers, and computer specialists employed by such companies as McDonnell Douglas, General Dynamics, and Monsanto are involved in research, development, and application of high technology in industry. Among the high-technology facilities in metropolitan St. Louis are the St. Louis Technology Center, the Missouri Research Park, and University Park at Southern Illinois University—Edwardsville. St. Louis is a leader in health care, at both the regional and national levels, numbering sixty-five metropolitan area hospitals and two highly regarded medical schools in the area.

As the nation sank into a recession in the late 1980s and early 1990s and the Pentagon began major spending cutbacks, the St. Louis area economy was jolted by massive layoffs. McDonnell Douglas, manufacturer of fighter jets, missiles, and commercial airliners, laid off nearly a quarter of its work force in 1990; it then cut its payroll from 113,000 workers industry-wide to 99,000 during the twelve-month period ending June 1992. The company then announced that it would streamline its six defense lines into two units. Hundreds of subcontractors in the area felt the effects. General Dynamics Corporation, the nation's second largest military contractor, announced in late 1991 that it would move its corporate headquarters to Falls Church, Virginia. The biggest gains in employment in recent years have been in health care, reflecting the city's growing role as a center of medical research. Manufacturing jobs have been declining steadily since 1973, while the number of service jobs increased 47 percent from 1973 to 1990.

Items and goods produced: meat, bread, beer, flour, granary products, malt, liquors, chemicals, drugs, paints and varnish, machinery, refrigerators, clothing, iron and steel, street and railroad cars, shoes, paper products, hardware, millinery, trucks, automotive parts, petroleum and coal, non-ferrous metals, stone, clay and glass, furniture, aircraft, aerospace equipment

Incentive Programs—New and Existing Companies

State programs—St. Louis has been rated among the top business climates in the country. Financing, taxation, and incentive programs available through the states of Missouri and Illinois include community development block grants, urban development action grants, municipal bonds for industrial development, and urban enterprise zones. Other features are property and sales tax exemptions, tax abatements, and tax increment financing. Customized employee-training programs and grants, including Job Training Partnership Act training funds, are offered to qualifying businesses. Missouri operates a higher-education research assistance program, and makes loans and other financing available through the Industrial Development Board, the Major Industry Fund, a neighborhood assistance program, and seed capital funds.

Local programs—Locally, the St. Louis Development Corporation (SLDC) offers financial assistance, site assembly assistance, and job training and placement; SLDC also operates the Business Assistance Center, which facilitates permit and license applications and provides business information.

With further major cuts in military spending expected in the coming years, many economists feel that helping small military contractors is the St. Louis region's most pressing priority. St. Louis officials are trying to attract new companies and industries to the area, using tactics ranging from advertising to personal calls from politicians.

Development Projects

Since 1970 St. Louis has undergone extensive rehabilitation and new development with the construction of office buildings, hotels, shops and stores, manufacturing sites, and transportation facilities. Among the projects is Metropolitan Square, which has added more than one million square feet of downtown office space, and the $34 million addition of office, retail, and entertainment space at historic Union Station.

The long neglected theater district, once called the Broadway of the Midwest, is undergoing a renovation that is expected to make it a model redevelopment project to rival Lincoln Center in New York. The $125 million project, known as Grand Center, is scheduled for completion at the turn of the century and will include construction of up to six new performance spaces for dance, theater, and music in new and existing buildings, as well as restaurants, art galleries, and the like. Grand Central hopes to lure the area's public broadcasting station to build its new facility there.

Economic Development Information: St. Louis Development Corp., 330 North Fifteenth St., St. Louis, MO 63103; telephone (314)622-3400

Commercial Shipping

St. Louis is a primary national center for air, land, and water transportation networks. Among the commodities shipped through the city are coal, grain, cement, petroleum products, and chemicals. The nation's third-largest rail freight hub, St. Louis is served by ten trunkline railroads and three switching lines; seventeen piggyback terminals have trailer on flat car facilities and three provide container on flat car services. Four interstate highways converge in St. Louis, affording more than one hundred trucking companies overnight to third-morning access to markets throughout the country. Ninety of these firms maintain terminals within the Commercial Truck Zone, which covers all or portions of a seven-county area. St. Louis is the nation's second-largest inland port, as well as the country's northernmost port with ice-free access year round; the port connects St. Louis via the Mississippi, Illinois, and Missouri river system with New Orleans and international waterways. Air freight service is available at Lambert-St. Louis International Airport. Two Foreign Trade Zones are located in the metropolitan region.

Labor Force and Employment Outlook

Skilled, affordable, productive workers are plentiful in such industries as aircraft, automobiles, fabricated metals, food, chemicals, nonelectrical machinery, and primary metals. Other sectors with high labor availability are clerical, machine trades, benchwork, and structural work. Local experts are cautiously optimistic about the St. Louis economy's ability to absorb the shock of the upheaval caused by the recession and military spending cuts. Many of the small military contractors are expected to wean themselves from the Pentagon by diversifying into other areas. The economy continues to create jobs, especially in the service sector.

Two labor-management committees—PRIDE in the Missouri metropolitan area counties and IMAGE in the Illinois counties—have achieved a significant reduction in work stoppages due to strikes. Labor-management disputes in St. Louis involving one thousand or more workers average 22 percent below the national rate. Applying the same cooperative approach in manufacturing, retailing, distribution, and other unionized businesses is the New Spirit of St. Louis Labor-Management Committee.

The following is a summary of data regarding the St. Louis metropolitan area labor force as of September 1992.

Size of non-agricultural labor force: 1,162,200

Number of workers employed in . . .
  mining: not reported
  construction: 50,800
  manufacturing: 202,500
  transportation and public utilities: 77,500
  wholesale and retail trade: 270,400
  finance, insurance, and real estate: 72,700
  services: 341,700
  government: 146,600

Average hourly earnings of production workers employed in manufacturing: $13.84

Unemployment rate: 5.8%

Largest employers	Number of employees
McDonnell Douglas	26,000
Southwestern Bell Corp.	10,000 (full time)
Washington University	8,013
Barnes Hospital	7,025
St. Louis University	6,685
Anheuser-Busch	5,500
Union Electric Co.	4,713

Cost of Living

The following is a summary of data regarding several key cost of living factors in the St. Louis area.

1992 (2nd Quarter) ACCRA Cost of Living Index: 96.5 (U.S. average = 100.0)

1992 (2nd Quarter) ACCRA Average House Price: $101,504

State income tax rate: graduated from 1.5% to 6.0%

State sales tax rate: 4.225%

Local income tax rate: 1.0%

Local sales tax rate: 1.5%

Property tax rate: $6.248 per $100 assessed valuation; assessed at 19% of true market value

Economic Information: St. Louis Regional Commerce and Growth Association, 100 South Fourth Street, Suite 500, St. Louis, MO 63102; telephone (314)231-5555

Education and Research

Elementary and Secondary Schools

The St. Louis Public Schools are administered by a twelve-member, nonpartisan, elected board of education that appoints a superintendent and serves a six-year term without compensation. Dozens of St. Louis public schools have been renovated in recent years at a cost of well over $100 million; two to five new school buildings are planned. The system operates magnet schools and schools for the gifted and talented.

The following is a summary of data regarding St. Louis public schools as of the 1992-1993 school year.

Total enrollment: 42,278

Number of facilities
  elementary schools: 70
  middle schools: 22
  senior high schools: 11
  other: 7

Student/teacher ratio: elementary, 22:1; middle school, 24:1; secondary, 26:1

Teacher salaries
  minimum: $22,165
  maximum: $42,575

Funding per pupil: $6,926.41 (1991-1992)

More than thirty private elementary and secondary schools offer educational alternatives in the St. Louis area; the city has a tradition of neighborhood parochial education.

Public Schools Information: Board of Education, St. Louis Public Schools, 911 Locust Street, St. Louis, MO 63101; telephone (314) 231-3720, ext. 220

Colleges and Universities

St. Louis is home to five major universities, three of them private and two public. Washington University, a private independent institution, grants degrees in 120 undergraduate and 166 graduate programs in such fields as business, architecture, engineering, social work, and teacher education; the university operates schools of medicine, dentistry, and law. Sixteen Nobel Laureates have been associated with Washington University. Saint Louis University, established in 1818 and affiliated with the Roman Catholic Church, also operates schools of medicine and law and offers graduate and undergraduate curricula in nearly 120 areas. Webster University, located in suburban Webster Groves, awards baccalaureate and master's degrees in nine disciplines. The University of Missouri at Saint Louis is both a graduate and undergraduate institution and part of the state university system; Southern Illinois University at Edwardsville, also a state university, is in neighboring Edwardsville, Illinois.

Fontbonne College, Harris-Stowe State College, Maryville University, Metropolitan College of St. Louis University, Missouri Baptist College, and St. Louis College of Pharmacy are four-year institutions locat-

The Gateway Arch to the West, an equilateral triangle measuring 630 feet tall and 630 feet wide at its base, is said to be the tallest person-made object in the country.

ed in the St. Louis area; the St. Louis Conservatory of Music offers both graduate and undergraduate programs. Theological schools in the city include Concordia Seminary and Eden Theological Seminary.

Libraries and Research Centers

Approximately ninety-five public and private libraries are maintained in St. Louis by various organizations and institutions. The Saint Louis Public Library operates a main facility with holdings of 1.7 million book volumes and bound periodicals, nearly seven thousand periodical titles, and records, tapes, slides, maps, and art reproductions; special collections include black history, genealogy, architecture, and federal and state documents. Fifteen branches and a bookmobile are also part of the library system. The Saint Louis County Library, with sixteen branches and nineteen bookmobiles, maintains a primary facility housing more than 2 million books and federal, state, and county documents. The Missouri Historical Society holds a reference collection on topics pertaining to regional and state history.

Most area colleges and universities maintain substantial campus libraries; among the most extensive is the Washington University Libraries system. Its central facility alone holds 2.7 million books and its ten department libraries house separate collections. The Washington University East Asian Library maintains more than 100,000 volumes in humanities-oriented collections on Chinese and Japanese subjects.

Government agencies operating libraries in St. Louis include the Federal Reserve Bank, the Metropolitan Police Department, and the United States Army, Court of Appeals, and Department of Defense. Anheuser-Busch Company, McDonnell Douglas, Monsanto Company, and Pet Incorporated are among major St. Louis-area corporations that maintain sizeable libraries. Other specialized libraries in the area are affiliated with churches and synagogues, hospitals, and such cultural organizations as the Missouri Botanical Garden, the National Museum of Transport, and the National Bowling Museum and Hall of Fame, which houses published materials relating to bowling.

Concordia Historical Institute is the largest American research center on Lutheranism in the country. Centers affiliated with St. Louis-area colleges and universities conduct research in such fields as computer-aided engineering, space sciences, medicine, urban studies, archaeology, and telecommunications. Research expenditures total nearly $80 million annually.

Public Library Information: Saint Louis Public Library, 1301 Olive Street, St. Louis, MO 63103-2389; telephone (314)241-2288

Health Care

As one of the country's leading medical care centers, St. Louis is served by twenty-six hospitals, two of which—the Washington University Medical Center and the St. Louis University Hospital—are top-rated teaching facilities. Providing a range of general and specialized services is the Barnes Hospital Group. In a survey of more than one thousand leading doctors conducted by *U.S. News & World Report* and reported in June 1992, Barnes Hospital was chosen best in the country for care in endocrinology. Specializing in the treatment of children are Cardinal Glennon Memorial Hospital for Children and Shriner's Hospital. The St. Louis College of Pharmacy and a number of schools of nursing, hospital administration, and allied health services train health care professionals. Nearly five thousand physicians practice in all specialties in St. Louis; over 9,600 beds are supplied by hospitals in the city.

Recreation

Sightseeing

The Gateway Arch, which rises 630 feet above the banks of the Mississippi River, is the starting point of a tour of St. Louis. Designed by Eero Saarinen and commemorating the nineteenth-century westward movement and St. Louis's role in settling the frontier, the Gateway Arch is the nation's tallest memorial. Beneath the Arch is the Old Courthouse, where the Dred Scott case was heard. A proud Greek revival structure, its dome was a forerunner of the style in public architecture that would sweep the country. The building holds displays relating to the Scott case and is home to the Museum of Westward Expansion, which documents the westward movement and life in St. Louis in the 1800s. The St. Louis Zoo is located in an 83-acre garden-like setting that houses nearly three thousand animals in naturalistic settings. The zoo's Big Cat Country with lions, tigers, and leopards, and the Jungle of the Apes with gorillas, chimpanzees, and orangutans, are two of the most popular animal habitats. The Living World is an educational center at the St. Louis Zoo.

A Digistar computerized planetarium projector, hands-on science exhibits, and outdoor science exhibits are featured at the St. Louis Science Center in Forest Park. The Missouri Botanical Garden is considered one of the most beautiful botanical gardens in the United States. Sightseers can view one of the nation's two contemporary sculpture parks at the Laumeier Sculpture Park. The St. Louis Carousel provides a rare opportunity to ride an authentic carousel at its Faust County Park location. Operated by Anheuser-Busch, Grant's Farm features a cabin built by General Grant in 1856; the farm's miniature zoo features a Clydesdale stallion barn and bird and elephant shows. Jefferson Barracks Historical Park combines military history and recreation with two museums and a number of sports fields; Robert E. Lee and Ulysses S. Grant are two of the many famous American military leaders whose service included a stay at Jefferson Barracks.

St. Louis museums include the National Museum of Transport, which specializes in pre-automobile modes of transportation; the Dog Museum, which relocated from New York in 1987 and presents exhibits on the dog through history; and the Soldiers' Memorial Military Museum.

The American Institute of Architects is located in St. Louis and provides complete information about this architecturally rich city. Among some of the significant structures are the Cathedral of St. Louis (New Cathedral), which houses one of the largest collections of mosaic art in the West; Christ Church Cathedral, the first Episcopal church west of the Mississippi; and Old Cathedral, the city's first church.

Arts and Culture

St. Louis is a major cultural center for the Midwest. The award-winning St. Louis Symphony Orchestra, ranked one of the two best in the country by *Time* magazine, presents a season of classical music concerts with internationally known guest artists at Powell Symphony Hall. In the summer the orchestra plays a series of pops concerts at Greensfelder Recreation Center. Theater is presented year round in St. Louis by a diverse range of organizations. The Repertory Theater of St. Louis performs a season of plays on two stages, including modern drama, musicals, and comedies. The Opera Theater of St. Louis performs its four productions of classical and new opera in English during a month-long season beginning in late May. The Fabulous Fox Theater was restored in 1982 and now sponsors a Broadway series, ballet, and pop music concerts. The Muny in Forest Park is a twelve-thousand-seat outdoor amphitheater that stages Broadway musical theater during the summer.

According to a local critic, the city's "most consistently exciting theater "is presented by the Black Repertory Company, which performs at the 450-seat Grandel Square Theater, a handsome 1883 structure that was once a church and has undergone extensive renovation. The Grandel also serves as a home theater for the Theater Project Company. Other theater companies and organizations in St. Louis include the Theater Factory, New York Theater, and Stages Production Company. The Goldenrod Showboat, a historic landmark, presents dinner theater and off-Broadway shows.

Dance St. Louis sponsors concerts with local, national, and international companies, and offers a dance education program. The First Street Forum is a multipurpose arts center that sponsors exhibitions, performances, lectures, and symposia.

The St. Louis Art Museum in Forest Park was the Fine Arts Palace of the 1904 World's Fair and is today ranked among the top ten art museums in the United States. Washington University's Gallery of Art was the first museum west of the Mississippi River. At the Jefferson Memorial Building the Missouri Historical Society recaptures the major events and individuals in St. Louis history from the first settlers to Charles Lindbergh. The Concordia Historical Institute maintains an authentic collection of American Lutheran historical documents as well as Protestant Reformation artifacts. Among St. Louis's other museums are the Mercantile Money Museum, which answers questions about the nature of money; the Golden Eagle River Museum, which is dedicated to preserving the lore of America's rivers and boats; the McDonnell Douglas Prologue Room, which is an aerospace museum documenting that industry's history from 1920; and the Eugene Field House and Toy Museum, which presents an extensive collection of antique toys and dolls.

St. Louis Union Station, once the largest passenger rail terminal in the world, is now a marketplace.

Festivals and Holidays

Major venues for celebrations in St. Louis are the Missouri Botanical Gardens and Jefferson Barracks Historical Park. At the Botanical Gardens, an orchid show in January features over eight hundred plants. The Spring Floral Display begins in March. An International Festival of Festivals celebrates different cultures on weekends throughout August. November brings a Fall Floral Display, giving way to a Poinsettia Display in December.

Jefferson Barracks Historical Park presents a World War II Reenactment in April and American Indian Days in May. May is also the month for arts and crafts displays at Laumeier Sculpture Park and Tilles County Park. Parades and other events at various locales mark St. Patrick's Day, Independence Day, Veterans' Day, and Christmas.

Sports for the Spectator

The St. Louis Cardinals compete in the Western Division of the Major League Baseball Association's National League and play their home games in Busch Stadium. The St. Louis Cardinals Hall of Fame, inside the stadium, houses displays and movies on baseball, football, basketball, hockey, golf, bowling, and soccer. The National Bowling Hall of Fame is located nearby. The St. Louis Blues compete in the National Hockey League and play home games in the Arena, also home to the Major Soccer League's St. Louis Storm. World-championship Grand Prix power boat racing occurs each year.

American and Canadian drivers compete in the Creve Couer Classic Drag Boat Races in June. Balloonists compete in the Great Forest Park Balloon Race scheduled in September. For two weeks in September horse owners and trainers from around the country participate in the St. Louis National Charity Horse Show at Queeny County Park.

Sports for the Participant

A city of parks and sports enthusiasts, St. Louis offers attractive outdoor facilities and a selection of major and minor sports for the individual, including golf, tennis, bicycling, and softball, and water sports such as swimming, water skiing, and boating. Two of the most successful amateur sports programs are in boxing and soccer. Forest Park offers recreational opportunities, including skating and tennis, on over 1,300 acres. Budweiser sponsors a St. Patrick's Day Parade costumed run in St. Louis.

Shopping and Dining

The St. Louis Centre in the city's downtown encompasses 1.7 million square feet of shopping and dining space on four levels, making it the largest enclosed downtown mall in the nation. The Centre is topped by a vaulted skylight that permits indoor shoppers to enjoy a view of the city's architecture. The St. Louis Union Station has been transformed into a festival marketplace, with a Grand Hall, a man-made lake, and more than 17 acres of specialty shops and restaurants in a giant train shed. Frontenac Plaza is anchored by Neiman-Marcus and Saks Fifth Avenue.

The St. Louis Galleria in Richmond Heights consists of three levels, 180 stores, eighteen restaurants, an Italian marble interior, and a one-hundred-foot-high atrium. West Port Plaza is modelled after a European village and Laclede's Landing, an antiques and art center, is a renovated historic warehouse district on the riverfront north of the Gateway Arch. Soulard Farmer's Market, established in 1779, is a favorite Saturday morning destination for locals.

Diners in St. Louis can choose from among hundreds of fine restaurants, including Cafe de France, Domenic's, Faust's, Fio's la Fourchette, Giovanni's, Station Grill, and Tony's, which *Food and Wine* magazine named Distinguished Restaurants of North America for 1992-1993. The city boasts an Italian district, known as "the Hill," that offers a number of fine moderately priced Italian eateries. Chinese, German, and other ethnic restaurants are located throughout the city. Regional specialties available in St. Louis include barbecued lamb, ribs, pork, ham, and sausage; pecan pie; and sweet potato pie.

Visitor Information: St. Louis Convention and Visitors Commission, 10 South Broadway, Suite 1000, St. Louis, MO 63102; telephone (314)421-1023 or (800)325-7962; and, St. Louis Visitor Center, 308 Washington, St. Louis, MO; telephone (314)241-1764; and, Downtown St. Louis, Inc., telephone (314)436-6500

Convention Facilities

The major convention facility in St. Louis is the Cervantes Convention Center. Opened in 1977, the center is undergoing the second phase of an expansion that is scheduled for completion in the fall of

1995. The first phase, opened in 1993, added two exhibit halls, an executive conference center, a twenty-eight-thousand-square-foot ballroom, and a fifteen-hundred fixed-seat lecture hall, and expanded exhibit space to 340,000 square foot. The second phase will add 175,000 square feet of exhibit space and seating for 70,000 people.

Kiel Auditorium and the Arena are also available for meeting purposes. Ample hotel space is available in the metropolitan area; several luxury hotels have been built in recent years.

Convention Information: St. Louis Convention and Visitors Commission, 10 South Broadway, Suite 1000, St. Louis, MO 63102; telephone (314)421-1023 or (800)325-7962

Transportation

Approaching the City

One of the busiest airports in the country, Lambert-St. Louis International Airport, which has been vastly expanded, is the domestic hub for Trans World Airlines and Ozark. Lambert is served by fifteen additional commercial airlines. Three general aviation facilities are located in the metropolitan region. Rail transportation to St. Louis is provided by Amtrak.

St. Louis, with a geographically central location, is easily accessible from points throughout the United States via four interstate highways that converge in the city: I-44, I-55, I-64, and I-70.

Traveling in the City

St. Louis's public bus system is operated by Bi-State Transit system, which offers service free in some downtown areas. Market Street downtown is the dividing point for north and south addresses.

Communications

Newspapers and Magazines

The city's major daily newspaper is the *St. Louis Post Dispatch.* The *St. Louis Business Journal* is a business weekly. Thirty-five other newspapers circulate daily and weekly in the area. The Associated Press and United Press International operate offices in St. Louis.

St. Louis Magazine focuses on topics of interest to metropolitan readers. More than sixty specialized magazines and journals are based in St. Louis; the majority are journals published for medical professionals by the C. V. Mosby Company and other firms. In addition to health care, subjects include religion, agriculture, engineering, environmental issues, business, insurance, and building trades.

Television and Radio

Television viewers in metropolitan St. Louis tune in broadcasts from six stations: three commercial network affiliates, one Public Broadcasting System outlet, and two independent stations. A complete range of radio programming—including classical, jazz, classic rock, "oldies," Christian, and gospel music, as well as news and public interest features—is offered by twenty-eight AM and FM radio stations. The St. Louis Symphony Orchestra is featured weekly on National Public Radio.

Media Information: St. Louis Post-Dispatch, 900 North Tucker Boulevard, St. Louis, MO 63101-9990; telephone (314)622-7000; and, *St. Louis Magazine,* American City Business Journals, 612 North Second Street, P.O. Box 88908, St. Louis, MO 63118-1908; telephone (314)991-1699

Selected Bibliography

Twain, Mark, *The Adventures of Huckleberry Finn* (New York: Puffin, 1988, 1953)

Twain, Mark, *The Adventures of Tom Sawyer* (Hartford, Conn.: The American Publishing Co., 1876)

Springfield

The City in Brief

Founded: 1830 (incorporated, 1838)

Head Official: City Manager Thomas Finnie (since 1990)

City Population
 1970: 120,096
 1980: 133,116
 1990: 140,494
 Percent change, 1980–1990: 5.5%
 U.S. rank in 1980: 118th
 U.S. rank in 1990: 126th

Metropolitan Area Population
 1970: 168,053
 1980: 207,704
 1990: 240,593
 Percent change, 1980–1990: 15.8%
 U.S. rank in 1980: Not available
 U.S. rank in 1990: Not available

Area: 68.0 square miles (1990)

Elevation: 1,268 feet above sea level

Average Annual Temperature: 55.9° F

Average Annual Precipitation: 41 inches (15 inches of snow)

Major Economic Sectors: Services, wholesale and retail trade, manufacturing, government

Unemployment Rate: 5.4% (September 1992)

Per Capita Income: $11,878 (1989)

1992 (2nd Quarter) ACCRA Average House Price: $88,000

1992 (2nd Quarter) ACCRA Cost of Living Index: 90.2 (U.S. average = 100.0)

1991 FBI Crime Index Total: 11,905

Major Colleges and Universities: Southwest Missouri State University

Daily Newspaper: *The News-Leader*

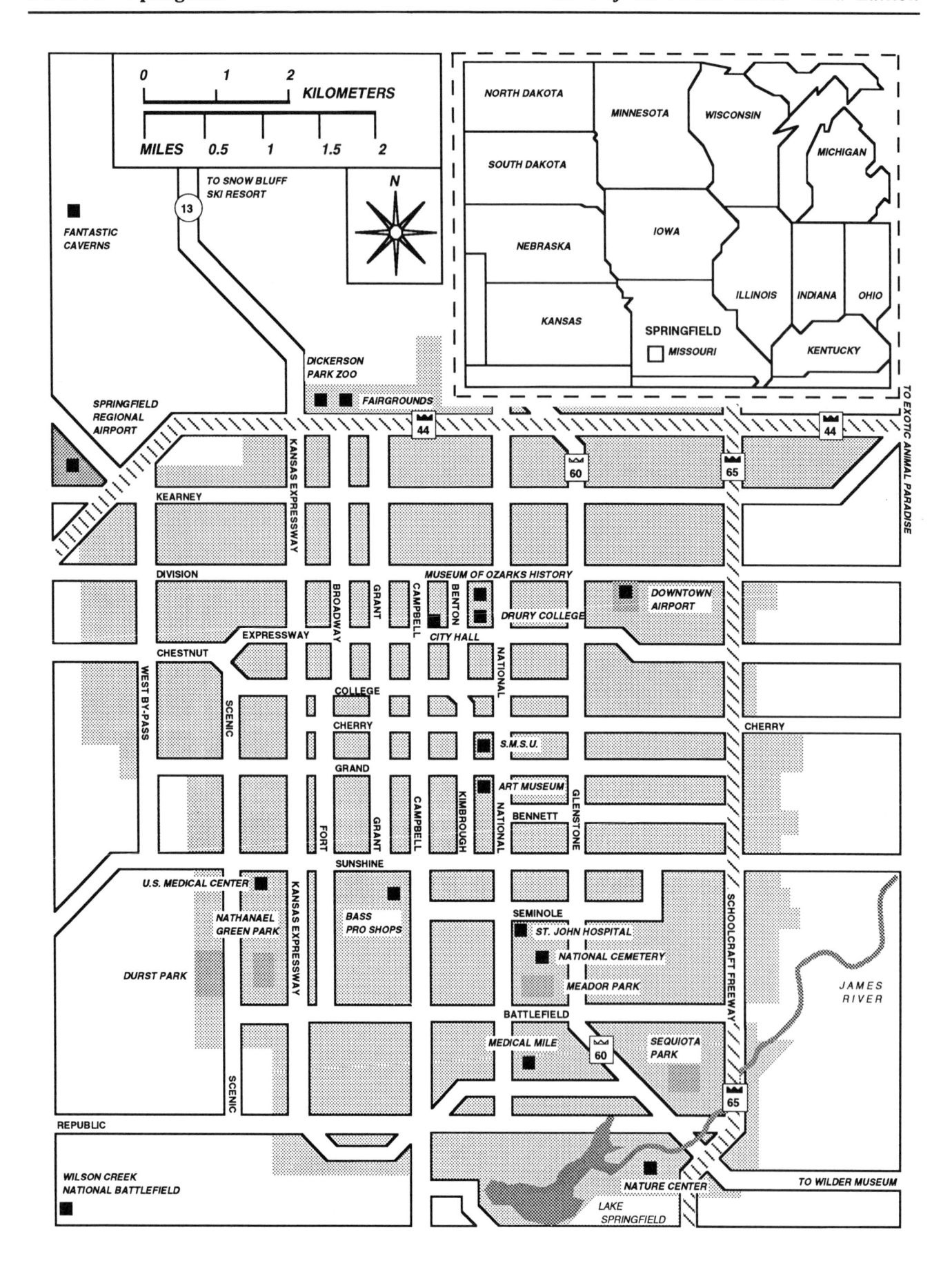

Missouri—Springfield

Introduction

Springfield is the seat of Missouri's Greene County and the center of a metropolitan statistical area that includes Christian and Greene counties. Termed the Gateway to the Ozark Mountains, Springfield is part of a resort area whose primary attractions are the largest cave in North America, an outdoor exotic animal park, and Bass Pro Shop, said to be the most-visited tourist attraction in the state. The Battle of Wilson's Creek was fought in the first year of the American Civil War near Springfield and is now a national battlefield site. Today the city is a regional agribusiness center and a dairy-product shipping center. Springfield was one of ten cities vying with the top fifteen for job growth and livability on *Kiplinger's Personal Finance Magazine*'s 1991 list.

Geography and Climate

Surrounded by flat or gently rolling tableland, Springfield is set atop the crest of the Missouri Ozark Mountain plateau. The climate is characterized as a plateau climate, with a milder winter and a cooler summer than in the upland plain or prairie. Springfield occupies a unique location for natural water drainage: the line separating two major water sheds crosses the north-central part of the city, causing drainage north of this line to flow into the Gasconade and Missouri Rivers; drainage to the south flows into the White and Mississippi Rivers. The average annual temperature range is over 140 degrees with lowest temperatures below minus twenty-five degrees and highest temperatures above 115 degrees.

Area: 68.0 square miles (1990)

Elevation: 1,268 feet above sea level

Average Temperatures: January, 31.5° F; July, 78.0° F; annual average, 55.9° F

Average Annual Precipitation: 41 inches (15 inches of snow)

History

Removal of Delaware Tribe Opens Farmland

Pioneer Thomas Patterson attempted, in 1821, to make the first permanent settlement on the site of present-day Springfield; however, the Delaware people arrived the following year to claim the land as a federal Indian reservation. James Wilson was the lone settler to remain, and after the further relocation of the Delaware in 1830 he farmed land in the area. New settlers followed immediately. Among them was John Polk Campbell, who staked a claim in 1830 on a site that was then called Kickapoo Prairie; he carved his initials in an ash tree where four springs unite to form Wilson's Creek. This location was well situated and a settlement soon grew up around the Campbell homestead.

Campbell was made county clerk when Missouri's Greene County was organized in 1833, and two years later he and his wife deeded land for a townsite. The origin of Springfield's name is not clear, although one version maintains that Campbell picked it because the geography of the area. Springfield was incorporated in 1838 and chartered in 1847.

Springfield's location and commercial base made it a military target during the Civil War. Sentiments regarding the war were split in the town, with the professional classes descended from Tennessee slave-holders supporting the Southern cause and rural settlers favoring the North. The Battle of Wilson's Creek was fought on August 10, 1861, resulting in a victory for the Confederate army; Union forces won the next battle in February, 1862, however, and held the area until the end of the war. Among the soldiers based at the Union Army's Springfield headquarters was James Butler Hickok, nicknamed Wild Bill, who served as a scout and spy. During a gun fight in July, 1865 with his former friend, gambler Charles Tutt, Hickok shot Tutt through the heart. Hickok was acquitted in a trial in which he was defended by John S. Phelps, a future Missouri governor.

Railroad Brings Expansion, New Business

In 1870 land speculators persuaded the Atlantic & Pacific Railroad to build a railroad through a new town north of Springfield despite the protests of Springfield citizens who claimed that the new route violated the original charter. Nonetheless, the Ozark Land Company was organized and the new town was deeded to the company. As both communities grew, they were consolidated in 1887.

During the first half of the twentieth century Springfield became an agricultural and distribution center; after World War II, population grew rapidly as the result of the expansion of Eastern manufacturing companies into the West. The city's proximity to the Ozark Mountains makes it a popular tourist destination.

Population Profile

Metropolitan Area Residents
1970: 168,053
1980: 207,704
1990: 240,593
Percent change, 1980–1990: 15.8%
U.S. rank in 1980: Not available
U.S. rank in 1990: Not available

City Residents
1970: 120,096
1980: 133,116
1990: 140,494 (of which, 66,406 were males and 74,088 were females)
Percent change, 1980–1990: 5.5%
U.S. rank in 1980: 118th
U.S. rank in 1990: 126th (State rank: 3rd)

Density: 2,069.1 people per square mile (1990)

Racial and ethnic characteristics (1990)
  White: 134,384
  Black: 3,527
  American Indian, Eskimo, Aleut: 939
  Asian and Pacific Islander: 1,264
  Hispanic (may be of any race): 1,339

Percent of residents born in state: 65.3% (1990)

Age characteristics (1990)
  Population under 5 years old: 8,698
  Population 5 to 9 years old: 8,220
  Population 10 to 14 years old: 7,572
  Population 15 to 19 years old: 12,138
  Population 20 to 24 years old: 17,429
  Population 25 to 29 years old: 12,219
  Population 30 to 34 years old: 10,922
  Population 35 to 39 years old: 9,732
  Population 40 to 44 years old: 8,413
  Population 45 to 49 years old: 6,760
  Population 50 to 54 years old: 5,600
  Population 55 to 59 years old: 5,528
  Population 60 to 64 years old: 5,934
  Population 65 to 69 years old: 6,156
  Population 70 to 74 years old: 5,102
  Population 75 to 79 years old: 4,283
  Population 80 to 84 years old: 3,092
  Population 85 years and over: 2,696
Median age: 33.7 years

Births (1988)
  Total number: 1,890

Deaths (1988)
  Total number: 1,452 (of which, 23 were infants under the age of 1 year)

Money income (1989)
  Per capita income: $11,878
  Median household income: $21,577
  Total households: 57,365
  Number of households with income of . . .
    less than $5,000: 4,786
    $5,000 to $9,999: 7,518
    $10,000 to $14,999: 7,422
    $15,000 to $24,999: 13,097
    $25,000 to $34,999: 9,789
    $35,000 to $49,999: 7,859
    $50,000 to $74,999: 4,540
    $75,000 to $99,999: 1,036
    $100,000 to $149,999: 711
    $150,000 or more: 607
  Percent of families below poverty level: 11.6% (71.2% of which were female householder families with related children under 5)
1991 FBI Crime Index Total: 11,905

Municipal Government

The city of Springfield, which is also the seat of Greene County, is administered by a council-manager form of government. Nine council members, one of whom serves a two-year term as mayor, are elected to four-year terms.

Head Official: City Manager Thomas Finnie (since 1990)

Total Number of City Employees: 1,300 (1993)

City Information: City Hall, telephone (417)864-1000

Economy

Major Industries and Commercial Activity

Principal industries in Springfield include agriculture and dairy farming, manufacturing, and shipping and distribution; services is the largest economic sector, with retailing ranking third after manufacturing. The Springfield area is rich in natural resources such as stone, lime, zinc, barium, coal, marble, sand, gravel, and lead. Abundant hardwood forests yield white oak, post oak, black oak, scarlet oak, hickory, maple, and black walnut. Indigenous wildlife include deer, furbearing animals, quail, rabbits, squirrels, doves, and waterfowl.

As an agribusiness center, the city is home to Springfield Regional Stockyards, the nation's sixth largest stockyards and feeder cattle facility, which posts sales of more than $100 million each year. Other agriculture-related firms are creameries, meatpacking plants, and flour mills. Springfield is also a shipping center for poultry, eggs, and milk. Diversified manufacturing, the second-largest economic sector, comprises nearly one-fourth of the metropolitan area employment base; major manufacturers include Advanced Circuitry Division-Litton, General Electric, Kraft, Paul Mueller, and Zenith.

Springfield is a regional hub for retailing, financial services, and health care as well as a popular tourist destination. The third largest retail market in Missouri—sales total more than $1.6 billion annually—Springfield ranks in the top 170 markets in the nation. The city's twelve banks and seven savings and loan associations, with combined assets of over $2.6 million, serve the population of Southwest Missouri. Two medical centers, which are among Springfield's top employers, form the basis of the major health care system in the area. As the gateway to the Ozark Mountain Country, the city receives millions of visitors each year.

Items and goods produced: flour, dairy products, clothing, paper cups and containers, furniture, plastics, trucks and trailers, iron and steel, concrete products, feed, fertilizers, typewriters

Incentive Programs—New and Existing Companies

According to the Springfield Chamber of Commerce, the business incentive in place in late 1992 was the Urban Enterprise Zone. In the launching process at that time were a business incubator and an industrial park with a shell building.

Economic Development Information: Springfield Business and Development Corporation, 320 North Jefferson, P.O. Box 1687, Springfield, MO 65801; telephone (417)862-5567

Commercial Shipping

Springfield is linked with national and international markets by a network of air, rail, and motor freight carriers. Exporting has become an integral part of the local economy; because Springfield is the site of a Port of Entry operated by the United States Customs Service, national companies can provide customs house and freight forwarding services. Air cargo services are available at Springfield Regional Airport. Rail transportation is provided by Burlington Northern and Missouri Pacific railroads; Burlington Northern maintains an intermodal hub for piggyback trailer shipping in the city. Forty-two trucking companies, twenty-two with terminals in Springfield, offer express delivery.

Labor Force and Employment Outlook

Springfield's population is growing—the city was second on Ryder Truck's 1992 list of places where more people were moving in than out. The labor force is described as possessing a Midwestern work ethic, and there is ample access to training and retraining facilities.

The following is a summary of data regarding the Springfield metropolitan area labor force as of September 1992.

Size of non-agricultural labor force: 123,400

Number of workers employed in . . .
  mining: not available
  construction: 5,200
  manufacturing: 19,300
  transportation and public utilities: 7,600
  wholesale and retail trade: 34,600
  finance, insurance, and real estate: 5,400
  services: 35,700
  government: 15,600

Average hourly earnings of production workers employed in manufacturing: $10.24

Unemployment rate: 5.4%

Largest employers	*Number of employees*
Lester E. Cox Medical Centers	More than 3,000
St. John's Regional Health Center	More than 3,000
Bass Pro Shops	From 2,000 to 3,000
Springfield Public Schools	From 2,000 to 3,000

Cost of Living

Salaries are low in Springfield, but so are living costs, according to *Kiplinger's Personal Finance Magazine*.

The following is a summary of data regarding several key cost of living factors in the Springfield area.

1992 (2nd Quarter) ACCRA Cost of Living Index: 90.2 (U.S. average = 100.00)

1992 (2nd Quarter) ACCRA Average House Price: $88,000

State income tax rate: graduated from 1.5% to 6%

State sales tax rate: 4.225%

Local sales tax rate: None

Property tax rate: $4.09 per $100 of assessed valuation at 19% of true value (1990)

Economic Information: Springfield Area Chamber of Commerce, P.O. Box 1687, Springfield, MO 65801-1687; telephone (417)862-5567

Education and Research

Elementary and Secondary Schools

Public elementary and secondary schools in Springfield are part of the School District of Springfield R-12, the third-largest system in Missouri. A six-member, nonpartisan school board selects a superintendent. More than 70 percent of teachers hold a master's degree or higher. Special schools are offered for the gifted and for early childhood education.

The following is a summary of data regarding the Springfield public schools as of the 1991–1992 school year.

Total enrollment: 23,800

Number of facilities
  elementary schools: 40
  junior high schools: 8
  senior high schools: 5
  other: 3

Student/teacher ratio: elementary, 24.9:1; junior high, 23.8:1; senior high, 23.9:1 (1988–1989)

Teacher salaries
  minimum: $19,380
  maximum: $38,189

Funding per pupil: $4,163

Seven private schools, including six church-related institutions, supplement the public school system.

Public Schools Information: School District of Springfield R-12, 940 North Jefferson, Springfield, MO 65802; telephone (417) 864-3980

Colleges and Universities

Southwest Missouri State University is Springfield's largest institution of higher learning. A public-supported university, it enrolls more than twenty-thousand students and awards associate, baccalaureate, and master's degrees in a range of programs, including chemistry, music, nursing, social work, and teacher education. Private, church-related colleges are: Assemblies of God Graduate School of Theology, Baptist Bible College, Central Bible College, Drury College, and Evangel College; all offer a predominantly liberal arts curriculum at the undergraduate level, while Assemblies of God and Drury College grant graduate degrees. Phillips Junior College, Heart of the Ozarks Technical College, and several specialty schools provide vocational and technical education.

Libraries and Research Centers

The Springfield-Greene County Library system operates a main facility and five branches; holdings total about 430,000 volumes in addition to periodicals and special collections in such areas as genealogy and Missouri history, and Ozarks folklore. Southwest Missouri State University maintains the Duane G. Meyer Library, which houses a collection of about 514,000 volumes and more than forty-five hundred periodicals, as well as the Greenwood Laboratory School Library, a music department library, and a campus library in West Plains. Assemblies of God Graduate School, Baptist Bible College, Central Bible College, Drury College, and Evangel College house holdings ranging from approximately fifty-five thousand to over 165,000 volumes. Specialized libraries located in the city are operated by the Missouri State Court of Appeals and the Springfield Art Museum among other organizations.

Public Library Information: Springfield-Greene County Library, 397 East Central, Springfield, MO 65801; telephone (417)869-4621

Health Care

Springfield's health care community serves the area with 550 medical doctors practicing in all fields of specialization. Providing a combined total of over 2,100 beds, the city's six hospitals are: Lester E. Cox Medical Center North, Lester E. Cox Medical Center South, Springfield Community Hospital, Springfield General Hospital, Lakeland Regional Hospital, and St. John's Regional Health Care Center. St. John's, the state's second largest private health care facility, maintains centers specializing in the heart, cancer, sports medicine and rehabilitation, fitness, emergency trauma, and burn care. The many health care facilities located on South National Avenue have given rise to the nickname Medical Mile, where more than $200 million has been invested.

Health Care Information: Greene County Medical Society, telephone (417)887-1017

Recreation

Sightseeing

One of Springfield's major sightseeing attractions is Wilson's Creek National Civil War Battlefield, the site of the first battle between Union and Confederate armies in Missouri and west of the Mississippi. An automobile tour of nearly 5 miles encompasses all the major points with historic markers and exhibits. Springfield National Cemetery is the only cemetery where soldiers from both the North and South are buried side by side.

Fantastic Caverns, a natural wonder, is the only cave in North America and one of three in the world that is so large visitors must tour it in motorized vehicles. Exotic Animal Paradise, 12 miles east of Springfield in Buena Vista, is a 400-acre park that is home to more than three-thousand wild and exotic animals and birds. Springfield's Dickerson Park Zoo, nationally known for its elephant herd, offers elephant rides to children.

Arts and Culture

The Springfield Symphony Orchestra and the Little Theater are the city's two oldest cultural organizations, with beginnings in 1934. Among the city's other performance arts institutions are the Springfield Regional Opera (performing at the 1909 Landers Theater, a historic landmark), the Springfield Ballet, and Chameleon Puppet Theater. Performing Arts presents a variety of cultural performances, and Southwest Missouri State University offers a summer series at its Tent Theater. Within the area, twenty-two country music theaters, such as the Roy Clark Celebrity Theater and the Ray Price Show, entertain country-music lovers. The Shepherd of the Hills is an outdoor theater that attracts a large audience each season with its stories on Ozark mountain families. Twenty local museums and other historic points of interest increase cultural awareness in the Springfield area. The Museum of Ozarks' History is in the Bentley House, a Queen Anne-style mansion built by Springfield banker J. F. G. Bentley. Nearby Mansfield is home to the Laura Ingalls Wilder Museum.

Festivals and Holidays

Bass Pro Shops, "the world's greatest sporting goods store," presents a World's Fishing Fair in Springfield in March. Historic Walnut Street is the site of a May Artsfest. A balloon race and Firefall—a fireworks display accompanied by the Springfield Symphony—are popular Fourth of July events. The Ozark Empire Fair in August also attracts large crowds. The Springfield Art Museum hosts a national "Watercolor USA" show each summer. In nearby Silver Dollar City the Mountain Folks Music Festival is held the third week of June. Ozark Empire Fair, Missouri's second largest and one of the top rated fairs in the country, is held in late July. Wilson's Creek National Battlefield sponsors special programs each year on Memorial Day, Independence Day, August 10, and Labor Day. The Ozark Auto Show, a collector car auction, draws vintage automobile buffs to nearby Branson on the last weekend of October.

Arts and Culture Information: Springfield Area Arts Council, Vandivort Center, 305 East Walnut, #312, Springfield, MO 65806; telephone (417)869-8380

Sports for the Spectator

Six local colleges and universities field a variety of teams in intercollegiate sports competition. The Drury Panthers and the Southwest Missouri State University Bears basketball teams frequently compete in national tournament play, as do the Lady Bears, who competed in the Final 4 in the 1992 Basketball NCAA finals.

Sports for the Participant

Forty-five city parks are located throughout Springfield. Nearby is the Mark Twain National Forest and Mincy Wildlife area. A number of lakes within close proximity to Springfield provide opportunities for fishing, swimming, boating, and water skiing. For the golfer Springfield offers three municipal courses. The city maintains fifty-six tennis courts and six city pools. A variety of sports programs are sponsored by the city. Skiing in the Ozark Mountains is possible year-round.

Recreation Information: Parks Department, telephone (417)864-1049

Shopping and Dining

One of the state's largest shopping malls, with 150 shops and five anchor department stores, is located in Springfield. A popular shopping district is a nineteenth-century village consisting of renovated buildings with shops offering quilts, crafts, and folk art. An antique mall and flea market houses more than seventy dealers in a three-story building, the largest such enterprise in the Ozarks. This antique mart sells everything from comic books and baseball cards to antique coins, dolls, toys, jewelry, furniture, and furnishings. A large reproduction shop is also on the premises. Nearby Silver Dollar City features products made by resident craftsmen using nineteenth-century skills. Bass Pro Shops, billing itself as the world's largest sporting goods store, is located in Springfield and specializes in equipment for anglers, hunters, and others. This unusual shop sports a two-story log cabin with water wheel, a four-story waterfall, fresh water and salt water aquariums, and daily fish feedings by divers.

The more than three-hundred restaurants in Springfield specialize in a variety of cuisines that include authentic ethnic foods and Southern cooking. One of the more popular dining establishments serves fish one night and prime rib the next, in addition to an eclectic menu that offers Ozark dishes. Another restaurant is known for its mesquite-grilled steaks and seafood.

Visitor Information: Springfield Convention and Visitors Bureau, P.O. Box 1687, Springfield, MO 65801-1687; telephone (417)881-5300 or (800)678-8767

Convention Facilities

Two principal meeting sites in Springfield cater to a full range of meeting needs, from small parties to merchandise shows. The Shrine Mosque features a 19,600-square-foot auditorium with variable capacity that includes up to sixty exhibit booths and seating for 3,355 people in a theater setting and 900 people for banquets. A lower-level, 15,000-square-foot exhibit area can contain as many as 96 additional booths and accommodate up to 2,500 people for a reception.

Centrally located near the Southwest Missouri State University (SMSU) campus is the University Plaza Trade Center, a two-level complex that provides a combined total of more than sixty-six thousand square feet of multipurpose space. The facility's meetings rooms host functions for 30 to 180 participants; banquet capacity for the first level is 1,824 people and 1,248 people for the second. A parking garage for 550 vehicles is attached.

Hammons Student Center and McDonald Arena on the SMSU campus, designed principally for university use, are frequently available for special events. The

Ozark Empire Fairgrounds can be rented April 1 through November 15 for meetings and conventions. Several Springfield area hotels and motels offer meeting accommodations; more than four-thousand lodging rooms are available in metropolitan Springfield.

Convention Information: Springfield Convention and Visitors Bureau, 3315 E. Battlefield Road, Springfield, MO 65801-1109; telephone (417)881-5300 (800)678-8767

Transportation

Approaching the City

Six commercial airlines schedule regular daily flights into Springfield Regional Airport. Principal highway routes into Springfield are I-44, U.S. 60, 65, 66, 160, and 266, and Missouri 13.

Traveling in the City

Springfield City Utilities operates the public bus transportation system.

Communications

Newspapers and Magazines

Springfield's daily newspaper is *The News-Leader,* which appears in daily and Sunday editions. The *Springfield Business Journal* is a weekly publication. The monthly *Springfield! Magazine* features articles on topics of local and community interest.

The General Council of the Assemblies of God Gospel Publishing House, which produces a variety of religious magazines and journals for Assemblies of God church leaders and members, is based in Springfield.

Television and Radio

Five television stations, including three network affiliates, one independent, and one public network outlet, plus cable, are received in Springfield. Fifteen AM and FM radio stations schedule music, religious, and news and information programming.

Media Information: The News-Leader, P.O. Box 798, Springfield, MO 65801; telephone (417)836-1100; and, *Springfield! Magazine,* P.O. Box 4749, Springfield, MO 65808; telephone (417)831-1600

NEBRASKA

Lincoln ....327 Omaha 341

The State in Brief

Nickname: Cornhusker State
Motto: Equality before the law

Flower: Goldenrod
Bird: Western meadowlark

Area: 77,358 square miles (1990; U.S. rank: 15th)
Elevation: Ranges from 840 feet to 5,426 feet above sea level
Climate: Continental, with wide variations of temperature: intensely hot summers and severely cold winters. Rainfall twice as heavy in east as in west

Admitted to Union: March 1, 1867
Capital: Lincoln
Head Official: Governor Ben Nelson (D) (until 1995)

Population
  1970: 1,485,333
  1980: 1,570,000
  1990: 1,593,000
  Percent change 1980–1990: 0.9%
  U.S. rank in 1990: 36th
  Percent of residents born in state: 71.4% (1990)
  Density: 20.5 people per square mile (1990) (U.S. rank: 42nd)
  1991 FBI Crime Index Total: 69,361

Racial and Ethnic Characteristics (1990)
  White: 1,578,000
  Black: 3.6%
  American Indian, Eskimo, Aleut: 0.79%
  Asian and Pacific Islander: 0.79%
  Hispanic origin (may be of any race): 2.34%

Age Characteristics (1990)
  Population under 5 years old: 120,000
  Population 5 to 17 years old: 315,000
  Percent of population 65 years and older: 14.1%
  Median age: 32.4 years
  Voting-age population (1988): 1,183,000 (55.9% of whom cast votes for president)

Vital Statistics
  Total number of births (1992): 23,003
  Total number of deaths (1992): 14,852 (of which, 154 were infants under the age of 1 year)
  AIDS cases reported, 1981–1990: 160 (U.S. rank: 43rd)

Economy
  Major industries: Finance, insurance, and real estate; trade; manufacturing; services
  Unemployment rate: 2.9% (September 1992)
  Per capita income: $12,452 (1989)
  Median household income: $26,016 (1989)
  Total number of families: 418,471 (8.0% of which had incomes below the poverty level) (1989)
  Income tax rate: graduated from 2.37% to 7.35% (1990–1991; rate set yearly by state legislature
  Sales tax rate: 5.0%

Lincoln

The City in Brief

Founded: 1861 (incorporated, 1869)

Head Official: Mayor Mike Johanns (R) (since 1991)

City Population
 1970: 150,000
 1980: 171,932
 1990: 191,972
 Percent change, 1980-1990: 11.7%
 U.S. rank in 1980: 81st
 U.S. rank in 1990: 81st

Metropolitan Area Population
 1970: 167,972
 1980: 192,864
 1990: 213,641
 Percent change, 1980-1990: 10.8%
 U.S. rank in 1980: Not available
 U.S. rank in 1990: Not available

Area: 63.3 square miles (1990)
Elevation: 1,167 feet above sea level
Average Annual Temperature: 50.4° F
Average Annual Precipitation: 26.92 inches

Major Economic Sectors: Government, services, wholesale and retail trade, manufacturing
Unemployment Rate: 2.4% (September 1992)
Per Capita Income: $13,720 (1989)
1992 (2nd Quarter) ACCRA Average House Price: $93,000
1992 (2nd Quarter) ACCRA Cost of Living Index: 90.5 (U.S. average = 100.0)
1991 FBI Crime Index Total: 14,954

Major Colleges and Universities: University of Nebraska—Lincoln

Daily Newspapers: *Star; Journal*

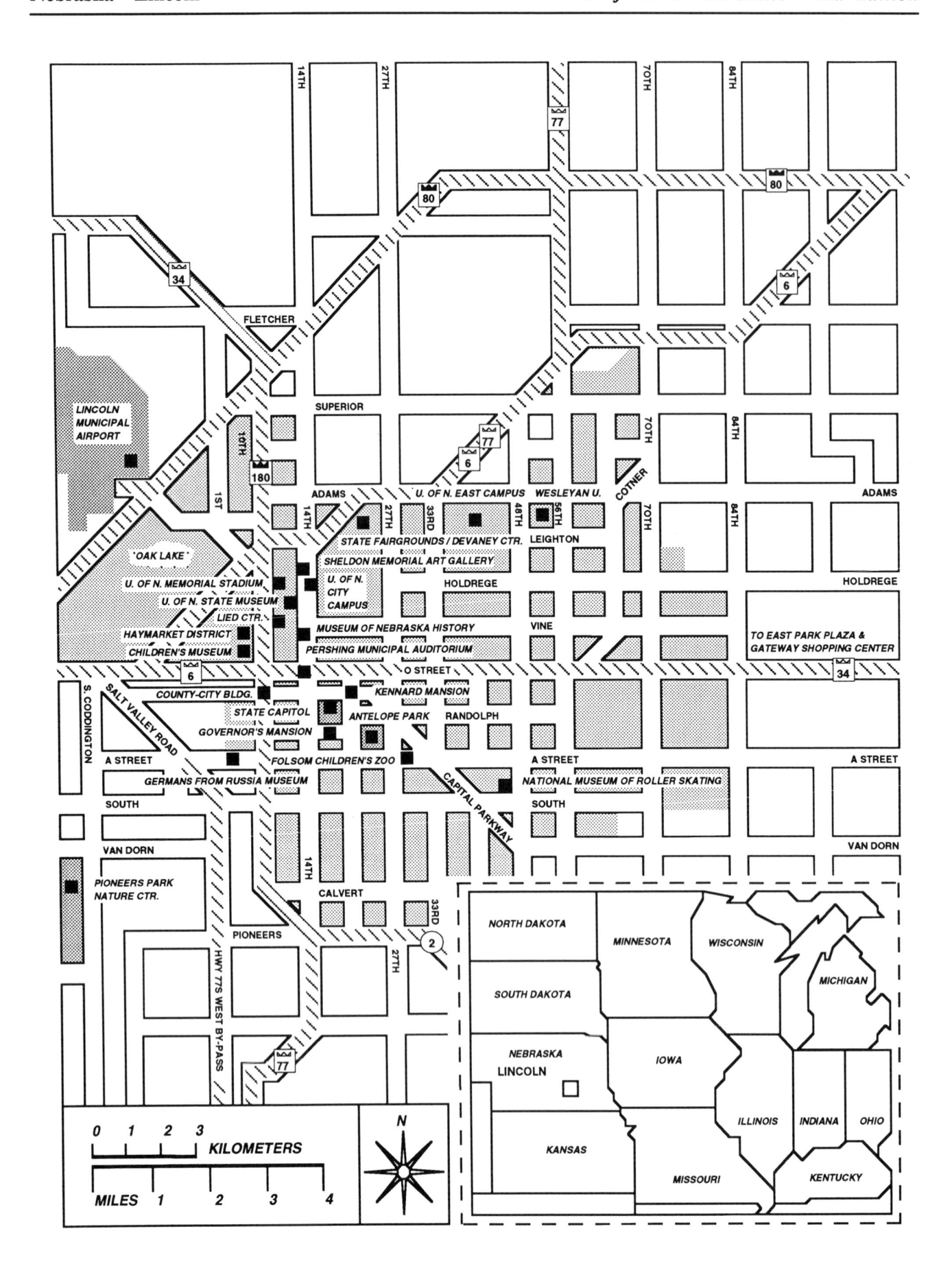

Nebraska—Lincoln

Introduction

Lincoln is the capital of Nebraska and the seat of Lancaster County. Lincoln and Lancaster County form a metropolitan statistical area, which serves as a commercial, educational, and government center for a grain and livestock producing region. Named after President Abraham Lincoln, the city was an important railroad junction for major western routes during the nineteenth century. William Jennings Bryan dominated the political life of Lincoln when he ran for president three times. The Nebraska state Capitol building, a modern structure rising four-hundred feet above the prairie, was designed to symbolize the spirit of the Plains.

Geography and Climate

Set near the center of Lancaster County in southeastern Nebraska, Lincoln is surrounded by gently rolling prairie. The western edge of the city lies in the valley of Salt Creek, which flows northeastward to the lower Platte River. The upward slope of the terrain to the west causes instability in moist easterly winds. Humidity remains at moderate to low levels except during short summer periods when moist tropical air reaches the area. Summer sunshine averages 64 percent of possible duration; high winds combined with hot temperatures occasionally cause crop damage. A chinook or foehn effect often produces rapid temperature rises in the winter. Annual snowfall is approximately twenty-five inches, though it has sometimes exceeded fifty-nine inches.

Area: 63.3 square miles (1990)

Elevation: 1,167 feet above sea level

Average Temperatures: January, 19.6° F; July, 77.6° F; annual average, 50.4° F

Average Annual Precipitation: 26.92 inches

History

Saline Deposits Attract First Settlers

In 1859 settlers attracted to the area surrounding present-day Lincoln because of saline deposits decided to name a town there after Lancaster County in Pennsylvania. But the new Lancaster existed only on paper, and the first county homestead is credited not to those settlers but to Captain W. T. Donovan, a salt company representative, who settled at Yankee Hill in 1861. The town was eventually platted in 1864. Lancaster's survival as a municipality was assured when Nebraska was admitted to the Union in 1867 and Lancaster was chosen as the site for the state capital.

Lancaster was a compromise choice between North Platters—who favored Omaha, the capital since 1854—and South Platters—who vied for a capital site south of the Platte River. Ultimately Lancaster was chosen and a new name proposed: "Capital City." Lancaster was finally renamed Lincoln, after President Abraham Lincoln. August F. Harvey, a state surveyor, replatted Lincoln in 1867, setting up a grid system of streets lettered from A to Z, with O as the division point, and north and south blocks numbered. In the heart of downtown were four square blocks for the state Capitol and a proposed university. The city plan also called for the planting of more than two million trees, mostly oak, which would line boulevards and parks. The attention to the natural landscaping of the city is a civic responsibility each generation of Lincolnites since has taken seriously.

In December 1868, the state government moved its property in covered wagons to hide the transfer of power from armed Omahans upset with the relocation. Local investors feared that Lincoln would not remain the state capital long since it numbered just thirty inhabitants in 1867, but within a year 500 people lived there, and new businesses started to develop. One event in Lincoln's history at this time symbolized the early difficulties. A herd of one-thousand Texas longhorns collapsed the wooden bridge over Salt Creek at O Street, but the wild herd blocked local officials from locating the cattle's owner and monetary restitution for the bridge's reconstruction was never obtained.

State Capital Weathers Troubled Times

At the first meeting of the Nebraska legislature in Lincoln in 1869, immediate action was taken to authorize land grants for railroad construction and a bill was passed to establish the University of Nebraska. The Burlington & Missouri River railroad line reached Lincoln in 1870, the same year the population reached 2,500 people. One popular rumor of the time was that Lincoln was built over an underground ocean that would provide a source of saline springs with commercial potential, but nothing of this sort materialized.

In the 1870s Lincoln suffered a difficult period. The state's first governor was impeached, a depression hit the local economy, and the legality of transferring the capital was questioned. Grasshoppers infested the area for more than three years. Saloons, gambling, and prostitution flourished, prompting the formation of the Women's Temperance Union, which set a moral tone that dominated local politics until Prohibition. Lincoln reversed its fortunes in the 1880s, as public services were introduced, businesses prospered, and a reform party was victorious in 1887. But as the new mayor and city council began cleaning up the local government, a crooked judge had them arrested and convicted in a circuit court case that was eventually reversed by the U.S. Supreme Court.

Twentieth Century Brings New Challenges

At the turn of the century William Jennings Bryan dominated the political life of Lincoln, running unsuccessfully for president as the Democratic candidate in 1896, 1900, and 1908. Bryan published *The Commoner,* a weekly newspaper with a circulation of more than one-hundred thousand after his defeat in 1900. Bryan was an oddity—a radical Democratic in conservative Lincoln. During World War I, segments of Lincoln's German population openly supported the Central Powers. A misplaced sense of American patriotism gripped the Lincoln populace and local German culture was shunned. The University Board of Regents conducted a hearing in which eighty professors faced charges of "lack of aggressive loyalty" and three were asked to resign.

The Capitol structure built in Lincoln in the 1880s began to settle into the ground, and one corner had sunk eight inches by 1908. Serious concern for the state of the Capitol prompted a contest to select the best new cost-effective design. All the entries except two involved the traditional federal dome style. The winning design featured a four-hundred-foot tower that could be built around the old Capitol, saving Nebraska nearly $1 million in office rental and making it possible to defray the costs of construction by the time the new capitol was completed in 1932. Its design revolutionized public and government buildings by ushering in a modernist style.

Lincoln in the 1990s is a typical "All-American" city, boasting clean, healthy air and safe streets.

Historical Information: Nebraska State Historical Society, 1500 R Street, P.O. Box 82554, Lincoln NE 68501; telephone (402)471-4745 or (800)833-6747; and, American Historical Society of Germans from Russia, 631 D Street, Lincoln, NE 68502-1199; telephone (402)474-3363

Population Profile

Metropolitan Area Residents
1970: 167,972
1980: 192,864
1990: 213,641
Percent change, 1980–1990: 10.8%
U.S. rank in 1980: Not available
U.S. rank in 1990: Not available

City Residents
1970: 150,000
1980: 171,932
1990: 191,972 (of which, 93,327 were males and 98,645 were females)
Percent change, 1980–1990: 11.7%
U.S. rank in 1980: 81st
U.S. rank in 1990: 81st (State rank: 2nd)

Density: 3,032.7 people per square mile (1990)

Racial and ethnic characteristics (1990)
  White: 181,320
  Black: 4,515
  American Indian, Eskimo, Aleut: 1,150
  Asian and Pacific Islander: 3,288
  Hispanic (may be of any race): 3,764

Percent of residents born in state: 71.0% (1990)

Age characteristics (1990)
  Population under 5 years old: 13,813
  Population 5 to 9 years old: 13,352
  Population 10 to 14 years old: 11,557
  Population 15 to 19 years old: 15,261
  Population 20 to 24 years old: 22,774
  Population 25 to 29 years old: 18,293
  Population 30 to 34 years old: 17,727
  Population 35 to 39 years old: 15,816
  Population 40 to 44 years old: 12,919
  Population 45 to 49 years old: 9,013
  Population 50 to 54 years old: 7,077
  Population 55 to 59 years old: 6,710
  Population 60 to 64 years old: 6,655
  Population 65 to 69 years old: 6,289
  Population 70 to 74 years old: 5,009
  Population 75 to 79 years old: 4,094
  Population 80 to 84 years old: 2,939
  Population 85 years and over: 2,674
  Median age: 30.3 years

Births (1988)
  Total number: 2,675

Deaths (1988)
  Total number: 1,386 (of which, 28 were infants under the age of 1 year)

Money income (1989)
  Per capita income: $13,720
  Median household income: $28,056
  Total households: 75,530
  Number of households with income of . . .
    less than $5,000: 3,917
    $5,000 to $9,999: 6,882
    $10,000 to $14,999: 7,705
    $15,000 to $24,999: 14,843
    $25,000 to $34,999: 13,386
    $35,000 to $49,999: 14,739
    $50,000 to $74,999: 9,752
    $75,000 to $99,999: 2,560
    $100,000 to $149,999: 1,123
    $150,000 or more: 623
  Percent of families below poverty level: 6.5% (53.8% of which were female householder families with related children under 5)
1991 FBI Crime Index Total: 14,954

Municipal Government

The city of Lincoln is governed by a mayor and seven-member council, all of whom are elected to four-year terms on a nonpartisan ballot. In a survey of twenty-four comparably sized cities, Lincoln's police department was ranked first in overall efficiency.

Head Official: Mayor Mike Johanns (R) (since 1991; current term expires 1995)

Total Number of City Employees: 1,800 (1993)

City Information: City of Lincoln, 555 South 10 St., Lincoln, NE 68508; telephone (402)471-7171

Economy

Major Industries and Commercial Activity

Located in a grain and livestock producing region, Lincoln has since its founding been a communications, distribution, and wholesaling hub. Important industries are the manufacture and repair of locomotives, flour and feed milling, grain storage, meat packing, dairy production, and diversified manufacturing. State government and the University of Nebraska constitute approximately 28 percent of the city's economy. Lincoln is also the corporate headquarters of several insurance companies.

During the 1980s Lincoln experienced sustained growth that is expected to continue at a rate of 1 percent per year throughout the 1990s. Growth has brought economic expansion, with the employment base increasing 2.5 percent annually. Retail trade, for example, has flourished since 1984, growing about 5 percent each year, a rate substantially above other metropolitan areas in the state. Manufacturing has also shown growth above the state average.

A number of Lincoln's local companies conduct business throughout the United States and in foreign countries. Among them are Ameritas Financial Services, Selection Research Inc./Gallup Poll, Lester Electrical, and Cook Family Foods. Peed Corporation, publishers of national trade magazines, moved its facilities to Lincoln in 1985. Harris Laboratories, a pharmaceutical testing and research firm that serves all fifty states and twenty-seven nations abroad, underwent a major expansion in 1988, adding between four-hundred and five-hundred jobs to its payroll. Norden Laboratories supplies veterinary products in the United States and sixty foreign countries.

Items and goods produced: creamery products, farm machinery, farm belts, veterinary supplies, radiator hoses, telephone equipment, biological products, pharmaceutical supplies, plumbing supplies, pumps, motors, motor scooters, wax, filing equipment and office supplies, and printing, lithographic, engraving, metal, stone, and concrete products

Incentive Programs—New and Existing Companies

State programs—The state of Nebraska, emphasizing its commitment to revitalized economic growth in all parts of the state, in 1987 passed a ground-breaking series of laws designed to make the state a better place to do business. Firms can now earn a series of tax credits and refunds for investment and new job creation through the provisions of the Employment and Investment Growth Act (LB 775), as well as the Employment Expansion and Investment Incentive Act (LB 270).

Local programs—The Lincoln Independent Business Association, the Chamber of Commerce, Southeast Community College, the University of Nebraska-Lincoln, and the city of Lincoln operate a small business resource center that helps businesses secure financing, permits, and information about other resources. Seven major established industrial parks cover over 1,000 acres and are designed for both heavy industry and multiple use. The City of Lincoln Research and Development Department, with assistance from the Nebraska Research and Development Authority, provides block grant funds to aid startup businesses. The state provides an aggressive tax incentive policy.

Development Projects

Lincoln's downtown business district is thriving, the result of ambitious development during the 1980s that included a $20 million performing arts center, a hotel and conference center, office-to-residential conversions, office construction and renovation, expansion of the skywalk system, and a movie theater. More than one-hundred companies expanded operations in Lincoln during the 1980s and fifteen companies moved to Lincoln then; nine new expansions were announced in 1990, adding one-thousand jobs.

Economic Development Information: Lincoln Chamber of Commerce, Economic Development Division, 1221 N Street, Lincoln, NE 68508; telephone (402)476-7511

Commercial Shipping

Lincoln is connected with national and world markets via two major railroads—Burlington Northern and Union Pacific—that provide piggyback transportation; twenty-two interstate and fifteen intrastate motor freight companies; and fourteen air express and freight carriers. The city is also conveniently situated within 50 miles of water transportation at Mississippi River terminals.

Labor Force and Employment Outlook

Lincoln's labor force is described as dependable, productive, and highly skilled, with an average of 12.9 years of schooling. Employers may draw from a large student population. Work stoppages are rare, with unionization estimated at about 15 percent. As agriculture declines, more rural laborers are seeking jobs in the city.

A diversified economy has enabled employment in Lincoln to remain resilient since the nationwide recession during the 1980s and to demonstrate an annual growth rate of 2.5 percent. Employment in the manufacture of both durable and nondurable goods in particular has expanded. Among non-manufacturing categories, Lincoln has been strong in construction, wholesale and retail trade, and services.

The following is a summary of data regarding the Lincoln metropolitan area labor force as of September 1992.

Size of non-agricultural labor force: 126,300

Number of workers employed in . . .
   mining: not available
   construction: 5,600
   manufacturing: 15,100
   transportation and public utilities: 7,400
   wholesale and retail trade: 25,600
   finance, insurance, and real estate: 8,700
   services: 29,500
   government: 34,400

Average hourly earnings of production workers employed in manufacturing: $11.64

Unemployment rate: 2.4%

The Nebraska State Capitol.

Largest employers	Number of employees
Lincoln Public Schools	Over 2,500
State of Nebraska	Over 2,500
University of Nebraska	Over 2,500
Bryan Memorial Hospital	1,000 to 2,499
City of Lincoln	1,800
Goodyear Tire & Rubber Co.	1,800
SmithKline Beecham-Norden Division	675
Kawasaki Motor Corps. USA	600

Cost of Living

Utility rates for both residents and industries are among the lowest in the country. Lincoln boasts a low tax burden with a high quality of services.

The following is a summary of data regarding several key cost of living factors in the Lincoln area.

1992 (2nd Quarter) ACCRA Cost of Living Index: 90.5 (U.S. average = 100.0)

1992 (2nd Quarter) ACCRA Average House Price: $93,000

State income tax rate: Graduated from 2.37% to 7.35% (1990–1991; rate set yearly by state legislature

State sales tax rate: 5.0%

Local income tax rate: None

Local sales tax rate: 1.5%

Property tax rate: $2.7253 per $100 of actual value (1990–1991)

Economic Information: Lincoln Chamber of Commerce, 1221 N Street, Lincoln, NE 68508; telephone (402) 476-7511

Education and Research

Elementary and Secondary Schools

The Lincoln Public Schools system is the second-largest district in the state of Nebraska. A seven-member, nonpartisan board of education selects a superintendent. Lincoln's students consistently score above the national average on standardized tests, and the system's high school graduation rate is the fourth highest in the country.

The following is a summary of data regarding the Lincoln public schools as of the 1991–1992 school year.

Total enrollment: 28,806

Number of facilities
 elementary schools: 34
 junior high schools: 8
 senior high schools: 4
 other: 1

Student/teacher ratio: 23:1

Teacher salaries
 minimum: $19,205
 maximum: $42,795

Funding per pupil: $4,997

The city is served by fifteen private and parochial schools, including four high schools.

Public Schools Information: Lincoln Educational Service Unit #18, P.O. Box 82889, Lincoln, NE 68501-2889; telephone (402)436-1000

Colleges and Universities

The University of Nebraska-Lincoln (UNL), with an enrollment of more than twenty-four thousand students, maintains two campuses in Lincoln. UNL offers 130 undergraduate and 105 graduate programs and also operates a law school and a dental college. Two liberal arts colleges, Nebraska Wesleyan University and Union College, schedule courses leading to the baccalaureate degree. Union, which is affiliated with the Seventh Day Adventist church, offers summer graduate study as a satellite campus of Loma Linda University in California; the functioning one-room George Stone School on campus permits education majors to acquire small-class teaching experience. Wesleyan sponsors the Wesleyan Institute for Lifelong Learning, an evening adult-education program.

Technical and vocational schools located in the Lincoln area include Southeast Community College-Lincoln Campus, The Lincoln School of Commerce, and Lincoln Airplane and Flying School, where Charles Lindbergh learned to fly.

Libraries and Research Centers

Lincoln is home to twenty-nine libraries associated with a wide range of institutions and organizations. The Lincoln City Libraries system, based downtown, operates six branches and a bookmobile and maintains holdings of more than 552,000 volumes, eighteen hundred periodicals, and microfiche, recordings, slides, and art reproductions. Special collections feature Nebraska authors; the library is a depository for state documents. The Nebraska Library for the Blind and Physically Handicapped provides 970 Braille volumes, 43,915 recorded cassettes, 50,433 recorded discs, and recorded magazines and talking books.

The Love Library at the University of Nebraska-Lincoln holds 2.1 million books and special collections in such fields as Czechoslovakian studies, folklore, military history, Plains materials, and twentieth-century Russia. The library, a federal and state documents depository, operates smaller branches in academic departments and provides services for the blind. Union College, Nebraska Wesleyan University, and Southeast Community College-Lincoln Campus operate campus libraries.

Several federal and state agencies maintain libraries in Lincoln; among them are the National Park Service, the Nebraska Game and Parks Commission, the Nebraska Gasohol Committee, the Nebraska Legislative Council, the Nebraska Library Commission, and the Nebraska State Historical Society. The American Historical Society of Germans from Russia, as well as hospitals, churches and synagogues, and corporations, also operate libraries in the city.

The University of Nebraska-Lincoln is a center for specialized research; facilities include the Berkeley Center for speech therapy and hearing impaired study, the Engine Technology Center, the Nebraska Food Processing Center, and the UNL Mass Spectrometry Center. The Nebraska Technology Development Corporation and the Nebraska Research and Development Authority provide links between research and commercial product development.

Public Library Information: Lincoln City Libraries, 136 South Fourteenth Street, Lincoln, NE 68508-1899; telephone (402)471-8500

Health Care

Money magazine's survey ranking Lincoln as the country's tenth most livable city noted its "abundant medical care." Bryan Memorial Hospital, the city's largest medical facility, specializes in cardiac and pulmonary care and rheumatology, oncology, dialysis, and ophthalmology services; Bryan Memorial is a regional apnea center and maintains a school of nursing. Lincoln General Hospital has been designated a regional trauma center; among the hospital's specialized units are an Alzheimer's disease assessment clinic and an oncology center. St. Elizabeth Community Health Center operates a regional burn care unit and a neonatal care center. Lincoln is also home to a Veterans Administration Hospital. The Lincoln medical community is comprised of more than three-hundred doctors, more than two-thousand nurses, and more than 140 dentists.

Recreation

Sightseeing

The Nebraska State Capitol Building was designed to reflect the spirit of the state of Nebraska: its large square base represents the Plains and its four-hundred-foot tower is meant to convey the dreams of the pioneers. Described as "the nation's first truly vernacular state Capitol," the building features an interior enhanced with mosaics, paintings, and murals that depict the history of Nebraska. On the Capitol grounds is Chester French's sculpture of Abraham Lincoln.

Folsom Children's Zoo and Botanical Gardens presents over two-hundred exotic animals from around the world on grounds that are lined with seven-thousand annual flowers and more than thirty varieties of trees. Antelope Park stretches throughout the city and contains the Sunken Gardens with thousands of flowers, lily pools, and a waterfall. The Prairie Interpretive Center in Pioneers Park focuses on animals and prairie grasses native to 1850s Nebraska; animal exhibits include deer, elk, goats, wild turkeys, and wild buffalo.

Historic houses on view in Lincoln include Kennard House, home of Nebraska's first U.S. secretary of state; Fairview, residence of William Jennings Bryan;

A scene at Folsom Children's Zoo and Botanical Gardens.

the governor's mansion, which features a collection of dolls depicting Nebraska's first ladies in their inaugural gowns; and Ferguson mansion, built in 1910 and furnished with period pieces.

Arts and Culture

Lincoln is highly rated for the quality of the cultural activities in a city its size. The Lincoln Symphony opens its season with a pops concert followed by a subscription series of classical music at Lied Center, which also hosts performances by Lincoln City Ballet/Ballet Midwest. Other local music offerings include the Nebraska Chamber Orchestra, Abendmusik, and the Kimball Series at the University of Nebraska. Lincoln's Zoo Bar is one of the nation's oldest blues clubs booking touring blues bands and rock artists.

Designed by Phillip Johnson, the Sheldon Memorial Art Gallery is located on the campus of the University of Nebraska and exhibits American art from the eighteenth through the twentieth centuries with an emphasis on the realist tradition and abstract expressionism. The gallery also sponsors film showings and a chamber music series.

The State Museum of History exhibits capture the history of Nebraska from prehistoric times through the native American tribes of the Great Plains to pioneer days. The world's largest fossil elephant is on display at the University of Nebraska State Museum, which is also home to a planetarium and presents laser shows. The American Historical Society of Germans from Russia Museum traces the history and culture of this ethnic group that settled in Lincoln in the nineteenth century. Lincoln is also home to the National Museum of Roller Skating, Great Plains Art Collection, and the Children's Museum.

Arts and Culture Information: Lincoln Arts Council Hotline, (402)477-3333

Festivals and Holidays

The Haymarket Heydays, celebrating the state's railroad heritage, brings artists to Lincoln's downtown to sell their work in a street fair featuring food, musical events, and activities for children, is held the end of June. July Jamm brings jazz and fine artists and restaurateurs from around the state for a three-day event. The Nebraska State Fair begins on the Friday prior to Labor Day and runs for ten days; the fair features national performers of country and rock music, midway rides, livestock shows, and agricultural and industrial exhibits. The Christmas season begins during Thanksgiving week with Tannenbaum Festival, followed by the Star City Holiday Parade, a colorful event with floats and costumed characters, held on the first Saturday in December.

Sports for the Spectator

When the University of Nebraska Corn Huskers football team plays home games at Lincoln's Memorial Stadium on fall Saturday afternoons, the crowd of more than 73,500 fans becomes the state's third largest "city." Nicknamed Big Red because of their bright red uniforms, the team competes in the Big Eight conference and has won nine or more games each season and played in a bowl game each season since 1972. The University of Nebraska also fields competitive teams in wrestling and men's and women's basketball. Lincoln is the site of the high school state championships in basketball, wrestling, volleyball, gymnastics, and swimming and diving. Thoroughbred horse racing with parimutuel betting permitted takes place at the State Fair Park.

Sports for the Participant

The Lincoln Parks and Recreation Department oversees sixty-nine city parks on 5,000 acres and sponsors team and league sports for all age levels. The Lincoln Track Club sponsors the Lincoln Marathon each May. The Cornhusker State Games, attracting nearly seventeen thousand competitors, consists of twenty-eight sports such as badminton, biathlon, fencing, tae kwon do, archery, and wrestling. Wilderness Park, Lincoln's largest park, maintains bridle trails, jogging and exercise trails, and cross country ski trails. Holmes Lake Park offers sailboats, canoes, and paddlewheel boats for use on its large lake; it also features an observatory. Chet Ager Nature Center's 56 acres include 2.5 miles of trails. Lincoln is surrounded by the seven Salt Valley Lakes with recreational areas providing opportunities for such pursuits as fishing, camping, and boating. Ten state recreation areas are within a thirty-minute drive.

Shopping and Dining

The nation's longest main street is Lincoln's O Street, which runs all the way through the city; a number of retail centers are located along the route. Antiques, art galleries, and specialty shops are the focus in the Central Business District and Historic Haymarket District. Local dining specialties include barbecue ribs and chicken as well as traditional American fare.

Visitor Information: Lincoln Convention and Visitors Bureau, 1221 N Street, Lincoln, NE 68508; telephone (402)476-7511 or 1-800-423-8212 (outside Nebraska)

Convention Facilities

Meeting and convention planners may choose from three major facilities that accommodate a full range of group functions. Pershing Auditorium, located downtown on Centennial Mall, houses an arena with more than twenty-eight thousand square feet of exhibit space and a capacity for 150 booths. The arena will also seat 2,000 people for a banquet and 3,000 people in a theater setting; four separate meeting rooms seat from fifty to two-hundred participants. Other amenities include concession facilities, catering services, and sound and lighting systems. Devaney Sports Center and Nebraska State Fair Park host trade shows, exhibitions, and athletic events as well as banquets and meetings; ample parking is provided at both sites. Lodging is available at downtown and metropolitan area hotels and motels offering a total of nearly three-thousand rooms; several also provide meeting facilities.

Convention Information: Lincoln Convention and Visitors Bureau, 1221 N Street, Lincoln, NE 68508; telephone (402)476-7511 or 1-800-423-8212 (outside Nebraska)

Transportation

Approaching the City

Lincoln Municipal Airport is served by six commercial air carriers with regularly scheduled daily direct and connecting flights from major United States cities as well as points throughout the world. Commuter service is also provided from cities in central and western Nebraska. Amtrak provides railway transportation into Lincoln.

An efficient highway system permits easy access into Lincoln. I-80 approaches from the northeast and exits due west; U.S. 6 also bisects the city from northeast to west. U.S. 34 runs northwest to south, in the center of downtown joining U.S. 77, which extends from the south, and joining Nebraska 2, which approaches from the southeast.

Traveling in the City

Lincoln's streets are laid out on a grid pattern, with lettered streets running east and west and numbered streets running north and south. The main north-south thoroughfare is O Street, which is also U.S. 6 and U.S. 34. Public bus service is provided by the Lincoln Transportation System.

Communications

Newspapers and Magazines

Lincoln's daily newspapers are the morning *Star,* the evening *Journal,* and the Sunday *Journal-Star.* Several neighborhood newspapers and shopping guides are distributed weekly.

A number of special-interest magazines are based in Lincoln. The Peed Corporation publishes four national trade magazines, and the Christian Record Braille Foundation, Inc., publishes magazines for blind adults and children. Other publications pertain to such subjects as agriculture, medicine, education, outdoor recreation and conservation, Nebraska history, and literature.

Television and Radio

Seven television channels are received in the city. A locally operated company supplies subscription cable service. Fourteen Lincoln radio stations, including thirteen AM and FM and one cable, schedule a complete range of musical programming such as rock and roll, classical, country, big band, jazz, blues, and gospel. Lincoln radio listeners can also tune into a several Omaha stations.

Media Information: Journal Star Printing Company, 926 P Street, Box 81609, Lincoln, NE 68506; telephone (402)475-4200

Selected Bibliography

Cather, Willa, *O Pioneers!* (Boston, New York, Houghton Mifflin, 1913)

Cather, Willa, *The Song of the Lark* (Boston, New York, Houghton Mifflin, 1915)

Keteyian, Armen, *Big Red Confidential: Inside Nebraska Football* (Chicago: Contemporary Books, 1989)

Neihardt, John Gneisenau, *The End of the Dream and Other Stories* (Lincoln: University of Nebraska Press, 1991)

Osborne, Tom, *More Than Winning* (Nashville: T. Nelson, 1985)

Omaha

The City in Brief

Founded: 1854 (incorporated, 1857)

Head Official: Mayor P. J. Morgan (R) (since 1989)

City Population
 1970: 346,929
 1980: 314,255
 1990: 335,795
 Percent change, 1980–1990: 7.0%
 U.S. rank in 1980: 48th
 U.S. rank in 1990: 48th

Metropolitan Area Population
 1970: 556,000
 1980: 585,122
 1990: 618,262
 Percent change, 1980–1990: 5.7%
 U.S. rank in 1980: 57th
 U.S. rank in 1990: 63rd

Area: 100.7 square miles (1990)
Elevation: 1,309 feet above sea level
Average Annual Temperature: 51.0° F
Average Annual Precipitation: 28.54 inches

Major Economic Sectors: Services, wholesale and retail trade, government, manufacturing
Unemployment Rate: 3.6% (September 1992)
Per Capita Income: $13,957 (1989)
1992 (2nd Quarter) ACCRA Average House Price: $92,415
1992 (2nd Quarter) ACCRA Cost of Living Index: 90.8 (U.S. average = 100.0)
1991 FBI Crime Index Total: 24,004

Major Colleges and Universities: University of Nebraska at Omaha, Creighton University, University of Nebraska Medical Center

Daily Newspaper: *Omaha World-Herald*

Nebraska—Omaha

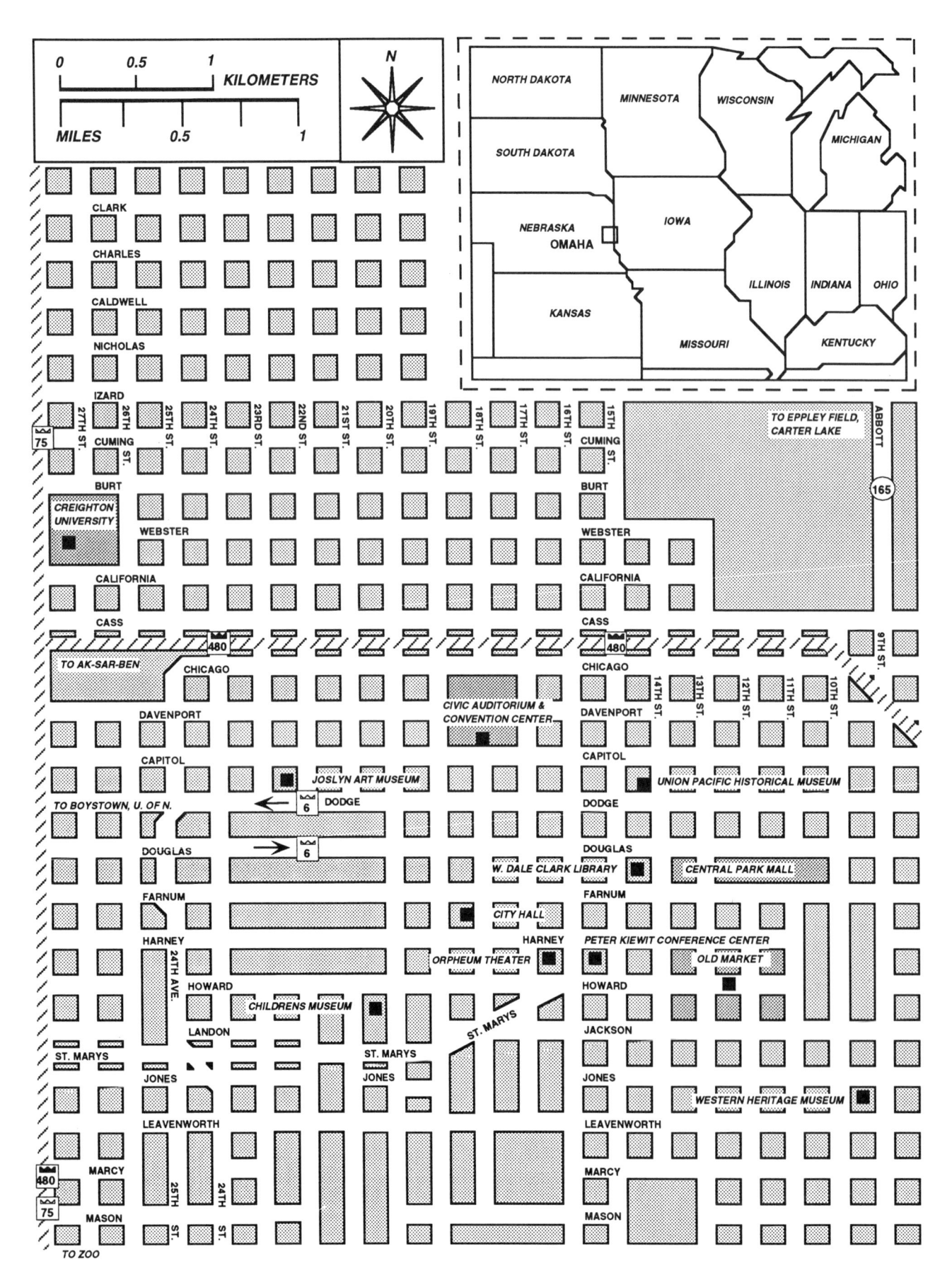

Cities of the United States • 2nd Edition

Introduction

Omaha, the seat of Douglas County, is the focus of a metropolitan statistical area that includes Douglas, Sarpy, and Washington counties in Nebraska and Pottawattamie County in Iowa. The city's development as a railroad center was augmented by the Union Stockyards and the meat-packing industry. Throughout its history Omaha has benefitted from the civic commitment of its citizens. Reverend Edward J. Flanagan's establishment of Boys Town in the Omaha area brought national recognition to the plight of homeless children. Today, Omaha is an insurance and telecommunications center, home to the U.S. Air Force Strategic Command, and notable for its inexpensive housing, good schools, and relatively few social and environmental problems.

Geography and Climate

Omaha is located on the bank of the Missouri River, surrounded by rolling hills. The area's continental climate, which produces warm summers and cold, dry winters, is influenced by its position between two zones: the humid east and the dry west. Low pressure systems crossing the country also affect the weather in Omaha, causing periodic and rapid changes, especially during the winter. Only 10 percent of the total annual precipitation falls during Omaha's winters, which are relatively cold. Sunshine occurs fifty percent of the possible time in the winter and 75 percent in the summer.

Area: 100.7 square miles (1990)

Elevation: 1,309 feet above sea level

Average Temperatures: January, 21.9° F; July, 77.4° F; annual average, 51.0° F

Average Annual Precipitation: 28.54 inches

History

Omaha Furthers Westward Expansion

The first people to live in the area surrounding present-day Omaha were the Otoe, Missouri, and Omaha tribes, who roamed and hunted along the Missouri River, which divides Iowa and Nebraska. The Mahas, a Nebraska plains tribe, lived where Omaha now stands. Meriwether Lewis and William Clark, on their mission to chart the Louisiana Purchase, reached the future site of Omaha in the summer of 1804, and held council with Otoe and Missouri native Americans. As early as the War of 1812, Manual Lisa established a fur-trading post in the area.

Mormon pioneers set up camp in Florence, a small settlement north of Omaha, in the winter of 1846 to 1847. Six hundred residents died during that harsh winter, and the Mormon Pioneer Cemetery today contains a monument by sculptor Avard Fairbanks that marks the tragedy. Florence, later annexed by Omaha, served for years as a Mormon way station in the westward journey to Utah. Omaha served as the eastern terminus and outfitting center for pioneers headed to the west to find their fortune in the California gold fields or to settle available inexpensive land.

A rush for land officially began in the area on June 24, 1854, when a treaty with the Omaha native Americans was concluded. The Council Bluffs & Nebraska Ferry Company, the town's founders, named the new town Omaha, from the Maha word meaning "above all others on the stream" or "up-river people." When it seemed likely that a Pacific Railroad line was to be constructed out of Omaha, the new town was proposed as the site of the future state capital. The first territorial legislature did meet in Omaha on January 16, 1855. Omaha was incorporated in 1857, but Lincoln was designated the capital when Nebraska was admitted to the Union in 1867.

Rail Transport Establishes Omaha's Future

The city's early years were full of incidents that prompted the administering of so-called frontier justice, including lynchings, fist and gun fights, and an arbitration body calling itself the Claim Club. Ignoring Federal land laws in favor of local interpretations, the Claim Club even went so far as to construct a house on wheels that could be used to protect the claims of people in need of a home to retain possession of the land. The U.S. Supreme Court in later rulings decided not to go against land title disputes made during this colorful but lawless time.

The fortunes of Omaha took a positive turn when President Abraham Lincoln selected Council Bluffs,

Iowa, for the terminus of the Pacific Railroad, which was subsequently relocated on Omaha's side of the Missouri River. Actual construction began in 1863, the first step in Omaha's development into one of the nation's largest railroad centers.

The historic trial that gave native Americans their citizenship took place in Omaha and was decided by Judge Elmer Dundy of the U.S. District Court for Nebraska on May 12, 1879; the case is known as *Standing Bear* v. *Crook.* The Poncas, after accepting a reservation in southeastern South Dakota, decided to return to their homeland. Led by Chief Standing Bear, they were arrested by a detachment of guards sent by Brigadier General George Crook, commander of the Department of the Platte, who was based at Ft. Omaha. General Crook, a veteran fighter in the Indian campaigns, was nonetheless an advocate of fair treatment of Indians. He cooperated fully in the trial, and some evidence indicates he even instigated the suit. Thomas Henry Tibbles, an editor of the *Omaha Daily Herald,* publicized the case nationwide, focusing attention on Omaha and on the humanitarian sentiments of General Crook and Tibbles, who was an abolitionist-turned-journalist.

Meatpacking Industry Spurs New Growth

The establishment of the Union Stockyards and the great packing houses in the 1880s invigorated the Omaha economy and drew to the city immigrants from Southern Europe and an assortment of colorful individuals who figured prominently in the city's growth. After a flood in 1881, residents relocated to the other side of the Missouri River, triggering another real estate boom. Fifty-two brickyards were by that time in operation, producing more than 150 million bricks each year. Omaha's first skyscraper, the New York Life Insurance Building, dates from this era.

The Knights of Ak-Sar-Ben (Nebraska spelled backwards), Omaha's leading civic organization, was created in 1895 to promote the city; they organized the Trans-Mississippi Exposition in 1898, bringing more than one million people to a city of less than one hundred thousand in a year-long event. The Omaha Grain Exchange was established at the turn of the century, helping the city develop as a grain market. Agriculture has proved to be the city's economic base, augmented by insurance.

The Reverend Edward J. Flanagan founded Boys TownBoys Town, NE in the Omaha area in 1917 with ninety dollars he borrowed and with the philosophy that "there is no such thing as a bad boy." This internationally famous boys' home, which was incorporated as a village in 1936, is located west of the city and now provides a home for boys and girls alike. After World War II, Omaha native and aviation pioneer Arthur C. Storz, son of brewing giant Gottlieb Storz, lobbied to have Omaha designated the headquarters of the U.S. Air Force. Today, Omaha's Offutt Air Force Base serves as headquarters of the Strategic Command.

Telecommunications Replaces Meatpacking

During the 1980s, while other cities were trying to attract industries, Omaha began a highly successful campaign to attract telecommunications companies. Promoting advantages like cheap real estate, comparatively low wages and cost of living, and its educated and reliable work force, Omaha succeeded to the point that by 1991 its telecommunications jobs were more than twice the number of meatpacking jobs. Today, Omaha is home to three of the nation's largest telemarketers.

Historical Information: Douglas County Historical Society, General Crook House, Thirtieth and Fort Streets, Omaha, NE 68110; telephone (402)455-9990

Population Profile

Metropolitan Area Residents
1970: 556,000
1980: 585,122
1990: 618,262
Annual average percent change, 1980–1988: 0.7%
U.S. rank in 1980: 57th
U.S. rank in 1990: 63rd

City Residents
1970: 346,929
1980: 314,255
1990: 335,795 (of which, 160,392 were males and 175,403 were females)
Percent change, 1980–1990: 7.0%
U.S. rank in 1980: 48th
U.S. rank in 1990: 48th (State rank: 1st)

Density: 3,337.9 people per square mile (1990)

Racial and ethnic characteristics (1990)
  White: 281,603
  Black: 43,989
  American Indian, Eskimo, Aleut: 2,274
  Asian and Pacific Islander: 3,412
  Hispanic (may be of any race): 10,288

Percent of residents born in state: 65.2% (1990)

Age characteristics (1990)
  Population under 5 years old: 25,711
  Population 5 to 9 years old: 24,580
  Population 10 to 14 years old: 22,266
  Population 15 to 19 years old: 22,699
  Population 20 to 24 years old: 27,563
  Population 25 to 29 years old: 32,198
  Population 30 to 34 years old: 29,243
  Population 35 to 39 years old: 25,736
  Population 40 to 44 years old: 21,740
  Population 45 to 49 years old: 17,078
  Population 50 to 54 years old: 14,754
  Population 55 to 59 years old: 14,462
  Population 60 to 64 years old: 14,468
  Population 65 to 69 years old: 13,714
  Population 70 to 74 years old: 10,634
  Population 75 to 79 years old: 8,313
  Population 80 to 84 years old: 5,656
  Population 85 years and over: 4,980
  Median age: 32.1 years

Births (1988)
  Total number: 5,783

Deaths (1988)
  Total number: 3,200 (of which, 67 were infants under the age of 1 year)

Money income (1989)
  Per capita income: $13,957
  Median household income: $26,927
  Total households: 133,888
  Number of households with income of . . .
    less than $5,000: 8,326
    $5,000 to $9,999: 13,172
    $10,000 to $14,999: 13,452
    $15,000 to $24,999: 26,988
    $25,000 to $34,999: 22,745
    $35,000 to $49,999: 23,612
    $50,000 to $74,999: 16,730
    $75,000 to $99,999: 4,453
    $100,000 to $149,999: 2,672
    $150,000 or more: 1,738
  Percent of families below poverty level: 9.6% (62.0% of which were female householder families with related children under 5)

1991 FBI Crime Index Total: 24,004

Municipal Government

The city of Omaha operates under a mayor-council form of government. The mayor, who does not serve on the council, and seven council members are all elected to four-year terms.

Head Official: Mayor P.J. Morgan (R) (since 1989; current term expires June 1997)

Total Number of City Employees: 2,900 (1991)

City Information: Mayor's Office, 1819 Farnam Street, Suite 300, Omaha, NE; telephone (402)444-5000

Economy

Major Industries and Commercial Activity

There are more than fifteen-thousand businesses located in the four-county metropolitan area, reflecting a growth rate of 22 percent for the period 1986-1991. The region is home to five Fortune 500 industrial companies: ConAgra, Peter Kiewit Sons, Berkshire Hathaway, AG Processing, and Valmont Industries. More than thirty other Fortune 500 companies have manufacturing plants in the metropolitan area.

The headquarters of nearly thirty insurance companies call Omaha home. Over half of the two dozen telemarketing/direct response/reservation centers operating in Omaha also have their corporate headquarters located in the metropolitan area. Numerous other large firms have their headquarters in Omaha, including Mutual of Omaha Companies, Union Pacific Railroad, Lozier Corporation, First Data Resources, I T I Marketing Services, Omaha Steaks International, Pamida, and Godfather's Pizza, Inc.

The Omaha economy is well diversified, with no industry sector accounting for more than 30 percent of total employment. Omaha has a higher concentration of its employment in finance, insurance and real estate; transportation, communications, and utilities; and services and trade jobs than does the country on average. This is offset by a relatively smaller share of total employment in the manufacturing, construction, and government sectors. Since 1980 the industry sectors that have shown the fastest growth within the Omaha metropolitan area are services, trade, and finance, insurance, and real estate.

Items and goods produced: a variety of food items from raw products like meat and flour to finished consumer goods like frozen dinners and cereal; irrigation equipment; phone apparatus; store fixtures; hydraulic motors and pumps; paper boxes and packaging materials; furniture; computer components

Incentive Programs—New and Existing Companies

State programs—In addition to receiving conventional financing from banks and other lending institutions, qualified Omaha businesses can take advantage of state and local programs. Among them are the Nebraska Business and Development Center and the Nebraska Technical Assistance Center, which provide technical and research assistance. The Nebraska Venture Capital Network, managed by the Nebraska Business Development Center at the University of Nebraska at Omaha, introduces entrepreneurs to individual investors and venture capital firms. Federal and state programs include the Minority Enterprise Small Business Investment Corporation, the Nebraska Investment Finance Authority, various Small Business Administration loans, the Nebraska Research and Development Authority, the Small Business Innovation Research Program, and the Urban Development Action Grant.

The state of Nebraska, emphasizing its commitment to revitalized economic growth in all parts of the state, in 1987 passed a ground-breaking series of laws designed to make the state an even better place to do business. Firms can now earn a series of tax credits and refunds for investment and new job creation through the provisions of the Employment and Investment Growth Act (LB 775), as well as the Employment Expansion and Investment Incentive Act (LB 270). Between 1987 and 1991, over 130 projects associated with LB 775 were announced by Omaha firms, with anticipated investment of over $1.2 billion and expected creation of more than thirteen-thousand new jobs through 1998.

Local programs—Assisting in the expansion of new and existing business at the local level are the Small Business Council, the Omaha Small Business Network, Inc., and the Omaha Regional Minority Purchasing Council. Among other finance programs are community development block grants, improvement financing, industrial development revenue bonds, and a range of local and state tax credits.

Development Projects

During the 1980s and early 1990s, many development projects were successfully completed in Omaha. In the early 1980s, the Central Park Mall was created, giving residents a place to enjoy nature in the heart of downtown. Recent revitalization of the city's historic riverfront area included the extension of the Central Mall into the new Heartland of America Park; the construction of the worldwide headquarters of ConAgra; a state of the art central dispatch center for Union Pacific Railroad; and a five-state computer billing center for U S West. These projects have transformed the eastern edge of downtown Omaha and given the local economy a boost.

The western edge of the city was also given a boost with the completion in 1991 of Phase I of the Oakview Mall. Also recently completed was the largest indoor tropical rain forest in the world, the Lied Jungle at the Henry Doorly Zoo.

Economic Development Information: Economic Development Council, Greater Omaha Chamber of Commerce, 1301 Harney Street, Omaha, NE 68102; telephone (402)346-5000

Commercial Shipping

The Port of Omaha, linking the city to the Gulf of Mexico and the Atlantic Ocean via the Missouri River and through the St. Lawrence Seaway, is an important factor in the local economy. The channel was recently expanded to a width of three-hundred feet and a depth of nine feet, thus accommodating larger commercial barges. Served by a number of barge lines, the port processes more than six million tons of goods annually. The Union Pacific and four other major railroads provide freight service that is coordinated with many of the ninety trucking companies serving the metropolitan area. Four air-cargo carriers maintain facilities at Eppley Airfield.

Labor Force and Employment Outlook

The Omaha labor force is described as trainable, possessing an old-fashioned work ethic, and lacking a regional accent, so workers are considered excellent for the phone operations jobs proliferating there.

The following is a summary of data regarding the Omaha metropolitan area labor force as of September 1992.

Size of non-agricultural labor force: 329,400

Number of workers employed in . . .
  mining: not reported
  construction: 14,900
  manufacturing: 34,900
  transportation and public utilities: 24,200
  wholesale and retail trade: 79,300
  finance, insurance, and real estate: 28,600
  services: 100,200
  government: 47,300

Average hourly earnings of production workers employed in manufacturing: $10.89

Unemployment rate: 3.6%

Largest employers	Number of employees
Strategic Air Command (U.S. Air Force)	Over 10,000
Mutual of Omaha/United of Omaha (insurance)	5,000 to 9,999
Omaha Public Schools	5,000 to 9,999
University of Nebraska Medical Center	5,000 to 9,999
First Data Resources (credit card processors)	3,000 to 4,999
US WEST Communications	3,000 to 4,999
Union Pacific Railroad	3,000 to 4,999

Cost of Living

The following is a summary of data regarding several key cost of living factors in the Omaha area.

1992 (2nd Quarter) ACCRA Cost of Living Index: 90.8 (U.S. average = 100.0)

1992 (2nd Quarter) ACCRA Average House Price: $92,415

State income tax rate: Graduated from 2.37% to 7.35% (1990-1991; rate set yearly by state legislature

State sales tax rate: 5.0%

Local income tax rate: None

Local sales tax rate: 1.5%

Property tax rate: $2.62549 per $100 of assessed valuation

Economic Information: Greater Omaha Chamber of Commerce, 1301 Harney Street, Omaha, NE 68102; telephone (402)346-5000

Education and Research

Elementary and Secondary Schools

The Omaha Public Schools, District 1, is the largest elementary and secondary public education system in Nebraska. A nonpartisan, twelve-member board of education appoints a superintendent.

The following is a summary of data regarding the Omaha public schools as of the 1992-1993 school year.

Total enrollment: 43,050

Number of facilities
  elementary schools: 56
  junior high schools: 10
  senior high schools: 7
  other: 4

Student/teacher ratio: 15:1

Teacher salaries
  minimum: $21,362 (with a bachelor's degree)
  maximum: $45,188 (with a doctorate)

Funding per pupil: $4,600

An extensive parochial school system as well as a number of private schools provide complete curricula, including religious instruction, for students in kindergarten through twelfth grade. The most notable private institution is Boys Town, a residential facility founded in 1917 as the "city of little men" by Monsignor E. J. Flanagan.

Public Schools Information: Omaha Public Schools, 3215 Cuming Street, Omaha, NE 68131; telephone (402)554-1111

Colleges and Universities

The University of Nebraska at Omaha, with an enrollment of more than fifteen-thousand students, awards graduate and undergraduate degrees in such fields as business, chemistry, engineering, social work, criminal justice, elementary education, and fine and dramatic arts. Affiliated with the university is the University of Nebraska Medical Center, which offers programs at all degree levels from associate to doctorate in areas that include dental hygiene, dentistry, medical technology, medicine, nuclear medicine technology, nursing, pharmacy, physical therapy, physician's assistant, radiation technology, and radiologic technology.

Creighton University is a private institution with colleges of arts and sciences and business administration and schools of law, nursing, pharmacy and allied health, dentistry, medicine, and graduate study. Creighton awards associate through doctorate degrees. Among the colleges located in the Omaha area are the College of Saint Mary, Grace College of the Bible, and Metropolitan Community College. Area vocational schools offer specialized and technical training.

Libraries and Research Centers

The Omaha Public Library operates a main downtown facility, the W. Dale Clark Library, and ten branches while also providing services for the deaf and blind. With holdings totalling over 613,000 volumes, more than twenty-three hundred periodical titles, and records, tapes, compact discs, and art reproductions, the library is also a depository for federal and state documents. Extensive main and departmental libraries are located on the campuses of all colleges and universities in the city. Other libraries in Omaha are associated with government agencies, corporations, hospitals, religious groups, arts organizations, and the local newspaper.

Research centers affiliated with Omaha-area colleges and universities conduct studies in such fields as cancer, allergies, gerontology, human genetics, and neonatology. The Eppley Institute for Research in Cancer and Allied Diseases, funded by the National Cancer Institute and housed at the University of Nebraska Medical Center, conducts research programs in biochemistry, biology, chemistry, immunology, nutrition, pathology, pharmacology, and virology.

Public Library Information: Omaha Public Library, 215 South Fifteenth Street, Omaha, NE 68102-1004; telephone (402)444-4800

Health Care

The health care industry, which consists of sixteen hospitals, several clinics, and a number of other medical facilities, is one of Omaha's largest employers. The city is a center for medical education and research, with medical schools at Creighton University and the University of Nebraska Medical Center, a dental school, and a number of schools of nursing.

St. Joseph Hospital is the teaching hospital for the Creighton University School of Medicine, specializing in renal dialysis, metabolic research, cardiac diagnosis and treatment, and cancer care. Adjacent to St. Joseph is the Boys Town National Institute for Communication Disorders in Children, a national diagnostic, treatment, and research facility for children with hearing, speech, or learning disorders. The University of Nebraska Hospital and Clinic, the teaching hospital for the University of Nebraska School of Medicine, operates units for pediatric cardiology, cancer therapy, and high-risk newborn care, and a pain rehabilitation institute.

Recreation

Sightseeing

Omaha received national attention when the Hollywood movie "Boys Town," starring Spencer Tracy and Mickey Rooney, was released in 1937. Today Tracy's Academy Award Oscar is on display in the Hall of History Museum on the Boys Town campus. The Hall traces the history of the country's most famous institution for the care of homeless children, presenting exhibits on the history of juvenile delinquency and of social programs designed to address it.

The PhilaMatic Museum exhibits stamp, coin, and currency collections for the hobbyist. General Crook House, a restored Victorian house on the grounds of Ft. Omaha, was the home of General George Crook, head of the Army of the Platte, who gained fame for his testimony in the trial of Chief Running Bear. The Gerald Ford Birthplace, an outdoor park and rose garden, contains a replica of the home where former President Ford was born as well as memorabilia from his White House years.

The Joslyn Art Museum, built in 1931 in honor of business leader George Joslyn, houses a permanent collection emphasizing European, American, and Western art.

The U.S. Air Force Strategic Air Command Museum in nearby Bellevue charts the history of the United States Air Force in indoor and outdoor exhibits; the museum displays thirty vintage and modern airplanes year round. The Henry Doorly Zoo houses more than two-hundred animal species, including rare white Siberian tigers; the zoo's aviary is the largest in the western hemisphere. The recently completed Lied Jungle at the zoo, winner of *Time* magazine's 1992 design award, was described by the magazine as "architecturally stupendous. . .and zoologically thrilling." It features a half-mile maze of trails offering views of exotica such as Malayan tapirs and pygmy hippos in an authentic rain forest atmosphere. The Mutual of Omaha Wild Kingdom wildlife pavilion presents the theme of animal adaptation for survival. Ak-Sar-Ben Aquarium, the only aquarium between Chicago and the West Coast, is open year-round and exhibits fifty species of fresh-water fish.

The Mutual of Omaha Dome exhibits memorabilia from the Mutual of Omaha's "Wild Kingdom" television program; the Dome is an underground facility topped by the largest glass dome of its kind. Completely redesigned, the Union Pacific Historical Museum at the Union Pacific Railroad's headquarters building traces the history of the company's railroad.

North of Omaha the DeSoto Bend National Wildlife Refuge offers opportunities in the spring and fall to view thousands of migrating birds that use the Missouri Valley flyway for their seasonal migration. Fontennel Forest in North Bellevue is a 1,300-acre sylvan area within the city. Peony Park, Nebraska's largest amusement park, combines amusement park rides, shows in an outdoor amphitheater, and the state's largest swimming pool.

Arts and Culture

Omaha Community Playhouse, one of the nation's largest and most recognized community theaters—whose alumni include Henry Fonda and Dorothy McGuire—schedules year-round productions in three performance areas. Main-stage productions as well as studio and experimental theater are presented in what is physically the largest amateur theater facility in the country. Omaha's other theater organizations include Center Stage, which presents African-American musicals and drama; Emmy Gifford Children's Theater, a professional company offering original adaptations of classic children's literature; and Omaha Magic Theater, which concentrates on world premieres and original experimental dramas and musicals. The Firehouse Dinner Theater presents Broadway productions. The Nebraska State Repertory Company performs in nearby Dundee; and at Diner Theater, original drama written by an Omaha native is produced in a real diner.

Omaha Ballet presents four productions a year at the Orpheum Theater; the Omaha Symphony Orchestra plays a season of classical, pop, and chamber music; and Opera Omaha sponsors three productions. The Joslyn Chamber Music Series and the Tuesday Musical Concert Series bring guest chamber ensembles and other artists to the Josyln's concert hall.

The Joslyn Art Museum, built in 1931 in honor of business leader George Joslyn, is an art deco facility on three levels that houses a permanent collection emphasizing European, American, and Western art. The Western Heritage Museum is housed in the restored Union Train depot. The museum charts the city's history from pioneer days to the 1950s and features a vintage soda fountain manned by volunteer soda jerks. The Great Plains Black Museum chronicles the contributions and achievements of African-Americans in the Midwest. Designed for children to interact with the exhibits, the Omaha Children's Museum features art projects that complement the displays. John Raimondi's *Dance of the Cranes* at Eppley Airfield, the largest bronze sculpture in North America, is a five-story fifteen-ton sculpture depicting sandhill cranes in a ritual dance.

Festivals and Holidays

Omaha sponsors festivals and special indoor and outdoor events year round. The major cultural institutions of the city host many of these festivals in honor of the city's heritage. The Food Fair in early February brings one hundred exhibitors to the Civic Auditorium to demonstrate food and food-related products; local and national cooking celebrities attend the two-day event. During the second weekend in February a softball tournament held throughout the city raises money for the March of Dimes. In mid-March Triumph of Agriculture, one of the largest farm equipment shows in the world, draws participants to the Civic Auditorium, where in mid-April the Ethnic Folk Festival presents ethnic food, entertainment, and costumes in colorful displays. The Soda Jerk Reunion, held in mid-May at the Western Heritage Museum's restored soda fountain, is the only soda-jerk reunion in the world.

Nearly two-hundred artists and craftspeople are featured at the Summer Arts Festival, held at the Civic Center in late June. Also in late June the American Sokol Slet and Czechoslovakian Festival is presented at the Civic Auditorium. In August the Offutt Air Force Base open house and air show enjoys the participation of the 55th Strategic Reconnaissance Wing. The Omaha Federation of Labor sponsors Septemberfest in honor of Omaha's working men and women over Labor Day weekend. This is also when La Festa Italiana brings music, dance, and food to a celebration at Peony Park.

The Great Missouri River Raft Regatta is held on September 3. Ak-Sar-Ben Rodeo and Livestock Exposition on the third weekend in September is the world's largest 4-H livestock show; the rodeo attracts the nation's top rodeo competitors. Dickens in the Market takes place the first weekend in December at Old Market and features costumed entertainers performing holiday music and vignettes of Charles Dickens' novels.

Sports for the Spectator

Omaha hosts the National Collegiate Athletic Association College baseball World Series each June at Rosenblatt Stadium. The Omaha Royals, the Triple-A farm team of professional baseball's American League Kansas City Royals, compete in the International League and play their home season at Rosenblatt Stadium. Ak-Sar-Ben has been presenting thoroughbred horseracing since 1927. The recently renovated track operates its season from May to August. A nonprofit organization, Ak-Sar-Ben contributes its proceeds to local and statewide communities. Major races are the Gold Cup, Queen's Handicap, and Cornhusker Handicap. Bluffs Run in Council Bluffs opened in 1986 and offers greyhound dog racing with individual televisions in the clubhouse for viewing each race.

Late-model stock race racing takes place at Sunset Speedway May through October. College sports are played by the Creighton Bluejays and the University of Nebraska at Omaha Mavericks; the Mavericks rank high among the nation's most competitive wresting teams. The Midwest Amateur Golden Gloves Boxing Tournament is held each February in Omaha.

Sports for the Participant

The Omaha Parks and Recreation Department administers more than 7,000 acres of city parks and recreation areas, thirteen neighborhood recreation centers, and various recreational leagues. The most popular is the summer softball program; Omaha claims the title of "Softball Capital of the World." The city boasts more than twenty public and private golf courses, more than twenty-five public and private pools, outdoor and indoor tennis courts, and facilities for hockey and ice skating. Three figure-skating clubs offer instruction. Two downhill skiing facilities operate despite the area's relative flatness.

Shopping and Dining

Omaha's Old Market in its earliest days was a warehouse district where pioneers purchased the goods they needed for the journey to the West. In 1968 Old Market began renovation, first converting to an artists colony; today it is a thriving shopping and restaurant district as well as a fruit and vegetable marketplace. A number of downtown locations have been renovated into malls as part of the revitalization of Omaha's downtown commercial district. Omaha claims the largest retail jewelry store in the United States. Possibly the city's most visited store is the Nebraska Furniture Mart, which records the nation's largest volume of furniture sales.

Some of the best beefsteaks in the world are served in Omaha restaurants; the city is also noted for Continental, French, East Indian, and Creole cuisine. *Food and Wine* magazine named Omaha's Le Cafe de Paris a 1992-1993 Distinguished Restaurant of North America. A local Chinese restaurant replicates Beijing's imperial palace. "Runza," a dough pocket filled with ground beef and cabbage, is a local specialty served at Runza Huts. Godfather's Pizza, one of the largest pizza chains in the country, originated in Omaha.

Visitor Information: Greater Omaha Convention and Visitors Bureau, 1819 Farnam, Suite 1200, Omaha, NE 68183; telephone (402)444-4660 or 1-800-332-1819 (outside Nebraska)

Convention Facilities

Centrally located downtown, within easy access of sightseeing, entertainment, shopping, dining, and lodging, the Omaha Civic Auditorium is a popular site for regional events as well as national conventions, trade shows, and meetings. The main exhibi-

Old Market, formerly a warehouse district where pioneers purchased the goods they needed for the journey to the West, now houses shops and restaurants.

tion hall, with more than seventy-two thousand square feet of space, accommodates up to three-hundred booths and can be partitioned into separate meeting rooms. The multipurpose, twenty-five-thousand-square-foot convention hall, providing space for 176 booths, hosts banquets and large meetings.

The Peter Kiewit Conference Center, located in the new mall area, is operated by the College of Continuing Studies of the University of Nebraska at Omaha. Accommodations include an auditorium with a seating capacity of over 500 people, eighteen meeting rooms for groups of five to 500 people, dining and catering service, and teleconferencing and computer access. Additional convention and meeting facilities are available at two clusters of hotels at 72nd and Grover Streets and 108th and L Streets; some of these offer a selection of meeting rooms for functions involving from thirty-five to eighteen hundred participants.

Convention Information: Greater Omaha Convention and Visitors Bureau, 1919 Farnam, Suite 1200, Omaha, NE 68183; telephone (402)444-4660 or 1-800-444-4660 (outside Nebraska)

Transportation

Approaching the City

The newly expanded terminal at Eppley Airfield, 4 miles northeast of downtown Omaha, is served by eight airlines with direct flights to most major United States cities and connecting flights to points throughout the world. Eppley East, on the east side of the main airfield, and Millard Airport, a reliever facility for Eppley Airfield, receive general aviation traffic.

Principal highway routes providing access to the Omaha metropolitan area are I-80 and I-29; U.S. 6, 30, 75, and 275; and Nebraska 36, 38, 50, 64, 85, 92, 131, 133, and 370.

Traveling in the City

Omaha's streets are arranged in a grid pattern, with Dodge Street dividing the city into north and south sectors. Streets running north-south are numbered; east-west streets are named. Public bus transportation is provided by Metro Area Transit Authority (MAT), which operates routes in Omaha, Council Bluffs, Bellevue, Papillion, Ralston, Boys Town, Carter Lake, La Vista, and Northeast Sarpy County. MAT schedules morning and evening express service; reduced fares for students and elderly and handicapped passengers are available.

Communications

Newspapers and Magazines

Omaha's daily newspaper is the *Omaha World-Herald*. *The Daily Record,* a legal newspaper established in 1886, appears Monday through Friday mornings; the *Midlands Business Journal* is a business-oriented weekly. Several special-interest newspapers and magazines are also published in Omaha. Among them are *American Dane Magazine, The Catholic Voice, Jewish Press, Nebraska Bird Review,* and *Home and Away.*

Television and Radio

Five television stations—three network affiliates, one independent, and one educational channel—broadcast from Omaha; two additional channels are received from Lincoln. Three companies supply cable television service to the metropolitan area. Radio programming that includes a range of musical formats such as rock, classical, jazz, and religious, as well as educational, information, and news features, is provided by thirteen AM and FM stations based in Omaha.

Media Information: Omaha World-Herald, World-Herald Square, Omaha, NE 68102; telephone (402)444-1000

Selected Bibliography

Crary, Margaret, *Susette La Flesche: Voice of the Omaha Indians* (New York: Hawthorn Books, 1973)

Oursler, Fulton, *Father Flanagan of Boys Town,* by Fulton Oursler and Will Oursler (New York: Doubleday, 1949)

NORTH DAKOTA

Fargo 357   Grand Forks..367

The State in Brief

Nickname: Flickertail State; Sioux State; Peace Garden State
Motto: Liberty and Union, now and forever, one and inseparable

Flower: Wild prairie rose
Bird: Western meadowlark

Area: 70,704 square miles (1990; U.S. rank: 19th)
Elevation: Ranges from 750 feet to 3,506 feet above sea level
Climate: Continental, with a wide variety of temperatures; brief, hot summers; winter blizzards; semi-arid in the west and twenty-two inches average rainfall in the east

Admitted to Union: November 2, 1889
Capital: Bismarck
Head Official: Governor Ed Schafer (R) (until 1997)

Population
  1970: 617,792
  1980: 653,000
  1990: 635,000
  Percent change 1980–1990: −2.1%
  U.S. rank in 1990: 47th
  Percent of residents born in state: 74.3% (1990)
  Density: 9.3 people per square mile (1990; U.S. rank: 46th)
1991 FBI Crime Index Total: 17,741

Racial and Ethnic Characteristics (1990)
  White: 94.6%
  Black: 0.6%
  American Indian, Eskimo, Aleut: 4.06%
  Asian and Pacific Islander: 0.54%
  Hispanic origin (may be of any race): 0.73%

Age Characteristics (1990)
  Population under 5 years old: 46,000
  Population 5 to 17 years old: 127,000
  Percent of population 65 years and older: 14.5%
  Median age: 32.9 years
  Voting-age population (1988): 484,000 (61.4% of whom cast votes for president)

Vital Statistics
  Total number of births (1992): 8,935
  Total number of deaths (1992): 5,797 (of which, 70 were infants under the age of 1 year)
  AIDS cases reported, 1981–1990: 20 (U.S. rank: 49th)

Economy
  Major industries: Agriculture, manufacturing, mining
  Unemployment rate: 4.4% (September 1992)
  Per capita income: $11,051 (1989)
  Median household income: $23,213 (1989)
  Total number of families: 168,023 (8.0% of which had incomes below the poverty level) (1989)
  Income tax rate: 14.0% of total federal tax liability
  Sales tax rate: 5.0%

Fargo

The City in Brief

Founded: 1871 (incorporated 1875)

Head Official: Mayor Jon Lindgren (D) (since 1978)

City Population
 1970: 53,365
 1980: 61,383
 1990: 74,111
 Percent change, 1980–1990: 20.7%
 U.S. rank in 1980: 329th
 U.S. rank in 1990: 297th

Metropolitan Area Population
 1970: 120,261
 1980: 137,574
 1990: 153,296
 Percent change, 1980–1990: 11.4%
 U.S. rank in 1980: Not available
 U.S. rank in 1990: Not available

Area: 29.8 square miles (1990)

Elevation: 970 feet above sea level

Average Annual Temperature: 40.5° F

Average Annual Precipitation: 19.59 inches (20 inches of rain and 35 inches of snow annually)

Major Economic Sectors: Wholesale and retail trade, services, government

Unemployment Rate: 3.0% (September 1992)

Per Capita Income: $13,554 (1989)

1992 (2nd Quarter) ACCRA Average House Price: Not reported ($118,000 in Minot, ND)

1992 (2nd Quarter) ACCRA Cost of Living Index: 93.6 (U.S. average = 100.0)

1991 FBI Crime Index Total: Not reported

Major Colleges and Universities: North Dakota State University

Daily Newspaper: *The Forum*

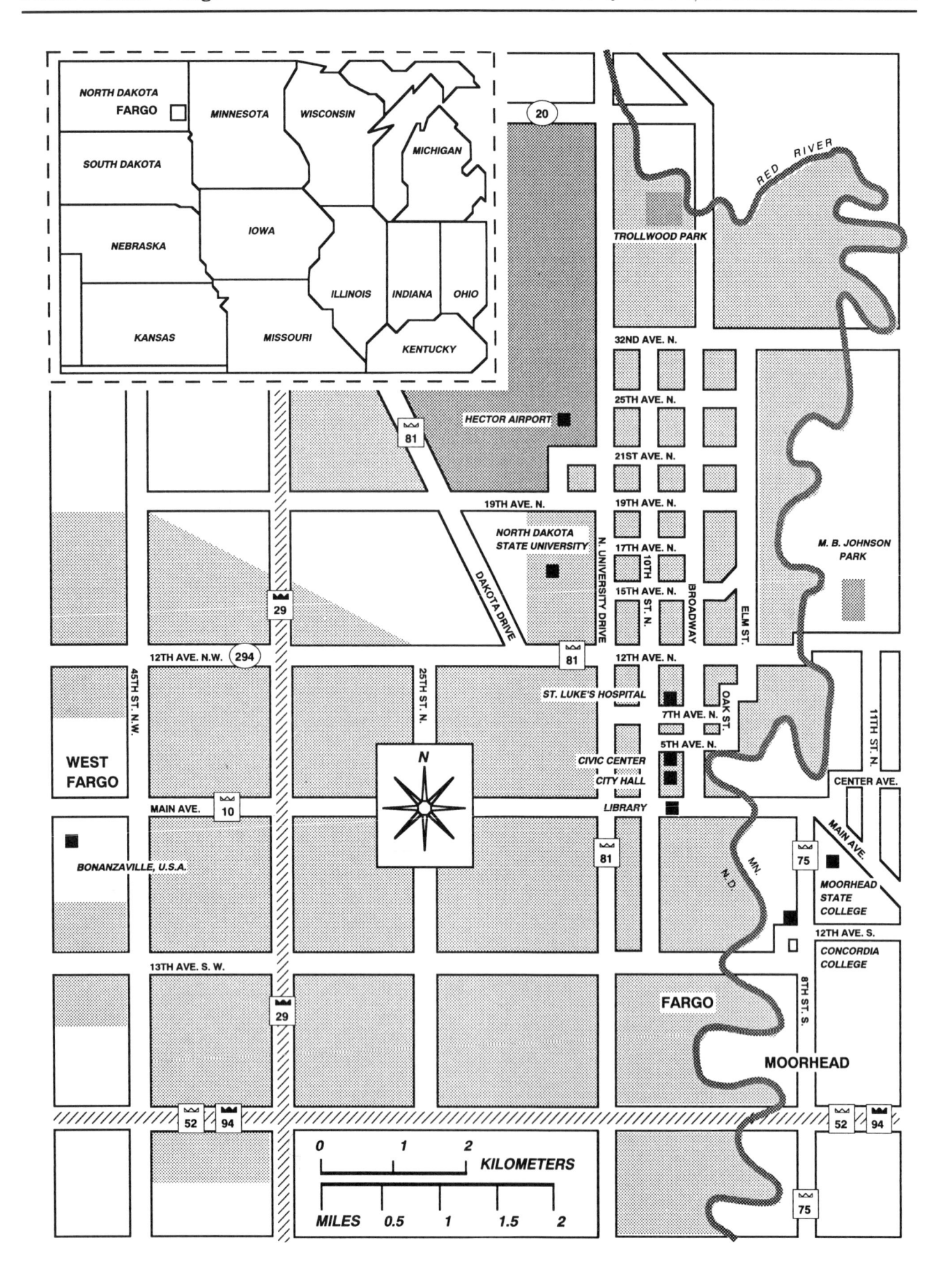

North Dakota—Fargo *Cities of the United States • 2nd Edition*

Introduction

Fargo is the largest city in North Dakota and the seat of Cass County. It is the focus of a metropolitan statistical area that extends over Cass County, North Dakota, and Clay County, Minnesota, where Fargo's sister city, Moorhead, is located. Founded by the Northern Pacific Railway, the city was an important transportation and marketing point for the surrounding fertile wheat-growing region. Today it is an agribusiness and agricultural research center. *Money Magazine* selected Fargo as the nation's fifth most livable city in 1992, noting that it was a safe city and a "booming regional center for health care and financial services." The city was declared a "Great Plains success story, with locally grown high-tech firms and a state university" by *Kiplinger's Personal Finance Magazine* in 1991.

Geography and Climate

Flat and open terrain surrounds Fargo, which is situated on the eastern boundary of North Dakota opposite Moorhead, Minnesota, in the Red River Valley of the North. The Red River, part of the Hudson Bay drainage area, flows north between the two cities.

Precipitation is Fargo's most significant climatic feature, since the valley lies in an area where lighter amounts fall to the west and heavier amounts to the east. Seventy-five percent of the precipitation, accompanied by electrical storms and heavy rainfall in a short period of time, occurs during the growing season, April to September. Summers are comfortable, with low humidity, warm days, and cool nights. Winters are cold and dry, the temperatures remaining at zero or below approximately half of the time; snowfall is generally light. The legendary Dakota blizzards result from drifting of even minimal snowfall, caused by strong winds that blow unimpeded across the flat terrain.

Area: 29.8 square miles (1990)

Elevation: 970 feet above sea level

Average Temperatures: January, 4.3° F; July, 70.6° F; annual average, 40.5° F

Average Annual Precipitation: 19.59 inches (20 inches of rain and 35 inches of snow annually)

History

Railroad Route Creates Townsite

The city of Fargo was founded by the Northern Pacific Railway in 1871 in expectation of the railroad track to be built across the Red River of the North. This particular location was selected as a safeguard against flooding because it represented the highest point on the river. The city was named for William G. Fargo, founder of the Wells-Fargo Express Company and a director of the Northern Pacific Railway. When the railroad announced in 1871 that a track would be laid from Lake Superior to the Pacific Ocean, land speculators sought to capitalize on the opportunity. Thus ensued attempts on the part of both the railroad and the speculators to outwit one another and to gain first possession of the land. For a time the railroad staked a claim but after much litigation decided to withdraw.

During the winter of 1871 to 1872, the settlement was divided into two distinct communities. One of them, "Fargo on the Prairie," became headquarters of the Northern Pacific engineers and their families. Although they lived in tents, the accommodations were the best available given the conditions. The other, "Fargo in the Timber," was much cruder and more primitive, consisting of huts, log houses, dugouts, and riverbank caves. The Timber community became known for its hard-drinking, gun-carrying men who had a rough sense of humor and enjoyed practical jokes. A delivery of potatoes to the Prairie community was once sabotaged by the Timber men who loosened the wagon endgates and shot their guns to scare the horses. The potatoes that spilled onto the ground turned out to be the only supply available for the winter.

Fargo was located in what was still legally native American territory, and the railroad company claimed the Timber residents were illegal squatters on native American land and were selling illegal liquor. In February of 1872, federal troops surrounded the Timber settlement, issuing warrants for the arrest of those accused of selling liquor and ordering the others to leave under threat of destruction of their crude homes. The settlers appealed to the government, claiming their land rights had been violated. A treaty was negotiated with the native tribes that opened the land to settlement and those who had not broken the law were able to retain their land.

Agricultural Prosperity Survives Disasters

Law and order followed with the arrival of new settlers on the first train of the Northern Pacific to cross the Red River on June of 1872. Soon residents were surprised to learn that Fargo was situated on rich wheat land. With the reduction of freight rates in 1873, farming became economically profitable and the town prospered. Two decades later Fargo suffered a severe fire, which began on one of the main streets and consumed the entire business district as well as the northwestern sector. This tragedy led to many civic improvements and put an end to wood construction.

Near disaster struck again four years later, when the Red River, dammed by ice north of Fargo, began rising. It continued to rise for a week; in order to save the railroad bridges, locomotive and threshing machines were placed on them. Citizens were forced to evacuate through second-story windows, and the flood carried away eighteen blocks of sidewalk and twenty blocks of wooden street paving.

During the first thirty years of the twentieth century, Fargo prospered from an influx of Norwegian immigrants who were attracted by the promise of a better life and a free farm. Fleeing economic depression in their own country, they introduced their customs to the upper Red River Valley, thus helping to shape the character of present-day Fargo. The city remains an important agricultural center as well as a regional distribution and transportation hub.

Historical Information: Cass County Historical Society, P.O. Box 719, West Fargo, ND 58078; telephone (701)282-2822

Population Profile

Metropolitan Area Residents
1970: 120,261
1980: 137,574
1990: 153,296
Percent change, 1980–1990: 11.4%
U.S. rank in 1980: Not available
U.S. rank in 1990: Not available

City Residents
1970: 53,365
1980: 61,383
1990: 74,111 (of which, 36,786 were males and 37,325 were females)
Percent change, 1980–1990: 20.7%
U.S. rank in 1980: 329th
U.S. rank in 1990: 297th (State rank: 1st)

Density: 2,486.9 people per square mile (1990)

Racial and ethnic characteristics (1990)
  White: 97.1%
  Black: 0.4%
  American Indian, Eskimo, Aleut: 1.1%
  Asian and Pacific Islander: 1.3%
  Hispanic (may be of any race): 0.7%

Percent of residents born in state: 60.0%

Age characteristics (1990)
  Population under 5 years old: 5,241
  Population 5 to 9 years old: 4,904
  Population 10 to 14 years old: 4,165
  Population 15 to 19 years old: 5,391
  Population 20 to 24 years old: 10,417
  Population 25 to 29 years old: 7,843
  Population 30 to 34 years old: 7,023
  Population 35 to 39 years old: 6,087
  Population 40 to 44 years old: 4,734
  Population 45 to 49 years old: 3,213
  Population 50 to 54 years old: 2,651
  Population 55 to 59 years old: 2,545
  Population 60 to 64 years old: 2,442
  Population 65 to 69 years old: 2,149
  Population 70 to 74 years old: 1,729
  Population 75 to 79 years old: 1,406
  Population 80 to 84 years old: 1,078
  Population 85 years and over: 1,093
  Median age: 29.4 years

Births (1988)
  Total number: 1,060

Deaths (1989)
  Total number: 492 (of which, 13 were infants under the age of 1 year)

Money income (1989)
  Per capita income: $13,554
  Median household income: $25,326
  Total households: 30,340
  Number of households with income of . . .
    less than $5,000: 1,866
    $5,000 to $9,999: 3,516
    $10,000 to $14,999: 3,365
    $15,000 to $24,999: 6,243
    $25,000 to $34,999: 5,249
    $35,000 to $49,999: 4,997
    $50,000 to $74,999: 3,314
    $75,000 to $99,999: 911
    $100,000 to $149,999: 519
    $150,000 or more: 360
  Percent of families below poverty level: 7.9% (59.5% of which were female householder families with related children under 5)
1991 FBI Crime Index Total: Not reported

Municipal Government

Fargo, the seat of Cass County, is governed by a city commission comprised of five at-large members, one of whom serves as mayor. Commissioners are elected to a four-year term. After 1992, all commissioners and mayors are subject to a limit of three consecutive terms.

Head Official: Mayor Jon G. Lindgren (D) (since 1978; current term expires May 1994)

Total Number of City Employees: 485 (1991)

City Information: City Commission, 200 Third Street North, Fargo, ND 58102; telephone (701)241-1310

Economy

Major Industries and Commercial Activity

The Fargo economy is based on education, the medical industry, agricultural equipment manufacturing, retailing, and services. Because of its central location, the city is a transportation hub for the northern Midwest region. Agriculture has long been of primary importance to Fargo, as the Red River Valley area contains some of the richest farmland in the world; related industries include agribusiness and agricultural research.

The principal manufacturing employer is Case I H, makers of heavy-duty tractors. Terminals for two oil pipeline systems—Standard Oil Company of Indiana and Great Lakes Pipeline Company of Oklahoma— are located in Fargo-Moorhead. The Standard Oil pipeline is connected with the company's refinery in Whiting, Indiana, which produces more than thirty thousand barrels of oil a day.

Items and goods produced: food, concrete, dairy and meat products, fur coats, jewelry, luggage, neon signs, electrical apparatus, sweet clover and sunflower seeds

Incentive Programs—New and Existing Companies

A forum for agricultural customers, commodity traders, technical experts, and processors and producers, the Northern Crops Institute (NCI) on the North Dakota State University campus provides short courses and seminars designed to promote crops grown in the northern plains region. NCI is funded by North Dakota, South Dakota, and Minnesota state governments as well as private corporations; it is administered by a council consisting of thirteen members representing government, education, and private industry. Since its inception in 1980, NCI has developed a worldwide market for regional crops by hosting participants and delegations from forty foreign countries.

New business and industry are actively promoted in Fargo through programs administered by lending institutions and local and state government. Two major industrial parks provide facilities with easy access to utilities and transportation networks; industrial sites and buildings are also available throughout the city and county.

Expansion of business and industry in Fargo is encouraged by a variety of programs, including the Job Partnership Act, Targeted Job Credit, the North Dakota Municipal Industrial Development Act, the Small Business Administration 504 Loan Program, and the Bank of North Dakota Risk Capital Program. The state of North Dakota and the city of Fargo also offer property tax and income tax exemptions.

Economic Development Information: Fargo-Cass County Economic Development Corporation, 471 Main Avenue, Fargo, ND 58103; telephone (701)237-6132

Commercial Shipping

Fargo is served by the Burlington Northern Railroad, which maintains a facility for daily switching and container loading and unloading. More than forty motor freight carriers transport goods to and from Fargo.

Labor Force and Employment Outlook

Kiplinger's Personal Finance Magazine placed Fargo on its 1991 list of the top fifteen cities in the country for job growth and livability.

The following is a summary of data regarding the Fargo metropolitan area labor force as of September 1992.

Size of non-agricultural labor force: 82,100

Number of workers employed in . . .
  mining: not reported
  construction: 4,400
  manufacturing: 6,200
  transportation and public utilities: 4,600
  wholesale and retail trade: 24,300
  finance, insurance, and real estate: 5,100
  services: 22,500
  government: 15,000

Average hourly earnings of production workers employed in manufacturing: $8.88 (September 1992)

Unemployment rate: 3.0% (September 1992)

Largest employers	Number of employees
North Dakota State University	3,500
Fargo Public School District #1	1,635
St. Luke's Hospital	1,450
Fargo Clinic	1,300
Dakota Hospital	969
Northern Improvement Co.	700

Cost of Living

The following is a summary of data regarding several key cost of living factors in the Fargo area.

1992 (2nd Quarter) ACCRA Cost of Living Index: 93.6 (U.S. average = 100.0)

1992 (2nd Quarter) ACCRA Average House Price: Not available ($118,000 in Minot, ND)

State income tax rate: 14.0% of federal tax liability

State sales tax rate: 5.0%

Local income tax rate: None

Local sales tax rate: 1.0% (3.0% lodging tax)

Property tax rate: 414.92 mills total; city share, 61.92 mills (1.6% of estimated value)

Economic Information: Fargo-Cass County Economic Development Corp., 417 Main Avenue, Fargo, ND 58103; telephone (701)237-6132

Education and Research

Elementary and Secondary Schools

Public elementary and secondary schools in Fargo are part of Fargo Public School District #1. A superintendent is appointed by a nine-member, nonpartisan school board.

The following is a summary of data regarding Fargo public schools as of the 1992-1993 school year.

Total enrollment: 10,885

Number of facilities
  elementary schools: 13
  junior high schools: 2
  senior high schools: 3

Student/teacher ratio: 25:1

Teacher salaries
  minimum: $19,829
  maximum: $40,307

Funding per pupil: $4,008

Parochial schools, kindergarten through high school, are operated by the Catholic and Lutheran churches in Fargo.

Public Schools Information: Fargo Public Schools, 1104 Second Avenue South, Fargo, ND 58103; telephone (701)241-4868

Colleges and Universities

The Fargo-Moorhead community is served by three universities as well as several vocational schools. North Dakota State University in Fargo, with an enrollment of more than nine-thousand students, awards baccalaureate, master's, and doctorate degrees in a wide range of disciplines; colleges within the university are humanities and social sciences, agriculture, engineering and architecture, home economics, pharmacy, science and mathematics, and teacher education. Located on the university campus is Tri-College University, a consortium of area colleges and universities. Technical schools in Fargo include Interstate Business College and Dakota Aero Tech. Concordia College, Moorhead State University, and Moorhead Technical College are located in Moorhead.

Libraries and Research Centers

The Fargo Public Library maintains holdings that include more than 146,000 volumes along with periodicals, films, tapes, records, and art reproductions. A depository for state documents, the library operates a bookmobile and offers reciprocal borrowing with Moorhead and West Fargo. The North Dakota State University Library houses more than 437,000 books, nearly twenty-three hundred periodicals, and microfilm, records, tapes, slides, and maps. Special collections include bonanza farming, the North Dakota Biography Index, North Dakota Pioneer Reminiscences, and the North Dakota Historical Manuscript, Photograph and Book Collection; the library is also a depository for federal and state documents. Specialized libraries in the city are affiliated with hospitals, fraternal societies, and religious organizations.

Completed in 1988 on the North Dakota State University campus, the Northern Crop Science Laboratory is a division of the Agricultural Research Service of the United States Department of Agriculture. Government and university scientists conduct cooperative research on barley, hard red spring wheat, durum wheat, flax, sunflowers, and sugar beets; the goal is to expand and retain profitable production of these crops through the use of the most advanced equipment and research techniques.

Public Library Information: Fargo Public Library, 102 North Third Street, Fargo, ND 58102-4808; telephone (701) 241-1490

Health Care

Fargo, the primary health care center for the region between Minnesota and the West Coast, is served by eight hospitals, thirty-one medical clinics, and seventeen nursing homes and retirement living facilities. Among the larger care facilities are St. Luke's Hospital, Dakota Medical Center, and Fargo Clinic. The medical community includes 409 physicians, over ninety dentists, over thirty-two chiropractors, and over twenty-one optometrists.

Recreation

Sightseeing

Bonanzaville, USA, is a recreated pioneer village of forty-five restored buildings on a 15-acre site; the structures were relocated from a number of small North Dakota towns and represent various types of architecture. Included among them are a drugstore, general store, sod and farm houses, district courtroom, and barber shop. Vintage automobiles, farm machinery, and airplanes are also on exhibit. The Red River and Northern Plain Regional Museum houses one of the largest and most complete Plains Indians collections. The center of attraction at Moorhead's Heritage Hjemkomst Interpretive Center is the sailing ship the late Robert Asp of Moorhead modelled after ancient Viking vessels. Housed in an architecturally distinctive building that also includes the Clay County Historical Museum, the ship made a journey from Duluth, Minnesota, to Bergen, Norway, in 1982.

The Solomon G. Comstock Historic House in Moorhead is the former home of this prominent Fargo-Moorhead figure who was a financier and political and cultural force in the community. The authentically restored Victorian house contains its original furnishings. The Roger Maris Museum in the West Acres Shopping Center pays tribute to the city's most famous athlete, who broke Babe Ruth's single-season home run record in 1961 when he hit sixty-one home runs. Maris donated all of his trophies and sports memorabilia to the museum as a tribute to the city in which he grew up. The Children's Museum at Yunker Farm, a century-old farm house, presents participatory learning exhibits in the physical, natural, and social sciences. At Moorhead State University the planetarium and the Regional Science Center, an outdoor lab for science education, present public programs.

Arts and Culture

The Fargo Theatre, a landmark movie theater built in 1926 in the art moderne style, has been fully restored and is the site of film showings as well as live theater, music, and dance performances. On weekends, the Mighty Wurlitzer organ performs before each show at the theater. The Fargo-Moorhead Community Theater stages six annual productions at the Emma K. Herbst Playhouse in Island Park. Other local performing groups are the Fargo-Moorhead Symphony Orchestra, the Fargo-Moorhead Civic Opera, Red River Dance and Performing Company, and Straw Hat Players. IMAGINE youth theater is housed at the 27-acre Trollwood Culture and Arts Park.

The Plains Art Museum in Moorhead's former post office contains more than 1,500 objects in its permanent collection of regional art and historically valuable art objects. The museum's exhibits showcase the work of artists with local and regional roots and contemporary Native American art.

Arts and Culture Information: Lake Agassiz Arts Council, telephone (701)237-6133

Festivals and Holidays

On weekends in mid-July the Red River Valley Fair in downtown Fargo features the works of artisans and craftsmen. Bonanzaville, U.S.A., holds Pioneer Days in August, when more than one-hundred demonstrators revive the skills and crafts of the past; it also hosts Christmas on the Prairie. Threshermen's Hill at Rollag, Minnesota, holds the annual Western Minnesota Steam Threshers Reunion over Labor Day weekend. The Big Iron agricultural exposition fills the Red River Valley Fairgrounds on the second weekend in September, bringing the latest farm products and services from four hundred agribusiness exhibitors. The annual winter festival celebration is held for ten days in the middle of February.

Sports for the Spectator

The Fargo-Moorhead Fever, a College Basketball Association team, debuted in 1992. The North Dakota State University Bison, six-time winners of the National Collegiate Athletic Association (NCAA) Division II national championship, the Moorhead State University Dragons, and the Concordia College Cobbers present a complete schedule of men's and women's major and minor sports. Fargo, Moorhead, and West Fargo field competitive American League baseball teams. Red River Valley Fair Association presents stock car racing.

Sports for the Participant

The Fargo Park District sponsors an extensive program of sports for all age groups. League and tournament competition as well as beginning classes are available. Winter sports are particularly popular with ice skating, figure skating, and youth and adult hockey available at both indoor and outdoor facilities; outdoor rinks are equipped with warming houses. Other recreational pursuits include volleyball, basketball, track, soccer, walking, cross-country skiing, ballroom dancing, table tennis, and broom ball. Two private and seven public golf courses are located in the Fargo-Moorhead area, including four tree-shaded courses next to the meandering Red River of the North.

Charitable and cultural organization sponsor gaming operations at forty-five casinos in Fargo-Moorhead's public establishments. Profits benefit the programs of the sponsoring organizations, and fraternal groups allocate profits to public causes. Games include blackjack, paper slot machines, bingo, and tri-wheel.

Shopping and Dining

Fargo is home to sixteen shopping centers and one of the largest malls between Minneapolis and the West Coast. Dining in historic settings is offered at Runck Chateau Ranch, a working cattle ranch, and at The White House, District 31—Victoria's, and The Conservatory.

Visitor Information: Greater Fargo-Moorhead Convention and Visitors Bureau, 701 Main Avenue, Box 2164, Fargo, ND 58107; telephone (701)237-6134

Convention Facilities

Fargo's newest convention/multipurpose facility, the $48 million FargoDome, opened in 1993. FargoDome seats up to 19,300 people; its eighty-thousand square feet make it the largest contiguous exhibit hall space in the state.

Constructed in 1960, the Fargo Civic Memorial Auditorium hosts a variety of events, including state

Sodbuster, created by Luis Jimenez for the city of Fargo, was presented by its citizens to the Plains Art Museum. It symbolizes the heritage of the Plains homesteader and traditional farmer.

political conventions, concerts, trade exhibitions, sporting events, and business gatherings. The eleven-thousand-square-foot arena accommodates up to 3,333 persons for sports events and concerts and 1,200 people in a banquet setting. The exhibition hall, measuring forty feet by one-hundred fifty feet, seats 600 people for both theater-style and banquet functions; the hall can be divided into four rooms for private meetings.

The Red River Valley Fairgrounds offers facilities for agricultural expositions, trade shows, conventions, and entertainment. A number of the area's twenty-eight hotels and motels maintain meeting and banquet rooms accommodating from 10 to 1500 participants; among the largest facilities are the Holiday Inn and Doublewood Inn in Fargo.

Convention Information: Greater Fargo-Moorhead Convention and Visitors Bureau, Box 2164, Fargo, ND 58107; telephone (701)237-6134; and, F. Roger Newton, Executive Director, FargoDome, P.O. Box 226, Fargo, ND 58107-0226; telephone (701)237-5198

Transportation

Approaching the City

Hector International Airport is situated ten minutes northwest of downtown Fargo. Three major airlines schedule daily flights; regular commuter service is available between Fargo and Minneapolis-St. Paul, Minnesota. Rail transportation is provided by Amtrak and bus transportation by Greyhound.

Highways serving metropolitan Fargo include I-94, extending east to west through the south sector of the city, and I-29, which runs north to south and intersects I-94. This is the only intersection of two interstate highways between western Montana and Sault Sainte Marie, Michigan. U.S. 10 and 52 are east-west routes, and U.S. 81 extends through the city from north to south. State routes serving Fargo are 20 and 294, both running east to west.

Traveling in the City

Except for streets following the configuration of the Red River, Fargo is laid out on a grid pattern. The city is divided into quadrants; roadways running north to south are designated "street," while those running east to west are labelled "avenue." First Avenue and Main Avenue are major thoroughfares crossing the river to connect Fargo with Moorhead, Minnesota.

Public bus transportation in Fargo-Moorhead is provided by Metropolitan Area Transit (MAT). A small fee is charged for transfers between Fargo and Moorhead. Senior citizens, handicapped persons, and students pay reduced fares.

Communications

Newspapers and Magazines

Fargo's daily newspaper is *The Forum*. Other newspapers include *The New Earth*, a Catholic Diocese publication, and *Spectrum*, a bi-weekly North Dakota State University student tabloid. *The Area Woman* is a free quarterly magazine.

Television and Radio

Five television stations—three commercial, one public, and one independent—broadcast in Fargo, and cable service is available. Eleven AM and FM radio stations, three of them based in the city, schedule a variety of programming.

Media Information: The Fargo Forum, Forum Publishing Company, Box 2020, Fargo, ND 58107; telephone (701)235-7311

Grand Forks

The City in Brief

Founded: 1875

Head Official: Mayor Michael Polovitz (D) (since 1988)

City Population
 1970: 39,008
 1980: 43,765
 1990: 49,425
 Percent change, 1980–1990: 12.9%
 U.S. rank in 1980: Not available
 U.S. rank in 1990: 511th (State rank: 2nd)

Metropolitan Area Population
 1970: Not available
 1980: 66,100
 1990: 70,683
 Percent change, 1980–1990: 6.9%
 U.S. rank in 1980: 280th
 U.S. rank in 1990: 279th

Area: 14.4 square miles (1990)

Elevation: 885 feet above sea level

Average Annual Temperature: 41.3° F

Average Annual Precipitation: 20.02 inches

Major Economic Sectors: Trade, government, services

Unemployment Rate: 3.0% (September 1992)

Per Capita Income: $11,902 (1989)

1992 (2nd Quarter) ACCRA Average House Price: Not reported

1992 (2nd Quarter) ACCRA Cost of Living Index: Not reported

1991 FBI Crime Index Total: 2,594

Major Colleges and Universities: University of North Dakota

Daily Newspaper: *Grand Forks Herald*

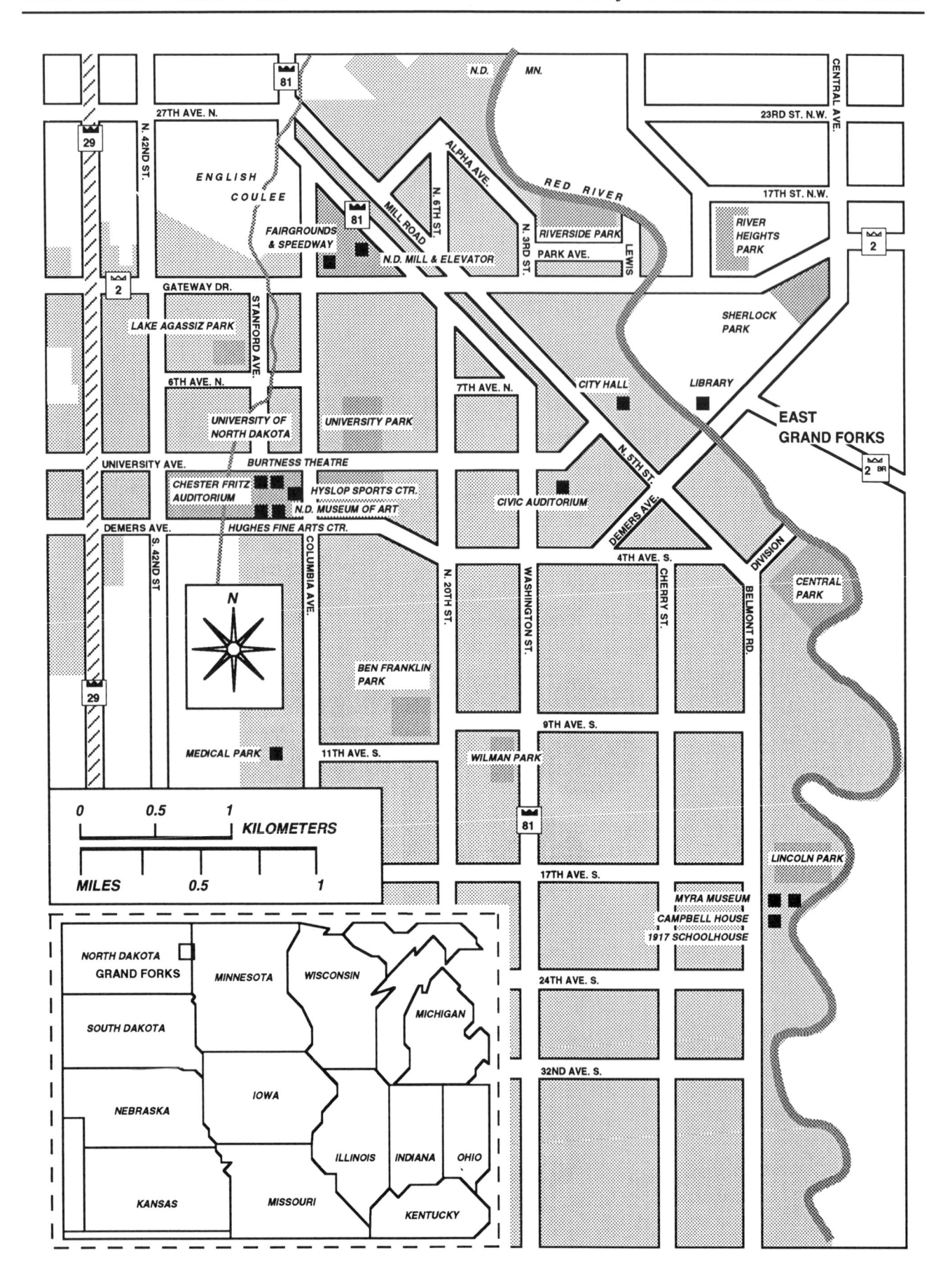

North Dakota—Grand Forks · Cities of the United States • 2nd Edition

Introduction

Since the 1870s when the juncture of the Red River of the North and the Red Lake River became a crossroads for people and their river-oriented business, the cities of Grand Forks and East Grand Forks have been a focal point of trade and services between the plains of North Dakota and the pine forests of northern Minnesota. Located 75 miles south of the Canadian border, the city is centered in one of the world's richest agricultural regions. The business community is deeply rooted in agriculture and its related enterprises. Today more than 300,000 people in an eighteen-county area come to Greater Grand Forks for the commercial, recreational, and cultural services it has to offer, which include nearly forty arts organizations. The city is headquarters for a major university and boasts a key military installation which has an important economic impact on the local economy.

Geography and Climate

Flat and open terrain surrounds Grand Forks, which is just 75 miles south of the Canadian border, and situated on the western boundary of the Red River Valley of the North. Seventy-five percent of the precipitation accompanied by electrical storms and heavy rainfall in a short period of time occurs during the growing season, April through September. Summers are comfortable with low humidity, warm days and cool nights. Winters are cold and dry with temperatures remaining at zero or below approximately half the time. Snowfall is generally light. The legendary Dakota blizzards result from drifting of even minimal snowfall caused by strong winds that blow unimpeded across the flat terrain.

Area: 14.4 square miles (1990)

Elevation: 885 feet above sea level

Average Temperatures: January, 4.2° F; July, 69.2° F; annual average, 41.3° F

Average Annual Precipitation: 20.02 inches

History

Railroads Stimulate Growth of City

Located at the junction of the Red Lake River and the Red River of the North, the area of Grand Forks served as a camping and trading site for native American for centuries. French, British, and American fur traders peddled their wares in and around "La Grand Fourches," as the French named it, meaning "the great forks."

In the 1850s, furs and trade goods passed through the Forks on oxcarts enroute between Winnipeg, Canada, and St. Paul, Minnesota. Steamboats replaced oxcarts in 1859. The shallow-draft steamboats could operate in less than three feet of water as they negotiated the Red River from Fargo to Winnipeg. Alexander Griggs, an experienced Mississippi River steamboat captain, established the town site of Grand Forks in 1870. Griggs teamed up with James J. Hill in the Red River Transportation Line of steamboats in the 1870s.

Grand Forks really began to grow after James J. Hill's Great Northern Railroad came to town in 1880. The Northern Pacific Railroad also built tracks to the city in 1882 and business boomed. Early arrivals who stayed in the region were mostly of northern European background including Scandinavian, German, and Polish immigrants.

Wheat and Lumber Anchor Economy

Wheat farming served as the basis of the Red River Valley prosperity. In 1893 Frank Amidon, chief miller at the Diamond Mills in Grand Forks, invented "Cream of Wheat." George Clifford, George Bull, and Emery Mapes financed the new breakfast porridge venture, and the city became a part of a national breakfast legend.

From the 1880s to 1910, pine logs were floated down the Red Lake River or brought in by rail to sawmills in the city. Many houses in Grand Forks were built of the majestic white pines from the vast forests of northern Minnesota. The University of North Dakota, founded in 1883, became the premier liberal arts institution in the state. The city grew from the river toward the college campus to the west. The Metropolitan Theatre opened in 1890 and for the next twenty-five years it presented quality productions of music and drama. During the period of the "Gilded Age" at the end of the last century, spacious and elegant houses were built along historic Reeves Drive and South Sixth Street for the local elite.

By 1900, Grand Forks had a population of almost 10,000 people. The wealth from the lumber companies, wheat farms, and railroads enabled the community to take its place as a leading city of the "Great Northwest." After his arrival in the early 1880s, local architect Jon W. Ross designed many of the area's most beautiful buildings. In 1902, Joseph Bell Deremer, trained at Columbia University, began to make his mark upon the community through the new buildings he designed.

The North Dakota Mill and Elevator, the only state-owned flour mill in the country, opened in 1923. The mill allowed North Dakota farmers to bypass Minneapolis-based railroads and milling monopolies. The mill distributed free flour to needy people during the Great Depression of the 1930s. Even today, the mill sends its trademark flour "Dakota Maid" around the world.

Grand Forks grew as a regional trade center in the twentieth century.

Historical Information: Grand Forks County Historical Society, 2405 Belmont Road, Grand Forks, ND 58201; telephone (701)775-2216

Population Profile

Metropolitan Area Residents
  1970: Not available
  1980: 66,100
  1990: 70,683
  Percent change, 1980–1990: 6.9%
  U.S. rank in 1980: 280th
  U.S. rank in 1990: 279th

City Residents
  1970: 39,008
  1980: 43,765
  1990: 49,425 (of which, 24,690 were females and 24,735 were males)
  Percent change, 1980–1990: 12.9%
  U.S. rank in 1980: Not available
  U.S. rank in 1990: 511th (State rank: 2nd)

Density: 3,432.3 per square mile (1990)

Racial and ethnic characteristics (1990)
  White: 47,194
  Black: 395
  American Indian, Eskimo, Aleut: 1,115
  Asian and Pacific Islander: 529
  Hispanic (may be of any race): 586
  Other: 192

Percent of residents born in state: 64.1% (1990)

Age characteristics (1990)
  Population under 5 years old: 3,625
  Population 5 to 17 years old: 7,901
  Population 18 to 20 years old: 5,109
  Population 21 to 24 years old: 5,786
  Population 25 to 44 years old: 15,740
  Population 45 to 54 years old: 3,743
  Population 55 to 59 years old: 1,531
  Population 60 to 64 years old: 1,465
  Population 65 to 74 years old: 2,404
  Population 75 to 84 years old: 1,488
  Population 85 years and older: 633
  Median age: 27.3 years

Births (1988)
  Total number: 711

Deaths (1988)
  Total number: 299 (12 of which were infants under the age of 1 year)

Money income (1989)
  Per capita income: $11,902 (1989)
  Median household income: $25,456
  Total households: 18,646
  Number of households with income of . . .
    less than $5,000: 1,460
    $5,000 to $9,999: 2,119
    $10,000 to $14,999: 2,024
    $15,000 to $24,999: 3,534
    $25,000 to $34,999: 3,469
    $35,000 to $49,999: 3,193
    $50,000 to $74,999: 2,055
    $75,000 to $99,999: 425
    $100,000 to $149,999: 249
    $150,000 or more: 118
  Percent of families below poverty level: 9.9% (72.6% of which were female householder families with related children under 5)
1991 FBI Crime Index Total: 2,594

Municipal Government

Grand Forks has a mayor-council form of government.

Head Official: Mayor Michael Polovitz (D) (since 1988; current term expires April 1996)

Total Number of City Employees: 385 (1992)

City Information: City of Grand Forks, 122 South Fifth Street, P.O. Box 1518, Grand Forks, ND 58206-1518; telephone (701) 746-2616

Economy

Major Industries and Commercial Activity

Grand Forks has a stable, agriculturally-based economy which has been expanding and diversifying since the early 1980s. Abundant moisture assists the growth of the hard spring wheat, corn, oats, sunflowers, durum, barley, potatoes, sugar beets, dry edible beans, and soybeans that represent its major crops, and in all its years of existence there has never been a crop failure. Cattle, sheep and hogs also contribute to the local farm economy. Plants operate for the processing of potatoes, for the conversion of locally grown mustard seed for table and commercial use, for the refining of beets into sugar, and for the pearling of barley. Much of the area's durham wheat is marketed through the North Dakota State Mill and Elevator.

While in the early 1980s almost all businesses were agriculturally based, other enterprises such as high-technology firms, a wood products company, and concrete firms now play an important role in the local economy. Some important local firms include: J. R. Simplot, which processes potatoes and other foods; American Woods, a relatively new company that produces outdoor lawn furniture; Strata Corporation, which produces ready-mix concrete and handles asphalt and masonry; the American Crystal Sugar refinery; Young Manufacturing, which custom designs, engineers, and manufactures metal products; Energy Research Center, which conducts research on energy-related products; and R. D. O., which deals in processed foods. In the 1990s, a new Grand Forks growth fund has distributed $2.7 million to twelve businesses that created five hundred new jobs and over $6 million in new payroll.

Due to the U.S.-Canada free trade agreement, North Dakota exports have nearly doubled from $128 million in 1988 to $246 million in 1990. Canadian tourism contributed $85.3 million to the Grand Forks economy in 1990.

The University of North Dakota (UND) is a major contributor to the city's economic life as well as its cultural and entertainment life. UND is the second largest employer in the state.

Grand Forks U.S. Air Force Base, which is in danger of being closed or severely reduced by government cutbacks, is a major employer, with an annual civilian labor force of more than 600 people and an annual payroll of more than $135 million.

Items and goods produced: farm crops, fertilizer, chemicals, seeds, wood products, metal products, concrete, computer software

Incentive Programs—New and Existing Companies

Local Programs—New businesses may negotiate with the city or county of Grand Forks for up to five years full or partial exemption from local real property taxes and state income taxes. The Growth Fund, the portion of the sales tax revenue set aside for economic development purposes, provides gap and incentive financing for new or expanding businesses which have the capacity to create new primary sector jobs and to contribute to the local tax base. The city and/or county is authorized to issue either general obligations and/or revenue bonds.

State Programs—If a new business does not take advantage of the local tax exemption described above, it alternatively may claim a state income tax credit equivalent to 1 percent of the firm's expenditures of wages and salaries for the first three years and 0.5% for the fourth and fifth years of its operation.

Other Programs—Grand Forks has a designated Foreign Trade Zone which provides an incentive for freight businesses to locate in the area.

Development Projects

When University Technology Park, a business incubator, is built in 1994, its first building will be the National Weather Service. Ecolab, Inc., a developing high-technology firm, will also be a tenant. In 1990 a twenty-five-thousand-square-foot pasta plant was opened in Grand Forks and the same year the Stone Container Corporation completed a twenty-thousand-square-foot expansion of its facilities.

Economic Development Information: Grand Forks Region Economic Development Corporation, 202 North Third Street, Suite 300, Grand Forks, ND 58203; telephone (701)780-9915

Commercial Shipping

Greyhound, Triangle and Star bus lines carry limited freight on each of their two daily runs. Fifteen motor carriers and three package service carriers are located in the city.

Labor Force and Employment Outlook

The following is a summary of data regarding the Grand Forks metropolitan area labor force as of September 1992.

Size of civilian non-agricultural labor force: 32,650

Number of workers employed in . . .
  mining and construction: 1,550
  manufacturing: 1,600
  transportation and public utilities: 1,750
  wholesale and retail trade: 9,700
  finance, insurance, and real estate: 1,200
  services: 7,750
  government: 8,850

Average hourly earnings of production workers employed in manufacturing: $8.88 (Fargo-Moorhead)

Unemployment rate: 3.0%

Largest employers	Number of employees
Grand Forks Air Force Base	5,446
University of North Dakota	3,000
The United Hospital	1,500
J. R. Simplot	425
City/County Government of Grand Forks	390

Cost of Living

The following is a summary of data regarding several key cost of living factors in the Grand Forks area.

1992 (2nd Quarter) ACCRA Cost of Living Index: Not reported

1992 (2nd Quarter) ACCRA Average House Price: Not reported

State income tax rate: 2.67% to 12.0%

State sales tax rate: 5.0%

Local income tax rate: None

Local sales tax rate: 1.0%

Property tax rate: 512.9 mills per $1,000 of assessed valuation; assessment ratio = 100% for residential

Economic Information: Grand Forks Chamber of Commerce, 202 North Third Street, Suite 100, P.O. Box 1177, Grand Forks, ND 58206-1177; telephone (701)772-7271

Education and Research

Elementary and Secondary Schools

The following is a summary of data regarding Grand Forks's public schools as of the 1992–1993 school year.

Total enrollment: 9,800

Number of facilities
  elementary schools: 13
  junior high/middle schools: 4
  senior high schools: 3

Student/teacher ratio: 16:1

Teacher salaries
  minimum: $19,500
  maximum: $40,000

Funding per pupil: $3,650

Public Schools Information: Grand Forks Public Schools #1, 314 Demers Avenue, Grand Forks, ND 58201; telephone (701)746-2200

Colleges and Universities

The University of North Dakota, with almost twelve thousand students, is the largest institution of higher learning in the Dakotas, Montana, Wyoming, and Idaho. Founded in 1883, the university has a strong

Cities of the United States • 2nd Edition   North Dakota—Grand Forks

The Myra Museum consists of buildings and exhibits which depict Grand Forks's past.

liberal arts course and a constellation of professional and specialized colleges and schools. Academic programs are offered in more than 170 fields, and the curriculum spans arts and sciences, aviation, business, fine arts, engineering, human resources, education, nursing, law, medicine, and graduate studies. Aakers Business College in downtown Grand Forks trains students in secretarial, clerical, and accounting programs. The Technical Institute in East Grand Forks provides vocational technical education geared to train high school graduates as well as students who want to enroll in retraining programs.

Libraries and Research Centers

The Grand Forks Public City-County Library houses 110,000 volumes and subscribes to more than 260 periodicals. Its Grand Forks Collection includes books, pictures, and oral history of the local area. Within Greater Grand Forks's libraries are more than 2.1 million volumes as well as periodicals, reports, microfilms, and documents.

The University of North Dakota houses numerous research projects that examine such areas as aerospace studies, economics, education, governmental affairs, health, biology, energy, chemistry, ecological studies, psychology, social science, and nutrition.

Public Library Information: Grand Forks Public Library, 2110 Library Circle, Grand Forks, ND 58201; telephone (701)772-8116

Health Care

Grand Forks Medical Park serves an eighteen-county area with facilities including: The United Hospital, a large regional hospital; Medical Center Rehabilitation Hospital, a state-operated rehabilitation hospital; United Recovery Center, a chemical dependency treatment center; three clinics offering primary and specialized health services; and a nursing home. The School of Medicine of the University of North Dakota operates a student health center and a family practice center.

Recreation

Sightseeing

The Grand Forks County Historical Society grounds feature the Myra Museum, which displays the heritage of the Grand Forks area through its exhibits and displays, including: the Quiet Room, which contains furnishings from the 1700s; the Chapel, with its stained glass windows and objects from original local churches; and the Lake Agasssiz display, which offers a history lesson in the ancient lake that produced the rich Red River Valley soil. The 1879 Campbell House displays furnishings of family life including a working loom, toys, and a summer kitchen. A 1917 School House, and the 1870s post office are some of the first buildings constructed in the town.

Arts and Culture

Grand Forks offers a variety of arts programs for citizens and visitors. The Chester Fritz Auditorium on the University of North Dakota (UND) campus presents a diversity of national, regional, and local theatrical productions and is home of the Grand Forks Symphony Orchestra. The campus's Burtness Theatre is the site of excellent college dramatic productions. The Fire Hall Theatre is the new home of the Greater Grand Forks Community Theatre, which presents five plays annually.

The UND Music Department has a number of affiliated performing ensembles, including: the Concert Choir, Women's Chorus and Varsity Bards, the Wind Ensemble, the University Band, and the Jazz Band. Many of these concerts take place at the Campbell Recital Hall at UND's Hughes Fine Arts Center. The Grand Forks Master Chorale performs contemporary choral works as well as works of the great masters. The North Country Traditional Music and Dance Society provides lessons in traditional dance and music. The North Dakota Ballet Company presents preprofessional training in classical ballet and other dance styles as well as dance performances.

The North Dakota Museum of Art, the state's official art gallery, serves as the center of cultural life for a five-state region. The museum exhibits national and international contemporary art with shows changing every six to eight weeks. The Hughes Fine Arts Center Gallery on the UND campus exhibits the works of national and regional artists as well as students. The UND Witmer Art Center displays quality works by professional artists.

Activities at *Friends and Neighbors Day* bring local citizens to Grand Forks Air Force Base.

Festivals and Holidays

February's Winterthing is a two-day indoor art festival with demonstrations and music. Guest writers and poets from across the nation come to the city in March for the Writer's Conference. April's Time Out/WACIPI, sponsored by the Native American Studies Department at UND, offers a variety of activities and entertainment focused on native American life. During three weekends in June, July, and August, Summerthing in the Park presents Music in the Park, Kids Days, and Artfest. In June, the Greater Grand Forks Fair and Exhibition offers carnival rides, concerts, 4-H entries, and races. July's Catfish Days is an event for those who love to catch or eat fish or even just enjoy watching the entertainment in the evenings. The Potato Bowl, in September, features football games, a queen pageant, and a golf tournament among other activities. A popular Grand Forks U.S. Air Force Base event, Friends and Neighbors Day, brings thousands of people to watch aerial demonstrations and to peer into cockpits. Crazy Days offers bargain shopping at many local marketplaces in August, and later in the month the two-day Heritage Days Festival includes old time threshing demonstrations and antique machinery.

Sports for the Participant

There are thirty-three parks, more than 12.5 miles of biking jogging lanes and paths, four golf courses, five ice arenas, four swimming pools, a waterslide, twenty-eight tennis courts, five indoor tennis courts, and four racquetball courts in Grand Forks and East Grand Forks.

Shopping and Dining

Consumers can purchase their necessities as well as indulge their whims at the city's seven major shopping areas, which feature national chain outlets, along with locally owned enterprises. Specialty shops and grocery supermarkets dot the two Forks cities, and a wide range of merchandise and foodstuffs can be found in its many retail outlets.

The Grand Forks area has more than eighty-five restaurants. From fast food to gourmet—one can find it all, including Chinese, Mexican, Bavarian, and Italian fare as well as the Midwest staple steak and potatoes dinner.

Visitor Information: Greater Grand Forks Convention and Visitors Bureau, 202 North Third Street, Suite 200, Grand Forks, ND 58203; telephone (701)746-0444, (800)866-4566

Convention Facilities

The Grand Forks Civic Auditorium, the most versatile civic and convention center in the state, has large rooms for up to 2,000 people and thirteen smaller rooms for more intimate meetings. The Auditorium can serve over twelve hundred guests on the main floor and 840 on its lower level. The Hyslop Sports Center on the University of North Dakota campus contains more than 250,000 square feet of space. The Arena seats 7,600 people and has been used for sporting events, concerts, circuses, and other special events. The Ralph Engelstad Arena is a site for concerts, rodeos, and other activities with permanent seating for 6,100 people. The Chester Fritz Auditorium offers twenty-four hundred concert seats, plus a lower level that can accommodate 150 people in a classroom setting, 250 people for banquets or 400 people in auditorium seating.

Convention Information: Greater Grand Forks Convention and Visitors Bureau, 202 North Third Street, Suite 200, Grand Forks, ND 58203; telephone (701)746-0444 or (800)866-4566

Transportation

Approaching the City

Grand Forks is accessible by two major highways, Interstate 29 which runs north and south, and U.S. Highway 2 which runs east and west. Grand Forks's Mark Andrews International Airport, located 4.5 miles west of the city, is served by Northwest Airlines, Mesaba Airlink, and Great Lakes Airlines, with ten arrivals and departures daily. Amtrak operates fourteen passenger trains per week. Interstate bus service is provided by Greyhound, Triangle, and Star bus lines, with two daily runs in each direction.

Traveling in the City

Scheduled bus service is provided to both Grand Forks and East Grand Forks on a Monday through

Saturday basis. Dial-a-Ride service is available for the physically handicapped.

Communications

Newspapers and Magazines

The city's daily newspaper is the *Grand Forks Herald* and the University of North Dakota *Student* publishes twice weekly during the fall and spring semesters. East Grand Forks's weekly is *The Exponent.*

Television and Radio

Residents of Grand Forks receive programming from one public and one commercial television station and from ten AM and FM radio stations.

Media Information: Grand Forks Herald, 120 North Fourth Street, P.O. Box 6008, Grand Forks, ND 58206-6008; telephone (701)780-1100

OHIO

Cincinnati 381
Cleveland 397
Columbus 409
Dayton 421
Toledo 433

The State in Brief

Nickname: Buckeye State
Motto: With God, all things are possible

Flower: Scarlet carnation
Bird: Cardinal

Area: 44,828 square miles (1990; U.S. rank: 35th)
Elevation: Ranges from 433 feet to 1,550 feet above sea level
Climate: Temperate and continental; humid with wide seasonal variation

Admitted to Union: March, 1, 1803
Capital: Columbus
Head Official: Governor George Voinovich (R) (until 1995)

Population
  1970: 10,657,423
  1980: 10,798,000
  1990: 10,939,000
  Percent change 1980–1990: 0.5%
  U.S. rank in 1990: 7th
  Percent of residents born in state: 75.9% (1990)
  Density: 264.9 people per square mile (1990; U.S. rank: 9th)
  1991 FBI Crime Index Total: 550,560

Racial and Ethnic Characteristics (1990)
  White: 9,522,000
  Black: 0.6%
  American Indian, Eskimo, Aleut: 0.19%
  Asian and Pacific Islander: 0.84%
  Hispanic (may be of any race): 1.29%

Age Characteristics (1990)
  Population under 5 years old: 796,000
  Population 5 to 17 years old: 2,023,000
  Percent of population 65 years and older: 13.1%
  Median age: 33.3 years
  Voting-age population (1988): 8,059,000 (54.5% of whom cast votes for president)

Vital Statistics
  Total number of births (1992): 169,067
  Total number of deaths (1992): 99,601 (of which, 1,474 were infants under the age of 1 year)
  AIDS cases reported, 1981–1990: 2,121 (U.S. rank: 11th)

Economy
  Major industries: Trade; finance, insurance, and real estate; services
  Unemployment rate: 6.3% (September 1992)
  Per capita income: $13,461 (1989)
  Median household income: $28,706 (1989)
  Total number of families: 2,915,439 (9.7% of which had incomes below the poverty level; 1989)
  Income tax rate: Graduated from 0.743% to 6.9%
  Sales tax rate: 5.0%

Cincinnati

The City in Brief

Founded: 1789 (incorporated, 1819)

Head Official: City Manager Gerald Newfarmer (since 1990)

City Population
 1970: 454,000
 1980: 385,457
 1990: 364,040
 Percent change, 1980–1990: −5.5%
 U.S. rank in 1980: 32nd
 U.S. rank in 1990: 45th

Metropolitan Area Population (CMSA)
 1970: 1,613,000
 1980: 1,660,000
 1990: 1,744,124
 Average annual percent change, 1980–1988: 0.4% (PMSA)
 U.S. rank in 1980: 20th
 U.S. rank in 1990: 23rd

Area: 77.2 square miles (1990)
Elevation: 869 feet above sea level
Average Annual Temperature: 53.3° F
Average Annual Precipitation: 40.14 inches

Major Economic Sectors: Services, wholesale and retail trade, manufacturing, government
Unemployment Rate: 5.2% (September 1992)
Per Capita Income: $12,547 (1989)
1992 (2nd Quarter) ACCRA Average House Price: $120,005
1992 (2nd Quarter) ACCRA Cost of Living Index: 106.3 (U.S. average = 100.0)
1991 FBI Crime Index Total: 35,693

Major Colleges and Universities: University of Cincinnati; Xavier University

Daily Newspapers: *The Cincinnati Enquirer; The Cincinnati Post*

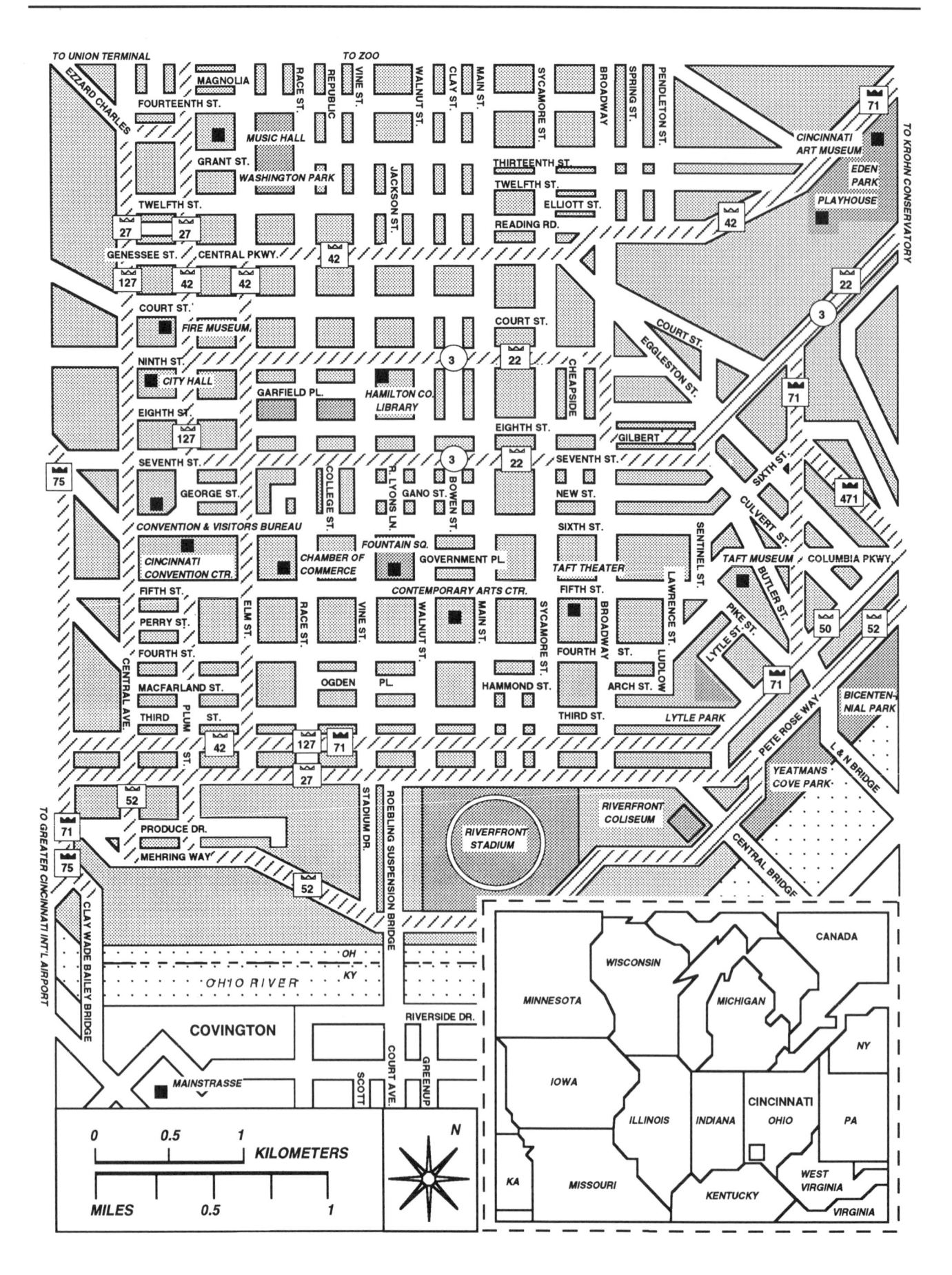

Ohio—Cincinnati — *Cities of the United States • 2nd Edition*

Introduction

Cincinnati, the seat of Hamilton County, is Ohio's third largest city and the center of a metropolitan statistical area comprised of Clermont, Hamilton, and Warren counties in Ohio, Kenton County in Kentucky, and Dearborn County in Indiana. Praised by Charles Dickens and Winston Churchill among others, Cincinnati is noted for its attractive hillside setting overlooking the Ohio River. The city enjoys a rich cultural history, particularly in choral and orchestral music, dating from German settlement in the nineteenth century. Once the nation's pork capital and the country's largest city, Cincinnati today is home to several leading national corporations.

Geography and Climate

Cincinnati is set on the north bank of the Ohio River in a narrow, steep-sided valley on the Ohio-Kentucky border in southwestern Ohio. The city is spread out on hills that afford beautiful vistas of downtown and give the city a picturesque landscape. The area's continental climate produces a wide range of temperatures from winter to summer. Winters are moderately cold with frequent periods of extensive cloudiness; summers are warm and humid with temperatures reaching ninety degrees about nineteen days each year.

Area: 77.2 square miles (1990)

Elevation: 869 feet above sea level

Average Temperatures: January, 28.9° F; July, 75.3° F; annual average, 53.3° F

Average Annual Precipitation: 40.14 inches

History

Ohio River Crossing Part of Northwest Territory

The Ohio River basin first served as a crossing point for native Americans travelling south. It is believed that Robert Cavelier, sieur de La Salle, was the first explorer to reach this spot on the Ohio River as early as 1669. Part of the Northwest Territory that the newly formed United States government received from England at the conclusion of the Revolutionary War, Cincinnati became a strategic debarkation point for settlers forging a new life in the wilderness.

Congressman John Cleves Symmes of New Jersey purchased from the Continental Congress one million acres of land between the two Miami rivers, and three settlements were platted. In February 1789, John Filson named one of the settlements Losantiville, meaning "the place opposite the Licking [River]." The next year, General Arthur St. Clair, governor of the Northwest Territory, renamed the village Cincinnati in honor of the Roman citizen-soldier Lucius Quinctius Cincinnatus and after the Society of the Cincinnati, an organization of American Revolutionary army officers. He made Cincinnati the seat of Hamilton County, which he named after Alexander Hamilton, then president general of the Society of Cincinnati.

River Traffic Swells City's Population

Fort Washington was built in the area in 1789 as a fortification from which action was mounted against warriors of the Ohio tribe, but the military efforts proved unsuccessful until General Anthony Wayne trained an army that defeated the Ohio at Fallen Timbers in 1794, securing the area for settlement. Cincinnati was chartered as a town in 1802 and as a city in 1819. The introduction of the river paddlewheeler on the Ohio River after the War of 1812 turned Cincinnati into a center of river commerce and trade. The opening of the Miami Canal in 1827 added to the town's economic growth. William Holmes McGuffey published his Eclectic Readers in Cincinnati in 1836, and eventually 122 million copies were sold. The first mass migration of Germans in 1830 and Irish a decade later swelled Cincinnati's population to 46,338 people.

The economy continued to boom as the South paid cash for foodstuffs produced in the city, and by 1850 Cincinnati was the pork-packing capital of the world. More than eight-thousand steamboats docked at Cincinnati in 1852. Cincinnati merchants protested the cutoff of Southern trade at the outbreak of the Civil War, but federal government contracts and the city's role as a recruiting and outfitting center for Union soldiers righted the economy. Cincinnati was a major stop on the Underground Railroad, a secret network of cooperation aiding fugitive slaves in reaching sanctuary in the free states or Canada prior to 1861. Cincinnati also served as a center of Copperhead political activity during the Civil War; Copperheads were Northerners sympathetic to the Southern cause. The city's proximity to the South spread fear of invasion by the Confederate Army, and martial law was decreed in 1862 when raiders led by Edmund Kirby-Smith, a Confederate commander, threatened invasion.

Cincinnati residents played an important role in the Abolitionist cause. James G. Birney, who published the abolitionist newspaper *The Philanthropist,* and Dr. Lyman Beecher of the Lane Theological Seminary were leading Northern antislavery activists. Dr. Beecher's daughter, Harriet Beecher Stowe, lived in Cincinnati from 1832 to 1850 and wrote much of her best seller, *Uncle Tom's Cabin,* there. African Americans have in fact been prominent in Cincinnati's history since its founding. The city's first African-American church was built in 1809 and the first school in 1825. African-Americans voted locally in 1852, eighteen years before the passage of the Fifteenth Amendment. The first African-American to serve on city council was elected in 1931, and two African-Americans have served as mayor.

Prosperity Follows End of Civil War

A suspension bridge designed by John R. Roebling connected Ohio and Kentucky upon its completion in 1867. Cincinnati prospered after the Civil War, and, with a population that grew to 200,000 people became the country's largest city before annexing land to develop communities outside the basin. Cincinnati's most revered public monument, the Tyler Davidson Fountain, was unveiled in 1871 in the heart of downtown. During this period Cincinnati's major cultural institutions were founded, including the art museum and art academy, the conservatory of music, the public library, the zoo, and Music Hall. Two of the city's most cherished traditions also date from this time: the May Festival of choral music at Music Hall and the first professional baseball team, the Cincinnati Red Stockings.

In reaction to the decline of riverboat trade in the 1870s, the city of Cincinnati built its own southern rail line—it was the first and only city to do so—at a cost of $20 million, rushing to complete the project in 1880. The era of boss-rule in the municipal government was introduced in 1884 when newly elected Governor Joseph B. Foraker appointed George Barnsdale Cox, a tavern keeper, to head the Board of Public Affairs. With control of more than two-thousand jobs, Cox and his machine ruled Cincinnati through a bleak period of graft and corruption, which finally came to an end with a nonpartisan reform movement that won election in 1924. The city's new charter corrected the abuses of the Cox regime.

On the national scene, a political dynasty was established when Cincinnatian William Howard Taft was elected President and then became the only President to be appointed Chief Justice of the U.S. Supreme Court. Taft's son, Robert A. Taft, was elected to three Senate terms; and his grandson, Robert Taft, Jr., was elected to the U.S. House of Representatives.

City Retains Vitality in Twentieth Century

Cincinnati weathered the Great Depression better than most American cities of its size, largely because of a resurgence of inexpensive river trade. The rejuvenation of downtown began in the 1920s and continued into the next decade with the construction of Union Terminal, the post office, and a large Bell Telephone building. The flood of 1937 was one of the worst in the nation's history, resulting in the building of protective flood walls. After World War II, Cincinnati unveiled a master plan for urban renewal that resulted in modernization of the inner city. Riverfront Stadium and the Coliseum were completed in the 1970s, as the Cincinnati Reds baseball team emerged as one of the dominant teams of the decade. Tragedy struck the Coliseum in December 1981 when eleven people were killed in a mass panic prior to The Who rock and roll concert. In 1989, the two-hundredth anniversary of the city's founding, much attention was focused on the city's Year 2000 plan, which involves further revitalization.

Historical Information: Cincinnati Historical Society, Museum Center, 1301 Western Avenue, Cincinnati, OH 45203; telephone (513)287-7000

Population Profile

Metropolitan Area Residents (CMSA)
 1970: 1,613,000
 1980: 1,660,000
 1990: 1,744,124
 Annual average percent change, 1980-1988: 0.4% (PMSA)
 U.S. rank in 1980: 20th
 U.S. rank in 1990: 23rd

City Residents
 1970: 454,000
 1980: 385,457
 1990: 364,040 (of which, 169,305 were males and 194,735 were females)
 Percent change, 1980-1990: -5.5%
 U.S. rank in 1980: 32nd
 U.S. rank in 1990: 45th (State rank: 3rd)

Density: 4,715.5 people per square mile (1990)

Racial and ethnic characteristics (1990)
 White: 220,285
 Black: 138,132
 American Indian, Eskimo, Aleut: 660
 Asian and Pacific Islander: 4,030
 Hispanic (may be of any race): 2,386

Percent of residents born in state: 72.1%

Age characteristics (1990)
 Population under 5 years old: 30,595
 Population 5 to 9 years old: 26,275
 Population 10 to 14 years old: 22,233
 Population 15 to 19 years old: 24,648
 Population 20 to 24 years old: 34,826
 Population 25 to 29 years old: 37,287
 Population 30 to 34 years old: 33,338
 Population 35 to 39 years old: 26,659
 Population 40 to 44 years old: 20,585
 Population 45 to 49 years old: 15,318
 Population 50 to 54 years old: 13,100
 Population 55 to 59 years old: 13,603
 Population 60 to 64 years old: 14,847
 Population 65 to 69 years old: 14,196
 Population 70 to 74 years old: 12,029
 Population 75 to 79 years old: 10,616
 Population 80 to 84 years old: 7,655
 Population 85 years and over: 6,230
 Median age: 30.8

Births (1988)
 Total number: 7,138

Deaths (1988)
 Total number: 4,479 (of which, 79 were infants under the age of 1 year)

Money income (1989)
 Per capita income: $12,547
 Median household income: $21,006
 Total households: 154,243
 Number of households with income of . . .
 less than $5,000: 20,837
 $5,000 to $9,999: 20,930
 $10,000 to $14,999: 16,497
 $15,000 to $24,999: 29,828
 $25,000 to $34,999: 22,628
 $35,000 to $49,999: 21,692
 $50,000 to $74,999: 13,643
 $75,000 to $99,999: 4,153
 $100,000 to $149,999: 2,255
 $150,000 or more: 1,780
 Percent of families below poverty level: 20.7% (71.2% of which were female householder families with related children under 5)
1991 FBI Crime Index Total: 35,693

Municipal Government

The nine-member city council, from which a mayor is chosen, appoints a city manager who is the administrative head of Cincinnati city government. Council members are elected to two-year terms; the city manager serves for an indefinite period.

Head Official: City Manager Gerald Newfarmer (since 1990)

Total Number of City Employees: 7,562 (1991)

City Information: City Hall, Ninth and Plum Streets, Cincinnati, OH 45202; telephone (513)352-3000

Economy

Major Industries and Commercial Activity

Cincinnati's diversified economic base includes manufacturing, wholesale and retail trade, insurance and finance, health services, and transportation. Known worldwide for Procter & Gamble soap products and U.S. Playing Cards, the city ranks high nationally in the value of manufacturing shipments, which totalled more than $21 billion in 1986. Fortune 500 companies that have established headquarters in Cincinnati include Procter & Gamble, Penn Central, Cincinnati Milacron Inc., Federated Department Stores Inc., Kroger Company, and U.S. Shoe Corporation. More than 340 other Fortune 500 companies maintain operations in Cincinnati. Companies that have recently relocated headquarters there include Heinz Pet Products, James River Corp., and Mercantile Stores. Retail sales average $2.6 billion annually. Banking assets total over $17 billion.

Five hundred area firms have contributed to Cincinnati's position as an international trade center, generating approximately $3 billion in sales to markets outside the United States each year. Among the export products are jet engines, machine tools, computer software, paper, and consumer goods; products imported into the city average around $2 billion yearly. Foreign investment in the local economy is increasing; ninety Cincinnati-area firms are presently owned by companies in Japan, England, Western Europe, and Canada.

Federal agencies with regional centers located in the city are the United States Postal Service, the U.S. Internal Revenue Service, the U.S. Environmental Protection Agency, and the National Institute for Occupational Safety and Health.

Items and goods produced: aircraft engines, auto parts, motor vehicles, chemicals, valves, alcoholic beverages and soft drinks, food and kindred products, playing cards, drugs, cosmetics, toiletries, detergents, building materials, cans, metalworking and general industrial machinery, toys, apparel, mattresses, electric motors, robotics, electronic equipment, housewares, shoes, printing and publishing

Incentive Programs—New and Existing Companies

Local programs—Business and industrial activity is encouraged by local economic development programs, small business forums, government forums, the Cincinnati Institute for Small Enterprise, and the Business Solutions Center. The Institute for Advanced Manufacturing Sciences Inc. (IAMS), a nonprofit organization formed by the business community, city government, and the University of Cincinnati , promotes manufacturing research, development, technological transfer, and training. One hundred acres are available in the area for location and expansion of light manufacturing and research firms.

International commerce is stimulated by the World Trade Association; foreign trade zone status, which lowers import duty and tax expenses, is extended to firms engaged in international trade in the Greater Cincinnati area.

Job training programs—Great Oaks Joint Vocational School District, the largest job training program of its kind in the world, offers nearly seventy programs. Job training is also offered by the Private Industry Council.

Development Projects

Cincinnati's Union Terminal, recently restored at a cost of $68 million, houses major cultural institutions. Airport projects include a new $65 million runway and a $315 million expansion by Delta airlines. Construction of offices downtown and in surrounding areas, as well as housing and shopping complexes, is robust. A performing arts center has been proposed.

Economic Development Information: Greater Cincinnati Chamber of Commerce, 300 Carew Tower, 441 Vine Street, Cincinnati, OH 45202-2812; telephone (513)579-3181 or 3136; and, Institute for Advanced Manufacturing Sciences Inc., telephone (513)948-2000

Commercial Shipping

The Port of Cincinnati is served year round by thirty-six barge lines that ship forty-six million tons of cargo through the port annually. The Ohio River barge system handles over 195 million tons of cargo annually. Connecting the city with national and world markets are three major railroads: C S X Transportation, Norfolk Southern Corporation, and Conrail; fifty-one interstate trucking companies; twenty-nine freight forwarders; and three air cargo carriers.

Labor Force and Employment Outlook

Productivity among Cincinnati's workers ranks consistently above the national average. Area educational institutions assure employers of well-trained managers and professionals as well as semi-skilled and highly skilled workers. The city considers itself well positioned for economic growth in the 1990s, citing its outstanding airport service and quality of life among other positive factors. It is projected that foreign trade will continue to grow, as will investment by suppliers to new Japanese auto plants.

Cities of the United States • 2nd Edition   Ohio—Cincinnati

Historic Fountain Square in downtown Cincinnati.

The following is a summary of data regarding the Cincinnati metropolitan area labor force as of September 1992.

Size of non-agricultural labor force: 741,100

Number of workers employed in . . .
  mining: 400
  construction: 34,000
  manufacturing: 141,800
  transportation and public utilities: 40,800
  wholesale and retail trade: 189,800
  finance, insurance, and real estate: 43,400
  services: 197,600
  government: 93,300

Average hourly earnings of production workers employed in manufacturing: $12.99

Unemployment rate: 5.2%

Largest employers	*Number of employees*
General Electric Company- Aircraft Engines	17,500
U.S. Government	14,841
The Procter & Gamble Company	13,400
University of Cincinnati	11,568
The Kroger Company	10,000
Internal Revenue Service	8,839
City of Cincinnati	7,562
Cincinnati Public Schools	6,328
Armco, Inc.	6,000
Hamilton County	5,973

Cost of Living

The following is a summary of data regarding several key cost of living factors in the Cincinnati area.

1992 (2nd Quarter) ACCRA Cost of Living Index: 106.3 (U.S.average = 100.0)

1992 (2nd Quarter) ACCRA Average House Price: $120,005

State income tax rate: graduated from 0.743% of Ohio taxable income of $5,000 or less to 6.900% plus $4,606.20 on taxable income over $100,000

State sales tax rate: 5.0%

Local income tax rate: 2.1%

Local sales tax rate: 0.5%

Property tax rate: ranges from $34.07 to $61.63 per $1,000 of assessed valuation; assessed at 35% of market value

Economic Information: Greater Cincinnati Chamber of Commerce, 300 Carew Tower, 441 Vine Street, Cincinnati, OH 45202-2812; telephone (513)579-3181 or 3136

Education and Research

Elementary and Secondary Schools

The third-largest school system in the state of Ohio, the Cincinnati City School District is administered by a seven-member board that appoints a superintendent. Following the suggestion of the city's business community, the superintendent announced in 1992 the total reorganization of the school district, a move that reduced the number of administrators in the central office from 127 to sixty-two and was expected to save $16 million over two years, money that would be put back into the schools.

The following is a summary of data regarding the Cincinnati public schools as of the 1988-1989 school year.

Total enrollment: 51,606

Number of facilities
  elementary schools: 60
  junior high schools: 9
  senior high schools: 10

Student/teacher ratio: elementary, 18.9:1; junior high, 15.2:1; senior high, 18.1:1

Teacher salaries
  minimum: $17,538.98
  maximum: $40,790.57 (doctorate; 27 years' experience)

Funding per pupil: $4,314 (general fund); $4,929 (all funds)

A parochial school system operated by the Catholic Diocese as well as several private schools throughout the Greater Cincinnati area provide instruction from kindergarten through twelfth grade.

Public Schools Information: Cincinnati Public Schools, 230 East Ninth Street, Cincinnati, OH 45202; telephone (513)369-4000

Colleges and Universities

The University of Cincinnati, part of Ohio's state higher education system, enrolls more than thirty-six thousand students and grants degrees at all levels, from associate through doctorate, in a complete range of fields. The university is a nationally recognized research institution known for its professional schools, notably the colleges of medicine, engineering, law, business, applied science, and architecture. Cooperative education originated at the University of Cincinnati in 1906. Cincinnati is also home to Xavier University, a Jesuit institution, which offers graduate and undergraduate programs in such areas as chemistry, health services administration, nursing, social work, and radiologic technology.

Hebrew Union College-Jewish Institute of Religion, a graduate rabbinical seminary, awards associate, master's, and doctorate degrees; branch campuses are located in Los Angeles, New York, and Jerusalem. Other colleges in Cincinnati are the Art Academy of Cincinnati, housed at the Cincinnati Art Museum, and Cincinnati Bible Seminary. Several local hospitals as well as the University of Cincinnati operate schools of nursing. Colleges and universities in the metropolitan area include Miami University in Oxford, known for its business school; Northern Kentucky University; Thomas More College; St. Thomas Institute; and College of Mount St. Joseph. Vocational and technical education is available at a variety of institutions such as Cincinnati Technical College and Southern Ohio College.

Libraries and Research Centers

Approximately seventy public, private, and specialized libraries are maintained in Cincinnati. The Public Library of Cincinnati and Hamilton County operates a downtown facility, forty-two branches, a library for the blind and physically handicapped, an exceptional children's division, bookmobiles, and a books-by-mail service. The main branch houses more than four million volumes in addition to more than fourteen thousand periodicals, and records, tapes, films, slides, maps, and compact disks. Special collections cover a range of topics, among them inland rivers, sacred music, patents from 1790 to the present, nineteenth and twentieth century illustrators, and Bibles and English language dictionaries; the library is a depository for federal documents. The Cincinnati Historical Society houses a reference library, which was founded in 1831.

Cincinnati-area colleges and universities also maintain campus libraries. The largest is the University of Cincinnati Libraries, which include a central facility with nearly two million volumes and eleven department libraries; the law school and the University of Cincinnati Medical Center operate separate library systems. The Hebrew Union College-Jewish Institute of Religion Klau Library is an important center for such subject interests as Hebraica, Judaica, ancient and near-Eastern studies, and rabbinical studies. Several cultural and scientific organizations operate libraries, including the Art Museum, the Museum of Natural History, the Taft Museum, and the Zoological Society.

United States government agencies with libraries open to the public in Cincinnati include the U.S. Army Corps of Engineers, the U.S. Department of Health and Human Services, and the U.S. Food and Drug Administration. Research libraries are operated by the Environmental Protection Agency and the James N. Gamble Institute of Medical Research. Collections of more than 200,000 volumes are maintained by the Cincinnati Law Library Association and the Young Men's Mercantile Library Association. Among corporations housing libraries for their own personnel and researchers are Procter & Gamble Company, Merrill Dow Research Institute, General Electric Company, Quantum Chemical Corporation, and Cincinnati Milacron. Other specialized libraries are affiliated with hospitals and churches and synagogues. The federal government operates environmental and occupational health and safety research centers.

Public Library Information: Public Library of Cincinnati and Hamilton County, Library Square, 800 Vine Street, Cincinnati, OH 45202-2701; telephone (513)369-6900

Health Care

The Cincinnati medical community, a regional health care center, has gained prominence for education, treatment, and research. The University of Cincinnati maintains the oldest teaching hospital/medical center in the country and is the place where Albert Sabin developed the first polio vaccine and

Leon Goldman performed the first laser surgery for the removal of cataracts. Children's Hospital Medical Center, one of the nation's largest and most respected pediatric hospitals, also operates the largest pediatric residency program and developed the first heart-lung machine.

More than thirty hospitals provide about 9,500 beds, and more than twenty-nine hundred physicians practice in the area. Among the general care and specialized facilities are the Shriners Burns Institute, Good Samaritan, Jewish, Bethesda, Christ, Deaconess, Providence, St. Elizabeth, St. Francis-St. George, and St. Luke hospitals.

Recreation

Sightseeing

A tour of Cincinnati can begin downtown at Fountain Square, the site of the Tyler Davidson Fountain, one of the city's most revered landmarks, which was made in Munich, Germany, and erected in 1871. Several historic monuments, including statues in honor of three United States presidents—James A. Garfield, William Henry Harrison, and Abraham Lincoln—are also located in the downtown area.

Eden Park in Mt. Adams, one of Cincinnati's oldest hillside neighborhoods and named after President John Quincy Adams, provides a panoramic view of the city and of northern Kentucky across the Ohio River. In Eden Park the Irwin M. Krohn Conservatory maintains one of the world's largest public greenhouses. The Cincinnati Zoo is recognized worldwide for the breeding of animals in captivity; the zoo park introduced the nation's first insect world exhibit. The zoo's big-cat canyon is the home of rare Bengal tigers.

Historic houses open for public viewing include the former homes of John Hauck, a nineteenth-century brewer; Harriet Beecher Stowe, author of *Uncle Tom's Cabin;* and William Howard Taft, twenty-seventh President of the United States. Dayton Street on Cincinnati's West End features restored nineteenth-century architecture. The Spring Grove Cemetery and Arboretum, a national historic landmark, contains one thousand labeled trees on 733 landscaped acres lined with statuary and sculpture.

Kings Island Theme Park, twenty minutes north of Cincinnati, features more than one hundred amusement attractions, including professional musical shows, and is known nationally for its daring rollercoaster and water rides. The College Football Hall of Fame is also located at Kings Island. Sharon Woods Village is an outdoor museum of restored nineteenth-century southwestern Ohio buildings. Meier's Wine Cellar, Ohio's oldest and largest winery, offers tours.

Arts and Culture

Many of Cincinnati's cultural institutions date from the mid-nineteenth century and the city takes particular pride in their longevity and quality. Music Hall, restored to its nineteenth-century elegance, is home to the Cincinnati Symphony Orchestra, the POPS, Cincinnati Ballet, and Cincinnati Opera. The symphony performs classical and pops concert series. The ballet company offers a number of subscription performances each season, presenting both classical and contemporary dance. The opera company, the second oldest in the United States, mounts four productions during a summer season, all with narratives translated into English and projected onto an overhead screen.

Riverbend Music Center, an amphitheater designed by noted architect Michael Graves, is the summer performance quarters for the Cincinnati Pops Orchestra and Symphony Orchestra, as well as the site for concerts by visiting artists. Two popular local traditions are the Matinee Musicale and the Cincinnati Chamber Music Series. The Kool Festival presents black artists performing contemporary works by black composers at Riverbend.

Cincinnati Playhouse in the Park, a professional regional theater, is housed in a modern facility in Eden Park. The Playhouse presents a season of comedies, dramas, and musicals on a main stage and in a smaller theater. The University of Cincinnati's College—Conservatory of Music presents more than three hundred concerts a year and is most noted for its philharmonic orchestra concerts, operas, and musical theater productions. It also sponsors a summer season of musicals at Corbett Theater on campus and at the Showboat Majestic, a restored nineteenth-century showboat on the Ohio River Public Landing. The School for the Creative and Performing Arts, an alternative public school, presents musicals and theater for the general public.

Music in Cincinnati is not limited to the classical tradition. Cincinnati and nearby Covington, Ken-

Basilica of the Assumption in Covington, Kentucky, is a replica of Notre Dame Cathedral in Paris.

tucky, support an active jazz club scene. Bogart's, a rock club near the University of Cincinnati, books rock, jazz, and blues performers.

In addition to music, art is an integral part of the city's cultural heritage. The Woman's Art Museum Association was responsible for the construction of the Cincinnati Art Museum in 1871; the museum houses more than one hundred galleries. Downtown's Taft Museum, built in 1820 and formerly the home of Charles P. Taft and his wife, was presented as a gift to the city in 1932; the museum holds paintings, porcelains, and enamels. The Contemporary Arts Center, also located downtown, presents changing exhibitions of modernist art in a variety of forms. A number of art galleries occupy converted warehouses near the shopping district.

Union Terminal, declared a masterpiece of art deco construction when it opened in 1933, has recently been restored and is the new home of the Museum of Natural History (featuring a children's discovery center), the library and museum of the Cincinnati Historical Society, and an Omnimax theater, one of only fourteen nationwide. The Cincinnati Fire Museum, located in a 1907 firehouse, exhibits the history of fire fighting in Cincinnati.

Festivals and Holidays

Each year Cincinnati presents a number of festivals that celebrate the city's heritage and institutions. The nation's professional baseball season opens in the spring with the Cincinnati Reds game at Riverfront Stadium. Preceding the game is an Opening Day Parade originating at historic Findlay Market. The Taste of Cincinnati celebration held over Memorial Day weekend downtown affords the city's best restaurants an opportunity to feature some of their favorite menu items. One of the largest of the local ethnic celebrations, the Greek Panegyri Festival fills three days in June. Summerfair brings an arts and crafts show to the city's riverfront the second weekend in June. The day-long Riverfest celebration on Labor Day is capped by a spectacular fireworks display. Oktoberfest Zinzinnati in October features German food, customs, dancing, and beer; downtown streets are blocked off for the festivities.

Popular Christmas-holiday events in Cincinnati include the annual tree-lighting on Fountain Square, the Festival of Lights at the Cincinnati Zoo, the Cincinnati Gas and Electric Company Christmas time train display, and the Krohn Conservatory's annual Christmas exhibit, featuring a live manger scene and a poinsettia tree.

Events are held throughout the year in nearby Sharon Woods Village and in the MainStrasse Village in Covington, Kentucky, across the Ohio River.

Sports for the Spectator

The Cincinnati Reds baseball team play their home schedule at Riverfront Stadium, competing in the western division of the National League. The Cincinnati Bengals, an expansion team in the old American Football League, played twice in the Super Bowl game in the 1980s, representing the American Conference of the National Football League. The Cincinnati Cyclones are in the East Coast Hockey League and play at Cincinnati Gardens. The University of Cincinnati and Xavier University provide a schedule of college sports teams and cross-town rivalry in basketball, in which both schools enjoy strong traditions and some national prominence.

Thoroughbred racing takes place April through September at River Downs Racetrack in Cincinnati and Turfway Park in Florence, Kentucky. The Association of Tennis Professionals compete in tournament play each August at Jack Nicklaus Sports Center adjacent to Kings Island.

Sports for the Participant

Cincinnati maintains more than 4,000 acres of park land in attractive urban settings. Alms Park and Eden Park offer dramatic views of the Ohio River and northern Kentucky, and these parks, as well as others, attract joggers because of their natural beauty and challenge for runners. The city's recreation department sponsors an array of sports from softball to soccer for all age groups and manages neighborhood swimming pools and tennis courts throughout the summer. Sawyer Point on the Ohio River provides facilities for pier fishing, rowboating, skating, tennis, and volleyball.

Shopping and Dining

Cincinnati's skywalk system connects downtown stores, hotels, and restaurants, and Riverfront Stadium and Coliseum, allowing visitors to explore the shopping district free of traffic and weather concerns. The new downtown Tower Place mixes local and nationally known stores with specialty shops in a compact area. Cincinnati consists of distinct neighborhoods within the city, where shopping districts provide an atmosphere not found in many cities

The steamboat *Mississippi Queen* cruises past Cincinnati's Riverfront Stadium, home of the Reds and the Bengals.

today. Other shopping opportunities include large regional malls, factory outlets, discount houses, and museum stores.

Cincinnati restaurants have been rated highly by critics and travel guides. The city is home to the Maisonette, one of the nation's most critically acclaimed French restaurants. *Food and Wine* magazine named Maisonette, as well as Orchids and The Palace 1992-1993 Distinguished Restaurants of North America. Both the number and variety of first-rate restaurants are impressive. Besides moderately priced German cuisine, Cincinnati offers Chinese and Italian restaurants. Cincinnati restaurateurs also have been successful in opening establishments in architecturally interesting buildings, such as firehouses, police precincts, or riverboat paddle-wheelers. A locally made ice cream is widely popular, as is a downtown New York-style deli known for its corned beef. The city's oldest tavern, opened in 1861, is still in business as a bar and grill. Cincinnati chili, Greek in origin, is flavored with cinnamon and chocolate as the "secret" ingredients and served over spaghetti; 3-way, 4-way, or 5-way chili choices consist of various combinations of grated cheese, onions, beans, and oyster crackers.

Visitor Information: Greater Cincinnati Convention and Visitors Bureau, 300 West Sixth Street, Cincinnati, OH 45202; telephone (513)621-2142; or, (800)582-5804 in Ohio, (800)543-2613 elsewhere in the U.S.

Convention Facilities

The Dr. Albert B. Sabin Cincinnati Convention Center is conveniently situated downtown and connected via the twenty-block Skywalk system with shops and stores, restaurants, entertainment and cultural activities, and hotels. The architecturally interesting entrance to the post-modern style Convention Center features the preserved facade of the historic Albee Theatre, which once stood near Fountain Square and was demolished several years ago.

The complex consists of three levels: the exhibit level contains three halls with 162,000 square feet of combined space that will accommodate up to 15,000 meeting participants; on the second level forty-one separate rooms provide banquet and meeting capacities ranging from 30 to 2,300 people; the third level is comprised of three ballrooms that combine to offer thirty thousand square feet of space. Convention center amenities include a banquet kitchen, teleconferencing facilities, handicapped access, and adjacent parking for five thousand vehicles.

Meeting and convention accommodations can also be found at several luxury hotels clustered downtown near the Convention Center and at other hotels and motels throughout the Greater Cincinnati area. More than fifteen thousand lodging rooms are available, with more than twenty-eight hundred of them located within three blocks of the convention center.

Convention Information: Greater Cincinnati Convention and Visitors Bureau, 300 West Sixth Street, Cincinnati, OH 45202; telephone (513)621-2142; or, (800)582-5804 in Ohio, (800)543-2613 elsewhere in the U.S.

Transportation

Approaching the City

The Cincinnati/Northern Kentucky International Airport is located in northern Kentucky, about 12 miles from the Cincinnati center city. Served by eight major commercial airlines that schedule well over six hundred commercial flights daily (including nonstop service to London, Paris, and Frankfurt), the airport is one of five Delta Airlines hubs in the United States. Highways providing access to downtown and the metropolitan region are: Interstates 71, 74, 75, 275, and 471; U.S. 22, 25, 27, 42, 50, 52, and 127; and several state and county routes.

Passenger rail service into renovated Union Terminal is available through Amtrak; bus transportation is provided by Greyhound and Southeastern Trailways.

Traveling in the City

The public transit bus system is operated by Queen City Metro, which schedules regular routes in the city and the suburbs.

Communications

Newspapers and Magazines

Cincinnati's major daily newspapers are *The Cincinnati Enquirer,* circulated mornings and Sundays, and the evening *The Cincinnati Post.* The *Cincinnati Business Courier,* a business tabloid, *The Greater Cincinnati Business Record,* and the *Cincinnati Herald,* an African-American oriented newspaper, appear weekly. Both the Associated Press and United Press International maintain offices in Cincinnati. *Cincinnati Magazine* is a monthly publication focusing on topics of community interest.

A number of nationally circulated magazines are published in Cincinnati; among them are *Writer's Digest, Dramatics Magazine,* and *St. Anthony Messenger.* Cincinnati-based Standard Publishing Company produces religious magazines. Specialized publications originating in the city are directed toward readers with interests in business, medicine, pharmacy, insurance, engineering, the arts, crafts, and other fields.

Television and Radio

Cincinnati is the broadcast media center for southwestern Ohio, northern Kentucky, and southeastern Indiana. Eight commercial, public, and independent television stations are received in the city; cable service is available. Twenty-five AM and FM radio stations broadcast educational, cultural, and religious programming as well as rock and roll, contemporary, classical, gospel, blues, jazz, reggae, and country music.

Media Information: The Cincinnati Enquirer, 617 Vine Street, Cincinnati, OH 45202; telephone (513)721-2700; and, *Cincinnati Magazine,* C. M. Media Inc., 409 Broadway, Cincinnati, OH 45202; telephone (513)421-4300; and, *Cincinnati Herald,* Porter Publishing, 836 Lincoln Avenue, Cincinnati, OH 45206; telephone (513)221-5440

Selected Bibliography

Chambrun, Clara Longworth, Comtesse de, *Cincinnati: Story of the Queen City* (New York, London: Scribner, 1939)

Fuller, John Grant, *Are the Kids All Right?: The Rock Generation and Its Hidden Death Wish* (New York: Times Books, 1981)

Howells, William Dean, *A Boy's Town: Described for "Harper's Young People"* (New York: Harper & Brothers, Franklin Square, 1890)

Howells, William Dean, *My Year in a Log Cabin* (New York, Harper & Brothers, 1893)

Lewis, Sinclair, *Babbitt* (New York: Harcourt, Brace, 1922)

Cleveland

The City in Brief

Founded: 1796 (incorporated, 1836)

Head Official: Mayor Michael White (D) (since 1989)

City Population
 1970: 751,000
 1980: 573,822
 1990: 505,616
 Percent change, 1980–1990: −11.9%
 U.S. rank in 1980: 18th
 U.S. rank in 1990: 23rd

Metropolitan Area Population (CMSA)
 1970: 3,000,000
 1980: 2,834,000
 1990: 2,759,823
 Percent change, 1980–1990: −0.3% (PMSA)
 U.S. rank in 1980: 11th
 U.S. rank in 1990: 13th

Area: 77.0 square miles (1990)

Elevation: most of the city is on a level plain 60 to 80 feet above Lake Erie

Average Annual Temperature: 49.6° F

Average Annual Precipitation: 35.40 inches

Major Economic Sectors: Services, wholesale and retail trade, manufacturing, government

Unemployment Rate: 6.2% (September 1992)

Per Capita Income: $9,258 (1989)

1992 (2nd Quarter) ACCRA Average House Price: $124,200

1992 (2nd Quarter) ACCRA Cost of Living Index: 110.0 (U.S. average = 100.0)

1991 FBI Crime Index Total: 45,610

Major Colleges and Universities: Case Western Reserve University; Cleveland State University

Daily Newspaper: *Plain Dealer*

Ohio—Cleveland

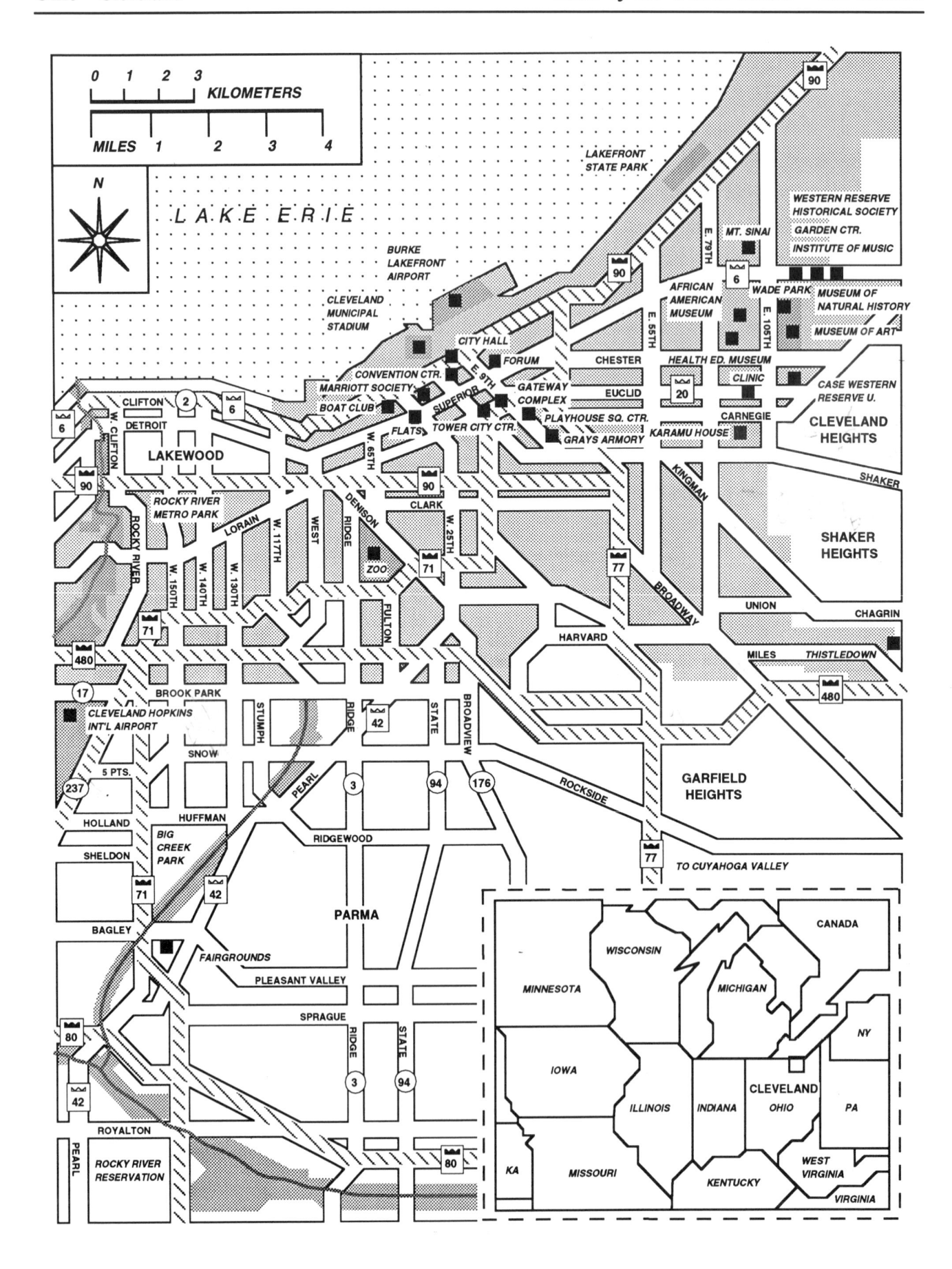

Introduction

The seat of Cuyahoga County, Cleveland, Ohio's second largest city, is the focus of a metropolitan statistical area that encompasses Cuyahoga, Geauga, Lake, and Medina counties. The city's location on Lake Erie accounts for its success as a transportation, industrial, and commercial center. Cleveland contributed a number of industrial discoveries that benefitted national growth and prosperity in the nineteenth century. In the early twentieth century, the local political system set a standard for reform that contributed to the general welfare of its citizens. Today Cleveland's revitalized central business and commercial districts complement its cultural institutions and major professional sports teams.

Geography and Climate

Extending 31 miles along the south shore of Lake Erie, Cleveland is surrounded by generally level terrain except for an abrupt ridge that rises five hundred feet above the shore on the eastern edge of the city. Cleveland is bisected from north to south by the Cuyahoga River. The continental climate is modified by west to northerly winds off Lake Erie, which lower summer temperatures and raise winter temperatures. Summers are moderately warm and humid, winters relatively cold and cloudy. Snowfall fluctuates widely, ranging from forty-five inches in west Cuyahoga County to ninety inches in the east. Thunderstorms often bring damaging winds of 50 miles per hour or greater; tornadoes occur frequently.

Area: 77.0 square miles (1990)

Elevation: most of the city is on a level plain 60 to 80 feet above Lake Erie

Average Temperatures: January, 25.5° F; July, 71.6° F; annual average, 49.6° F

Average Annual Precipitation: 35.40 inches

History

Lake Erie Port Attracts Development

U.S. General Moses Cleaveland was sent in 1796 by the Connecticut Land Company to survey the Western Reserve, a one-half million acre tract of land in northeastern Ohio, which was at that time called "New Connecticut." General Cleaveland platted a townsite on Lake Erie at the mouth of the Cuyahoga River, copying the New England style of town square layout. The settlement was abandoned, however, when dysentery and insects drove Cleaveland and his company back to New England. The eventual taming of the Western Reserve wilderness has been credited to Lorenzo Carter, who arrived at General Cleaveland's original townsite in 1799. Carter, a man of impressive ability and stature, brought stability to the primitive setting and established friendly relations with the native Americans in the area. The revived settlement was named for its initial founder; the current spelling of the name can be traced to a newspaper compositor who dropped the first "a" from Cleaveland in order to fit the name on the newspaper masthead. Cleveland's geographic position as a Lake Erie port made it ideally situated for development in transportation, industry, and commerce.

By 1813 the port was receiving shipments from the cities in the East. Cleveland was chosen as the northern terminus of a canal system connecting the Ohio River and Lake Erie; it was completed in 1832. Cleveland was incorporated in 1836 as its population increased dramatically. Telegraph lines were installed in 1847, and shortly thereafter Western Union telegraph service was founded in Cleveland by Jeptha H. Wade. The opening of the Soo Canal in 1855 and the arrival of the railroad soon thereafter strengthened Cleveland's position as a transportation center.

The city played a significant role in the Civil War. Clevelanders generally opposed slavery, and a prominent local lawyer defended abolitionist John Brown. As a principal stop along the Oberlin-Wellington Trail, Cleveland was active in the Underground Railroad. While the city sent its share of volunteers to fight for the Union cause, during the Civil War the ironworks industry grew, aided by the discovery of soft coal in canal beds. After the war the iron industry continued to expand in Cleveland, and local fortunes were made in steel and shipping; those who benefitted created the Cleveland residential district known as "Millionaires Row."

Industry and Reform Spell Progress

John D. Rockefeller's Standard Oil Company, organized in 1870, put Cleveland on the map as the nation's first oil capital. A rise in trade unionism paralleled Cleveland's industrialization. The Brotherhood of Locomotive Engineers established headquarters in the city, which was the site of national labor meetings that eventually led to walkouts and brought about better conditions for workers. Inventors found a hospitable environment in Cleveland. Charles F. Brush, originator of the carbon arc lamp, founded the Brush Electric Light and Power Company and installed arc lamps throughout the city. He also invented and manufactured the first practical storage battery. Worcester R. Warner and Ambrose Swasey perfected automotive gear improvements and designed astronomy instruments, bringing about innovations in both industries.

Cleveland gained a reputation as a reform city during the five-term administration of Thomas Loftin Johnson, a captain of the steel and transportation industries. Johnson was influenced by the American social philosopher Henry George, and his administration won high praise from muckraking journalist Lincoln Steffens, who called Johnson the nation's "best mayor" and Cleveland "the best governed city in the United States." First elected to office on the "three-cent fare program," Johnson fought to overcome the entrenched political interests of his nemesis, Mark Hanna, who used his power to work against Johnson's reforms. Johnson, a mentor to a generation of young politicians, improved life in Cleveland by building new streets and parks, creating a municipal electric company to curb the abuses of private utilities, and introducing city-owned garbage and refuse collection. He also set standards for meat and dairy products, and even took down "keep off the grass" signs in city parks.

Cleveland's Cuyahoga River became a national joke when its polluted waters caught fire in 1969; by 1979 the city was a national synonym for urban collapse. Cleveland's numerous twentieth-century urban renewal efforts date back to nineteenth-century actions to eliminate slums and to revitalize the downtown core. Revitalization efforts carried out in the 1980s have produced a modern metropolis that is the envy of and a model for decaying rust-belt cities. Cleveland has enjoyed the distinction of being the first major United States city to elect to office an African-American mayor, Carl Stokes, and of being a three-time winner of the all-American city award.

Historical Information: Western Reserve Historical Society, 10825 East Boulevard, Cleveland, OH 44106-1788; telephone (216)721-5722; Great Lakes Historical Society Museum and Library, 480 Main Street, Vermillion, OH; telephone (216)967-3467

Population Profile

Metropolitan Area Residents (CMSA)
1970: 3,000,000
1980: 2,834,000
1990: 2,759,823
Percent change, 1980–1990: –0.3% (PMSA)
U.S. rank in 1980: 11th
U.S. rank in 1990: 13th (State rank: 2nd)

City Residents
1970: 751,000
1980: 573,822
1990: 505,616 (of which, 237,211 were male, and 268,405 were female)
Percent change, 1980–1990: –11.9%
U.S. rank in 1980: 18th
U.S. rank in 1990: 23rd

Density: 6,566.4 people per square mile (1990)

Racial and ethnic characteristics (1990)
  White: 250,234
  Black: 235,405
  American Indian, Eskimo, Aleut: 1,562
  Asian and Pacific Islander: 5,115
  Hispanic (may be of any race): 23,197

Percent of residents born in state: 70.8% (1990)

Age characteristics (1990)
  Population under 5 years old: 44,156
  Population 5 to 9 years old: 38,593
  Population 10 to 14 years old: 34,287
  Population 15 to 19 years old: 34,017
  Population 20 to 24 years old: 38,494
  Population 25 to 29 years old: 46,120
  Population 30 to 34 years old: 45,128
  Population 35 to 39 years old: 36,019
  Population 40 to 44 years old: 28,401
  Population 45 to 49 years old: 22,483
  Population 50 to 54 years old: 21,487
  Population 55 to 59 years old: 22,029
  Population 60 to 64 years old: 23,649
  Population 65 to 69 years old: 23,051
  Population 70 to 74 years old: 18,265
  Population 75 to 79 years old: 14,206
  Population 80 to 84 years old: 8,619
  Population 85 years and over: 6,612
  Median age: 31.8 years

Births (1988)
  Total number: 10,521

Deaths (1989)
  Total number: 6,297 (of which, 176 were infants under the age of 1 year)

Money income (1989)
  Per capita income: $9,258
  Median household income: $17,822
  Total households: 199,617
  Number of households with income of . . .
    less than $5,000: 33,323
    $5,000 to $9,999: 31,029
    $10,000 to $14,999: 22,925
    $15,000 to $24,999: 38,904
    $25,000 to $34,999: 29,632
    $35,000 to $49,999: 25,866
    $50,000 to $74,999: 14,060
    $75,000 to $99,999: 2,568
    $100,000 to $149,999: 916
    $150,000 or more: 394
  Percent of families below poverty level: 25.2% (71.4% of which were female householder families with related children under 5)
1991 FBI Crime Index Total: 45,610

Municipal Government

Cleveland city government is administered by a mayor and a twenty-one member council. Councilpersons and the mayor, who is not a member of council, are elected to four-year terms.

Head Official: Mayor Michael White (D) (since 1989; current term expires November 1993)

Total Number of City Employees: 8,000 (1993)

City Information: Cleveland City Hall, 601 Lakeside Avenue, Cleveland, OH 44144; telephone (216)664-2000

Economy

Major Industries and Commercial Activity

Diversified manufacturing is a primary economic sector, resting on a traditional base of heavy industry in particular. In 1990, for example, nearly 22 percent of the workforce was engaged in manufacturing, a figure that ranks above the national average. Consistent with a nationwide trend, the services industry—transportation, health, insurance, retailing, utilities, commercial banking, and finance—is emerging as a dominant sector. As the nation's twelfth-largest consumer market, the city is headquarters for twenty-eight major corporations, both industrial and nonindustrial. Among the firms based in Cleveland are National City Corporation, Society Corporation, Goodyear Tire and Rubber, Firestone Tire and Rubber, and B. F. Goodrich, B P America, Roadway Services, Leaseway Transportation, T R W, Sherwin-Williams Company, and American Greetings Corporation. Nearly seventy corporate headquarters with 1990 revenues of more than $250 million are located there.

Northeastern Ohio has become one of the top three polymer research and development centers in the United States. The polymer industry is expected to expand to the $100 billion level by the year 2000, and forecasts position the Cleveland metropolitan area in the forefront. Currently, between six hundred and seven hundred polymer-related companies employ thirty thousand workers in Cleveland, and more than seventy-five firms are engaged in polymer research and development. Local corporate centers for polymer-related industry include Goodyear Tire and Rubber, T R W, Standard Oil, GenCorp, B. F. Goodrich Company, and Lubrizol.

Items and goods produced: automobile parts, bolts and nuts, machine tools, paints and lacquers, chemicals, rayon, foundry and machine shop products, electrical machinery and appliances, men's and women's clothing, oil products, iron and steel

Development Projects

Cleveland's Cuyahoga River waterfront, long notorious for pollution and the ugliness of its architecture, has undergone a major transformation. As monuments to their faith in the city's revival, developers continue to erect new buildings in Cleveland. Among the most visible recent projects are the Cleveland Convention Center; Tower City Center, an elegant office and retail restoration covering thirty-four acres in the center of the city; the renovation of three theaters at Playhouse Square; and the $362 million Gateway sports/entertainment complex, to include a ballpark for the Cleveland Indians and an arena for the Cleveland Cavaliers, and scheduled to open in 1994. Cleveland will be the site of the $98 million Rock 'n Roll Hall of Fame, a futuristic complex designed by I. M. Pei and scheduled to open in 1996.

Economic Development Information: Research Department, Greater Cleveland Growth Association, 200 Tower City Center, Cleveland, OH 44113; telephone (216)621-3300

Commercial Shipping

Cleveland is at the center of the nation's largest concentration of industrial and consumer markets. The Port of Cleveland, a Foreign Trade Zone, is the third-largest on the Great Lakes and the primary general cargo facility on Lake Erie. The city is served by three rail freight carriers—Conrail, Norfolk & Southern, and C S X Corp.—that integrate services with several of the trucking companies that ship goods to and from the metropolitan area. Air cargo facilities are located at Cleveland Hopkins International Airport and Burke Lakefront Airport.

Labor Force and Employment Outlook

Employment in the service sector, especially health services, is expected to increase dramatically by the year 2000. The new sports/entertainment complex will act as an economic stimulus, creating jobs and attracting visitors.

The following is a summary of data regarding the Cleveland metropolitan area labor force as of September 1992.

Size of non-agricultural labor force: 915,400

Number of workers employed in . . .
 mining: 700
 construction: 32,400
 manufacturing: 189,400
 transportation and public utilities: 38,300
 wholesale and retail trade: 215,700
 finance, insurance, and real estate: 60,300
 services: 261,600
 government: 116,900

Average hourly earnings of production workers employed in manufacturing: $12.94

Unemployment rate: 6.2%

Largest employers	Number of employees
Ford Motor Co.	12,500
Cleveland Clinic Foundation	9,400
L T V Steel Co.	8,200
First National Supermarkets	6,451
Goodyear Tire & Rubber Co.	6,400
Centerior Energy Corp.	6,200
Ohio Bell Telephone Co.	6,200

Cost of Living

Cleveland's taxes are moderately high and are very dependent on the payroll tax. The Cleveland Chamber of Commerce pioneered a project that helps small businesses offer cheaper health care policies to workers.

The following is a summary of data regarding several key cost of living factors in the Cleveland area.

1992 (2nd Quarter) ACCRA Cost of Living Index: 110.0 (U.S. average = 100.0)

1992 (2nd Quarter) ACCRA Average House Price: $124,200

State income tax rate: Graduated from 0.743% to 6.9%

State sales tax rate: 5.0%

Local income tax rate: 2.0%

Local sales tax rate: 2.0%

Property tax rate: 81 mills per $1,000 of assessed value

Economic Information: Research Department, Greater Cleveland Growth Association, 690 Huntington Building, Cleveland, OH 44115; telephone (216)621-3300; and, County Tax Assessor, telephone (216)443-7418

Education and Research

Elementary and Secondary Schools

The Cleveland City School District, administered by a seven-member nonpartisan board that appoints a superintendent, enrolls the largest student population of any Ohio school system. It is one of thirty-one districts in Cuyahoga County. More than three hundred businesses and other organizations have joined in a partnership with the city's 127 schools; one of these is NASA Lewis Research Center.

The following is a summary of data regarding Cleveland public schools as of the 1990–1991 school year.

Total enrollment: 67,835

Number of facilities
  elementary schools: 89
  junior high schools: 19
  senior high schools: 19

Student/teacher ratio: 44.17 classroom personnel per 1,000 students

Teacher salaries
  minimum: $22,982
  maximum: $48,746

Funding per pupil: $5,628.47

More than thirty parochial and private schools offer a range of educational alternatives at the pre-school, kindergarten, elementary, and secondary levels in the Cleveland metropolitan area.

Public Schools Information: Cleveland Public Schools, 1380 East Sixth Street, Cleveland, OH 44114; telephone (216) 574-8159

Colleges and Universities

Cleveland State University, predominantly a commuter institution, enrolls more than eighteen thousand students. The university grants undergraduate and graduate degrees in sixty fields, including doctoral programs in regulatory biology, chemistry, engineering, urban studies, and urban education. Case Western Reserve University offers undergraduate, graduate, and professional education in sixty areas of study such as medicine, dentistry, nursing, law, management, and applied social sciences. Case Western Reserve is a major research institution and receives more than $60 million annually for research projects.

The Cleveland Institute of Art operates a five-year bachelor of fine arts program. The Cleveland Institute of Music grants baccalaureate, master's, and doctoral degrees in various music fields in conjunction with Case Western Reserve University, which provides the academic curriculum. Other colleges in Cleveland include Dyke College and Cuyahoga Community College (CCC), which is the city's largest college and the fourth largest in the state. It offers career education leading to an associate degree and enrolls more than twenty-four thousand students at its Metropolitan, Eastern, and Western campuses. Among the programs available are allied health, business technologies, engineering technologies, early childhood education, law enforcement, and mental health.

Among the colleges and universities enrolling more than one thousand students and located in the surrounding area or within commuting distance of Cleveland are Kent State University, University of Akron, Lakeland Community College, Lorain County Community College, Baldwin-Wallace College, John Carroll University, Oberlin College, and Ursuline College, which offers the nation's only program tailored to the way women learn.

Libraries and Research Centers

Approximately eighty libraries are operated in Cleveland by a diverse range of public agencies, private corporations, and other organizations. The Cleveland Public Library maintains twenty-eight branches with separate holdings plus a Library for the Blind and Physically Handicapped, in addition to a main facility that houses well over two million volumes, more than five thousand periodicals, and microfiche, records, tapes, and films. The library is a depository for federal, state, United Nations, and Organization of American States documents. The Cleveland Public Library for the Blind and Physically Handicapped offers Braille books, cassettes, and discs; materials on visual and physical disabilities is included in the special collections.

The Cuyahoga County Public Library, which is based in the city, houses 1.8 million books and operates twenty-seven branches in communities throughout the county. The Western Reserve Historical Society, the Cleveland Museum of Art, and the Cleveland Museum of Natural History maintain reference libraries. As a major research institution, Case Western Reserve University maintains holdings of more than 1.5 million books, nearly fourteen thousand periodical subscriptions, and approximately thirty-five special collections in such fields as literature, history, philosophy, urban studies, psychology, and the sciences; six departmental libraries are also located on campus. The Cleveland Health Sciences Library is operated by Case Western Reserve University and the Cleveland Medical Library Association. Other colleges and universities, as well as several corporations, hospitals, and religious organizations, maintain libraries in the city.

More than four hundred public and private research centers are based in the Cleveland metropolitan area. Among them are the Lewis Research Center of the National Aeronautics and Space Administration (NASA), the Cleveland Clinic Educational Foundation, and the Cleveland Psychoanalytic Institute.

Public Library Information: Cleveland Public Library, 325 Superior Avenue, Cleveland, OH 44114-1271; telephone (216) 623-2800

Health Care

Cleveland is home to a number of the nation's top institutions providing health care, medical education, and medical research and technology. The Cleveland metropolitan area is served by forty-four hospitals furnishing over 12,000 beds; more than seventy-five thousand health care professionals serve the community.

The Cleveland Clinic, which pioneered kidney transplants and open-heart surgery, is a 1,030-bed treatment and referral center for patients throughout the United States and the world. In a survey of more than one thousand leading doctors conducted by *U.S. News & World Report* and reported in June 1992, Cleveland Clinic was rated best in the country for care in cardiology, gastroenterology, neurology, orthopedics, and urology. In the same survey, Rainbow Babies and Childrens Hospital was rated best in pediatrics.

Case Western Reserve University School of Medicine provides medical education, and University Hospitals leads in research. Among other facilities in the medical forefront are St. Vincent Charity Hospital, which participated in the development of the first heart-lung machines, and Metropolitan General Hospital, which operates technologically advanced perinatal care and burn treatment units.

Other major health care facilities located in Cleveland proper include Marymount Hospital and Mt. Sinai Medical Center.

Health Care Information: Cleveland Health Education Museum, 8911 Euclid Avenue; Cleveland, OH; telephone (216)231-5010

Recreation

Sightseeing

Public Square is a good place to begin a walking tour through the downtown historic district, the adjacent Warehouse District, and the riverfront Flats. A trolley tour also offers views of landmark buildings and historic neighborhoods and will take the visitor to University Circle, where a number of museums are located. Among them are the three museums operated by the Western Reserve Historical Society, one concentrating on local history and the others displaying American and European furnishings and tracing the history of the automobile's development in Cleveland. The African-American Museum aims to correct errors of omission in black history.

Union Terminal, declared a masterpiece of art deco construction when it opened in 1933, has recently been restored and is the new home of the Cleveland Museum of Natural History, which features exhibits on the natural history of the region that include a seventy-foot dinosaur display; the most complete skeleton of the oldest human, nicknamed "Lucy," is also displayed there. Also at Union Terminal are the library and museum of the Cincinnati Historical Society, and an Omnimax theater, one of only fourteen in the country.

Steamer William G. Mather Museum is a floating ship museum and cargo boat containing a hands-on discovery center. The Cleveland Metroparks Zoo in Brookside Park simulates natural habitats for wild animals. In Rockefeller Park the Cleveland Greenhouse cultivates outdoor gardens. The Garden Center of Greater Cleveland maintains a horticultural library and plant exhibits and presents lectures on gardening and flower shows in a new modern buildings on landscaped grounds.

The NASA-Lewis Visitor Center presents programs on space exploration, aircraft propulsion, satellites, and alternative energy sources. Two of Cleveland's best-known monuments are the Garfield Monument in Lakeview Cemetery and the National Shrine of Our Lady of Lourdes, which resembles the original shrine in France and is located 10 miles east of the city.

Arts and Culture

University Circle, located 4 miles east of downtown, boasts the largest concentration of cultural institutions and museums in the country. Among the groups performing there is the Cleveland Orchestra, considered to be one of the nation's top orchestras. The Cleveland Orchestra plays a season of concerts at Severance Hall from September to May; the summer season is scheduled at the open-air Blossom Music Center from June to August. Blossom also hosts opera, classical, pop, jazz, rock, and folk concerts during the summer months. The Cleveland Chamber Music Society and the Cleveland Chamber Symphony offer a schedule of chamber music each year. The internationally acclaimed Cleveland Quartet was founded in the city and gives performances throughout the world.

One of the nation's premier dance companies, the Cleveland Ballet performs an October to May concert season at the State Theater. Two other dance companies perform in Cleveland: Dance Cleveland and North Coast Ballet Theatre. Cleveland's three opera companies, Opera Cleveland at the State Theater, Lyric Opera, and Cleveland Institute of Music's Opera Theater, stage operatic presentations.

Cleveland supports a number of theater companies. Cleveland Playhouse, the country's first professional resident company, presents a season of classical drama and new works in the Playhouse Square area, where three theaters have been restored. One of these, the Ohio, is home to the Great Lakes Theater Festival; the others host touring Broadway shows as well as opera and ballet companies. Karamu House, from the Swahili for "a center of enjoyment, a place to be entertained," has earned a national reputation as a center of black culture. Its theater presents the works of African-American playwrights as well as classics of black theater.

The Cleveland Museum of Art exhibits an impressive collection including well-known Far Eastern holdings as well as works of the masters.

Festivals and Holidays

Cleveland schedules a full calendar of annual events. Each year Cleveland organizes a sizeable St. Patrick's Day parade for March 17. Regularly on the Sunday following March 15, seventy-five buzzards return to nearby Hinckley, Ohio, from their winter habitat in the Smokey Mountains, and this natural oddity is celebrated each year. Cleveland begins its Parties in the Park in May at various downtown locations. Other May events include the Revco-Cleveland Marathon and the National Rib Cook-Off.

July highlights are the Cuyahoga Valley Folk Festival, the BP America Riverfest in the Flats, and the Fourth of July weekend Sunday at the Market at the West Side Market. The Cuyahoga County Fair in August is one of the state's largest fairs. On Labor Day weekend the Cleveland National Air Show brings an end to summer events. The Apple Butter Festival in Century Village, and Oktoberfests at Geauga Lake Park and in Painesville are among the area's many fall festivals. The Christmas season marks its start with the Holiday Light-Up on Public Square the day after Thanksgiving.

Sports for the Spectator

Cleveland, a major league city, supports professional teams in four sports. The Cleveland Indians compete in the eastern division of the Major League Baseball Association's American League. The Cleveland Browns, named for their first coach, the legendary Paul Brown, are part of the National Football League's American Conference. Both the Indians and Browns will play home games at Municipal Stadium (also known as Cleveland Stadium) on the lakefront until the new Gateway complex is completed in 1994, at which time the Indians and the Cavaliers will move there. The Cleveland Cavaliers of the National Basketball Association currently play home games at the Coliseum, as does the Cleveland Crunch, an indoor professional soccer team. Cloverleaf Speedway provides a venue for auto racing fans. Thistledown Racing Club is a facility for thoroughbred racing, and Northfield Park schedules harness races.

The Cleveland Polo Club offers a sporting alternative, as do two local rugby clubs, the Cleveland Rovers and the Cleveland Rugby Football Club. On the Fourth of July weekend the Budweiser Cleveland Grand Prix Race takes place at Burke Lakefront Airport.

Sports for the Participant

Cleveland's Metroparks system, consisting of 19,000 acres that surround the city's core, represents one of the nation's largest concentrations of park land per capita. Facilities are available for hiking, cycling, tennis, swimming, golf, boating, and horseback riding. Winter activities include cross-country skiing, tobogganing, ice skating, and ice fishing. Downhill skiing is available at three nearby resorts. Greater Cleveland encompasses more than seventy public and private golf courses. One hundred miles of Lake Erie shoreline, as well as inland lakes, reservoirs, rivers, and streams, make fishing a favorite pastime; the annual catch in Lake Erie equals that of the other four Great Lakes combined. Cleveland Lakefront State Park, Huntington Beach, and Mentor Headlands State Park are popular summer spots for water sports enthusiasts.

Shopping and Dining

More than six hundred retail businesses are located in downtown Cleveland. Downtown's newest retail center is The Avenue, located in the elegant Tower City complex and offering shopping and dining at more than one hundred establishments. The Galleria is an upscale complex of retail shops and stores, fast food eateries, and a restaurant area named The Court. Unique shopping opportunities can be found throughout the city. Antique Row on Lorain Avenue attracts antique buyers, and The Powerhouse in The Flats district on the waterfront is known for its interesting shops. The Arcade is a nineteenth-century marketplace containing more than one hundred shops and restaurants. Elegant dining is possible at Classics, named by *Food and Wine* magazine a 1992–1993 Distinguished Restaurant of North America. West Side Market sells fresh fish and meats, vegetables and fruits, cheeses, and ethnic foods.

Visitor Information: Convention and Visitors Bureau of Greater Cleveland, 3100 Terminal Tower, Cleveland, OH 44113; telephone (216)621-4110 or (800)321-1001

Convention Facilities

The Cleveland Convention Center, located downtown, contains 375,000 square feet of flexible exhibit space that can be divided into four separate meeting halls and can accommodate up to fifteen hundred exhibitors. The Public Auditorium provides a banquet capacity of 2,700 people and theater seating for 10,000 people. The lower level of the complex features a number of meeting rooms for large and small groups. Parking for six thousand cars is available nearby. The International Exposition Center is set on a 175-acre site next to Cleveland Hopkins International Airport and contains 2.5 million square feet of space. The complex can be used for a variety of events. A nineteen-thousand-square-foot conference center can be divided into nine classrooms and a lobby area for groups ranging from 25 to 425 people. On-site parking for ten thousand vehicles and a range of services and amenities are available.

Other convention and meeting facilities are located throughout the Greater Cleveland area; among them are the Boat Club, Cleveland State University Convocation Center, the Forum, Grays Armory, Playhouse Square Center, and Unified Technologies Center. In neighboring Richfield, thirty minutes south of Cleveland, the Coliseum offers thirty-one thousand square feet of continuous exhibit space, 6 meeting rooms, a banquet room, and a restaurant. Five major and luxury hotels are located downtown; three modern or restored lodging facilities are located at University Circle.

Convention Information: Convention and Visitors Bureau of Greater Cleveland, 3100 Terminal Tower, Cleveland, OH 44113; telephone (216)621-4110 or (800)321-1001

Transportation

Approaching the City

Cleveland Hopkins International Airport, the major commercial air facility in the metropolitan region, is served by fourteen carriers that schedule direct and connecting flights throughout the United States and to major foreign cities. As one of the nation's major airports, Hopkins served more than 8.7 million passengers in 1990. A rapid transit system connects the airport to downtown. Commuter air service to regional cities is available at Burke Lakefront Airport; business and general aviation traffic is handled at Cuyahoga County Airport. Twenty-one other general aviation facilities are located in the metropolitan area.

Interstate highways leading into Cleveland are east-west I-80 (the Ohio Turnpike) and I-90, which are major national routes, and I-71 and I-77 from the south; I-271 and I-480 form bypasses around the city. Other principal routes are U.S. 6, U.S. 20, and S.R. 2, which extend east to west, and U.S. 42, S.R. 8, and S.R. 21, which approach from the south.

Amtrak provides rail transportation service into Cleveland.

Traveling in the City

The Regional Transit Authority (RTA) operates Cleveland's extensive mass transit system. Public Square is the center of the city and is the starting point for east-west numbered streets. Trolley tours and riverboat cruises are available. Average intracity commuting time is under twenty-four minutes.

Communications

Newspapers and Magazines

Cleveland's major daily newspaper is the *Plain Dealer.* Numerous community newspapers, including the *Call & Post,* a black community newspaper, also circulate in the city. *Cleveland Magazine,* for readers in the Cleveland metropolitan area, features articles on politics, crime, urban and suburban contemporary and events. *Northern Ohio LIVE,* a monthly magazine describing entertainment opportunities, and *Crain's Cleveland Business* are also published there.

About eighty specialized magazines and trade and professional journals are published in Cleveland on such subjects as local history, fraternal organizations, lawn care, ethnic culture, business and economics, religion, medicine, welding and metal production, food service, and building trades.

Television and Radio

Cleveland is the broadcast media center for northeastern Ohio. Greater Cleveland television viewers tune into programming scheduled by six stations based there: five commercial and one public. Eight AM and fourteen FM radio stations broadcast a wide range of listening choices, from religious and inspirational features to news and talk shows to all major musical genres.

Media Information: Plain Dealer, 1801 Superior Avenue, NE, Cleveland, OH 44114; telephone (216)344-4500; and, *Cleveland Magazine,* 1422 Euclid Avenue, Cleveland, OH 44115; telephone (216)771-2833; and, *Northern Ohio LIVE,* 11320 Juniper Road, Cleveland, OH 44106; telephone (216)721-1800

Selected Bibliography

Chapman, Edmund H., *Cleveland, Village to Metropolis: A Case Study of Problems of Urban Development in Nineteenth-Century America* (Cleveland, Ohio: Western Reserve Historical Society, 1964)

Grubb, Davis, *The Night of the Hunter* (New York: Harper & Row, 1953)

Grubb, Davis, *Oh Beulah Land: A Novel* (New York: Viking, 1956)

Jones, Jennie, *Cleveland: A Celebration in Color* (2nd ed., Cleveland, OH: Cleveland Stock Images, 1987)

Columbus

The City in Brief

Founded: 1797 (incorporated, 1834)

Head Official: Mayor Gregory Lashutka (R) (since 1992)

City Population
 1970: 540,000
 1980: 564,871
 1990: 632,910
 Percent change, 1980–1990: 12.0%
 U.S. rank in 1980: 19th
 U.S. rank in 1990: 16th

Metropolitan Area Population
 1970: 1,149,000
 1980: 1,244,000
 1990: 1,377,419
 Percent change, 1980–1990: 10.7%
 U.S. rank in 1980: 28th
 U.S. rank in 1990: 29th

Area: 190.9 square miles (1990)

Elevation: Ranges from 685 to 893 feet above sea level

Average Annual Temperature: 51.6° F

Average Annual Precipitation: 37.0 inches

Major Economic Sectors: Services, wholesale and retail trade, government, manufacturing

Unemployment Rate: 4.9% (September 1992)

Per Capita Income: $13,151 (1989)

1992 (2nd Quarter) ACCRA Average House Price: $129,140

1992 (2nd Quarter) ACCRA Cost of Living Index: 107.7 (U.S. average = 100.0)

1991 FBI Crime Index Total: 64,778

Major Colleges and Universities: The Ohio State University; Capital University

Daily Newspaper: *The Columbus Dispatch*

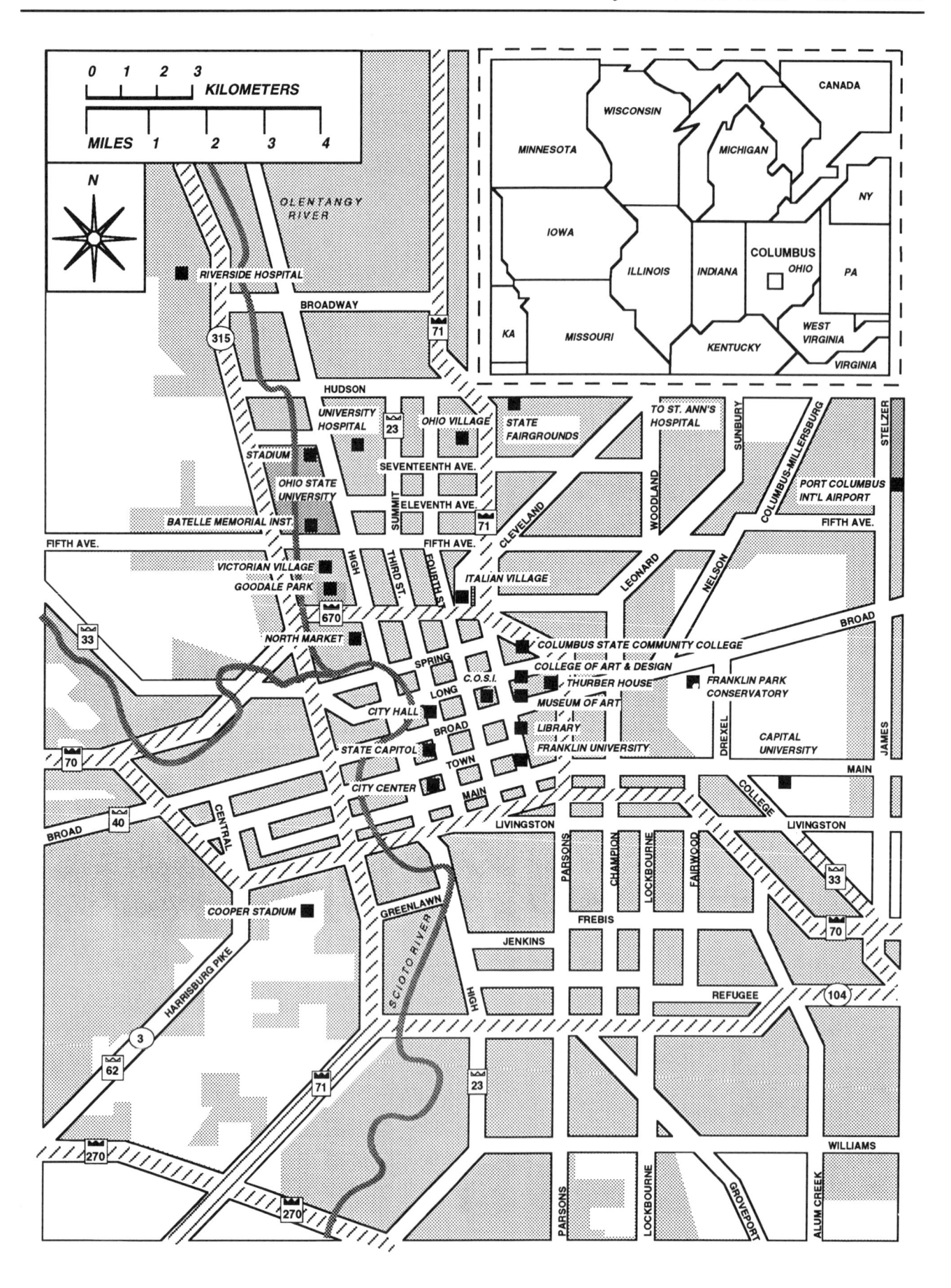

Ohio—Columbus *Cities of the United States • 2nd Edition*

Introduction

Columbus, the capital of Ohio and the state's largest city, is the seat of Franklin County. The focus of an urban complex comprised of Grandview Heights, Upper Arlington, Worthington, Bexley, and Whitehall, Columbus is the center of the metropolitan statistical area that includes Delaware, Fairfield, Franklin, Licking, Madison, Pickaway, and Union counties. Chosen by the Ohio General Assembly as the state capital because of its central location, Columbus developed in the nineteenth century as an important stop on the National Highway and as a link in the nation's canal system. Today, the city is a leader in research, education, technology, and insurance. Columbus is the only midwestern city to consistently place in the top fifty fastest-growing U.S. cities in *Inc.* magazine's annual survey; the magazine describes Columbus as "clean, with good schools, reasonably priced housing, and a college-town atmosphere that helps attract and retain young people."

Geography and Climate

Situated in central Ohio in the drainage area of the Ohio River, Columbus is located on the Scioto and Olentangy rivers; two minor streams running through the city are Alum Creek and Big Walnut Creek. Columbus's weather is changeable, influenced by air masses from central and southwest Canada; air from the Gulf of Mexico reaches the region during the summer and to a lesser extent in the fall and winter. The moderate climate is characterized by four distinct seasons. Snowfall averages around twenty-seven inches annually.

Area: 190.9 square miles (1990)

Elevation: Ranges from 685 to 893 feet above sea level; average elevation is 777 feet

Average Temperatures: January, 30.0° F; July, 75.0° F; annual average, 51.6° F

Average Annual Precipitation: 37.0 inches

History

Central Location Makes Columbus Ohio's Capital

After Ohio gained statehood in 1803, the General Assembly set out to find a geographically centralized location for the capital. Congress had enacted the Ordinance for the Northwest Territory in 1787 to settle claims from the American Revolution and a grant was given to Virginia for lands west of the Scioto River. Lucas Sullivant, a Virginia surveyor, established in 1797 the village of Franklinton, which quickly turned into a profitable trading center. In 1812 plans for a state Capitol building and a penitentiary at Franklinton were drawn up and approved by the legislature, which also agreed to rename the settlement Columbus. Construction of the state buildings was delayed for four years by the War of 1812.

During its early history the major threat to Columbus was a series of fever and cholera epidemics that did not subside until swamps close to the center of town were drained. With the opening in 1831 of the Ohio & Erie Canal, which was connected to Columbus by a smaller canal, and then the National Highway in 1833, Columbus was in a position to emerge as a trade and transportation center. Then, on February 22, 1850, a steam engine pulling flat cars made its maiden run from Columbus to Xenia, 54 miles away, and Columbus entered the railroad age. Five locally financed railroads were in operation by 1872.

Columbus, with a population of 20,000 people in 1860, became a military center during the Civil War. Camp Jackson was an assembly center for recruits and Columbus Barracks—renamed Fort Hayes in 1922—served as an arsenal. Camp Chase, also in the area, was the Union's largest facility for Confederate prisoners, and the Federal Government maintained a cemetery for the more than two thousand soldiers who died there.

Academic Prominence Precedes High-Technology Growth

Columbus prospered economically after the Civil War, as new banks and railroad lines opened and horse-and-buggy companies manufactured twenty thousand carriages and wagons a year. The city's first waterworks system and an extended streetcar service were built during this period. In 1870 the Ohio General Assembly created, through the Morrill Land Grant Act, the Ohio Agricultural and Mechanical

College, which became a vital part of the city's life and identity. This coeducational institution, renamed The Ohio State University in 1878, is now one of the country's major state universities. The Columbus campus consists of nearly four hundred permanent buildings on more than 3,500 acres of land. Today, the university's research facilities, coupled with the Battelle Memorial Institute, comprise the largest private research organization of its kind in the world.

Two events prior to World War I shook Columbus's stability. The streetcar strike of 1910 lasted through the summer and into the fall, resulting in riots and destruction of street cars and even one death. The National Guard was called out to maintain order, and when the strike finally ended, few concessions were made by the railway company. Three years later, the Scioto River flood killed 100 people and left 20,000 people homeless; property damages totalled $9 million.

Traditionally a center for political, economic, and cultural activity as the state capital, Columbus is today one of the fastest-growing cities in the east central United States. The downtown area has undergone a complete transformation, and the economy is surging as high-technology development and research companies, among other industries, move into the metropolitan area. Columbus was the scene in 1992 of a massive international celebration of the quincentennial of Christopher Columbus's voyage to the New World; as part of that project, the shallow Scioto River was dredged to make way for a replica of the *Santa Maria*.

Historical Information: Ohio Historical Society, 1985 Velma Avenue, Columbus, OH 43211; telephone (614)297-2300

Population Profile

Metropolitan Area Residents
1970: 1,149,000
1980: 1,244,000
1990: 1,377,419
Annual average percent change, 1980–1988: 0.9%
U.S. rank in 1980: 28th
U.S. rank in 1990: 29th

City Residents
1970: 540,000
1980: 564,871
1990: 632,910 (of which, 305,574 were males and 327,336 were females)
Percent change, 1980–1990: 12.0%
U.S. rank in 1980: 19th
U.S. rank in 1990: 16th (State rank: 1st)

Density: 3,315.4 people per square mile (1990)

Racial and ethnic characteristics (1990)
  White: 471,025
  Black: 142,748
  American Indian, Eskimo, Aleut: 1,469
  Asian and Pacific Islander: 14,993
  Hispanic (may be of any race): 6,741

Percent of residents born in state: 71.9%

Age characteristics (1990)
  Population under 5 years old: 50,122
  Population 5 to 9 years old: 42,564
  Population 10 to 14 years old: 36,467
  Population 15 to 19 years old: 44,754
  Population 20 to 24 years old: 75,267
  Population 25 to 29 years old: 75,609
  Population 30 to 34 years old: 64,740
  Population 35 to 39 years old: 50,330
  Population 40 to 44 years old: 39,853
  Population 45 to 49 years old: 27,877
  Population 50 to 54 years old: 23,469
  Population 55 to 59 years old: 22,018
  Population 60 to 64 years old: 21,907
  Population 65 to 69 years old: 19,464
  Population 70 to 74 years old: 14,607
  Population 75 to 79 years old: 10,688
  Population 80 to 84 years old: 7,189
  Population 85 years and over: 5,981
  Median age: 29.4 years

Births (1988)
  Total number: 11,139

Deaths (1989)
  Total number: 4,709 (of which, 137 were infants under the age of 1 year)

Money income (1989)
  Per capita income: $13,151
  Median household income: $26,651
  Total households: 257,376
  Number of households with income of . . .
    less than $5,000: 20,529
    $5,000 to $9,999: 23,378
    $10,000 to $14,999: 24,790
    $15,000 to $24,999: 51,204
    $25,000 to $34,999: 45,305
    $35,000 to $49,999: 46,573
    $50,000 to $74,999: 32,069
    $75,000 to $99,999: 8,650
    $100,000 to $149,999: 3,514
    $150,000 or more: 1,364
  Percent of families below poverty level: 12.6% (60.1% of which were female householder families with related children under 5)
  1991 FBI Crime Index Total: 64,778

Municipal Government

The city of Columbus is governed by a mayor and a council comprised of seven members who are elected at large to a four-year term.

Head Official: Mayor Gregory Lashutka (R) (since 1992; current term expires December 1995)

Total Number of City Employees: 6,871 (1992)

City Information: City Hall, Mayor's Office, Columbus, OH 43215-4184; telephone (614)645-7671

Economy

Major Industries and Commercial Activity

Columbus's diversified economy is balanced among the services, trade, government, and manufacturing sectors. State government, education, banking, research, insurance, and data processing in particular have helped the city to resist recession in the 1980s and 1990s. Telecommunications, retailing, health care, and the military are other strong employment areas. Home to more than seventy insurance companies, Columbus ranks among the insurance capitals of the United States. The city is the corporate headquarters for several nationwide firms such as Ashland Chemical, Borden Inc., Battelle Memorial Institute, Bob Evans Foods Inc., Motorists Insurance Companies, Nationwide Insurance, Producers Livestock Association, Wendy's International Inc., and White Castle Systems Inc. Twenty of Columbus's largest financial institutions operate more than four hundred offices throughout the metropolitan region. Columbus is especially attractive to foreign companies; by 1990 at least sixty had relocated or invested there.

The Federal Government is the city's second largest employer; it operates the Defense Construction Supply Center, whose seven thousand employees operate a massive central storehouse that ships up to ten thousand items a day to military posts around the world. Manufacturing comprises about sixteen percent of the metropolitan Columbus economic base, the main production categories being machinery, fabricated metal, printing and publishing, and food processing. Local industry profits from proximity to coal and natural gas resources. Limestone and sandstone quarries operate in the area.

Items and goods produced: airplanes, auto parts, appliances, telephone components, computer equipment, glass, coated fabrics, shoes, and food products

Incentive Programs—New and Existing Companies

State of Ohio incentive programs include loans, loan guarantees, and industrial revenue bonds. The Columbus Development Department incentive programs focus on small business lending and inner-city revitalization. The Columbus Area Chamber of Commerce oversees very successful public and private partnerships and small business programs to ensure the success of the region's businesses. Training programs are available through the Small Business Administration and the Central Ohio Industrial Training Program.

Development Projects

Columbus is one of the nation's fastest-growing cities. Fueling this expansion is downtown development, which during the 1980s involved an investment increase of more than 100 percent—in excess of $1 billion—since the previous decade. Principal projects include Capitol Tower, the Greater Columbus Convention Center, the Brewery District revitalization, and the Columbus City Center retail mall, along with construction of hotels and office buildings around the State Capitol and redevelopment of the Scioto riverfront. Another recent project has been the revitalization of the Short North area, involving restoration of neighborhoods, Goodale Park, and historic North Market; artists' galleries, shops, and theaters have sprung up in the area.

Economic Development Information: City of Columbus, Development Department, Economic Development Division, 99 North Front St., Columbus, OH 43215; telephone (614)645-8172; and ColumbusAmerica, Columbus Area Chamber of Commerce, 37 North High St., Columbus, OH 43215; telephone (614)225-6940

Commercial Shipping

Located within 51 percent of the country's population and served by an excellent transportation system, Columbus is a marketing, distribution, and warehouse center. An important link in the import/export shipping network is Rickenbacker Air/Industrial Park, which has been designated a free trade zone. Forty-two air carriers serve Port Columbus International Airport and two others in Franklin County. Three major railroads operate routes through Columbus; all provide piggyback and rail car shipping and two have export-import containerization facilities. Completing the ground transportation system are more than one-hundred thirty motor freight companies. One of three inland ports in the United States, Columbus receives and ships U.S. Customs-sealed containers to the Pacific Rim.

Labor Force and Employment Outlook

Local educational institutions assure employers abundant skilled labor, especially those trained in technology and engineering. Among Ohio's ten largest cities, Columbus is the only one whose population increased in the 1980s. Seventy-three percent of the labor force are high school graduates and more than 20 percent have college degrees. The presence of government, The Ohio State University, corporate headquarters, and large financial institutions will continue to lend stability to the local economy.

The following is a summary of data regarding the Columbus metropolitan area labor force as of September 1992.

Size of non-agricultural labor force: 721,600

Number of workers employed in . . .
  mining: 800
  construction: 28,900
  manufacturing: 102,800
  transportation and public utilities: 30,900
  wholesale and retail trade: 177,400
  finance, insurance, and real estate: 61,800
  services: 189,000
  government: 130,000

Average hourly earnings of production workers employed in manufacturing: $13.31

Unemployment rate: 4.9%

Largest employers	Number of employees
State of Ohio	24,989
Federal Government	15,516
The Ohio State University	12,678
Columbus Public Schools	7,684
City of Columbus	6,871
A T & T	6,693
Franklin County	5,044

Cost of Living

Most city revenue comes from income taxes, which averaged 8 percent growth annually between 1984 and 1989; fiscal 1990 and 1991 saw a slippage in that growth to a little below 5 percent.

The following is a summary of data regarding several key cost of living factors in the Columbus area.

1992 (2nd Quarter) ACCRA Cost of Living Index: 107.7 (U.S. average = 100.0)

1992 (2nd Quarter) ACCRA Average House Price: $129,140

State income tax rate: Graduated from 0.743% to 6.9%

State sales tax rate: 5.0%

Local income tax rate: 2.0%

Local sales tax rate: 5.5%

Property tax rate: 43.0159 mills of assessed valuation (35%) (1989)

Economic Information: Columbus Area Chamber of Commerce, 37 North High Street, Columbus, OH 43215; telephone (614)225-6940; Ohio Bureau of Employment Services, Labor Market Information

The old and the new juxtaposed in downtown Columbus.

Bureau, 145 South Front St., P.O. Box 1618, Columbus, OH 43216-1618

Education and Research

Elementary and Secondary Schools

The Columbus Public Schools are administered by a seven-member board of education that supports a superintendent. The system's Alexander Graham Bell School for the hearing impaired is considered one of the nation's finest. Alternative/magnet schools and a high school for the performing arts are also among the system's offerings.

The following is a summary of data regarding the Columbus public schools as of the 1991-1992 school year.

Total enrollment: 63,866

Number of facilities
  elementary schools: 89
  middle schools: 26
  senior high schools: 17 plus 4 career centers

Student/teacher ratio: 15:1

Teacher salaries
  minimum: $24,096
  maximum: $49,896

Funding per pupil: $5,548

Columbus is also served by twelve private and parochial schools that offer a range of curricula, including special education programs.

Public Schools Information: Columbus Public Schools, 270 East State Street, Columbus, OH 43215; telephone (614) 365-5000

Colleges and Universities

The Ohio State University, a major institution of higher learning at both the state and national levels, with an enrollment of more than fifty thousand students, awards undergraduate through doctorate degrees. In addition to its Columbus campus, the university maintains four regional campuses and a two-year branch facility. The Ohio State system includes eight schools and eighteen colleges that administer 165 instructional areas, more than two hundred undergraduate majors, and 108 graduate programs. Capital University schedules courses leading to undergraduate and graduate degrees in such fields as arts and sciences, music, nursing, business administration, and law; the university also operates an adult education division.

Other four-year institutions located in the Columbus area include the Columbus College of Art and Design, Devry Institute of Technology, Franklin University, and Ohio Dominican College. Columbus State Community College, enrolling more than eleven thousand students, grants two-year associate degrees in business, health, public service, and engineering technologies.

Libraries and Research Centers

Columbus is home to more than sixty libraries that are maintained by a range of institutions, corporations, government agencies, and organizations. The Columbus Metropolitan Library (formerly Public Library of Columbus and Franklin County) operates twenty-one branches in Columbus and throughout Franklin County in addition to the main facility and a bookmobile. Housing a total of more than a million volumes, nearly eighteen hundred periodical titles, and films, records, tapes, slides, maps, and charts, the library maintains special collections on local and state history and federal and state documents. The Ohio State University Libraries hold more than 4.6 million book volumes and operates numerous department libraries and five campus facilities. Included in the more than twenty-five special collections are the American Association of Editorial Cartoonist Archives, American playwrights' theater records, film scripts, Ohio News Photographers Association Archives, and various author collections featuring the works of such writers as Miguel di Cervantes, Emily Dickinson, Nathaniel Hawthorne, Edith Wharton, James Thurber, and Samuel Beckett. The library is a depository for federal, state, and European Economic Community documents.

As the state capital, Columbus is the site of libraries associated with state governmental divisions, including the Supremc Court of Ohio, the Ohio Department of Transportation, the Ohio Environmental Protection Agency, the Ohio Legislative Service Commission, and the Public Utilities Commission of Ohio. The *Columbus Dispatch,* all local colleges and universities, most major hospitals, several churches and synagogues, and cultural organizations maintain libraries in the city. Private corporations and law firms provide library facilities for both employee and public use. Among the research institutions that house libraries are Battelle Columbus Laboratories, Chemical Abstracts Service, National Center for Research in Vocational Education, and Institute of Polar Studies.

Columbus is home to the headquarters of Battelle Memorial Institute, considered the world's largest independent research organization, which conducts research, analysis, testing, design, and consultation in fields that include energy, environmental quality, health sciences, engineering and manufacturing technology, and national security. The American Ceramic Society performs educational, technical, scientific, and information services for the international ceramic community. The Online Computer Library Center (OCLC) maintains an automated information and cataloging system for more than six thousand libraries in the United States.

More than fifty research centers at The Ohio State University provide research, testing, analysis, design, and consultation services. Other research facilities located in Columbus are Chemical Abstracts Service of the American Chemical Society, The Applied Information Technologies Research Center, Edison Welding Institute, Honda of America Transportation Research Center, and several engineering, pharmaceutical, and chemical firms.

Public Library Information: Columbus Metropolitan Library, 96 South Grant Avenue, Columbus, OH 43215; telephone (614) 645-2275

Health Care

The Columbus and Franklin County metropolitan region is served by fifteen hospitals offering almost 6,000 beds. Nationally recognized for its faculty, educational resources, and diversity of medical specialties, The Ohio State University Hospital is a referral center for Ohio and the Midwest; the hospital complex houses The Ohio State University Comprehensive Cancer Center, one of twenty-three such facilities authorized by the National Cancer Act.

Children's Hospital, the country's second-largest children's health care institution, conducts research on childhood illnesses and specializes in burn treatment. Among the other hospitals in Columbus are Riverside Methodist Hospital (which recently expanded and added an ambulatory care center), Mt. Carmel Medical Center, Grant Medical Center, Saint Anthony Medical Center, and Doctors Hospital, the largest osteopathic teaching facility in the nation.

Recreation

Sightseeing

At the center of Columbus's downtown is the State Capitol Building, an example of Greek Doric architecture. Several blocks south of the Capitol, German Village, one of the city's major attractions, is a restored community in a 230-acre area settled by German immigrants in the early 1800s. The largest privately funded restoration in the United States, the district features German bakeries, outdoor beer gardens, restaurants, and homes.

The Center of Science and Industry (COSI) is one of only twenty-two such science and technology centers in the world; COSI maintains hands-on exhibits in health, history, science, and technology for all ages. The Columbus Zoo displays animals in natural habitats and has gained a reputation for successfully breeding endangered species, including gorillas, cheetahs, snow leopards, polar bears, and eagles. The zoo houses the world's largest reptile collection and is the home of four generations of gorillas.

Franklin Park Conservatory and Garden Center cultivates tropical, subtropical, and desert plants. Columbus's Park of Roses, the world's largest municipal rose garden, displays 450 varieties of roses. Located seven minutes from downtown, the Ohio Historical Center and Ohio Village recreate a nineteenth-century Ohio town, where period dishes are served at the Colonel Crawford Inn. Costumed craftspersons add to the authenticity of the exhibits. The Mid-Ohio Historical Museum displays antique dolls and toys. Hanby House, a station on the Underground Railroad, is now a memorial to Ben Hanby, who composed "Darling Nelly Gray."

Arts and Culture

Columbus is a national leader in local government support of the arts. The Columbus Arts Council distributes $3 million annually to fine-arts institutions, and the city provides an additional $2 million to a $30 million cultural industry. The focus of cultural activities are the Martin Luther King, Jr.

Center for the Performing and Cultural Arts and the Columbus Cultural Arts Center. The King center showcases African-American cultural events, while the Cultural Arts Center, located in a renovated arsenal, hosts visual and performing arts events.

Two elegant theaters are also the scene of cultural activity in Columbus. The Palace Theatre, opened in 1926, has been completely renovated and now houses Opera Columbus and presents Broadway touring musicals and plays, concerts, and films. The Ohio Theatre, a restored 1928 movie palace and the official theater for the state of Ohio, is the home of the Columbus Symphony Orchestra, BalletMet, the new Broadway series, and presentations sponsored by the Columbus Association for Performing Arts.

The Actors Repertory Theatre, the Contemporary American Theatre Company, Players Theatre Columbus, the Gallery Players, and the theater department at The Ohio State University stage live theater performances ranging from world premieres to revivals of classic plays.

The Columbus Museum of Art houses a sculpture garden and a permanent collection of European and American art works. The restored Thurber House, the home of James Thurber during his years as a student at Ohio State, is now a writers' center that displays Thurber memorabilia.

Festivals and Holidays

A major event in Columbus is the Ohio State Fair, the nation's largest state fair; held in August, the fair features livestock shows, agricultural and arts exhibitions, horse shows, rides, and concessions. Music in the Air, sponsored by the city Recreation and Parks Department, is the country's largest free outdoor concert series; two hundred concerts are presented at Columbus parks beginning in late May and concluding on Labor Day weekend. The Columbus Arts Festival, which draws 500,000 people to the city, begins the summer season on Memorial Day and continues through June 10. In June and July laser light shows are presented in the evenings, with animated stories choreographed to popular music. The city's Independence Day Parade is followed by one of the largest fireworks displays in the Midwest. The Hot Ribs and Cool Jazz festival draws participants to downtown locations the last weekend in July.

The German Village Oktoberfest is held the second weekend in September in historic German Village with German music, food, arts and crafts, and free rides. Columbus Day is celebrated in grand style in Columbus on the first weekend in October with dozens of events commemorating the history of the largest United States city named after the reputed discoverer of America. Columbus International Festival recognizes more than fifty regions and countries of the world with crafts, food, music, dance, and song on the second weekend in November at Veterans Memorial Hall. The Santa Claus Parade, held the Saturday before Thanksgiving, raises money for charity and opens the Christmas season.

Sports for the Spectator

The Big Ten conference Ohio State Buckeyes, one of the nation's top college football teams, play a home schedule to soldout crowds on fall Saturday afternoons in the ninety-thousand-seat Ohio Stadium. The Buckeyes also field men's and women's basketball teams that play home games at St. John's Arena. The Columbus Clippers, a Triple-A affiliate of baseball's professional New York Yankees, play a seventy-game home schedule at fifteen-thousand-seat Cooper Stadium.

The Banc One Marathon attracts four thousand runners from around the world. Harness racing is on view at Scioto Downs, where more than a dozen world records have been set in a season that runs from early May to mid-September. The Little Brown Jug, the year's biggest harness race, is held at the Delaware County Fairgrounds. Columbus's most important golf event, the Jack Nicklaus Memorial Tournament, is sometimes referred to as the "fifth major;" competitors tee-off in nearby Dublin at the Muirfield Village course that Nicklaus designed.

Sports for the Participant

Columbus city parks number over 165 on 5,400 acres; ten metroparks cover an additional 9,400 acres. Water sports can be enjoyed on two major rivers and three lakes in the city; among the area's popular activities are fishing, boating, sailing, water skiing, and paddleboating. The city maintains municipal tennis courts; indoor tennis and racquetball courts are available at private clubs. The city's scenic commuter routes are popular among joggers and cyclists. Year-round recreational programs for all age groups are available at the city parks.

Shopping and Dining

Columbus City Center downtown offers 130 upscale stores. Among the distinctive shopping districts in Columbus is German Village, where small shops and stores offer specialty items. Short North exhibits and sells the works of Columbus and national artists as well as clothing and home furnishings.

Diners in Columbus can choose from among a number of German restaurants as well as those serving contemporary American, European, and ethnic cuisine. *Food and Wine* magazine has named The Refectory a 1992–1993 Distinguished Restaurant of North America. Several restaurants are housed in architecturally interesting buildings such as railroad cars, churches, and firehouses. The renovated North Market features local produce and German and Italian delicatessens. Columbus is also home base for Wendy's and Bob Evans, the national restaurant chains.

Visitor Information: Greater Columbus Convention and Visitors Bureau, 10 West Broad Street, Suite 1300, Columbus, OH 43215; telephone (614)221-6623 or (800)345-4FUN

Convention Facilities

Convention and meeting planners are offered a wide range of facilities in the metropolitan Columbus area. The new Greater Columbus Convention Center, which opened in 1993, added 216,000 square feet of exhibit space, a twenty-five-thousand-square-foot ballroom, and fifty-seven meeting rooms to the ninety thousand square feet of exhibit space at the former Ohio Center, which is now included in the new complex. The nearby Ohio Center Mall is an added attraction. Other meeting facilities include Franklin County Veterans Memorial, Ohio Expositions Center (site of the Ohio State Fair), Aladdin Auditorium, the Palace and Ohio theaters, and a number of accommodations offered by The Ohio State University Department of Conferences and Institutes. First-class downtown hotels maintain a complete range of meeting and banquet facilities.

Convention Information: Greater Columbus Convention and Visitors Bureau, 10 West Broad Street, Suite 1300, Columbus, OH 43215; telephone (614)221-6623

Transportation

Approaching the City

Fifteen commercial domestic and international airlines schedule daily flights into Port Columbus International Airport, located fifteen minutes east of downtown Columbus. More than forty thousand landings are made at the newly expanded and renovated airport each year. General aviation facilities are provided at Don Scott Field and Bolton Field.

Two interstate highways—north-south I-71 and east-west I-70—intersect in the city; I-270 serves as a bypass, and I-670 is a downtown innerbelt. Several other major highways provide convenient access into and out of Columbus.

Traveling in the City

Columbus streets conform to a grid pattern, the principal thoroughfares being Broad Street (U.S. 40/62) and High Street (U.S. 23 south of I-70), which form the main downtown intersection and divide north-south streets and east-west avenues. Efficient traffic flow into the center city permits commuting time of no more than forty-five minutes from outlying areas.

The public bus system is operated by Central Ohio Transit Authority (COTA).

Communications

Newspapers and Magazines

The principal daily newspaper in Columbus is *The Columbus Dispatch* (morning). *Business First,* a business weekly, presents current news as well as analyses of local commerce. Several suburban newspapers also have a wide circulation in the metropolitan area.

Columbus is the publishing base for magazines and journals with extensive state and national distribution. Especially popular with Ohio readers is *Ohio Magazine,* which contains articles on local and state topics. *The Ohio Farmer,* an agricultural magazine established in 1848, is widely read by farmers in the state. A number of professional organizations publish their official journals in the city; among them are the

Ohio Academy of Science, the Ohio State Bar Association, the Ohio Historical Society, and the Ohio Education Association. Other specialized publications are directed toward Ohio readers with interests in such fields as agriculture, religion, education, library science and communications, banking, business and industry, and sports.

Magazines with extensive circulation include *AAA Magazine Today*, *FUR-FISH-GAME*, *Ceramics Monthly*, and *Online Today*, a magazine for subscribers to the CompuServe Information Service. Columbus is also home to membership publications of several national organizations, including Business Professionals of America and the American Society for Nondestructive Testing. The Ohio State University Press publishes several scholarly journals in such fields as theoretical geography, higher education, banking, and urban planning; several academic departments and colleges also issue publications.

Television and Radio

Columbus is the broadcast media center for central Ohio. Four commercial network affiliates and one public station—all locally based—provide television programming for viewers in the city and surrounding communities. Cable service is also available. Radio listeners tune into music, news, special features, and public-interest programs scheduled by eighteen locally-based AM and FM radio stations.

Media Information: The Columbus Dispatch, 34 South Third Street, Columbus, OH 43216; telephone (614)461-5000; and, *Columbus Monthly*, 171 East Livingston Avenue, Columbus, OH 43215; telephone (614)464-4567

Selected Bibliography

Howells, William Dean, *Years of My Youth* (New York and London: Harper & Brothers, 1916)

Dayton

The City in Brief

Founded: 1795 (incorporated, 1829)

Head Official: Mayor Richard Clay Dixon (D) (since 1986)

City Population
 1970: 243,000
 1980: 203,371
 1990: 182,044
 Percent change, 1980-1990: -5.9%
 U.S. rank in 1980: 70th
 U.S. rank in 1990: 89th

Metropolitan Area Population
 1970: 975,000
 1980: 942,000
 1990: 951,270
 Percent change, 1980-1990: 1.0%
 U.S. rank in 1980: 39th
 U.S. rank in 1990: 44th

Area: 55.0 square miles (1990)

Elevation: 750 feet above sea level

Average Annual Temperature: 51.9° F

Average Annual Precipitation: 36.71 inches

Major Economic Sectors: Wholesale and retail trade, manufacturing, services, government

Unemployment Rate: 5.7% (September 1992)

Per Capita Income: $9,135 (1987)

1992 (2nd Quarter) ACCRA Average House Price: $117,148

1992 (2nd Quarter) ACCRA Cost of Living Index: 99.8 (U.S. average = 100.0)

1991 FBI Crime Index Total: 21,602

Major Colleges and Universities: University of Dayton; Wright State University

Daily Newspaper: *Dayton Daily News*

Ohio—Dayton

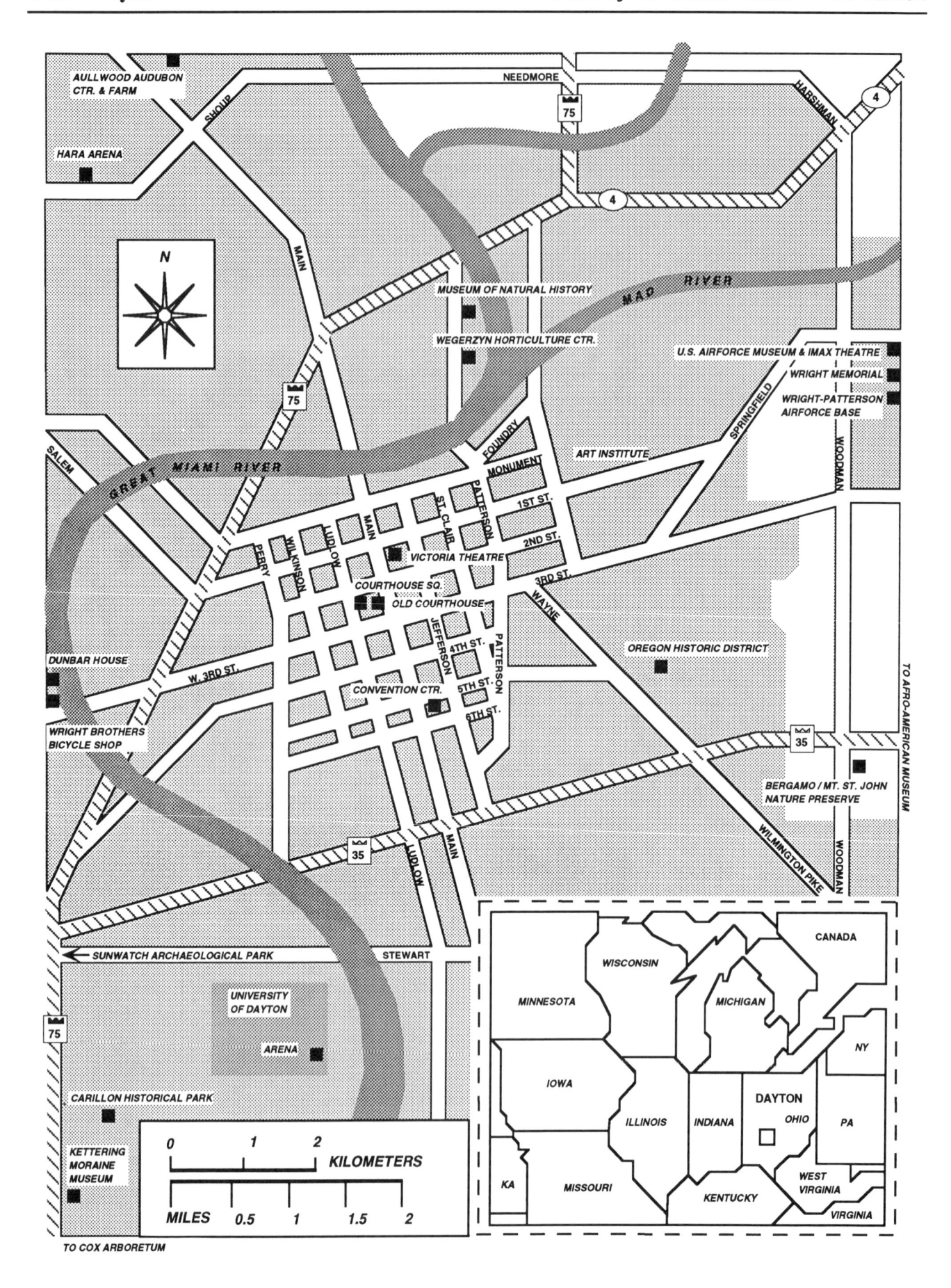

Introduction

Dayton, the seat of Ohio's Montgomery County, is the focus of a two-county metropolitan statistical area that includes Montgomery and Greene counties and the cities of Kettering, Miamisburg, Xenia, Fairborn, Oakwood, and Vandalia. World-famous through the pioneering efforts of the Wright brothers, today Dayton is an aviation center and home of Wright-Patterson Air Force Base, headquarters of the United States Air Force bomber program. Dayton, once vulnerable to severe flooding, was the site of the first comprehensive flood control project of its kind. Today the city is at the center of industrial and high-technology development, serving traditional and new markets.

Geography and Climate

Surrounded by a nearly flat plain that is fifty to one hundred feet below the elevation of the adjacent rolling countryside, Dayton is situated near the center of the Miami River Valley. The Mad River, the Stillwater River, and Wolf Creek, all tributaries of the Miami River, join the master stream within the city limits. The Miami Valley is a fertile agricultural region because of evenly distributed precipitation and moderate temperatures. High relative humidity throughout the year can cause discomfort to people with allergies. Winter temperatures are moderated by the downward slope of the Miami River; cold polar air from the Great Lakes produces extensive cloudiness and frequent snow flurries, but snow accumulation averages only nine inches annually.

Area: 55.0 square miles (1990)

Elevation: 750 feet above sea level

Average Temperatures: January, 26.6° F; July, 74.7° F; annual average, 51.9° F

Average Annual Precipitation: 36.71 inches

History

Town Planned Despite Flood Danger

The point where the Mad River flows into the Great Miami was a thoroughfare for native tribes on their way from Lake Erie to Kentucky and for frontier heroes such as George Rogers Clark, Simon Kenton, Daniel Boone, and Anthony Wayne. Revolutionary War veterans General Arthur St. Clair, General James Wilkinson, Colonel Israel Ludlow, and Jonathan Dayton of New Jersey, for whom Dayton is named, purchased 60,000 acres in the area from John Cleves Symmes. Ludlow surveyed the town plot in the fall of 1795, and the first settlers arrived on April 1, 1796. In spite of well-founded native American warnings against the danger of floods, settlers occupied the area where Dayton now stands at the confluence of four rivers and creeks.

Ohio gained statehood in 1803, and two years later Dayton was incorporated as a town and became the seat of Montgomery County. The opening of the Miami & Erie Canal in 1828 brought booming cannons and cheering crowds in celebration of future economic prosperity. That year 100,000 people descended upon Dayton, whose population then numbered 6,000 people, to hear William Henry Harrison, Whig presidential candidate. A year later Dayton was incorporated as a city. In 1851 the Mad River & Lake Erie Railroad reached Dayton, motivating Daytonians to establish new industries that were expanded during the Civil War boom years. Local Congressman Clement L. Vallandigham was head of the anti-Lincoln Copperhead faction in the North, which brought riots, murder, and the destruction of the Republican *Dayton Journal* newspaper office. Vallandigham was banished from the Union for treason.

Industrial Innovation Characterizes Dayton

Dayton entered its golden age of invention and business acumen when John Patterson bought James Ritty's cash register company and his "mechanical money drawer" in 1884. Two years later, Patterson introduced the "daylight factory," a new work environment in which 80 percent of the walls were glass. National Cash Register soon set the standard for this indispensable business device. Dayton-based inventors Wilbur and Orville Wright taught themselves aerodynamics by reading every book on the subject in the Dayton public library. They experimented with kites and gliders and built the world's first wind tunnel to test their ideas. Then on December 17, 1903, the Wright brothers made aviation history at Kitty Hawk, North Carolina, when their flying machine made its first successful flight. The Wrights' commonsensical approach to solving the centuries-old problem of heavier-than-air flight is considered one of the great engineering achievements in history.

The next inventor and engineer to make his mark in Dayton was Charles "Boss" Kettering, who began his career at National Cash Register by inventing an electric cash register. Kettering and a partner founded the Dayton Engineering Laboratories Company (Delco), which became a subsidiary of General Motors in 1920 when Kettering was appointed a vice president and director of research at General Motors. Kettering repeatedly revolutionized the automobile industry; he designed the motor for the first practical electric starter, developed tetraethyl lead that eliminated engine knock and led to ethyl gasoline, and, with chemists, discovered quick-drying lacquer finishes for automobile bodies. Kettering is considered to have demonstrated the value of industrial research and development.

Reform, Cooperation Meet City's Challenges

Newspaper publisher James Cox bought the *Dayton News* in 1898 and then purchased other newspapers in Ohio, Florida, and Atlanta, Georgia. Cox turned to politics in 1909, serving as Dayton's congressman, then as Ohio governor, and running for the presidency in 1920 on the Democratic ticket but losing to Warren G. Harding. As governor, Cox initiated a number of reforms, including the initiative and referendum, minimum wage, and worker's compensation.

Destructive floods had frequently plagued Dayton during the city's first one hundred years. Total devastation came on March 25, 1913, when the Great Miami River, swollen by a five-day downpour that brought ten inches of rain, burst through protective levees and flooded the city. So powerful was the flood that houses were literally wrenched from their foundations and sent down the Great Miami. The water level did not recede until March 28, by which time 361 people had died and property damage had reached $100 million.

The flood forced citizens to find a solution to this perennial threat; they responded by raising $2 million in sixty days. Arthur E. Morgan, a self-taught engineer who was then head of the Tennessee Valley Authority—and later became the president of Antioch College in nearby Yellow Springs—was charged with the responsibility of finding solutions. A systematic plan of flood protection consisting of five huge dams and retaining basins was proposed. The Miami Conservancy District, the first comprehensive flood-control project of its kind in the United States, was established by the state legislature on June 18, 1915. Construction was completed in 1922. In another response to the flood crisis, Dayton turned to the nonpartisan, democratically controlled commission-manager form of government, becoming the first major American city to do so and inspiring other cities to follow suit.

Historical Information: Montgomery County Historical Society, Seven North Main, Dayton, OH 45402; telephone (513) 228-6271

Population Profile

Metropolitan Area Residents
1970: 975,000
1980: 942,000
1990: 951,270
Average annual percent change, 1980–1988: 0.1%
U.S. rank in 1980: 39th
U.S. rank in 1990: 44th

City Residents
1970: 243,000
1980: 203,371
1990: 182,044 (of which, 85,675 were males and 96,369 were females)
Percent change, 1980–1990: –5.9%
U.S. rank in 1980: 70th
U.S. rank in 1990: 89th (State rank: 6th)

Density: 3,309.9 people per square mile (1990)

Racial and ethnic characteristics (1990)
   White: 106,258
   Black: 73,595
   American Indian, Eskimo, Aleut: 410
   Asian and Pacific Islander: 1,157
   Hispanic (may be of any race): 105,526

Percent of residents born in state: Not reported

Age characteristics (1990)
  Population under 5 years old: 15,403
  Population 5 to 9 years old: 13,412
  Population 10 to 14 years old: 11,735
  Population 15 to 19 years old: 13,485
  Population 20 to 24 years old: 17,181
  Population 25 to 29 years old: 16,732
  Population 30 to 34 years old: 16,023
  Population 35 to 39 years old: 13,154
  Population 40 to 44 years old: 10,428
  Population 45 to 49 years old: 7,820
  Population 50 to 54 years old: 7,338
  Population 55 to 59 years old: 7,375
  Population 60 to 64 years old: 8,029
  Population 65 to 69 years old: 8,045
  Population 70 to 74 years old: 6,220
  Population 75 to 79 years old: 4,767
  Population 80 to 84 years old: 2,837
  Population 85 years and over: 2,060
  Median age: 30.9

Births (1988)
  Total number: 3,674

Deaths (1988)
  Total number: 2,185 (49 of which were infants under the age of 1 year)

Money income
  Per capita income: $9,135 (1987)
  Effective buying income (EBI), Dayton MSA (1990)
  Total number of households: 365,200 (1990)
  Median household EBI: $27,773 (1990)
  Percent of households with income of . . .
    Less than $10,000: 15.8% (1990)
    $10,000 to $19,999: 19.8% (1990)
    $20,000 to $34,999: 27.1% (1990)
    $35,000 to $49,999: 18.9% (1990)
    $50,000 or more: 18.4% (1990)
  Number of households with an EBI above $50,000: 67,200
    Source: *Sales & Marketing Management, 1991 Survey of Buying Power*
1991 FBI Crime Index Total: 21,602

Municipal Government

The Dayton city government is administered by a five-member council, from which a mayor is chosen; council members are elected to a four-year term.

Head Official: Mayor Richard Clay Dixon (D) (since 1986; current term expires January 1, 1994)

Total Number of City Employees: 3,100 (1992)

City Information: City Hall, 101 West Third, Dayton, OH 45402; telephone (513)443-3636

Economy

Major Industries and Commercial Activity

Dayton's balanced economy is supported principally by manufacturing, wholesale and retail trade, and services. Nine of the nation's largest manufacturing companies have established headquarters in the city. The Dayton area is experiencing economic expansion with the establishment of multinational firms such as A G A, Burdox, Marconi Avionics, Honda, Fujitech Industries Inc., and Pioneer Electronics.

The transportation equipment industry, employing one fifth of manufacturing workers, has been established for many years in Dayton. Two major auto makers operate divisions in the city: six General Motors plants make small trucks, diesel engines, braking systems, and other automotive components, and a Chrysler subsidiary produces air conditioning units. Dayton has also become the site of extensive investment by Japanese auto makers.

More than fifteen hundred other firms in the Dayton area manufacture accounting systems, bicycles, castings and forgings, compressors, concrete products, washing machines, generators, hoists and jacks, industrial belts, machine tools, name plates, paints and varnishes, paper and paper-making machinery, plastics, precision gauges, tools and dies, and meat products.

Wright-Patterson Air Force Base, the research and development arm of the U.S. Air Force, is the headquarters of the Air Force Logistics Command, Air Force Material Command, and the Aeronautical Systems Division (A S D), in addition to more than one hundred other Department of Defense divisions. The new U.S. Defense Department Joint Logistics Systems Center, affiliated with Wright-Patterson, oversees the installation of new computer systems for all military services; the center is expected to generate numerous private sector jobs. The A S D at Wright-Patterson manages the U.S. Air Force bomber program; also housed at the base is the Center for Artificial Intelligence Applications (C A I A). In addition to attracting C A I A, Wright-Patterson is credited with bringing to Dayton one of the highest concentrations of aerospace/high-technology firms in the nation. More than 830 such firms employ more than twenty-three thousand scientists, engineers, technicians, and specialists actively involved in development and application in both the private and public sectors. A vital factor in the metropolitan area economy is the Miami Valley Research Park, supported by the Miami Valley Research Foundation, a private, nonprofit corporation; the 1,500-acre park is the site of corporate and government research firms.

Incentive Programs—New and Existing Companies

The State of Ohio grants direct low interest loans, industrial revenue bonds, and financial assistance for research and development to companies creating or retaining jobs in Ohio. Technical and financial assistance for job training is provided through the Ohio Industrial Training Program. Locally, the County Corporation provides loan packaging assistance, administers the SBA 504 program, and extends direct business loans within Montgomery County. The City Wide Development Corporation offers business and real estate development consulting, financial packaging, and direct loans within city limits; the organization also administers the Urban Development Action Grant and SBA 504 programs. Other incentives in Dayton and Montgomery County include tax abatement on property improvements, exemption of real property taxes on improved city-owned land, and the Urban Enterprise Zone Program.

Economic Development Information: Research Department, Dayton Development Council, Chamber Plaza, Fifth and Main, Dayton, OH 45402-2400; telephone (513)226-8222 or (800)221-8234 (in Ohio) and (800)221-8235 (outside Ohio)

Commercial Shipping

Dayton International Airport, ranking among the nation's busiest air-freight facilities, is the midwestern hub for Emery Worldwide and a base for three other air cargo carriers. Dayton's central location places its over-the-road market of more than 5.6 million people, one of the largest in the country, within a ninety-minute drive from the city. Thirty trucking companies maintain terminals in the metropolitan area; most are located at the intersection of I-70 and I-75, twenty minutes from the airport.

Three Class I rail systems furnish rail cargo transportation, including trailer on flat car service; both C S X and Conrail operate switching yards in the city. Because of its transportation system, which affords direct access to major markets, Dayton has become an important warehouse and distribution center.

Labor Force and Employment Outlook

Dayton educational institutions provide employers with skilled workers. A job growth rate of 18.6 percent for engineers and engineering technicians is predicted for the period 1988-2000; a 10.8 percent job growth rate for aeronautical and astronautical engineers is predicted for the same period. Job growth generally during that period is predicted at 10.4 percent, especially in health and business services.

The following is a summary of data regarding the Dayton metropolitan area labor force as of September 1992.

Size of non-agricultural labor force: 445,000

Number of workers employed in . . .
  mining: 500
  construction: 15,000
  manufacturing: 94,400
  transportation and public utilities: 17,700
  wholesale and retail trade: 102,400
  finance, insurance, and real estate: 11,300
  services: 75,900
  government: 44,700

Average hourly earnings of production workers employed in manufacturing: $14.51

Unemployment rate: 5.7%

Largest employers	*Number of employees*
Wright-Patterson Air Force Base	30,000
General Motors Corp. (several divisions)	20,740
NAVISTAR Corporation	5,530
N C R Corporation	5,200
Montgomery County	4,500

Largest employers	Number of employees
Miami Valley Hospital	3,950
U.S. Postal Services	3,500
Airborne Express	3,500

Cost of Living

The following is a summary of data regarding several key cost of living factors in the Dayton area.

1992 (2nd Quarter) ACCRA Cost of Living Index: 99.8 (U.S. average = 100.0)

1992 (2nd Quarter) ACCRA Average House Price: $117,148

State income tax rate: Graduated from 0.743% to 6.9%

State sales tax rate: 5.0%

Local income tax rate: 2.25%

Local sales tax rate: 6.5% (state and Montgomery County)

Property tax rate: $86.30 per $1,000 assessed valuation (1993)

Economic Information: Dayton Area Chamber of Commerce, Chamber Plaza, Fifth and Main, Dayton, OH 45402-2400; telephone (513)226-1444

Education and Research

Elementary and Secondary Schools

The Dayton City Schools system, the sixth largest district in the state of Ohio, is administered by a seven-member, nonpartisan board of education that appoints a superintendent. The system supports magnet schools, a Partners in Education program, and a Challenger Learning Center. The aerospace industry supports a District Space Symposium.

The following is a summary of data regarding Montgomery County public schools as of the 1990-1991 school year.

Total enrollment: 85,955

Student/teacher ratio: 16.7:1

Teacher salaries
  average: $32,321

Funding per pupil: $4,704

Catholic, Jewish, Baptist, Seventh Day Adventist, Church of God, and nondenominational groups also operate schools in the region.

Colleges and Universities

A wide range of higher learning resources are available within driving distance of Dayton. Located in the area are twenty-six colleges and universities, and ten vocational and technical schools that offer curricula for traditional as well as nontraditional students. The largest state-funded institution is Wright State University, with an enrollment of more than seventeen thousand students in one hundred undergraduate and thirty graduate and professional degree programs; Wright State operates schools of law, medicine, pharmacy, and nursing.

The University of Dayton, founded in 1850, is the state's largest independent university and grants associate, baccalaureate, master's, and doctorate degrees in 120 fields of study. The university operates professional schools in education, business administration, engineering, and law. The United Theological Seminary, affiliated with the United Methodist Church, offers graduate programs in theology. Based near Dayton in Yellow Springs is Antioch University; founded by Horace Mann in 1852, Antioch has long been respected for its innovative role in alternative and cooperative education. Central State University, in neighboring Wilberforce, is Ohio's only public university with a traditionally African-American student enrollment.

Sinclair College, located in downtown Dayton, awards two-year associate degrees in such areas as allied health, business, engineering technologies, and fine and applied arts. The school is known for its robotics program, operated in association with General Motors Fanacu. The Air Force Institute of Technology (A F I T) at Wright-Patterson Air Force Base is operated by the Air Force for military personnel. Designed primarily as a graduate school, AFIT also offers upper-level baccalaureate study as well as continuing education for civilians. Included among A F I T graduates are twenty-five United States astronauts.

Libraries and Research Centers

Dayton is home to nearly thirty libraries operated by a variety of institutions, businesses, and organizations. The Dayton and Montgomery County Library is the largest facility in the Miami Valley. Containing more than 1.5 million books, more than one thousand periodicals, and records, tapes, films, and slides, the library operates nineteen branches; special collections include local history and federal and state documents. All of the colleges and universities in the area maintain substantial campus libraries with holdings in a wide range of fields. Most specialized libraries are affiliated with hospitals, law firms, major corporations, and government agencies.

Dayton's higher education community is involved in technological research of national scope. The University of Dayton Research Institute works in association with Wright-Patterson Air Force Base; human-computer interaction is studied at the university's Information System Laboratory. The engineering department at Central State University conducts projects for the National Aeronautics and Space Administration and for high-technology firms. Wright State University School of Medicine's Cox Heart Institute has received recognition for the development of diagnostic and surgical treatment of heart disease. Also located in Dayton is the Hipple Cancer Research Center, one of twenty-two independent cancer research facilities in the country.

Public Library Information: Dayton and Montgomery County Public Library, 215 East Third Street, Dayton, OH 45402-2103; telephone (513) 227-9500)

Health Care

Eighteen hospitals, four of which are teaching hospitals, and a medical community that comprises the third largest employment sector in the Miami Valley combine to make Dayton a primary health care center for southwestern Ohio. Miami Valley Hospital, providing 772 beds, is the city's largest medical facility; Miami Valley operates an air ambulance service and maintains a Level 1 regional trauma center as well as units specializing in kidney dialysis, burn treatment, maternity services, and women's health programs.

In addition to furnishing in-patient and out-patient care, 560-bed Good Samaritan Hospital houses the Family Birthing Center, the Marie-Joseph Living Care Center, and a substance abuse treatment center. St. Elizabeth Medical Center, founded in 1878 near downtown Dayton, provides 631 beds and specializes in family medicine, physical therapy, sports medicine, women's health programs, and senior health care. In suburban Kettering, the Kettering Memorial Hospital/Sycamore Hospital provides 630 beds. Among other medical facilities in Dayton are Children's Medical Center, Grandview Hospital, Dartmouth Hospital, and Veterans Affairs Medical Center.

Recreation

Sightseeing

The Dayton Museum of Natural History maintains a planetarium and observatory, and operates SunWatch, a twelfth-century native American village restoration south of the city, which is considered the most complete prehistoric settlement of any culture east of the Mississippi. The United States Air Force Museum is the world's largest military aviation museum. Historic Dayton buildings and collections of artifacts from the city's golden age of invention are presented at the Kettering Moraine Museum. The National Afro-American Museum and Cultural Center, located in Wilberforce, a stop on the Underground Railroad, consists of the museum and renovated Carnegie Library.

At Carillon Historical Park, on 65 acres next to the Great Miami River, the carillon bells that are a Dayton landmark are among the featured displays, which also include the Wright Flyer III and the Barney & Smith railroad car. The Cox Arboretum is a 160-acre public garden set in native woodlands. Five miles of trails wind through woods and meadows containing more than 150 indigenous Ohio plant species at Aullwood Audubon Center, a 200-acre nature sanctuary. Other nature preserves in the Dayton area include Wegerzyn Horticultural Center and Bergamo/Mt. St. John.

The Paul Laurence Dunbar House, the restored home of one of the country's great African-American poets, is open to the public. The Wright Memorial commemorates the spot where the Wright brothers tested

The Wright Brothers Bicycle Shop in Dayton is a national historic landmark.

their airplane during its invention; the Wright Brothers Bicycle Shop is a National Historic Landmark. At the center of Dayton's downtown district, the Montgomery County Historical Society is housed in the Old Courthouse, which was built in 1850 and is considered one of the nation's finest examples of Greek Revival architecture.

Arts and Culture

Dayton supports an active cultural community. The Arts Center Foundation was created in 1986 to plan and fund new facilities to house Dayton's major arts institutions. The restoration and renovation of Victoria Theatre, a historically significant structure, was recently completed as part of a new performing arts complex. The Dayton Art Institute, founded in 1919, sponsors exhibition programs, Sunday afternoon musicales, twilight concerts, gallery talks, and studio classes. Artworks by the members of the Dayton Society of Painters and Sculptors, Inc., are exhibited in two galleries at the society's Victorian mansion quarters in the historic St. Anne's Hill district.

The Dayton Philharmonic Orchestra, founded as a chamber orchestra in 1933, is now an eighty-five-member orchestra performing classical, pops, chamber, and a summer band concert series at Memorial Hall and other Dayton locations. Dayton Opera, founded in 1960, presents three fully staged operas at Memorial Hall and shares productions with Michigan Opera Theatre and Opera Pacific in Southern California. Dayton Ballet's season of four productions includes traditional and new ballet works. Dayton Contemporary Dance Company, nationally acclaimed for innovative work, presents three performances a year at Memorial Hall in addition to national tours.

The Dayton Music Club celebrated its centennial in 1988; it sponsors free music programs at various city locations with performances by local and national artists. Other regularly scheduled musical events include the chamber concert Vanguard Series, the Soirees Musical piano performances, the Bach Society choral productions, the CityFolk ethnic and folk music series, and concerts at area churches.

Theater companies offering full seasons of traditional and experimental works include the Dayton Playhouse, the Human Race, and the Dayton Theatre Guild. The Victoria Theatre, which opened in 1865 as Dayton's first theatrical house for live entertainment, sponsors touring companies' productions as well as a season of children's drama. Wright State University, the University of Dayton, Sinclair Community College, and Antioch College stage theater performances for the general public. The Muse Machine, a Dayton organization designed to inform young people about the arts and culture, each year stages a theatrical production showcasing student performers. *Blue Jacket,* an outdoor drama about the white Shawnee war chief, is presented each summer at a facility 6 miles southeast of neighboring Xenia.

Festivals and Holidays

Art in the Park in May attracts artists from around the nation for an outdoor fine arts and crafts show. At A World A'Fair, held in May at the Convention Center, thirty-five countries share their native culture, cuisine, and costumes. Dave Hall Plaza Park hosts music festivals in the summer.

The U.S. Air and Trade Show, one of the largest of its kind in the world, draws more than two-hundred thousand spectators to the Dayton International Airport in June of even-numbered years. Arts and crafts, ethnic foods, music and dancing, and special children's activities are featured at Oktoberfest, held in late September on the grounds of the Dayton Art Institute. Each year the Dayton Holiday Festival begins the day after Thanksgiving with a tree-lighting ceremony at Courthouse Square. Ohio Renaissance Festival is held on weekends in August and September near Waynesville.

Sports for the Spectator

Dayton sports fans support both the Cincinnati Reds baseball team and the Cincinnati Bengals football team. The University of Dayton Flyers field a football team in National Collegiate Athletic Association (NCAA) Division III, as does Wittenberg University in nearby Springfield. The Flyers' basketball team has a record of successful competition on the national level and is now in the Midwestern Collegiate Conference. Wright State University and Central State University also host sports events. The Dayton Dynamos play their home games at Hara Arena in the American Indoor Soccer Association. The Dayton Polo Club competes in the Mid-States Polo League, playing sixteen matches from June to October.

Sports for the Participant

The Dayton Recreation and Parks Department sponsors sports programs for preschoolers to senior citizens at seventy-eight parks and ten recreation centers. Programs include soccer and tennis camps, summer-day camps for children, and softball leagues. Swimming, canoeing, golf, tennis, basketball, volleyball, boating, sailing, fishing, and winter sports are also available. Among the facilities managed by the department are the Jack Nicklaus Sports Center, the Wesleyan Nature Center, and the Horace M. Huffman River Corridor Bikeway, a 24-mile path along the Great Miami River.

Shopping and Dining

Downtown, the Merchants Row District offers jewelry, antiques, books, and more. The Oregon Historic District is a twelve-block area near downtown that features shops, restaurants, and clubs among restored turn-of-the-century homes. There are nearly thirty shopping centers in the region, the largest being Dayton Mall and Salem Mall. Between 1989 and 1992, five Wal-Marts and five Meijers were added to the shopping possibilities.

Dining choices in Dayton include Japanese, Chinese, Mexican, Italian, Indian, and American cuisine. One critically acclaimed restaurant, which specializes in French and continental cuisine, is known for its rack of lamb, duck, and fresh seafood. Another serves authentic German dishes. One of the city's most popular eateries is a traditional steak and chop house that does not take reservations or serve desserts.

Visitor Information: Dayton/Montgomery County Convention and Visitors Bureau, Chamber Plaza, Fifth and Main, Dayton, OH 45402; telephone (800)221-8234 (in Ohio) and (800)221-8235 (outside Ohio)

Convention Facilities

Situated in the central business district, the Dayton Convention Center is within walking distance of hotels, restaurants, shopping, and entertainment. The Convention Center was built in 1969, then renovated in 1988 in a $9 million project that doubled the available meeting space. Two exhibit halls, with capacities of forty-seven thousand square feet and 21,300 square feet, can be combined to accommodate from 3,600 to 9,970 people in a variety of settings. Also part of the complex are twenty-two meeting rooms, a 674-seat theater, a fully equipped kitchen, and teleconferencing, sound, and lighting systems. Hara Arena Conference and Exhibition Center, the second-largest facility of it kind in the state of Ohio, contains a total of 165,575 square feet of space, which includes an eight-thousand-seat arena. On the Wright State University campus is the multi-purpose Ervin J. Nutter Center, which seats up to 300 people in fifty-five hundred square feet of space.

Dayton-area hotels and motels offer meeting and banquet accommodations for large and small groups; more than seventy-five hundred lodging rooms can be found in the Dayton-Montgomery County area.

Convention Information: Dayton/Montgomery County Convention and Visitors Bureau, Chamber Plaza, Fifth and Main, Dayton, OH 45402-2400; telephone (800)221-8234 (in Ohio) and (800)221-8235 (outside Ohio); and, Dayton Convention Center, telephone (513)443-4700

Transportation

Approaching the City

The destination for the majority of air traffic into Dayton is the Dayton International Airport, near the junction of I-70 and I-75 north of the city. Dayton International is served by eleven airlines and two commuter companies. About four million passengers are enplaned and deplaned yearly on more than two hundred daily flights. Seven general aviation airports are located throughout the Miami Valley.

Highways into metropolitan Dayton include two major interstate freeways, east-west I-70 and north-south I-75; I-675, a bypass connects these highways and provides direct access to the city from Columbus and Cincinnati. U.S. 35 extends from east to west through the southern sector of Dayton. State routes leading into Dayton from points throughout the state and the immediate vicinity are 4, 202, 48, 49—all with a general north-south orientation.

Traveling in the City

Regional Transit Authority (R T A) provides regularly scheduled mass transit bus service throughout Montgomery County and in parts of Greene County; R T A operates special routes to Wright-Patterson Air Force Base and Wright State and Central State Universities.

Communications

Newspapers and Magazines

Established in 1808 and merged with the *Journal Herald* in 1988, the *Dayton Daily News* is the city's daily morning newspaper. More than twenty suburban newspapers plus local college and university publications circulate weekly. Special-interest magazines published in Dayton cover such subjects as religion, African-American culture, and management.

Television and Radio

Dayton is the primary center for television and radio north of Cincinnati in southwestern Ohio. Five television stations—three commercial affiliates, one public, and one independent—broadcast from Dayton; cable service is available. Between thirteen and seventeen AM and FM radio stations schedule a variety of programs such as jazz, gospel, Celtic and folk, African-American, contemporary, and classical music, educational features, and news.

Media Information: Dayton Newspapers Inc., 45 South Ludlow Street, Dayton, OH 45401; telephone (513)225-2085

Selected Bibliography

Szathmary, Louis, *Midwestern Home Cookery* (New York: Promontory Press, 1974) (Reprint of the 1875 ed. of the Presbyterian Cook Book, compiled by the ladies of the First Presbyterian Church, Dayton, Ohio; and of the 3d ed., 1906, of the Capital City Cook Book, compiled by the Women's Guild of Grace Church, Madison, Wis.)

Toledo

The City in Brief

Founded: 1817 (incorporated, 1837)

Head Official: City Manager Thomas Hoover (since 1990)

City Population
 1970: 383,000
 1980: 354,635
 1990: 332,943
 Percent change, 1980-1990: -6.1%
 U.S. rank in 1980: 40th
 U.S. rank in 1990: 49th

Metropolitan Area Population
 1970: 606,000
 1980: 617,000
 1990: 614,128
 Percent change, 1980-1990: -0.4%
 U.S. rank in 1980: 55th
 U.S. rank in 1990: 64th

Area: 80.6 square miles (1990)
Elevation: 669 feet above sea level
Average Annual Temperature: 48.5° F
Average Annual Precipitation: 31.78 inches

Major Economic Sectors: Services, wholesale and retail trade, manufacturing, government
Unemployment Rate: 6.7% (September 1992)
Per Capita Income: $11,894 (1989)
1992 (2nd Quarter) ACCRA Average House Price: $119,250
1992 (2nd Quarter) ACCRA Cost of Living Index: 106.7 (U.S. average = 100.0)
1991 FBI Crime Index Total: 31,907

Major Colleges and Universities: University of Toledo; Medical College of Ohio; Owens Technical College

Daily Newspaper: *The Toledo Blade*

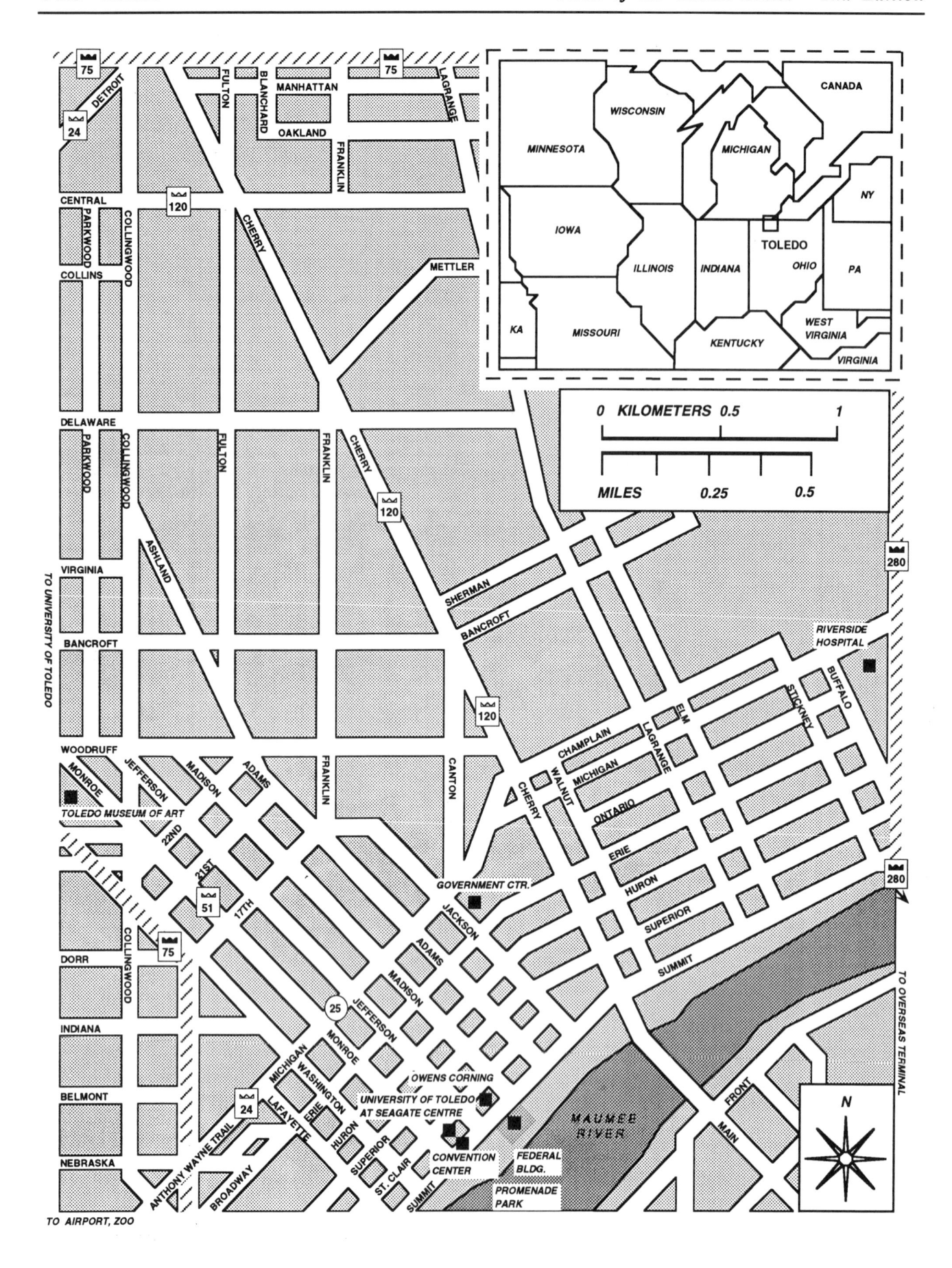

Ohio—Toledo *Cities of the United States • 2nd Edition*

Introduction

Toledo, the seat of Ohio's Lucas County, is the focus of a metropolitan complex comprised of Ottawa Hills, Maumee, Oregon, Sylvania, Perrysburg, and Rossford. The Toledo metropolitan statistical area encompasses the counties of Fulton, Lucas, and Wood. The city played a strategic role in the War of 1812, after which the victorious Americans enjoyed unimpeded settlement of the Northwest Territory. The site of pioneer advancements in the glass-making industry, today Toledo continues to be headquarters of international glass companies. The Port of Toledo is a major Great Lakes shipping point.

Geography and Climate

Toledo is located on the western end of Lake Erie at the mouth of the Maumee River, surrounded by generally level terrain. The soil is quite fertile, particularly along the Maumee Valley toward the Indiana state line. The nearness of Lake Erie moderates temperatures; humidity is high throughout the year and is accompanied by an excessive amount of cloudiness. Severe and damaging windstorms occur frequently, and flooding is often produced by heavy rains. Snowfall in Toledo is normally light.

Area: 80.6 square miles (1990)

Elevation: 669 feet above sea level

Average Temperatures: January, 23.1° F; July, 71.8° F; annual average, 48.5° F

Average Annual Precipitation: 31.78 inches

History

French, British Settle Maumee Valley

As early as 1615 Etienne Brule, Samuel de Champlain's French-Canadian scout, discovered the Erie tribe of native Americans living at the mouth of the Maumee River, the largest river that flows into the Great Lakes. Robert Cavelier, sieur de La Salle, claimed the territory in the name of France's King Louis XIV in 1689, and French trading posts were subsequently established in the Maumee Valley. A century later the British built Fort Miami there. Following the French and Indian War in 1763, France ceded all claims in the territory to Britain, who annexed the region to the Canadian Province of Quebec in 1774. At the end of the American Revolution, the region became part of the United States and was designated as part of the Northwest Territory in 1787. Renegade agents incited native American warriors to attack settlers in the area; when American military forces were sent there in 1790, the native tribes prevailed. Four years later, General Anthony Wayne defeated two thousand native Americans at the Battle of Fallen Timbers southwest of present-day Toledo. General Wayne then directed the building of several forts, of which one was Fort Industry, constructed at the present site of Toledo.

At the outbreak of the War of 1812 the few settlers in the vicinity fled. In January, 1813, General William Henry Harrison, later President of the United States, erected Fort Meigs, a massive fortification enclosing nine acres, which became known as the "Gibraltar of the Northwest." In the Battle of Lake Erie, off Put-In-Bay, the U. S. Navy's young Commodore Perry defeated the British naval force, followed by Harrison's defeat of General Proctor at the Battle of the Thames. These victories re-secured the Northwest Territory for the United States. After the war, a permanent settlement was formed on the northwest side of the Maumee River near the mouth of Swan Creek. In 1817 an Indian treaty conveyed most of the remaining land in the area to the federal government. The village of Port Lawrence near Fort Industry was formed by a Cincinnati syndicate in 1817, but it failed in 1820 and was then revived. Port Lawrence voted in 1835 to consolidate with the settlement of Vistula, one mile away, and the two were incorporated as Toledo in 1837.

The choice of the name of Toledo for the new city is shrouded in local legend. Popular versions give credit to a merchant who suggested Toledo because it "is easy to pronounce, is pleasant in sound, and there is no other city of that name on the American continent." Whatever the source, friendly relations with the city of Toledo, Spain, have resulted. The Hispanic government awarded *The Toledo Blade,* the city's oldest newspaper, the royal coat of arms, and the University of Toledo has permission to use the arms of Spain's Ferdinand and Isabella as its motif.

Border Dispute Precedes Industrial Growth

The "Toledo War" of 1835-36 between Ohio and Michigan over their common boundary did not involve bloodshed but it did result in federal intervention to resolve the dispute. Governor Robert Lucas of Ohio led a force of one thousand soldiers to Perrysburg in March 1835, with the intent of driving Michigan militia from Toledo, but emissaries sent by President Andrew Jackson arranged a truce. Governor Lucas held a special session of the legislature in June, creating Lucas County out of the land in Wood County involved in the dispute. The new county held court in Toledo on the first Monday of September, which proved it had exercised jurisdiction over the disputed territory by holding a Court of Common Pleas in due form of law. Finally, Congress settled the issue by stipulating that the condition of Michigan's entrance into the Union would award Ohio the contested land and Michigan, in compensation, would receive what is now the state's Upper Peninsula.

Toledo in the mid-nineteenth century benefitted from the opening of new canals, the establishment of businesses along the river bank to accommodate trade and new shipping industries, and the arrival of the railroad. Prosperity continued during the Civil War, and by the end of the century the city became a major rail center in the United States. During the 1880s Toledo's industrial base, spurred by the discovery of inexpensive fuel, attracted glass-making entrepreneurs. Edward Libbey established a glassworks in Toledo, and then hired Michael Owens to supervise the new plant. The two pioneers revolutionized the glass business with inventions that eliminated child labor and streamlined production. Edward Ford arrived in the Toledo region in 1896 to found the model industrial town of Rossford and one of the largest plate-glass operations of its time.

Two politicians stand out in the history of Toledo. Samuel M. "Gold Rule" Jones was elected mayor on a nonpartisan ticket and emerged as a national figure. His reform efforts in city government introduced one of the first municipal utilities, the eight-hour workday for city employees, and the first free kindergartens, public playgrounds, and band concerts. Mayor Brand Whitlock continued Jones's reforms by securing a state law for the nonpartisan election of judges and Ohio's initiative and referendum law in 1912.

John Willys moved his Overland automobile factory from Indianapolis to Toledo in 1908, and, in time, automotive-parts manufacture flourished in the area; the industry was firmly established by such firms as Champion Spark Plug and Warner Manufacturing Company, maker of automobile gears. A strike by Auto-Lite workers in 1934 was marred by violence and prompted the intervention of U.S. troops and the Federal Department of Labor; the resolution of this strike, which received national attention, helped contribute to the unionization of the automotive industries. The Toledo Industrial Peace Board, set up in 1935 to resolve labor disputes by round-table discussion, served as a model for similar entities in other cities.

Historical Information: Maumee Valley Historical Society, 1031 River Road, Maumee, OH; telephone (419) 893-9602

Population Profile

Metropolitan Area Residents
1970: 606,000
1980: 617,000
1990: 614,128
Percent change, 1980-1990: —0.4%
U.S. rank in 1980: 55th
U.S. rank in 1990: 64th

City Residents
1970: 383,000
1980: 354,635
1990: 332,943 (of which, 157,941 were males and 175,002 were females)
Percent change, 1980-1990: —6.1%
U.S. rank in 1980: 40th
U.S. rank in 1990: 49th (State rank: 4th)

Density: 4,130.8 people per square mile (1990)

Racial and ethnic characteristics (1990)
  White: 256,239
  Black: 65,598
  American Indian, Eskimo, Aleut: 920
  Asian and Pacific Islander: 3,487
  Hispanic (may be of any race): 13,207

Age characteristics (1990)
　Population under 5 years old: 27,159
　Population 5 to 9 years old: 24,498
　Population 10 to 14 years old: 22,101
　Population 15 to 19 years old: 25,023
　Population 20 to 24 years old: 27,749
　Population 25 to 29 years old: 29,920
　Population 30 to 34 years old: 28,752
　Population 35 to 39 years old: 24,547
　Population 40 to 44 years old: 20,675
　Population 45 to 49 years old: 15,430
　Population 50 to 54 years old: 13,549
　Population 55 to 59 years old: 13,212
　Population 60 to 64 years old: 15,127
　Population 65 to 69 years old: 14,474
　Population 70 to 74 years old: 11,662
　Population 75 to 79 years old: 8,774
　Population 80 to 84 years old: 5,870
　Population 85 years and over: 4,421
　Median age: 31.7 years

Births (1988)
　Total number: 6,225

Deaths (1988)
　Total number: 3,541 (of which, 68 were infants under the age of 1 year)

Money income (1989)
　Per capita income: $11,894
　Median household income: $24,819
　Total households: 130,774
　Number of households with income of . . .
　　less than $5,000: 13,033
　　$5,000 to $9,999: 15,924
　　$10,000 to $14,999: 12,555
　　$15,000 to $24,999: 24,253
　　$25,000 to $34,999: 20,816
　　$35,000 to $49,999: 22,419
　　$50,000 to $74,999: 15,962
　　$75,000 to $99,999: 3,718
　　$100,000 to $149,999: 1,460
　　$150,000 or more: 634
　Percent of families below poverty level: 15.4% (72.0% of which were female householder families with related children under 5)
1991 FBI Crime Index Total: 31,907

Municipal Government

The city of Toledo is administered by a city manager form of government. Nine council members, one of whom is the mayor, are elected to two-year terms. The mayor and council appoint the city manager, who serves a term of indefinite length.

Head Official: City Manager Thomas Hoover (since 1990)

Total Number of City Employees: approximately 3,000 (1993)

City Information: telephone (419)245-1010

Economy

Major Industries and Commercial Activity

Manufacturing comprises approximately one fourth of Toledo's economic base. Nearly one thousand manufacturing facilities, many of them automotive-related, are located in the metropolitan area. Toledo is home to the headquarters of such corporations as TRINOVA Corporation, Libbey-Owens-Ford Company, Owens-Corning Fiberglas Corporation, and Owens-Illinois, Inc. With thirteen major financial institutions, Toledo is also a banking and finance center for northwestern Ohio.

Medical and technologically oriented businesses are a major force in the local economy; Lucas County ranks among the fifty counties in the United States that account for 50 percent of medical industry production. Several private testing laboratories and manufacturers of medical instruments and allied products are located in the Toledo area. In addition, more than four hundred plastics, metalworking, and electronics companies adapt engineering and production capabilities to the medical device and instrument industries. Education is also an economic pillar.

Items and goods produced: spark plugs, automotive and truck components, health care products, glass products, fiberglass, packaged foods, plastic and paper products, building materials

Incentive Programs—New and Existing Companies

The Economic Development Division of the Toledo-Lucas County Port Authority is the principal agency for facilitating business expansion and location in the Toledo metropolitan area. Primary emphasis is placed on industry and manufacturing, which have traditionally been an integral part of the area economic base. Working in cooperation with public and private development agencies, the Port Authority matches sites and vacant buildings with business needs, evaluates public services and costs, and provides financial packaging assistance through the Northwest Ohio Bond Fund. Among the participants in the bond program are Teledyne CAE, designers and manufacturers of small gas turbines for military applications, and Solar Cells, Inc., makers of photovoltaic cells for converting sunlight to electricity.

Economic Development Information: Toledo-Lucas County Port Authority, One Maritime Plaza, Toledo, OH 43604-1866; telephone (419)243-8251

Development Projects

Major projects of the University of Toledo include the $10 million Center for the Visual Arts, an addition to the Toledo Museum of Art, which was designed by Frank Gehry and is itself considered an architectural work of art. A $9.25 million Academic Centre and a $1.2 million Student Medical Center have been built, and the Ohio Board of Regents has approved $26 million in capital improvements at the university. A proposed research and development park there will include a new business incubator.

Commercial Shipping

Toledo is situated at the center of a major market area; located within 500 miles of the city are 43 percent and 47 percent, respectively, of U.S. and Canadian industrial markets. A commercial transportation network, consisting of a river port, railroads, interstate highways, and an international airport, provides access to this market area as well as points throughout the nation and the world.

The Port of Toledo, on the Maumee River, is a 150-acre domestic and international shipping facility that includes a general cargo center, mobile cargo handling gear, and covered storage space. An average of ten to fifteen million tons of coal and iron ore, grain, and general cargo are processed through the port each year; designated as a Foreign Trade Zone, the complex affords shippers deferred duty payments and tax savings on foreign goods.

Toledo is served by five railroad systems, which provide direct and interline shipping; Conrail maintains piggyback terminal facilities in the city. More than 110 truck firms link Toledo with all major metropolitan areas in the United States and points throughout Canada. Commercial air freight carriers operate out of Toledo Express Airport, where Burlington Air Express recently added a $75 million air cargo hub.

Labor Force and Employment Outlook

Manufacturing accounts for approximately 20 percent of the jobs in metropolitan Toledo. The traditional manufacturing base, comprised of glass and auto companies, whose employees are well-paid and unionized, is shrinking. Low-skill, low-paying jobs in nonunion retail stores, service businesses, and small manufacturing companies are expanding. Meijer department stores, and Burlington Air Express, the area's two new big employers, reportedly are offering only part-time work at low wages. The University of Toledo reported in 1993 that 30 percent of its graduates were accepting contingent jobs, compared to 10 percent in 1990.

The following is a summary of data regarding the Toledo metropolitan area labor force as of September 1992.

Size of non-agricultural labor force: 282,100

Number of workers employed in . . .
  mining: 200
  construction: 11,300
  manufacturing: 55,600
  transportation and public utilities: 13,100
  wholesale and retail trade: 70,000
  finance, insurance, and real estate: 11,300
  services: 75,900
  government: 44,700

Average hourly earnings of production workers employed in manufacturing: $14.89

Unemployment rate: 6.7%

Largest manufacturing/ utility employers	Number of employees
Jeep/Eagle Division, Chrysler Corp.	5,300
Power Train Division/General Motors Corp.	4,200
Owens-Illinois, Inc.	3,100

Wolcott House Museum in Maumee depicts life in the Maumee Valley from 1840 to 1860.

Largest manufacturing/ utility employers	Number of employees
Toledo Edison Co.	2,545
The Andersons (grain storage/ processing)	2,100

Cost of Living

The following is a summary of data regarding several key cost of living factors in the Toledo area.

1992 (2nd Quarter) ACCRA Cost of Living Index: 106.7 (U.S. average = 100.0)

1992 (2nd Quarter) ACCRA Average House Price: $119,250

State income tax rate: Graduated from 0.743% to 6.9%

State sales tax rate: 5.0%

Local income tax rate: 2.25%

Local sales tax rate: 1.5% (county)

Property tax rate: Ranges in the Toledo area from $40 to $58 per $1,000 of assessed valuation; assessed at 35.0%

Economic Information: Toledo Area Chamber of Commerce, 218 North Huron Street, Toledo, OH 43604; telephone (419)243-8191

Education and Research

Elementary and Secondary Schools

Public elementary and secondary schools in Toledo are administered by the Toledo Public Schools system, the fourth largest of 615 districts in the state of Ohio. Five partisan board of education members select a superintendent. Washington Local Schools serve much of the northwest area of the city.

The following is a summary of data regarding Toledo public schools as of the 1992–1993 school year.

Total enrollment: 39,415

Number of facilities
elementary schools: 43
junior high schools: 8
senior high schools: 8

Student/teacher ratio: 22:1

Teacher salaries
minimum: $21,321
maximum: $44,881

Funding per pupil: $5,087

The Catholic Diocese of Toledo operates an extensive parochial school system in the city and surrounding area. Other private and church-related schools also offer educational alternatives.

Public Schools Information: Toledo Public Schools, Manhattan and Elm Streets, Toledo, OH 43608; telephone (419)729-8231

Colleges and Universities

Five institutions of higher learning are located in metropolitan Toledo. The University of Toledo's eight colleges enroll about twenty-five thousand students and offer degrees in undergraduate and graduate fields, including engineering and pharmacy. The University of Toledo Community and Technical College provides two-year technical training in such areas as engineering technology, electronics technology, and plastics engineering. The Medical College of Ohio (M C O) grants a medical degree as well as graduate degrees in medical science and industrial hygiene; M C O conducts joint educational programs and collaborative research with area businesses and educational institutions. Owens Technical College offers two-year programs in biomedical equipment, computer-integrated manufacturing, and glass engineering, among others.

Within commuting distance of Toledo are Bowling Green State University and the University of Michigan.

Libraries and Research Centers

Toledo is home to twenty-four libraries operated by public agencies and private organizations and corporations. The Toledo—Lucas County Public Library houses about 1.9 million books as well as about 2,161 periodical titles, audio and video tapes, films, slides, and maps; the library system includes eighteen branches and two bookmobiles located throughout the city and the county. The University of Toledo, the Medical College of Ohio at Toledo, and Owens Technical College maintain campus libraries. Other libraries are associated with the Toledo Museum of Art, companies such as Libbey-Owens-Ford, law firms, hospitals, and churches and synagogues.

The Medical College of Ohio (M C O) in Toledo is active in medical research and development. M C O has created the Health Technology Park to house college facilities and the Northwest Ohio Health Technology Center (N O H T C), which serves as a research and development incubator for private companies and academic institutions. Among the projects affiliated with N O H T C are work in high resolution, flat (plasma) panel display; detection of bacterial growth in liquid culture media, without time lags; development of artificial lung material and other products; and a computer-based therapeutic drug monitoring program. The M C O Image Analysis Center utilizes the most advanced equipment to consolidate information from existing and emerging imaging technologies for greater accessibility to physicians and other professionals.

Research and development is also conducted at the University of Toledo's Polymer and Thin Films Institute and Eitel Institute for Silicate Research as well as at Edison Industrial Systems Center. Under construction in 1992 was the federally-funded National Center for Tooling and Precision Products research at the University of Toledo. The National Drosophilia Species Resource Center, affiliated with nearby Bowling Green State University, is internationally known for fruit-fly research.

Public Library Information: Toledo-Lucas County Public Library, 325 Michigan Street, Toledo, OH 43624-1614; telephone (419)259-5200

Health Care

Ten hospitals, providing more than 3,000 beds, serve the metropolitan Toledo area with complete general, specialized, and surgical care. The largest facilities are Toledo Hospital, with 775 beds, and St. Vincent Medical Center, with 588 beds; other hospitals include Flower Memorial Healthplex, Mercy Hospital, St. Charles Hospital, Riverside Hospital, and St. Luke's Hospital. A valuable resource in the community is the Medical College of Ohio, which operates three hospitals and provides training for health care professionals.

Health Care Information: Academy of Medicine referral services, telephone (419)473-3200

Recreation

Sightseeing

Fort Meigs, located near Toledo along the southern bank of the Maumee River west of Perrysburg, was the largest walled fortification in North America. Built in 1813 under the direction of General William Henry Harrison(who later became president of the United States), Fort Meigs is an impressive structure of earthworks and timber. Toledo's Old West End, covering twenty-five blocks, is one of the largest collections of late-Victorian architecture in the country; Frank Lloyd Wright studied the Old West End in preparing his plans for Oak Park, Illinois. Blair Museum of Lithophanes and Carved Waxes is located in Old West End.

The freighter *William B. Boyer* was first launched in 1911 and served for many years on the Great Lakes as the largest ship of its type. Now restored, it is docked at International Park. The Sauder Farm and Craft Village, a living-history museum in nearby Archibald, recaptures life in northwest Ohio in the 1830s. Wolcott House Museum in Maumee depicts life in the Maumee Valley from 1840 to 1860.

The 30-acre Toledo Zoo is comprised of thirteen major buildings that were constructed during the Great Depression to provide work for unemployed designers and laborers. Today, it is one of the nation's highest rated zoological parks, with well-known survival programs for endangered species including orangutans, gorillas, snow leopards, and cheetahs. Two thousand animals representing four hundred species are on exhibit in facilities that include a conservatory, a botanical garden, one of the country's largest aquariums, a children's zoo, and the Museum of Science with its hands-on exhibit.

The nine Metroparks of the Toledo area preserve sand dunes, tall grass prairies, upland woody swamp forests, and oak savannahs. The parks offer elevated views of the Maumee River Valley. Oak Openings Preserve protects threatened and endangered plant species, while Pearson Preserve protects one of the

Toledo Museum of Art.

few remnants of the Great Black Swamp. The Metroparks present many free nature and history programs and recapture the natural beauty of the area at the time it was first settled. At Side Cut Metropark visitors can examine massive limestone locks that were part of the mid-nineteenth century canal system. Providence Metropark's Isaac Ludwig Mill, which first ground grain in 1846, has been restored as a waterpower interpretive center. The Ohio Baseball Hall of Fame is at Lucas County Recreation Area.

Located in a firehouse that dates from around 1920, the Toledo Firefighters Museum preserves 150 years of fire fighting in the city. Thousands of items are on exhibit, including many of large pieces of vintage fire fighting equipment. Crosby Gardens cultivates herbs, roses, azalea, rhododendron, and wildflowers; artists' studios and galleries are maintained on the grounds.

Arts and Culture

The Toledo Museum of Art was founded in 1912 when Edward Libbey made a contribution of money and land to help initiate the museum's first stage of construction. Today, the museum's permanent collection represents holdings from diverse cultures and periods, including ancient Egyptian tombs, a medieval cloister, a French chateau, glass, furniture, silver, tapestries, and paintings by world masters. The Toledo Symphony Orchestra presents a full season of concerts in Peristyle Hall at the Toledo Museum of Art.

The Masonic Auditorium hosts performances by the Toledo Opera Association and touring Broadway shows. Two community theater groups, Toledo Repertoire Theatre and the Village Players, stage several productions annually, while Junior Theatre Guild stages four annual professional family-oriented shows. The Toledo Ballet Association presents local and guest performers, sometimes in collaboration with the opera and symphony. Both the University of Toledo and Bowling Green State University schedule plays and other cultural events, many featuring well-known performing artists and speakers.

Festivals and Holidays

Many festivals celebrate Toledo's history and its ethnic diversity, including International Folk Festivals, sponsored in May by the International Institute. Toledo's recreational boating season is officially opened each year on Memorial Day weekend with four days of entertainment, food, drink, and activities. Through the summer, Rallies by the River sponsors music and refreshments at Promenade Park on Friday afternoons. In early June the Old West End Spring Festival opens restored Victorian homes to the public. The Crosby Festival of the Arts is held in late June at Toledo Botanical Gardens. The annual Toledo fireworks display takes place downtown on the river on July 3. Also downtown, in Promenade Park, the Northwest Ohio Rib-Off is scheduled for August; the six-day Lucas County Fair is also held in August. Toledo's largest summer street fair is held on Labor Day weekend.

Sports for the Spectator

The Toledo Mud Hens, the Triple A farm team for professional baseball's Detroit Tigers, compete in the International League with home games at Ned Skeldon Stadium in Maumee. Beginning in October, the Toledo Storm, East Coast Hockey League affiliates for the National Hockey League's Detroit Red Wings, entertain fans at Toledo Sports Arena. Raceway Park presents harness racing on a spiral-banked five-eighths mile track from March to December. Stock car racing is on view at Toledo Speedway. The University of Toledo Rockets and the Bowling Green State University Falcons field teams in Mid-American Conference sports. The Inverness Club hosts PGA and LPGA tournament play. U.S. Formula One Grand Prix racing is held on the Maumee River during Labor Day weekend.

Sports for the Participant

Toledo, the largest port on Lake Erie, offers some of the best fishing in the world. Walleye season runs from May to August, followed by perch in the fall; white and smallmouth bass are other popular catches. Ice fishing is available in January and February. Toledo maintains one of Ohio's best park systems, setting aside 147 areas for sports and relaxation. The Lucas County Recreation Department provides facilities for swimming, tennis, track, handball, and softball; it also operates two blue-water swimming quarries. Toledo Area Metroparks offers boating, cycling, hiking, jogging, water and field sports, and fitness trails on over 6,600 acres. Toledo boasts some of the finest golf courses in the country.

Shopping and Dining

Portside Festival Marketplace, located at the downtown waterfront, combines shopping and dining in a two-story glass-enclosed marketplace. Unique shopping opportunities include glass factory outlet stores, featuring all types and styles of glassware; flea markets; the renovated Farmer's Market; and art galleries. At least five major shopping centers are located in the area, and in early 1993, the Meijer chain was building four giant stores there.

Among Toledo's five hundred to seven hundred restaurants is Tony Packo's Cafe, celebrated by Corporal Klinger, a character on the television program "M*A*S*H." Featuring an extensive Tiffany lamp collection, the restaurant serves a distinctive hot dog, Hungarian hamburgers, and a vegetable soup with Hungarian dumplings.

Visitor Information: The Greater Toledo Convention and Visitors Bureau, 401 Jefferson Avenue, Toledo, OH 43604; telephone (419)321-6404 or (800)243-4667

Convention Facilities

The principal meeting and convention site in Toledo is the SeaGate Centre, situated downtown one block from the Maumee River; connected to the convention center is the University of Toledo at SeaGate Centre facility. When combined, the three-level complex features seventy-five thousand square feet of multipurpose space, which can be divided into three separate halls, and twenty-five meeting rooms. SeaGate Centre is linked to downtown restaurants, hotels, stores, and the Portside Festival Marketplace by Citiwalk, a network of enclosed tunnels and walkways.

Hotels and motels provide additional meeting space, accommodating groups ranging from twelve to eight hundred participants. Unique conference facilities include the Franciscan Life Center, located in nearby Sylvania on the campus of Lourdes College, and the $60 million resort and conference center at Maumee Bay State Park.

Convention Information: The Greater Toledo Convention and Visitors Bureau, 401 Jefferson Avenue, Toledo, OH 43604; telephone (419)321-6404 or (800)243-4667

Transportation

Approaching the City

Toledo Express Airport is served by seven commercial airlines providing direct and connecting flights to major cities throughout the United States. The airport also handles corporate and private aircraft. Additional general aviation services are available at Metcalf Field, operated by the Port Authority and located south of the city. Detroit Metropolitan Airport, less than an hour's drive from Toledo, is served by international as well as domestic flights.

A network of interstate, federal, and state highways facilitates access into and around the city and links Toledo to points in all sectors of the nation. Interstate 75 extends north through Michigan and south through Florida; the Ohio Turnpike (I-80 and I-90) connects Toledo with the East and West Coasts. Other highways include U.S. 24, 25, 20, and 23.

Amtrak provides east-west rail service to Toledo plus daily service from Detroit. Greyhound and Trailways buses travel into the city.

Traveling in the City

Streets in the city of Toledo are laid out on a grid pattern; downtown streets are tilted on a northwest-southeast axis to conform to the Maumee River. Toledo's bus-based public transportation system, TARTA, schedules routes throughout the city and suburban areas. Boat, train, trolley, and horse-drawn carriage tours are available.

Communications

Newspapers and Magazines

The major daily newspaper in Toledo is *The Toledo Blade. Toledo Business Journal* is a business monthly focusing on finance, travel, real estate, and other related topics. Several neighborhood newspapers, as well as scholarly, academic, and religious journals, and special-interest tabloids and magazines are also published in the city, including the *Toledo Union Journal,* a bimonthly labor newspaper.

Television and Radio

Toledo is the broadcast media center for northwestern Ohio and parts of southeastern Michigan. Television viewers receive programs from five stations—one public and four commercial—based in the city. Thirteen AM and FM radio stations schedule a complete range of music, news, information, and public interest features; one broadcasts performances by local cultural groups.

Media Information: The Toledo Blade Company, 541 Superior Street, Toledo, OH 43660; telephone (419)245-6000; and, *Metropolitan,* Greater Toledo Publications, Inc., 317 Tenth Street, Toledo, OH 43624; telephone (419)244-3015

Selected Bibliography

Geha, Joseph, *Through and Through: Toledo Stories* (Saint Paul: Graywolf Press, 1990)

SOUTH DAKOTA

Rapid City 449   Sioux Falls 461

The State in Brief

Nickname: Coyote State, Sunshine State
Motto: Under God the people rule

Flower: Pasque flower
Bird: Ringnecked pheasant

Area: 77,121 square miles (1990; U.S. rank: 17th)
Elevation: 962 feet to 7,242 feet above sea level
Climate: Continental, characterized by seasonal extremes of temperature as well as persistent winds, low humidity, and scant rainfall

Admitted to Union: November 2, 1889
Capital: Pierre
Head Official: Governor Walter Dale Miller (R) (until 1995)

Population
  1970: 666,000
  1980: 691,000
  1990: 703,000
  Percent change 1980–1990: 0.8%
  U.S. rank in 1990: 45th
  Percent of residents born in state: 71.0% (1990)
  Density: 9.2 people per square mile (1990)
  1991 FBI Crime Index Total: 21,647

Racial and Ethnic Characteristics (1990)
  White: 638,000
  Black: 0.5%
  American Indian, Eskimo, Aleut: 7.27%
  Asian and Pacific Islander: 0.45%
  Hispanic (may be of any race): 0.75%

Age Characteristics (1990)
  Population under 5 years old: 54,000
  Population 5 to 17 years old: 146,000
  Percent of population 65 years and older: 14.7%
  Median age: 33.5 years
  Voting-age population (1988): 518,000 (60.4% of whom cast votes for president)

Vital Statistics
  Total number of births (1992): 11,281
  Total number of deaths (1992): 6,927 (of which, 113 were infants under the age of 1 year)
  AIDS cases reported, 1981–1990: 18 (U.S. rank: 50th)

Economy
  Major industries: Finance, insurance, and real estate; wholesale and retail trade; services
  Unemployment rate: 2.8% (September 1992)
  Per capita income: $10,661 (1989)
  Median household income: $22,503 (1989)
  Total number of families: 182,205 (11.6% of which had incomes below the poverty level; 1989)
  Income tax rate: None
  Sales tax rate: 4.0%

Rapid City

The City in Brief

Founded: 1876 (incorporated, 1882)

Head Official: Mayor Edward McLaughlin (R) (since 1991)

City Population
 1970: 43,836
 1980: 46,492
 1990: 54,523
 Percent change, 1980–1990: 17.3%
 U.S. rank in 1980: Not available
 U.S. rank in 1990: 445th

Metropolitan Area Population
 1970: Not a metropolitan area at that time
 1980: 70,361
 1990: 81,343
 Percent change, 1980–1990: 15.6%
 U.S. rank in 1980: 276th
 U.S. rank in 1990: 274th

Area: 35.0 square miles (1990)

Elevation: 3,200 feet above sea level

Average Annual Temperature: 46.6° F

Average Annual Precipitation: 17.0 inches (38.0 inches of snowfall)

Major Economic Sectors: Agriculture, wholesale and retail trade, services, government

Unemployment Rate: 3.6% (September 1992)

Per Capita Income: $12,469 (1989)

1992 (2nd Quarter) ACCRA Average House Price: $81,900

1992 (2nd Quarter) ACCRA Cost of Living Index: 95.1 (U.S. average = 100.0)

1991 FBI Crime Index Total: 4,200

Major Colleges and Universities: South Dakota School of Mines and Technology, Western Dakota Vocational Technical Institute, National College

Daily Newspaper: *Rapid City Journal*

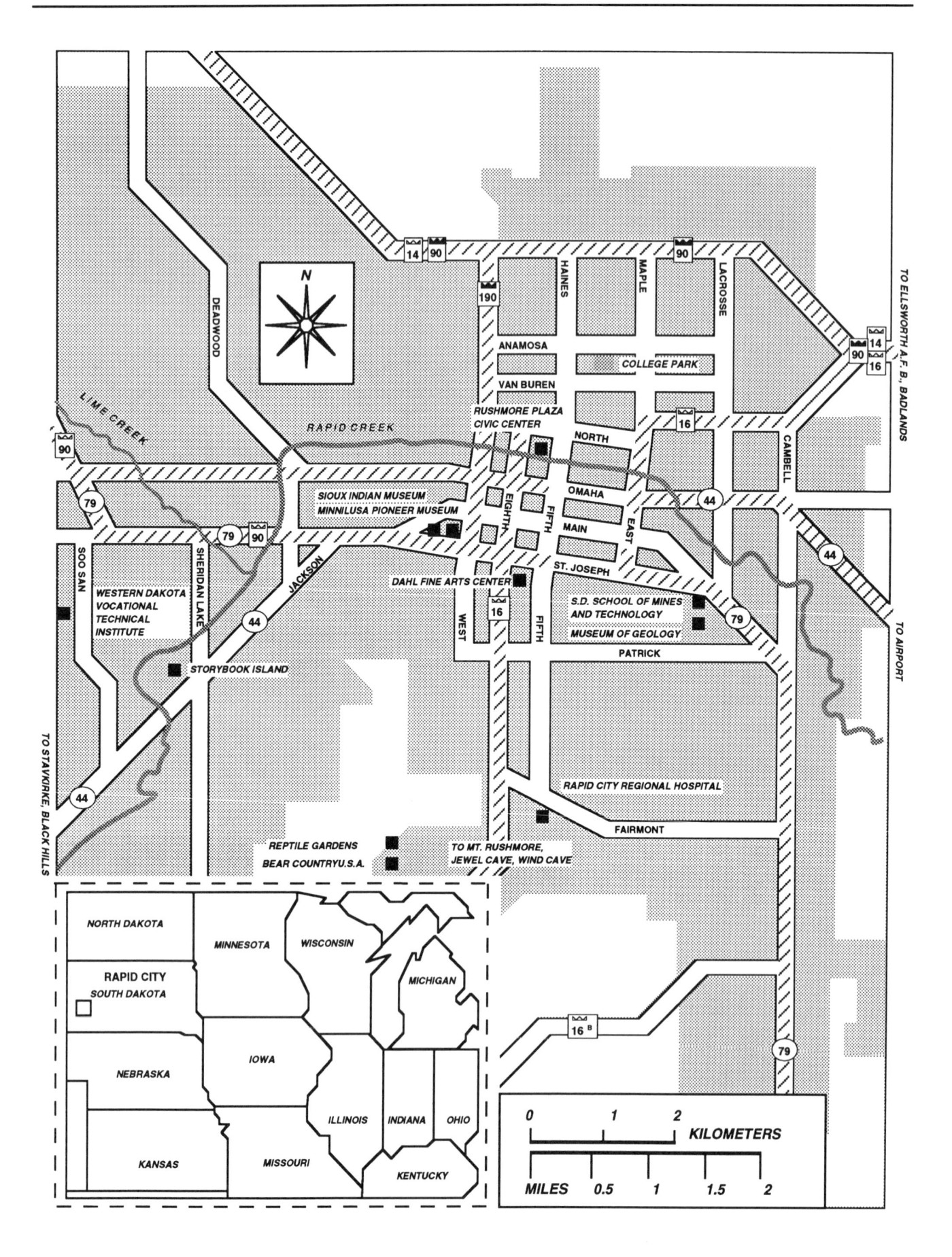

South Dakota—Rapid City *Cities of the United States • 2nd Edition*

Introduction

Rapid City is a diverse, thriving small midwestern city that refers to itself as "The Star of the West." Tourists are drawn to the area, which was celebrated in the 1990 award-winning film *Dances With Wolves*, to see the presidents' busts carved into Mount Rushmore and to visit the Black Hills. The city enjoys a thriving economy based on the farmers who have been raising beans, wheat, and alfalfa since the turn of the last century. A regional center for retail shopping and medical facilities, the city is home to the South Dakota School of Mines and Technology as well as Ellsworth Air Force Base. Ten percent of Rapid City's population is made up of native Americans and Indian arts and crafts abound in the city's shops. Locals like to say that the city has the quality of life of a small town with the business and cultural benefits of a city.

Geography and Climate

Rapid City, the natural eastern gateway to the great growing empire known as the West River Region, is surrounded by contrasting land forms. The forested Black Hills rise immediately west of the city, while the other three edges of the city look out on the prairie. Protected by the six-thousand to seven-thousand foot peaks of the Black Hills, Rapid City enjoys an enviable climate, free of the icy blizzards and scorching summers typical of much of the rest of the Dakotas. Summers are warm but dry and autumn is noted for its delightful "Indian summer" weather. Mild, sunny days are common throughout the winter and occasional "chinook" or warm winds frequently follow a stint of snowy weather. Snowfall is normally light with the greatest monthly average less than eight inches. Spring is characterized by wide variations in temperature and occasionally some wet snowfall. Low humidity levels, infrequent precipitation, and northwesterly winds prevail in the city.

Area: 35.0 square miles (1990)

Elevation: 3,200 feet above sea level

Average Temperatures: January, 21.9° F; July, 72.6° F; annual average, 46.6° F

Average Annual Precipitation: 17.0 inches (38.0 inches of snowfall)

History

New City Becomes Regional Trade Center

The discovery of gold in 1874 brought an influx of settlers into the Black Hills region of South Dakota. Rapid City was founded in 1876 by a group of disappointed miners, who promoted their new city as the "Gateway to the Black Hills." John Brennan and Samuel Scott, with a small group of men, laid out the site of the present Rapid City, which was named for the spring-fed Rapid Creek that flows through it. A square mile was measured off and the six blocks in the center were designated as a business section. Committees were appointed to bring in prospective merchants and their families to locate in the new settlement. Although it began as a hay camp, the city soon began selling supplies to miners and pioneers. By 1900 Rapid City had survived a boom and bust and was establishing itself as an important regional trade center.

Tourism and the Military Spur Economy

The invention of the automobile brought tourists to the Black Hills. Gutzon Borglum, the famous sculptor, began work on Mount Rushmore in 1927, and his son, Lincoln Borglum, continued the carving of the presidents' faces in rock following his father's death. The massive sculpture was completed in 1938. Although tourism sustained the city throughout the Great Depression of the 1930s, the gas rationing of World War II had a devastating effect on the tourist industry in the town.

The city benefited greatly from the opening of Ellsworth Air Force Base, an Army Air Corps base. As a result, the population of the area nearly doubled between 1940 and 1948, from almost 14,000 to nearly 27,000 people. Military families and civilian personnel soon took every available living space in town, and mobile parks proliferated. Rapid City businesses profited from the military payroll.

Rapid City Since Mid-Century

In 1949 city officials envisioned the city as a retail and wholesale trade center for the region and designed a plan for growth that focused on a civic center, more downtown parking places, new schools, and paved streets. A construction boom continued into the 1950s. Growth slowed in the 1960s, but the worst natural disaster in Rapid City's history led to another building boom a decade later. On June 9, 1972, heavy rains caused massive flooding of the Rapid Creek. More than two hundred people were killed and more than $100 million in property was destroyed.

The devastation of the flood and the outpouring of private donations and millions of dollars in federal aid led to the completion of one big part of the 1949 plan—clearing the area along the Rapid Creek and making it a public park. New homes and businesses were constructed to replace those that had been destroyed. Rushmore Plaza Civic Center and a new Central High School were built in part of the area that had been cleared. In 1978, Rushmore Mall was built, adding to the city's position as a retail shopping center.

In recent times, Rapid City has been rated no lower than third overall in the nation six years in a row for its manufacturing climate. A hard-working labor force and a governmental structure deeply rooted in the concept of being a partner in the success of its business community remain major assets.

Population Profile

Metropolitan Area Residents
 1970: Not a metropolitan area at that time
 1980: 70,361
 1990: 81,343
 Percent change, 1980–1990: 15.6%
 U.S. rank in 1980: 276th
 U.S. rank in 1990: 274th

City Residents
 1970: 43,836
 1980: 46,492
 1990: 54,523 (of which 27,862 were female and 26,661 were males)
 Percent change, 1980–1990: 17.3%
 U.S. rank in 1980: Not available
 U.S. rank in 1990: 445th

Density: 1,600 people per square mile (1990)

Racial and ethnic characteristics (1990)
 White: 48,082
 Black: 691
 American Indian, Eskimo, Aleut: 4,852
 Asian and Pacific Islander: 541
 Hispanic (may be of any race): 1,215

Percent of residents born in state: 56.2% (1990)

Age characteristics (1990)
 Population under 5 years old: 4,676
 Population 5 to 17 years old: 10,337
 Population 18 to 20 years old: 2,594
 Population 21 to 24 years old: 3,760
 Population 25 to 44 years old: 17,785
 Population 45 to 54 years old: 4,895
 Population 55 to 59 years old: 2,148
 Population 60 to 64 years old: 2,075
 Population 65 to 74 years old: 3,488
 Population 75 to 84 years old: 2,105
 Population 85 years and older: 660
 Median age: 30.9 years (1990)

Births (1988)
 Total number: 1,078

Deaths (1988)
 Total number: 380 (of which, 15 were infants under the age of 1 year)

Money income (1989)
  Per capita income: $12,469 (1989)
  Median household income: $25,740
  Total households: 21,206
  Number of households with income of . . .
    less than $5,000: 1,350
    $5,000 to $9,999: 2,121
    $10,000 to $14,999: 2,093
    $15,000 to $24,999: 4,714
    $25,000 to $34,999: 4,028
    $35,000 to $49,999: 3,686
    $50,000 to $74,999: 2,230
    $75,000 to $99,999: 445
    $100,000 to $149,999: 335
    $150,000 or more: 204
  Percent of families below poverty level: 10.6% (70.6% of which were female householder families with related children under 5 years)
1991 FBI Crime Index Total: 4,200

Municipal Government

Rapid City has a mayor-council form of government with an elected, full-time mayor and two part-time council members from each of the city's five wards, who are elected to staggered two-year terms. All positions are non-partisan.

Head Official: Mayor Edward McLaughlin (R) (since 1991; current term expires May 1995)

Total Number of City Employees: 500 (1992)

City Information: City of Rapid City, 300 Sixth Street, Rapid City, SD 57701; telephone (605)394-4110

Economy

Major Industries and Commercial Activity

Agriculture, tourism, and Ellsworth Air Force Base are the major factors in Rapid City's economy. The area is also known for the manufacture of high-value, low-bulk items that can be swiftly shipped to market or assembly centers in other parts of the nation.

Agriculture, and all that goes with it, is the number one industry in South Dakota, and Rapid City is the regional trade center for farm-ranch activity in the southwest part of the state and neighboring counties in Montana, Wyoming, and Nebraska. Cattle and sheep production dominate the agricultural scene, as well as processing and packing of meat and meat byproducts, but the cultivation of small grains is also important. Services offered to area farmers and ranchers include selling of new and used farm equipment, spare parts and repairs, and flour milling.

The South Dakota Cement Plant, a state-owned facility, is equipped with high capacity, environmentally sound equipment to produce high-quality cement for multi-state distribution. Other important industrial and employment institutions include several large construction companies, rock quarries, steel fabrication firms, and trucking firms. Several light industries and services located in the city include manufacturing of computer parts, printing, Indian crafts, and headquarters for insurance companies and other businesses. Regional or headquarters facilities of many state and federal offices also operate in the city.

Within half a day's drive of Rapid City are five of the country's most famous national park areas: Mount Rushmore National Memorial, Devil's Tower National Monument, Badlands National Park, Jewel Cave National Monument, and Wind Cave National Park. With its variety of restaurants, more than twenty-seven hundred hotel/motel rooms and many modern campgrounds, Rapid City benefits from a large annual tourist trade.

Each year the $69.8 million payroll for workers at Ellsworth Air Force Base, the largest employer in the state, boosts the local economy. Community leaders are working together to counter the loss of military personnel as the federal government implements its military reductions.

Items and goods produced: computer components, jewelry, cement, processed foods, steel products, printing, wood products

Incentive Programs—New and Existing Companies

The city of Rapid City, along with Pennington County and the Governor's Office of Economic Development, offers a number of financial inducements to aid industry looking to establish operations in the area.

Local programs—Rapid City rebates the tax increment created by investments in real property for up to fifteen years. Pennington County has a real estate tax incentive offered to new industrial or commercial structures, or new non-residential agricultural structures.

State programs—The South Dakota REDI Fund lends money at 3 percent interest to companies creating new jobs in the state. The money can be used for almost any capital purchase or operating financing for which a company qualifies under standard banking guidelines. The South Dakota Futures Fund provides matching funds, dollar for dollar, for research projects done at state universities such as the South Dakota School of Mines & Technology.

Other programs—Federal Small Business Administration (SBA) participation loans and SBA Direct loans are available.

Job Training programs—Western Dakota Vocational-Technical Institute's Business and Industry Training Program specializes in customized training for new and expanding industries.

Development Projects

Rapid City has two growing industrial parks, Rushmore and Lombardy. The Rushmore Plaza Civic Center completed a $12 million expansion in the early 1990s. Major local structures completed in the 1990s include a $6.5 million city school administrative center, a $10 million airport terminal, and a $2.5 million outdoor sports complex for adult soccer and softball. The Rushmore Plaza Holiday Inn opened in 1990, as did Black Hills Packing Company, and Spiegel, Inc. In 1991 Custom Packaging began operations, with one hundred employees to be added in two years, and Hi-Qual Manufacturing was slated to open in 1993. Since 1990 the city has experienced more than $15 million of building activity.

Economic Development Information: Rapid City Area Economic Development Office, P.O. Box 747, Rapid City, SD 57709; telephone (605)343-1880

Commercial Shipping

Rapid City is served by the Chicago Northwestern Railroad and offers piggyback service with daily switching service. Nearly forty motor freight carriers, as well as terminals, are located in Rapid City. Parcel service is provided by United Parcel.

Labor Force and Employment Outlook

Adult dependents from nearby Ellsworth Air Force Base offer a ready-made source of potential employees to augment other local people. Engineering graduates from the South Dakota School of Mines and Technology and other skilled workers trained by local institutions also make the area attractive to potential industrial and commercial newcomers.

The following is a summary of data regarding the Rapid City metropolitan area labor force as of September 1992.

Size of civilian non-agricultural labor force: 41,400

Number of workers employed in . . .
  mining: not reported
  construction: 2,800
  manufacturing: 4,400
  transportation and public utilities: 2,000
  wholesale and retail trade: 12,500
  finance, insurance, and real estate: 1,400
  services: 11,100
  government: 7,200

Average hourly earnings of production workers employed in manufacturing: $8.95

Unemployment rate: 3.6%

Largest employers	Number of employees
Ellsworth Air Force Base	6,800
Rushmore National Health System	1,800
Rapid City School District	1,700
City of Rapid City	800
SCI Systems Inc.	615

Cost of Living

The cost of living in Rapid City is substantially below that of many cities of similar size around the country.

The following is a summary of data regarding several key cost of living factors in the Rapid City area.

1992 (2nd Quarter) ACCRA Cost of Living Index: 95.1 (U.S. average = 100.0)

1992 (2nd Quarter) ACCRA Average House Price: $81,900

State income tax rate: None

State sales tax rate: 4.0%

Local income tax rate: None

Local sales tax rate: 2.0%

Property tax rate: approximately $29.00 per $1,000 of assessed valuation; assessment ratio = 100% for residential

Economic Information: Rapid City Area Chamber of Commerce, P.O. Box 747, 444 North Mount Rushmore Road, Rapid City, SD 57709; telephone (605)343-1744

Education and Research

Elementary and Secondary Schools

Rapid City's school district, which covers a 30-mile radius, has a separate building and staff for youngsters who require special education. At Ellsworth Air Force Base, the Douglas School District has 2,827 students, four elementary schools, one middle school and one high school.

The following is a summary of data regarding Rapid City's public schools as of the 1991–1992 school year.

Total enrollment: 14,332

Number of facilities
elementary schools: 19
junior high/middle schools: 5
senior high schools: 4

Student/teacher ratio: Kindergarten-three, 24:1; four–six, 26:1

Funding per pupil: $3,206

Parochial schools include St. Elizabeth Seton Elementary School, plus several other church-related elementary schools.

Public Schools Information: Rapid City Area School District, 300 Sixth Street, Rapid City, SD 57701; telephone (605)394-4031

Colleges and Universities

South Dakota School of Mines and Technology (SDSM&T) has long been recognized as one of the best science and engineering colleges in the county. SDSM&T, which enrolls almost twenty-three hundred students, is known for its technological expertise and innovation, as well as for its world-famous Museum of Geology. Western Dakota Vocational Technical Institute, located on the eastern edge of the city, provides diplomas and Associate in Applied Science degrees in more than twenty business, construction trades, agricultural, electronics, human services, and mechanical career fields. Western Dakota Vo-Tech works closely with the local business community to provide student training programs. With approximately one thousand students on the main campus and two thousand at its several branches, National College near downtown, offers twenty major career fields.

Libraries and Research Centers

The Rapid City Public Library, with more than 112,000 volumes, has strong collections in business and audio-visual materials, and operates one bookmobile. Its South Dakota collection includes many items for historical research. The library subscribes to more than four hundred magazines and newspapers and houses the collection of the Rapid City Society for Genealogical Research Inc. South Dakota Schools of Mines and Technology (SDSM&T), the National College, and Rapid City Regional Hospital also have libraries.

SDSM&T has been involved in providing research services for government, industry, and business for the past century, with a primary emphasis on energy, the environment, and mineral development.

Public Library Information: Rapid City Public Library, 610 Quincy Street, Rapid City, SD 57701; (605)394-4171

Health Care

Rushmore National Health System and its subsidiaries Rapid City Regional Hospital, Black Hills Reha-

South Dakota—Rapid City — Cities of the United States • 2nd Edition

The Rapid City Area is known for its spectacular natural scenery such as the rocks overlooking Lake Pactola.

bilitation Hospital (BHRH), Rushmore Community Health Resources (RCHR), and American Business Enterprises provide comprehensive acute care services to South Dakota and portions of North Dakota, Nebraska, Wyoming, and Montana. Rapid City Regional Hospital served more than eighty thousand patients from five states in 1991. A 338-bed facility, the hospital offers a full range of medically oriented programs. The 51-bed BHRH, the only freestanding rehabilitation hospital between Minneapolis and Denver, is available for the disabled or those recovering from illness or accidents. Special treatment programs include those for patients with: arthritis, diabetes, pulmonary disease, neurological disorders, amputations, and spinal cord injuries. Recent additions encompass sports medicine, pulmonary rehabilitation, and classes for people with back trouble. RCHR provides outreach services to the region including: home health care, hospice care, and homemaker services, as well as alcohol and drug treatment, and psychiatric care. The city is home to 148 physicians. Black Hills Regional Eye Institute provides modern services to a multi-state region, as well as offering teaching and research in the structure, function, and diseases of the eye.

Recreation

Sightseeing

The Visitor Information Center at the Rushmore Plaza Civic Center, with its maps and brochures, is a good first stop on a trip to Rapid City. Story Book Island is an 11-acre park with free attractions for youngsters. It is filled with dozens of larger-than-life sets that depict children's nursery rhymes and tales, including Yogi Bear's picnic basket and the Crooked Man's house. The Pioneer Museum depicts the area's history through its exhibits and displays featuring American and European glass and porcelain. The unique Stavkirke, an exact replica of the famous 830-year-old Borgund Church in Norway, features intricate woodcarvings, strange dragon heads, and ingenious pegged construction. Fossil skeletons of giant, prehistoric marine reptiles command attention at the Museum of Geology at the South Dakota Schools of Mines and Technology. The museum also houses the world's finest exhibits of Badlands fossils and an extensive collection of rare and beautiful rocks, gems, and minerals from the Black Hills. Seven life-size concrete replicas of monstrous prehistoric reptiles are located in the outdoor park-like setting at Dinosaur Park. Discovered in 1900, Jewel Cave, a national monument, contains more than 80 miles of passageways in an underground labyrinth that offers rare and unusual calcite crystal formations. Wind Cave, the first cave designated as part of the National Park systems, provides more than 53 miles of mapped corridors and halls, making it the fourth-longest cave in the world. With its jagged cliffs, deep canyons, flat-topped buttes, and rich fossils, Badlands National Park is one of the most stunning geological displays on earth. Reptile Gardens, founded in 1937, gives spectators the opportunity to observe colorful birds and reptiles surrounded by thousands of orchids and other tropical and desert plants in its Skydome. The gardens also feature miniature horses and donkeys; the Wings of Adventure Bird Program featuring hawks, owls, eagles, parrots, and other birds; an alligator show; and the Snake Program. Bear Country U.S.A., a drive-through wildlife park, features the world's largest collection of black bears plus a large and varied collection of North American wildlife including grizzly bears, timber wolves, mountain lions, buffalo, moose, elk, and more. The Air and Space Museum, at the entrance of Ellsworth Air Force Base, features the HONDA Stealth bomber model and twenty-two other vintage aircraft. Several tour companies offer guided tours to some of the memorable sites featured in the award-winning film *Dances With Wolves*.

Arts and Culture

The Dahl Fine Arts Center features rotating exhibits of paintings and sculptures by local artists, especially local native American artists. A two-hundred-foot-long and ten-foot-high Cyclorama of American History tells the story of the nation from the landing of Columbus to the Space Age. The Group Theatre, Inc., the city's only community theater, is based in the Dahl Center's 150-seat auditorium. The nearby Black Hills Playhouse at Custer State Park is a professional theater and training center. Two puppet theaters entertain the community. Black Hills Dance Theatre, Inc. engages a variety of regionally and nationally recognized dance companies. Other community arts attractions include the Black Hills Symphony Orchestra, the Blacks Hills Chamber Music Society, Black Hills Chorale, the Black Hills Voices in Concert, and other musical groups.

The Sioux Indian Museum provides exhibits including traditional and contemporary Native American art and historic artifacts. The Minnilusa Pioneer Museum next door features exhibits of Rapid City's rich history and heritage.

Festivals and Holidays

Music is the focus of The Black Hills Bluegrass and Acoustic Music Festival, which is held in June. July's Black Hills Heritage Festival and Arts Fair celebrates the cultural heritage of the Black Hills. The Northern Plains Indian Exposition and Pow-Wow, also in July, features championship singing and dancing contests, an arts exhibition and trade show. The Fine Arts Festival provides art, music, and theater entertainment for the South Dakota School of Mines and Technology campus as well as the community. The Central States Fair, a week-long extravaganza that entertains crowds from all over the region, occurs in August. October's Buffalo Roundup is held annually at nearby Custer State Park. Rodeo fun is the attraction at January's Black Hills Stock Show and Rodeo.

Sports for the Spectator

The Rushmore Plaza Civic Center Arena plays host to the Continental Basketball Association basketball league's Rapid City Thrillers.

Sports for the Participant

Rapid City has twenty-seven parks, playgrounds and special outdoor public facilities spanning 500 acres inside the city limits. The largest, Sioux Park, boasts 220 acres. A 13.5-mile bicycle path spans the town, which boasts eight golf courses, thirty-two tennis courts, four swimming pools, five wading pools, thirty-one ball fields, six soccer fields, six skating rinks, and a Frisbee court. Blue ribbon trout fishing and many types of hunting are also available.

Shopping and Dining

Since its inception, Rapid City has been a commercial center for miners, ranchers, the military, and tourists. Downtown Rapid City, with more than four hundred businesses, is a diverse mix of retail stores, financial institutions, service businesses, and lodging. Other local shopping areas include Baken Park, the city's first shopping center; Eastside Family Thrift Shopping Center; Northgate Shopping Center; Rushmore Mall; Steele Plaza; Times Square Plaza; Haines Station; and the Sturgis Road shopping area. A number of Rapid City shops specialize in fine handcrafted paintings, pottery, jewelry, and museum quality reproductions created by the seventy thousand Sioux who live in the region.

Many fine restaurants are located throughout the city, featuring sizzling steaks cut from prime South Dakota beef.

Visitor Information: Rapid City Convention and Visitors Bureau, P.O. Box 747V, Rapid City, SD 57709; telephone (800)888-1417

Convention Facilities

The Rushmore Plaza Civic Center, located near the heart of downtown Rapid City, contains twelve separate meeting rooms with seating capacities from 80 to 400 people. The Exhibit Halls consist of one-hundred and twenty thousand square feet of exhibit space, with seating capacities from 500 to 2,500 people. The versatile arena can be used for concerts, sports events, and other special events. Floor area is twenty-four thousand square feet. A $12 million expansion, completed in the 1990s, provides an additional one-hundred and twenty thousand square feet of space to the facility. A new exhibit hall with twenty-seven thousand square feet and a food service building with eleven thousand square feet complete the facility.

Convention Information: Rapid City Convention and Visitors Bureau, P.O. Box 747V, Rapid City, SD 57709; telephone (800)888-1417

Transportation

Approaching the City

The new Rapid City Regional Airport, 10 miles east of the city, is the third most active airport in the Northern Rockies. It offers nearly fifty flights a day to and from Sioux Falls, Minneapolis, Salt Lake City, Chicago, and Denver. The airport had more than three-hundred thousand boardings and departures in 1991. Three fixed-base operators provide charter service. Several wide, modern highways intersect in the city including Interstate 90, which runs east and west; State Highway 79, which runs north and south; U.S. Highway 14, which cuts through the city on an angle running northwest to southeast; and U.S. Highway 16, which approaches the city center from the south. Six highways lead from the north, west, and south into the canyons and mountains. Bus service is provided by Jack Rabbit Lines, Stagecoach West, and Gray Line of the Black Hills.

Traveling in the City

The city is divided into three main areas named by locals according to compass direction: South Robbinsdale, North Rapid City, and West Rapid. Two inter-city bus lines serve Rapid City, and Rapid Ride, a fixed-route bus system which takes passengers to more than two hundred stops along five city routes, was established in the early 1990s. City bus service is offered by the Rapid Transit System.

Communications

Newspapers and Magazines

The city's daily newspaper is the *Rapid City Journal*. Other local newspapers include *The Rapid City Prospector*, and *The Plainsman*. The *Visitor-Quarterly* magazine and the *Investment Report*, a monthly magazine, are published in Rapid City.

Television and Radio

Rapid City is served by four television stations: three networks and one public station. The city has eight FM and five AM radio stations.

Media Information: Rapid City Journal, 507 Main Street, P.O. Box 450, Rapid City, SD 57701; telephone (605)394-830

Sioux Falls

The City in Brief

Founded: 1870 (incorporated, 1889)

Head Official: Mayor Jack White (R) (since 1986)

City Population
 1970: 72,468
 1980: 81,343
 1990: 100,814
 Percent change, 1980–1990: 12.2%
 U.S. rank in 1980: 223rd
 U.S. rank in 1990: 194th

Metropolitan Area Population
 1970: 95,209
 1980: 109,435
 1990: 123,809
 Percent change, 1980–1990: 13.1%
 U.S. rank in 1980: 270th
 U.S. rank in 1990: Not available

Area: 45.1 square miles (1990)
Elevation: 1,395 feet above sea level
Annual Average Temperature: 45.3° F
Average Annual Precipitation: 24.23 inches

Major Economic Sectors: Wholesale and retail trade, services, manufacturing
Unemployment Rate: 2.3% (September 1992)
Per Capita Income: $13,677 (1989)
1992 (2nd Quarter) ACCRA Average House Price: $92,232
1992 (2nd Quarter) ACCRA Cost of Living Index: 94.1 (U.S. Average = 100.0)
1991 FBI Crime Index Total: 5,184

Major Colleges and Universities: Augustana College; University of South Dakota School of Medicine; Sioux Falls College

Daily Newspaper: *Argus Leader*

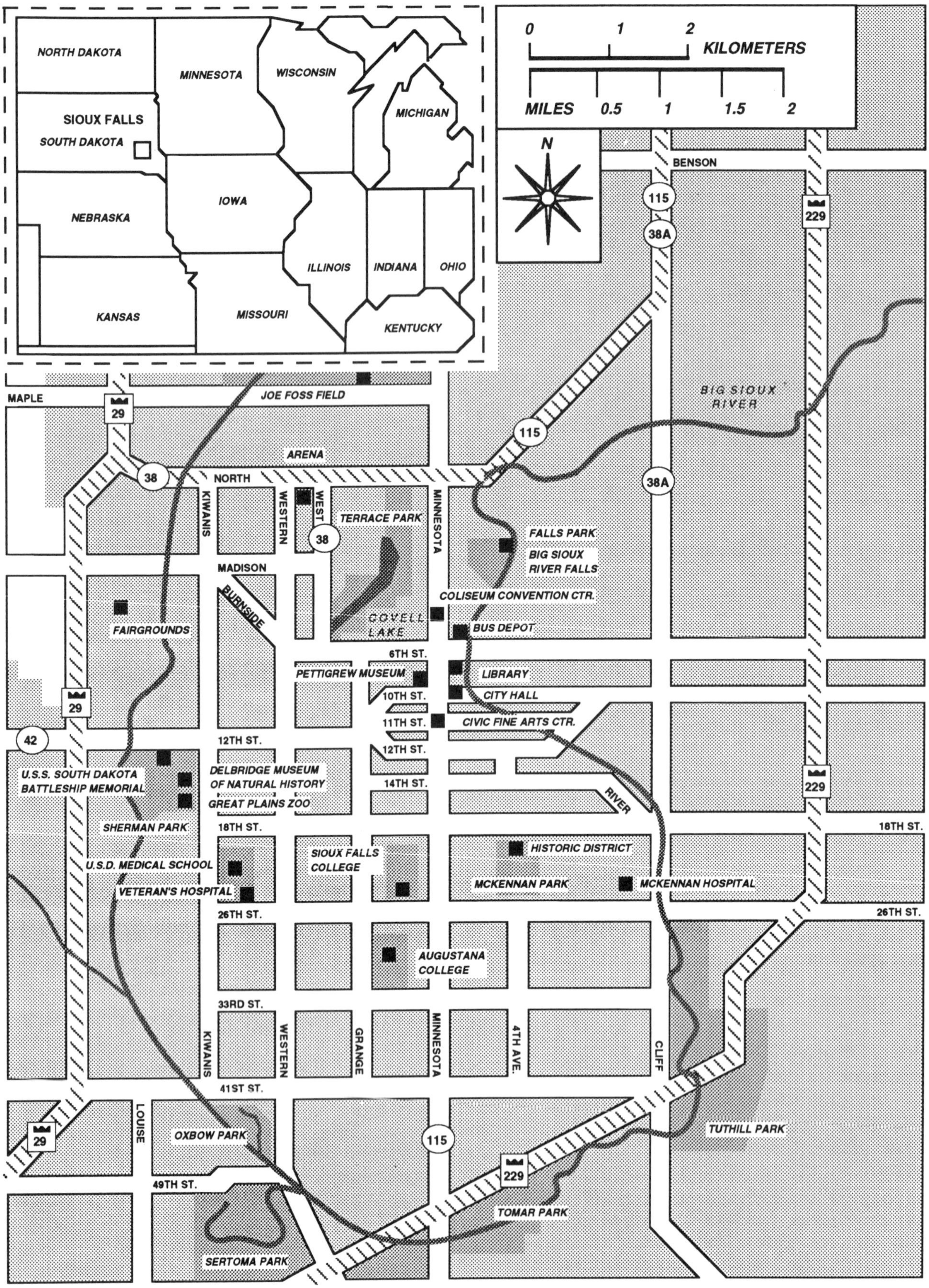
NORTH DAKOTA
MINNESOTA
WISCONSIN
MICHIGAN
SIOUX FALLS
SOUTH DAKOTA
NEBRASKA
IOWA
ILLINOIS
INDIANA
OHIO
KANSAS
MISSOURI
KENTUCKY
0 1 2 KILOMETERS
MILES 0.5 1 1.5 2
N
BENSON
115
38A
229
BIG SIOUX RIVER
MAPLE
29
JOE FOSS FIELD
ARENA
38
NORTH
KIWANIS
WESTERN
WEST
MINNESOTA
TERRACE PARK
FALLS PARK
BIG SIOUX RIVER FALLS
MADISON
BURNSIDE
COLISEUM CONVENTION CTR.
FAIRGROUNDS
COVELL LAKE
BUS DEPOT
6TH ST.
PETTIGREW MUSEUM
LIBRARY
10TH ST.
CITY HALL
11TH ST.
CIVIC FINE ARTS CTR.
42
12TH ST.
12TH ST.
U.S.S. SOUTH DAKOTA BATTLESHIP MEMORIAL
DELBRIDGE MUSEUM OF NATURAL HISTORY
GREAT PLAINS ZOO
14TH ST.
RIVER
SHERMAN PARK
18TH ST.
18TH ST.
SIOUX FALLS COLLEGE
HISTORIC DISTRICT
U.S.D. MEDICAL SCHOOL
MCKENNAN PARK
MCKENNAN HOSPITAL
VETERAN'S HOSPITAL
26TH ST.
26TH ST.
AUGUSTANA COLLEGE
33RD ST.
GRANGE
4TH AVE.
CLIFF
41ST ST.
LOUISE
OXBOW PARK
TUTHILL PARK
49TH ST.
TOMAR PARK
SERTOMA PARK

Introduction

Sioux Falls, seat of South Dakota's Minnehaha County, is the largest city in the state and the center of the metropolitan statistical area that includes both Sioux Falls and Minnehaha County. The city first grew during the Dakota boom years of the late nineteenth century as the arrival of the railroad made possible the nationwide transportation of granite quarried in Sioux Falls. Sioux Falls was selected by *Money* magazine in 1992 as the best place to live in America. Mentioned was the city's "down-home feel even though Citibank and Sears have transformed it into a booming financial services center."

Geography and Climate

Located in the Big Sioux River Valley in southeast South Dakota, Sioux Falls is surrounded by gently rolling terrain that slopes to higher elevations approximately 100 miles to the north-northeast and to the south. The city's climate is continental, exhibiting frequent weather changes from day to day and from week to week as differing air masses move into the area. During the late fall and winter, strong winds cause abrupt drops in temperature, but cold spells are usually of short duration. Snowfall and sleet average 39.8 inches yearly, and one or two heavy snows fall each winter, with blizzard conditions sometimes resulting. Thunderstorms are common in late spring and summer; tornadoes can occur in July. Flooding from melting snow runoff in the spring along the Big Sioux River and Skunk Creek is reduced by a diversion canal around the city.

Area: 45.1 square miles (1990)

Elevation: 1,395 feet above sea level

Average Temperatures: January, 12.4° F; July, 74.0° F; annual average, 45.3° F

Average Annual Precipitation: 24.23 inches

History

Falls on Big Sioux River Attract Settlers

Attracted by the economic potential of the Sioux Falls on the Big Sioux River, Dr. George M. Staples of Dubuque, Iowa, organized Western Town near the falls in 1856. Staples and his group hoped that the settlement would become the capital of the Territory of Dakota, but it was not chosen. Instead, in the winter of 1856, the Legislature of Minnesota Territory chartered the Dakota Land Company and established the town of Sioux Falls.

In August 1862, the settlers, fearing violence from the local Native Americans, abandoned the village. Raiders did burn the buildings and destroyed everything, including an old Smith printing press used by the *Sioux Falls Democrat* that was dumped in the Big Sioux River after it was stripped of decorative items. Fort Dakota, a military post, was established in the area in May 1865, to help assure the resettlement of Sioux Falls. Another incentive came when the water power of the falls was harnessed in 1873. A scourge of grasshoppers in 1874 hurt resettlement, but by 1876 Sioux Falls claimed a population of 600 people. Sioux Falls was incorporated as town in 1877 and as a city in 1889.

In the last decades of the nineteenth century Northern European immigrants were attracted to the Territory of Dakota, which resembled their homeland. The establishment of rail transport in the area in 1878 enabled locals to begin shipping "Sioux Falls granite," a pink quartzite bedrock second only to diamond in hardness. The city's two church-affiliated private schools date from this period; Augustana College, a Lutheran school, was founded in 1860 and Sioux Falls College, a Baptist school, was opened in 1883.

Agriculture Provides Economic Base

Life on the Plains was a test of endurance. During the winter of 1880 to 1881 snow began falling in October and continued until the spring, isolating residents and forcing them to burn corn, wheat, hay, and railroad ties for heat sources. In spite of hardship, Sioux Falls gained in economic importance. South Dakota's lenient divorce law brought outsiders into Sioux Falls until the law was changed in 1908. One memorable case unfolded when the wife of heavyweight boxing champion Bob Fitzsimmons sought a divorce in Sioux Falls. Her distraught husband followed her and managed to change her mind. To celebrate their reunion, Fitzsimmons forged horseshoes and passed them out to admirers; in the process, the local blacksmith shop's floor gave way, injuring a young boy. Fitzsimmons then organized a benefit performance and gave the proceeds to the boy's family.

In 1942 the U.S. War Department leased Sioux Falls land for the construction of the Air Force Technical Radio School, invigorating the local economy and social life. Sioux Falls native Joe Foss won the Congressional Medal of Honor for shooting down thirty-one enemy airplanes in the Pacific campaign of World War II; after the war, Foss returned to Sioux Falls, becoming a successful businessman and commander of the South Dakota Air National Guard.

Today Sioux Falls, through the processing of agricultural products, serves as a distribution center for farms in Iowa, Minnesota, and South Dakota. Financial services and medicine have also emerged as primary industries.

Historical Information: Siouxland Heritage Museums, Pettigrew Museum Library, 131 North Duluth, Sioux Falls, SD 57104-3021; telephone (605)339-7097

Population Profile

Metropolitan Area Residents
1970: 95,209
1980: 109,435
1990: 123,809
Percent change, 1980–1990: 13.1%
U.S. rank in 1980: 270th
U.S. rank in 1990: Not available

City Residents
1970: 72,468
1980: 81,343
1990: 100,814 (of which, 48,020 were males, and 52,794 were females)
Percent change, 1980–1990: 23.9%
U.S. rank in 1980: 223rd
U.S. rank in 1986: 194th (State rank: 1st)

Density: 2,235.3 people per square mile (1990)

Racial and ethnic characteristics (1990)
  White: 97,627
  Black: 733
  American Indian, Eskimo, Aleut: 1,574
  Asian and Pacific Islander: 688
  Hispanic (may be of any race): 571

Percent of residents born in state: 66.2%

Age characteristics (1990)
  Population under 5 years old: 7,987
  Population 5 to 9 years old: 7,811
  Population 10 to 14 years old: 6,768
  Population 15 to 19 years old: 6,510
  Population 20 to 24 years old: 8,581
  Population 25 to 29 years old: 10,342
  Population 30 to 34 years old: 9,593
  Population 35 to 39 years old: 8,296
  Population 40 to 44 years old: 6,626
  Population 45 to 49 years old: 4,827
  Population 50 to 54 years old: 3,961
  Population 55 to 59 years old: 3,875
  Population 60 to 64 years old: 3,862
  Population 65 to 69 years old: 3,590
  Population 70 to 74 years old: 2,955
  Population 75 to 79 years old: 2,198
  Population 80 to 84 years old: 1,512
  Population 85 years and over: 1,520
  Median age: 31.2 years

Births (1988)
  Total number: 1,674

Deaths (1989)
  Total number: 721 (of which, 12 were infants under the age of 1 year)

Money income (1989)
  Per capita income: $13,677
  Median household income: $27,286
  Total households: 39,923
  Number of households with income of . . .
    less than $5,000: 2,147
    $5,000 to $9,999: 3,328
    $10,000 to $14,999: 3,904
    $15,000 to $24,999: 8,577
    $25,000 to $34,999: 7,683
    $35,000 to $49,999: 7,692
    $50,000 to $74,999: 4,465
    $75,000 to $99,999: 1,041
    $100,000 to $149,999: 571
    $150,000 or more: 515
  Percent of families below poverty level: 5.5% (48.5% of which were female householder families with related children under 5)

1991 FBI Crime Index Total: 5,184

Municipal Government

The administrative branch of the Sioux Falls city government is composed of a five-member commission, one of whom is the mayor. Voters elect the mayor and commissioners at large to staggered five-year terms. Sioux Falls is considered one of the safest communities in the United States, employing 166 police personnel as well as 167 fire personnel.

Head Official: Mayor Jack White (R) (since 1986; current term expires 1996)

Total Number of City Employees: 920 (1991)

City Information: Mayor's Office, 224 West Ninth, Sioux Falls, SD 57102; telephone (605)339-7200

Economy

Major Industries and Commercial Activity

The Sioux Falls economy—comprised of a diversity of sectors, including finance, health care, retailing, agriculture, and wholesale distribution—continues a steady expansion. Evidence can be found in figures for new construction, which showed an increase of 150 percent between 1980 and 1992.

The city is the national headquarters for the finance services divisions of several large companies. Citibank (South Dakota), N.A., the international credit card processing facility for Citibank, employs 2,800 people. Credit card and financial services operations of Bank of New York, Dial Bank, and Sears Payment Systems are also located in Sioux Falls. The main offices of state and regional banks, as well as brokerage and insurance firms with nationwide connections, are based in the downtown financial district.

The medical industry figures significantly in the city's economic stability. Sioux Falls has emerged as a regional health care center, with the two major hospitals ranking among the top ten employers in the metropolitan area; private physician clinics employ more than one thousand workers. Retailing is another important sector; sales between 1982 and 1992 increased over 70 percent, and taxable sales now exceed $1.3 billion per year.

Set in a fertile agricultural region and the site of one of the world's largest stockyards, Sioux Falls has traditionally been a center for the agricultural industry: John Morrell & Company, a meat packer, is the city's largest employer, for instance, and agricultural cash receipts now top $3 billion annually. Among the agriculture-related activities are meat processing and packing, the production of dairy and bakery items, livestock feed milling, and the manufacture of farm implements and equipment. General manufacturing and granite quarries also contribute to the local economy.

Items and goods produced: fabricated steel, concrete blocks and prestressed concrete, millwork, sewn items, microwave appliances, electronic test equipment, corrugated boxes, computer components, window sash balances

Incentive Programs—New and Existing Companies

To encourage economic expansion, the Sioux Falls Development Foundation and the Chamber of Commerce jointly undertook a long-range marketing program in 1987 titled "Forward Sioux Falls," which was implemented by a fourteen-member committee representing more than three hundred businesses. The program goals included: diversification of the local and state economies, creation of new enterprises, expansion of existing businesses, growth of the tax base through capital investment, and continued development of medical services, food processing, and retailing. Between 1987 and 1991, "Forward Sioux Falls'" efforts resulted in the creation of six thousand jobs and investment of nearly $300 million in the community. Accordingly, "Forward Sioux Falls II" was launched as a new four-year initiative to create jobs and stimulate capital investment.

The 520-acre Sioux Empire Development Park offers assessment-free industrial sites with direct access to an air, rail, and ground transportation system that links the city to national and world markets. State and local tax incentives and abatements along with Private Industry Council employee training programs are also designed to encourage economic development in Sioux Falls.

Economic Development Information: Sioux Falls Development Foundation, P.O. Box 907, Sioux Falls, SD 57102; telephone (605)339-0103 or (800)658-3373

Development Projects

Infrastructure and transportation improvements include a new interchange for I-229, with other transportation projects planned at a cost of more than $90 million, and renovation of the airport. Retail space continues to be added, and medical and educational facilities are being expanded; in the 1990s, an elementary school and two high schools were added to the system. Existing-business expansions have also bolstered the economy.

Commercial Shipping

Wholesale distributing remains a primary industry in Sioux Falls, which has long been a hub for the distribution of automobiles, trucks, food, fuel, oil, gasoline, machinery, plastics, and paper products. The city is served by the Chicago & Northwestern and Ellis & Eastern railroads. Thirty-eight motor freight carriers transport goods through Sioux Falls to markets throughout the United States. Air freight tonnage out of Joe Foss Field was up more than 400 percent from 1987 to 1992.

Labor Force and Employment Outlook

The Sioux Falls unemployment rate is consistently well below the national average. An atmosphere of employer-employee cooperation in Sioux Falls is augmented by South Dakota's right-to-work law. Considered one of the top business climates in the country, Sioux Falls creates almost seven jobs per day.

The following is a summary of data regarding the Sioux Falls metropolitan area labor force as of September 1992.

Size of non-agricultural labor force: 81,300

Number of workers employed in . . .
  mining: not reported
  construction: 4,400
  manufacturing: 10,100
  transportation and public utilities: 5,000
  wholesale and retail trade: 23,200
  finance, insurance, and real estate: 8,000
  services: 22,600
  government: 8,000

Average hourly earnings of production workers employed in manufacturing: $9.50

Unemployment rate: 2.3%

Largest employers	Number of employees
John Morrell & Company	2,800
Citibank (South Dakota), N.A.	2,800
Sioux Valley Hospital	2,716
McKennan Hospital	2,159
Midwest Coast Transport	988
Sunshine Food Stores	866
Hutchinson Technology	860

Cost of Living

The following is a summary of data regarding several key cost of living factors in the Sioux Falls area.

1992 (2nd Quarter) ACCRA Cost of Living Index: 94.1 (U.S. average = 100.0)

1992 (2nd Quarter) ACCRA Average House Price: $92,232

State income tax rate: None

State sales tax rate: 4.0%

Local income tax rate: None

Local sales tax rate: 2.0%

Property tax rate: $25.2370 per $1,000 of assessed valuation (taxed at 100% of full and true value)

Economic Information: Sioux Falls Development Foundation, P.O. Box 907, Sioux Falls, SD 57102; telephone (605)339-0103 or (800)658-3373

Education and Research

Elementary and Secondary Schools

Public elementary and secondary schools in Sioux Falls are in Sioux Falls School District 49-5, which enrolls the highest number of students in the state. A five-member, nonpartisan school board appoints a superintendent.

The following is a summary of data regarding Sioux Falls public schools as of the 1992–1993 school year.

Total enrollment: 17,077

Number of facilities
  elementary schools: 23
  junior high schools: 4
  senior high schools: 3
  other: 4

Student/teacher ratio: elementary, 23:1; overall average, 16:1

Teacher salaries
  minimum: $19,475
  maximum: $40,036

Funding per pupil: $4,097

Fifteen parochial and private elementary and secondary schools provide alternative educational curricula. Special schools in the city include a vocational school for the handicapped, a school and hospital for the disabled, and a school for the deaf.

Public Schools Information: Sioux Falls School District #49-5, 201 East 38th Street, Sioux Falls, SD 57117; telephone (605) 331-7900

Colleges and Universities

Sioux Falls is home to Augustana College, affiliated with the American Lutheran Church and the largest private institution of higher learning in the state of South Dakota. The college awards a baccalaureate degree in more than forty fields of study and a Master of Arts in Teaching degree. Also located in the city are Sioux Falls College and North American Baptist Seminary, both affiliated with the American Baptist Church; Sioux Falls College offers degrees in thirty-one fields and two-year programs in seven areas. The University of South Dakota School of Medicine in Sioux Falls provides education and training for health care professionals. Other colleges in the area include Nettleton College, National College, and Killian Community College.

Libraries and Research Centers

The Sioux Falls Public Library maintains holdings of about 224,000 volumes, five hundred periodical titles, and records, tapes, slides, and maps. The library, a depository for federal and state documents, operates four bookmobiles and houses special collections in South Dakota history and oral history. The Mikkelsen Library and Learning Resources Center at Augustana College holds more than two-hundred thousand volumes; the Center for Western Studies, a special collection within the library system, brings together thirty thousand volumes pertaining to the Upper Great Plains and oral history.

Twelve other libraries and research centers are operated by colleges, hospitals, Siouxland Heritage Museums, and government agencies such as the Sioux Falls Police Department, the South Dakota State Penitentiary, and the United States Geological Survey.

Public Library Information: Sioux Falls Public Library, 201 North Main Avenue, Sioux Falls, SD 57102-0386; telephone (605)339-7120

Health Care

Sioux Falls has emerged as a major center for health care in a four-state region of the Upper Midwest. The medical industry, employing fully 25 percent of Sioux Falls workers, is also an important factor in the local economy. Central to the health care community is the University of South Dakota School of Medicine; several of the city's more than 350 practicing physicians serve on the faculty of the School of Medicine, which maintains an association with four hospitals in the area. Providing a total of 1,331 beds are Sioux Valley Hospital, Veteran's Hospital, Crippled Children's Hospital, and McKennan Hospital. The new Dakota Midwest Cancer Institute at McKennan offers advanced care and conducts research. Charter Hospital provides psychiatric care. Available at these facilities and at specialized clinics or treatment centers are such services as mental health, wellness, and trauma care, poison control, rehabilitation, open-heart surgery, hospice programs, oncology care, a burn center, a critical care nursery, outreach programs, and helicopter ambulance transportation.

Recreation

Sightseeing

Local sightseeing revolves around the natural beauty and history of Sioux Falls. Falls Park is located where the Sioux River forms the Falls, a natural phenomenon from which the city takes its name. Falls Park preserves the Queen Bee Mill, a flour mill built in the nineteenth century that proved to be too large for the river's typical water flow. The Memorial to the Pioneers at the junction of North Drive and North Cliff Avenue marks the spot where pioneers from Iowa first saw the Falls of the Sioux.

The Great Plains Zoo is home to more than 240 live reptiles, birds, and mammals from around the world. The adjoining Delbridge Museum of Natural History features an extensive display of mounted animals. Created between 1928 and 1936, the Shoto-teien Japanese Gardens near Covell Lake have been restored. The Pettigrew Home and Museum is the renovated home of one of South Dakota's first two United States Senators. The Battleship *South Dakota* Memorial honors the most decorated battleship of World War II. At EROS Data Center, a United States Department of Interior research and development facility near Sioux Falls, millions of satellite and aircraft photos of the earth are on display together with a pictorial history of Sioux Falls from 1937 to the present.

Arts and Culture

The Sioux Falls Community Playhouse stages a season of theater productions at the Orpheum Theatre; these range from drama to musicals and children's shows and draw casts from local performers. The Old Town Theatre in Worthing presents dinner theater. The drama departments at Augustana College and Sioux Falls College mount productions during the school year. Sioux Falls is the home of the South Dakota Symphony, which presents classical and pops concerts featuring guest artists and soloists. The Sioux Falls Municipal Band entertains with summer concerts at three outdoor locations. Local cultural groups sponsor touring dance, musical, and Broadway performances at Sioux Falls College's Jeschke Fine Arts Center and at the Sioux Falls Coliseum.

The Civic Fine Arts Center, holding a number of exhibits each year, is the region's only contemporary museum that shows works by regional artists. Exhibits at the Siouxland Heritage Museums and Center for Western Studies capture the culture of the area's Plains tribes and the city's early settlers. The Old Courthouse Museum features a restored 1890s courtroom and law library. Represented at the Jim Savage Western Art Gallery and Memorial Studio is art from more than fifty of the nation's top western artists, including work by the late Jim Savage; Sioux culture items are also on display. Minnehaha County's historic rural churches offer a chance to examine nineteenth-century church architecture and religious customs imported to the western frontier from Norway, Sweden, and other Scandinavian countries.

Festivals and Holidays

The Sioux Empire Farm Show at the Lyon Fairgrounds is scheduled for four days in late January. Spring events include the Western Mall Arts and Crafts Show at the Western Mall the second weekend in March, the Sioux Empire Home Show for four days in April at the Sioux Falls Arena, and the Dakotas Traditional Folk Art Festival in June. For five days in late August the Lyon Fairgrounds hosts the Sioux Empire Fair, during which the Sioux Valley Restoration Society opens by appointment its authentic frontier village. The Sidewalk Arts Festival is held in early September, and the Festival of Bands invites thirty of the top area high school bands for a one-day competition in early October. The Savage Centennial Art Show is scheduled for the last weekend in October.

Sports for the Spectator

The Augustana College football team is one of the most successful small college teams in the country. Augustana, along with Sioux Falls College, fields teams in most collegiate sports, including the College Basketball Association team the Sioux Falls Skyforce, which plays a five-month season at the Sioux Falls Arena. State high school basketball tournament competition takes place at Sioux Falls Arena in March. Sioux Falls softball and baseball fields and the Sioux Falls Baseball Stadium, host local, regional, and national competition throughout the season. The acclaimed Howard Wood Field hosts track and football events; motor sports and greyhound racing events are on view at other local facilities. The National Street Rod Association holds mid-America nationals in May.

Sports for the Participant

Sioux Falls maintains sixty-three parks and outdoor recreation centers, where in addition to the usual park facilities can be found golf courses, swimming pools, and cross-country ski trails. The 13-mile Greenway system of bicycle and hiking trails is a popular attraction. Karts West/Wild Water West water park, Austad's golfers' supply store (offering video golfing), and one of the world's largest walleye fisheries are located in or near Sioux Falls.

Cities of the United States • 2nd Edition   South Dakota—Sioux Falls

The Sioux Falls, origin of the city's name, are the focal point of scenic Falls Park. The falls are shown here at night.

Shopping and Dining

Four shopping malls and a redeveloped downtown retail district in Sioux Falls offer shoppers options ranging from small specialty shops to major retail outlets. The Empire Mall contains 180 retail establishments and twelve restaurants. The Prairie Star features Plains tribes art, artifacts, jewelry, collectibles, and wearable items.

Restaurants numbered at between 150 and 340 provide menu choices that include Japanese, Chinese, French, Mexican, and Greek dishes. The local specialty is beefsteak, and one of the city's steakhouses is rated among the region's ten best.

Visitor Information: Sioux Falls Convention and Visitors Bureau, Box 1425, Sioux Falls, SD 57101; telephone (605) 336-1620

Convention Facilities

Convention and meeting planners may choose from two major facilities as well as accommodations at several area hotels and motels. The Sioux Falls Arena, located 3 miles from the business district and 1.5 miles from the airport, provides thirty-three thousand square feet of exhibit space, four meeting rooms, catering for up to 2,500 persons, and parking for twenty-five hundred vehicles.

The Convention Center adjoining the Sioux Falls Coliseum accommodates meeting or convention participants in more than nineteen thousand square feet of exhibit space in addition to five separate meeting rooms with capacities of 80 to 400 persons; the Coliseum seats around 1,900 people. Meeting facilities are also operated by hotels and motels that provide twenty-five hundred guest rooms in metropolitan Sioux Falls.

Convention Information: Sioux Falls Convention and Visitors Bureau, Box 1425, Sioux Falls, SD 57101; telephone (605)336-1620

Transportation

Approaching the City

The largest air facility in South Dakota, Sioux Falls Regional Airport at Joe Foss Field, is the destination for air traffic into Sioux Falls. Six commercial carriers schedule daily flights at remodeled Costello Terminal, providing direct or connecting service to most major cities in the country.

East-west I-90, joining Boston and Seattle, and north-south I-29, connecting metropolitan Kansas City with Winnipeg, Canada, intersect northwest of Sioux Falls. I-229, a beltway around the eastern sector of the city, links I-90 and I-29. U.S. highways 18 and 81 also serve the area.

Traveling in the City

Sioux Falls Transit, operating out of a new transfer facility downtown, provides bus transportation and a trolley available for special tours. Sioux Falls Paratransit provides service to the elderly and disabled.

Communications

Newspapers and Magazines

The Sioux Falls daily newspaper is the *Argus Leader*, which is part of the Gannett chain and is distributed every morning. Other newspapers, including a farm tabloid and college publications, appear weekly and bimonthly.

Several magazines are published in Sioux Falls on such subjects as education, wool growing, trucking, knitting and weaving, and poetry.

Television and Radio

Six television stations are received in Sioux Falls; cable channels are available by subscription. Radio listeners tune in programs on seventeen AM and FM radio stations in the city, which also receives radio broadcasts from Florence and Reliance, South Dakota.

Media Information: Argus Leader, 200 South Minnesota Avenue, P.O. Box 5034, Sioux Falls, SD 57117-5034; telephone (605)331-2200

Selected Bibliography

Brown, Dee Alexander, *Bury My Heart at Wounded Knee: An Indian History of the American West* (New York, Holt, Rinehart & Winston, 1971, 1970)

Cook-Lynn, Elizabeth, *The Power of Horses and Other Stories* (New York: Arcade Pub., 1990)

Landau, Elaine, *The Sioux* (New York: F. Watts, 1989)

LaPointe, Frank, *The Sioux Today* (New York: Crowell-Collier Press, 1972)

Turner, Ann Warren, *Grasshopper Summer* (New York: MacMillan, 1989)

Wilder, Laura Ingalls, *By the Shores of Silver Lake* (New York: Harper & Row, 1971)

Wood, Ted, *A Boy Becomes a Man at Wounded Knee: Ted Wood with Wanbli Numpa Afraid of Hawk* (New York: Walker, 1992)

WISCONSIN

Green Bay 475
Madison 487
Milwaukee 501
Racine 515

The State in Brief

Nickname: Badger State
Motto: Forward

Flower: Wood violet
Bird: Robin

Area: 65,503 square miles (1990; U.S. rank: 23rd)
Elevation: Ranges from 581 feet to 1,952 feet above sea level
Climate: Tempered by the Great Lakes, with winters more severe in the north and summers warmer in the south

Admitted to Union: May 29, 1848
Capital: Madison
Head Official: Governor Tommy G. Thompson (R) (until 1995)

Population
  1970: 4,417,821
  1980: 4,706,000
  1990: 4,955,000
  Percent change, 1980–1990: 4.0%
  U.S. rank in 1990: 16th
  Percent of residents born in state: 78.4% (1990)
  Density: 90.1 people per square mile (1990; U.S. rank: 24th)
  1991 FBI Crime Index Total: 221,283

Racial and Ethnic Characteristics (1990)
  White: 4,513,000
  Black: 5.0%
  American Indian, Eskimo, Aleut: 0.81%
  Asian and Pacific Islander: 1.10%
  Hispanic (may be of any race): 1.91%

Age Characteristics (1990)
  Population under 5 years old: 362,000
  Population 5 to 17 years old: 949,000
  Percent of population 65 years and older: 13.3%
  Median age: 32.6 years
  Voting-age population (1988): 3,593,000 (61.0% of whom cast votes for president)

Vital Statistics
  Total number of births (1992): 69,878
  Total number of deaths (1992): 41,807 (of which, 496 were infants under the age of 1 year)
  AIDS cases reported, 1981–1990: 559 (U.S. rank: 29th)

Economy
  Major industries: Manufacturing; finance, insurance, and real estate; wholesale and retail trade; services
  Unemployment rate: 5.4% (September 1992)
  Per capita income: $13,276 (1989)
  Median household income: $29,442 (1989)
  Total number of families: 1,284,297 (7.6% of which had incomes below the poverty level; 1989)
  Income tax rate: 6.93%
  Sales tax rate: 5.0%

Green Bay

The City in Brief

Founded: 1701 (incorporated, 1854)

Head Official: Mayor Samuel J. Halloin (NP) (since 1979)

City Population
 1970: 87,809
 1980: 87,899
 1990: 96,466
 Percent change, 1980-1990: 9.7%
 U.S. rank in 1980: 200th
 U.S. rank in 1990: 205th

Metropolitan Area Population
 1970: 158,244
 1980: 175,280
 1990: 194,594
 Percent change, 1980-1990: 11.0%
 U.S. rank in 1980: Not available
 U.S. rank in 1990: Not available

Area: 43.8 square miles (1990)

Elevation: 582 feet above sea level

Average Annual Temperature: 43.6° F

Average Annual Precipitation: 28.0 inches

Major Economic Sectors: Wholesale and retail trade, services, manufacturing

Unemployment Rate: 5.2% (September 1992)

Per Capita Income: $12,969 (1989)

1992 (2nd Quarter) ACCRA Average House Price: $107,420

1992 (2nd Quarter) ACCRA Cost of Living Index: 97.5 (U.S. average = 100.0)

1991 FBI Crime Index Total: 4,982

Major Colleges and Universities: University of Wisconsin-Green Bay; St. Norbert College; Northeast Wisconsin Technical College

Daily Newspapers: *Green Bay Press-Gazette*; *Green Bay News-Chronicle*

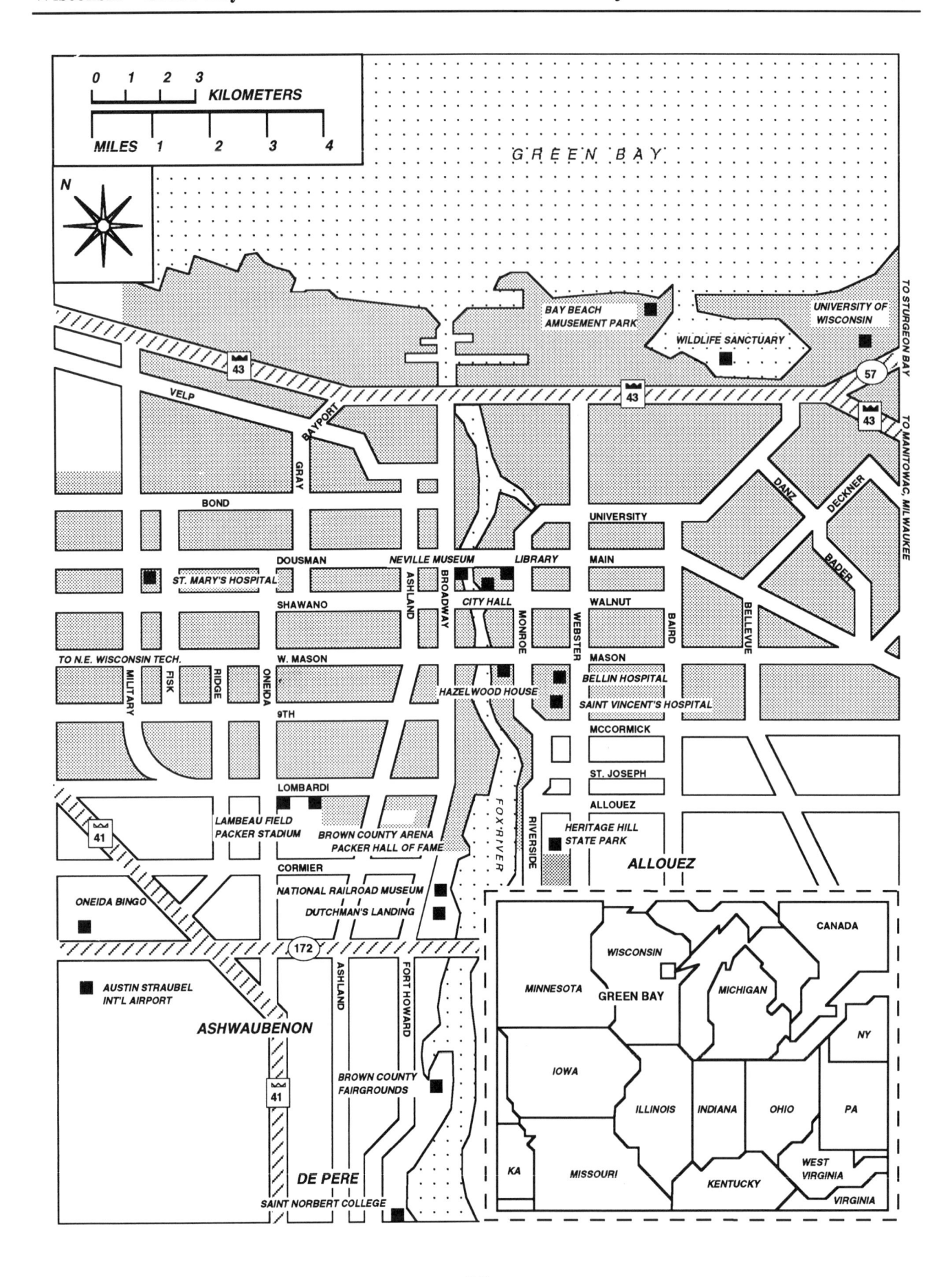

Wisconsin—Green Bay *Cities of the United States • 2nd Edition*

Introduction

Green Bay is the seat of Wisconsin's Brown County and the center of a metropolitan statistical area that includes the entire county. The oldest permanent settlement in Wisconsin, Green Bay began as a French fur-trading post and mission that was important to the exploration of the Upper Midwest in the early seventeenth century. Since the nineteenth century the local economy has been based on the lumbering, meat packing, and paper making industries, with a currently expanding service sector. Today Green Bay is known as "the tissue paper capital of America" and is home to the famous Green Bay Packers professional football team. Green Bay was cited in *Kiplinger's Personal Finance Magazine* in 1991 as a "growth spot with affordable housing and a host of new employers."

Geography and Climate

Green Bay is located at the mouth of the Fox River, one of the largest northward-flowing rivers in the United States, which empties into the south end of Lake Michigan's Green Bay. The surrounding topography—the bay, Lakes Michigan and Superior, and to a lesser extent the slightly higher terrain terminating in the Fox River Valley—modifies the continental climate. The lake effects and the limited hours of sunshine, caused by cloudiness, produce a narrow temperature range. Three-fifths of the total annual rainfall occurs during the growing season, May through September; the high degree of precipitation, combined with the low temperature range, is conducive to the development of the dairy industry. Long winters with snowstorms are common, though winter extremes are not so severe as would be indicated by Green Bay's northern latitude location. Snowfall averages 44.8 inches each year.

Area: 43.8 square miles (1990)

Elevation: 582 feet above sea level

Average Temperatures: January, 13.9° F; July, 69.5° F; annual average, 43.6° F

Average Annual Precipitation: 28.0 inches

History

Great Lakes-Mississippi Water Link Sought

On a mission for Samuel de Champlain, the governor of New France, Jean Nicolet was charged with finding a route from the Great Lakes to the Mississippi River; in 1634 he arrived at La Baye des Puans, where the Fox River empties into Lake Michigan, and claimed the region for France. But La Baye did not gain importance until 1669 when Jesuit missionary Father Claude Allouez, who established a mission there, traveled the length of the Fox River and discovered a waterway to the Mississippi River, indirectly linking the St. Lawrence and the Gulf of Mexico.

La Baye became a fur-trading center and its future importance was secured when Nicolas Perrot was made commandant of La Baye. Perrot was an effective diplomat who made alliances and trade agreements with native Americans. The lands of the upper Mississippi became the possession of the French Empire when a formal agreement was signed at Fort St. Antoine in 1689, turning a lucrative fur trading region over to the French. But when Perrot was recalled to France in 1716, his diplomatic policy was replaced by a military regime. The resulting tensions developed into warfare with the Fox Indians that continued until 1740, when fur trading again prospered and permanent housing was constructed.

In 1745 Augustin de Langlade established a trading center on the bank of the Fox River; his relations with native Americans were built on trust and respect. Langlade's large family controlled the region's trade, owned large parcels of land, married Menominee tribe women, and lived independent of French rule. During the French and Indian War, the Langlades left La Baye to fight against the British in Ohio and Canada. The British gained control of what was known as the Northwest Territory and captured Fort La Baye, which they rebuilt and renamed Fort Edward August. The British also renamed the area Green Bay, after the green-tinted streaks that stripe the bay in springtime. Trade flourished for both French and English settlers during the period of British rule and continued to prosper after the Northwest Territory was transferred to the U.S. government after the Revolutionary War.

City Develops With Lumber, Professional Sports

It was not until after the War of 1812 that financier John Jacob Astor's American Fur Company secured control of the fur trade. Fort Howard at Green Bay and Fort Crawford at Prairie du Chine were built to protect U.S. commercial interests. The opening of the Erie Canal, linking the Great Lakes to New England, further advanced Green Bay as a trading center. Daniel Whitney platted one part of present-day Green Bay in 1829 and named it Navarino while Astor platted an opposite section and built the Astor Hotel to attract settlers. Astor priced his land too high and when the hotel burned down in 1857 his company relinquished claims on the land. Farming was soon replaced by lumber as the dominant economic activity in Green Bay and in 1853, the year the city was incorporated, eighty million feet of pine lumber was milled.

Today, Green Bay is known as the smallest city in the United States to sponsor a professional football team. The Green Bay Packers were founded in 1919 by Early "Curly" Lambeau and George Calhoun, sports editor of the *Green Bay Press-Gazette,* and the team takes its name from the Indian Packing Corporation, which purchased the team's first uniforms. The Packers joined the National Football League in 1919 and have had a distinctive history. Under coach Vince Lombardi in the 1960s the Packers set a standard of team performance and dedication that other teams in the league have come to emulate in the modern football era. The Packers won the first two Super Bowl games in 1967 and 1968, and Lombardi and his players became national heroes. Green Bay was cited in *Kiplinger's Personal Finance Magazine* in 1991 as a "growth spot with affordable housing and a host of new employers."

Population Profile

Metropolitan Area Residents
1970: 158,244
1980: 175,280
1990: 194,594
Percent change, 1980–1990: 11.0%
U.S. rank in 1980: Not available
U.S. rank in 1990: Not available

City Residents
1970: 87,809
1980: 87,899
1990: 96,466 (of which, 46,070 were males, and 50,396 were females)
Percent change, 1980–1990: 9.7%
U.S. rank in 1980: 200th
U.S. rank in 1990: 205th (State rank: 3rd)

Density: 2,202.4 people per square mile (1990)

Racial and ethnic characteristics (1990)
  White: 90,888
  Black: 453
  American Indian, Eskimo, Aleut: 2,448
  Asian and Pacific Islander: 2,234
  Hispanic (may be of any race): 1,063

Percent of residents born in state: 83.0% (1990)

Age characteristics (1990)
  Population under 5 years old: 7,787
  Population 5 to 9 years old: 7,241
  Population 10 to 14 years old: 6,377
  Population 15 to 19 years old: 6,567
  Population 20 to 24 years old: 7,889
  Population 25 to 29 years old: 9,729
  Population 30 to 34 years old: 9,055
  Population 35 to 39 years old: 7,793
  Population 40 to 44 years old: 6,316
  Population 45 to 49 years old: 4,535
  Population 50 to 54 years old: 3,779
  Population 55 to 59 years old: 3,475
  Population 60 to 64 years old: 3,735
  Population 65 to 69 years old: 3,418
  Population 70 to 74 years old: 1,062
  Population 75 to 79 years old: 2,565
  Population 80 to 84 years old: 1,778
  Population 85 years and over: 1,355
  Median age: 31.3 years

Births (1988)
  Total number: 1,644

Deaths (1989)
  Total number: 786 (of which, 10 were infants under the age of 1 year)

Statues of an unidentified Native American, Jesuit Missionary Father Claude Allouez, and French fur trader Nicholas Perrot stand before the Brown County Courthouse.

Money income (1989)
  Per capita income: $12,969
  Median household income: $26,770
  Total households: 38,516
  Number of households with income of . . .
    less than $5,000: 1,616
    $5,000 to $9,999: 4,773
    $10,000 to $14,999: 4,112
    $15,000 to $24,999: 7,537
    $25,000 to $34,999: 6,861
    $35,000 to $49,999: 7,511
    $50,000 to $74,999: 4,428
    $75,000 to $99,999: 891
    $100,000 to $149,999: 402
    $150,000 or more: 295
  Percent of families below poverty level: 10.0% (71.5% of which were female householder families with related children under 5)
1991 FBI Crime Index Total: 4,982

Municipal Government

The Green Bay city government is administered by a mayor and twenty-three aldermen. The mayor is elected to a four-year term; the aldermen are elected for two years and also serve as Brown County supervisors.

Head Official: Mayor Samuel J. Halloin (NP) (Since 1979; current term expires in 1995)

Total Number of City Employees: 960 (1991)

City Information: City Clerk's Office, 100 North Jefferson, Green Bay, WI 54301; telephone (414)448-3014

Economy

Major Industries and Commercial Activity

Manufacturing, with an annual payroll in excess of $618 million, comprises more than one-fourth of the Green Bay and Brown County economy. The primary industry is paper making; eleven paper mills operate in the area, and nearly 40 percent of manufacturing activity is related to paper making. Food processing is the second-largest industry; twenty-four plants make cheese, meat, dairy, and vegetable products for domestic and foreign markets. Pizzas, baked goods, and candy are also made in Brown County. Green Bay is the largest meat-packing center east of the Mississippi.

Brown County is among the top four jobbing, wholesale, and distribution points in Wisconsin. Green Bay is the site of a petroleum storage terminal. The city ranks as a major retailing center for northeastern Wisconsin and Upper Michigan. The strongest economic growth has occurred in the retail sector in recent years, and health care is also a fast-growing sector.

Items and goods produced: tissue paper and paper products, cheese, food products, lumber, woodwork, paper mill machinery, paper boxes, clothing, steel furniture, auto parts, dairy products, gloves, fertilizers, foundry products, brick tile, sheet metal, awnings

Incentive Programs—New and Existing Companies

The principal economic development organization in Green Bay is Advance, a publicly and privately supported branch of the Green Bay Chamber of Commerce. Advance is targeting biotechnology companies and suppliers of existing local firms for location in the area. City Centre Council is a coalition of downtown business people devoted to maintaining the vitality of the central business district through redevelopment and new construction projects.

Wisconsin Public Service Corporation (WPS), the largest utility company in northeastern Wisconsin, has invested $2.5 million in Utech Venture Capital Corporation for placement in ventures that provide goods and services to the utility industry. WPS also has initiated Partners in Regional Industrial Development (PRIDE), a program for the recruiting of new businesses and retaining existing businesses in its service territory.

State programs—The state of Wisconsin extends tax exemptions for manufacturing machinery and equipment, inventories, and pollution control equipment; tax credits for research and development and energy conservation; and a 60 percent exclusion of state capital gains held for twelve months. The state provides labor training, infrastructure, asset-based lending, and high-technology awards.

Development Projects

Several development projects have been initiated or are in the planning stages for Green Bay and the surrounding area. An especially successful venture is the Business Development Center, an incubator set up by Advance, which has been instrumental in initiating a number of local small businesses. Among them are a manufacturer of magnetic cylinders used in the printing industry, a maker of ceramic tile inlays, a commercial printer, a supplier of portable radio communications systems, an electrical contractor, a seafood wholesaler and distributor, and a food testing laboratory.

Fort Howard Corporation, the city's largest employer, has added a $180 million paper machine, generating one hundred jobs and increasing productivity by 20 percent in what was the largest expansion in the company's history. The Edward W. Weidner Center for the Performing Arts at the University of Wisconsin-Green Bay opened in 1992.

Economic Development Information: Advance, Green Bay Area Economic Development, P.O. Box 1660, Green Bay, WI 54305-1660; telephone (414)437-8704

Commercial Shipping

The Port of Green Bay is an international and domestic port with a navigation season extending from April through December. More than two hundred commercial vessels transport cargo through the channel each year; port tonnage averages 1.6 million tons annually. Linking the port with inland markets are an interstate highway, air cargo service, forty motor freight carriers and the Green Bay & Western, Soo Line, Chicago & Northwestern, and Escanaba & Lake Superior railroads.

Labor Force and Employment Outlook

Surveys indicate that the job growth rate, especially in services and retail trade, in Green Bay will be second only to LaCrosse in the state of Wisconsin throughout the 1990s and into the second decade of the twenty-first century.

The following is a summary of data regarding the Green Bay metropolitan area nonagricultural labor force as of September 1992.

Size of non-agricultural labor force: 111,800

Number of workers employed in . . .
  mining: not reported
  construction: 5,300
  manufacturing: 26,000
  transportation and public utilities: 8,500
  wholesale and retail trade: 26,400
  finance, insurance, and real estate: 6,600
  services: 26,400
  government: 12,500

Average hourly earnings of production workers employed in manufacturing: $12.60

Unemployment rate: 5.2%

Largest employers	Number of employees
Fort Howard Corporation	3,223
St. Vincent Hospital	2,139
Employers Health Insurance Company	2,024
Proctor & Gamble Paper Products	1,800
Bellin Memorial Hospital	1,600
Schneider National	1,321
Wisconsin Public Service Corp.	1,289
James River Corporation	1,271

Cost of Living

The cost of living in Green Bay ranks consistently below the national average in health care, utilities, housing, food, and miscellaneous goods and services.

The following is a summary of data regarding several key cost of living factors in the Green Bay area.

1992 (2nd Quarter) ACCRA Cost of Living Index: 97.5 (U.S. average = 100.0)

1992 (2nd Quarter) ACCRA Average House Price: $107,420

State income tax rate: 6.93%

State sales tax rate: 5.0%

Local income tax rate: None

Local sales tax rate: None

Property tax rate: $27.60 per $1,000 of equalized or full market value (1990)

Economic Information: Advance, Green Bay Area Economic Development, P.O. Box 1660, Green Bay, WI 54305-1660; telephone (414)437-8704

Education and Research

Elementary and Secondary Schools

The Green Bay Area Public School District, the fourth largest school system in the state of Wisconsin, includes, in addition to the city of Green Bay, the towns of Allouez and Scott and parts of the towns of Bellevue, DePere, Eaton, and Humboldt. A seven-member, nonpartisan board hires a superintendent.

The following is a summary of data regarding the Green Bay public schools as of the 1990-1991 school year.

Total enrollment: 18,369

Number of facilities
  elementary schools: 24
  middle schools: 4
  senior high schools: 4

Student/teacher ratio: elementary, 23:1; middle, 22.52:1; senior high, 23.16:1

Teacher salaries (1988-1989)
  minimum: $20,176
  maximum: $45,078

Funding per pupil: $4,204 (1988-1989)

Twenty-seven parochial schools, including Catholic and Lutheran, enroll students in kindergarten through twelfth grade curricula.

Public Schools Information: Green Bay Area Public School District, P.O. Box 1387, Green Bay, WI 54305; telephone (414)497-4000

Colleges and Universities

Part of the statewide university system, the University of Wisconsin-Green Bay grants associate, undergraduate, and graduate degrees in such areas as arts and sciences, business, and natural and biological sciences. St. Norbert College is a four-year liberal arts institution operated by the Norbertine Fathers. Vocational, technical, and adult education is provided by the Northeast Wisconsin Technical College as well as trade schools specializing in particular skills.

Libraries and Research Centers

The largest library in Green Bay is the Brown County Library, which holds about 340,000 volumes; holdings also include 46,495 paperback books, records, films, slides, and art reproductions. Special collections pertain to Brown County history, genealogy, Wisconsin history, and oral history; the library is a depository for state documents. Eight branch libraries and one bookmobile are located in communities throughout Brown County. The Nicolet Federated Library is a regional library, serving a population of approximately 330,000. The University of Wisconsin-Green Bay Library Learning Center, with 295,000 volumes, is the area research center for local history. Libraries are also maintained by Northern Wisconsin Technical College, county agencies, health care organizations, churches, and corporations.

Public Library Information: Brown County Library, 515 Pine Street, Green Bay, WI 54301; telephone (414) 497-3452

Health Care

Green Bay is served by three major hospitals providing more than 1,200 beds, several clinics and health care agencies, and twenty nursing homes. St. Vincent Hospital, with 542 beds, is the city's largest hospital and a regional center for cancer treatment, perinatal care, and poison information. Bellin Memorial Hospital, a 242-bed general care facility that specializes in the treatment of heart disease, operates the four-year Bellin School College of Nursing. St. Mary's Hospital houses one of the state's largest twenty-four-hour emergency wards; other services include an alcohol and drug abuse program and a sick child day care program.

The Curative Workshop-Rehabilitation Center treats handicapped, severely disabled, and elderly patients. The Visiting Nurses Association and the Green Bay Health Department provide free immunization and testing services in the public schools and at local clinics. Also located in Green Bay is the Brown County Mental Health Center.

Recreation

Sightseeing

The Green Bay Packer Hall of Fame, opposite Lambeau Field in the Brown County Expo Centre

Heritage Hill Living History Museum in Green Bay.

complex, is one of Green Bay's most popular attractions. Trophies, memorabilia, and mementos of the Green Bay Packers are on exhibit, including the Vince Lombardi collection and the league championships and Super Bowl victories. Forty-acre Heritage Hill State Park Living History Museum features furnished historical buildings grouped according to four heritage themes: pioneer, small town, military, and agricultural. Among them are a 1762 fur trader's cabin, a reproduction of Wisconsin's first courthouse, Wisconsin's oldest standing house, Fort Howard buildings dating from the 1830s, and a Belgian farmhouse.

Hazelwood, a home built by Morgan L. Martin, president of the second Wisconsin Constitutional Convention, dates from 1837 and contains the table on which Wisconsin's constitution was drafted. The National Railroad Museum is a locomotive museum that exhibits locomotives and cars from the steam and diesel eras, including "Big Boy," one of the world's largest locomotives. Special attractions are U.S. Army General Dwight D. Eisenhower's World War II staff train and British Prime Minister Winston Churchill's traveling car.

Arts and Culture

The Green Bay Symphony performs a four-concert season. The Peoples Ballet presents dance concerts and the Pamiro Opera Company stages one opera each year. Both classic and modern plays are mounted in the Community Theater's season series. The Civic Music Association sponsors visiting artists. St. Norbert College hosts a performing Arts Series and college theater productions, and the new Edward W. Weidner Center for the Performing Arts at the University of Wisconsin-Green Bay hosts a variety of entertainments, including ballet performances and Broadway musicals.

Brown County's Neville Public Museum houses six galleries of art, history, and science exhibits; the "On the Edge of the Inland Sea" exhibit traces thirteen thousand years of northeast Wisconsin history. The Oneida Nation Museum captures the history of the Oneida Utopian community's life after it moved from New York to Wisconsin.

Festivals and Holidays

Artstreet is Green Bay's annual celebration of the performing and visual arts, held in the downtown district. Other annual celebrations include Arti Gras, Bayfest, Celebrate Americafest, the Oneida Indian Pow Wow, Fox Riverfest, Brown County Fair, and the Holiday Parade.

Sports for the Spectator

The Green Bay Packers, the oldest modern professional football team, enjoy one of the most heralded histories in professional sports and play in the midwest division of the National Conference of the National Football League. They compete at home at Lambeau Field against perennial rivals—the Detroit Lions, Chicago Bears, and Minnesota Vikings. In college athletics, St. Norbert College provides small-college football and baseball in nearby DePere. The University of Wisconsin-Green Bay supports a successful soccer program and competes in Division I basketball. The Green Bay Blue Ribbons compete on the semi-professional baseball circuit.

Sports for the Participant

The Green Bay parks and recreation department sponsors sports leagues for all age groups. Facilities include courts for indoor tennis and racquetball, indoor and outdoor public swimming pools, ice skating and hockey rinks, outdoor tennis courts, and ski and toboggan hills. Soccer and rugby teams compete in leagues. Boating facilities are available along Green Bay. Green Bay, Fox River, and Lake Michigan provide fishermen with pike, bass, salmon, trout, muskie, and panfish. Hunters can obtain licenses to bag duck, deer, and small game. Children enjoy rides and other activities at Dutchman's Landing Family Fun Park and Bay Beach Amusement Park. Across the street from the amusement park at Wildlife Sanctuary, a 700-acre urban wildlife refuge, the visitor can observe native fauna and hike the nature trails. The Oneida native American Tribe presents bingo and other games of chance, while parimutuel betting is permitted at Fox Valley Greyhound Park in Kaukauna.

Shopping

The Green Bay area is the regional shopping center for northeaster Wisconsin. Shoppers may choose from among four major shopping malls, mini-malls, and numerous craft stores.

Visitor Information: Green Bay Area Visitor and Convention Bureau, P.O. Box 10596, Green Bay, WI 54307; telephone (414)494-9507 or (800)236-3976

A statue entitled *The Receiver* stands at the entrance to the Green Bay Packer Hall of Fame.

Convention Facilities

A popular meeting site in Green Bay is the Brown County Expo Centre Complex, which includes the Brown County Veterans Memorial Arena, the Exposition Hall—offering a combined total of 60,680 square feet of exhibition space—and the Green Bay Packer Hall of Fame. Providing modern equipment and facilities, the complex accommodates a variety of functions such as trade and consumer shows, conventions, and banquets, in addition to sports events. Brown County Veterans Memorial Arena features a number of floor layout options, ranging from 185 exhibit booths to portable seating for nearly 3,000 people. The Exposition Hall also offers multiple layouts, with a maximum of 255 exhibit booths and a seating capacity of 2,500 people for dining and 3,000 people in a theater setting. The Green Bay Packer Hall of Fame hosts breakfast meetings, cocktail receptions, and banquets for groups of 50 to 500 people. Parking for seven thousand automobiles is available on the grounds.

A number of downtown and suburban hotels and motels provide complete meeting accommodations; more than 2,670 guest rooms are available in the Green Bay metropolitan area.

Convention Information: Green Bay Area Visitor and Convention Bureau, P.O. Box 10596, Green Bay, WI 54307; telephone (414)494-9507 or (800)236-3976

Transportation

Approaching the City

Four commercial airlines schedule forty daily flights into Austin Straubel Airfield, operated by Brown County and located in Ashwaubenon on the outskirts of the city.

As the transportation hub for northeastern Wisconsin, Green Bay is served by motor routes linked by the state's only complete beltline. Interstate 43, connecting Green Bay with Milwaukee, circles the east side of the city from northwest to southeast and is linked with the north-south U.S. 41 on the west side by Highway 172. Other principal highways are U.S. 141 and state 29, 32, 54, and 57.

Traveling in the City

Intracity public bus transportation is available Monday through Saturday on regularly scheduled routes throughout Green Bay.

Communications

Newspapers and Magazines

The major daily newspapers in Green Bay are the *Green Bay Press-Gazette,* published evenings and Saturday and Sunday mornings, and the *Green Bay News-Chronicle,* published every morning except Sunday. Eight neighborhood and regional newspapers appear weekly. *Musky Hunter,* a magazine for anglers, is published six times a year.

Television and Radio

Six television stations—including three network affiliates, two independent, and one public—broadcast in Green Bay; subscription cable service is available. Six AM and FM radio stations schedule music programming such as country and western, easy listening, and contemporary, along with public interest features. Radio stations broadcasting from DePere and Escanaba, Michigan, are also received.

Media Information: Green Bay News-Chronicle, P.O. Box 2467, Green Bay, WI 54306; telephone (414)432-2941; and, *Green Bay Press-Gazette,* 435 East Walnut, P.O. Box 19430, Green Bay, WI 54307-9430; telephone (414)435-4411

Selected Bibliography

The Door County Peninsula (Marina del Rey, CA: Bennett Marine Video, 1991. Videorecording)

Madison

The City in Brief

Founded: 1836 (incorporated, 1856)

Head Official: Mayor Paul Soglin (R) (since 1989)

City Population
 1970: 171,809
 1980: 170,616
 1990: 191,262
 Percent change, 1980–1990: 12.1%
 U.S. rank in 1980: 84th
 U.S. rank in 1990: 82nd

Metropolitan Area Population
 1970: 290,000
 1980: 324,000
 1990: 367,085
 Percent change, 1980–1990: 13.5%
 U.S. rank in 1980: 100th
 U.S. rank in 1990: 99th

Area: 57.8 square miles (1990)

Elevation: 845.6 feet above sea level (average)

Average Annual Temperature: 45.2° F

Average Annual Precipitation: 30.16 inches

Major Economic Sectors: Government, services, wholesale and retail trade

Unemployment Rate: 3.0% (September 1992)

Per Capita Income: $15,143 (1989)

1992 (2nd Quarter) ACCRA Average House Price: Not reported

1992 (2nd Quarter) ACCRA Cost of Living Index: Not reported

1991 FBI Crime Index Total: 12,884

Major Colleges and Universities: University of Wisconsin-Madison

Daily Newspapers: *Wisconsin State Journal; The Capital Times*

Wisconsin—Madison

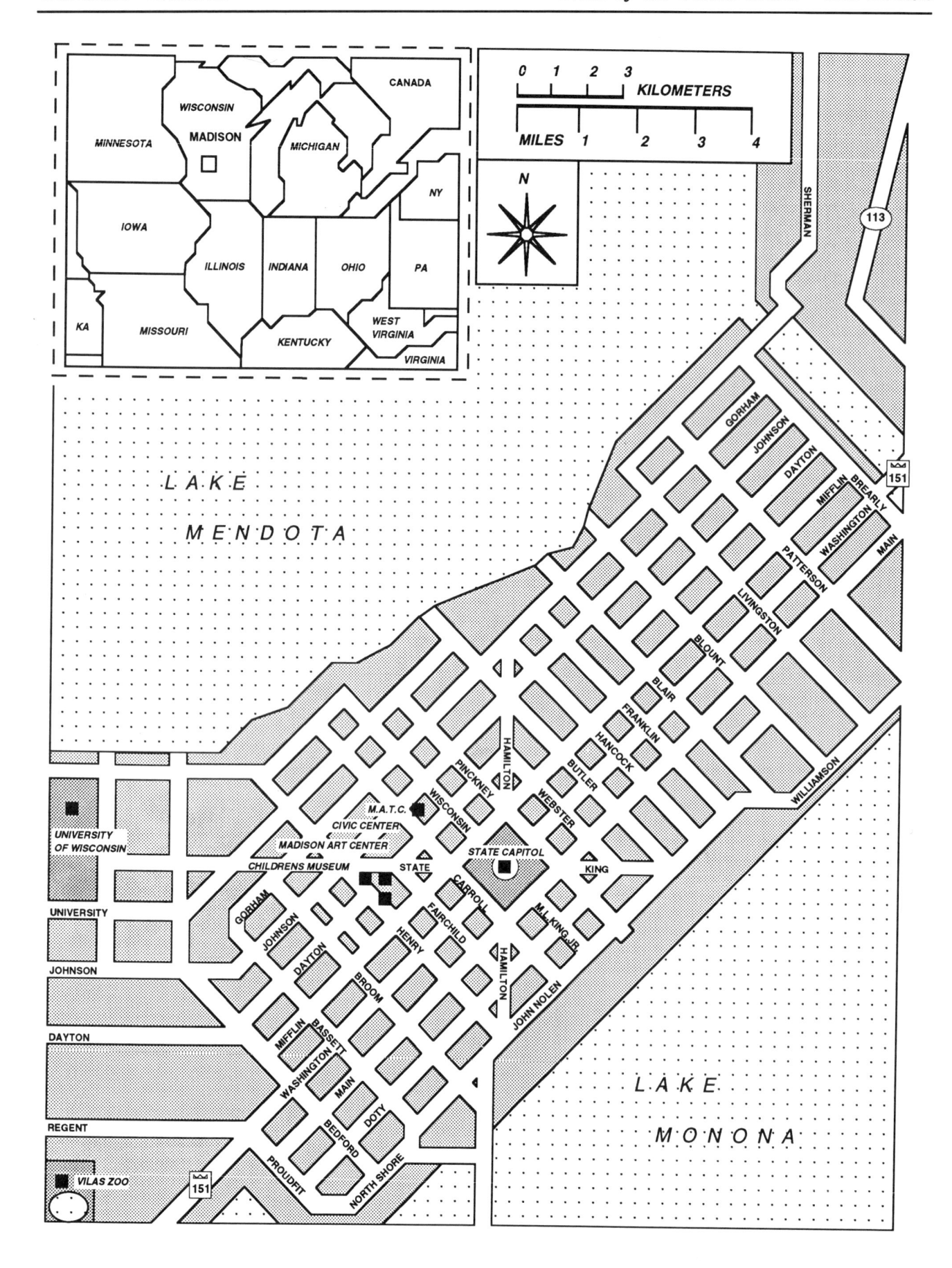

Cities of the United States • 2nd Edition

Introduction

The capital of Wisconsin, Madison is also the seat of Dane County and the focus of a metropolitan statistical area that includes the entire county. The city was founded as the state capital, where no other permanent settlement had previously existed, on a unique geographic site, a narrow isthmus of land called Four Lakes Isthmus between two lakes. Since Madison was founded, the natural beauty of its setting has been enhanced by parks and boulevards with an impressive State Capitol Building and plaza at the center of the city. Madison is the base of the University of Wisconsin, a nationally respected research institution, which is known for a tradition of academic excellence.

Geography and Climate

Set on a narrow isthmus of land between Lake Mendota and Lake Monona, Madison is surrounded by a network of lakes and rivers. The topography is rolling. The continental climate is consistent with the city's location in interior North America; the temperature range is wide, with an extreme winter low of minus forty degrees and an extreme summer high of one-hundred ten degrees. Tornadoes can be prevalent during spring, summer, and fall; moderate temperatures and humidity prevail during a generally pleasant summer. Annual average snowfall is thirty-seven inches; the growing season is approximately 175 days.

Area: 57.8 square miles (1990)

Elevation: 845.6 feet above sea level (average)

Average Temperatures: January, 15.6° F; July, 70.6° F; annual average, 45.2° F

Average Annual Precipitation: 30.16 inches

History

Land Speculator Prevails in State Capital Bid

The Winnebago tribe were the first inhabitants of the area where the city of Madison now stands; these native Americans lived off the land's bounty and camped alongside Lake Monona and Lake Mendota. Madison owes its founding to James Doty, a native New Yorker who served as circuit judge of the Western Michigan Territory, which included Wisconsin and points as far west as the Dakotas and Iowa. Doty became a land agent for fur trader and financier John Jacob Astor and in August 1835, he started buying land around the site that was to become Madison; soon he owned over 1,200 acres on the Four Lakes isthmus.

When the Wisconsin Territorial legislature convened for the first time in October 1836, with the task of selecting the site for the capital, land speculators flocked to the village with "paper" towns for the legislators to consider. In all, eighteen townsites were considered, but Doty's vision proved to be the most persuasive. Doty had selected the name Madison in honor of James Madison, the former United States President, for the state capital. The recently deceased Madison had been the last surviving signer of the U.S. Constitution. Doty's design of Madison, with a square in the middle housing the Capitol and streets radiating diagonally from it like spokes in a wheel, was the same as Pierre Charles L'Enfant's street plat of Washington, D.C. The widest street was to be named Washington, and the other streets named after the other signers of the Constitution. When the legislators complained of being cold during their meetings, Doty dispatched a man to Dubuque, Iowa, to purchase Buffalo robes to warm the freezing public officials.

Eben and Rosaline Peck and their son Victor were the first non-native American family to settle in Madison, arriving in the spring of 1837. They built a crude log inn and named it Madison House, which became the center of early activity and boarded the workmen who had arrived to begin work on the new capitol. Augustus A. Bird supervised a crew of workmen who first built a steam-driven sawmill and then proceeded to try to complete the capitol building before the first legislative session. In November 1838, the legislators arrived to find the statehouse incomplete; when they finally moved into the new statehouse, the conditions were terrible: inkwells were frozen, ice coated the interiors, and hogs squealed in the basement. Legislators threatened to move the capital to Milwaukee but better accommodations could not be guaranteed. The statehouse was not completed until 1848.

Growth and Development Preserve Natural Setting

Improvements were slow to come to Madison and the living conditions remained crude until the arrival of Leonard J. Farwell in 1849. Farwell, a successful Milwaukee businessman, began developing the land by channelling a canal between Lakes Mendota and Monona, damming one end of Lake Mendota, building a grist and flour mill, and opening streets and laying sidewalks. But even as late as 1850, when Madison's population numbered more than 1,600 people, the isthmus thickets were still dense and impenetrable.

The University of Wisconsin was founded in 1848, the year Wisconsin was admitted to the Union. The first graduating class, in 1854, numbered two men. That year the first railroad service arrived in Madison and during the decade before the Civil War, Madison's business economy began to grow. The Madison Institute sponsored a successful literary lyceum and boasted thirteen hundred volumes in its library. Streets were gas-illuminated by 1855, when three daily and five weekly newspapers were published in the new capital and the population had increased to more than 6,800 people. The city was incorporated in 1856. The following year Madison's citizens voted to donate $50,000 in city bonds to enable the legislature to enlarge and improve the Capitol building.

The Madison Park and Pleasure Drive Association was organized in 1894 and citizens donated lakeshore and forest-bluff tracts as well as money to create scenic drives, parks, and playgrounds in the city. Four years later, the city council started annual contributions to the park association. By 1916, the park association had spent more than $300,000 on improvements to the shoreline and parks. In February 1904, a fire destroyed much of the Capitol's interior. A new Capitol was constructed in stages between 1906 and 1917 on the site of the old one, featuring the only granite state Capitol dome in the United States. As both a state capital and home to a major state university, Madison has experienced a stable economic and educational base.

Historical Information: State Historical Society of Wisconsin, 816 State Street, Madison, WI 53706; telephone (608)264-6535

Population Profile

Metropolitan Area Residents
1970: 290,000
1980: 324,000
1990: 367,085
Annual average percent change, 1980-1990: 1.1%
U.S. rank in 1980: 100th
U.S. rank in 1990: 99th

City Residents
1970: 171,809
1980: 170,616
1990: 191,262 (of which, 93,179 were males, and 98,083 were females)
Percent change, 1980-1990: 12.1%
U.S. rank in 1980: 84th
U.S. rank in 1990: 82nd (State rank: 2nd)

Density: 3,309.0 people per square mile (1990)

Racial and ethnic characteristics (1990)
 White: 173,504
 Black: 8,109
 American Indian, Eskimo, Aleut: 752
 Asian and Pacific Islander: 7,471
 Hispanic (may be of any race): 3,877

Percent of residents born in state: 66.9%

Age characteristics (1990)
 Population under 5 years old: 11,863
 Population 5 to 9 years old: 10,387
 Population 10 to 14 years old: 8,527
 Population 15 to 19 years old: 16,297
 Population 20 to 24 years old: 30,670
 Population 25 to 29 years old: 20,777
 Population 30 to 34 years old: 18,220
 Population 35 to 39 years old: 16,257
 Population 40 to 44 years old: 13,124
 Population 45 to 49 years old: 8,864
 Population 50 to 54 years old: 6,605
 Population 55 to 59 years old: 5,917
 Population 60 to 64 years old: 5,923
 Population 65 to 69 years old: 5,459
 Population 70 to 74 years old: 4,354
 Population 75 to 79 years old: 3,399
 Population 80 to 84 years old: 2,408
 Population 85 years and over: 2,211
 Median age: 29.3 years

Births (1988)
 Total number: 2,666

Cities of the United States • 2nd Edition   Wisconsin—Madison

A 13-acre park surrounds Wisconsin's State Capitol Building. The park is only eight inches smaller than the one surrounding the nation's Capitol Building in Washington, D.C.

Deaths (1989)
  Total number: 1,212 (of which, 21 were infants under the age of 1 year)

Money income (1989)
  Per capita income: $15,143
  Median household income: $29,420
  Total households: 76,673
  Number of households with income of . . .
    less than $5,000: 4,458
    $5,000 to $9,999: 7,063
    $10,000 to $14,999: 6,964
    $15,000 to $24,999: 13,793
    $25,000 to $34,999: 12,684
    $35,000 to $49,999: 13,904
    $50,000 to $74,999: 11,259
    $75,000 to $99,999: 3,715
    $100,000 to $149,999: 1,825
    $150,000 or more: 1,008
  Percent of families below poverty level: 6.6% (56.2% of which were female householder families with related children under 5)
1991 FBI Crime Index Total: 12,884

Municipal Government

The city of Madison operates under a mayor-alderman form of government; twenty-two aldermen, representing the city districts, and the mayor, who is not a member of council, are chosen for a two-year term in a nonpartisan election.

Head Official: Mayor Paul Soglin (R) (since 1989; current term expires April 1995)

Total Number of City Employees: 2,500 (1991)

City Information: City Hall, 210 Martin Luther King, Jr. Boulevard, Madison, WI 53710; telephone (608)266-4615

Economy

Major Industries and Commercial Activity

The principal economic sectors in Madison are manufacturing, agriculture, services, and government. Meat packing and the production of agriculture and dairy equipment have long been established industries in the city; among other items produced by area manufacturing firms are hospital equipment, advanced instrumentation, storage batteries, and air circulating fixtures. Diversified farming contributes significantly to the Madison economy; nearly one-sixth of all Wisconsin farms are located within the Greater Madison market region. Dane County ranks among the top ten counties in the nation for agricultural production, the primary products being corn, alfalfa, tobacco, oats, eggs, cattle, hogs, and dairy foods.

The home offices of more than thirty insurance companies are located in Madison; included among them are American Family, CUNA Mutual Insurance Group, and General Casualty. The city is also the world headquarters of RAYOVAC Corporation and Ohmeda and Nicolet Instrument Corporation; Oscar Mayer headquarters are located in Madison as well. Government and education are major economic sectors; about one third of the area work force is employed in federal, state, and local government jobs, and the University of Wisconsin employs more than thirty-six thousand workers. Madison is a banking and finance center, serving the metropolitan region with more than 120 banks, credit unions, and savings and loan institutions. Other service areas important to the local economy are health care and research and development.

Items and goods produced: dry cell batteries, farm machinery, hospital equipment, optical instruments, lenses, fabricated structural steel

Incentive Programs—New and Existing Companies

Grants, venture capital, and loans are available to businesses interested in reaching research and development goals, and the resources of the University of Wisconsin-Madison are available to businesses interested in accessing research facilities and programs.

State programs—The state of Wisconsin extends tax exemptions for manufacturing machinery and equipment, inventories, and pollution control equipment; tax credits for research and development and energy conservation; and a 60 percent exclusion of state capital gains held for twelve months. The state provides labor training, infrastructure, asset-based lending, and high-technology awards.

Commercial Shipping

Madison is served by the Chicago & Northwestern, Soo/Milwaukee, and Wisconsin & Calumet Rail-

Frank Lloyd Wright's Hillside School in Taliesin draws young architects from around the world to study Wright's designs and teachings.

roads. More than forty motor freight carriers link the city with markets throughout the nation via an extensive interstate highway system. Air cargo is shipped through Dane County Regional Airport by three companies; over eleven million pounds of freight were handled at the airport in 1989 alone.

Labor Force and Employment Outlook

The following is a summary of data regarding the Madison metropolitan area labor force as of September 1992.

Size of non-agricultural labor force: 232,900

Number of workers employed in . . .
  mining: not reported
  construction: 9,600
  manufacturing: 25,600
  transportation and public utilities: 7,700
  wholesale and retail trade: 50,000
  finance, insurance, and real estate: 21,300
  services: 52,100
  government: 66,600

Average hourly earnings of production workers employed in manufacturing: $10.93

Unemployment rate: 3.0%

Largest employers	Number of employees
University of Wisconsin-Madison	36,000
State of Wisconsin	9,067
University of Wisconsin Hospitals & Clinics	5,000
Madison Metropolitan School District	3,230
U.S. Government	2,122
Madison Area Technical College	1,800
Dane County Government	1,600
U.S. Postal Service	1,417
William S. Middleton Memorial Veterans Hospital	1,064

Cost of Living

The following is a summary of data regarding several key cost of living factors in the Madison area.

1992 (2nd Quarter) ACCRA Cost of Living Index: Not reported

1992 (2nd Quarter) ACCRA Average House Price: Not reported

State income tax rate: 6.93%

State sales tax rate: 5.0%

Local income tax rate: None

Local sales tax rate: 0.5% (Dane County)

Property tax rate: Net tax rate $31.6612 per $1,000 of assessed valuation; assessed at 0.9933% of market value (1989)

Economic Information: Economic Research Coordinator, Greater Madison Chamber of Commerce, P.O. Box 71, Madison, WI 53701-0071; telephone (608)256-8348

Education and Research

Elementary and Secondary Schools

Public elementary and secondary schools in Madison are part of the Madison Metropolitan School District, the third largest system in the state of Wisconsin. A superintendent is appointed by a seven-member, nonpartisan board of education.

The following is a summary of data regarding Madison public schools as of the 1992–1993 school year.

Total enrollment: 24,288

Number of facilities
  elementary schools: 29
  middle schools: 9
  high schools: 4
  other: 1 alternative

Student/teacher ratio: 23.5:1

Teacher salaries
  minimum: $23,406
  maximum: $60,856

Funding per pupil: $6,500

Parochial elementary and secondary school systems are operated by the Roman Catholic and Lutheran churches; three private schools in Dane County provide a kindergarten through grade eight curriculum; and four interdenominational schools offer instruction at all grade levels.

Public Schools Information: Madison Metropolitan School District, 545 West Dayton Street, Madison, WI 53703-1967; telephone (608)266-6270

Colleges and Universities

The University of Wisconsin-Madison, chartered in 1848, enrolls over forty-three thousand students and grants undergraduate and graduate degrees in a full range of disciplines, including agriculture, allied health professions, education, environmental studies, law, pharmacy, medicine, veterinary medicine, and nursing. As a major research institution, the university is known for work in a variety of fields such as agriculture, bacteriology, chemistry, engineering, forest products, genetics, land use, medicine, nuclear energy, and physics. Edgewood College is a private liberal arts college awarding associate and baccalaureate degrees; a cooperative program in medical technology with area schools and limited cross-registration with the University of Wisconsin-Madison are available. Vocational training is provided by Madison Area Technical College and Madison Business College; areas of specialization include aviation, cosmetology, dance, electronics, music, nursing, recreation, and television.

Libraries and Research Centers

Madison is home to 180 public, governmental, special, and academic libraries. The Madison Public Library, with a centrally located main facility, operates seven branches throughout the city. Holdings include more than 615,000 volumes, over two thousand periodicals, and tapes, slides, films, maps, charts, and art reproductions; the library is a depository for federal and city documents. The University of Wisconsin-Madison Memorial Library is a major research facility, housing nearly five million volumes, with more than eighty special collections in a wide range of scholarly fields. The State Historical Society library specializes in Wisconsin lore and is in the process of assembling archives of material relating to the civil rights movement.

As the state capital, Madison is the site for libraries affiliated with governmental agencies; among them are the Wisconsin Department of Justice Law Library, the Wisconsin Legislative Reference Bureau, the Wisconsin Department of Public Instruction, the Public Service Commission of Wisconsin, the Wisconsin Department of Transportation Library, and the Wisconsin State Law Library. Several county agencies also maintain libraries in the city. Other specialized libraries are operated by colleges, public interest groups, labor organizations, churches, hospitals, corporations, museums, and newspapers.

Madison is an important center for research; most projects are conducted through the University of Wisconsin at the University Research Park. Government research laboratories located in Madison include the U.S. Forest Products Lab, the U.S. Fish and Wildlife Laboratory, the Space Science and Engineering Center, the Waisman Center on Mental Retardation and Human Development, the Enzyme Institute, the Sea Grant Institute, Air Pollution Lab, and the U.S. Department of Agriculture Research Service. A number of private research and testing centers, such as Hazelton Laboratories America, Inc., are also based in Madison.

Public Library Information: Madison Public Library, 201 West Mifflin Street, Madison, WI 53703; telephone (608)266-6300

Health Care

Medical service in Dane County is provided by eight hospitals, more than one hundred clinics and urgent care centers, a mental health institute, a center for the developmentally disabled, one hospice, nine home health care centers, and five health maintenance organizations. Among the principal facilities are Madison General Hospital, Methodist Hospital, St. Mary's Hospital, the University of Wisconsin Hospitals and Clinics, Dean Urgent Care Center, and Jackson Clinic. Approximately fourteen hundred physicians practice in major areas of specialization in the Madison metropolitan region. The University of Wisconsin Medical School has gained a national reputation for medical research, particularly in the treatment of cancer.

Recreation

Sightseeing

The starting point for sightseeing in Madison is the State Capitol building located between Lakes Mendota and Monona. The dome is topped with Daniel Chester French's gilded bronze statue, *Wisconsin*. The Capitol's interior features forty-three varieties of stone and murals, glass mosaics, and hand-carved wood furniture. The State Historical Society on the Capitol Concourse recaptures the history of Wisconsin with exhibits on native American tribal life from prehistoric times to the present, pioneer days, paintings and statues. The Grand Army of the Republic Hall in the capitol building displays a gallery of guns, uniforms, and flags from the major American wars.

The architect Frank Lloyd Wright, who resided in nearby Spring Green, designed two buildings that are open to the public in Madison. The First Unitarian Society Meeting House was completed by Wright in 1951; the Taliesin Hillside Home School and Fellowship, located in Spring Green, is used by Taliesin Associates for training young architects studying in the Wright tradition. Wright designs that can be viewed from the outside in Madison are the Robert Lamp House, the E. A. Gilmore Residence, Jacobs I and Jacobs II, the John C. Pew House, the Van Tamelen Residence, and the Rudin House.

The University of Wisconsin Arboretum, maintained for research and instruction by the institution, consists of 1,200 acres of natural forests, prairie, and orchards inside the city; 250 varieties of lilacs and a number of effigy mounts highlight the Arboretum's park trails. Olbrich Park Botanical Gardens, a 52-acre park, displays annuals, perennials, shrubs, and spring bulbs. The Tenney Park Locks and Dam connect Lakes Mendota and Monona, providing passageway for almost twenty thousand watercraft each season and a popular spot for fishing or feeding ducks. The University of Wisconsin Carillon Tower and Bells on Observatory Drive is the only carillon to be supported at a university by gifts of senior classes.

The Henry Vilas Park Zoo, bordering the shore of Lake Wingra, is home to hundreds of species of exotic animals. Tours are offered at the U.S. Forest Products Laboratory, which researches new and improved uses for wood and wood-based productions. The first laboratory of its kind in the world, it is equipped to test the strength and durability of new wood building materials, experiment, and find new uses for wood and other wood products.

Arts and Culture

The Madison Civic Center, a comprehensive arts facility, is the performance and exhibition space for the city's major arts institutions. The Madison Art Center maintains six galleries and concentrates on modern and contemporary visual art by local, regional, and national artists; the center sponsors twenty changing exhibitions each year. The Madison Civic Center, home to the Madison Symphony Orchestra, consists of the Oscar Mayer Theatre and the smaller Isthmus Playhouse where the Madison Repertory Theatre performs. Summer performances of Shakespeare and other classics by the American Players Theater are held in Spring Green.

The University of Wisconsin Elvehjem Museum of Art maintains an eclectic permanent collection ranging from native American miniatures, Japanese prints, and European medals to Soviet paintings and European and American art. The university's other museums concentrate in the fields of geology and zoology. Exhibits at the Madison Children's Museum involve children in learning about science, culture, and art.

Festivals and Holidays

The Capitol Concourse is the center of many of Madison's special events and activities. In June "Cows on the Concourse" celebrates dairy month. The Badger States Games are held in June, attracting from throughout the state thousands of amateur athletes who participate in eighteen different sports. Art Fair on the Square, held the second weekend in July, brings nearly five hundred artists to the Capitol Concourse to exhibit their works. The Maxwell Street Days, a bazaar of bargains, music, German bratwurst and beer is another popular event, as is the Paddle 'N Portage Canoe Race.

Two of the city's biggest events are Taste of Madison, held on Labor Day weekend, when area restaurants serve their most exotic and popular dishes, and farmers' markets, held on Wednesday and Saturday mornings around the picturesque Capitol. Concerts on the Square, held on Wednesday summer nights, are an opportunity to picnic on the Capitol grounds and listen to music performed by the Wisconsin Chamber Orchestra.

Little Norway in Blue Mounds features a Norwegian Church, built in Norway for the 1893 World's Columbian Exhibition in Chicago.

Sports for the Spectator

The University of Madison Badgers compete in the Big Ten athletic conference in twelve sports; the football and hockey teams consistently draw large crowds. Speed skating, ski jumping, and bicycle racing are also popular spectator sports in Madison.

Sports for the Participant

Water sports are particularly attractive in Greater Madison, where four lakes provide ideal conditions for swimming, fishing, boating, canoeing, windsurfing, and ice skating in winter. Year-round fishing is popular, with typical catches including muskie, northern pike, walleye, bass, panfish, and cisco. The Madison Parks Department maintains 7,213 acres of park land. Forty parks maintain ice skating ponds, the majority of which are lighted for evening skating; many provide warming houses. Cross country ski trails line city parks. Many of the parks are equipped with outdoor tennis courts.

In a city where bicycles may outnumber automobiles, 100 miles of bicycle paths are provided for cycling enthusiasts. Favorite routes circle Lake Monona and the University of Wisconsin Arboretum, cutting through Madison's historic residential district, the zoo, and Lake Wingra. Public golf courses, of varying lengths and difficulties for golfers of all ability levels, are located in Madison. The Springs Golf Course is a highly rated eighteen-hole course designed by Robert Trent Jones.

Shopping and Dining

Madison numbers almost seventy distinct shopping areas with as few as five stores and as many as seventy individual stores. The Antiques Mall of Madison offers an abundance of purchases for the antique enthusiast or serious collector. The State Capitol district offers a selection of restaurants and stores in a park setting. The pedestrian State Street Mall connects the Capitol Concourse with the University of Wisconsin; the lower section of the Mall is populated by street vendors selling crafts and food. Specialty shops and some of the city's finest restaurants are located on State Street. Friday night fish fries are a local custom, and one restaurant caters to specialties native to Wisconsin. The Farmers' Market comes highly recommended for purchasing fresh produce from local growers.

Visitor Information: Greater Madison Convention and Visitors Bureau, 615 East Washington Avenue, P.O. Box 71, Madison, WI 53701-0071; telephone (608)255-2537 or (800)373-6376

Convention Facilities

The Madison Civic Center, situated downtown on State Street Mall, has received national awards and recognition for design and resources. The Civic Center complex consists of two theaters—the Oscar Mayer Theatre and the Isthmus Playhouse—meeting and banquet rooms, and an art museum. A range of functions can be accommodated, including entertainment events and meetings for 25 to 250 participants; large receptions are held in the "Crossroads," a multi-storied lobby area. Two downtown hotels providing meeting and convention facilities are The Concourse, with three ballrooms and several meeting rooms, and The Edgewater, with five meeting rooms.

The Forum at the Dane County Exposition Center, southeast of the city, features twenty-five thousand square feet of dividable space for meetings, receptions, trade shows, conventions, and banquets. Adjacent to the Exposition Center is the Dane County Coliseum, which hosts conventions, trade shows, and exhibitions for groups of 4,000 to 10,000 people. Ample parking is provided for both facilities.

Additional meeting accommodations are available on the campus of the University of Wisconsin-Madison, as well as at numerous hotels and motels throughout metropolitan Madison.

Convention Information: Greater Madison Convention and Visitors Bureau, 615 East Washington Avenue, P.O. Box 71, Madison, WI 53701-0071; telephone (608)255-2537 or (800)373-6376

Transportation

Approaching the City

The Dane County Regional Airport, east of the city, is served by seven commercial airlines with regularly scheduled daily flights.

I-90 and I-94, two of Wisconsin's interstate highways, pass through Madison, connecting the city with Chicago, Minneapolis, and Milwaukee. The highway

Wollersheim Winery in Prairie du Sac produces ten varieties of wine from vineyards planted in the 1840s.

system also includes U.S. routes 12, 14, 18, 51, and 151 and state roads 30 and 113. The West Beltline, formed by U.S. 18, 151, 12, and 14, bypasses the city.

Traveling in the City

Madison is long and narrow, following a northeast-southwest orientation along the shores of Lakes Mendota and Monona. Within this configuration, downtown streets radiate from the Capitol hub; principal thoroughfares are Washington, Johnson, and Williamson, which run northeast and southwest, and State Street and University Avenue, which extend due east.

Intracity public bus transportation is operated by Madison Metro Bus Company, which provides Metro Plus service for elderly and handicapped patrons.

Communications

Newspapers and Magazines

Daily newspapers in Madison are the morning and Sunday *Wisconsin State Journal* and the evening (Monday through Friday; mornings on Saturday) *The Capital Times.* Several other newspapers also circulate in the city; among them are the alternative weekly *Isthmus,* and University of Wisconsin student dailies.

Madison is the center of extensive magazine and journal publishing activity. Magazines with wide circulation focus on such subjects as agriculture, athletics, money management, economic justice, and Wisconsin recreation. Several academic journals are based at the University of Wisconsin, and numerous specialized magazines and journals, many affiliated with government agencies, are printed in Madison.

Television and Radio

Five television channels—four commercial and one public—broadcast from Madison, which also receives programming from Green Bay and Wausau. Cable service is available. Several television production firms are located in the city.

Fourteen AM and FM radio stations serve Greater Madison with a variety of programming that includes classical music, jazz, easy listening, farm news, and topics of public interest.

Media Information: The Capital Times, 1901 Fish Hatchery Road, P.O. Box 8060, Madison, WI 53708; telephone (608)252-6400; and, *Wisconsin State Journal,* 1901 Fish Hatchery Road, P.O. Box 8058, Madison, WI 53708; telephone (608)252-6100

Selected Bibliography

Guide to Archives and Manuscripts in the University of Wisconsin, Green Bay Area Research Center/State Historical Society of Wisconsin (Madison, WI: State Historical Society of Wisconsin. University of Wisconsin-Green Bay, 1982)

Szathmary, Louis, *Midwestern Home Cookery* (New York: Promontory Press, 1974) (Reprint of the 1875 ed. of the Presbyterian Cook Book, compiled by the ladies of the First Presbyterian Church, Dayton, Ohio; and of the 3d ed., 1906, of the Capital City Cook Book, compiled by the Women's Guild of Grace Church, Madison, Wis.)

Milwaukee

The City in Brief

Founded: 1839 (incorporated, 1846)

Head Official: Mayor John O. Norquist (D) (since 1988)

City Population
 1970: 717,000
 1980: 636,212
 1990: 628,088
 Percent change, 1980–1990: –1.3%
 U.S. rank in 1980: 16th
 U.S. rank in 1990: 17th

Metropolitan Area Population
 1970: 1,575,000
 1980: 1,570,000
 1990: 1,607,183
 Percent change, 1980–1990: 2.4%
 U.S. rank in 1980: 23rd
 U.S. rank in 1990: 24th

Area: 96.1 square miles (1990)
Elevation: 581 feet above sea level
Average Annual Temperature: 46.1° F
Average Annual Precipitation: 31 inches

Major Economic Sectors: Services, wholesale and retail trade, manufacturing
Unemployment Rate: 5.0% (September 1992)
Per Capita Income: $11,106 (1989)
1992 (2nd Quarter) ACCRA Average House Price: Not reported
1992 (2nd Quarter) ACCRA Cost of Living Index: Not reported
1991 FBI Crime Index Total: 57,551

Major Colleges and Universities: University of Wisconsin-Milwaukee; Marquette University

Daily Newspapers: *Milwaukee Sentinel*; *The Milwaukee Journal*

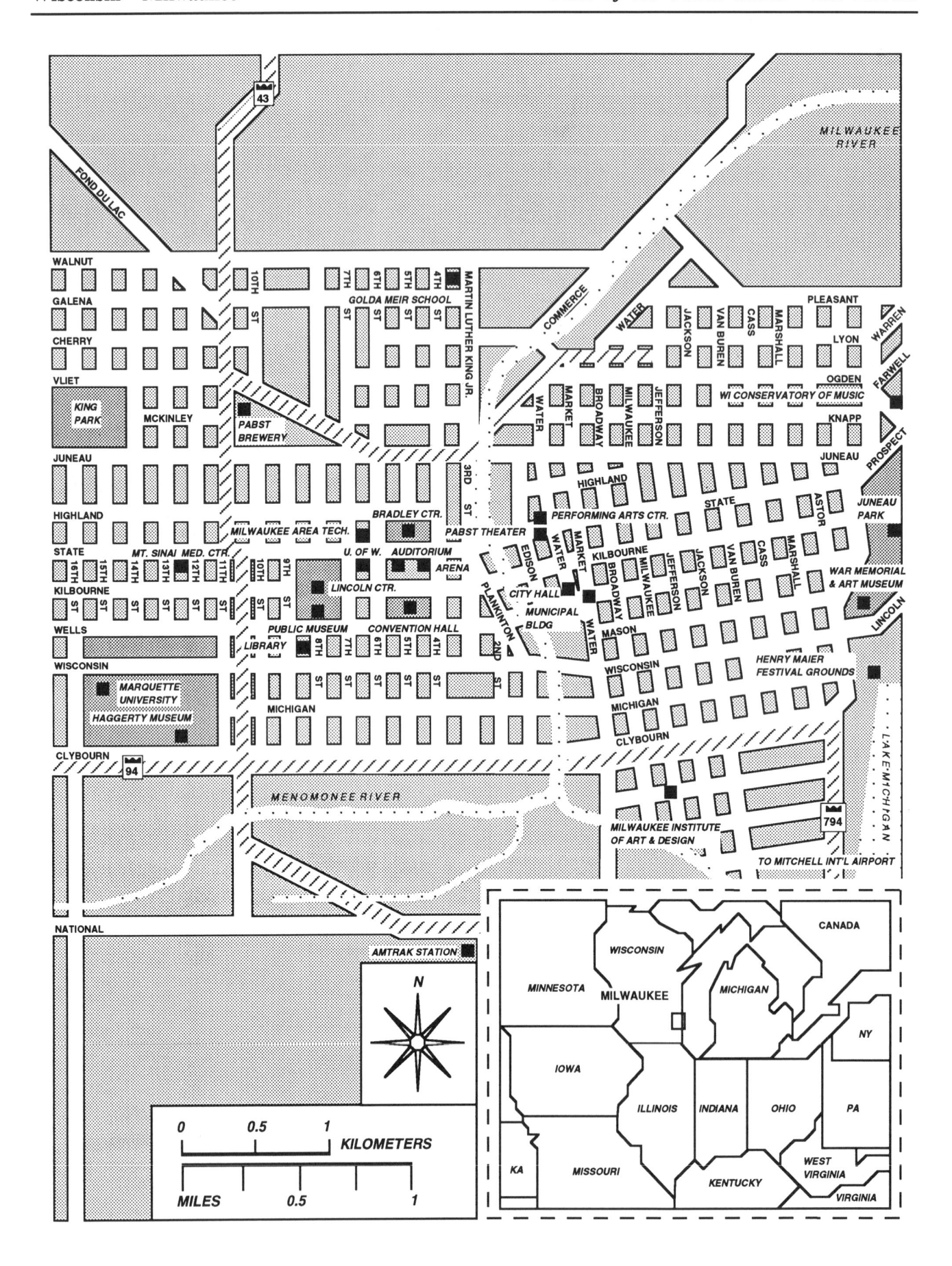

Wisconsin—Milwaukee

Introduction

Milwaukee, the seat of Milwaukee County, is the largest city in Wisconsin and the focus of a metropolitan statistical area comprised of Milwaukee, Ozaukee, Washington, and Waukesha counties. Mid-nineteenth century German immigration laid the foundation for Milwaukee's "golden age," when cultural and political life flourished, culminating in the election of the country's first socialist mayor in 1912. The city is a major Great Lakes port, traditionally known for manufacturing and breweries. Milwaukee has in recent years reemerged as a primary cultural and entertainment center for the Upper Midwest. The *Kiplinger Washington Letter* reported in 1992 that it is "workhorse cities such as Milwaukee [that] will carry the nation's economy."

Geography and Climate

Situated on the western shore of Lake Michigan at the confluence of the Milwaukee, Menomonee, and Kinikinnic rivers, Milwaukee experiences a continental climate characterized by a wide range of temperatures. The frequently changeable weather is influenced by eastward-moving storms that cross the middle section of the nation. Severe winter storms often produce ten inches of snow, and incursions of arctic air result in several days of bitterly cold weather. The Great Lakes influence the local climate during all seasons, modifying air masses before they reach the city; Lake Michigan, in particular, causes dramatic shifts in temperature. Summer temperatures seldom exceed one hundred degrees, although a combination of high temperatures and humidity occasionally develops.

Area: 96.1 square miles (1990)

Elevation: 581 feet above sea level

Average Temperatures: January, 18.6° F; July, 70.5° F; annual average, 46.1° F

Average Annual Precipitation: 31.0 inches (47.0 inches of snow)

History

Tribal Meeting Place Draws Permanent Settlement

Mahn-a-waukee Seepe, a native American word meaning "gathering place by the river," was the name given to the land next to the natural bay where the Milwaukee, Menomonee, and Kinnickinnic rivers flow into Lake Michigan and where a number of tribes met to hold counsel. The Potawatomi was the largest of the local tribes and they, along with the Menominee, were under French control in the seventeenth century. As white traders moved into the territory, the native Americans withdrew into the wilderness. The Menominee gave up land east and north of the Milwaukee River in 1831, and the United Nation of Chippewa, Ottawa, and Potawatomi signed a treaty in Chicago in 1833 that relinquished a large section of land south and west of the Milwaukee River.

In 1835 three men bought at a land auction in Green Bay the first land holdings in Milwaukee. French trader Solomon Juneau had operated a trading post near the Milwaukee River since 1818, and he purchased the land between the Milwaukee River and Lake Michigan that he named Juneautown. Byron Kilbourn named his western tract Kilbourntown, and George H. Walker claimed a southern section. Juneau accrued great wealth through his trading business; he also served as an interpreter and peacemaker between the Native Americans and white settlers. Juneau sold some of his land, and he and the new investors established a village that they named Milwaukee. The first population wave took place when Irish and New England settlers and German immigrants arrived. In 1838 the Potawatomi were relocated to Kansas.

A feud called the Bridge War, notorious in Milwaukee history, began in 1840 when the villages of Juneautown and Kilbourntown, which were consolidated in 1839, disputed payments for river bridges required by the legislature. This feuding continued for five years and in 1845 erupted in violence. The Bridge War was finally resolved when the legislature ordered that costs be shared equally between the two founding communities. The next year the city charter was ratified, and Solomon Juneau was elected the first mayor of Milwaukee.

By that time the city's population numbered 10,000 people, half of them German and a higher percentage

Catholic. John Martin Henni was appointed bishop of the new diocese, becoming the first German Catholic bishop in America. In 1848 the arrival of the "forty-eighters," German intellectuals forced to flee their homeland after their rebellion failed, helped to influence the direction of Milwaukee history. These men wanted to establish a free German republic but settled for improving the cultural and political life of the city by creating theaters and musical societies, and generally upgrading Milwaukee's intellectual life. Between 1850 and 1851 Milwaukee's population more than doubled to 46,000 people. The economy prospered during the Civil War as local industries grew rapidly and filled in the gaps created by the closing of southern markets.

Progress Continues Despite Setbacks

Several disasters threatened Milwaukee's progress. In 1867, the city's first major labor union, the Knights of St. Crispin, was formed in the shoe industry. As the economy expanded so did the labor movement, which received a setback when state troops fired on labor demonstrators in 1886, killing five. Almost 300 people drowned in 1859 when the *Lady Elgin* collided with the *Augusta*; Milwaukee again mourned when a fire at the Newhall House in 1883 took at least sixty-four lives. Both events were commemorated in popular ballads. In 1892 sixteen residential and business blocks between the Milwaukee River and Lake Michigan were destroyed by fire. Despite this tragedy, the decade of the 1890s in Milwaukee was described as the "golden age," marked by the flourishing of German theater and musical societies.

The rise of Milwaukee's brand of socialism dates from this period, when Socialist leader Victor L. Berger forged an alliance with labor, bringing the Social Democratic party into existence. Emil Seidel was elected the first Socialist mayor in 1910 and Berger became the first Socialist in the U.S. House of Representatives. The "bundle brigade" delivered campaign pamphlets in twelve languages to rally votes. In addition to Seidel, Daniel W. Hoan and Frank P. Zeidler later also served as Socialist mayors. In keeping with anti-German sentiments during World War I, the statue of *Germania* was removed from the Brumder Building and Berger was convicted of conspiracy to violate the Espionage Act. This decision was, however, reversed by the U.S. Supreme Court in 1921.

Milwaukee has been a shipping center and industrial giant in the Midwest, noted in the nineteenth century for wheat and then in the twentieth century for manufacturing, primarily the metal trades, meat packing, tanning and leather goods, brewing, and durable goods. Milwaukee industry has contributed to national and international progress with steam shovels to dig the Panama Canal, turbines to harness Niagara Falls, and agricultural equipment to farm the world's land.

Historical Information: Milwaukee County Historical Society, 910 North Third Street, Milwaukee, WI 53203; telephone (414)273-8288

Population Profile

Metropolitan Area Residents
1970: 1,575,000
1980: 1,570,000
1990: 1,607,183
Percent change, 1980–1990: 2.4%
U.S. rank in 1980: 23rd
U.S. rank in 1990: 24th

City Residents
1970: 717,000
1980: 636,212
1990: 628,088 (of which, 296,837 were males, and 331,251 were females)
Percent change, 1980–1990: –1.3%
U.S. rank in 1980: 16th
U.S. rank in 1990: 17th (State rank: 1st)

Density: 6,535.8 people per square mile (1990)

Racial and ethnic characteristics (1990)
  White: 398,033
  Black: 191,255
  American Indian, Eskimo, Aleut: 5,858
  Asian and Pacific Islander: 11,817
  Hispanic (may be of any race): 39,409

Percent of residents born in state: 72.4% (1990)

Age characteristics (1990)
   Population under 5 years old: 54,276
   Population 5 to 9 years old: 49,719
   Population 10 to 14 years old: 44,078
   Population 15 to 19 years old: 44,902
   Population 20 to 24 years old: 55,767
   Population 25 to 29 years old: 61,344
   Population 30 to 34 years old: 57,728
   Population 35 to 39 years old: 47,375
   Population 40 to 44 years old: 37,032
   Population 45 to 49 years old: 26,374
   Population 50 to 54 years old: 23,125
   Population 55 to 59 years old: 23,259
   Population 60 to 64 years old: 24,964
   Population 65 to 69 years old: 23,125
   Population 70 to 74 years old: 19,402
   Population 75 to 79 years old: 15,711
   Population 80 to 84 years old: 10,690
   Population 85 years and over: 8,781
   Median age: 30.3 years

Births (1988)
   Total number: 12,191

Deaths (1989)
   Total number: 6,061 (of which, 169 were infants under the age of 1 year)

Money income (1989)
   Per capita income: $11,106
   Median household income: $23,627
   Total households: 240,962
   Number of households with income of . . .
     less than $5,000: 15,173
     $5,000 to $9,999: 36,004
     $10,000 to $14,999: 26,936
     $15,000 to $24,999: 48,083
     $25,000 to $34,999: 39,908
     $35,000 to $49,999: 42,108
     $50,000 to $74,999: 25,496
     $75,000 to $99,999: 4,946
     $100,000 to $149,999: 1,449
     $150,000 or more: 859
   Percent of families below poverty level: 18.5% (70.9% of which were female householder families with related children under 5)

1991 FBI Crime Index Total: 57,551

Municipal Government

Milwaukee is governed by a sixteen-member council and a mayor, who is not a member of council; all are elected to a four-year term. Mayor Norquist, working with the state legislature and the governor, modified state law to create a cabinet form of government for Milwaukee to ensure greater accountability, coordination, and planning among managers and departments. This reorganization resulted in savings in the city budget of $11 million in 1989 and $7 million in 1990, increasing productivity and allowing for municipal tax-rate cuts without reducing services. *FW* magazine in 1992 declared Milwaukee "a nicely managed city [that] continues to improve with new financial/strategic plan for future."

Head Official: Mayor John O. Norquist (D) (since 1988; current term expires April 1996)

Total Number of City Employees: 8,700 (1991; includes seasonal workers)

City Information: City Hall, 200 East Wells, Milwaukee, WI 53202; telephone (414)278-3200

Economy

Major Industries and Commercial Activity

Milwaukee, a commercial and industrial hub for the Great Lakes region, is home to several Fortune 500 industrial companies, banks, and diversified service companies as well as one of the nation's ten largest insurance firms. The city places among the top manufacturing centers in the United States, although it recently has lost eighty-five thousand manufacturing jobs due to the flight of factories abroad. The economy is dominated by small- to medium-size firms with representatives in nearly every industrial classification.

Metropolitan area firms are engaged primarily in the manufacture of machinery; contrary to Milwaukee's reputation as a brewery capital, less than one percent of the city's industrial output is related to brewing. Major products include industrial controls, X-ray apparatus, steel, mining machinery, hoists, industrial cranes and monorails, speed changers, and drives and gears. Milwaukee companies are also in the forefront of science and technology, producing such items as computers, aircraft components, medical instruments, water desalination systems, electronic circuit boards, and industrial robots.

Milwaukee's foundries rank among the most productive in the nation; they turn out iron, steel, aluminum, brass, and copper castings. Milwaukee is known worldwide for sausage making. Other principal industries include food processing; the manufacture of paper, plastic, rubber, and leather products; and advertising, printing, publishing, and graphic arts. The service sector, which increased substantially in the 1980s, accounts for more than one-fourth of the city's economic base, surpassing manufacturing as the main source of employment. A number of large service firms serving national markets are headquartered in Milwaukee. The service sector, including finance, insurance, and real estate, and retail trade, employs more than sixty-one percent of the area's non-farm workforce.

Nearly a quarter of the state's high-tech firms, employing over one-third of Wisconsin's technology industry staff, are located in Milwaukee County.

Items and goods produced: automobile frames and parts, heavy pumping machinery, gas engines, heavy lubricating and agricultural equipment, large mining shovels, dredges, saw mill and cement machinery, malt drinks and products, packaged meat, boots, shoes, leather products, knit goods, women's sportswear, gloves, children's clothes, diesel engines, motorcycles, outboard motors, electrical equipment, products of iron and steel foundries, metal fabricators

Incentive Programs—New and Existing Companies

Milwaukee is known for its harmonious working relationship with the business community throughout the entire area. Its Milwaukee Economic Development Corporation (MEDC), the first municipally-sponsored economic development division in the country, offers unconventional financing to businesses and redevelopment projects in the city. Its staff also assists in securing state of Wisconsin business development funds for Milwaukee firms. MEDC works with the city's Redevelopment Authority to issue bonds on behalf of area businesses, administer several of the city's tax incremental financing districts, provide formal business training, and attract and retain businesses. MEDC is very supportive of minority-owned businesses.

Milwaukee's Land Bank program stimulates new business investment through acquisition and development of sites. Continued demand for Land Bank sites led to the opening in 1990 of the 100-acre Granville Woods Business Park. The city also assists the Milwaukee Enterprise Center is its mission of incubating small businesses by providing capital funding.

State programs—The state of Wisconsin extends tax exemptions for manufacturing machinery and equipment, inventories, and pollution control equipment; tax credits for research and development and energy conservation; and a 60 percent exclusion of state capital gains held for twelve months. The state provides labor training, infrastructure, asset-based lending, and high-technology awards.

Other programs and incentives—The Milwaukee industrial and business community profits from area educational institutions, which provide technology transfer, research services, and training programs. The Milwaukee Area Technical College, recognized for its computer graphics program, offers on-site and quick-start training. The new Technology/Innovation Center at Milwaukee County Research Park assists new technology-based businesses.

Development Projects

During the 1980s MEDC assisted in financing more than 240 projects, representing over $300 million in total investment and affecting more than fifty-seven hundred jobs. Its programs continue to create jobs and stimulate investment in the 1990s. Public and private investment between 1987 and 1993 saw the construction of such significant projects as a $100 million theater district, a $94 million hockey and basketball arena, and the $13 million renovation of the Performing Arts Center. Projects announced during the 1990s include new office buildings, apartments, and other housing options; a $130 million new home for the Milwaukee Brewers; and a $95 million chocolate factory to be built on a site in Menomonee Falls that was annexed by the city in a display of city/suburban cooperation.

Economic Development Information: Milwaukee Economic Development Corporation, 809 North Broadway, P.O. Box 324, Milwaukee, WI 53201; telephone (414)223-5840

Milwaukee skyline with one of the city's Lake Michigan marinas in the foreground.

Commercial Shipping

Because of its location near the nation's population center—nearly 65 million people and 33 percent of U.S. manufacturing are within 600 miles of the city—Milwaukee is a major commercial shipping hub. Of vital importance to both the local and state economies is the Port of Milwaukee, a shipping and receiving point for international trade as well as the primary heavy-lift facility on the Great Lakes. A protected harbor permits year-round navigation through the port from three rivers in addition to Lake Michigan. With access to the eastern seaboard via the St. Lawrence Seaway and to the Gulf of Mexico through the Mississippi River, the Port of Milwaukee processes more than 2.5 million tons of cargo annually and is the only major port on the Great Lakes to turn a profit in recent years.

More than 350 multi-service motor freight carriers are engaged in shipping goods from Milwaukee to markets throughout the country. Three railroads provide rail freight service to the metropolitan area. More than two hundred million pounds of cargo and mail are handled annually by air freight carriers at General Mitchell Airport.

Labor Force and Employment Outlook

With a stable, diversified economy that protects against pronounced shifts in employment, the Milwaukee labor force ranks high nationally in terms of manufacturing output per capita and average hours worked per week. Cooperation between businesses and educational institutions produces a pool of highly skilled technicians for industries and businesses.

Business development and expansion is expected to be relatively robust in Milwaukee in the 1990s. Among the city's leading companies are nationally and internationally known firms participating in dynamic and growing markets such as energy management, aerospace, and C A D/C A M production processes including the robotics industry. The service sector, especially the expanding insurance industry, will continue to increase employment. Aggressive overseas and Canadian promotion is expected to result in expanded exports of Milwaukee's goods and services.

The following is a summary of data regarding the Milwaukee metropolitan area labor force as of September 1992.

Size of non-agricultural labor force: 755,100

Number of workers employed in . . .
  mining: not available
  construction: 26,100
  manufacturing: 167,100
  transportation and public utilities: 37,600
  wholesale and retail trade: 170,200
  finance, insurance, and real estate: 52,200
  services: 213,800
  government: 88,200

Average hourly earnings of production workers employed in manufacturing: $12.96

Unemployment rate: 5.0%

Largest manufacturing employers	*Number of employees (1989 average)*
Allen-Bradley Co. (div. of Rockwell International)	5,076
Wisconsin Bell	4,349
Marshall & Ilsley Bank	3,926
Firstar Corp. (bank-holding)	3,853
Wisconsin Electric Power Co.	3,693
A. O. Smith Corp. (manufacturing)	3,674
Godfrey Co. (groceries)	3,400
P. A. Bergner & Co. (Boston Stores)	3,125
The Marcus Corp. (entertainment)	3,000

Cost of Living

The median price of an existing Milwaukee-area home averages 16 percent less than the U.S. average. The selling price for starter homes in the metropolitan area ranges from $45,000 to $90,000.

The following is a summary of data regarding several key cost of living factors in the Milwaukee area.

1992 (2nd Quarter) ACCRA Cost of Living Index: Not reported

1992 (2nd Quarter) ACCRA Average House Price: Not reported

State income tax rate: Ranges from 4.90% to 6.93% of total income less the standard deduction

State sales tax rate: 5.0%

Local income tax rate: None

Local sales tax rate: None

Property tax rate: $38.73 per $1,000 assessed valuation (100% of market value); tax rate includes levies for city, county, sewerage, school board, and technical colleges

Economic Information: Metropolitan Milwaukee Association of Commerce, Business Development Division, 765 North Milwaukee Street, Milwaukee, WI 53202; telephone (414)273-3000

Education and Research

Elementary and Secondary Schools

The Milwaukee Public Schools system, the largest district in the state of Wisconsin, is administered by an nine-member, nonpartisan board of school directors that appoints a superintendent. Milwaukee's public- and private-school choice plan is a national model. The city's secondary schools are part of the College Board's "Pacesetter" pilot program, which uses the latest consensus by educators on what students should know in mathematics, English, science, Spanish, and world history to develop a curriculum and test for high school students.

The Milwaukee Association of Commerce has set up a $13 million fund at five Milwaukee center-city high schools to guarantee higher education funding to any student who earns a 2.5 grade point average.

The following is a summary of data regarding the Milwaukee public schools as of the 1991–1992 school year.

Total enrollment: 99,233

Number of facilities
 elementary schools: 111
 middle schools: 20
 senior high schools: 15

Student/teacher ratio: elementary, 26:1; middle and high, 30:1

Teacher salaries
 minimum: $23,113
 maximum: $46,907

Funding per pupil: $6,298

More than one hundred private elementary and secondary schools serve metropolitan Milwaukee.

Public Schools Information: Milwaukee Public Schools, Administration Building, 5225 West Vliet Street, P.O. Drawer 10K, Milwaukee, WI 53201-8210; telephone (414)475-8393

Colleges and Universities

Several institutions of higher learning are located in Milwaukee. The University of Wisconsin-Milwaukee grants baccalaureate, master's, and doctorate degrees in a full range of programs such as the health fields, business administration, fine arts, education, architecture and urban planning, and library and information science. Marquette University offers undergraduate and graduate curricula in arts and sciences, business, dentistry, education, engineering, journalism, law, medicine, and nursing, among other fields.

The Medical College of Wisconsin is one of the nation's largest private medical schools. Other colleges in the city are Alverno College (one of the Midwest's top liberal arts colleges), Cardinal Stritch College, Milwaukee Institute of Art and Design, Milwaukee School of Engineering, Mount Mary College, and Wisconsin Conservatory of Music. Vocational and technical training is available at Milwaukee Area Technical College.

Libraries and Research Centers

In addition to its main facility, the Milwaukee Public Library operates twelve branches throughout the city and a bookmobile. Total library holdings include more than two million books, over five thousand periodicals, and films, records, art reproductions, sheet music, and art objects. Special collections are maintained on a wide range of subjects, such as Great Lakes ships and shipping, Milwaukee artists, motion picture posters, and historical recordings. The library is a depository for federal and state agency documents. The Golda Meir Library at the University of Wisconsin-Milwaukee maintains holdings of more than nine-hundred thousand books as well as special collections in many scholarly fields; separate departmental libraries include the American Geographical Society Collection, numbering more than two-hundred thousand books in addition to other items.

The Medical College of Wisconsin Libraries house more than 191,000 books pertaining to basic sciences, clinical medicine, and nursing; the main library is a depository for World Health Organization publications. The Medical College is recognized as a leading center for research in such fields as interferon, obesity, allergies, eye disorders, arthritis, heart disease, childhood cancer, and diagnostic imaging.

The University of Wisconsin-Milwaukee maintains the Office of Industrial Research and Technology Transfer, the Management Research Center, the International Business Center, and the Laser Laboratory. Marquette University operates the Robotics Control System Laboratory and conducts in-house training programs in management development, computer technology, and industrial technology. The recently established Biological and Biomedical Research Institute at Marquette University stimulates collaborative research by scientists in the life sciences. The Milwaukee School of Engineering houses the Applied Technology Center, the nationally known Fluid Power Institute, and the Biomedical Research Institute.

Public Library Information: Milwaukee Public Library, 814 West Wisconsin Avenue, Milwaukee, WI 53233-2385; telephone (414)278-3020

Health Care

Milwaukee has been ranked by *Health Magazine* as the fourth-healthiest city in the country. Residents have access to thirty-seven hospitals, many of them nationally known. New on the health care scene in Milwaukee are the Milwaukee Regional Medical Center and the Newtowne Medical Center. The Regional Medical Center is a consortium of private, nonprofit, and governmental institutions formed to deliver state-of-the-art patient care, medical research, and education of health personnel in a 250-acre park-like location. Members of this consortium are The Blood Center of Southeastern Wisconsin, Children's Hospital of Wisconsin, Curative Rehabilitation Center, Froedtert Memorial Lutheran Hospital, Medical College of Wisconsin, Milwaukee County Medical Complex, Milwaukee Mental Health Complex, and the Trauma Center.

The Newtowne Medical Center is a $3 million facility opened in 1990. Clement J. Zablocki Veterans Affairs Medical Center is working with the Medical College of Wisconsin on a human growth hormone to reverse aspects of the aging process. St. Luke's Medical Center specializes in cardiac care, while St. Mary's concentrates on the treatment of burns and cardiovascular diseases. The International Health Training Center is also located in Milwaukee.

Recreation

Sightseeing

Milwaukee successfully mixes old and new architectural styles that tell the history of the city from its beginning to the present. Kilbourntown House, the 1844 home of one of the city's founding fathers, is furnished with mid-nineteenth century furniture and decorative arts. The Jeremiah Curtin House, built in 1846, is an example of Irish cottage architecture, while the Lowell Damon House, built a year later, exemplifies the colonial style. Two structures of Flemish Renaissance design from the 1890s are of special note: Milwaukee City Hall, completed in 1895, features carved woodwork, leaded glass, stencilled ceilings, and stained-glass windows; and Pabst Mansion, built in 1893, contains decorative woodwork and ironwork.

Milwaukee is noted for its church architecture. St. Joan of Arc Chapel at Marquette University is a reconstructed fifteenth-century French chapel. Under its dome, modeled after St. Peter's in Rome, St. Josaphat's Basilica displays a collection of relics and portraits. St. Sava Serbian Orthodox Cathedral was built in a Byzantine style with imported mosaics and stained-glass windows. St. Stephen's Catholic Church is the last remnant of the 1840 German settlement of New Coeln, and the church's wood carvings are said to be world famous. Trinity Evangelical Lutheran Church, an ornamental Victorian gothic structure, is on the National Register of Historic Places.

Cities of the United States • 2nd Edition Wisconsin—Milwaukee

Downtown Milwaukee's *Bastille Days* festival, one of a dozen ethnic festivals held there.

The Milwaukee County Zoo, recently renovated, was one of the first U.S. zoos to separate its animals with hidden moats in a natural environment. The Mitchell Park Horticultural Conservatory, known as the Domes, cultivates tropical, arid, and seasonal plant displays. The Boerner Botanical Gardens at Whitnall Park displays perennials, wildflowers, annuals, and herbs, and features a highly praised rose garden. The Wehr Nature Center is designed to foster environmental awareness as a "living laboratory" consisting of woodlands and wetlands and a small lake.

Arts and Culture

Milwaukee's cultural heritage dates to the nineteenth century when German immigrants established the city's first music societies and theater groups. Today the Milwaukee Symphony Orchestra performs a season of classical and pop concerts at the Performing Arts Center, which is also the home of the Milwaukee Ballet Company, Milwaukee Repertory Theater, and the Florentine Opera Company. The Milwaukee Symphony Orchestra's summer season takes place at two locations: Uihlein Hall at the Performing Arts Center, an indoor summer facility, and Marcus Amphitheater on Lake Michigan, which is the largest covered outdoor summer facility used by any U.S. orchestra. The Skylight Opera Theatre presents a season of productions ranging from Mozart to Gilbert and Sullivan.

The Milwaukee Repertory Theater's six-play season is produced in a new complex that includes a Mainstage theater, the Stackner Cabaret, and the Pabst Theater, a Victorian structure built in 1895. Riverside Theater presents theatrical shows and musical performances. The Milwaukee Chamber Theater produces America's only Shaw Festival.

Milwaukee's museums present a variety of choices for the art enthusiast. The Milwaukee Art Museum on Lake Michigan is housed in the War Memorial Center designed by Eero Saarinen. The Museum's permanent collection consists of nineteenth and twentieth century painting and sculpture, extensive Haitian art holdings, and the Bradley gift of modern art displayed in a wing built in 1975. The Charles Allis Art Museum houses its collection of American and European paintings in a 1911 Edwardian mansion. The American Geographical Society Collection at the University of Wisconsin-Milwaukee exhibits material related to geography, exploration, cartography, and the earth and social sciences.

Other Milwaukee museums include the Discovery World Museum with hands-on exhibits; Greene Memorial Museum with minerals, crystals, and fossils; the Haggerty Museum of Art; the Milwaukee County Historical Center; the Milwaukee Public Museum (featuring a Tropical Rain Forest); Black Holocaust Museum; and the University of Wisconsin-Milwaukee Art Museum. The Villa Terrace, overlooking Lake Michigan, displays decorative art.

Festivals and Holidays

Milwaukee, dubbed the "City of Festivals," is the site of a wide variety of events. The U.S. snow sculpting competition takes place in early January at the Milwaukee County Zoo; the subsequent international competition is held later in the month at Pierre Marquette Park. Most events are scheduled in the summer, beginning with RiverSplash in June; Rainbow Summer, a musical celebration held June through August at Peck Pavilion; Summerfest; Bastille Days; and Independence Day Celebrations.

Milwaukee's City of Festivals Parade in June and the Great Circus Parade in July attract a combined total of more than 1.2 million spectators. The Great Circus Parade is a four-mile processional along Milwaukee's main streets with restored circus wagons, circus animals—including the Budweiser Clydesdales—clowns, and marching bands. Another popular event in Milwaukee is the State Fair in August that attracts just under one million people. Miller Maritime Festival is held on Labor Day.

Sports for the Spectator

Major league baseball's Milwaukee Brewers compete in the Eastern Division of the American League and play their home games at Milwaukee County Stadium. The Milwaukee Bucks of the National Basketball Association are based at the Bradley Center, a privately funded $94 million sports and concert facility that provides the city with one of the nation's most architecturally significant and functional sports facilities. Bradley Center is also home to the Marquette Warriors basketball team, the Milwaukee Admirals of the International Hockey League, and the Milwaukee Wave professional soccer team. The Green Bay Packers host three home games at Milwaukee County Stadium.

The Bavarian Club soccer team schedules a season of games from spring through the fall. Marquette University and the University of Wisconsin-Milwaukee Panthers field teams in most collegiate sports.

Jetrockets, wheelstanders, and funny cars are featured in a season of competition at the Great Lakes Dragway from April through November. The Milwaukee Mile at the Wisconsin State Fair track attracts nationally known drivers.

Sports for the Participant

The Milwaukee County Park System maintains 140 parks on over 14,000 acres. Indoor and outdoor recreational activities offered year-round include rugby, soccer, softball, baseball, swimming, tennis, golf, ice skating, tobogganing, and boating. Public skating is available at the new Pettit National Ice Center, which contains the country's first indoor 400-meter racing oval, one of only five worldwide. The center hosted the 1993 U.S. Olympic Trials and will host the 1995 World Sprint championships. Milwaukee's location on Lake Michigan offers a myriad of recreational opportunities.

Shopping and Dining

Milwaukee is one of a few midwestern cities with a skywalk system connecting the downtown commercial district; one section, called Riverspan, bridges the Milwaukee River. The Grand Avenue is an enclosed multi-level four-block marketplace of 160 shops and restaurants and five historic buildings forming the core of the glass skywalk system. The Market Place Shopping Village, Old World Third Street, and Stonewood Village feature shops that offer crafts, foods, and specialty items in unique and historical settings. Several neighborhood and regional shopping malls also serve the metropolitan area. There are two city-owned farmers' markets that operate year-round.

Some of the best German restaurants in the country are located in Milwaukee, such as Karl Ratzsch's, named by *Food and Wine* magazine a 1992-1993 Distinguished Restaurant of North America. Dining in Milwaukee is not limited to award-winning German cuisine, however; besides Continental, Italian, and Chinese restaurants, Milwaukee offers a surprising mix of other ethnic choices, such as Czechoslovakian, East Indian, Polynesian, Serbian, and Thai. One of the city's highest rated restaurants specializes in early American food. Three local French restaurants combine French delicacies with indigenous fare such as Wisconsin reindeer and salmon.

Visitor Information: Greater Milwaukee Convention and Visitors Bureau, Inc., 756 North Milwaukee Street, Milwaukee, WI 53202; telephone (414) 273-3950

Convention Facilities

The Milwaukee Exposition and Convention Center and Arena (MECCA) houses a convention hall, an auditorium, and an arena; the complex contains a total of 250,000 square feet of exhibit and meeting space in addition to an adjacent parking area for thirteen thousand vehicles. The MECCA Convention Hall, the largest of the facilities, provides 132,000 square feet of multi-use, divisible space, as well as twenty-nine banquet and meeting rooms. Bruce Hall in the Auditorium seats up to 6,100 persons, and the MECCA Arena features a total seating capacity of 12,000 people. The convention center is linked to the downtown Grand Avenue shopping mall via an enclosed, weather-protected skywalk.

Additional meeting and banquet accommodations are available at a number of first-class downtown hotels and at hotel-motel convention centers located near the airport. Area hotels and motels offer approximately eleven thousand sleeping rooms. As Milwaukee's popularity as a convention site grows, consideration is being given to major expansion of MECCA and downtown hotel facilities.

Convention Information: Greater Milwaukee Convention and Visitors Bureau, Inc., 756 Milwaukee Street, Milwaukee, WI 53202; telephone (414)273-3950

Transportation

Approaching the City

General Mitchell International Airport is the destination for most air traffic into Milwaukee. Situated adjacent to I-94, 8 miles south of downtown, Mitchell Airport is served by seventeen commercial airlines. The terminal accommodates more than 4 million passengers each year and is highly regarded by frequent travelers. Based at General Mitchell International Airport is Midwest Express Airlines, ranked one of the best airlines in the country, which provides nonstop commuter service to Milwaukee from several major United States cities. The principal general aviation facility for Milwaukee is Timmerman Field.

A 160-mile freeway system permits direct access to central Milwaukee within twenty minutes from points throughout a 10-mile radius, except during the peak rush-hour period.

Amtrak provides passenger rail service into Milwaukee.

Traveling in the City

The city of Milwaukee lies along the shore of Lake Michigan and is intersected from north to south by the Milwaukee River. Streets are laid out on a grid pattern; Lincoln Memorial Drive runs along the lake shore downtown. North-south streets are numbered and east-west streets are named.

The Milwaukee County Transit System, which ranks among the nation's largest all-bus transportation systems, operates sixty-five bus routes in Milwaukee County. Additional services include express routes from park-ride lots and special routes to the university area and the stadium.

Communications

Newspapers and Magazines

The major daily newspapers in Milwaukee are the morning (Monday through Saturday) *Milwaukee Sentinel* and the evening (Monday through Saturday; mornings on Sunday) *The Milwaukee Journal.* Several other newspapers, including *The Business Journal Serving Greater Milwaukee,* circulate biweekly or weekly.

At least thirty-five trade and special-interest magazines and journals are published in Milwaukee; they cover such subjects as personal improvement, religion, hobbies, the social sciences, business and finance, computers, railroads, construction and building trades, and archaeology.

Television and Radio

Seven commercial, two public, and one Christian television stations broadcast in Milwaukee. Thirty-nine AM and FM radio stations are received in the county. The Milwaukee Symphony Orchestra produces national radio broadcasts.

Media Information: Journal/Sentinel, Inc., 333 West State Street, Milwaukee, WI 53201-0661; telephone (414)224-2000; and, *Milwaukee Magazine,* Monthly Milwaukee, Inc., 312 East Buffalo, Milwaukee, WI 53202; telephone (414) 273-1101

Selected Bibliography

Derleth, August William, *The Wind Leans West* (New York: Candlelight Press, 1969)

Wright, Betty Ren, *The Scariest Night* (New York: Holiday House, 1991)

Racine

The City in Brief

Founded: 1834 (chartered, 1848)

Head Official: Mayor N. Omen Davis (NP) (since 1987)

City Population
 1970: 95,162
 1980: 85,725
 1990: 84,298
 Percent change, 1980–1990: −1.7%
 U.S. rank in 1980: Not available
 U.S. rank in 1990: 248th

Metropolitan Area Population
 1970: 1,575,000
 1980: 1,570,152
 1990: 1,607,183
 Percent change, 1980–1990: 2.4%
 U.S. rank in 1980: 23rd
 U.S. rank in 1990: 24th

Area: 15.4 square miles (1990)

Elevation: 626 feet above sea level

Average Annual Temperature: 47.4° F

Average Annual Precipitation: 39.35 inches (38.6 inches of snowfall)

Major Economic Sectors: Manufacturing, services, trade

Unemployment Rate: 6.3% (September 1992)

Per Capita Income: $11,858 (1989)

1992 (2nd Quarter) ACCRA Average House Price: $124,500

1992 (2nd Quarter) ACCRA Cost of Living Index: 104.9 (U.S. average = 100.0)

1991 FBI Crime Index Total: 8,072

Major Colleges and Universities: University of Wisconsin-Parkside, Gateway Technical College

Daily Newspaper: *Journal-Times*

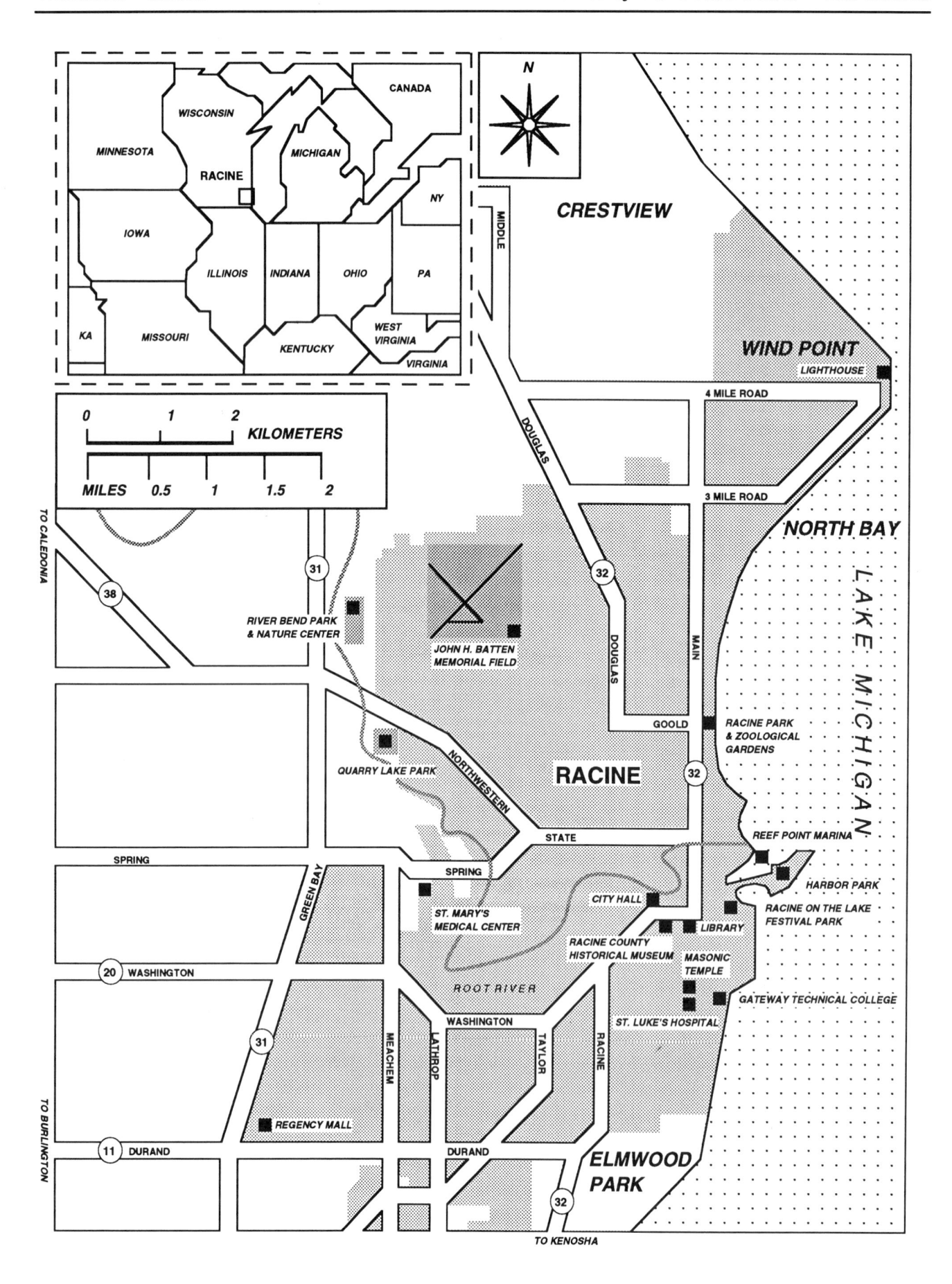

Wisconsin—Racine *Cities of the United States • 2nd Edition*

Introduction

Located on the corridor between Milwaukee and Chicago, the lakeside city of Racine has been primarily manufacturing-oriented for the past one hundred years. With the construction in the 1980s of the largest recreational boat harbor on Lake Michigan, Racine has diversified its economy from one based on durable goods to one that embraces tourism. The marina and its restaurant, the development of bed and breakfast inns, a charming lakefront zoo, and one of the largest and most prestigious furniture galleries in the midwest add to the city's attractions. Racine County hosts more than 130 festivals, concerts, carnivals, fairs, parades, sporting events, picnics and celebrations annually, which also boosts tourism to the "Belle City of the Lakes."

Geography and Climate

Racine is located on the western shore of Lake Michigan in southeastern Wisconsin about 65 miles north of Chicago and 25 miles south of Milwaukee. Racine's weather is influenced to a considerable extent by Lake Michigan, especially when the temperature of the lake differs markedly from the air temperature. During spring and early summer a wind shift from westerly to easterly can cause a ten to fifteen degree drop in temperature. In autumn and winter the relatively warm water of Lake Michigan prevents nighttime temperatures from falling as low as they do a few miles inland from shore.

Area: 15.4 square miles (1990)

Elevation: 626 feet above sea level

Average Temperatures: January, 21° F; July, 70° F; annual average, 47.4° F

Average Annual Precipitation: 39.35 inches (38.6 inches of snowfall)

History

City Settled by Yankees

The first known visit by white men to the Root River area, the site of present-day Racine, occurred in 1679 when explorers LaSalle and Tonti stopped there on their search for a route to the Mississippi River. Prior to the 1830s, the area of southeastern Wisconsin was inhabited by the Potowatomi tribe, whose rights to the lands were recognized by the federal government. By 1833 the U.S. government made an agreement with the Potowatomi to purchase five million acres of land including the area where Racine is located. Soon after the Potowatomi were moved by the government to areas in the western United States. The first settlers arrived in what came to be Racine County about 1820 and established trading posts along the Root River in the present day cities of Racine and Caledonia.

In 1834 Gilbert Knapp settled at the mouth of the Root River and blazed out a 160-acre claim. From 1834 to 1836 the community was named Root for the river on which the city was settled, (Root being the English translation for the name the Potowatomi called the river). After 1836 the name was changed to Racine, the French word for root, but the English word was retained for the name of the river. From the spot at the mouth of the river and spreading westward across the entire county, commercial and industrial enterprises sprang up. In 1834 and 1835 hundreds of settlers migrated west to the newly open lands. Northern Europeans settled along waterways throughout Racine County, utilizing them for transportation and power.

Shortly after Racine's founding, a saw mill was constructed, which proved to be a real convenience to the settlers. By 1840, 337 settlers lived in the area and by 1844 the city had 1,100 people. The government built a lighthouse in 1839, a $10,000 courthouse in 1840, and several bridges and a major hotel. Between 1844 and 1860 the government assisted in the completion of the harbor. A large elevator was built in 1867 to load the ships with wheat that was brought to Racine and stored in dozens of grain warehouses. It was destroyed by a fire in 1882.

Manufacturing Anchors Local Economy

The young city was supported by a large farming community who came to town for manufactured goods. The city's growth coincided with the invention and development of agriculture machinery and other labor-saving devices. A flour and feed business was Racine's first. Other early industries were boots and shoes, tanneries, clothing, wagons and carriages, soap and candles, saddles, trucks, harnesses, and blacksmithing. By 1860 boat building and brick making were added.

Racine's first school was built in 1836. During the Civil War, the Camp Utley federal war camp was built in Racine. In 1884 the first ship entered the newly built harbor. That same year, upon the city's fiftieth birthday, a monument that still stands in Monument Square was erected to honor city's the city's Civil War soldiers.

Over the years, as waterways declined in importance, railroads became the major transport for freight. The first railroad to reach Racine arrived in 1853 and the first steam engine came into use in 1867.

A number of local industries have had a vital relation to the growth and prosperity of the city itself. The J. I. Case Plow Threshing Machine Works was established in 1844. In 1886 S. C. Johnson began a parquet flooring manufacturing operation which diversified over the years and is now the city's largest employer. Gold Metal Camp Furniture was started in 1892, the Racine Rubber Company in 1910, Mitchell Motor Car Company in 1903, and Western Publishing in 1908.

The Great Depression of the 1930s was especially severe in the agricultural sector and the sale of farm machinery drastically declined. By 1937 recovery had begun, and World War II accelerated that recovery. However, from 1945 through 1960 the business community, always sensitive to national business cycles, experienced slow post-war growth. In the 1960s, the voluntary desegregation of the schools became a national model. During the 1960s and 1970s Racine manufacturing entered a growth cycle, and printing, publishing, and chemical production became more predominant.

During the 1970s there was an increased movement of industry from central Racine to the outlying areas. In 1971 the University of Wisconsin-Parkside was founded in a rural setting between Racine and the nearby city of Kenosha.

The construction of the multimillion dollar Racine On The Lake Festival Park marina complex in the 1980s spurred the growth of tourist visits to the city, particularly from the Chicago and Milwaukee areas.

Historical Information: Racine County Historical Museum, 701 Main Street, Racine, WI 53406; telephone (414)636-3926

Population Profile

Metropolitan Area Residents
1970: 1,575,000
1980: 1,570,152
1990: 1,607,183
Average annual percent change, 1980–1988: less than 0.5%
Percent change, 1980–1990: 2.4%
U.S. rank in 1980: 23rd
U.S. rank in 1990: 24th

City Residents
1970: 95,162
1980: 85,725
1990: 84,298 (of which 44,313 were females and 39,985 were males)
Percent change, 1980–1990: −1.7%
U.S. rank in 1980: Not available
U.S. rank in 1990: 248th (State rank: 4th)

Density: 5,473.9 per square mile (1990)

Racial and ethnic characteristics (1990)
  White: 64,378
  Black: 15,551
  American Indian, Eskimo, Aleut: 273
  Asian and Pacific Islander: 458
  Hispanic (may be of any race): 6,853

Percent of residents born in state: 74.0% (1990)

Age characteristics (1990)
  Population under 5 years old: 7,4079,295
  Population 18 to 20 years old: 3,179
  Population 21 to 24 years old: 4,791
  Population 25 to 44 years old: 26,909
  Population 45 to 54 years old: 7,131
  Population 55 to 59 years old: 3,260
  Population 60 to 64 years old: 3,526
  Population 65 years and older: 11,033
  Median age: 31.4 years (1990)

Births (1988)
  Total number: 1,510

Downtown's Monument Square was the center of activity in early Racine.

Deaths (1988)
　Total number: 758 (18 of which were infants under the age of 1 year)

Money income (1989)
　Per capita income: $11,858 (1989)
　Median household income: $26,540
　Total households: 31,758
　Number of households with income of . . .
　　less than $5,000: 1,481
　　$5,000 to $9,999: 4,024
　　$10,000 to $14,999: 3,374
　　$15,000 to $24,999: 6,132
　　$25,000 to $34,999: 5,267
　　$35,000 to $49,999: 6,169
　　$50,000 to $74,999: 3,988
　　$75,000 to $99,999: 945
　　$100,000 to $149,999: 322
　　$150,000 or more: 83
　Percent of families below poverty level: 10.6% (65.2% of which were female householder families with related children under 5)

1991 FBI Crime Index Total: 8,072

Municipal Government

The city of Racine has a mayor-council form of government.

Head Official: Mayor N. Owen Davies (NP) (since 1987; current term expires April 1995)

Total Number of City Employees: 956 (1992)

City Information: City of Racine, 730 Washington Avenue, Racine, WI 53403; telephone (414)636-9103

Economy

Major Industries and Commercial Activity

The recent history of the city of Racine is a story of downtown revitalization. During the 1980s Racine County lost an average of one thousand jobs per year and many downtown retailers closed or moved to new outlying malls or elsewhere. A group of local business leaders marshalled private, county, and city support in their efforts to turn a declining downtown area with a failing commercial harbor into a vital, attractive harbor complex that would attract tourism and convention activity. The project includes a 110-acre 921-slip luxury harbor/marina; a 16-acre county park; and a 6-acre city-owned festival park that contains both indoor and outdoor facilities designed for year-round use. The city, county, and private sector have pumped more than $25 million into the projects. By the early 1990s, fifty new retailers had moved to the central city and more than one-hundred thousand square feet of first-class office space was added to the downtown. In addition, the revitalized lakefront has spurred more than $30 million in private investment, including a seventy-six-unit lakefront condominium.

Presently, there are more than three hundred established manufacturing firms across Racine County, a number of them based in the city of Racine. Racine is world headquarters of S. C. Johnson Wax, one of the world's leading manufacturers of chemical specialty products for home care, insect control, and personal care. One of the largest privately-held family controlled businesses in the United States, it is the city's major employer. Another important local firm is In-Sink-Erator, the world's largest manufacturer of food waste disposers. The first food disposer was created in 1927 in Racine by John W. Hammes, founder of the company which began operations in 1937. Today the company also markets hot water dispensers, water heaters, dishwashers, and trash compactors.

In 1844 J. I. Case began a threshing machine works in Racine, and today is known worldwide for its quality agricultural and construction equipment. With origins in the city dating back more than seventy years, Master Appliance Corporation has become one of the world's leading designers, manufacturers and marketers of heat tools for industry. Western Publishing Company, the nation's largest publisher and producer of children's storybooks, was founded in Racine in 1907 as a small printing company. The company is also a major producer of puzzles, games, and youth electronic books and products, and ranks among the largest commercial printers in the U.S. Founded in Racine more than seventy years ago, Jacobsen Textron has built a worldwide reputation for delivering the finest in turf maintenance equipment, from precision greenmowers to giant sixteen-foot rotary mowers.

Items and goods produced: paper products, electric and electronic products, rubber and plastic products, fabricated metal products, wood products, apparel, transportation equipment, printing and publishing

Incentive Programs—New and Existing Companies

Local programs—The Racine County Economic Development Corporation (RCEDC) offers loans for purposes such as purchase of land, buildings machinery and equipment and new construction or relocation, working capital, inventory and fixed assets; RCEDC also administers Small Business Innovations programs for product research projects and associated market studies; the city of Racine offers loans for rehabilitation of exterior facades of buildings in the downtown area.

State Programs—The Wisconsin Development Fund and the Farmers Home Administration offer loans for fixed assets for inventory and working capital; the Wisconsin Housing and Economic Development Authority provides below-market, fixed-rate loans to manufacturers through banks via sale of tax-exempt bonds as well as loans for energy conservation improvements and energy-based process efficiency; the State of Wisconsin Investment Board offers loans for general corporate purposes; the Wisconsin Department of Development offers loans for research and development leading to product in two years for already existing firms.

Job training programs—The Wisconsin Department of Development offers Customized Labor Training grants for training or retraining of in-state workers, providing an economic contribution to the area; the Racine County Department of Human Service has programs to provide employees to qualified and trained participants and subsidiaries for up to nine months; Gateway Technical College grants provide technical, educational, and other related services to businesses and residents of the state; through the Job Training Partnership Act the Southeastern Wisconsin Private Industry Council provides trained employees and customized training to unskilled adults and youths for entry into the labor force and offers on-the-job training with 50 percent wage reimbursement offered to employers along with summer youth programs. Lakeshore Job Service assists area businesses by recruiting, screening and referring qualified applicants to available openings at no charge.

Development Projects

The most important project in recent years occurred in 1988 with the construction of Racine On The Lake Festival Park, a $25 million public/private economic development project located on the shore of Lake Michigan.

Economic Development Information: Racine County Economic Development Corporation, 6929 Mariner Drive #B, Racine, WI 53406; telephone (414)886-6723

Commercial Shipping

Rail freight service is provided by the Chicago & North Western Transportation Company, the Wisconsin Central Ltd., and the Soo Line Railroad Company. There are ninety-five widely distributed trucking and warehousing establishments in Racine County. The city is located 30 miles south of the Port of Milwaukee.

Labor Force and Employment Outlook

The following is a summary of data regarding the Racine metropolitan area labor force as of September 1992.

Size of civilian non-agricultural labor force: 74,100

Number of workers employed in . . .
  mining: not reported
  construction: 2,200
  manufacturing: 24,600
  transportation and public utilities: 2,600
  wholesale and retail trade: 15,800
  finance, insurance, and real estate: 2,300
  services: 17,400
  government: 9,100

Average hourly earnings of production workers employed in manufacturing: $12.66

Unemployment rate: 6.3%

Largest employers	Number of employees
S. C. Johnson & Son, Inc.	2,628
J. I. Case Company	2,500
Western Publishing Company, Inc.	1,575
Twin Disc, Inc.	917
St. Luke's Hospital	911

Cost of Living

The following is a summary of data regarding several key cost of living factors in the Racine area.

1992 (2nd Quarter) ACCRA Cost of Living Index: 104.9 (U.S. average = 100.0)

1992 (2nd Quarter) ACCRA Average House Price: $124,500

State income tax rate: 4.9% to 6.93%

State sales tax rate: 5.0%

Local income tax rate: None

Local sales tax rate: None

Property tax rate: 37.99 mills per $1,000 of assessed valuation; assessment ratio = 100% for residential

Economic Information: Racine Area Manufacturing and Commerce, 300 Fifth Street, Racine, WI 53403; telephone (414)634-1931

Education and Research

Elementary and Secondary Schools

Racine's Unified School District is a composite of city, suburban, and rural areas contained in a 99-square-mile area. Racine County is known for having outstanding schools, and many innovative, statewide models have been developed in the school districts. Special schools include three magnet elementary, one alterative mid/high school, one middle school academy, MACK Achievement Center, and Garfield Early Childhood Center.

The following is a summary of data regarding Racine's public schools as of the 1992-1993 school year.

Total enrollment: 21,806

Number of facilities
  elementary schools: 23
  junior high/middle schools: 7
  senior high schools: 4
  other: 7

Student/teacher ratio: 25.6:1

Teacher salaries
  minimum: $23,030
  maximum: $45,081

Funding per pupil: $5,381

Public Schools Information: School/Community Relations Office, Racine Unified School District, 2220 Northwestern Avenue, Racine, WI 53404; telephone (414)631-7057

Colleges and Universities

The University of Wisconsin-Parkside, part of the University of Wisconsin system, serves more than fifty-one hundred undergraduate and two hundred graduate students on its 700-acre campus located between the cities of Racine and Kenosha. The University has schools of Liberal Arts and Science and Technology, and offers undergraduate course work in twenty-eight major fields of study. The school also offers Master of Business Administration programs and a Master of Science degree in applied science. Gateway Technical College offers associate degree, diploma, and certificate programs, as well as educational classes offered to specifically meet area employment needs.

Libraries and Research Centers

The Racine Public Library contains more than a quarter of a million volumes, subscribes to nearly 650 publications, and has more than five thousand microfilms and films. The library has two bookmobiles. The library's special collections include works on Racine history and the Early Childhood Resource Collection.

At the University of Wisconsin-Parkside Center for Survey and Marketing Research in Kenosha, studies on travel and tourism and product and market feasibility are conducted.

Public Library Information: Racine Public Library, 75 Seventh Street, Racine, WI 53403; telephone (414)636-9241

Health Care

Racine's two hospitals are St. Luke's Hospital, which has 230 beds and is operated by the Wheaton Franciscan Services, and St. Mary's Medical Center, which has 226 beds. St. Mary's offers general inpatient service for AIDS, cardiac catheterization, open heart surgery, angioplasty, chronic obstructive pulmonary disease, Alzheimer Diagnosis/assessment services, emergency response, a geriatric acute care unit, patient education, community health, intensive care units, a histopathology lab, occupational health services, and pediatric and psychiatric services, as well as an emergency department and fitness center.

Recreation

Sightseeing

Racine has an impressive collection of more than fourteen blocks of homes and buildings on the National Register of Historic Places. Of special interest are the English Gothic-style buildings at the DeKoven Center Retreat/Conference Center. The Henrietta Benstead Hall, built in the Colonial Revival style, incorporates the classical details of the Queen Anne style, and features Tiffany windows and quality furnishings. Across the street is the Italianate style Masonic Temple, built circa 1856. The mansion contains two operable theaters and features a unique Egyptian motif in the style of the 1920s. Both structures are lavishly lighted and decorated during the Christmas season and are open for tours.

A favorite local site for picnic outings and observation of more than three hundred resident animals is the 32-acre Racine Zoological Gardens, located on the shores of Lake Michigan. During the holiday season the zoo is decorated with hundreds of thousands of lights. The Firehouse 3 Museum, in an authentic fire house, features antique fire fighting equipment. The Modine-Benstead Observatory is open to the public to examine the skies when visibility allows.

The beautiful grounds of the S. C. Johnson Wax Company, the city's largest employer, house the Golden Rondelle Theater, the center for the company's guest relations and public tour program. Originally designed as S. C. Johnson's pavilion at the 1964 World's Fair, it features the film *To be Alive!*, which summarizes the joys of living through sight and sound. After the fair, the theater was relocated to Racine, where the structure was refashioned to complement the Frank Lloyd Wright-designed Administration Building and Research Tower which is open for tours. The theater, which is also open to the public, features films on flight, ecology, and U.S. history.

Arts and Culture

Since 1937 the Racine Theatre Guild has produced an outstanding selection of plays as part of its six play season. The Malt House Theater, in nearby Burlington, is home of the Haylofters, Wisconsin's oldest community theater group.

Racine Symphony Orchestra, the oldest continuous symphony orchestra in the state, performs four concerts annually in addition to a Summer Lakeside Pops series.

Racine's Charles A. Wustum Museum of Fine Arts for more than fifty years has provided changing exhibits, classes, tours, and lectures. The Racine County Historical Museum, a registered historic landmark, is devoted to the preservation of county artifacts and archives through its exhibits, events, and other educational programs.

Festivals and Holidays

May's Lakefront Artist's Fair features original art and handicrafts by more than one hundred artists. Harbor Fest in June at Festival Park is a four-day lakefront celebration of music, food, and entertainment. In September the Racine Antiques Fair at the County Fair Grounds offers one of the Midwest's finest collections of antiques, while later that month Preservation Racine's annual Tour of Historic Homes features tours of houses of historical interest. November and December's Christmas House for Cancer features turn-of-the-century mansions transformed into holiday fantasies with magnificent displays and furnishings. The Festival of Trees at the Racine Civic Centre Festival Hall displays more than one hundred professionally decorated Christmas trees, wreaths, and gingerbread houses. February's Racine Area Winter Carnival at Johnson Park features broomball tournaments, softball and volleyball tournaments and other outdoor sports fun for all ages. Thousands are drawn to May's Chocolate City Festival in nearby Burlington which features outdoor music, a city bike ride, parade, and many chocolate exhibits—with tasting encouraged.

Sports for the Spectator

Professional baseball, hockey, soccer, basketball, and football sporting events can be found in Racine, Kenosha,, Milwaukee, and Chicago. The Racine Raiders stir up semi-pro football excitement.

Wisconsin—Racine   *Cities of the United States • 2nd Edition*

Windpoint Lighthouse is believed to be the oldest and tallest lighthouse on the Great Lakes.

Sports for the Participant

Riverbend Nature Center, an 80-acre year-round nature and recreation center, offers hiking, bird watching, demonstrations, nature studies, and canoe rental. Quarry Lake Park is a mecca for scuba divers and a great place for swimmers looking for spring-fed waters. The 40-acre park has an eighteen-acre lake which varies in depth up to one hundred feet and an expansive sandy beach. North Beach provides more than a mile of clean, white sandy beach with lifeguards and picnic areas. Thirteen-acre Racine County Harbor Park, which extends out into Lake Michigan, offers fishing, a modern fish-cleaning station and an observation deck with spectacular views. Visitors can enjoy a peaceful stroll around the Reefpoint Marina.

Racine County is home to six eighteen-hole golf courses, 2,200 acres of county parklands, 2,520 acres of inland lakes, 17.3 miles of off-road bicycle trails, and 7 miles of cross country ski trails. There are twenty-five baseball diamonds in the city alone, and Shane Rawley Sports Complex hosts both state and national softball tournaments. Lake Michigan provides opportunities for both boating and game fishing.

Shopping and Dining

The city and county of Racine offer many shops filled with antiques, resale items, and collectibles. A waterfront showplace, downtown Racine, which is linked with the Racine Civic Centre complex and the nearly one-thousand-slip Reefpoint Marina, has many beautifully renovated buildings housing fine jewelry shops and unique collections of sportswear, quality clothing, fine furniture, and specialty shops. Porter's of Racine, a fine furniture store with twelve model room displays, is recognized throughout the region and may be the oldest retail establishment in the Midwest. Regency Mall, anchored by five major department stores, offers more than one hundred boutiques, specialty stores and eateries. The county is home to The Seven Mile Fair, Wisconsin's largest flea market.

No visit to Racine would be complete without sampling the local delicacy, Danish Kringle, a flaky, oval-shaped coffee cake made of traditional Danish pastry and filled with a variety of fruits or nuts. Mid-priced family restaurants share the local spotlight with ethnic eateries, including Italian and Chinese, as well as places offering meat and potatoes or the catch of day from the Great Lakes.

Visitor Information: Racine County Convention and Visitors Bureau, 345 Main Street, Racine, WI 53403; telephone (414)634-3293

Convention Facilities

Situated on 5 acres on the shores of Lake Michigan, Racine On The Lake Festival Park is the city's newest multi-use facility. Opened in 1987, Festival Park can accommodate conventions, trade shows, meetings, art exhibits, and concerts. Facilities include Festival Hall, a 15,700 square foot area with a theater that can seat 1,500 people, a classroom that can accommodate 1,000 and banquet space for 1,200 people; the Green Room, designed for private gatherings, a 1,050-square-foot space that can handle 75 people in theater-style seating, 50 people in classroom-style and 60 people for banquets; the Collonade, a free-standing covered structure measuring nearly nine thousand square feet under its canopy; and a forty by eighty foot stage with a forty-three-thousand-square-foot concert area.

Overlooking Lake Michigan, Memorial Hall is the location for many concerts, crafts, and various local functions. Built in 1938 by Frank Lloyd Wright as a private residence, Wingspread is a private international conference facility operated by the Johnson Foundation.

Convention Information: Racine County Convention and Visitors Bureau, 345 Main Street, Racine, WI 53403; telephone (414)634-3293

Transportation

Approaching the City

General Mitchell International Airport, located 7 miles north of the city in Milwaukee, is the nearest airport. Chicago's O'Hare International Airport is 60 miles to the south.

Interstate 94, situated 8 miles west of the city, links Racine County with Milwaukee and Chicago. State highways 11, 20, 31, 32, and 38 also serve the city. Passenger service is provided by Amtrak and by two intracity bus companies, Wisconsin Coach Lines,

Inc. and Greyhound Lines, Inc., which provide services in the Chicago-to-Milwaukee corridor.

Traveling in the City

The city of Racine owns and operates the Belle Urban System. Downtown Racine Lakefront Trolleys, with clanging bells, shuttle visitors to shops and sites along the lakefront.

Communications

Newspapers and Magazines

Racine's *Journal-Times*, is the city's daily paper. The city is also served by the *Racine Labor*, a biweekly, and the *Communicator News*, which publishes weekly.

Television and Radio

Racine receives four network, one independent, and two public television stations from Milwaukee, as well as several Chicago stations. The city has three FM stations and one AM station and receives many stations from Milwaukee and Chicago.

Media Information: Journal-Times, 212 Fourth Street, Racine, WI 53404; telephone (414)634-3322

Cumulative Index

The one hundred fifty-four cities featured in *Cities of the United States,* Volume 1: *The South,* Volume 2: *The West,* Volume 3: *The Midwest,* and Volume 4: *The Northeast,* along with names of individuals, organizations, historical events, etc., are designated in this Cumulative Index by the name of the appropriate regional volume, or volumes, followed by the page number(s) on which the term appears in that volume. For example, the index term **Grant, Ulysses S. Midwest: 139; 311; South: 280; 400** indicates that term appears on pages 139 and 311 of *Cities of the United States,* Volume 3: *The Midwest* and on pages 280 and 400 of Volume 1: *The South.*

Abilene, TX **Midwest**: 181
Absecon Island, NJ **Northeast**: 229; 235
Acadia National Park **Northeast**: 87; 90; 94
Acadia, ME **Northeast**: 87
Acworth, GA **South**: 167; 176
Adams, John Quincy **Midwest**: 390
Admiralty Island, AK **West**: 31
Aetna Life and Casualty Company **Northeast**: 32
Alameda, CA **West**: 121; 129
Albany, CA **West**: 129
Albany, NY **Northeast**: 291
Albuquerque, NM **West**: 339
Allatoona, GA **South**: 167; 176
Allen, Ethan **Northeast**: 477; 478; 493
Allentown, PA **Northeast**: 359
Alta, UT **West**: 418
American Fork, UT **West**: 405; 406
Ames, IA **Midwest**: 144
Amherst, MA **Northeast**: 159; 163
Amherst, NY **Northeast**: 307; 310
Amoskeag Manufacturing Company **Northeast**: 193; 199
Anaheim, CA **West**: 81
Anchorage, AK **West**: 5
Ankeny, IA **Midwest**: 142
Ann Arbor, MI **Midwest**: 193; 205
Annapolis, MD **West**: 357
Anthony, Susan B. **Northeast**: 335; 340
Appleseed, Johnny **Midwest**: 63; 71
Aquidneck Island, RI **Northeast**: 449; 452; 456
Archibald, OH **Midwest**: 441
Arlington, TX **South**: 488; 495; 498; 500
Arnold, Benedict **Northeast**: 17; 48; 451; 477
Arnold, MD **South**: 262
Atlanta, GA **South**: 149; 167; 168; 170; 171; 174; 175; 178
Atlanta University Center **South**: 149; 156
Atlantic City, NJ **Northeast**: 227

Auburn Hills, MI **Midwest**: 215
Auburn, IN **Midwest**: 71
Auburn, ME **Northeast**: 99; 100; 101; 102; 103
Augusta, ME **Northeast**: 75
Auke Lake, AK **West**: 33
Austell, GA **South**: 167
Austin, TX **South**: 465
Bal Harbor, FL **South**: 91
Baltimore, MD **South**: 255
Bangor, ME **Northeast**: 85
Barnum, P(hineas) T(aylor) **Northeast**: 7; 11
Barre, VT **Northeast**: 489; 492; 493
Barrow, Clyde **South**: 482
Basie, Count **Midwest**: 297
Bates College **Northeast**: 97; 102; 103
Baton Rouge, LA **South**: 225
Battelle Memorial Institute **Midwest**: 412; 413; 417
Bayou La Batre, AL **South**: 30; 31
Beiderbecke, Bix **Midwest**: 130; 134
Bel Air, MD **South**: 262
Bellevue, NE **Midwest**: 350
Benedict College **South**: 379
Berkeley, CA **West**: 121; 176; 190
Bernhardt, Sarah **South**: 374; 534
Bethel, ME **Northeast**: 104
Bethlehem, PA **Northeast**: 361; 363; 364; 365; 367; 368
Bethlehem Steel **Northeast**: 363; 382
Bettendorf, IA *See* Quad Cities
Beverly Hills, CA **West**: 105; 112; 114; 204
Bexley, OH **Midwest**: 411
Biddeford, ME **Northeast**: 112
Billings, MT **West**: 289
Birmingham, AL **South**: 5
Bloomfield Hills, MI **Midwest**: 211; 214
Bloomington, MN **Midwest**: 268; 282
Boblo Island, MI **Midwest**: 213
Boeing Company **Midwest**: 183; 184; 185

527

Boise, ID **West**: 275
Bonner Springs, MO **Midwest**: 164
Boone, Daniel **South**: 590
Boston Garden **Northeast**: 135
Boston, MA **Northeast**: 121; **West**: 157
Boulder, CO **West**: 209
Bowdoin College **Northeast**: 112
Bowie, Jim **South**: 525
Bowling Green State University **Midwest**: 440; 441
Boyington, W. W. **Midwest**: 146
Boys Town **Midwest**: 347; 348
Bradley University **Midwest**: 29; 30; 31
Bradley, ME **Northeast**: 92
Brewer, ME **Northeast**: 94
Bridgeport, CT **Northeast**: 5
Brigham Young University **West**: 399; 401; 405; 406
Brockport, NY **Northeast**: 339
Bronx, NY **Northeast**: 318; 325; 327; 329; 332
Brooklyn, NY **Northeast**: 318; 322; 325; 326; 327
Brown University **Northeast**: 459; 464; 466; 467
Brown, John **Midwest**: 163; 206; 399
Bryan, William Jennings **Midwest**: 329; 330; 335
Bryant, Paul "Bear" **South**: 15; 17
Buena Park, CA **West**: 88; 114; 204
Buena Vista, MO **Midwest**: 321
Buffalo, NY **Northeast**: 303
Bulfinch, Charles **Northeast**: 31; 34; 82; 132
Bulls Island, SC **South**: 376
Bunker Hill, Battle of **Northeast**: 181
Bunyan, Paul **Northeast**: 87; 93; 94
Burlington, VT **Northeast**: 475
Burlington, WI **Midwest**: 523
Busch Gardens/The Dark Continent **South**: 138
Butte, MT **West**: 299
Cadillac, Antoine de la Mothe **Midwest**: 205
Calder, Alexander **Midwest**: 15; 228
Caldwell, ID **West**: 282
Caledonia, WI **Midwest**: 517
Calendar Islands, ME **Northeast**: 113
Cambridge, MA **Northeast**: 131; 134; 136
Camden, ME **Northeast**: 81
Campobello Island, Canada **Northeast**: 92
Canaan, ME **Northeast**: 82; 92
Capone, Alphonse **Midwest**: 8
Carlisle, PA **Northeast**: 386; 388; 389

Carnegie Mellon University **Northeast**: 419; 423; 424; 426; 428
Carnegie, Andrew **Northeast**: 421; 428
Carson City, NV **West**: 332
Case Western Reserve University **Midwest**: 212; 403; 404
Catalina Island, CA **West**: 114
Cavelier, Robert **Midwest**: 383; 435; **South**: 23; 41; 237; 431
Cayce, SC **South**: 390
Cedar Rapids, IA **Midwest**: 113
Cessna Aircraft Company **Midwest**: 183
Cezanne, Paul **South**: 128; 458
Champlain, Samuel de **Midwest**: 435; **Northeast**: 87; 477
Chapel Hill, NC **South**: 319; 325
Chapman, John *See* Johnny Appleseed
Charleston, SC **South**: 363
Charleston, WV **South**: 587
Charlestown, MA **Northeast**: 124; 129; 134
Charlotte, NC **South**: 287
Chattanooga, TN **South**: 397
Chautauqua, NY **Northeast**: 375
Chelsea, MA **Northeast**: 126
Cheney, WA **West**: 444
Chesapeake, VA **South**: 561
Cheyenne, WY **West**: 463
Chicago Board of Trade **Midwest**: 8; 10
Chicago, IL **Midwest**: 5
Chicopee, MA **Northeast**: 158
Chisholm Trail **Midwest**: 181; 186
Churchill, Winston **Midwest**: 484
Cincinnati, OH **Midwest**: 381; **West**: 296
Cisneros, Henry **South**: 526
Citadel Military College of South Carolina, The **South**: 363; 366; 371; 374
Clark, George Rogers **South**: 211; 216
Clark, William **Midwest**: 157; 289; 304; 343; **West**: 291; 375
Clay, Henry **South**: 204
Clearwater, FL **South**: 121
Cleveland, OH **Midwest**: 397
Clinton, William Jefferson (Bill) **South**: 42
Clovis, CA **West**: 101
Coconut Grove, FL **South**: 91
Cody, William (Buffalo Bill) **Midwest**: 130; 133
Colchester, VT **Northeast**: 482
Colorado Springs, CO **West**: 219
Columbia College **South**: 379
Columbia Falls, ME **Northeast**: 92
Columbia, SC **South**: 379
Columbus, OH **Midwest**: 409

Concord, Battle of **Northeast**: 181
Concord, NH **Northeast**: 179
Cook Inlet, AK **West**: 8
Cook, James, Captain **West**: 7; 261
Cooperstown, NY **Northeast**: 353
Coral Gables, FL **South**: 91
Costa Mesa, CA **West**: 88; 114
Council Bluffs, IA **Midwest**: 343
Covington, KY **Midwest**: 392
Crockett, Davy **South**: 525; 526
Cromwell, CT **Northeast**: 35
Cross Lanes, WV **South**: 597
Custer, George (General) **West**: 291
Cuttingsville, VT **Northeast**: 503
Dali, Salvador **South**: 128
Dallas, TX **South**: 479; 495; 498; 505
Danbury, CT **Northeast**: 15
Dauphin Island, AL **South**: 28; 30; 31; 33
Davenport, George **Midwest**: 129; 134
Davenport, IA **Midwest**: 127
Davis, Jefferson **South**: 158; 554
Dayton, OH **Midwest**: 421
de Soto, Hernando **South**: 41; 399; 431
Dearborn, MI **Midwest**: 211; 213; 214
Deepwater, WV **South**: 593
Denver, CO **West**: 231
Des Moines, IA **Midwest**: 137
Detroit, MI **Midwest**: 195; 203; 306
Dillinger, John **Midwest**: 8; **South**: 388
Disney, Walt **West**: 84
Disney World **South**: 107; 108; 109; 111; 112; 113; 116; 138
Disneyland **West**: 83; 84; 86; 87; 88; 90; 92
Dodge City, KS **Midwest**: 181
Douglas, AK **West**: 31
Douglas Island, AK **West**: 29
Douglas, Stephen **Midwest**: 26
Douglass, Frederick **Midwest**: 206; **Northeast**: 335; 340; **South**: 573; 580
Drum Island, SC **South**: 377
Dublin, OH **Midwest**: 418
Duluth, MN **Midwest**: 247
Dundee, NE **Midwest**: 350
du Pont, Eleuthere I. **South**: 60; 62; 63; 64; 68
Durham, NC **South**: 319; 325; 328
East Boston, MA **Northeast**: 124
East Brunswick, NJ **Northeast**: 272
East Cambridge, MA **Northeast**: 128; 129
East Grand Forks, ND **Midwest**: 369; 374; 376
East Lansing, MI **Midwest**: 233; 238; 240
East Los Angeles, CA **West**: 106; 110

East Moline, IL **Midwest**: 134
Eastern Michigan University **Midwest**: 196
Eastman, George **Northeast**: 335; 339; 340
Eastman Kodak Company **Northeast**: 81; 335; 336; 337; 338; 339
Eastman School of Music **Northeast**: 339; 340
Easton, PA **Northeast**: 361; 363; 368
Eastover, SC **South**: 385
Eddy, Mary Baker **Northeast**: 181; 182
Edison, Thomas **Midwest**: 214; **South**: 216
Egg Harbor City, NJ **Northeast**: 236
Eisenhower, Dwight D. **Midwest**: 484; **South**: 42
Eklutna, AK **West**: 12
Ellsworth, ME **Northeast**: 92
Emeryville, CA **West**: 121
Emory University **South**: 149; 156
Ephrata, PA **Northeast**: 401
Erie, PA **Northeast**: 369
Ester, AK **West**: 24
Eugene, OR **West**: 365
Evansville, IN **Midwest**: 49
Fairbanks, AK **West**: 7; 17
Fairbanks, Charles **West**: 19
Fairborn, OH **Midwest**: 423
Fairfield County, CT **Northeast**: 7; 8; 11; 53; 55; 56; 59
Falls Church, VA **Midwest**: 306
Fargo, ND **Midwest**: 357
Farmington, CT **Northeast**: 33
Faubus, Orval E. **South**: 42
Fernandina Beach, FL **South**: 86
Fitzgerald, F. Scott **Midwest**: 278; 283
Flanagan, Edward J. (Father) **Midwest**: 344
Flint, MI **Midwest**: 206
Florence, KY **Midwest**: 392
Folly Beach, SC **South**: 377
Folsom, CA **West**: 151
Ford, Gerald R. **Midwest**: 199; 227; 348
Ford, Henry **Midwest**: 205; 206; 213; 214
Fort George Island, FL **South**: 84
Fort Wayne, IN **Midwest**: 61
Fort Worth, TX **South**: 481; 492; 493
Fountain Hills, AZ **West**: 58
Fox, AK **West**: 19
Foxboro, MA **Northeast**: 135
Franklin, Benjamin **Northeast**: 132; 293; 406; 411; 413; 415
Franklin, VA **South**: 561
Freeport, ME **Northeast**: 104; 109; 116
Fremont, CA **West**: 190
Fresno, CA **West**: 93

Frick, Henry Clay **Northeast:** 421
Frick Museum, Henry Clay **Northeast:** 430
Fuller, R. Buckminster **Midwest:** 186
Galveston, TX **South:** 509; 510; 518
Garden Grove, CA **West:** 88
Garfield, James A. **Midwest:** 390
Gary, IN **Midwest:** 73
Gatlinburg, TN **South:** 418; 423
Gauguin, Paul **South:** 128
General Electric Corporation **Northeast:** 481; 482; 499; 500; 501
Genoa, NV **West:** 332
George II King of England **South:** 289
Georgetown University **South:** 571; 578; 579; 582
Georgia Institute of Technology **South:** 149; 156; 170
Gershwin, George **South:** 374
Gilbert, Cass **Midwest:** 275; 280
Gilbert, SC **South:** 390
Gillespie, Dizzy **South:** 312
Grafton, MA **Northeast:** 171
Grand Forks, ND **Midwest:** 367
Grand Prairie, TX **South:** 488; 495; 500
Grand Rapids, MI **Midwest:** 219
Grandview Heights, OH **Midwest:** 411
Grant, Ulysses S. **Midwest:** 139; 311; **South:** 280; 400
Green Bay, WI **Midwest:** 475
Greensboro, NC **South:** 301
Greenwich, CT **Northeast:** 53; 55; 59
Grosse Pointe Shores, MI **Midwest:** 213
Guilderland, NY **Northeast:** 301
Hallowell, ME **Northeast:** 77; 84; 94
Hamburg, NY **Northeast:** 312
Hamilton, Alexander **Midwest:** 383
Hammond, IN **Midwest:** 80
Hampton, VA **South:** 561; 567; 569
Hamtramck, MI **Midwest:** 214
Harding, Warren G. **Midwest:** 424
Harris, Joel Chandler **South:** 159
Harrisburg, PA **Northeast:** 379
Harrison, Benjamin **Midwest:** 94
Harrison, NJ **Northeast:** 248
Harrison, William Henry **Midwest:** 63; 390; 423; 435; 441
Harrodsburg, KY **South:** 197
Hartford, CT **Midwest:** 142; **Northeast:** 25
Harvard University **Northeast:** 121; 128; 131; 132; 134; 136
Hawthorne, Nathaniel **Midwest:** 416
Hazel Park, MI **Midwest:** 215
Hennepin, Louis (Father) **Midwest:** 25; 259

Henry, Patrick **South:** 545; 546; 553
Hershey, PA **Northeast:** 386; 387; 388; 389
Heyward, DuBose **South:** 373; 374
Hialeah, FL **South:** 91
Hickok, James Butler (Wild Bill) **Midwest:** 317
High Point, NC **South:** 303
Hilo, HI **West:** 247
Hinckley, OH **Midwest:** 405
Hoboken, NJ **Northeast:** 248
Holbrook, Hal **South:** 312
Holland, MI **Midwest:** 228
Hollywood, CA **West:** 105; 112
Honolulu, HI **West:** 259
Hoover, Herbert **Midwest:** 123
Houston, Sam **South:** 510; 526
Houston, TX **South:** 507
Howard University **South:** 571; 578; 579
Hudson, Henry **Northeast:** 293; 317; 405
Hudson, NH **Northeast:** 210
Hummelstown, PA **Northeast:** 388
Humphrey, Hubert H. **Midwest:** 8
Hunterdon, NJ **Northeast:** 267
Huntington, WV **South:** 595
IBM Corporation **Northeast:** 478; 481
Idaho City, ID **West:** 282
Independence, MO **Midwest:** 164; 289; 295
Indiana University Northwest **Midwest:** 73
Indianapolis, IN **Midwest:** 83
Indianola, IA **Midwest:** 144
International Correspondence School (PA) **Northeast:** 433; 440
International Museum of Photography **Northeast:** 339; 342
Iowa City, IA **Midwest:** 118; 120; 123; 124; 133; 139
Irving, TX **South:** 486; 488; 489; 495; 500
Isle of Palms, SC **South:** 377
Ives, Charles **Northeast:** 22
Jackson, Andrew **Midwest:** 436; **South:** 77; 244; 275; 431; 448; 579
Jackson Memorial Hospital **South:** 98
Jackson, MS **South:** 273
Jackson, Thomas "Stonewall" **South:** 158; 554
Jacksonville Civic Auditorium **South:** 86
Jacksonville, FL **South:** 75
James, Jesse **Midwest:** 164; 295
Jamestown, VA **South:** 561; 567
Jefferson City, MO **Midwest:** 304
Jefferson, Thomas **South:** 238; 545; 574
Jenney, James **Midwest:** 64
Jersey City, NJ **Northeast:** 239

Johns Hopkins University and Hospital **South**: 255; 259; 262; 264; 266
Johnson & Johnson **Northeast**: 263; 264; 265; 267
Johnson, Andrew **South**: 326
Johnson, Lyndon Baines **Midwest**: 195; **South**: 472; 474
Johnson, Philip **South**: 510
Johnson, S. C. **Midwest**: 518; 520
Joliet, Louis **Midwest**: 7; 25; **South**: 431
Juneau, AK **West**: 27
Kahn, Albert **Midwest**: 214
Kansas City, KS **Midwest**: 155
Kansas City, MO **Midwest**: 287
Kansas-Nebraska Act **Midwest**: 157
Kaukauna, WI **Midwest**: 484
Kennedy, John F. **Midwest**: 195; **South**: 482; 489
Kennesaw, GA **South**: 167; 168; 174
Kennesaw State College **South**: 165
Kenosha, WI **Midwest**: 522; 523
Kettering, OH **Midwest**: 423
Kiawah Island, SC **South**: 376
Killington, VT **Northeast**: 499; 503
Kilmer, Alfred Joyce **Northeast**: 263
King Louis XV of France **South**: 237
King, Martin Luther, Jr. **South**: 7; 8; 10; 60; 158; 162; 326; 432; 574; **West**: 127
Kissimmee, FL **South**: 115
Kittery, ME **Northeast**: 215; 219; 221; 222
Kitty Hawk, NC **Midwest**: 80; 424
Knott's Berry Farm **West**: 83; 88; 90; 201
Knox, Henry **South**: 416
Knoxville, TN **South**: 413
L'Enfant, Pierre **South**: 574
La Guardia, Fiorello **Northeast**: 318
Lafayette, Mortier de, **South**: 197
Lafitte, Jean **South**: 509
Lamy, NM **West**: 355; 361
Lancaster, PA **Northeast**: 391
Landis Valley Museum (PA) **Northeast**: 399
Lansing, MI **Midwest**: 231
Laramie, WY **West**: 469
Largo, FL **South**: 145
Las Vegas, NV **West**: 313
Laurel, MT **West**: 296
League of New Hampshire Craftsmen **Northeast**: 188; 200; 211
Learjet Corporation **Midwest**: 183
Ledyard, CT **Northeast**: 48
Lee, Robert E. **Midwest**: 311; **Northeast**: 382; **South**: 158; 553; 554
Lehigh University **Northeast**: 359; 364; 365

Lehigh Valley (PA) **Northeast**: 361; 363; 364; 365; 367; 368
Leon, Ponce de **South**: 121
Lewis, Meriwether **Midwest**: 157; 289; 304; 343; **West**: 291; 375
Lewiston, ID **West**: 377
Lewiston, ME **Northeast**: 97
Lexington, Battle of **Northeast**: 181
Lexington County, SC **South**: 385; 388
Lexington, KY **South**: 195
Libbey, Edward **Midwest**: 436; 443
Liberty, MO **Midwest**: 295
Lilly and Company, Eli **Midwest**: 86; 90; 94
Lincoln, Abraham **Midwest**: 8; 14; 26; 30; 37; 41; 58; 64; 69; 106; 329; 335; 343; 390; **Northeast**: 247; 398; **South**: 182; 320; 366; 574; 580
Lincoln, Mary Todd **South**: 204
Lincoln National Life Insurance Company **Midwest**: 64; 65; 69
Lincoln, NE **Midwest**: 327
Lincoln, RI **Northeast**: 467
Lind, Jenny **South**: 374
Lindbergh, Charles **Midwest**: 334; **Northeast**: 82; 301; **South**: 580
Lindsay, Vachel **Midwest**: 42
Litchfield Hills, CT **Northeast**: 17
Little Rock, AR **South**: 39
Livonia, MI **Midwest**: 211; 215
London, Jack **Midwest**: 140
Long Beach, CA **West**: 110
Long Island, NY **Northeast**: 317; 318; 329
Long Island Sound **Northeast**: 7; 11; 12; 41; 53; 58
Longfellow, Henry Wadsworth **Midwest**: 266; **Northeast**: 77; 107; 125; 155
Los Alamos, NM **West**: 342; 355
Los Angeles, CA **West**: 103
Loudon, NH **Northeast**: 200
Louisiana Purchase **Midwest**: 304; 343
Louisville, KY **South**: 209
Low, Juliette Gordon **South**: 182
Lowell, MA **Northeast**: 141
Lynchburg, TN **South**: 408
Lynn, Loretta **South**: 459
Madeira Beach, FL **South**: 129
Madison Muskies **Midwest**: 228
Madison, Dolley **South**: 312
Madison, James **Midwest**: 489
Madison, WI **Midwest**: 487
Manchester, NH **Northeast**: 191
Manitou Springs, CO **West**: 221
Manoa, HI **West**: 266

Mansfield, MO **Midwest**: 321
Marietta, GA **South**: 165
Marina Del Ray, CA **West**: 114
Marion, IA **Midwest**: 115
Maris, Roger **Midwest**: 363
Marquette, Jacques (Pere) **Midwest**: 7; 25; 75; 139; **South**: 431
Massachusetts Bay Colony **Northeast**: 27; 99; 123; 181; 193; 205; 210; 215
Massachusetts General Hospital **Northeast**: 128; 131; 132
Masters, Edgar Lee **Midwest**: 42
Maumee, OH **Midwest**: 435
Mayport, FL **South**: 84
Mays Landing, NJ **Northeast**: 234
McCormick, Cyrus **Midwest**: 8
Medical University of South Carolina **South**: 363; 369; 370; 371
Memphis State University **South**: 429; 436; 438; 439; 440
Memphis, TN **South**: 429
Mencken, H. L. **South**: 262; 264
Menninger Foundation **Midwest**: 170; 174; 175
Menotti, Gian Carlo **South**: 374
Mercer, Johnny **South**: 188
Merrimack, NH **Northeast**: 210
Miami Beach, FL **South**: 91
Miami, FL **South**: 89
Miamisburg, OH **Midwest**: 423
Michener, James A. **South**: 472
Michigan City, IN **Midwest**: 80
Michigan State University **Midwest**: 224; 227; 233; 236; 237; 238; 240; 241; 242
Middlebury, VT **Northeast**: 502; 503
Middletown, RI **Northeast**: 450; 452; 454; 456
Milford, CT **Northeast**: 58
Milford, NH **Northeast**: 210
Millerton, CA **West**: 95
Milwaukee, WI **Midwest**: 501
Minneapolis, MN **Midwest**: 257
Minnesota North Stars **Midwest**: 268
Mishawaka, IN **Midwest**: 101
Mobile, AL **South**: 21
Moline, IL *See* Quad Cities
Moncks Corner, SC **South**: 376; 378
Monmouth, OR **West**: 391
Monroe, James **South**: 374; 554
Montpelier, VT **Northeast**: 487
Moore, Henry **Midwest**: 266; 295
Moorhead, MN **Midwest**: 359; 363; 364
Morgan, Thomas Hunt **South**: 204

Mount Vernon, IA **Midwest**: 123
Mt. Angel, OR **West**: 393
Mt. Pleasant, SC **South**: 376; 377; 378
Mt. Vernon, IN **Midwest**: 53
Muscle Beach, CA **West**: 114
Muskegon, MI **Midwest**: 224; 229
Mutual of Omaha **Midwest**: 345; 347; 350
Nampa, ID **West**: 282
Nashua, NH **Northeast**: 203
Nashville, TN **South**: 445
National Life Insurance Company (VT) **Northeast**: 489; 490; 492
Neal, Patricia **South**: 423
New Britain, CT **Northeast**: 35; 37
New Brunswick, NJ **Northeast**: 261
New England Culinary Institute **Northeast**: 487; 493
New Harmony, IN **Midwest**: 56; 58
New Haven, CT **Northeast**: 39
New Orleans, LA **South**: 235
New York, NY **Northeast**: 315
Newark, NJ **Northeast**: 249
Newbury, NH **Northeast**: 188
Newport Beach, CA **West**: 204
Newport News, VA **South**: 561; 569
Newport, RI **Northeast**: 447
Niagara Falls, NY **Northeast**: 305; 307; 311; 312; 313
Norfolk, VA **South**: 561; 562; 567; 568
North Bellevue, NE **Midwest**: 350
North Carolina Agricultural and Technical State University **South**: 301; 309; 310; 312; 313
North Carolina State University **South**: 317; 319; 321; 323; 324; 325; 326; 328
North Dakota State University **Midwest**: 361; 362; 363; 364
North Kingston, RI **Northeast**: 452
North Pole, AK **West**: 22; 23
North Sacramento, CA **West**: 145
Northern Pacific Railway **Midwest**: 359
Northville, MI **Midwest**: 215
Northwest Territory **Midwest**: 383
Norwalk, CT **Northeast**: 17; 20; 53; 55; 58; 59
O'Keefe, Georgia **South**: 458; **West**: 239
Oak Park, IL **Midwest**: 441
Oak Ridge, TN **South**: 415; 418; 423; 424; 425
Oakland, CA **West**: 119; 185
Oakwood, OH **Midwest**: 423
Ocean Beach, CA **West**: 177
Ogden, UT **West**: 414

Ohio State University, The **Midwest**: 412; 414; 416; 417; 418; 419
Oklahoma City, OK **South**: 335
Old Town, ME **Northeast**: 87; 92; 94
Oldenburg, Claes **Midwest**: 15; 148
Olds, R. E. **Midwest**: 240
Olmstead, William Law **Midwest**: 94
Olmsted, Frederick Law **Midwest**: 213; **Northeast**: 114; 340; 352; 454; 484
Omaha, NE **Midwest**: 341
Ontario, Canada **Midwest**: 251
Oracle, AZ **West**: 58
Orchard Park, NY **Northeast**: 312
Oregon City, OR **West**: 387
Oregon, OH **Midwest**: 435
Orem, UT **West**: 401; 402; 405; 406
Orlando, FL **South**: 105
Ottawa Hills, OH **Midwest**: 435
Owens, Jesse, Memorial Rose Garden **West**: 371
Owens, Michael **Midwest**: 436
Painesville, OH **Midwest**: 405
Palo Alto, CA **West**: 185; 190
Parker, Bonnie **South**: 482
Parker, Charlie (Bird) **Midwest**: 297
Parrish, Maxfield **South**: 68
Pasadena, CA **West**: 114
Patti, Adelina **South**: 374
Pawtucket, RI **Northeast**: 461; 467
Pease Air Force Base **Northeast**: 184; 197; 217; 218; 220
Pease International Trade Port *See* Pease Air Force Base
Pei, I. M. **Midwest**: 148; 402; **Northeast**: 114; 330; 352; **South**: 264; 510;
Pelion, SC **South**: 390
Penn, William **Northeast**: 361; 393; 405; 478; **South**: 59
Pennsylvania Dutch **Northeast**: 361; 367; 393; 396; 399; 401; 416
Peoria, IL **Midwest**: 23
Perry, Oliver H. **Midwest**: 205; 435; **Northeast**: 371; 375
Perrysburg, OH **Midwest**: 435; 436; 441
Philadelphia, PA **Northeast**: 403
Phoenix, AZ **West**: 39
Phyfe, Duncan **South**: 68
Picasso, Pablo **South**: 458
Pico, VT **Northeast**: 499; 502; 503
Piedmont, CA **West**: 121
Pierce, Franklin **Northeast**: 181; 182; 187; 210
Pigeon Forge, TN **South**: 418; 423

Pike, Zebulon Montgomery **West**: 221
Piscataway, NJ **Northeast**: 270; 272
Pittsburgh, PA **Northeast**: 419
Pittsford, NY **Northeast**: 342; 343
Pleasant Hill, IA **Midwest**: 139
Pleasure Island, AL **South**: 33
Plymouth, FL **South**: 111
Poe, Edgar Allan **Northeast**: 466; **South**: 262; 264; 555
Polk, James K. **South**: 296
Pomona, NJ **Northeast**: 231; 234; 236
Poquoson, VA **South**: 561
Port Authority of New York and New Jersey **Northeast**: 321; 322
Port Canaveral, FL **South**: 111
Portland, ME **Northeast**: 105
Portland, OR **West**: 373
Portsmouth, NH **Northeast**: 213
Portsmouth (NH) Naval Shipyard **Northeast**: 215; 217; 219; 220; 221
Portsmouth, RI **Northeast**: 449; 450; 452; 456
Portsmouth, VA **South**: 561; 562
Powder Springs, GA **South**: 167; 175
Prairie du Sac, WI **Midwest**: 499
Presley, Elvis **South**: 439; 440
Presque Isle, ME **Northeast**: 80; 95
Presque Isle State Park (PA) **Northeast**: 375
Prince Wales Island, AK **West**: 33
Prince William Sound, AK **West**: 8
Princeton University **Northeast**: 251; 256; 266; 282
Proctor, VT **Northeast**: 503
Providence, RI **Northeast**: 459
Provo, UT **West**: 399
Pullman, George **Midwest**: 8
Pyle, Howard **South**: 68
Quad Cities **Midwest**: 129; 130; 131; 133; 134
Quaker Oats **Midwest**: 115; 120; 121; 171
Queens College **South**: 287
Queens, NY **Northeast**: 318; 327; 329
Racine, WI **Midwest**: 515
Raleigh, NC **South**: 317
Rapid City, SD **Midwest**: 449
Reagan, Ronald **Midwest**: 30
Reedley, CA **West**: 101
Remington, Frederic **West**: 239
Reno, NV **West**: 325
Renoir, Pierre-Auguste **South**: 128; 458
Research Triangle Park **South**: 320; 321; 323; 325
Reuther, Walter **Midwest**: 206

Revere, MA **Northeast:** 126
Revere, Paul **South:** 68
Rhode Island School of Design **Northeast:** 459; 466; 467; 469
Rice University **South:** 507; 516; 518
Richmond Heights, MO **Midwest:** 313
Richmond, VA **South:** 543
Riverside, CA **West:** 131
Robinson, Bill "Mr. Bojangles", **South:** 554
Rochester, MI **Midwest:** 211; 213
Rochester, MN **Midwest:** 266
Rochester, NY **Northeast:** 333
Rock Island, IL *See* Quad Cities
Rockefeller, John D. **Midwest:** 13; 400
Rockne, Knute **Midwest:** 108
Rollag, MN **Midwest:** 364
Rollins College **South:** 105; 108; 112; 113; 115
Romulus, MI **Midwest:** 217
Roosevelt, Franklin D. **Midwest:** 8; **South:** 401; 574; **West:** 254
Roosevelt, Theodore **South:** 448; **West:** 19
Rossford, OH **Midwest:** 435
Rothsville, PA **Northeast:** 401
Royal Oak, MI **Midwest:** 213
Rutgers University **Northeast:** 249; 256; 257; 261; 263; 264; 265; 266; 269; 270; 272; 273; 280
Ruth, Babe **South:** 264
Rutland, VT **Northeast:** 497
Saarinen, Eero **Midwest:** 134; 310
Saarinen, Eliel **Midwest:** 148
Sabin, Albert **Midwest:** 389
Sacramento, CA **West:** 143
Saint Paul, MN **Midwest:** 251; 271
Salem, New Hampshire **Northeast:** 205
Salem, OR **West:** 385
Saline, MI **Midwest:** 201
Salt Lake City, UT **West:** 409
San Antonio, TX **South:** 523
San Bernardino, CA **West:** 133
San Diego, CA **West:** 155
San Francisco, CA **West:** 121; 122; 153; 169
San Jose, CA **West:** 180; 181; 183
San Juan Capistrano Mission, **West:** 83
San Leandro, CA **West:** 121
San Mateo, CA **West:** 192
Sandburg, Carl **Midwest:** 7; 80
Sanford, FL **South:** 111
Santa Ana, CA **West:** 197
Santa Cruz, CA **West:** 190
Santa Fe, NM **West:** 351
Santa Fe Trail **Midwest:** 289

Saratoga Springs, NY **Northeast:** 299
Savannah, GA **South:** 179
Schenectady, NY **Northeast:** 300; 301
Scott, Dred **Midwest:** 310
Scott-Fanton Museum **Northeast:** 18; 21; 22
Scottsdale, AZ **West:** 45; 51
Scranton, PA **Northeast:** 433
Seabrook Island, SC **South:** 377
Searsport, ME **Northeast:** 90
Seattle, WA **West:** 425
Second City **Midwest:** 17; 214
Selkirk, NY **Northeast:** 296
Sevierville, TN **South:** 418; 423
Seward, AK **West:** 7
Shakopee, MN **Midwest:** 282
Shelburne, VT **Northeast:** 484; 485
Sherman, William T. **South:** 151; 168; 174; 182; 187; 280; 382; 388
Silver Dollar City, MO **Midwest:** 322
Sioux Falls, SD **Midwest:** 461
Sitka, AK **West:** 29
Skidaway Island, GA **South:** 188
Smith, Bessie **South:** 400
Smith, John **South:** 545; 561
Smithville, NJ **Northeast:** 235; 236
Smyrna, GA **South:** 167; 174; 175
Somerset, NJ **Northeast:** 267; 270
Sonoma, CA **West:** 129
South Baltimore, MD **South:** 265; 269
South Bend, IN **Midwest:** 99
South Burlington, VT **Northeast:** 484
South Charleston, WV **South:** 589; 591; 592; 594; 595
South Dakota School of Mines and Technology **Midwest:** 449; 451; 454; 455
Southbury, CT **Northeast:** 18
Southern Research Institute **South:** 8; 11; 12; 14
Southfield, MI **Midwest:** 211
Sparks, NV **West:** 327; 334
Spokane, WA **West:** 439
Spring Green, WI **Midwest:** 496
Springfield (MA) Armory **Northeast:** 155; 157; 159
Springfield, IL **Midwest:** 35
Springfield, MA **Northeast:** 153
Springfield, MO **Midwest:** 315
Springfield, OH **Midwest:** 430
Springfield, OR **West:** 367; 369
Springville, UT **West:** 406
St. Albans, VT **Northeast:** 484
St. Augustine, FL **South:** 86

St. Jude Children's Research Hospital **South**: 438
St. Louis, MO **Midwest**: 301
St. Petersburg, FL **South**: 119; 140; 145
Stamford, CT **Northeast**: 51
Stanford University **West**: 185; 190
Staten Island, NY **Northeast**: 317; 318; 327
Stern, Isaac **South**: 312
Stieglitz, Alfred **South**: 458
Stillwater, MN **Midwest**: 282
Storrs, CT **Northeast**: 33
Stowe, Harriet Beecher **Midwest**: 384; 390; **Northeast**: 28; 34; 112
Stowe, VT **Northeast**: 495
Stratford, CT **Northeast**: 7; 12
Stratham, NH **Northeast**: 220
Studebaker, Clement and Henry **Midwest**: 101
Suffolk, VA **South**: 561
Sullivan, Louis **Midwest**: 15
Sullivan's Island, SC **South**: 377
Sweetwater, GA **South**: 167
Sweetwater, TN **South**: 408
Sylvania, OH **Midwest**: 435; 444
Syracuse, NY **Northeast**: 345
Tacoma, WA **West**: 449
Taft, William Howard **Midwest**: 384; 390
Tampa, FL **South**: 121; 122; 124; 126; 128; 129; 131
Tarkington, Booth **Midwest**: 95
Taylor, Zachary **South**: 216
Tchaikovsky, Peter I. **South**: 440
Tempe, AZ **West**: 45; 46; 53; 56; 58
Tennessee Valley Authority **Midwest**: 424
Texas Medical Center **South**: 512; 516; 517
Tijuana, Mexico **West**: 161; 164; 166; 167
Timonium, MD **South**: 266
Toledo, OH **Midwest**: 433
Tombstone, AZ **West**: 67
Tonowanda, NY **Northeast**: 312
Topeka, KS **Midwest**: 167
Toronto, Ontario, Canada **Northeast**: 307
Toulouse-Lautrec, Henri de **South**: 458
Townsend, TN **South**: 423
Trenton, NJ **Northeast**: 275
Troy, NY **Northeast**: 297; 299; 300
Truckee, NV **West**: 332
Truman, Harry S **Midwest**: 164; 295
Tubb, Ernest **South**: 459
Tucson, AZ **West**: 65
Tufts University **Northeast**: 121; 128; 131; 132; 159
Tulane University **South**: 235; 243; 244; 247

Tulsa, OK **South**: 347
Turner, Ted **South**: 151; 162
Tustin, CA **West**: 88
Twain, Mark **Northeast**: 28; 34; 310
Twitty, Conway **South**: 459
Tybee Island, GA **South**: 188; 191
Tyler, John **South**: 554
U.S. Naval War College (RI) **Northeast**: 449; 450; 453; 454
United Nations **Northeast**: 317; 318; 326; 327; 330
University of Alabama at Birmingham **South**: 5; 8; 12; 13; 14; 17
University of Alabama at Birmingham Medical Center **South**: 11; 12
University of Arkansas at Little Rock **South**: 39; 47; 50
University of Baltimore **South**: 255; 262
University of Bridgeport **Northeast**: 5; 9; 10; 11; 12; 57
University of Buffalo **Northeast**: 303; 307; 310; 311; 312
University of California, Riverside **West**: 136
University of Central Florida **South**: 105; 108; 109; 112; 115
University of Chicago **Midwest**: 12; 13; 14; 15; 21
University of Cincinnati **Midwest**: 386; 388; 389; 390; 392
University of Colorado **West**: 211
University of Houston **South**: 507; 512; 516; 518
University of Iowa **Midwest**: 116; 118; 120; 121; 123; 133
University of Kentucky **South**: 195; 198; 200; 201; 202; 204; 205; 206
University of Kentucky College of Medicine **South**: 202
University of Louisville **South**: 209; 216; 218; 220
University of Maine **Northeast**: 75; 81; 82; 85; 90; 91; 92; 94; 103; 112
University of Miami **South**: 89; 97; 100; 101
University of Michigan **Midwest**: 195; 196; 197; 198; 199; 200; 201; 202; 211; 212; 213; 234
University of Minnesota **Midwest**: 247; 252; 253; 254; 257; 261; 264; 266; 268; 271; 277; 278; 282
University of Missouri **Midwest**: 287; 294; 295; 308

University of Nebraska **Midwest:** 330; 331; 332; 334; 335; 337; 346; 347; 348; 351; 353
University of North Carolina at Charlotte **South:** 287; 294; 298
University of North Carolina at Greensboro **South:** 301; 309; 310; 312; 313
University of North Dakota **Midwest:** 367; 369; 371; 372; 374; 376
University of Notre Dame **Midwest:** 101; 105; 106; 108
University of Pittsburgh **Northeast:** 419; 423; 425; 426; 428
University of Rochester **Northeast:** 333; 338; 339; 340; 342
University of South Alabama **South:** 21; 28; 31
University of South Carolina **South:** 379; 381; 383; 386; 387; 388; 390; 391
University of South Florida **South:** 119; 126; 128; 131; 138; 140; 141; 143; 144
University of Southern Maine **Northeast:** 97; 101; 105; 109; 110; 112; 113
University of Tampa **South:** 131; 138; 140; 141; 143
University of Tennessee at Chattanooga **South:** 397; 406; 408; 410
University of Tennessee at Knoxville **South:** 413; 415; 418; 421; 422; 423; 424; 425
University of Texas Southwestern Medical Center **South:** 483; 486
University of Texas at Austin **South:** 465; 467; 468; 470; 471; 472; 474; 475; 476
University of Toledo **Midwest:** 435; 438; 440; 441; 443; 444
University of Vermont **Northeast:** 475; 480; 481; 482; 484; 485; 492
Upper Arlington, OH **Midwest:** 411
Urbandale, IA **Midwest:** 139
Valencia, CA **West:** 114
Valmont, CO **West:** 211
Van der Rohe, Ludwig Mies **Midwest:** 15
Vandalia, OH **Midwest:** 423
Vanderbilt University **South:** 445; 448; 452; 453; 455; 458; 460
Vanderbilt University Medical Center **South:** 453
Venice Beach, CA **West:** 114
Virginia Beach, VA **South:** 559; 561
Virginia City, NV **West:** 327; 332
Virginia Commonwealth University **South:** 543; 552; 555; 556
Walkerville, MT **West:** 307

Wang Laboratories Inc. **Northeast:** 144; 146; 147
Warwick, RI **Northeast:** 456; 469
Washington, D.C. **South:** 571
Washington, George **Midwest:** 63; **Northeast:** 28; 155; 159; 161; 246; 251; 263; 277; 282; 284; 318; 408; 421; 466; **South:** 374; 381; 573; 574
Washington University **Midwest:** 308; 310; 311
Waterbury, CT **Northeast:** 61
Waterbury, VT **Northeast:** 493
Waterford, NY **Northeast:** 296
Watertown, CT **Northeast:** 63
Waterville, ME **Northeast:** 80
Watervliet, NY **Northeast:** 300
Watkins Glen, NY **Northeast:** 353
Wayne, Anthony **Midwest:** 63; 205; 383; 423; 435; **Northeast:** 371; 375
Wayne State University **Midwest:** 211; 212
Waynesville, OH **Midwest:** 430
Weiser, ID **West:** 282
West Branch, IA **Midwest:** 123
West Des Moines, IA **Midwest:** 139
West Fargo, ND **Midwest:** 364
West Hartford, CT **Northeast:** 33; 36; 70
West Springfield, MA **Northeast:** 161; 162; 163
Western Connecticut State University **Northeast:** 15; 21; 22
Western Dakota Vocational Technical Institute **Midwest:** 449; 455
Western Michigan University **Midwest:** 224; 227
Wethersfield, CT **Northeast:** 10; 13; 53
Whistler, James Abbott McNeill **Midwest:** 200
Whitehall, OH **Midwest:** 411
Whitehall Township, PA **Northeast:** 363
Whitney, Eli **South:** 181
Wichita, KS **Midwest:** 179
Wilberforce, OH **Midwest:** 427; 428
Wilkes-Barre, PA **Northeast:** 433; 435; 438; 440; 441; 443
Williamsburg, VA **South:** 561; 567
Wilmington, DE **South:** 57
Wilson, Woodrow **South:** 388
Windsor Locks, CT **Northeast:** 24; 36; 71
Windsor, Ontario, Canada **Midwest:** 202; 210
Winston-Salem, NC **South:** 303
Winter Park, FL **South:** 108; 112; 113; 115; 116

Winthrop, MA **Northeast**: 126
Wood, Grant **Midwest**: 116; 121; 123; 134
Woodstock, VT **Northeast**: 499
Worcester, MA **Northeast**: 165
Worthing, SD **Midwest**: 468
Worthington, OH **Midwest**: 411
Wright, Frank Lloyd **Midwest**: 15; 41; 200; 228; 441; 493; 496; 523; 525; **Northeast**: 187; 311; 329; 422; 428; **West**: 45; 60; 114
Wright, Frank Lloyd Library **Northeast**: 365
Wright, Orville and Wilbur **Midwest**: 80; 214; 423; 428

Wright-Patterson Air Force Base **Midwest**: 423; 426; 427; 428
Xenia, OH **Midwest**: 423; 430
Xerox Corporation **Northeast**: 335; 336; 337; 338
Yeager, Charles S. **South**: 598
Yellow Springs, OH **Midwest**: 424; 427
Yermo, CA **West**: 114
Young, Brigham **West**: 401; 405
Ypsilanti, MI **Midwest**: 196; 198; 200
Zebulon, NC **South**: 328
Zeeland, MI **Midwest**: 223